Using Econometrics

A Practical Guide

Using Econometrics

A Practical Guide

A. H. STUDENMUND
Occidental College

HENRY J. CASSIDY
Federal Home Loan Mortgage Corporation

HarperCollins*Publishers*

Library of Congress Cataloging-in-Publication Data

Studenmund, A. H.
    Using econometrics.

    Accompanied by instructor's manual.
    Includes index.
    1. Econometrics.   2. Regression analysis.
I. Cassidy, Henry J.   II. Title
HB139 1987   330'.028   86-21382
ISBN 0-316-82010-5

Library of Congress Catalog Card No. 86-21382

ISBN 0-673-39137-X

9 8 7 6 5 4

MPC

Printed in the United States of America

Acknowledgments

Table B-1: Reprinted with permission of Macmillan Publishing Company from *Statistical Methods for Research Workers*, 14th Edition, by Ronald A. Fisher. Copyright © 1970 by University of Adelaide.

Tables B-2 and B-3: Abridged from M. Merrington and C. M. Thompson, "Tables of percentage points of the inverted beta (*F*) distribution," *Biometrika*, Vol. 33, 1943, p. 73. By permission of the Biometrika Trustees.

Tables B-4, B-5, and B-6: From J. Durbin and G. S. Watson, "Testing for serial correlation in least squares regressions," *Biometrika*, Vol. 38, 1951, pp. 159-77. By permission of the Biometrika Trustees.

Tables B-7 and B-8: Based on *Biometrika Tables for Statisticians*, Vol. 1, 3rd ed. (1966). By permission of the Biometrika Trustees.

Dedicated to our parents,
Betsy and Russ Studenmund
and
Catherine and Thomas Cassidy

Contents

Preface

"Econometric education is a lot like learning to fly a plane; you learn more from actually doing it than you learn from reading about it."

Using Econometrics represents a new approach to the understanding of elementary econometrics. It covers the topic of single-equation linear regression analysis in an easily understandable format that emphasizes real-world examples and exercises. As the subtitle, *A Practical Guide,* implies, the book is aimed not only at beginning econometrics students but also at regression users looking for a refresher and at experienced practitioners who want a convenient reference.

The material covered by this book is traditional, but there are four specific features that we feel distinguish *Using Econometrics:*

1. Our approach to the learning of econometrics is simple, intuitive, and easy to understand. We do not use matrix algebra, and we relegate proofs and calculus to the footnotes.

2. We include numerous examples and example-based exercises. We feel that the best way to get a solid grasp of applied econometrics is through an example-oriented approach.

3. Although most of this book is at a simpler level than previous econometrics texts, our two chapters on specification choice are among the most complete in the field. We think that an understanding of specification issues is vital for regression users.

4. We include a new kind of learning tool, called an interactive regression learning example, that helps students simulate econometric analysis by giving them feedback on various kinds of decisions without relying on computer time or much instructor supervision.

The formal prerequisites for using this book are few. Most importantly, readers are assumed to have some familiarity with macroeconomic and microeconomic theory; in addition, the book is easier to use if the reader has had a statistics course (even if he or she has forgotten most of it), or if the reader is not afraid of working with mathematical functions. While all the statistical concepts necessary for econometric study are covered in the text, they are covered only to the extent needed for an understanding of regression analysis. Because the prerequisites are few and the statistics material is self-contained, *Using Econometrics* can be used not only in undergraduate econometrics courses but also in MBA-level graduate courses in quantitative methods. We also anticipate that the book would be a helpful supplement for graduate-level econometrics courses.

The text is accompanied by an instructor's manual (that includes lecture notes, answers to odd-numbered exercises, sample examinations, and an additional interactive learning example) and a PC-compatible diskette that contains all the data used in the book's exercises. Instructors who adopt *Using Econometrics* can obtain either or both of these ancillaries free of charge by contacting Little, Brown directly. We have also prepared Vu-graphs for instructors who feel that the use of such devices will improve their classroom presentations by allowing them to focus their energies on teaching rather than continuously writing on the board. For information on the availability and cost of the Vu-graphs, contact Henry Cassidy, 3100 N. Oakland Street, Arlington, Virginia 22207.

Two previous books, those of Rao and Miller* and Cassidy† (both now out of print), played a major role in shaping our approach. We would like to thank the Reston Publishing Company for allowing us to use portions of the latter book.

While most authors express their gratitude to a number of individuals for their assistance in a book's preparation, we feel especially blessed in regard to the quantity and quality of help we have received. Of special assistance were Robby Moore of Occidental College (who helped inspire the project and who reviewed practically every chapter), Cynthia Schroeder of Occidental (who did much of the computer work), Carolyn Summers of the National Education Association (who reviewed the manuscript and wrote the index), and George Wang of the Federal Home Loan Bank Board (who wrote a preliminary draft of Section 13.3 and who also reviewed the text). Others whose ideas helped shape the manuscript were Kenneth D. Boyer, Michigan State University; Richard E. Caves, Harvard University; Edward Coulson, Pennsylvania State University; Mark Dynarski, University of California at Davis; John Geweke, Duke University; L. Jay Helms, University of California at Davis; Catherine Melfi, Indiana University; Gary Smith, Pomona College; David C. Stapleton, Dartmouth College; Larry Taylor, Lehigh University; Lowell Taylor, University of Texas at Austin; William G. Tomek, Cornell University; and Ronald S. Warren, University of Georgia. Heavily involved at the editorial and production end were Will Ethridge, Cynthia Chapin, Denise Clinton, Judy Gelman, Ann Manning, Betty Tracy, Cathy Wesche, and Laura Fillmore and the folks at Editorial Inc. The excellent ECSTAT regression package used throughout the text was provided by Insight Software (3 Risley Road, Winchester MA 01890). Finally, but perhaps most importantly, we owe a special debt of gratitude to our students and colleagues who provided us with feedback, examples, good humor, and the feeling that writing this book was worthwhile. Although it is impossible to name everyone, we'd like to especially single out Peter Adamson, Terri Behrle, Bill Edler, Mike Goldberg, Dan Springer, Jim Whitney, and Roxanne Wahler for going above and beyond the call of duty in their assistance to this project.

---

*Potluri Rao and Roger LeRoy Miller, *Applied Econometrics* (Belmont, California: Wadsworth, 1971).

†Henry J. Cassidy, *Using Econometrics: A Beginner's Guide* (Reston, Virginia: Reston, 1981).

1

An Overview of Regression Analysis

1.1 What Is Econometrics?

"Econometrics is too mathematical; it's the reason my best friend isn't majoring in economics."

"There are two things you don't want to see in the making—sausage and econometric research."[1]

"Econometrics may be defined as the quantitative analysis of actual economic phenomena."[2]

"It's my experience that 'economy-tricks' is usually nothing more than a justification of what the author believed before the research was begun."

It may be hard to believe, but these are actual quotations about econometrics. Obviously, econometrics has come to mean different things to different people. To beginning students, it must seem as if econometrics is an overly complex obstacle to an otherwise useful education. To skeptical observers, econometric results should only be trusted when the steps that produced those results are completely known. To professionals in the field, econometrics is a fascinating set of techniques that allows the measurement and analysis of economic phenomena and the prediction of future economic trends.

You're probably thinking that such diverse points of view sound like the statements of four blind people trying to describe an elephant based on what they happen to be touching, and you are at least partially right. Econometrics has both a formal definition and a larger context. While you can easily memorize the formal definition, you'll get a complete picture only by understanding the many uses of and alternative approaches to econometrics.

That said, we need a formal definition. **Econometrics,** literally "economic measurement," is the quantitative measurement and analysis of actual economic

1

and business phenomena. It attempts to quantify economic reality and bridge the gap between the worlds of economic theory and actual business activity. To many students, these worlds must seem far apart. On the one hand, economists theorize equilibrium prices based on carefully conceived marginal costs and marginal revenues, while on the other, many firms seem to operate as though they had never heard of such concepts. Econometrics allows us to examine data from real-world firms and to quantify the actions of these firms and other factors, such as the actions of consumers and governments. Such measurements have a number of different uses, and an examination of these uses is the first step to understanding the broader context within which econometrics operates.

1.1.1   Uses of Econometrics

Econometrics has three major uses:

1. the description of economic reality

2. the testing of hypotheses about economic theory

3. the forecasting of future economic activity.

The simplest use of econometrics is for *description.* We can use econometrics to quantify economic processes; econometrics allows us to put numbers in equations where previously we had only abstract symbols. For example, consumer demand for a particular commodity often can be thought of as a relationship between the quantity demanded (C) and the commodity's price (P), the price of substitute goods (P_j and P_k), and disposable income (Y_d). For most goods, the relationship between consumption and disposable income is expected to be positive, because an increase in disposable income will be associated with an increase in the consumption of the good. Econometrics actually allows us to estimate that relationship based upon reference to past consumption, income, and other relevant variables. In other words, a general and purely theoretical functional relationship:

$$C = f(P, P_j, P_k, Y_d) \qquad (1.1)$$

can become explicit:

$$C = 10.0 - 5.6P + 8.0P_j + 2.6P_k + 0.003Y_d \qquad (1.2)$$

This technique gives a much more specific and descriptive picture of the function.[3] Instead of expecting consumption merely to "increase" if there is an increase in disposable income, we now expect an increase of a specific amount (0.003 units for each dollar of increased income). The number 0.003 is called an estimated regression coefficient, and it is the ability to estimate these coefficients that makes econometrics valuable.

Perhaps the most common use of econometrics is for **hypothesis testing,** the testing of alternative theories through the use of quantitative evidence. Much of the science of economics involves building theoretical models and then testing them against the evidence, and hypothesis testing is vital to that scientific approach. For example, you could test the hypothesis that the product in Equation 1.1 is what economists call a *normal good* (one for which the quantity demanded increases when disposable income increases). You could do this by applying various statistical tests to the estimated coefficient (0.003) of disposable income (Y_d) in Equation 1.2. At first glance, the evidence would seem to support this hypothesis because the coefficient's sign is positive, but the "statistical significance" of that estimate would have to be investigated before such a conclusion could be justified. Even though the estimated coefficient 0.003 is positive, as expected, it may not be sufficiently different from zero to imply that the coefficient is indeed positive instead of zero. Unfortunately, tests of such hypotheses are not always easy, and there are times when two different researchers can look at the same set of data and come to different conclusions. Even given that possibility, the use of econometrics in testing hypotheses is probably its most important function.

The third and most difficult use of econometrics is to **forecast** or predict what is likely to happen next quarter, next year, or even farther into the future. For example, economists use econometric models to make forecasts of variables like sales, profits, Gross National Product, and the inflation rate. The accuracy of such forecasts is dependent in large measure on the degree to which the past is a good guide to the future. Business leaders and politicians tend to be especially interested in this use of econometrics, because they need to make decisions about the future, and the penalty for being wrong (bankruptcy for the entrepreneur and political defeat for the candidate) is high. To the extent that econometrics can shed light on the impact of their policies, business and government leaders will be better equipped to make decisions. For example, if the president of a company that sold the product modeled in Equation 1.1 wanted to decide whether to increase prices, forecasts of sales with and without the price increase could be calculated and compared to help make such a decision. In this way, the use of econometrics in forecasting can be used not only for forecasting but for policy analysis as well.

1.1.2 Alternative Econometric Approaches

There are many approaches to obtaining econometric estimates. For example, the fields of biology, psychology, and physics all face quantitative questions similar to the ones in economics and business, but these fields tend to use somewhat different techniques for analysis, because the nature of the problems differs among the fields. Different approaches also make sense within the field of economics. The kind of econometric tools used to quantify a particular function will depend in part on the uses to which that equation will be put. A model built solely for descriptive purposes might be different from one used for forecasting, for example.

To get a better picture of these approaches, look at the steps necessary for any kind of quantitative research. There are three important steps in such research:

1. specifying the models or relationships to be studied

2. collecting the data needed to quantify the models

3. quantifying the models with estimates obtained from the data.

Steps 1 and 2 are similar in all sorts of quantitative work, but the techniques used in step 3, the quantification of models, differ widely between and within disciplines. Choosing among techniques for the quantification of a model given a particular set of data, though, is often referred to as the "art" of econometrics; there are many different alternative approaches to quantifying the same equation, and each approach may give somewhat different results. The choice of approach is left to the individual econometrician (the researcher using econometrics), but each researcher should be able to justify that choice to others.

This book will focus primarily on one particular econometric approach: single-equation linear *regression analysis*. The following section will thus discuss only regression analysis, but it is important for every econometrician to remember that regression is one of many approaches to econometric quantification.

The importance of critical evaluation cannot be stressed too strongly; a good econometrician is one who can diagnose faults in a particular approach and who can figure out how to repair them. The limitations of the regression analysis approach must be fully perceived and appreciated by anyone attempting to use regression analysis or its findings. The possibility of missing or inaccurate data, incorrectly formulated relationships, poorly chosen estimating techniques, or improper statistical testing procedures implies that the results from regression analyses need to be viewed with some caution.

1.2   What Is Regression Analysis?

Econometricians use regression analysis to make quantitative estimates of economic relationships that previously had been completely theoretical in nature. After all, anybody can claim that the quantity of compact discs demanded will increase if the price of those discs goes down (holding everything else constant), but not many people can actually put numbers into an equation and estimate *by how many* compact discs the quantity demanded will increase for each dollar that price decreases. To predict the *direction* of the change, you need a knowledge of economic theory and the general characteristics of the product in question. To predict the *amount* of the change, though, you need a sample of data, and you need a way to estimate the relationship such as regression analysis.

1.2.1   Dependent and Independent Variables

Regression analysis is a statistical technique that attempts to "explain" movements in one variable, the **dependent variable**, as a function of movements in a set of other variables, called the **independent (*or* explanatory) variables,**

through the quantification of a single empirical equation. For example, in Equation 1.1, repeated below for convenience,

$$C = f(P, P_j, P_k, Y_d) \tag{1.1}$$

C is the dependent variable and P, P_j, P_k, and Y_d are the independent variables. Regression analysis is a natural tool for economists because most economic propositions can be stated in such single-equation[4] functional forms. For example, the level of production of a particular product (dependent variable) is a function of capital and labor inputs (independent variables), or the quantity demanded (dependent variable) is a function of price, income, and the prices of substitutes (independent variables).

Much of economics and business is concerned with cause-and-effect propositions: If the price of a good increases by one unit, then the quantity demanded decreases on average by a certain amount, depending on the price elasticity of demand (defined as the percentage change in the quantity demanded that is caused by a one percent change in price). Similarly, if the quantity of capital employed increases by one unit, then output increases by a certain amount, called the marginal productivity of capital. Propositions such as these pose an if-then, or causal, relationship that logically postulates a dependent variable having movements that are causally determined by movements in a number of specified independent variables.

Don't be deceived by the words dependent or independent, however. While many economic relationships are causal by their very nature, a regression result, no matter how statistically significant, cannot prove causality. All regression analysis can do is test whether a significant quantitative relationship exists. Judgments as to causality must also include a healthy dose of economic theory and common sense. For example, the fact that the bell on the door of a flower shop rings just before a customer enters and purchases some flowers by no means implies that the ringing of the bell causes the purchase! If events A and B are related statistically, it may be that A causes B, that B causes A, that some omitted factor causes both, or that a chance correlation exists between the two.

The cause and effect relationship is often so subtle that it fools even the most prominent economists. For example, in the late nineteenth century, English economist Stanley Jevons hypothesized that sunspots caused an increase in economic activity. To test this, he collected data on national output (the "dependent" variable) and sunspot activity (the "independent" variable) and showed that a significant positive relationship existed. This result led him, and some others, to jump to the conclusion that sunspots did indeed cause output to rise. Such a conclusion was unjustified because regression analysis cannot confirm causality; it can only test the strength and direction of the quantitative relationships involved.

1.2.2 Single-Equation Linear Models

The simplest single-equation linear regression model is:

$$Y = \beta_0 + \beta_1 X \tag{1.3}$$

Equation 1.3 states that Y, the dependent variable, is a single-equation linear function of X, the independent variable. The model is a single-equation model because no equation for X as a function of Y (or any other variable) has been specified. The model is linear because if you were to plot Equation 1.3 on graph paper, it would be a straight line rather than a curve or any other shape.

The βs are the **coefficients** (or **parameters**) that determine the coordinates of the straight line at any point. β_0 is the **constant** or **intercept** term; it indicates the value of Y when X equals zero. β_1 is the **slope coefficient,** and it indicates the amount that Y will change when X changes by one unit. Figure 1.1 illustrates the relationship between the coefficients and the graphical meaning of the regression equation. As can be seen from the diagram, Equation 1.3 is indeed linear.

The slope β_1 shows the response of the value of Y to changes in X. Since being able to explain and predict changes in the dependent variable is the essential reason for quantifying behavioral relationships, most of the emphasis in regression analysis is on slope coefficients such as β_1. In Figure 1.1 for example, if X were to increase from X_1 to X_2, the value of Y in Equation 1.3 would increase from Y_1 (the level of the dependent variable associated with X_1) to Y_2 (the level associated with X_2). For linear (i.e., straight-line) regression models, the response in the predicted value of Y due to a change in X is constant and equal to the slope coefficient β_1:

$$(Y_2 - Y_1)/(X_2 - X_1) = \Delta Y/\Delta X = \beta_1$$

where Δ is used to denote a change in the variables. Some readers may recognize this as the "rise" (ΔY) divided by the "run" (ΔX). For a linear model, the slope is constant over the entire function.

We must distinguish between an equation that is linear in the variables and one that is linear in the coefficients (or parameters). This distinction is necessary because while linear regressions need to be linear in the coefficients, they do not necessarily need to be linear in the variables. An equation is **linear in the variables** if plotting the function in terms of X and Y generates a straight line. For example, Equation 1.3, repeated for convenience:

$$Y = \beta_0 + \beta_1 X \qquad (1.3)$$

is linear in the variables, but Equation 1.4:

$$Y = \beta_0 + \beta_1 X^2 \qquad (1.4)$$

is not linear in the variables because if you were to plot Equation 1.4 it would be a quadratic, not a straight line. This difference can be seen in Figure 1.1.

An equation is **linear in the coefficients** (or parameters) only if the coefficients (the βs) appear in their simplest form—they are not raised to any powers (other than one), are not multiplied or divided by other coefficients, and do not themselves include some sort of function (like logs or exponents). For example, Equation 1.3 is linear in the coefficients, but Equation 1.5:

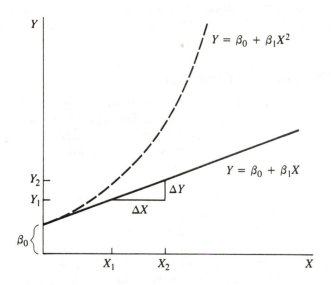

FIGURE 1.1 *Graphic Representation of the Coefficients of the Regression Line*
The graph of the equation $Y = \beta_0 + \beta_1 X$ is linear with a constant slope equal to
$\beta_1 = \Delta Y / \Delta X$. The graph of the equation $Y = \beta_0 + \beta_1 X^2$, on the other hand, is nonlinear
with an increasing slope (if $\beta_1 > 0$).

$$Y = \beta_0 + \beta_1^2 X \tag{1.5}$$

is not linear in the coefficients β_0 and β_1. Equation 1.5 is not linear because there
is no rearrangement of the equation that will make it linear in the βs of original
interest, β_0 and β_1. In fact, of all possible equations for a single explanatory
variable, *only* functions of the general form:

$$f(Y) = \beta_0 + \beta_1 f(X) \tag{1.6}$$

are linear in the coefficients β_0 and β_1. In essence, any sort of configuration of
the Xs and Ys can be used and the equation will continue to be linear in the
coefficients, but even a slight change in the configuration of the βs will cause
the equation to become nonlinear in the coefficients. For example, Equation 1.4
is not linear in the variables but *is* linear in the coefficients. The reason that Equation 1.4 is linear in the coefficients is that if you define $Z = f(X) = X^2$, then
Equation 1.4 fits into the general form of Equation 1.6.

All this is important because if linear regression techniques are going to be
applied to an equation, it *must be* linear in the coefficients. Linear regression
analysis can be applied to an equation that is nonlinear in the variables as long
as the equation can be formulated in a way that is linear in the coefficients.

Indeed, when econometricians use the phrase "linear regression," they usually mean "regression that is linear in the coefficients." The application of regression techniques to equations that are nonlinear in the coefficients is discussed in Section 7.6.

1.2.3 The Stochastic Error Term

Besides the variation in the dependent variable (Y) that is caused by the independent variable (X), there is almost always variation that comes from other sources as well. This additional variation comes in part from omitted explanatory variables (like X_2, X_3, etc.), but even if these extra variables are added to the equation, there still is going to be some variation in Y that simply cannot be explained by the model.[5] This variation probably comes from sources such as omitted influences, measurement error, incorrect functional form, or purely random and totally unpredictable occurrences.

Econometricians admit the existence of this inherent unexplained variation ("error") by explicitly including a stochastic (or random) error term in their regression models. A **stochastic error term** is a variable that is added to a regression equation to introduce into the model all the variation in Y that cannot be explained by the included Xs. It is, in effect, a symbol of the econometrician's ignorance or inability to model all the movements of the dependent variable. The error term is usually referred to with the symbol epsilon (ϵ), although others symbols (like u or v) are sometimes used.

The addition of a stochastic error term (ϵ) to Equation 1.3 results in a typical regression equation:

$$Y = \beta_0 + \beta_1 X + \epsilon \qquad (1.7)$$

It can be thought of as having two components, the *deterministic* component and the *stochastic* or random component. The expression $\beta_0 + \beta_1 X$ is called the deterministic component of the regression equation, because it indicates the value of Y that is determined by the given value of X, which is assumed to be nonstochastic. This deterministic component can also be thought of as the **expected value** of Y given X, the mean value of the Ys associated with a particular value of X. For example, if the average height of all 14-year-old girls is 5 feet, then 5 feet is the expected value of a girl's height given that she is 14. The deterministic part of the equation may be written:

$$E(Y|X) = \beta_0 + \beta_1 X \qquad (1.8)$$

which states that the expected value of Y given X, denoted as $E(Y|X)$, is a linear function of the independent variable (or variables if there are more than one).

Unfortunately, the value of Y observed in the real world is extremely unlikely to be exactly equal to the deterministic expected value $E(Y|X)$. After all, not all 14-year-old girls are exactly 5 feet tall. As a result, the stochastic element (ϵ) must be added to the equation:

$$Y = E(Y|X) + \epsilon = \beta_0 + \beta_1 X + \epsilon \tag{1.9}$$

The stochastic error term must be present in a regression equation because there are at least four sources of variation in Y other than the variation in the included Xs:

1. Many minor influences on Y are *omitted* from the equation (for example, because data are unavailable), and yet they still have effects on Y.

2. It is virtually impossible to avoid some sort of *measurement error* in at least one of the equation's variables.

3. The underlying theoretical equation might have a *different functional form* (or shape) than the one chosen for the regression. For example, the underlying equation might be nonlinear in the variables for a linear regression (or vice-versa).

4. All attempts to generalize human behavior must contain at least some amount of unpredictable or *purely random* variation.

Let's look at a consumption function (aggregate consumption as a function of aggregate disposable income) to get a better feeling for these components of (or reasons for including) the stochastic error term. First, consumption in a particular year may have been less than it would have been otherwise because of uncertainty over the future course of the economy, causing consumers to save more and to consume less than they would have if the uncertainty had not existed. Since this uncertainty is hard to measure, there might be no variable measuring consumer uncertainty in the equation; in such a case, the impact of the omitted variable (consumer uncertainty) would be likely to end up in the stochastic error term. Second, the observed amount of consumption may have been different from the actual level of consumption in a particular year due to an error (such as a sampling error) in the measurement of consumption in the National Income Accounts. Third, the underlying consumption function may be nonlinear, but a linear consumption function might be estimated. To see how this incorrect functional form would cause errors, see Figure 1.2. Fourth, the consumption function attempts to portray the behavior of people, and there is always an element of unpredictability in human behavior. At any given time, some random event might increase or decrease aggregate consumption in a way that might never be repeated and could hardly be anticipated.

Any or all of these possibilities may explain the existence of a difference between the observed values of Y and the values expected from the deterministic component of the equation, $E(Y|X)$. These sources of error will be taken up in more detail in the chapters that follow, but for now it is enough to recognize that in economics there will always be some stochastic or random element, and, for this reason, an error term must be included in all regression equations.

1.2.4 Extending the Notation

Our regression notation needs to be extended to include reference to the number of observations and to allow the possibility of more than one independent variable.

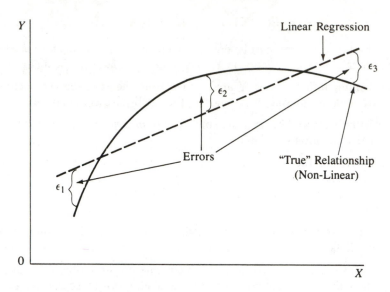

FIGURE 1.2 *Errors Caused by Using a Linear Regression to Model a Nonlinear Relationship*

One source of stochastic error is the use of an incorrect functional form. For example, if a linear regression is used when the underlying relationship is nonlinear, systematic errors (the ϵs) will occur. These nonlinearities are just one component of the stochastic error term. The others are omitted variables, measurement error, and purely random variation.

If we include the specific reference to the observations, the single-equation linear regression model may be written as:

$$Y_i = \beta_0 + \beta_1 X_i + \epsilon_i \quad (i = 1,2,\ldots,n) \tag{1.10}$$

where: Y_i = the ith observation[6] of the dependent variable
$\quad\quad$ X_i = the ith observation of the independent (or explanatory) variable
$\quad\quad$ ϵ_i = the error (or disturbance) term associated with the ith observation
$\quad\quad$ β_0, β_1 = the regression coefficients (or parameters)
$\quad\quad$ n   = the number of observations

This equation is actually n equations, one for each of the n observations:

$$Y_1 = \beta_0 + \beta_1 X_1 + \epsilon_1$$
$$Y_2 = \beta_0 + \beta_1 X_2 + \epsilon_2$$
$$Y_3 = \beta_0 + \beta_1 X_3 + \epsilon_3$$
$$\vdots$$
$$Y_n = \beta_0 + \beta_1 X_n + \epsilon_n$$

That is, the regression model is assumed to hold for each observation. The coefficients do not change from observation to observation, but the values of Y, X, and ϵ do change.

The second notational addition is to allow for more than one independent variable. Since more than one independent variable is likely to have an effect on the dependent variable, our notation should allow these additional explanatory Xs to be added. If we define:

X_{1i} = the ith observation of the first independent variable
X_{2i} = the ith observation of the second independent variable
X_{3i} = the ith observation of the third independent variable

then all three variables can be expressed as determinants of Y in a **multivariate** (more than one independent variable) linear regression model:

$$Y_i = \beta_0 + \beta_1 X_{1i} + \beta_2 X_{2i} + \beta_3 X_{3i} + \epsilon_i \qquad (1.11)$$

β_1 is now the effect of a one unit change in X_1 on the dependent variable Y, holding constant the other included independent variables (X_2 and X_3). Similarly, β_2 gives the effect of X_2 on Y, holding X_1 and X_3 constant. These multivariate regression coefficients (which are parallel in nature to partial derivatives in calculus) serve to isolate the impact on Y of a change in one variable from the impact on Y of changes in the other variables. This is possible because multivariate regression takes the movements of X_2 and X_3 into account when it estimates the coefficient of X_1. The result is quite similar to what we would obtain if we were capable of conducting laboratory experiments in which only one variable at a time was changed.

In the real world, though, it is almost impossible to run controlled experiments, because many economic factors change simultaneously, often in opposite directions. Thus the ability of regression analysis to measure the impact of one variable on the dependent variable, holding constant the influence of the other variables in the equation, is a tremendous advantage. Note that if a variable is not included in an equation, then its impact is *not* held constant in the estimation of the regression coefficients. This will be discussed in more depth in Chapter 6.

The general multivariate regression model with K independent variables is written as:

$$Y_i = \beta_0 + \beta_1 X_{1i} + \beta_2 X_{2i} + \cdots + \beta_K X_{Ki} + \epsilon_i \quad (i = 1,2,\ldots,n) \quad (1.12)$$

If the sample consists of a series of years or months (called a **time series**), then the subscript i is usually replaced with a t to denote time. It also does not matter if X_{1i}, for example, is written as X_{i1} as long as the appropriate definitions are presented. Often the observational subscript (i or t) is deleted entirely, and the reader is expected to understand that the equation holds for each observation in the sample.

1.2.5 The Estimated Regression Equation

Once a researcher has decided on a specific equation, he or she must attempt to actually quantify it. This version of the "true" regression equation is called the **estimated regression equation** and is obtained from a sample of Xs and Ys. While the true equation is purely theoretical in nature:

$$Y_i = \beta_0 + \beta_1 X_i + \epsilon_i \qquad (1.13)$$

the estimated regression equation has actual numbers in it, as in:

$$\hat{Y}_i = 103.40 + 6.38 X_i \qquad (1.14)$$

The observed values of X and Y are used to determine the coefficient estimates 103.40 and 6.38. These estimates are then used to determine $\hat{Y}$ (read as "Y-hat"), the *computed* or *fitted* value of Y_i. To allow this section to focus on the general characteristics of the estimated regression concept, we will postpone an explanation of how these estimates are obtained until the next chapter.

Let's look at the differences between a true regression equation and an estimated regression equation. First, the theoretical regression coefficients β_0 and β_1 in Equation 1.13 have been replaced with *estimates* of those coefficients like 103.40 and 6.38 in Equation 1.14. We can never actually observe the values of the true regression coefficients, so instead we must calculate estimates of those coefficients from the data. The **estimated regression coefficients,** more generally denoted by $\hat{\beta}_0$ and $\hat{\beta}_1$ (read as "beta-hats"), are empirical best guesses of the true regression coefficients and are obtained from a sample of the Ys and Xs. The expression

$$\hat{Y}_i = \hat{\beta}_0 + \hat{\beta}_1 X_i \qquad (1.15)$$

is the general applied empirical counterpart to the true regression Equation 1.13. The calculated estimates in Equation 1.14 are examples of estimated regression coefficients $\hat{\beta}_0$ and $\hat{\beta}_1$. For each sample we would calculate a different set of estimated regression coefficients.

$\hat{Y}_i$ is the *estimated value* of Y_i, and it represents the value of Y calculated from the estimated regression equation for the *i*th observation. As such $\hat{Y}_i$ is our prediction of Y_i from the regression equation, and the closer $\hat{Y}_i$ is to Y_i the better the fit of the equation. (The word fit is used here much as it would be used to describe how well clothes fit.)

The difference between the estimated value of the dependent variable ($\hat{Y}_i$) and the actual value of the dependent variable (Y_i) is defined as the **residual:**

$$e_i = Y_i - \hat{Y}_i \qquad (1.16)$$

Note the distinction between the residual in Equation 1.16 and the error term:

$$\epsilon_i = Y_i - E(Y_i|X_i) \qquad (1.17)$$

The *residual* is the difference between the observed Y and the estimated regression line ($\hat{Y}$), while the *error term* is the difference between the observed Y and the true regression equation (the expected value of Y). In other words, the error term is a theoretical value that can never be observed, but the residual is a real-world value that is calculated for each observation every time a regression is run. Indeed, most regression techniques not only observe the residual but also attempt to select values of $\hat{\beta}_0$ and $\hat{\beta}_1$ that keep the residual as low as possible. The smaller the residual, the better the fit, and the closer the $\hat{Y}$s will be to the Ys.

All these concepts are shown diagramatically in Figure 1.3. The (X,Y) pairs are shown as points on the diagram, and both the true regression equation (which cannot be seen in real applications) and an estimated regression equation are included. Notice that the estimated equation is close to but not equivalent to the true line. This is a typical result. As can be seen in the figure, $\hat{Y}_6$, the computed value of Y for the sixth observation, lies on the estimated (dashed) line, and it differs from Y_6, the actual observed value of Y for the sixth observation. The difference between the observed and estimated value is the residual, denoted by e_6. In addition, while we usually would not be able to see an error term, we have drawn the assumed true regression line here (the solid line) in order to see the error term for the sixth observation, ϵ_6, which is the difference between the true line and the observed value of Y.

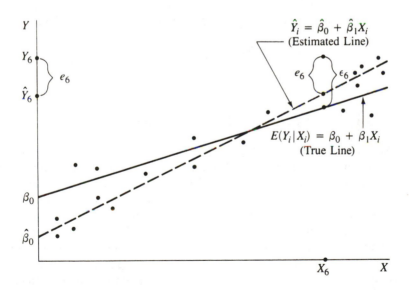

FIGURE 1.3 *True and Estimated Regression Lines*
The true relationship between X and Y (the solid line) cannot typically be observed, but the estimated regression line (the dotted line) can. The difference between an observed data point (for example, i = 6) and the true line is the value of the stochastic error term (ϵ_6). The difference between the observed Y_6 and the fitted value from the regression line ($\hat{Y}_6$) is the value of the residual e_6 for this observation.

Another way to state the estimated regression equation is to combine Equations 1.15 and 1.16, obtaining:

$$Y_i = \hat{\beta}_0 + \hat{\beta}_1 X_i + e_i \qquad (1.18)$$

Compare this equation to Equation 1.13. When we replace the theoretical regression coefficients with estimated coefficients, the error term must be replaced by the residual, because the error term, like the regression coefficients β_0 and β_1, is never observed. Instead, the residual is observed and measured whenever a regression line is estimated with a sample of Xs and Ys. In this sense, the residual can be thought of as an estimate of the error term, and e could have been denoted as $\hat{\epsilon}$.

The chart below summarizes the notation used in the true and estimated regression equations.

True Regression Equation	Estimated Regression Equation
β_0	$\hat{\beta}_0$
β_1	$\hat{\beta}_1$
ϵ_i	e_i

The estimated regression model can easily be extended to more than one independent variable by adding the additional Xs to the right side of the equation. The multivariate estimated regression counterpart of Equation 1.12 would thus be:

$$\hat{Y}_i = \hat{\beta}_0 + \hat{\beta}_1 X_{1i} + \hat{\beta}_2 X_{2i} + \cdots + \hat{\beta}_K X_{Ki} \qquad (1.19)$$

1.3   A Simple Example of a Regression

Let's look at a fairly simple example of regression analysis. Suppose you have accepted a summer job as a weight guesser at the local amusement park, Magic Flag Farm. Each of your customers pays 50 cents, which you get to keep if you guess their weight within ten pounds. If you miss by more than ten pounds, then you have to give the customer a small prize that you buy from Magic Flag Farm for 60 cents each. Luckily, the friendly managers of Magic Flag Farm have arranged a number of marks on the wall behind the customer so that you are capable of accurately measuring the customer's height. Unfortunately, there is a five-foot wall between you and the customer, so you can tell little about the person except for height and (usually) gender.

On your first day on the job, you do so poorly that you work all day and actually lose two dollars, so on the second day you decide to collect data in order to run a regression to formally estimate the relationship between weight and height. Since most of the participants are male, you decide to limit your sample to males. You hypothesize the following relationship:

$$Y_i = f(\overset{+}{X_i}) = \beta_0 + \beta_1 X_i + \epsilon_i \qquad (1.20)$$

where: Y_i = weight in pounds of the *i*th customer
X_i = height in inches (above 5 feet) of the *i*th customer
ϵ_i = the stochastic error term

In this case, the sign of the theoretical relationship between height and weight is believed to be positive (signified by the positive sign above X_i in the general theoretical equation), but you want to actually quantify that relationship in order to be able to estimate weights given heights. To do this, you need to collect a data set and you need to apply regression analysis to the data.

The next day you collect the data summarized in Table 1.1 and then run your regression on the Magic Flag Farm computer, obtaining the following estimates:

$$\hat{\beta}_0 = 103.40 \qquad \hat{\beta}_1 = 6.38$$

This means that the equation

Estimated Weight = 103.40 + 6.38 · Height (inches above five feet) (1.21)

Table 1.1 Data for and Results of the Weight Guessing Equation

OBSER- VATION i (1)	HEIGHT ABOVE 5' X_i (2)	WEIGHT Y_i (3)	PREDICTED WEIGHT $\hat{Y}_i$ (4)	RESIDUAL e_i (5)	$ GAIN OR LOSS (6)
1	5.0	140.0	135.3	4.7	+.50
2	9.0	157.0	160.8	−3.8	+.50
3	13.0	205.0	186.3	18.7	−.60
4	12.0	198.0	179.9	18.1	−.60
5	10.0	162.0	167.2	−5.2	+.50
6	11.0	174.0	173.6	0.4	+.50
7	8.0	150.0	154.4	−4.4	+.50
8	9.0	165.0	160.8	4.2	+.50
9	10.0	170.0	167.2	2.8	+.50
10	12.0	180.0	179.9	0.1	+.50
11	11.0	170.0	173.6	−3.6	+.50
12	9.0	162.0	160.8	1.2	+.50
13	10.0	165.0	167.2	−2.2	+.50
14	12.0	180.0	179.9	0.1	+.50
15	8.0	160.0	154.4	5.6	+.50
16	9.0	155.0	160.8	−5.8	+.50
17	10.0	165.0	167.2	−2.2	+.50
18	15.0	190.0	199.1	−9.1	+.50
19	13.0	185.0	186.3	−1.3	+.50
20	11.0	155.0	173.6	−18.6	−.60
				TOTAL =	$6.70

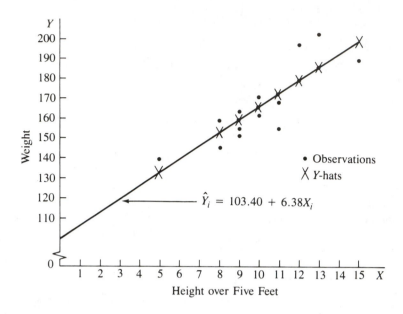

FIGURE 1.4 *A Weight-Guessing Equation*
If we plot the data from the weight guessing example and include the estimated regression line, we can see that the fitted $\hat{Y}$s come fairly close to the observed Ys for all but three observations. Find your own height and weight on the graph; how well does the regression equation work for you?

---

is worth trying as an alternative to just guessing the weights of your customers. Such an equation estimates weight with a constant base of 103.40 pounds and then adds 6.38 pounds for every inch of height over five feet. Note that the sign of $\hat{\beta}_1$ is positive, as you expected.

How well does the equation work? To answer this question, you need to calculate the residuals (Y_i minus $\hat{Y}_i$) from Equation 1.21 to see how many were greater than ten. As can been seen in the last column in Table 1.1, if you had applied the equation to these twenty people you wouldn't exactly have gotten rich, but at least you would have earned $6.70. Figure 1.4 shows not only Equation 1.21 but also the weight and height data on all twenty of the customers used as your sample.

Equation 1.21 would probably help a beginning weight guesser, but it probably could be improved on by adding other variables or collecting a larger sample. Such an equation is realistic, though, because it's likely that every successful weight guesser uses an equation like this in his or her mind and even makes judgments about the error term without consciously thinking about that concept.

Let us review the important concepts discussed in the previous section. Our goal with this equation was to quantify the theoretical weight/height equation, Equation 1.20, by collecting data (Table 1.1) and calculating an estimated regression (Equation 1.21). Although the true equation, like the actual stochastic error terms, can never be observed, we were able to come up with an estimated equation that had the sign we expected for $\hat{\beta}_1$ and that helped us in our job. Before you decide to quit school or your job and try to make your living guessing weights at Magic Flag Farm, though, there is quite a bit more to learn about regression analysis, so we had better move on.

1.4 Summary

1. Econometrics, literally "economic measurement," is a branch of economics that attempts to quantify theoretical relationships. Regression analysis is only one technique used in econometrics, but it is by far the most frequently used.

2. The major uses of econometrics are description, hypothesis testing, and forecasting. The precise econometric techniques employed may vary depending on the projected use of the econometric research.

3. While regression analysis specifies that a dependent variable is a function of one or more independent variables, regression analysis alone cannot be used to prove or even imply causality.

4. Linear regression can only be applied to equations that are *linear in the coefficients,* which means that the regression coefficients are in their simplest possible form. For an equation with two explanatory variables, this form would be:

$$f(Y_i) = \beta_0 + \beta_1 f(X_{1i}) + \beta_2 f(X_{2i}) + \epsilon_i$$

5. A stochastic error term must be added to all regression equations to account for variations in the dependent variable that are not completely determined by the independent variables. The components of (and reasons for) this error term include
   a. omitted or left-out variables
   b. measurement errors in the data
   c. an underlying theoretical equation that has a different functional form (shape) than the regression equation
   d. purely random and unpredictable events.

6. An estimated regression equation is an approximation of the true equation that is obtained by using data from a sample of actual Ys and Xs. Since we can never know the true equation, econometric analysis focuses on this estimated regression equation and the estimates of the regression coefficients. The difference between a particular observation and the estimated value from the regression equation is called the residual.

Exercises

(Answers to even-numbered exercises are in Appendix A.)

1. Write out the meaning of each of the following terms without reference to the book (or your notes) and then compare your definition with the version in the text for each:
   a. stochastic error term
   b. regression analysis
   c. linear in the variables
   d. slope coefficient
   e. multivariate regression model
   f. expected value
   g. residual

2. Decide whether you would expect relationships between the following pairs of dependent and independent variables (respectively) to be positive, negative, or ambiguous. Explain your reasoning.
   a. Aggregate net investment (in the U.S. in a given year) and Gross National Product (GNP) in that year.
   b. The amount of hair on the head of a male professor and the age of that professor.
   c. The number of acres of wheat planted in a season and the price of wheat at the beginning of that season.
   d. Aggregate net investment and the nominal rate of interest in the same year and country.
   e. The rate of growth of GNP in a year and the average skirt length in that year.
   f. The quantity of canned heat demanded and the price of a can of heat.

3. Review the four components of (reasons for) a stochastic error term.
   a. Can you think of other possible reasons for adding ϵ to the equation? What would they be? Why do you think they were omitted from the discussion in Section 1.2.3?
   b. If you were to run a regression on each of the pairs of dependent and independent variables in Question 2 above, for which regressions would an error term not be necessary? Why?

4. Look over the following equations and decide whether they are linear in the variables, linear in the coefficients, both, or neither.
   a. $Y_i = \beta_0 + \beta_1 X_i^3 + \epsilon_i$
   b. $Y_i = \beta_0 + \beta_1 \log X_i + \epsilon_i$
   c. $\log Y_i = \beta_0 + \beta_1 \log X_i + \epsilon_i$
   d. $Y_i = \beta_0 + \beta_1(\beta_2 X_i) + \epsilon_i$

    e. $Y_i = \beta_0/(\beta_1 X_i) + \epsilon_i$

    f. $Y_i = 1 + \beta_0(1 - X_i^{\beta_1}) + \epsilon_i$

    g. $Y_i = \beta_0 + \beta_1 X_{1i} + \beta_2 X_{2i}/10 + \epsilon_i$

5. Your friend estimates a simple equation of bond prices in different years as a function of the interest rate that year (for equal levels of risk) and obtains:

$$\hat{Y}_i = 101.40 - 4.78 X_i$$

where: Y_i = U.S. Government Bond Prices (per \$100 bond) in the ith year.
        X_i = The Federal funds rate (percent) in the ith year.

    a. Carefully explain the meanings of the two estimated coefficients. Are the estimated signs what you would have expected?

    b. Why is the left-hand variable in your friend's equation $\hat{Y}$ and not Y?

    c. Didn't your friend forget the stochastic error term in the estimated equation?

    d. What is the economic meaning of this equation? What criticisms would you have of this model? (Hint: The Federal funds rate is a rate that applies to overnight holdings in banks.)

6. Recall the weight-guessing regression in Section 1.3:

    a. Go back to the data set and identify the three customers who seem to be quite a distance from the estimated regression line. Would we have a better regression equation if we dropped these customers from the sample?

    b. Measure your own height and weight (or that of a male friend) and plug them into Equation 1.21. Does the equation come within ten pounds? If not, do you think you see why? Why does the estimated equation predict the same weight for all males of the same height when it is obvious that all males of the same height don't weigh the same?

    c. Look over the sample with the thought that it might not be a randomly drawn one. Does the sample look abnormal to you in any way? (Hint: Are the customers who choose to play such a game a random sample?) If the sample wasn't random, would this have an effect on the regression results and the estimated weights?

    d. Think of at least one other factor besides height that might be a good choice as a variable in the weight/height equation. How would you go about obtaining the data for this variable? What would the expected sign of your variable be if it were added to the equation?

---

[1] Attributed to Edward E. Leamer. Note that all footnotes have been placed at the end of the chapters to avoid distracting the reader.

[2] Paul A. Samuelson, T. C. Koopmans, and J. R. Stone, "Report of the Evaluative Committee for *Econometrica*," *Econometrica*, April 1954, p.141.

[3] The results in Equation 1.2 are from a model of the demand for coffee that is examined in more detail in Section 6.3.

[4] Often there are several related propositions that, when taken as a group, suggest a *system* of regression equations. An example is a two-equation model of supply and demand. Usually, these two equations must

be considered simultaneously instead of separately. The estimation of such simultaneous models is discussed in Chapter 12.

[5.] An exception would be the case where the data can be explained by some sort of physical law and are measured perfectly. Here, continued variation would clearly point to an omitted independent variable. A similar kind of problem is often encountered in astronomy, where planets have been discovered by noting that the orbits of known planets exhibit variations that could only have been caused by the gravitational pull of another heavenly body. Absent these kinds of physical laws, researchers in economics and business would be foolhardy to believe that *all* the variation in Y could be explained by a regression model because there are always elements of error in any behavioral relationship.

[6.] A typical observation is an individual person, year, or country. For example, a series of annual observations starting in 1950 would have $Y_1 = Y$ for 1950, Y_2 for 1951, etc.

2

Ordinary Least Squares

The bread and butter of regression analysis is the estimation of the coefficients of econometric models with a technique called Ordinary Least Squares (OLS). The first section of this chapter summarizes the reasoning behind and the mechanics of OLS. Regression users usually rely on computers to do the actual OLS calculations, so the emphasis here is on understanding what OLS attempts to do and how it goes about doing it.

How can you tell a good equation from a bad one once it has been estimated? One factor is the extent to which the estimated equation fits the actual data. The rest of the chapter is devoted to developing an understanding of the two most commonly used measures of this fit, R^2 and the adjusted R^2 ($\bar{R}^2$), called R-Bar-Squared. The use of $\bar{R}^2$ is not without perils, however, and the chapter concludes with an example of the misuse of that statistic.

2.1 Estimating the Coefficients of the Model with OLS

Once the variables have been specified and the data collected, the next step in regression analysis is to estimate the coefficients of the equation. In a sense, this estimation is what regression is all about; the purpose of regression analysis is to take a purely theoretical equation like:

$$Y = \beta_0 + \beta_1 X_1 + \beta_2 X_2 + \epsilon \tag{2.1}$$

and use a set of data to create an estimated equation like:

$$\hat{Y} = \hat{\beta}_0 + \hat{\beta}_1 X_1 + \hat{\beta}_2 X_2 \tag{2.2}$$

where the caret indicates a sample estimate of the "true" population value (in the case of Y, the "true population value" is $E[Y|X_1$ and $X_2]$.) The purpose of the estimation technique is to obtain numerical values of the coefficients of an otherwise completely theoretical regression equation.

21

The most widely used method of obtaining these estimates (or "running" a regression) from a sample is called Ordinary Least Squares (OLS). **Ordinary Least Squares** chooses estimates of the βs by minimizing the sum of the squared differences between the actual Ys and the estimated Ys (the $\hat{Y}$s in Equation 2.2). OLS estimates have become so standard that the results from other techniques are almost never presented without OLS as a point of reference.

2.1.1 Why Use Ordinary Least Squares?

OLS is the most-used estimation technique today, but it is not the only readily available estimation technique. Why use OLS? The reasons for the popularity of OLS are many, but there are two that stand out. First, Ordinary Least Squares is the simplest of the estimation techniques. Most others are extensions of OLS or involve complicated nonlinear estimation formulas. Second, OLS is defined so as to minimize the summed squared residuals, which most researchers agree is an appropriate goal for an estimation technique. Since we are attempting to explain a dependent variable, given information about independent variables, it makes sense to attempt to minimize the residuals

$$e_i = Y_i - \hat{Y}_i \quad (i = 1, 2, \ldots, n) \tag{2.3}$$

in one way or another.

What criteria might you choose for an estimation technique to do this? Since our goal is to minimize the residuals, it would seem logical to simply add up the residuals and choose that set of $\hat{\beta}$s that minimizes them. Unfortunately, positive residuals and negative residuals cancel each other out, so that both wildly inaccurate estimates and very accurate estimates have net residuals that sum to zero.

Two alternatives that have been proposed to "minimize the residuals" are:

1. Minimize the summed absolute residuals.
2. Minimize the summed squared residuals.

Minimizing the summed absolute residuals gets rid of the positive and negative signs attached to the residuals, but it has problems as well. First, absolute values are difficult to work with mathematically, since some mathematical operations do not provide unambiguous answers. Second, summing the absolute residuals gives no extra weight to extraordinarily large residuals. This may be desired if the regression is meant to portray the majority of data, but quite often, it matters not at all if a number of estimates are off by a small amount, but it matters quite a bit if one estimate is off by a large amount. For example, consider the weight guessing equation of Chapter 1; you lost only if you missed the customer's weight by ten or more pounds. In such a circumstance, you would want a mechanism that helped avoid large residuals.

The second alternative, Ordinary Least Squares, yields the set of $\hat{\beta}$s that minimizes the summed squared residuals given a particular sample of data. Squared functions pose no unusual mathematical difficulties in terms of manipulations, and the technique avoids the cancelling of positive and negative signs, because squared terms are always positive. In addition, squaring gives greater weight to large residuals than it does to small ones (because e_i^2 is relatively larger as e_i increases). For example, one residual equal to 4.0 is more serious than two residuals equal to 2.0 if residuals are squared.

Ordinary Least Squares estimates have three beneficial characteristics:

1. The estimated regression line (Equation 2.2) goes through the means of Y and the Xs; that is, if you substitute the arithmetic means $\bar{Y}$, $\bar{X}_1$, and $\bar{X}_2$ into Equation 2.2, the equation holds *exactly.*

2. The sum of the residuals is exactly zero.

3. As we will see in Chapter 4, OLS can be shown to be "the best" estimator available under a set of fairly realistic assumptions.

2.1.2 How Does OLS Work?

Recall the definition of the residual from Equation 2.3, repeated for convenience:

$$e_i = Y_i - \hat{Y}_i \quad (i = 1, 2, \ldots, n) \tag{2.3}$$

OLS selects estimates $\hat{\beta}_0$, $\hat{\beta}_1$, . . . , $\hat{\beta}_K$ that minimize the sum of squared residuals, summed over all the sample data points:[1]

$$\sum_{i=1}^{n} e_i^2 = \sum_{i=1}^{n} (Y_i - \hat{Y}_i)^2 \tag{2.4}$$

However, since $\hat{Y}_i = \hat{\beta}_0 + \hat{\beta}_1 X_{1i} + \cdots + \hat{\beta}_K X_{Ki}$, OLS actually minimizes:

$$\Sigma e_i^2 = \Sigma(Y_i - \hat{\beta}_0 - \hat{\beta}_1 X_{1i} - \cdots - \hat{\beta}_K X_{Ki})^2 \tag{2.5}$$

by choosing the $\hat{\beta}$s that do so. In other words, OLS yields the $\hat{\beta}$s that minimize Equation 2.5. For an equation with just one independent variable, these coefficients are:

$$\hat{\beta}_1 = \sum_{i=1}^{n} [(X_i - \bar{X}) \cdot (Y_i - \bar{Y})] / \sum_{i=1}^{n} (X_i - \bar{X})^2 \tag{2.6}$$

and

$$\hat{\beta}_0 = \bar{Y} - \hat{\beta}_1 \bar{X} \tag{2.7}$$

(where $\bar{X}$ = the mean of X or $\Sigma X/n$, and $\bar{Y}$ = the mean of Y or $\Sigma Y/n$). For an equation with more than one independent variable, the equations are similar but a bit more complicated.[2]

The purpose of Ordinary Least Squares estimation is to provide the researcher with estimates of the regression coefficients that are capable of producing estimates of the dependent variable that are adequately close to the actual values of the dependent variables in the sample. A comparison of the estimated values with the sample values can help the researcher get a feeling for the adequacy of the hypothesized regression model.

Various statistical measures can be used to assess the degree to which the $\hat{Y}$s approximate the corresponding sample Ys, but all of them are based on the degree to which the regression equation estimated by OLS explains the values of Y better than a naive estimator, the sample mean, denoted by $\bar{Y}$. That is, econometricians used the squared variations of Y around its mean as a measure of the amount of variation to be explained by the regression; this computed quantity is usually called the **total sum of squares,** or TSS, and is written as:

$$TSS = \sum_{i=1}^{n}(Y_i - \bar{Y})^2 \tag{2.8}$$

Rewriting Equation 2.3 as $Y_i = \hat{Y}_i + e_i$, we can see that Y is equal to the estimated value of Y plus the residual (because the residual is defined as the difference between Y and $\hat{Y}$). Thus Equation 2.8 can be rewritten as:

$$TSS = \sum_i(Y_i - \bar{Y})^2 = \sum_i[(\hat{Y}_i - \bar{Y}) + e_i]^2 \tag{2.9}$$

$$= \sum_i(\hat{Y}_i - \bar{Y})^2 + \sum_i e_i^2 + 2\sum_i(\hat{Y}_i - \bar{Y})e_i$$

For the estimation techniques dealt with in this text, it can be shown that the last term of Equation 2.9 equals zero. Thus, a few manipulations have allowed us to decompose the total sum of squares into two components, that which can be explained by the regression and that which cannot:

$$\sum_i(Y_i - \bar{Y})^2 = \sum_i(\hat{Y}_i - \bar{Y})^2 + \sum_i e^2 \tag{2.10}$$

Total Sum of Squares (TSS)	=	Explained Sum of Squares (ESS)	+	Residual Sum of Squares (RSS)

This decomposition is usually called the "decomposition of variance" or the decomposition of the squared deviations of Y_i from its mean.

Figure 2.1 illustrates the decomposition of variance for the simple regression model. All estimated values of Y_i lie on the estimated regression line $\hat{Y}_i = \hat{\beta}_0 + \hat{\beta}_1X_i$. The sample mean of Y is denoted by the horizontal line at $\bar{Y}$. The total deviation of the actual value of Y_i from its sample mean value is decomposed into two components, the deviation of $\hat{Y}_i$ from the mean and the deviation of the actual value of Y_i from the fitted value $\hat{Y}_i$. Thus, the first component of Equation 2.10 measures the amount of the squared deviation of Y_i from its mean that is explained by the regression line. In Figure 2.1 the fitted value $\hat{Y}_i$ lies closer to the value of Y_i than does $\bar{Y}$, thus explaining in a purely empirical sense a portion of the squared deviation of Y_i from its mean. This component of the

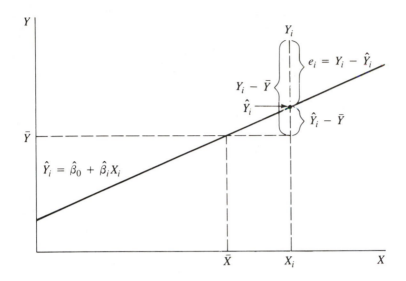

FIGURE 2.1 *Decomposition of the Variance in Y*
The variation of Y around its mean ($Y_i - \bar{Y}$) can be decomposed into two parts:
1. ($\hat{Y}_i - \bar{Y}$), the difference between the fitted value of Y ($\hat{Y}$) and the mean value of Y
($\bar{Y}$), and 2. ($Y_i - \hat{Y}_i$), the difference between the actual value of Y and the fitted value of
Y.

total sum of squared deviations, called the **explained sum of squares,** or ESS, is attributable to the fitted regression line.

The ESS is the explained portion of the total sum of squares. The unexplained portion, that is, unexplained in an empirical sense by the estimated regression equation, is called the **residual sum of squares** or RSS. Some authors denote the residual sum of squares with SSR and similarly replace TSS with SST and ESS with SSE, but the meanings are identical.

We can see from Equation 2.10 that the smaller the RSS is relative to the total sum of squares (TSS), the better the estimated regression line appears to fit the data. Thus, given the TSS, which no estimating technique can alter, researchers desire an estimating technique that minimizes the RSS and thus maximizes the ESS. That technique is OLS.

2.1.3   An Illustration of OLS Estimation

The equations specified for the calculation of regression coefficients by OLS computer programs might seem a little forbidding, but it is not hard to apply them yourself to datasets that have only a few observations and independent variables. While you will usually want to use regression software packages to do your estimation for you, you will understand OLS better if you work through the following illustration.

To keep things simple, let's attempt to estimate the regression coefficients of the height and weight data given in Section 1.3. For your convenience in following this illustration, the original data are reproduced in the spreadsheet in Table 2.1. As was noted in Section 2.1.2, the formulas for OLS estimation for a regression equation with one independent variable are:

$$\hat{\beta}_1 = \frac{\sum_{i=1}^{n} [(X_i - \bar{X}) \cdot (Y_i - \bar{Y})]}{\sum_{i=1}^{n} (X_i - \bar{X})^2} \tag{2.11}$$

$$\hat{\beta}_0 = \bar{Y} - \hat{\beta}_1 \bar{X} \tag{2.12}$$

If we undertake the calculations outlined in Table 2.1, and substitute them into Equations 2.11 and 2.12, we obtain the values:

$$\hat{\beta}_1 = \frac{590.20}{92.50} = 6.38$$

$$\hat{\beta}_0 = 169.4 - (6.38 \cdot 10.35) = 103.4$$

Table 2.1 The Calculation of Estimated Regression Coefficients for the Weight/Height Example

	Raw Data				Required Intermediate Calculations			
i (1)	Y_i (2)	X_i (3)	$(Y_i - \bar{Y})$ (4)	$(X_i - \bar{X})$ (5)	$(X_i - \bar{X})^2$ (6)	$(X_i - \bar{X}) \cdot (Y_i - \bar{Y})$ (7)	$\hat{Y}_i$ (8)	$e_i = Y_i - \hat{Y}_i$ (9)
1	140	5	−29.40	−5.35	28.62	157.29	135.3	4.7
2	157	9	−12.40	−1.35	1.82	16.74	160.8	−3.8
3	205	13	35.60	2.65	7.02	94.34	186.3	18.7
4	198	12	28.60	1.65	2.72	47.19	179.9	18.1
5	162	10	−7.40	−0.35	0.12	2.59	167.2	−5.2
6	174	11	4.60	0.65	0.42	2.99	173.6	0.4
7	150	8	−19.40	−2.35	5.52	45.59	154.4	−4.4
8	165	9	−4.40	−1.35	1.82	5.94	160.8	4.2
9	170	10	0.60	−0.35	0.12	−0.21	167.2	2.8
10	180	12	10.60	1.65	2.72	17.49	179.9	0.1
11	170	11	0.60	0.65	0.42	0.39	173.6	−3.6
12	162	9	−7.40	−1.35	1.82	9.99	160.8	1.2
13	165	10	−4.40	−0.35	0.12	1.54	167.2	2.8
14	180	12	10.60	1.65	2.72	17.49	179.9	0.1
15	160	8	−9.40	−2.35	5.52	22.09	154.4	5.6
16	155	9	−14.40	−1.35	1.82	19.44	160.8	−5.8
17	165	10	−4.40	−0.35	0.12	1.54	167.2	−2.2
18	190	15	20.60	4.65	21.62	95.79	199.1	−9.1
19	185	13	15.60	2.65	7.02	41.34	186.3	−1.3
20	155	11	−14.40	0.65	0.42	−9.36	173.6	−18.6
sum	3388	207	0.0	0.0	92.50	590.20	3388.3	−0.3
mean	169.4	10.35	0.0	0.0			169.4	0.0

If you compare these results, you will find that the manual calculation of the estimates of the coefficients yields exactly the same answers as the regression results summarized in Section 1.3. As can be seen in Table 2.1, the sum of the $\hat{Y}$s (column 8) equals the sum of the Ys (column 2), so that the sum of the residuals (column 9) equals zero (except for rounding). This result ($\Sigma e = 0$) is one of the properties of OLS estimates.

The figures in Table 2.1 can be used to derive values of the total sum of squares (TSS), the explained sum of squares (ESS), and the residual sum of squares (RSS). The total sum of squares equals $\Sigma(Y_i - \bar{Y})^2$, or the sum of the square of the values in column four, which equals 5,065. The explained sum of squares equals $\Sigma(\hat{Y}_i - \bar{Y})^2$, or the sum of the squared differences between the values in columns eight and two, which equals 3,765. The residual sum of squares Σe_i^2, is the sum of the square of the values in column nine, which equals 1,305. Note that TSS = ESS + RSS except for rounding.[3] For practice in the use of these concepts, see Exercise 4.

2.2   Evaluating the Overall Fit of the Estimated Model

Once the data on Y and the Xs are collected and the computer estimates of the coefficients have been obtained, the researcher must evaluate the results. There are two general questions in this evaluation process:

1. How well do the estimated coefficients conform to the researcher's expectations developed before the data were collected?

2. How well does the regression as a whole fit the data?

This section will deal with the second of these general questions, while the first will be investigated in Chapters 5 and 6.

In practice, a number of different regression models are sometimes specified and compared. These may differ from one another with respect to the independent variables included, the functional form of the equation, or the portion of the data set sampled. In general, it is good to avoid estimating numerous alternative models, because the final estimated equation can be dramatically influenced by which other equations have been estimated, tested, and compared. In addition, the more equations compared before the final model is chosen, the less statistically significant the results will be. The usual justification for estimating alternative models is that since the data contain information from the true economic model, the researcher should be able to discern the appropriate model from the inappropriate ones by comparing the properties of the alternative estimated equations. We can never be truly sure that one estimated model represents the truth any more than another one, but practically speaking, evaluating regression results is still essential to the choice of a particular formulation of the regression model. The second criterion for regression results is the quality of the fit of the equation, and the simplest commonly used measure of that fit is the coefficient of determination, R^2.

2.2.1 R^2, The Coefficient of Determination

An estimated regression equation should be capable of explaining the sample observations of the dependent variable Y with some degree of accuracy. That is, the better the fit of the equation, the closer the estimated Y will be to the actual Y.

The **coefficient of determination** is the ratio of the explained sum of squares to the total sum of squares:

$$R^2 = \frac{ESS}{TSS} = 1 - \frac{RSS}{TSS} = 1 - \frac{\Sigma e^2_i}{\Sigma (Y_i - \bar{Y})^2} \qquad (2.13)$$

The higher R^2 is, the closer the estimated regression equation fits the sample data; measures of this type are called "goodness of fit" measures. Since TSS, RSS, and ESS are all non-negative (being squared deviations), and since ESS $\leq$ TSS, R^2 must lie in the interval

$$0 \leq R^2 \leq 1 \qquad (2.14)$$

A value of R^2 close to one shows a "good" overall fit, whereas a value near zero shows a failure of the estimated regression equation to explain the values of Y_i better than could be explained by the sample mean $\bar{Y}$. In words, R^2 can be defined as the percentage of the variation of Y around $\bar{Y}$ that is explained by the regression equation. Since OLS selects the parameter estimates that minimize RSS, OLS provides the largest possible R^2, given the linear specification of the model.

Figures 2.2 through 2.4 demonstrate some extremes. Figure 2.2 shows X and Y that are related in a curvilinear fashion but not in a linear one. Thus, the fitted regression line might be $Y = \bar{Y}$, the same value it would have if X were omitted. As a result, the estimated linear regression is no better than the sample mean as an estimate of Y_i. The explained portion ESS = 0, and the unexplained portion RSS equals the total squared deviations TSS; thus, $R^2 = 0$. In this case, the residuals are large relative to the deviations in Y from its mean, implying that a regression line is not useful in describing the relationship between X and Y.

Figure 2.3 shows a relationship between X and Y that can be quite adequately "explained" by a linear regression equation: the value of R^2 is .95. This kind of result is typical of a time-series regression with a "good fit." Much of the variation has been explained, but there still remains a portion of the variation that is essentially random or unexplained by the model. "Goodness of fit" is relative to the topic being studied. If the sample is **cross-sectional,** that is, consisting of observations of many individuals, countries, or states for the same time period, an R^2 of .50 might be considered a good fit. In other words, there is no simple method of determining how high R^2 must be for the fit to be considered satisfactory. Instead, knowing when R^2 is relatively large or small is a matter of experience.

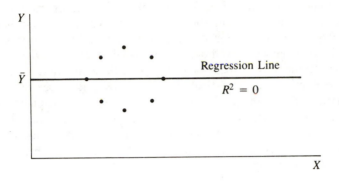

FIGURE 2.2
X and Y are related in a circular pattern; in such a case, R^2 would be 0.

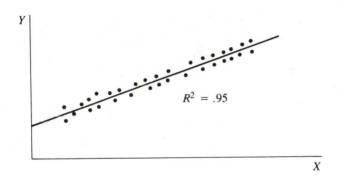

FIGURE 2.3
A set of data for X and Y that can be adequately explained with a regression line
($R^2 = .95$).

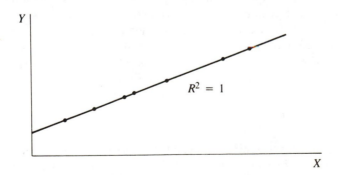

FIGURE 2.4
A perfect fit: all the data points are on the regression line, and the resulting R^2 is 1.

Figure 2.4 shows a perfect fit $R^2 = 1$. Such a fit implies that no estimation is required; the relationship is completely deterministic. In fact, reported equations with R^2s equal to (or very near) one should be viewed with suspicion; they very likely do not explain the movements of the dependent variable Y in terms of the causal proposition advanced even though they explain them empirically.

While the R^2 is a measure of the overall degree of fit, a slightly modified version, called the F-ratio, is a "statistical test" of the overall degree of fit of the estimated equation. The term "statistical test" is explained in Chapter 5, but for the application here, it can be briefly defined as a procedure by which the researcher can accept or reject the overall equation based on its ability to empirically explain the total sum of squares. The following is a rather mechanical explanation of how to use the F-ratio.

The **F-ratio** is defined as:

$$F = \frac{ESS/(K)}{RSS/(n - K - 1)} = \frac{\Sigma(\hat{Y}_i - \bar{Y})^2/(K)}{\Sigma e_i^2/(n - K - 1)} \tag{2.15}$$

It is the ratio of the explained to the unexplained portions of the total sum of squares, adjusted for the number of independent variables (K) and the number of observations in the sample (n). When the value of F is high, the estimated regression equation provides an adequate statistical explanation of the overall deviations of Y_i from $\bar{Y}$ (since ESS is large relative to RSS). The overall fit of the equation is considered statistically acceptable only if the computed value of the F-ratio is greater than a "critical value" found in the table of F-values (see Tables B-2 and B-3). Further discussion of the F-statistic is contained in Section 5.8; Exercises 6 and 7 contain examples of the use of the F-ratio.

2.2.2 $\bar{R}^2$, the Adjusted R^2

A problem with R^2 is that adding another independent variable to a particular equation can never decrease R^2. That is, if you compare two regressions that are identical in every way (same dependent variable and independent variables) except that one has an additional independent variable, the equation with the greater number of independent variables will always have a better (or equal) fit as measured by R^2. To see this, remember the equation for R^2:

$$R^2 = 1 - \frac{RSS}{TSS} = 1 - \frac{\Sigma e_i^2}{\Sigma(Y_i - \bar{Y})^2} \tag{2.16}$$

Since the dependent variable has not changed, TSS is still the same, and since most estimating techniques ensure that adding a variable will not increase the summed squared residuals, RSS will only decrease or stay the same. If RSS decreases, RSS/TSS will also decrease, and $1 - RSS/TSS$ will increase. Thus adding a variable to an equation virtually guarantees that R^2 will increase.[4]

Perhaps an example will make this clear. Let's return to our weight guessing regression (repeated below for convenience):

Estimated weight = 103.40 + 6.38 · (height over five feet)

The R^2 for this equation is .74. If we now add a completely nonsensical variable to the equation (say, the campus post office box number of each individual in question), then it turns out that the results become:

Estimated weight = 102.35 + 6.36 · (height over five feet) + 0.02 · (box#)

but the R^2 for this equation is .75! Thus an individual using R^2 alone as a measure of the quality of the fit of the regression would choose the second version as better fitting.

Besides adding a nonsensical variable, the inclusion of another variable requires the estimation of another coefficient. This lessens the **degrees of freedom,** or the excess of the number of observations (n) over the number of coefficients (including the intercept) estimated (K + 1). For instance, when the campus box number variable is added to the weight/height example, the number of observations stays constant at 20, but the number of estimated coefficients increases from two to three, so the number of degrees of freedom falls from 18 to 17. This decrease has a cost, since the lower the degrees of freedom, the less reliable the estimates are likely to be, thus the increase in the quality of the fit caused by the addition of a variable needs to be compared to the decrease in the degrees of freedom before a decision can be made with respect to the statistical impact of the added variable.

To incorporate the impact of changes in the number of independent variables, it is necessary to use $\bar{R}^2$ (pronounced R-Bar-Squared), which is R^2 adjusted for the degrees of freedom:

$$\bar{R}^2 = 1 - \frac{RSS/(n-K-1)}{TSS/(n-1)} = 1 - \frac{\Sigma e_i^2/(n-K-1)}{\Sigma(Y_i-\bar{Y})^2/(n-1)} \qquad (2.17)$$

Notice that the only difference between R^2 and $\bar{R}^2$ is that the latter has been adjusted to take account of the K degrees of freedom that were lost in the calculations of the estimated slope coefficients. As a result, it is no surprise to learn that one can be expressed in terms of the other. If we substitute Equation 2.16 into Equation 2.17, it turns out that $\bar{R}^2$ can be expressed as a function of R^2:

$$\bar{R}^2 = 1 - (1 - R^2) \cdot \frac{(n-1)}{(n-K-1)} \qquad (2.18)$$

$\bar{R}^2$ will increase, decrease, or stay the same when a variable is added to an equation depending on whether the improvement in fit caused by the addition of the new variable outweighs the loss of the degree of freedom. Indeed, the $\bar{R}^2$ for the weight guessing equation *decreases* from .73 to .72 when the mail box variable is added. The mail box variable, since it has no theoretical relation to weight, should not have been included in the equation, and the $\bar{R}^2$ measure supports this conclusion. Empirically, $\bar{R}^2$ can be used to compare the fits of equations with the same dependent variable and different numbers of independent variables. Because of this property, most researchers automatically use $\bar{R}^2$ instead of R^2 when evaluating the fit of their estimated regression equations; in fact, $\bar{R}^2$ has become so popular that it replaces R^2 in most reported regression results.

Finally, a warning is in order. Always remember that the quality of fit of an estimated equation is only one measure of the overall quality of that regression. As mentioned above, the degree to which the estimated coefficients conform to economic theory and the researcher's previous expectations about those coefficients are just as important as if not more important than the fit itself. For instance, an estimated equation with a good fit but with an implausible sign for an estimated coefficient might give implausible predictions and thus not be a very useful equation. Other factors, such as theoretical relevance and usefulness, also come into play. To help avoid the natural urge to maximize $\bar{R}^2$ without regard to the rest of the equation, you might find it useful to imagine the following conversation:

YOU: Sometimes I wish I could play the game of maximizing $\bar{R}^2$, that is, choosing the model that gives the highest $\bar{R}^2$.

YOUR CONSCIENCE: But that would be wrong.

YOU: I know that the goal of regression analysis is to obtain dependable estimates of the true population coefficients and not to get a high $\bar{R}^2$, but my results "look better" if my fit is good.

YOUR CONSCIENCE: Look better to whom? It's not at all unusual to get a high $\bar{R}^2$ but find that some of the regression coefficients have signs that are contrary to theoretical expectations.

YOU: Well, I guess I should be more concerned with the logical relevance of the explanatory variables than with the fit, huh?

YOUR CONSCIENCE: Right! If in this process we obtain a high $\bar{R}^2$, well and good, but if $\bar{R}^2$ is high, it doesn't mean that the model is good.

YOU: Amen.

2.3   An Example of the Misuse of $\bar{R}^2$

Perhaps the best way to visualize the dangers inherent in attempting to maximize $\bar{R}^2$ without regard to the economic meaning or statistical significance of an equation is to look at an example of such misuse. This is important because it is one thing for a researcher to agree in theory that "$\bar{R}^2$ maximizing" is bad, and it is another thing entirely for that researcher to be able to avoid trying subconsciously to maximize $\bar{R}^2$ on his or her own projects. It is easy to agree that the goal of regression is not to maximize $\bar{R}^2$, but many people find it hard to resist that temptation.

As an example, assume that you have been hired by the State of California to help the legislature evaluate a bill to provide more water to Southern California. This issue is important because a decision must be made on whether or not to ruin, through a system of dams, one of the state's best trout fishing areas. On one side of the issue are Southern Californians who claim that their desert-like environment requires more water, and on the other side of the issue are outdoors-lovers and environmentalists who want to retain the natural beauty for which California is famous. Your job is to forecast the amount of water demanded in Los Angeles County, the biggest user of water in the state.

Because the bill is about to come before the state legislature, you are forced to choose between two regressions that have already been run for you, one by the state econometrician and the other by an independent consultant.[5] You will base your forecast on one of these two equations:

The state econometrician's equation:

$$\hat{W} = 24{,}000 + 48{,}000PR + 0.40P - 370RF \qquad (2.19)$$
$$\bar{R}^2 = .859 \quad DF = 25 \ (\text{Annual: } 1950\text{-}1978)$$

The independent consultant's equation:

$$\hat{W} = 30{,}000 + 0.62P - 400RF \qquad (2.20)$$
$$\bar{R}^2 = .847 \quad DF = 26$$

where: W = the total amount of water consumed in L.A. County in a given year (measured in millions of gallons)

    PR = the price of a gallon of water that year (measured in real dollars)

    P = the population in L.A. County that year

    RF = the amount of rainfall that year (measured in inches)

    DF = degrees of freedom, which equal the number of observations (n = 29, since the years in the sample are 1950 through 1978) minus the number of coefficients estimated.

Look over these two equations carefully before going on with the rest of the section. What do you think the arguments of the state econometrician were for using his equation? What case did the independent econometrician make for her work?

The question is whether or not the increased $\bar{R}^2$ is worth the unexpected sign in the price of water coefficient in Equation 2.19. The state econometrician argued that given the better fit of his equation, it would do a better job of forecasting water demand. The independent consultant argued that it did not make sense to expect that an increase in price in the future would, holding the other variables in the equation constant, increase the quantity of water demanded in Los Angeles. Given the unexpected sign of the coefficient, she argued, it seemed much more likely that the demand for water was unrelated to price during the sample period or that some important variable (such as real per capita income) had been left out of both equations. Since the price of water was fairly low in comparison to other expenditures during the sample years, she pointed out, it was possible that the demand for water was fairly price-inelastic. The economic argument for the positive sign observed by the state econometrician is difficult to make; it implies that as the price of water goes up, so too does the quantity of water demanded.

Was this argument simply academic? The answer, unfortunately, is no, because if a forecast is made with Equation 2.19, it will tend to overforecast water demand in scenarios that foresee rapidly rising prices and underforecast water demand otherwise. In essence, the equation with the better fit would do a worse job of forecasting![6]

Thus, a researcher who uses $\bar{R}^2$ as the sole measure of the quality of an equation (at the expense of economic theory or statistical significance) increases the chances of ending up with an unrepresentative or misleading result. This practice should be avoided at all costs. No simple rule of econometric estimation is likely to work in all cases. Instead, a combination of theoretical competence, ethics, and common sense makes a good econometrician.

2.4 Summary

1. Ordinary Least Squares (OLS) is the most frequently used method of obtaining estimates of the regression coefficients from a set of data. OLS chooses those $\hat{\beta}$s that minimize the summed squared residuals (Σe_i^2) for a particular sample.

2. The coefficient of determination, R^2, is the simplest measure of the degree of statistical fit of an estimated equation. It can be thought of as the percentage of the variation of Y around its mean that has been explained by a particular regression equation and is defined as the explained sum of squares (ESS) divided by the total sum of squares (TSS). A major fault of R^2 is that it always increases (technically, never decreases) when a variable is added to an equation.

3. R-bar-squared ($\bar{R}^2$) is the coefficient of determination (R^2) adjusted for degrees of freedom. $\bar{R}^2$ increases when a variable is added to an equation only if the improvement in fit caused by the addition of the new variable more than offsets the loss of the degree of freedom that is used up in estimating the coefficients of the new variable. As a result, most researchers will automatically use $\bar{R}^2$ instead of R^2 when evaluating the fit of their estimated regression equations.

4. Always remember that the quality of fit of an estimated equation is only one of the measures of the overall quality of that regression. The degree to which the estimated coefficients conform to economic theory and expectations developed by the researcher before the data were collected are at least as important as the size of $\bar{R}^2$ itself.

Exercises

(Answers to even-numbered exercises are in Appendix A.)

1. Write out the meaning of each of the following terms without reference to the book (or your notes) and then compare your definition with the version in the text for each:
   a. ordinary least squares
   b. F-ratio
   c. total, explained, and residual sum of squares
   d. coefficient of determination
   e. degrees of freedom
   f. $\bar{R}^2$

2. It turns out that the F-ratio can be expressed as a function of R^2.
   a. As an exercise in learning to use these two concepts, substitute Equation 2.13 into Equation 2.15 to derive the exact relationship between F and R^2.
   b. If one can be expressed as a function of the other, why do we need both? What reason is there for computer regression packages to typically print out both R^2 and the F-ratio?

3. What's wrong with this kind of thinking?
   "I understand why R^2 is a bad measure of the quality of a regression equation; it always increases when a variable is added to the equation. Once we adjust for degrees of freedom by using $\bar{R}^2$, though, it seems to me that the higher the $\bar{R}^2$, the better the equation!"

4. Just as you are about to estimate a regression project (due tomorrow), massive sunspots cause magnetic interference that ruins all electrically powered machines (e.g., computers and calculators). Instead of giving up and flunking, you decide to calculate estimates from your data (on per capita income in thousands of U.S. dollars as a function of the percent of the labor force in agriculture in 10 developed countries in 1981) using methods like those used in Section 2.1.3 *without* a computer or calculator. Your data are:

Country	A	B	C	D	E	F	G	H	I	J
Income	6	8	8	7	7	12	9	8	9	10
Percent on Farms	9	10	8	7	10	4	5	5	6	7

   a. Calculate $\hat{\beta}_0$ and $\hat{\beta}_1$
   b. Calculate R^2, $\bar{R}^2$, and the F-ratio
   c. If the percentage of the labor force in agriculture in another developed country was 8 percent, what level of per capita income (in thousands of U.S. dollars) would you guess that country had?

5. Suppose that you have been asked to estimate an econometric model to explain the number of people jogging a mile or more on the school track in order to help decide whether to build a second track to handle all the "fitness craze" joggers. You collect data by living in the press box for all of the spring term, and you run two possible explanatory equations.

$$\text{Equation A:} \quad \hat{Y} = 125.0 - 15.0X_1 - 1.0X_2 + 1.5X_3 \quad \bar{R}^2 = .75$$

$$\text{Equation B:} \quad \hat{Y} = 123.0 - 14.0X_1 + 5.5X_2 - 3.7X_4 \quad \bar{R}^2 = .73$$

where: Y = the number of joggers on a given day
X_1 = inches of rain that day
X_2 = hours of sunshine that day
X_3 = high temperature for that day (in degrees F)
X_4 = the number of classes with term papers due the next day

a. Which of the two (admittedly hypothetical) equations do you prefer? Why?
b. How is it possible to get different estimated signs for the coefficient of the same variable using the same data?

6. *(Optional)* Test the overall significance of the Magic Flag Farm weight/height estimated equation in Section 1.3 by using the F-ratio and Statistical Table B-2 in the back of the book. (Hint: The first step is to calculate the F-ratio from the information given in Table 1.1, and the second step is to compare that number with the 5 percent critical F-value in Statistical Table B-2 for one degree of freedom in the numerator and 18 degrees of freedom in the denominator. For further hints, see the answer in the back of the book and the description that accompanies Table B-2).

7. *(Optional)* Test the overall significance of equations that have the following F-values the same way you did in Exercise 6 (Using Statistical Table B-2):
a. $F = 5.63$ with 4 degrees of freedom in the numerator and 30 degrees of freedom in the denominator
b. $F = 1.53$ with 3 degrees of freedom in the numerator and 24 degrees of freedom in the denominator
c. $F = 57.84$ with 5 degrees of freedom in the numerator and 60 degrees of freedom in the denominator

8. David Katz[7] studied faculty salaries as a function of their "productivity" and estimated a regression equation that had the following coefficients:

$$\hat{S}_i = 11,155 + 230B_i + 18A_i + 102E_i + 489D_i + 189Y_i + \ldots$$

where: S_i = the salary of the ith professor in 1969-70 in dollars per year
B_i = the number of books published, lifetime
A_i = the number of articles published, lifetime

E_i = the number of "excellent" articles published, lifetime
D_i = the number of dissertations supervised since 1964
Y_i = the number of years teaching experience

a. Do the signs of the coefficients match your prior expectations?
b. Do the relative sizes of the coefficients seem reasonable?
c. Suppose a professor had just enough time (after teaching, etc.) to either write a book or write two excellent articles or supervise three dissertations, which would you recommend? Why?
d. Would you like to reconsider your answer to Part b above? Which coefficient seems out of line? What explanation can you give for that result? Is the equation in some sense invalid? Why or why not?

[1.] The summation symbol, Σ, means that all terms to its right should be added up (or summed) over the range of the i values attached to the bottom and top of the symbol. In Equation 2.4, for example, this would mean adding up e_i^2 for all integer values between 1 and n:

$$\sum_{i=1}^{n} e_i^2 = e_1^2 + e_2^2 + \cdots + e_n^2$$

Often, the Σ notation is simply written as $\sum_i$, as in Equation 2.9, and it is assumed that the summation is over all observations from i = 1 to i = n. Sometimes, the i is omitted entirely, as in Note 2, and the same assumption is made implicitly.

[2.] For the case in which there are two independent variables, X_1 and X_2, these equations are:

$$\hat{\beta}_1 = \frac{(\Sigma y_i x_{1i})\,(\Sigma x_{2i}^2) - (\Sigma y_i x_{2i})\,(\Sigma x_{1i} x_{2i})}{(\Sigma x_{1i}^2)\,(\Sigma x_{2i}^2) - (\Sigma x_{1i} x_{2i})^2}$$

$$\hat{\beta}_2 = \frac{(\Sigma y_i x_{2i})\,(\Sigma x_{1i}^2) - (\Sigma y_i x_{1i})\,(\Sigma x_{1i} x_{2i})}{(\Sigma x_{1i}^2)\,(\Sigma x_{2i}^2) - (\Sigma x_{1i} x_{2i})^2}$$

where $y_i = Y_i - \bar{Y}$, $x_{1i} = X_{1i} - \bar{X}_1$, $x_{2i} = X_{2i} - \bar{X}_2$

(This is called the deviations-from-the-mean form of the variables)

and $\hat{\beta}_0 = \bar{Y} - \hat{\beta}_1 \bar{X}_1 - \hat{\beta}_2 \bar{X}_2$ as in Equation 2.7.

[3.] If there is no constant term in the equation, TSS will not necessarily equal ESS + RSS, nor will Σe necessarily equal zero. This will be covered in more detail in Section 7.4. Also, note that some authors use different definitions of TSS, RSS, and ESS or reverse the order of the letters, as in SSR.

[4.] You know that RSS will never decrease, because the OLS program could always set the coefficient of the added variable equal to zero, thus giving the same fit as the previous equation. The coefficient of the newly added variable being zero is the only circumstance in which R^2 will stay the same when a variable is added. Otherwise, R^2 will always increase when a variable is added to an equation.

[5.] The principle involved in this section is precisely the same one that was discussed during the actual research, but these coefficients are hypothetical, because the complexities of the real equation are irrelevant to our points.

[6.] A couple of caveats to this example are in order. First, the purpose of the rainfall variable in both equations was to explain past behavior. For forecasting purposes, average rainfall figures would likely be used. Second, the income variable suggested by the independent consultant turned out to have a relatively small coefficient because water expenditure is so minor in relation to the overall budget that the demand for water turned out to be fairly income-inelastic as well as fairly price-inelastic.

[7.] David A. Katz, "Faculty Salaries, Promotions, and Productivity at a Large University," *American Economic Review*, June 1973, pp. 469-477.

3

**Learning To Use
Regression Analysis**

3.1 The Measurement of Variables

3.2 Steps in Applied Regression

3.3 A More Complete Example of Applied Regression Analysis

3.4 Summary and Exercises

From a quick reading of Chapter 2, it would be easy to conclude that regression analysis is little more than the mechanical application of a set of equations (for coefficient estimation and $\bar{R}^2$ calculation) to a sample of data. Such a notion would be similar to deciding that all there is to golf is hitting a ball with a club. Just as golfers will tell you that hitting the ball is often less important than choosing the right club, direction, and type of swing, so will experienced econometricians speak less about the actual OLS estimation of an equation than about a number of other factors. Our goal in this chapter is to introduce some of those "real-world" concerns.

The first section focuses on the measurement of variables. Data collection, though usually frustrating and time-consuming, is seldom theoretically difficult, but a few generalizations about problems that do tend to come up frequently will save the reader time and effort later. This section is followed by an overview of the steps typically taken by researchers engaged in applied regression analysis. The purpose of suggesting these steps is not to discourage any researchers from using innovative or unusual approaches but rather to develop in the reader a sense of how regression is ordinarily done by professional economists and business analysts. The chapter concludes with a more complete example of applied regression analysis, a study of location analysis for the "Woody's" restaurant chain that is based on actual company data and to which we will return in future chapters to apply new tests and ideas.

3.1 The Measurement of Variables

Before any quantitative analysis can be done, data must be defined, collected, organized, and entered into a computer. Usually, this is a time-consuming and frustrating task because of the difficulty of finding data, definitional differences between theoretical variables and their empirical counterparts, and printing or typing errors. After some effort, though, a diligent researcher can usually find satisfactory data. In at least three cases, however, normal data collection techniques do not work. Instead, the methods of theoretically specified variables, proxy variables, or dummy variables are used.

3.1.1 Theoretically Specified Variables

In one sense, every variable in a regression is theoretically specified, since theory helps determine which variables belong in a given equation. In some instances, however, theory can also provide insights into how the variables themselves should be measured.

For example, if the dependent variable is the quantity of television sets demanded per year, then most independent variables should be measured annually as well. It would be inappropriate and possibly misleading to define the price of TVs as the price from a particular month; an average of prices over the year (usually weighted by the number of TVs sold per month) would be more meaningful. If the dependent variable includes all TV sets sold regardless of brand, then the price would appropriately be an aggregate based on prices of all brands. Calculating such aggregate variables, however, is not straightforward. The researcher typically makes his or her best effort to compute the respective aggregate variables and then acknowledges that problems may still remain. If the price data for all the various brands are not available, for example, the researcher may be forced to compromise and use the prices of one or a few of the major brands as a substitute for the proper aggregate price.

Another issue is suggested by the TV example. Over the years of the sample, it is likely that the market shares of particular kinds of TV sets have changed. For example, 19-inch color TV sets might have made up a majority of the market in one decade, while 13-inch black and white sets might have been the favorite ten years before. In cases like these where the composition of the market share, the size, or the quality of the various brands might have changed over time, it would make little sense to measure the dependent variable as the number of TV sets because a "TV set" from one year might have little in common with a "TV set" from another. The approach usually taken to deal with this issue is to measure the variable in dollar terms, under the assumption that value encompasses size and quality. Thus we would work with the dollar sales of TVs rather than the number of sets sold. Most often, it is best to state the variables in "real" (constant dollar) terms by selecting an appropriate price deflator, such as the Consumer Price Index, and adjusting the money (or nominal) value of sales by it.

As an example, the appropriate price index for Gross National Product is called the GNP deflator. Real GNP is calculated by multiplying money GNP by the ratio of the GNP deflator from the base year to the GNP deflator from the current year:

Real GNP = money GNP $\cdot$ (base year GNP deflator/current year GNP deflator)

In 1981, U.S. money GNP was $2925 billion and the GNP deflator (for a base year of 1972 = 100) was 193.7, so real GNP was:

$$\text{Real GNP} = \$2925 \cdot (100/193.7) = \$1510 \text{ billion}$$

That is, the goods and services produced in 1981 were worth $2925 billion if 1981 prices were used but only $1510 billion if 1972 prices were used.

Often in applied regression analysis, observations come from a cross-section instead of a time series. In a **cross-section,** all observations are from the same point in time and refer to different economic entities, such as people or countries. In a **time series,** the data are chronologically ordered observations from different time periods, such as months or years, for the same economic entity. Because of the distinction between time series and cross-sections, models must be constructed differently depending on the data used. The primary difference is that appropriate definitions of the independent variables often depend on whether the sample is a time series or a cross-section. To understand this, consider the TV set example once again. A time series model might study the sales of TV sets in the United States from 1950 to 1980, while a cross-sectional study might study the sales of TV sets by state for 1980. The time series data set would have 31 observations, each of which would refer to a particular year, while the cross-sectional data set would have 50 observations, each of which would refer to a particular state. A variable that might be appropriate for the time series model might be completely inappropriate for the cross-section model and vice versa; at the very least, it would have to be measured differently. National advertising in a particular year would be appropriate for the time-series model, for example, while 1980 advertising in or near each particular state would make more sense for the cross-sectional one.

3.1.2   Proxies

It sometimes happens that data for a theoretically relevant variable are not available. In such cases a **proxy variable** is often used. Proxy variables substitute for theoretically desired variables when data on the desired variables are incomplete or missing altogether. For example, the value of net investment is a variable that is not directly measured in a number of countries. As a result, a researcher might use an estimate of the value of gross investment as a proxy, the assumption being that the value of gross investment is directly proportional to the value of net investment. This proportionality (which is similar to a change in units) is all that is required because the regression analyzes the relationship between changes among variables, rather than the absolute levels of the variables.

In general, a proxy variable is a "good" proxy when its movements correspond relatively well to movements in the theoretically correct variable. Since the latter is unobservable whenever a proxy must be used, there is usually no easy way to examine a proxy's "goodness" directly. Instead, the researcher must document as well as possible why the proxy is likely to be a good or bad one. In some cases, proxies are admittedly of poor quality, but they are the only quantitative measures available and are used with the appropriate caveats being stated. Poor proxies and variables with large measurement errors constitute "bad" data. The degree to which the data are bad is a matter of judgment by the individual researcher.

In fact, a good regression project may be thwarted by the lack of adequate data. In many cases, even the simplest of regression techniques may not be appropriate, because the information is inaccurate. Sometimes it is measured with so much error that the researcher should only compose tables or graphs and make general inferences from these. By the way, tables and graphs are generally very useful adjuncts to the documentation of regression equations.

3.1.3 Dummy Variables

Some variables (for example, gender) defy explicit quantification and can only be expressed in a qualitative manner. One of the most common ways such variables are quantified is by binary or dummy variables. **Dummy variables** take on the values one or zero depending on whether some condition does or does not occur. The basic use of these variables is presented here; some frequently used extensions are discussed in Chapter 7.

As an illustration, suppose that Y_i represents the salary of the ith high school teacher, and that this depends primarily on the type of degree earned and the experience of the teacher. All teachers have a B.A., but some have an M.A. in addition. An equation representing the relationship between earnings and the type of degree might be:

$$Y_i = \beta_0 + \beta_1 X_{1i} + \beta_2 X_{2i} + \epsilon_i \qquad (3.1)$$

where: $X_{1i} = \begin{cases} 1 \text{ if the } i\text{th teacher has an M.A.} \\ 0 \text{ otherwise} \end{cases} \qquad (3.2)$

$X_{2i} = $ number of years teaching experience of the ith teacher

The variable X_1 only takes on values of zero or one. The variable X_1 is called a dummy variable, or just a dummy. Needless to say, the term has generated many a pun. In this case, the dummy variable represents the condition of having a Master's degree.

The coefficients of this regression equation are interpreted as follows:

(1) If the teacher has a B.A. only, X_1 is zero, and

$$E(Y_i|X_1) = \beta_0 + \beta_2 X_{2i} \qquad (3.3)$$

If the teacher has no experience, the coefficient β_0 equals $E(Y_i|X_1)$, so β_0 can be interpreted as the expected (or average) starting salary with a B.A. if no other variable besides X_2 belongs in the equation.

(2) If the teacher has an M.A., X_1 equals one, and

$$E(Y_i|X_1) = \beta_0 + \beta_1 + \beta_2 X_{2i} \qquad (3.4)$$

Thus, $\beta_0 + \beta_1$ is the expected starting salary for a teacher with an M.A.

Comparing these two equations, β_1 represents the additional average earnings gained by having the Master's degree as compared to the Bachelor's degree, holding experience constant. This interpretation is important because it allows the researcher to formulate an expectation concerning the sign of β_1 prior to estimation, and the ability to postulate the signs of coefficients is essential to regression analysis. Such a dummy variable is called an *intercept dummy* because it actually changes the intercept of the regression depending on whether or not the teacher in question has a Master's degree. Figure 3.1 shows this relationship graphically.

An alternative formulation of the regression model (Equation 3.1) would be to define X_{1i} as:

$$X_{1i} = \begin{cases} 0 \text{ if the } i\text{th teacher has an M.A.} \\ 1 \text{ otherwise} \end{cases} \qquad (3.5)$$

That is, the conditions are turned around. In this case, β_1 would be interpreted as the difference between the average earnings of a B.A. and those of an M.A., and its sign would be expected to be negative. While the β_1 of the redefined variable would have the opposite sign, it would have the same absolute magnitude as the β_1 of the original variable in Equation 3.1. The reason is that the two βs are measuring exactly the same thing (but in opposite directions). The definitions of dummy variables are, in this sense, arbitrary. Once they have been defined, though, only one interpretation can be placed on them. That is, in Equation 3.2, β_1 is expected to be positive while in Equation 3.5, β_1 is expected to be negative, although they have the same absolute magnitude. This works for estimated as well as theoretical models.

In general, one fewer dummy variable is constructed than conditions. The event not explicitly represented by a dummy variable, the **omitted condition,** forms the basis against which the included conditions are compared. Thus, for dual situations (e.g., B.A. and M.A.), only one variable is entered as an independent variable; the coefficient is interpreted as the effect of the included condition relative to the omitted condition. If a third condition (such as neither having a B.A. nor an M.A.) is to be included, then only two dummy variables should be used.

Beginners often err by including as many dummy variables as conditions, but such a model is useless because the dummies add up to a constant, which is perfectly multicollinear with the intercept term already in the equation. **Perfect multicollinearity** is defined as an exact linear relationship among some or all of the explanatory variables. This occurs because the sum of the three dummy variables (if there are only three conditions) equals one for each observation in the data set. Computer regression programs will produce no output under perfect multicollinearity unless there is rounding error.

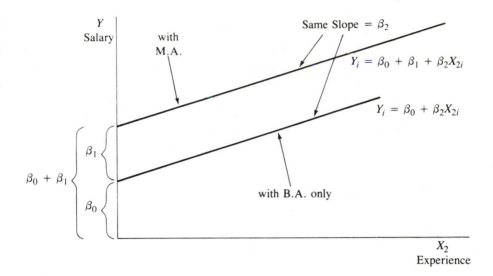

FIGURE 3.1 *Graphical Interpretation of an Intercept Dummy Variable (X_1)*
An intercept dummy changes the intercept of the regression equation depending on
whether the qualitative condition specified by the dummy variable is met. The difference
between the two intercepts is the estimated coefficient of the dummy variable.

Sometimes researchers use dummy variables to account for large deviations
(residuals) in the fitted model, but such a practice amounts to trying to maximize
$\bar{R}^2$ because such variables are not justified by theory and should be avoided.
Also, a dummy variable that has only a single observation with a value of one
while the rest of the observations are zeroes (or vice versa) is to be avoided even
if the variable is suggested by theory. Such a "one-time dummy" acts merely to
eliminate that observation from the data set, artificially improving the fit by setting the dummy's coefficient equal to the residual for that observation. One would
obtain exactly the same estimates of the other coefficients if that observation were
deleted, but the deletion of an observation is rarely if ever appropriate.

Sometimes dummy variables are used to account for seasonal variation in the
data in time-series models. For example:

$$X_{1t} = \begin{cases} 1 \text{ in quarter 1} \\ 0 \text{ otherwise} \end{cases} \tag{3.6}$$

$$X_{2t} = \begin{cases} 1 \text{ in quarter 2} \\ 0 \text{ otherwise} \end{cases} \tag{3.7}$$

$$X_{3t} = \begin{cases} 1 \text{ in quarter 3} \\ 0 \text{ otherwise} \end{cases} \tag{3.8}$$

in an equation

$$Y_t = \beta_0 + \beta_1 X_{1t} + \beta_2 X_{2t} + \beta_3 X_{3t} + \beta_4 X_{4t} + \cdots + \beta_K X_{Kt} + \epsilon_t \quad (3.9)$$

where $X_4, \ldots, X_K$ are the other independent variables and t indexes the quarterly observations. Notice that three dummy variables are required to represent four seasons. In this formulation, β_1 shows the extent to which the expected value of Y in the first quarter differs from its expected value in the fourth quarter, the omitted condition. Similarly for β_2 and β_3.

This procedure may be used if Y or any of the other variables $X_4, X_5, \ldots,$ X_K are not "seasonally adjusted" prior to estimation. Inclusion of a set of seasonal dummies deseasonalizes Y as well as any other independent variables that are not seasonally adjusted. Many scholars believe that the type of seasonal adjustment done prior to estimation distorts the data in unknown and arbitrary ways, but seasonal dummies have their own limitations such as remaining constant for the entire time period. As a result, there is no unambiguous best approach to deseasonalizing the data.

3.2 Steps in Applied Regression

While there are no hard and fast rules for conducting econometric research, most investigators commonly follow a set method for applied regression analysis. The relative emphasis and effort expended on each step may vary, but normally all the steps are considered necessary for successful research. The researcher must first select the dependent variable; this choice is determined by the purpose of the regression. After that, it is logical to follow this sequence:

1. Review the literature.
2. Specify the model: select the independent variables and the functional form.
3. Hypothesize the expected signs of the coefficients.
4. Collect the data.
5. Estimate and evaluate the equation.
6. Document the results.

3.2.1 Step 1: Review the Literature

Before developing a theoretical model too deeply (and certainly before estimating it) it is a good idea to review the scholarly literature. Researchers can find out if someone else has already examined a topic sufficiently to permit the use of previously generated results. On the other hand, they may disagree with the approach or assumptions used by previous authors or may want to apply their theoretical model to a different data set. In either event, researchers should not have to "reinvent the wheel"—they can start their investigation where earlier ones left off. Any research paper should begin with a comment on the extent and quality of previous research.

The most convenient approach to reviewing the literature is to obtain several recent issues of the *Journal of Economic Literature* or a business-oriented publication of abstracts, find and read several recent articles related to the selected topic, and trace back appropriate references cited in the literature.

3.2.2 Step 2: Specify the Model: Select the Independent Variables and the Functional Form

The most important step in applied regression analysis is the *specification* of the theoretical regression model. After selecting the dependent variable, the following components should be specified: the variables to be included as independent variables and how they should be measured, the functional (mathematical) form of the equation, and the type of error term in the equation.

A regression equation is specified when each of these elements is treated appropriately, but we will focus on the selection of the independent variables until the other two topics have been introduced more completely.

Each of the elements of specification is determined primarily on the basis of economic theory, rather than on the results of an estimated regression equation. Once the literature has been reviewed, choosing the correct specification of the model is the logical next step in regression analysis and the most crucial. A mistake in any of the three elements results in a **specification error.** Of all the kinds of mistakes that can be made in applied regression analysis, specification error is usually the most disastrous to the usefulness of the estimated equation. Thus, the more attention is paid to economic theory at the beginning of a project, the more satisfying the regression results are likely to be.

The emphasis in this text is on estimating behavioral equations, which describe the behavior of economic entities. The researcher selects independent variables based on economic theory concerning that behavior. An explanatory variable is chosen because it is a causal determinant of the dependent variable; it is expected to explain at least part of the variation in the dependent variable. Recall that regression gives evidence but does not *prove* economic causality. Just as an example does not prove the rule, a regression result does not prove the theory.

There are dangers in specifying the wrong number of independent variables. A researcher's goal is to specify only relevant explanatory variables, those expected theoretically to assert a "significant" influence on the dependent variable. Variables suspected of having virtually no effect should be excluded unless their possible effect on the dependent variable is of some particular (e.g., policy) interest.

For example, an equation that explains the quantity demanded of a consumption good might use the price of the product and consumer income or wealth as likely variables. Theory also indicates that complementary and substitute goods are important. Therefore, the researcher may select as independent variables the prices of these complements and substitutes, but the problem arises of which complements and substitutes to choose. Of course, selection of the closest complements and substitutes is appropriate, but how far should one go? The choice must be based on theoretical judgment.

When researchers decide that, for example, only the prices of two other goods need to be included, they are said to impose their *priors* (i.e., prior information) or their working hypotheses on the regression equation. Imposition of such priors is a common practice that determines the number and kind of hypotheses that the regression equation has to test. The danger is that a prior may be wrong and will diminish the usefulness of the estimated regression equation. Each of the priors should therefore be explained and justified in detail.

3.2.3   Step 3: Hypothesize the Expected Signs of the Coefficients

Once the variables are selected, it is important to hypothesize carefully the signs you expect their regression coefficients to have. For example, in the demand equation for a final consumption good, the quantity demanded (Q_d) is expected to be inversely related to its price (P) and the price of a complementary good (P_c), and positively related to consumer income (Y) and the price of a substitute good (P_s). The first step in the written development of a regression model usually is to express the equation as a function:

$$Q_d = f(\overset{-}{P}, \overset{+}{Y}, \overset{-}{P_c}, \overset{+}{P_s}) \tag{3.10}$$

The signs above the variables indicate the hypothesized sign of the respective regression coefficient in a linear model. This is a simple convention that has become increasingly popular.

In many cases, the basic theory is commonly understood, so that the reasons for each sign need not be discussed. However, if any doubt surrounds the selection of an expected sign, the researcher should document the difficulty or the opposing forces at work and the reasons for hypothesizing a positive or negative coefficient. Alternatively, if theory does not suggest an unambiguous sign, then a question mark may be placed above the respective variable. For example, if the dependent variable in a demand equation is one for which the impact of income on demand is ambiguous (like potatoes), the function may be written as:

$$Q_d = f(\overset{-}{P}, \overset{?}{Y}, \overset{-}{P_c}, \overset{+}{P_s}) \tag{3.11}$$

3.2.4   Step 4: Collect the Data

After the specification of the regression model, data collection may begin. This step entails more than a mechanical recording of data, though, because the type and size of the sample must also be chosen. Often, inductive reasoning applies as the researcher examines the data and begins to see unanticipated patterns or relationships.

A general rule regarding sample size is the more observations the better. Ordinarily, the researcher takes all the roughly comparable observations that are readily available. Even if a number of computations are necessary to quantify a variable, the burden is on the researcher to explain why he or she did not use as many observations as were available. In regression analysis, all the variables must have the same number of observations. They also should have the same frequency (monthly, quarterly, annual, etc.) and time period. Very often, the frequency selected is determined by the availability of data. However, if, for example, one variable is only available annually in an otherwise quarterly model, the researcher may make linear or nonlinear quarterly interpolations (i.e., estimates of the value of the variable between observed values) of that variable.[1] If it is a slow-moving variable, such as total population, this approach may be adequate, but extreme caution should always be exercised when "creating" data in any way and full documentation is required.

The reason there should be as many observations as possible concerns the statistical concept of **degrees of freedom.** Consider fitting a straight line to two points on an X,Y coordinate system, as in Figure 3.2. Such an exercise can be done mathematically without error. Both points lie on the line, and there is no estimation of the coefficients involved. The two points precisely determine the two parameters, the intercept and the slope. Estimation takes place only when a straight line is fitted to three or more points that were generated by some process that is not exact. The excess of the number of observations (three) over the number of parameters to be estimated (in this case two, the intercept and slope) is called the degrees of freedom. All that is necessary for estimation is a single degree of freedom, as in Figure 3.3, but the more observations there are, the less likely it is that the stochastic or purely random component of the equation (the error term) will significantly affect inferences about the deterministic portion, which is the portion of primary interest. This is because when the number of observations is large, every large positive error is likely to be balanced by a large negative error. With only a few points, the random element is likely to fail to provide such offsetting observations. For example, the more times a coin is flipped, the more likely it is that the observed proportion of heads will reflect the true underlying probability (namely 0.5).

Another area of concern has to do with the units of measurement of the variables. Does it matter if a variable is measured in dollars or thousands of dollars? Does it matter if the measured variable differs consistently from the true variable by 10 units? Surprisingly, such changes do not matter in terms of regression analysis except in interpreting the scale of the coefficients. All conclusions about signs, significance, and economic theory are independent of units of measurement.

Let us take as an example the case of a variable measured in dollars or thousands of dollars. If $Y = f(X$ or $Z)$ and $X = 1000Z$, then the following regression equations would be equivalent:[2]

$$Y = 20 + 30X \quad \text{which equals} \quad Y = 20 + 30{,}000Z \qquad (3.12)$$

A multiplicative factor does change the slope coefficient (30 vs. 30,000) but only by the exact amount necessary to compensate for the change in the units of

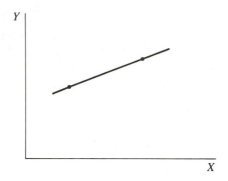

FIGURE 3.2 *Mathematical Fit of Line to Two Points*
If there are only two points in a data set, as in Figure 3.2, a straight line can be fitted
to those points mathematically without error, because two points completely determine
a straight line.

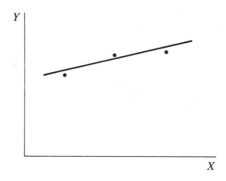

FIGURE 3.3 *Statistical Fit of Line to Three Points*
If there are three (or more) points in a data set, as in Figure 3.3, then the line must almost
always be fitted to the points statistically, using the estimation procedures of this chapter.

measurement in the independent variable. Similarly, a constant factor added to
a variable alters only the intercept term without changing the slope coefficient
itself. Recall the weight-height regression of Section 1.3. The explanatory variable
was measured as inches above five feet, so the 5 feet, or 60 inches, was just a
constant factor that was subtracted from each observation. If we re-estimate the
equation with the absolute height in inches (Z) as the independent variable, we
get $Y_i = -279.2 + 6.38Z_i$. Since the original equation was $Y_i = 103.4 +
6.38X_i$, only the constant term has changed, and for each height we would obtain
the exact same weight. The essential relationship between Y and Z is the same
as between Y and X. That is, adding a constant to a variable will not change the
slope coefficients of a linear equation. (But it will in most nonlinear equations.)

3.2.5 Step 5: Estimate and Evaluate the Equation

The Ordinary Least Squares (OLS) technique, discussed in Section 2.1, is the normally used estimating technique. Where alternative techniques might be appropriate, they should be used and the empirical estimates compared with OLS. The alternatively estimated equations must be evaluated carefully and judgment applied before a choice is made.

Once the model has been estimated, the data should be checked for errors. Data transformations and coefficient estimation are usually done in the same computer program, so it is wise to obtain a printout of the data set exactly as it was used in the regression estimation. Check one or two values of any variables that were transformed. If these values are correct, it may be assumed that the computer did not make any mistakes transforming the rest of the observations. Also obtain a printout or a plot of the data and look for outliers. An **outlier** is an observation that lies outside the range of the rest of the observations. Looking for outliers is a very economical way to look for typing or transcription errors, which often occur in preparation of data for the computer.

After checking for data errors, examine the signs and magnitudes and significance of the coefficients and the overall measures of fit. Regression results are rarely what one expects. Usually, additional model development is required or alternative estimating techniques are called for. Be sure to reevaluate the model and make any necessary changes before jumping into fancy regression "fix-up" routines. Sometimes these routines improve the overall measures of goodness of fit or some other statistic while playing havoc with the reliability of estimates of the model's parameters. A famous econometrician, Zvi Griliches, has warned that errors in the data coming from their measurement, usually computed from samples or estimates, imply that the fancier estimating techniques should be avoided because they are more sensitive to data errors than is OLS.[3] For a more detailed discussion of such *errors in the variables,* see Section 12.6. Also, when faced with unexpected regression results (which happen all too often), reexamination of the theoretical basis of the model is in order. However, one should avoid adjusting the theory merely to fit the data, thus introducing researcher bias. The researcher has to walk the fine line between making appropriate and inappropriate adjustments to the model. Choosing proper modifications is one of the artistic elements in applied regression analysis.

3.2.6 Step 6: Document the Results

A standard format is usually used to present estimated regression results:

$$Y_i = 103.40 + 6.38X_i \qquad (3.13)$$
$$(0.88)$$
$$t = 7.22$$
$$n = 20 \qquad \bar{R}^2 = .73$$

The number in parenthesis is the estimated standard error of the estimated coefficient, and the t-value is used to test the hypothesis that the true value of the coefficient is zero. These and other measures of the quality of the regression will be discussed in later chapters. What is important to note is that the documentation of regression results using an easily understood format is considered part of the analysis itself. For time-series data sets, the documentation also includes frequency (e.g. quarterly or annual) and the time period covered.

Most computer programs present statistics to eight or more digits, but it is important to recognize the difference between the number of digits computed and the number of *significant figures,* which may be as low as two or three. The number of significant figures is the number of meaningful digits in a result and is a function of the quality of the measurement of the data. Simply because the computer prints out a result to eight places is not an indication that all those digits have meaning. Indeed, it would be surprising if more than two or three did; only if data are known to be measured extremely accurately is there justification for an increase in the number of places presented.

One of the important parts of the documentation is the explanation of the model, the assumptions, and the procedures and data used. The written documentation must contain enough information so that the entire study can be exactly replicated[4] (except for rounding errors) by others. Unless the variables have been defined in a glossary or a table, short definitions of them should be presented along with the equations. If there is a series of estimated regression equations, then tables may be established providing the relevant information for each of them. All data manipulations as well as the data sources should be fully documented. When there is much to explain, this documentation is usually relegated to a "data appendix." If the data are not generally available or are available only after computation, the data set itself might also be included in this appendix.

3.3   A More Complete Example of Applied Regression Analysis

To solidify our understanding of the six basic steps of applied regression analysis, let's work through a complete regression example. Suppose that you have been hired to determine the best location for the next Woody's restaurant, where Woody's is a moderately priced, 24-hour, family restaurant chain. You decide to build a regression model to explain the gross sales volume at each of the restaurants in the chain as a function of various descriptors of the location of that particular branch. If you can come up with a sound equation to explain gross sales as a function of location, then you can use this equation to help Woody's decide which of the locations being considered for the newest eatery will have the highest potential for gross sales. Given data on land costs, building costs, and local building and restaurant municipal codes, the owners of Woody's will be able to make an informed decision.

1. *Review the literature.* You do some reading on the restaurant industry, but your review of the literature consists mainly of talking to various experts within the firm in order to get their hypotheses, based on experience, as to the particular attributes of a location that contribute to success at selling food at Woody's. The experts tell you that all of the chain's restaurants are identical (indeed, this is sometimes a criticism of the chain) and that all the locations are in what might be called "suburban, retail, or residential" environments (as distinguished from central cities or rural areas, for example). Because of this, you realize that many of the reasons that might help explain differences in sales volume in other chains do not apply in this case because all the Woody's locations are similar. (If you were comparing Woody's to another chain, this variable might be appropriate.)

   In addition, some discussion with the people in the Woody's strategic planning department convince you that price differentials and other consumption differences between locations are not as important as the number of customers a particular location attracts. This causes you to be concerned for a while because the variable you had originally planned to study, gross sales volume, would vary as prices changed between locations. Since your company controls these prices, you feel that you would rather have an estimate of the "potential" for such sales. As a result, you decide to specify your dependent variable as the number of customers served (actually, the number of checks or bills that your waiters and waitresses handed out) in a given location in the most recent year for which complete data are available.

2. *Specify the model: select the independent variables and functional form.* Your discussions and personal investigations lead to a number of suggested variables that should help explain the attractiveness of a particular site to potential customers. After a while, you realize that there are three major determinants of sales (customers) on which virtually everyone agrees. These are the number of people who live near the location, the general income level of the location, and the number of direct competitors close to the location. In addition, there are two other good suggestions for potential explanatory variables. These others are the number of cars passing the location per day and the number of months that the particular restaurant had been open at the time the data were collected. After some serious consideration of your alternatives, you decide not to include the last possibilities. All the locations have been open long enough to have achieved a stable clientele, so the number of months open would not be likely to be important. In addition, data are not available for the number of passing cars for all the locations. Should population prove to be a poor measure of the available customers in a location, you will have to decide whether or not to ask your boss for the money to collect more complete traffic data.

   The exact definitions of the variables you decide to include are:

   C = Competition − The number of direct market competitors within a two-mile radius of the Woody's location.

P = Population   – The number of people living within a three-mile radius of the Woody's location.

I = Income   – The average household income of the population measured in variable P.

Since you have no reason to suspect anything other than a linear functional form, that's what you decide to use.

3. *Hypothesize the expected signs of the coefficients.* After thinking about which variables to include, you expect the hypothesizing of signs will be easy, and for two of the variables, you are right. Everyone expects that the more competition, the fewer customers (holding constant the population and income of an area), and also that the more people that live near a particular restaurant, the more customers (holding constant the competition and income). You expect that the greater the income in a particular area, the more people will choose to eat away from home and the more people will choose to eat in a family restaurant instead of in the lower-priced fast-food chains, but people in especially high-income areas might want to eat in a restaurant that is even more expensive than a family restaurant. Some investigation reveals that it is virtually impossible to get zoning clearance to build a 24-hour facility in "ritzy" residential neighborhoods, but you remain slightly worried that the income variable might not be as unambiguous a measure of the appeal of a location as you had thought. To sum, you expect:

$$Y_i = f(\overset{-}{C}, \overset{+}{P}, \overset{+}{I}) = \beta_0 + \beta_c C_i + \beta_p P_i + \beta_I I_i + \epsilon_i$$

where the signs above the variables indicate the expected impact of that particular independent variable on the dependent variable, holding constant the other two explanatory variables, and ϵ_i is a typical stochastic error term.

4. *Collect the data.* You want to include every restaurant in the Woody's chain in your study, and, after some effort, you come up with data for your dependent variable and all your independent variables for all 33 locations. Since each manager measured each variable identically, since you've included each restaurant in the sample, and since all the information is from the same year, you are confident that the quality of your data is excellent. The data set for this regression is at the end of this section, along with a sample computer output for the regression estimated.

5. *Estimate and evaluate the equation.* You take the data set collected above and enter it into the computer. You then ask for an ordinary least squares regression on the data, but you do so only after thinking through your model once again to see if there are any hints that you have made theoretical mistakes. You end up admitting that while you cannot be sure you are right, you have done the best you can, and so you estimate the equation, obtaining:

$$\hat{Y}_i = 102{,}192 - 9075C_i + 0.3547P_i + 1.288I_i \qquad (3.14)$$

$$n = 33 \quad \bar{R}^2 = .579 \quad F = 15.65$$

This equation satisfies your needs in the short run. In particular, the estimated coefficients in the equation have the signs you expected, and the overall fit, while not outstanding, seems reasonable for such a diverse group of locations. In order to predict check volumes at potential locations, you obtain the values of C, P, and I for each location and then plug them into Equation 3.14. Other things being equal, the higher the predicted Y, the better the location from Woody's point of view.

Since we have yet to learn how to fully evaluate such a result, our job is complete. In future chapters, we will return to this example in order to apply various tests and ideas as we learn them. For more on this example, see Exercises 4 through 6.

6. *Document the results.* The results summarized in Equation 3.14 meet our documentation requirements (except for the exclusion of t-values, to be covered in Chapter 5). Unfortunately, it is sometimes difficult for a beginning researcher to find all the estimates needed for such documentation given the output of their computer's regression package. Even though computer programs vary tremendously, it will probably help you have an easier time reading your own system's printout if you "walk through" some of the output on the next two pages that our ECSTAT computer program produced for the Woody's example.

Page one of the computer output summarizes the input data. The first items listed are the actual data. This is followed by two tables that describe these data; the first lists means, standard deviations, and variances, and the second lists the simple correlation coefficients (to be covered in Chapter 5) between all pairs of variables in the data set. Numbers followed by "E+06" or "E−01" are expressed in a scientific notation that means that the printed decimal point should be moved 6 places to the right or one place to the left, respectively.

The second page summarizes the OLS estimates generated from the data. It starts with a listing of the estimated coefficients, their estimated standard errors, and the associated t-values, and follows with R^2, $\bar{R}^2$, the standard error of the regression, RSS, and the F-ratio. This is followed by a listing of the observed Ys, the predicted Ys and the residuals for each observation.

Table 3.1 Data for the Woody's Restaurants Example

OBSERV.	Y	C	P	I
1	107919.0	3.000000	65044.00	13240.00
2	118866.0	5.000000	101376.0	22554.00
3	98579.00	7.000000	124989.0	16916.00
4	122015.0	2.000000	55249.00	20967.00
5	152827.0	3.000000	73775.00	19576.00
6	91259.00	5.000000	48484.00	15039.00
7	123550.0	8.000000	138809.0	21857.00
8	160931.0	2.000000	50244.00	26435.00
9	98496.00	6.000000	104300.0	24024.00
10	108052.0	2.000000	37852.00	14987.00
11	144788.0	3.000000	66921.00	30902.00
12	164571.0	4.000000	166332.0	31573.00
13	105564.0	3.000000	61951.00	19001.00
14	102568.0	5.000000	100441.0	20058.00
15	103342.0	2.000000	39462.00	16194.00
16	127030.0	5.000000	139900.0	21384.00
17	166755.0	6.000000	171740.0	18800.00
18	125343.0	6.000000	149894.0	15289.00
19	121886.0	3.000000	57386.00	16702.00
20	134594.0	6.000000	185105.0	19093.00
21	152937.0	3.000000	114520.0	26502.00
22	109622.0	3.000000	52933.00	18760.00
23	149884.0	5.000000	203500.0	33242.00
24	98388.00	4.000000	39334.00	14988.00
25	140791.0	3.000000	95120.00	18505.00
26	101260.0	3.000000	49200.00	16839.00
27	139517.0	4.000000	113566.0	28915.00
28	115236.0	9.000000	194125.0	19033.00
29	136749.0	7.000000	233844.0	19200.00
30	105067.0	7.000000	83416.00	22833.00
31	136872.0	6.000000	183953.0	14409.00
32	117146.0	3.000000	60457.00	20307.00
33	163538.0	2.000000	65065.00	20111.00

MEANS, VARIANCES, AND CORRELATIONS
SAMPLE RANGE: 1-33

VARIABLE	MEAN	STANDARD DEV	VARIANCE
Y	125634.6	22062.02	4.86732E+08
C	4.393939	1.889996	3.572084
P	103887.5	55031.26	3.02844E+09
I	20552.58	5063.359	2.56376E+07

	CORRELATION COEFF		CORRELATION COEFF
Y,Y	1.000000	C,Y	-0.144225
C,C	1.000000	P,Y	0.392568
P,C	0.726251	P,P	1.000000
I,Y	0.537022	I,C	-0.031534
I,P	0.245198	I,I	1.000000

**Table 3.2 Actual Computer Output (Using the ECSTAT Program)
from the Woody's Regression**

```
ORDINARY LEAST SQUARES                    DEPENDENT VARIABLE IS Y
SAMPLE RANGE:        1-33

                     COEFFICIENT          STANDARD ERROR      T-STATISTIC
        CONST         102192.4             12799.83            7.983891
        C            -9074.674             2052.674           -4.420904
        P             0.354668             0.072681            4.879810
        I             1.287923             0.543294            2.370584

  R-squared           0.618154          Mean of depend var      125634.6
  Adjusted R-squared  0.578653          Std dev depend var      22404.09
  Std err of regress  14542.78          Residual sum            3.30806E-06
  Durbin Watson stat  1.758193          Sum squared resid       6.13328E+09
  F Statistic         15.64894
```

```
OUT OF SAMPLE FORECAST: Y

OBSERVATION       ACTUAL          PREDICTED
     1           107919.0         115089.6           -7170.559
     2           118866.0         121821.7           -2955.740
     3           98579.00         104785.9           -6206.864
     4           122015.0         130642.0           -8627.041
     5           152827.0         126346.5           26480.55
     6           91259.00         93383.88           -2124.877
     7           123550.0         106976.3           16573.66
     8           160931.0         135909.3           25021.71
     9           98496.00         115677.4          -17181.36
    10           108052.0         116770.1           -8718.094
    11           144788.0         138502.6           6285.425
    12           164571.0         165550.0           -979.0342
    13           105564.0         121412.3          -15848.30
    14           102568.0         118275.5          -15707.47
    15           103342.0         118895.6          -15553.63
    16           127030.0         133978.1           -6948.114
    17           166755.0         132868.1           33886.91
    18           125343.0         120598.1           4744.898
    19           121886.0         116832.3           5053.700
    20           134594.0         137985.6           -3391.591
    21           152937.0         149717.6           3219.428
    22           109622.0         117903.5           -8281.508
    23           149884.0         171807.2          -21923.22
    24           98388.00         99147.65           -759.6514
    25           140791.0         132537.5           8253.518
    26           101260.0         114105.4          -12845.43
    27           139517.0         143412.3           -3895.303
    28           115236.0         113883.4           1352.599
    29           136749.0         146334.9           -9585.906
    30           105067.0         97661.88           7405.122
    31           136872.0         131544.4           5327.620
    32           117146.0         122564.5           -5418.450
    33           163538.0         133021.0           30517.00
```

3.4 Summary

1. A proxy variable is one that substitutes for a theoretically relevant variable when data on the desired variable are incomplete or missing altogether. The more highly correlated the proxy variable is with the originally specified variable, the better a proxy it is.

2. A dummy variable takes on only the value of one or zero depending on whether or not some condition is met. An example of a dummy variable would be an X equals 1 when a particular individual is female and 0 if the person is male. One fewer dummy variable is constructed than there are qualitative conditions. It is arbitrary which condition is assigned which value, but once assigned, the interpretation of the coefficient is unambiguous.

3. Six steps typically taken in applied regression analysis are:
   a. review the literature
   b. specify the model: select the independent variables and functional form
   c. hypothesize the expected signs of the coefficients
   d. collect the data
   e. estimate and evaluate the equation
   f. document the results

Exercises

(Answers to even-numbered exercises are in Appendix A.)

1. Write out the meaning of each of the following terms without reference to the book (or your notes) and then compare your definition with the version in the text for each:
   a. proxy variable
   b. dummy variable
   c. omitted condition
   d. cross-section data set
   e. specification error

2. Contrary to their name, dummy variables are not always easy to understand without a little bit of practice:
   a. Specify a dummy variable that would allow you to distinguish between undergraduate students and graduate students in your econometrics class.
   b. Specify a regression equation to explain the grade (measured on a scale of 4.0 for an A grade) each student in your class received on his or her first econometrics test (Y) as a function of the student's grade in a previous course in statistics (G), the number of hours the student studied for the test (H), and the dummy variable you created above (D). Are there any other variables you would want to add? Explain your answer.

    c. What is the hypothesized sign of the coefficient of D? Does the sign depend on the exact way in which you defined D? How?

    d. Suppose that you collected the data and ran the regression and found an estimated sign of the coefficient in D that had the expected sign and an absolute value of 0.5. What would this mean in real-world terms? By the way, what would have happened if you had only undergraduates or only graduate students in your class?

3. For each of the following dependent variables, data for a particular independent variable are not available and the choice of a proxy variable must be considered:

    a. In an equation where the dependent variable is total sales ($) of Classic Cola (time series) and the desired independent variable is the amount of advertising by Dr. Popper (Classic Cola's main competitor), it would be hard to get the Dr. Popper folks to give advertising data to their arch-rivals. Would a good proxy variable be total advertising in the soft-drink industry? What about total sales of Dr. Popper? Explain your reasoning.

    b. In an equation where the dependent variable is the value of exports from the U.S. to Japan (time series) and the desired independent variable is the amount of bureaucratic red tape making such exports more difficult, the independent variable is so vaguely defined as to make its exact measurement impossible. Would a good proxy be the Japanese average tariff rate? What about the number of laws in Japan that apply to goods imported from the U.S.?

    c. In an equation where the dependent variable is the "reservation wage" (the lowest wage offer that an unemployed worker will accept) and the desired independent variable is the "expected wage" (the wage that the worker expects to end up with once he or she gets a job), data on expected wages are usually very hard to get. Would the worker's last wage be a good proxy? How about the average wage in the worker's profession? Explain your reasoning.

4. Return to the more complete regression example of Section 3.3.

    a. In any applied regression project there is the distinct possibility that an important explanatory variable has been omitted. Reread the discussion of the selection of independent variables and come up with a suggestion for an independent variable that has not been included in the model (other than the traffic variable already mentioned). Why do you think this variable was not included?

    b. What other kinds of criticisms would you have of the sample or independent variables chosen in this model?

    c. What's wrong with this kind of thinking? "I know that the coefficients in Equation 3.14 are wrong because if you just divide the average number of checks in the sample (125,635 as can be seen in the computer output at the end of Table 3.1) by the average population in the sample (103,888 from the same source) you get 1.21, a number that is much larger than the computer estimate of the same coefficient (0.3547). Therefore, it's easier and more accurate to just do the calculations yourself!"

5. Suppose you were told that, while data on traffic for Equation 3.14 is still too expensive to obtain, a variable on traffic, called T_i, *is* available that is defined as one if more than 45,000 cars per day pass the restaurant and zero otherwise. Further suppose that when the new variable (T_i) is added to the equation the results are:

$$\hat{Y}_i = 99,090 - 7,068C_i + .2863P_i + 1.059I_i + 15,483T_i$$

$$n = 33 \quad \bar{R}^2 = .661 \quad F = 18.07$$

a. Is the new variable a dummy variable or a proxy variable? Why?
b. What is the expected sign of the coefficient of the new variable?
c. Would you prefer this equation to the original one in Section 3.3? Why?
d. Does the fact that $\bar{R}^2$ is higher in the new equation mean that it is necessarily better than the old one?

6. Suppose that the population variable in Section 3.3 had been defined in different units as in:

P = Population − Thousands of people living within a three-mile radius of the Woody's location

a. Given this definition of P, what would the estimated slope coefficients in Equation 3.14 have been?
b. Given this definition of P, what would the estimated slope coefficients in the equation in Exercise 5 (above) have been?
c. Are any other coefficients affected by this change?

7. Develop your own regression equation to explain a dependent variable that relates directly to you and your immediate surroundings or personal interests. Your main focus here should be on choosing appropriate independent variables and on hypothesizing expected signs. Follow through the first three steps in applied regression analysis:
a. Write up a review of the relevant theory and research behind your chosen dependent variable.
b. Select your independent variables, being sure to be quite specific as to how they are defined and measured.
c. Hypothesize the expected signs of the coefficients of your independent variables and explain your reasoning.
At this point in your econometric career, it is probably a bit premature to attempt to estimate your equation, but if you are still interested in this dependent variable after completing Chapter 5, you might collect data and estimate the equation.

8. Consider the following two least-squares estimates[5] of the relationship between interest rates and the federal budget deficit in the U.S.:

Model A: $\hat{Y}_1 = 0.103 - 0.079X_1$ $R^2 = .00$

where: Y_1 = interest rate on Aaa corporate bonds
X_1 = the federal deficit as a percentage of GNP
(quarterly model: 1970—1983)

Model T: $\hat{Y}_2 = 0.089 + 0.369X_2 + 0.887X_3$ $R^2 = .40$

where: Y_2 = interest rate on 3-month Treasury bills
X_2 = federal budget deficit in billions of dollars
X_3 = rate of inflation in percent
(quarterly model: April 1970—September 1979)

a. What does "least squares estimates" mean? What is being estimated? What is being squared? In what sense are the squares "least?"
b. What does it mean to have an R^2 of .00? Is it possible for an R^2 to be negative?
c. Calculate $\bar{R}^2$ for both equations.
d. Compare the two equations. Which model has estimated signs that correspond to your prior expectations? Is model T automatically better because it has a higher R^2? If not, which model do you prefer and why?

9. Calculate the real price of a "Whitney GT" automobile for the following years:

	Money Price	CPI (current year)	CPI (base year)
a. 1965	$ 4,000	95	100
b. 1975	$10,000	160	100
c. 1985	$18,000	300	100

---

[1] Given an annual data series, quarterly estimates can sometimes be interpolated linearly or exponentially (using the geometric mean). Let X_0 and X_4 be the two observed annual data points one year apart between which it is desired to interpolate the quarterly numbers. The two procedures are as follows:

	Linear	Exponential
Adjustment Factor a:	$a = \dfrac{X_4 - X_0}{4}$	$a = \dfrac{1}{4} Ln(X_4/X_0)$
Interpolated Observations	$\begin{cases} \hat{X}_1 = X_0 + a \\ \hat{X}_2 = X_0 + 2a \\ \hat{X}_3 = X_0 + 3a \end{cases}$	$\begin{cases} \hat{X}_1 = X_0 e^a \\ \hat{X}_2 = X_0 e^{2a} \\ \hat{X}_3 = X_0 e^{3a} \end{cases}$

The exponential interpolation is usually used when the data values appear to be growing exponentially. For more extensive data manipulations or "massaging," see Michael D. Intriligator, *Econometric Models, Techniques, and Applications* (Englewood Cliffs, NJ: Prentice-Hall, 1978), pp. 67-70.

[2] To prove this to yourself, simply substitute 1000Z for X in Equation 3.12 to get Y = 20 + 30,000Z. The units of measurement of the dependent variable likewise do not alter the interpretation of the regression equation (except, as above, in interpreting the magnitude of the regression coefficients), hypothesis testing, or measures of fit such as $\bar{R}^2$.

[3] See Zvi Griliches, "Data and Econometricians—The Uneasy Alliance," *American Economic Review*, May 1985, p. 199.

[4] For example, the *Journal of Money, Credit and Banking* has requested authors to submit the actual data sets used so that regression results can be verified. See W. G. Dewald et. al., "Replication in Empirical Economics," *American Economic Review*, Sept. 1986, pp. 587-603.

[5] These estimates are simplified versions of results presented in the June/July 1984 issue of the *Review* of the Federal Reserve Bank of St. Louis (Model A) and the Summer 1983 issue of the *Review* of the Federal Reserve Bank of San Francisco (Model T).

4

The Classical Model

The classical model of econometrics has nothing to do with ancient Greece or even the classical economic thinking of Adam Smith. Instead, the term *classical* refers to a set of fairly basic assumptions required to hold in order for the ordinary least squares (OLS) procedure to be considered the best (minimum variance) linear unbiased estimator available for regression models. When one or more of these assumptions do not hold, other estimation techniques may sometimes be better than OLS.

As a result, one of the most important jobs in regression analysis is to decide whether the classical assumptions hold for a particular equation. If they do apply, the OLS estimation technique is the best available. Otherwise, the pros and cons of alternative estimation techniques must be weighed; these alternatives are usually adjustments to OLS that take into account the particular assumption that has been violated. In a sense, most of the rest of this book deals in one way or another with the question of what to do when one of the classical assumptions is not met. Since econometricians spend so much time analyzing violations of them, it is crucial that they know and understand these assumptions.

4.1 The Classical Assumptions

The classical assumptions must be met in order for OLS estimators to be the best available. Because of their importance in applied regression analysis, they are presented here in tabular form and standard statistical notation as well as in words. Subsequent chapters will investigate major violations of the assumptions and introduce estimation techniques that may provide better estimates in such cases.

An error term satisfying Assumptions I through V is called a **classical error term,** and if Assumption VII is added, the error term is called a **classical normal error term.**

The Classical Assumptions

I. The regression model is linear in the coefficients and the error term.

II. The error term has a zero population mean.

III. All explanatory variables are uncorrelated with the error term.

IV. The error term from one observation is independent of the error terms from the other observations (no serial correlation).

V. The error term has a constant variance (no heteroskedasticity).

VI. No explanatory variable is a perfect linear function of other explanatory variables (no perfect multicollinearity).

VII. The error term is normally distributed (this assumption is optional but is usually invoked).

I.   The regression model is linear in the coefficients and the error term. The regression model is assumed to be linear in the coefficients:

$$Y_i = \beta_0 + \beta_1 X_{1i} + \beta_2 X_{2i} + \cdots + \beta_K X_{Ki} + \epsilon_i \qquad (4.1)$$

On the other hand, the regression model does not have to be linear in the variables, because OLS can be applied to equations that are nonlinear in the variables. The good properties of OLS estimators hold regardless of the functional form of the *variables* as long as the form of the equation to be estimated is linear in the *coefficients*. For example, an exponential function:

$$Y_i = e^{\beta_0} X_i^{\beta_1} e^{\epsilon_i} \qquad (4.2)$$

where e is the base of the natural log, can be transformed by taking the natural log of both sides of the equation:

$$\ln(Y_i) = \beta_0 + \beta_1 \ln(X_i) + \epsilon_i \qquad (4.3)$$

The variables can be relabeled as $Y_i^* = \ln(Y_i)$ and $X_i^* = \ln(X_i)$, and the form of the equation is linear in the coefficients:

$$Y_i^* = \beta_0 + \beta_1 X_i^* + \epsilon_i \qquad (4.4)$$

In Equation 4.4, the good properties of the OLS estimator of the βs still hold because the equation is linear in the coefficients. Equations that are nonlinear in the coefficients will be discussed briefly in Section 7.6.

II.   The error term has a zero population mean. As was pointed out in Section 1.2.3, econometricians add a stochastic (random) error term to regression equations to account for variation in the dependent variable that is not explained by the model. The specific value of the error term for each observation is determined purely by chance. Probably the best way to picture this concept is to think of each error term as being drawn from a random variable distribution such as the one illustrated in Figure 4.1.

Classical Assumption II says that the mean of this distribution is zero, that is, when the entire population of possible values for the stochastic error term is considered, the average value of that population is zero. For a small sample of error terms, it is not likely that the mean would be zero, but as the size of the sample approaches infinity, the mean of the sample approaches zero.

To compensate for the chance that the mean of the population ϵ might not equal zero, the mean of ϵ_i for any regression is forced to be zero by the existence of the constant term in the equation. If the mean of the error term is not equal to zero, then this nonzero amount is implicitly (because error terms are unobservable) subtracted from each error term and added instead to the constant term. Such a change leaves the equation unchanged except that the new error term has a zero mean (and thus conforms to Assumption II), and the constant term has been changed by the difference between the sample mean of the error terms and zero. Partially because of this difference, it is risky to place much importance on the estimated magnitude of the constant term. In essence, the constant term equals the fixed portion of Y that cannot be explained by the independent variables, while the error term is the stochastic portion of the unexplained value of Y.

While it is true that the error terms can never be observed, it might be instructive to imagine that we can observe them, in order to see how the existence of a constant term forces the mean of the error terms to be zero even in a sample. Consider a typical regression equation:

$$Y_i = \beta_0 + \beta_1 X_i + \epsilon_i \qquad (4.5)$$

If the mean of ϵ_i is, for example, 3 instead of 0, then $E(\epsilon_i - 3) = 0$. If we add 3 to the constant term and subtract it from the error term, we obtain:

$$Y_i = (\beta_0 + 3) + \beta_1 X_i + (\epsilon_i - 3) \qquad (4.6)$$

Since Equations 4.5 and 4.6 are equivalent (do you see why?) and since $E(\epsilon_i - 3) = 0$, then Equation 4.6 can be written in a form that has a zero mean for the error term:

$$Y_i = \beta_0^* + \beta_1 X_i + \epsilon_i^* \qquad (4.7)$$

where the variables in Equation 4.7 correspond to those in Equation 4.6. As can be seen, Equation 4.7 conforms to Assumption II. This form is always assumed to apply for the true model. Therefore, the second classical assumption is assured as long as there is a constant term included in the equation. This statement is correct as long as all the other classical assumptions are met and as long as there are no specification errors in the equation.

III. All explanatory variables are uncorrelated with the error term. It is assumed that the observed values of the explanatory variables are determined independently of the values of the dependent variable and the error term. Explanatory variables (Xs) are considered to be determined outside the context of the regression equation in question.

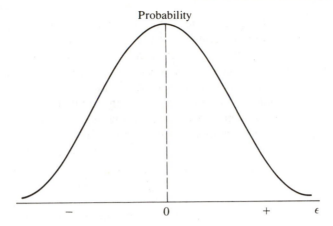

FIGURE 4.1 *A Zero-Meaned Stochastic Error Term Distribution*
Stochastic error terms are assumed to be drawn from a zero-meaned, symmetrical random variable distribution. If Classical Assumption II is met, the probability of a positive observation of the error term equals the probability of a negative observation because the expected value (the mean) of the error term is zero.

If an explanatory variable and the error term were indeed correlated with each other, the OLS estimates would be likely to attribute to the X some of the variation in Y that actually came from the error term. If the error term and X were positively correlated, for example, then the estimated coefficient of the variable in question will be higher than it would otherwise have been (biased upward), because the OLS program would mistakenly attribute the variation in Y caused by ϵ to have been caused by X instead (because X and ϵ are positively correlated with each other). As a result, it is important to assure that the explanatory variables are uncorrelated with the error term.

A common economic application that violates this assumption is any model that is simultaneous in nature. For example, in a simple Keynesian macroeconomic model, an increase in consumption (caused perhaps by an unexpected change in tastes) will increase aggregate demand and therefore aggregate income. An increase in income, however, will also increase consumption; income and consumption are interdependent. Note, however, that the error term in the consumption function (which is where an unexpected change in tastes would appear) and an explanatory variable in the consumption function (income) have now moved together. As a result, Classical Assumption III has been violated; the error term is no longer independent of all the explanatory variables. This will be considered in more detail in Chapter 12.

IV. The error term from one observation is independent of the error terms from the other observations. The values of the error term are drawn independently from the population distribution. If a systematic correlation exists between an error term for one observation and an error term for another, then this fact will make it more difficult for OLS to get precise estimates of the coefficients of the explanatory variables. For example, if the fact that the ϵ from one observation is positive increases the probability that the ϵ from another observation also is positive, then the two observations of the error term are said to be positively correlated. Such a lack of independence would violate Classical Assumption IV.

In economic applications, this assumption is most important in time series models. In such a context, Assumption IV says that an increase in the error term in one time period (a random shock, for example) does not show up in or affect in any way the error term in another time period. If, over all the observations of the sample, ϵ_{t+1} tends to show some correlation with ϵ_t, then the error terms are said to be **serially correlated** (or *autocorrelated*), and this assumption is violated. Violations of this assumption are considered in more detail in Chapter 9.

V.   The error term has a constant variance. The variance of the distribution from which the error terms are drawn is constant. That is, the error terms are assumed to be continually drawn from the same distribution (for example, the one pictured in Figure 4.1). The alternative would be for the variance of the distribution of the error terms to change for each observation or range of observation. In Figure 4.2, for example, the variance (or dispersion) of the error term is shown to increase as X increases; such a pattern violates Classical Assumption V. To see how such a violation makes precise estimation difficult, remember that a particular deviation from a mean (in this case an error term) can be called a statistically large or small deviation only when it is compared to the standard deviation (which is the square root of the variance) of the distribution in question. If you assume that all error terms are drawn from a distribution with a constant variance when in reality they are drawn from distributions with different variances, then the relative importance of changes in Y is very hard to judge. While the actual values of the error term are not directly observable, the lack of a constant variance for the distribution of the error term still causes OLS to generate imprecise estimates of the coefficients of the independent variables.

In economic applications, Assumption V is most important in cross-sectional data sets. For example, in a cross-sectional analysis of household consumption patterns, the variance (or dispersion) of the consumption of certain goods might be greater for higher-income households because they have more discretionary income than do lower-income households. Thus the absolute amount of the dispersion is greater even though the percentage dispersion is the same. The violation of Assumption V is referred to as **heteroskedasticity** and will be discussed in more detail in Chapter 10.

VI.   No explanatory variable is a perfect linear function of other explanatory variables. Perfect **collinearity** between two independent variables implies that they are really the same variable, except that one is a multiple of the other and/or a constant has been added to one of the variables. That is, the relative movements of one explanatory variable will be matched exactly by the relative movements of the other even though the absolute size of the movements might differ. Because every time one of the variables moves, it is exactly matched by a relative move-

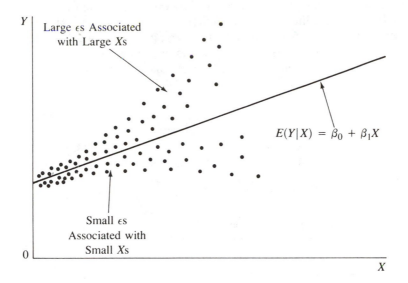

FIGURE 4.2 *Error Terms Whose Variance Increases as X Increases (Heteroskedasticity)*
One example of Classical Assumption V not being met is when the variance of the error
term increases as X increases. In such a situation (called heteroskedasticity), the observations are on average farther from the true regression line for large values of X than they
are for small values of X.

ment in the other, the OLS estimation procedure will be incapable of distinguishing
one variable from the other.

Many instances of perfect collinearity (or *multicollinearity* if more than two
independent variables are involved) are the result of the researcher not account-
ing for identities among the independent variables and can be corrected easily.
All that needs to be done is to drop one of the perfectly collinear variables from
the equation. Suppose you were attempting to explain home purchases and had
included both real and nominal interest rates as explanatory variables in your equation for a time period in which expected inflation was constant. In such an instance,
real and nominal interest rates would differ by a constant amount, and the OLS
procedure would not distinguish between them. Note that perfect multicollinearity
can be caused by an accident in the sample at hand. While real and nominal interest
rates would be perfectly multicollinear if inflation (and therefore expected inflation) were constant in a given sample, they would not be perfectly multicollinear
in samples where there was some change in inflation.

Similarly, perfect multicollinearity occurs when two independent variables always sum to a third. For example, the explanatory variables "games won" and "games lost" for a sports team with a constant number of games played and no ties will always sum to a constant, and perfect multicollinearity will exist. In such cases, the OLS computer program (or any other estimation technique) will be unable to estimate the coefficients unless there is a rounding error. The remedy is easy in the case of perfect multicollinearity; just delete one of the two perfectly correlated variables. It is quite unusual to encounter perfect multicollinearity; however, as we shall see in Chapter 8, even imperfect multicollinearity can cause problems for estimation.

VII. The error term is normally distributed. While we have already assumed that observations of the error terms are drawn independently (Assumption IV) from a distribution that is zero-meaned (Assumption II) and that has a constant variance (Assumption V), we have said little about the shape of that distribution. Assumption VII states that these error terms are drawn from a distribution that is normal, i.e., bell-shaped and generally following the pattern portrayed in Figure 4.1. This assumption of normality is not required for OLS estimation; its major use is in **hypothesis testing,** which uses the calculated regression statistics to accept or reject hypotheses about economic behavior. One example of such a test is deciding whether a particular demand curve is elastic or inelastic in a particular range. Hypothesis testing is the subject of Chapter 5.

4.2 The Normal Distribution of the Error Term

The only assumption that is optional to the definition of the classical model is that the error term is normally distributed. It is usually justified and advisable to add the assumption of normality to the other six assumptions for two reasons:

1. The error term ϵ_i can be thought of as the composite of a number of minor influences, or errors, and as the number of these minor influences gets larger, the distribution of the error term tends to approach the normal distribution. This tendency is called the Central Limit Theorem.

2. The *t* statistic developed in Chapter 5 and the *F* statistic developed in Section 5.8 are not truly applicable unless the error term is normally distributed.

In this section we briefly introduce the concept of the normal distribution and explain why the Central Limit Theorem tends to justify the assumption of normality for a stochastic error term.

4.2.1 A Description of the Normal Distribution

The normal distribution is a symmetrical, continuous, bell-shaped curve. The parameters that describe normal distributions and allow us to differentiate between various normal distributions are the **mean** μ (the measure of central tendency) and the **variance** σ^2 (the measure of dispersion). Two such normal distributions

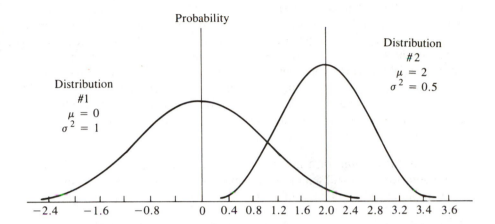

FIGURE 4.3 *Normal Distributions*
While all normal distributions are symmetrical and bell-shaped, they do not necessarily
have the same mean and variance. Distribution #1 has a mean of 0 and a variance of 1,
while distribution #2 has a mean of 2 and a variance of 0.5. As can be seen, the whole
distribution shifts when the mean is different, and the distribution gets fatter as the
variance increases.

are shown in Figure 4.3. In normal distribution #1, the mean is 0 and the variance
is 1, while in normal distribution #2, the mean is 2 and the variance is 0.5.

A quick look at Figure 4.3 will show how normal distributions differ when the
means and variances are different. When the mean is different, the entire distribution shifts; for example, distribution #2 is to the right of distribution #1 because
its mean, 2, is greater than the mean of distribution #1. When the variance is different, the distribution becomes fatter or skinnier. For example, distribution #2
is more compactly distributed around its mean than is distribution #1, because
distribution #2 has a smaller variance. Observations drawn at random from
distribution #2 will tend to be closer to the mean than those drawn from distribution
#1, while distribution #1 will tend to have a higher likelihood of observations quite
far from its mean.

In Figure 4.3, distribution #1 represents what is called the **standard normal
distribution** because it is a normal distribution with a mean equal to zero and
a variance equal to one. This is the usual distribution given in statistical tables,
such as Table B-7 in the back of this book. Often the parameters of a normal
distribution will be listed in a compact summary form: $N(\mu, \sigma^2)$. For distribution #1, this notation would be $N(0,1)$ and would stand for a normal distribution
with mean zero and variance one.

4.2.2   The Central Limit Theorem and the Normality of the Error Term

As was mentioned in Chapter 1, the error term in a regression equation is assumed to be caused in part by the omission of a number of variables from the equation. These variables are expected to have relatively small individual effects on the hypothesized regression equation, and it is not advisable to include them as independent variables. The error term represents the combined effects of these omitted variables. This component of the error term is usually cited as the justification of the assumption of normality for the error term. In general, a random variable generated by the combined effects of a number of omitted, individually unimportant variables will be normally distributed according to the **Central Limit Theorem** that states:

> The mean (or sum) of a number of independent, identically distributed random variables will tend to be normally distributed, regardless of their distribution, if the number of different random variables is large enough.

The Central Limit Theorem becomes more valid as the number of omitted variables approaches infinity, but even a few are sufficient to show the tendency toward the normal bell-shaped distribution. The more variables omitted, the more quickly the distribution of the error term approaches the normal distribution, because the various omitted variables will be more likely to cancel out extreme observations. As a result, it is good econometric practice to assume a normally distributed stochastic error term in a regression that must omit a number of minor unrelated influences. Purposely omitting a few variables to help achieve normality for the error term, however, should *never* be considered.

Here is an illustration of the Central Limit Theorem. Suppose that there are two relatively unimportant variables that have been omitted from a regression equation; assume further that each omitted variable is distributed uniformly (every value is equally and uniformly likely) and that either these two variables are the only cause of the error term in the regression (which is unlikely), or else the other causes are negligible in comparison to these (which is more realistic). Then the equation's error term is the sum of the random observations of the two omitted variables (multiplied by the impacts they would have on the dependent variable, holding constant the variables in the equation; we will assume for simplicity that these coefficients are equal to one). Figure 4.4 shows 10 computer-generated observations of a stochastic error term that is the sum of these two omitted variables.

Suppose that the error term consisted of ten such minor independent influences instead of just two. Then the error term would be the sum of the observations of all ten. Figure 4.5 shows ten computer-generated observations of a stochastic error term that is the sum of ten such variables. To see the effect of increasing the number of influences on the error term, compare the two figures. As we expect from the Central Limit Theorem, Figure 4.5 looks much more bell-shaped (normal) than does Figure 4.4. If we were to continue to add variables, the distribution would tend to look more and more like the normal distribution.

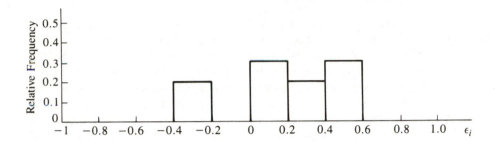

FIGURE 4.4 *Relative Frequency of the Error Term as an Average of 2 Omitted Variables from the Uniform Distribution: 10 Observations*

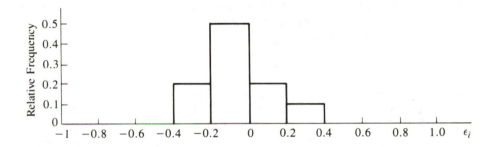

FIGURE 4.5 *Relative Frequency of the Error Term as an Average of 10 Omitted Variables from the Uniform Distribution: 10 Observations*

As the number of different omitted variables increases, the distribution of the sum of those variables approaches the normal distribution. This tendency (called the Central Limit Theorem) can be seen in Figures 4.4 and 4.5. As the number of omitted variables increases from 2 to 10, the distribution of their average does indeed become more symmetrical and bell-shaped.

These figures show the tendency of errors to cancel each other out as the number of omitted variables increases. Why does this occur? The averaging of the Xs, each of which is distributed according to the uniform distribution, bunches the observations toward the middle because extreme values of any X tend to be off-set by the others, resulting in a fairly normal distribution. The more Xs there are to be averaged, the more normal this distribution becomes.

By the way, the omitted variables do not have to conform to the uniform distribution to produce this result; they can follow *any* probability distribution. Indeed, if the omitted variables were normally distributed, the error term would be normally distributed by definition, since the sum (or average) of normally distributed variables is also a normally distributed variable.

4.3   The Sampling Distribution of $\hat{\beta}$

Just as the error terms follow a probability distribution, so the estimates of the true slope βs (the $\hat{\beta}$s or "β-hats") follow such a probability distribution. In fact, each different sample of data is capable of producing a different set of $\hat{\beta}$s. These $\hat{\beta}$s are usually assumed to be normally distributed, because the normality of the error term implies that the OLS estimator of the $\hat{\beta}$s in the simple linear regression model is normally distributed as well. The probability distribution of the $\hat{\beta}$s is called a **sampling distribution** because it is based on a number of sample drawings of the error term. To show this, we will discuss the general idea of the sampling distribution of the $\hat{\beta}$s and then use a computer-generated example to demonstrate that such distributions do indeed tend to be normally distributed.

4.3.1   Sampling Distributions of Estimators

We have noted that the purpose of regression analysis is to obtain good estimates of the true (or population) coefficients of an equation from a sample of that population. In other words, given an equation like:

$$Y_i = \beta_0 + \beta_1 X_{1i} + \beta_2 X_{2i} + \epsilon_i \tag{4.8}$$

we want to estimate βs by taking a sample of the population and calculating those estimates (typically by OLS if the classical assumptions of Section 4.1 are met). Since researchers usually only have one sample, beginning econometricians often assume that regression analysis can produce only one estimate of the βs. In reality, each different sample from a given population will produce a different set of estimates of the βs. For example, one sample might produce an estimate considerably higher than the true β while another might come up with a $\hat{\beta}$ which is lower. We need to discuss the properties of the distribution of these $\hat{\beta}$s, even though in most real applications we will encounter only a single draw from it.

A simplified example will help clarify this point. Suppose you were attempting to estimate the average age of your class from a sample of the class; let's say that you were trying to use a sample of five to estimate the average age of a class of thirty. The estimate you would get would obviously depend on the exact sample you picked. If your random sample happened to accidentally include the five youngest or the five oldest people in the class, then your estimated age would be dramatically different from the one you would get if your random sample were more centered. In essence, then, there is a distribution of all the possible estimates that will have a mean and a variance just as the distribution of error terms does. To illustrate this concept, assume that the population is uniformly distributed between 19 and 23. Here are three samples from this population:

sample #1: 19, 19, 20, 22, 23;   sample mean #1 = 20.6
sample #2: 20, 21, 21, 22, 22;   sample mean #2 = 21.2
sample #3: 19, 20, 22, 23, 23;   sample mean #3 = 21.4

Each sample yields an estimate of the true population mean (which is 21), and the distribution of the means of all the possible samples would have its own mean and variance. For a "good" estimation technique, we would want the mean of the distribution of sample estimates to be equal to the true population mean. This is called *unbiasedness*. While the mean of our three samples is a little over 21, it seems likely that if we took enough samples, the mean of our group of samples would eventually equal 21.0.

In a similar way, the $\hat{\beta}$s estimated by Ordinary Least Squares for Equation 4.8 form a distribution of their own. Each sample of observations of Y and the Xs will produce different estimates of the βs, but the distribution of these estimates for all possible samples has a mean and a variance just as any distribution. When we discuss the properties of estimators in the next section, it will be important to remember that we are discussing the properties of the distribution of estimates generated from a number of samples (a sampling distribution).

A desirable property of a distribution of estimates is that its mean equals the true mean of the item being estimated. An estimator that yields such estimates is called an unbiased estimator. (Technically, an *estimator* is a formula, such as the OLS formula in Equation 2.11, that tells you how to compute $\hat{\beta}_k$; an *estimate* is the value of $\hat{\beta}_k$ computed by that formula.) An **unbiased estimator** is an estimator whose sampling distribution is centered around the true value of β:

$$E(\hat{\beta}_k) = \beta_k \qquad (4.9)$$

A single estimate of β obtained for a particular sample from an unbiased estimator is called an unbiased estimate. Only one value of $\hat{\beta}$ is obtained in practice, but the property of unbiasedness is useful because a single estimate $\hat{\beta}$ drawn from an unbiased distribution is more likely to be near the true value (assuming identical variances of the $\hat{\beta}$s) than one taken from a distribution not centered around the true value. If an estimator produces $\hat{\beta}$s that are not centered around the true β, the estimator is referred to as a *biased estimator.*

We cannot insure that every estimate from an unbiased estimator is better than every estimate from a biased one because a particular unbiased estimate could, just by chance, be farther from the true value than a biased estimate might be. This could happen by chance, for example, or because the biased estimator has a smaller variance. Without any other information about the distribution of the estimates, however, we would always rather have an unbiased estimate than a biased one.

Just as we would like the distribution of the $\hat{\beta}$s to be centered around the true population β, so we would like that distribution to be as narrow (or precise) as possible. A distribution centered around the truth but with an extremely large variance might be of very little use because any given estimate would quite likely be far from the true β value. For a $\hat{\beta}$ distribution with a small variance, the estimates are likely to be close to the mean of the sampling distribution. To see this more clearly, compare distributions #1 and #2 (both of which are unbiased) in Figure 4.6. Distribution #1, which has a larger variance than distribution #2, is less precise

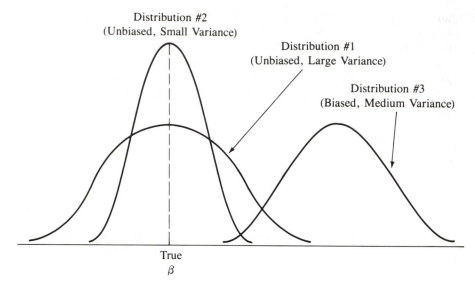

FIGURE 4.6 *Distributions of* $\hat{\beta}$

Different distributions of $\hat{\beta}$ can have different means and variances. Distributions #1 and #2, for example, are both unbiased, but distribution #1 has a larger variance than does distribution #2. Distribution #3, which is biased, has a smaller variance than distribution #1, but it is not centered around the true β.

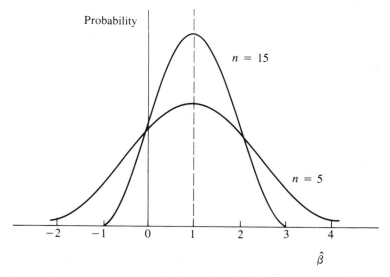

FIGURE 4.7 *Sampling Distribution of* $\hat{\beta}$ *for Various Values of the Number of Observations (n)*

As the size of the sample increases, the variance of the distribution of $\hat{\beta}$s calculated from that sample tends to decrease. In the extreme case (not shown) a sample size equal to the population would only yield an estimate equal to the mean of that distribution which (for unbiased estimators) would equal the true β, and the variance of the estimates would be zero.

than distribution #2. For comparison purposes, a biased distribution (distribution #3) is also pictured; note that the bias implies that the center of the distribution has moved to the right (or left) of the true β.

The variance of the distribution of the $\hat{\beta}$s can be decreased by increasing the size of the sample, which also increases the degrees of freedom, since the number of degrees of freedom equals the sample size minus the number of parameters estimated. As the number of observations increases, other things held constant, the distribution of $\hat{\beta}$s becomes more centered around its sample mean, and the variance of the sampling distribution (as well as the square root of the variance, called the *standard deviation*) tends to decrease. Thus the variance decreases as the sample size increases. Although it is not true that a sample of 15 will always produce estimates closer to the true β than a sample of 5, it is quite likely to do so, and such larger samples should be sought. Figure 4.7 shows illustrative sampling distributions of βs for 15 and 5 observations for OLS estimators of β when the true β equals one. The larger sample indeed produces a sampling distribution that is more closely centered around β. In econometrics, general tendencies must be relied on; the element of chance, a random occurrence, is always present in estimating regression coefficients, and some estimates may be far from the true value no matter how good the estimating technique is. However, if the distribution is centered around the true value and has as small a variance as possible, the element of chance is less likely to induce a poor estimate.

If the sampling distribution is centered around a value other than the true β—that is, if $\hat{\beta}$ is *biased*—then a lower variance implies that most of the sampling distribution of $\hat{\beta}$ is concentrated on the wrong value. However, if this value is not very different from the true value, which is usually not known in practice, then the greater precision will still be valuable. A final item of importance is that as the variance of the error term increases, so does the variance of the distribution of $\hat{\beta}$. The reason for the increased variance of $\hat{\beta}$ is that, with the larger variance of ϵ_i, the more extreme values of ϵ_i are observed with more frequency, and the error term becomes more important in determining the values of Y_i. Thus, the relative portion of the movements of Y_i explained by the deterministic component βX_i is less, and there are more unexplained changes in Y_i caused by the stochastic element ϵ_i. This implies that empirical inferences about the value of β are more tenuous. The R^2 of the equation will tend to decrease as the variance of the error term increases, symptomatic of this tendency.

4.3.2 A Demonstration That the $\hat{\beta}$s Are Normally Distributed

One of the properties of the normal distribution is that any linear function of normally distributed variables is itself normally distributed. Given this property, it is not difficult to prove mathematically that the assumption of the normality of the error terms implies that the $\hat{\beta}$s are themselves normally distributed. This proof is not as important as an understanding of the meaning of such a conclusion, however, and so this section presents a simplified demonstration of that property.

In order to demonstrate that normal error terms imply a normally distributed $\hat{\beta}$, we will use a computer to generate a number of samples and then calculate $\hat{\beta}$s from these samples in much the same manner as mean ages were calculated in the previous section. All the samples generated will conform to the same arbitrarily chosen true model, and the error term distribution used to generate the samples will be assumed to be normally distributed as is implied by the Central Limit Theorem. An examination of the distribution of $\hat{\beta}$s generated by this experiment not only shows their normality, it is a good review of the discussion of the sampling distribution of $\hat{\beta}$s. Computer-generated simulations of this kind are usually referred to as Monte Carlo experiments.[1]

For this demonstration, assume that the following model is true:

$$Y_i = \beta_0 + \beta_1 X_i + \epsilon_i = 0 + 1X_i + \epsilon_i \tag{4.10}$$

This is the same as stating that, on average, $Y = X$. If we now assume that the error term is (independently) normally distributed with mean zero and variance of 0.25, and if we further choose a sample size of 5 and a given set of fixed Xs, we can use the computer to generate a large number of random samples (data sets) conforming to the various assumptions listed above. We then can apply OLS and calculate a $\hat{\beta}$ for each of these samples, resulting in a distribution of $\hat{\beta}$s as discussed in this section. The sampling distribution for a large number[2] of such computer-generated data sets and OLS-calculated $\hat{\beta}$s is shown in Figure 4.8.

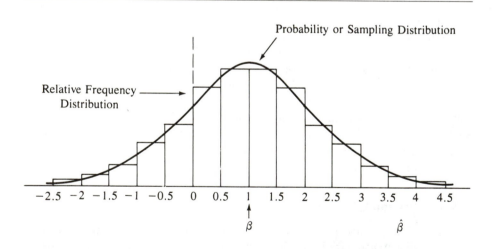

FIGURE 4.8 *Sampling Distribution of the OLS Estimator $\hat{\beta}$ for $\beta = 1$ and $\sigma^2 = 0.25$.* To demonstrate that the distribution of $\hat{\beta}$s is indeed normal, we calculated 5,000 estimates of $\hat{\beta}$ from 5,000 samples where the true β was known to be 1.0. As can be seen, the resulting distribution of the $\hat{\beta}$s was not only centered around 1.0, the true β, but it also was symmetrical and bell-shaped, as is the normal distribution.

Two conclusions can be drawn from an examination of this figure:

1. The distribution of $\hat{\beta}$s appears to be a symmetrical, bell-shaped distribution that is approaching a continuous normal distribution as the number of samples of $\hat{\beta}$s increases.

2. The distribution of the $\hat{\beta}$s is unbiased but shows surprising variation. $\hat{\beta}$s from -2.5 to $+4.5$ are observed even though the true value of β is 1.0. Such a result implies that any researcher who bases an important conclusion on a single regression result runs a severe risk of overstating the case. This danger depends on the variance of the error term, which decreases with the size of the sample. Note from Figure 4.7 that as the sample size increases from 5 to 15, the chance of observing a single $\hat{\beta}$ far from its true value falls; this demonstrates the preferability of larger samples.

4.4 The Gauss-Markov Theorem and the Properties of OLS Estimators

The Gauss-Markov Theorem derives the properties of Ordinary Least Squares estimators that meet the classical assumptions. This theorem is proven in all advanced econometrics textbooks, but for a regression user, it is more important to know what the theorem implies than to be able to prove it. The Gauss-Markov Theorem states that

> Given Classical Assumptions I through VI (Assumption VII, normality, is not needed for this theorem), the OLS estimate of β_k is the minimum variance, linear, unbiased estimator of β_k for k = 0,1,2,...,K.

The Gauss-Markov Theorem is perhaps the most easily remembered by stating that "OLS is BLUE" where BLUE stands for "*B*est (meaning minimum variance) *L*inear *U*nbiased *E*stimator." Students who might forget that "best" stands for minimum variance or maximum precision might be better served by remembering "OLS is MvLUE," but such a phrase is hardly catchy or easy to remember. (For an interpretation of the word "linear," see the answer to Exercise 4–8 in Appendix A.)

If an equation's estimation is unbiased (i.e., if each of the estimated slope coefficient is an unbiased estimate of the true population parameter), then:

$$E(\hat{\beta}_k) = \beta_k \quad (k = 0,1,2,...,K)$$

Best, as mentioned above, means that each $\hat{\beta}_k$ has the smallest variance of all the linear unbiased estimators of β_k. An unbiased estimator with the smallest variance is called **efficient,** and that estimator is said to have the property of efficiency.

Given the classical assumptions, the OLS estimators can be shown to have the following properties:

1. They are *unbiased*. That is, $E(\hat{\beta}) = \beta$. This means that the OLS estimates are centered around the true population values of the parameters being estimated.

2. They are *minimum variance*. The distribution of the estimates around the true parameter values is as tightly or narrowly distributed as is possible for an unbiased distribution. No other linear unbiased estimator has a lower variance for each estimated coefficient than OLS does. The combination of minimum variance with unbiasedness is called efficiency.

3. They are *consistent*. As the sample size approaches infinity, the estimates converge on the true population parameters. Put differently, as the sample size gets larger, the variance gets smaller, and each estimate approaches the true value of the coefficient being estimated.

4. They are *normally distributed;* the $\hat{\beta}$s are $N(\beta, \text{VAR}[\hat{\beta}])$. Thus various statistical tests based on the normal distribution may indeed be applied to these estimates, as will be done in Chapter 5.

If the seven classical assumptions are met and if Ordinary Least Squares is used to calculate the $\hat{\beta}$s, then it can be stated that an estimated regression coefficient is an unbiased, minimum variance estimate of the impact on the dependent variable of a one-unit change in a particular independent variable, holding constant all other independent variables in the equation. Such an estimate is drawn from a distribution of estimates that is centered around the true population coefficient and has the smallest possible variance for such unbiased distributions.

4.5   The Classical Assumptions in Standard Notation

We now formally introduce the notation that is typically used to represent the measures of central tendency and the degree of dispersion of sampling and probability distributions. Then we present the classical regression assumptions in this standard notation.

4.5.1   Standard Econometric Notation

While Section 4.3 portrayed graphically the notions of central tendency and dispersion, this section presents the standard notation used throughout the econometrics literature for these concepts.

The measure of the central tendency of the sampling distribution of $\hat{\beta}$, which can be thought of as the mean of the $\hat{\beta}$s, is denoted as $E(\hat{\beta})$, read as "the expected value of beta-hat." The expected value of a random variable is the population mean of that variable (with observations weighted by the probability of observation).

The variance of $\hat{\beta}$ is the typical measure of dispersion of the sampling distribution of $\hat{\beta}$. The variance operator has several alternative notational representations, including $\text{VAR}(\hat{\beta})$ and $\sigma^2(\hat{\beta})$. Each of these is read as the "variance of beta-hat" and represents the degree of dispersion of the sampling distribution of $\hat{\beta}$.

Table 4.1 presents various alternative notational devices used to represent the different population (true) parameters and their corresponding estimates (based on samples).

Table 4.1 Notation Conventions

Population Parameter (True Values, but Unobserved)		Estimate (Observed from Sample)	
Name	Symbol(s)	Name	Symbol(s)
Regression coefficient	β_k	Estimated regression coefficient	$\hat{\beta}_k$
Expected value of the estimated coefficient	$E(\hat{\beta}_k)$		
Variance of the error term	σ^2 or $VAR(\epsilon_i)$	Estimated variance of the error term	s^2 or $\hat{\sigma}^2$
Standard deviation of the error term	σ	Standard error of the equation	s or SEE
Variance of the estimated coefficient	$\sigma^2(\hat{\beta}_k)$ or $VAR(\hat{\beta}_k)$	Estimated variance of the estimated coefficient	$s^2(\hat{\beta}_k)$ or $\widehat{VAR}(\hat{\beta}_k)$
Standard deviation of the estimated coefficient	$\sigma_{\hat{\beta}_k}$ or $\sigma(\hat{\beta}_k)$	Standard error of the estimated coefficient	$\hat{\sigma}(\hat{\beta}_k)$ or $SE(\hat{\beta}_k)$
Error or disturbance term	ϵ_i	Residual (estimate of error in a loose sense)	e_i

To review Table 4.1, the true coefficient β_k is estimated by $\hat{\beta}_k$. The estimator is stochastic, or random, because its value depends on the values of the stochastic error term in the true function. Thus $\hat{\beta}$ has a sampling distribution based on the distribution of the ϵ_is. If the ϵ_is are normally distributed, as is usually assumed by invoking the Central Limit Theorem, then the $\hat{\beta}$s are normally distributed.

Two population parameters, the mean and the variance, fully describe the $\hat{\beta}$ distribution. The mean, the measure of central tendency of the sampling distribution, is $E(\hat{\beta}_k)$, which equals β_k if the estimator is unbiased. The variance (or, alternatively, the square root of the variance, called the **standard deviation**) is a measure of dispersion in the sampling distribution of $\hat{\beta}_k$. The variance of the estimates is a population parameter that is never actually observed in practice; instead, it is estimated with $\hat{\sigma}^2(\hat{\beta}_k)$, also written as $s^2(\hat{\beta}_k)$. Note, by the way, that the variance of the true β, $\sigma^2(\beta)$ is zero, since there is only one true β_k and there is no distribution around it. Thus the estimated variance of the estimated coefficient is defined and observed, the true variance of the estimated coefficient is unobservable, and the true variance of the true coefficient is zero.

4.5.2 The Classical Assumptions in Notational Form

Most econometrics texts and articles state the assumptions of the classical model in terms of expectation and variance operators. The classical assumptions typically stated in this notation (Assumptions II through V) are presented here:

$$\text{II.} \quad E(\epsilon_i) = 0$$

Assumption II states that the distribution of the error term has a central tendency or expected value of zero.

$$\text{III.} \quad E(X_{ki} \cdot \epsilon_i) = 0 \quad (k = 1,2,\ldots,K \text{ and } i = 1,2,\ldots,n)$$

Assumption III states that the error term and each explanatory variable are independent. This is typically summarized by stating that the expected value of the product of an independent variable and the error term from the same observation is zero. This results because the expected value of the error term is zero, and because if the values of the error term and the explanatory variables are indeed independent, the positive $X_{ki} \cdot \epsilon_i$ products will offset the negative ones. If X_{ki} and ϵ_i are not independent, then they will either be positively or negatively correlated, and the expected value of their product will no longer be zero. For example, a positive correlation would occur if values of any given X were above its mean when ϵ was positive.[3]

$$\text{IV.} \quad E(\epsilon_i \cdot \epsilon_j) = 0 \quad \text{for all } i,j = 1,2,\ldots,n \text{ except } i = j$$

Assumption IV states that the observations of the error term are similarly independent. If an error term was systematically related to another error term, then the expected value of their product would not be zero.

$$\text{V.} \quad VAR(\epsilon_i) = \sigma^2 \quad \text{a constant, for all } i = 1,2,\ldots,n$$

Assumption V states that the variance of the distribution of the error term is constant for all observations; that is, the value of the variance does not change with any observation of the error term. To make this clearer, note that the alternative to Assumption V (heteroskedasticity) would be that the variance of the distribution of the error term *does* depend on exactly which observation is being discussed, or:

$$VAR(\epsilon_i) = \sigma^2_i \quad (i = 1,2,\ldots,n) \tag{4.11}$$

The only difference between Assumption V and Equation 4.11 is that with homoskedasticity there is no subscript and with heteroskedasticity there is a subscript. This subscript implies that the variance of the error term in this situation differs from observation to observation, and Assumption V is violated.

4.6   Summary

1. The seven classical assumptions state that the regression model is linear with an error term which is zero-meaned, is independent of explanatory variables and other observations of the error term, has a constant variance, and is normally distributed (optional). In addition, the explanatory variables are assumed not to be perfect linear functions of each other.

2. The two most important properties of an estimator are unbiasedness and minimum variance. An estimator is unbiased when the expected value of the estimated coefficient is equal to the true value, and minimum variance holds when the estimating distribution has the smallest variance of all the estimators. An estimator that is unbiased and minimum variance is called efficient.

3. Given the classical assumptions, ordinary least squares (OLS) can be shown to be the minimum variance, linear, unbiased estimator (or BLUE, for best linear unbiased estimator) of the regression coefficients. This is the Gauss-Markov Theorem. When one or more of the classical properties do not hold (excluding normality), OLS is no longer BLUE, but it still may provide better estimates in some cases than the alternative estimation techniques discussed in subsequent chapters.

4. The sampling distribution of the OLS estimator $\hat{\beta}_k$, being BLUE, has desirable properties. Moreover, the variance, or the degree of dispersion of the sampling distribution of $\hat{\beta}_k$, decreases as the number of observations increases. The rule here is simple; if the cost of additional observations is within reason, obtain them and use them for estimation.

5. There is a standard notation used in the econometric literature. Table 4.1 presents this fairly complex set of notational conventions for use in regression analysis. This table should be reviewed periodically as a refresher.

6. An OLS-estimated regression coefficient from a model that meets the classical assumptions is an unbiased, minimum variance estimate of the impact on the dependent variable of a one-unit change in the independent variable in question, holding constant the other independent variables in the equation.

Exercises

(Answers to even-numbered exercises are in Appendix A)

1. Write out the meaning of each of the following terms without reference to the book (or to your notes) and then compare your definition with the version in the text for each:
   a. The Classical Assumptions
   b. classical error term
   c. standard normal distribution
   d. The Central Limit Theorem
   e. unbiased estimator
   f. BLUE

2. Think back to the assumption of linearity in the coefficients (Assumption I in Section 4.1) and the equation reproduced below:

$$\ln(Y_i) = \beta_0 + \beta_1 \ln(X_i) + \epsilon_i$$

a. What is the elasticity of Y with respect to X? (Elasticity is defined as the percentage change in Y brought about by a one-percent change in X.)

b. Would the above equation still be linear in the coefficients if it also included an additional (additive) term, $\beta_2 \ln(Z_i)$? Why or why not? What is the economic application of such an equation?

3. Suppose one of your friends said that "Assumptions III and IV don't really mean that much." After all, if ϵ is zero, then ϵ multiplied by something should be zero, and it's no big deal that:

$$E(X_{ki} \cdot \epsilon_i) = 0 \ \text{ or } \ E(\epsilon_i \cdot \epsilon_j) = 0$$

Would your friend be right or wrong? Why?

4. Which of the following pairs of independent variables would violate Assumption VI? (That is, which pairs of variables are perfect linear functions of each other?)

a. right shoe size and left shoe size (of students in your class)

b. consumption and disposable income (in the U.S. over the last thirty years)

c. X_i and $2X_i$

d. X_i and $(X_i)^2$

5. Consider the following estimated regression equation:

$$\hat{Y}_t = -120 + 0.10F_t + 5.33RS_t \qquad \bar{R}^2 = .50$$

where: Y_t = corn yield (bushels/acre) in year t
F_t = fertilizer intensity (pounds/acre) in year t
RS_t = rainfall (inches) in year t

a. Carefully state the meaning of the coefficients 0.10 and 5.33 in this equation in terms of the impact of F and RS on Y.

b. Does the constant term of -120 really mean that *negative* amounts of corn are possible? If not, what is the meaning of that estimate?

c. Suppose you were told that the true value of β_F is *known* to be 0.40. Does this show that the estimate is biased? Why or why not?

d. Suppose you were told that the equation does not meet all the classical assumptions and therefore is not BLUE. Does this mean that the true β_{RS} is definitely *not* equal to 5.33? Why or why not?

6. Consider a random variable that is distributed $N(0, 0.5)$; that is, normally distributed with a mean of zero and a variance of 0.5. What is the probability that a single observation drawn from this distribution would be greater than one or less than minus one? (Hint: To answer this question, you will need to convert this distribution to a standard normal one (with mean equal

to zero and standard deviation equal to one) and then refer to Table B-7 in the back of the book. That table includes a description of how to make such a transformation.)

7. Consider the following estimated regression equation for 78 cities:[4]

$$\hat{L}_i = 94.2 - 0.24U_i - 0.20E_i - 0.69I_i - 0.06S_i + 0.002C_i - 0.80D_i$$

where: L_i = percent labor force participation (males ages 25 to 54) in the ith city

U_i = percent unemployment rate in the ith city

E_i = average earnings (hundreds of dollars/year) in the ith city

I_i = average other income (hundreds of dollars/year) in the ith city

S_i = average schooling completed (years) in the ith city

C_i = percent of the labor force that is nonwhite in the ith city

D_i = dummy equal to 1 if the city is in the South and 0 otherwise

a. Interpret the estimated coefficients of C and D. What do they mean?

b. How likely is perfect collinearity in this equation? Explain your answer.

c. Suppose that you were told that the data for this regression were from 1950 and that estimates on the data from 1960 yielded a much smaller coefficient of the dummy variable. Would this imply that one of the estimates was biased? If not, why not? If so, how would you determine which year's estimate was biased?

d. Comment on the following statement. "I know that these results are not BLUE because the average participation rate of 94.2 percent is way too high." Do you agree or disagree? Why?

8. A typical exam question in a more advanced econometrics class is to prove the Gauss-Markov Theorem. How might you go about starting such a proof? What is the importance of such a proof? (Hint: If you're having trouble getting started answering this question, see Appendix A.)

---

[1] Monte Carlo experiments can be thought of as having seven steps:
1. Assume a "true" model.
2. Select values for the parameters and the independent variables.
3. Select the estimating technique (usually OLS, but for a comparison of techniques, select several).
4. Create various sets of values of the dependent variable, using the assumed model, by randomly generating error terms from the assumed distribution.
5. Compute the estimates of the βs from the various samples.
6. Evaluate the results.
7. Return to step #2 and choose other values for the parameters or the independent variables and compare these results with the first set (this step, which is optional, is called *sensitivity analysis*).

[2] The number of data sets was 5,000, but the exact number of $\hat{\beta}$s calculated is less important than the fact that the number is large enough for the sampling distribution to approach the underlying population distribution.

[3] Only when two variables are independent is the expected value of their product equal to the product of their expected values. Therefore, even if the expected value of epsilon is zero, the expected value of epsilon *times* X is not equal to zero unless epsilon and X are independent.

[4] W. G. Bowen and T. A. Finegan, "Labor Force Participation and Unemployment," in Arthur M. Ross (ed.), *Employment Policy and Labor Markets* (Berkeley: University of California Press, 1965), Table 4-2.

5

Hypothesis Testing and the *t*-Test

The most important use of econometrics for many researchers is in testing their theories with data from the real world, so hypothesis testing is far more meaningful to them than are the two other major uses of econometrics, description and forecasting. The present chapter introduces hypothesis testing from a general point of view and then focuses on the *t*-test, the statistical tool typically used for such testing in regression applications.

We are merely returning to the essence of econometrics—an effort to quantify economic relationships by analyzing sample data—and asking what conclusions we can draw from this quantification. Hypothesis testing goes beyond mere calculation of estimates of the true population parameters to a much more complex set of questions. Hypothesis testing asks what we can learn about the real world from this sample. Is it likely that our result could have been obtained by chance? Can our theories be rejected using the results generated by our sample? If our theory is correct, what are the odds that this particular sample would have been observed?

All approaches to hypothesis testing take into account that any particular estimate comes from a distribution of estimates and must be interpreted with respect to the standard error of that distribution before any importance can be attached to it. A single estimate of a regression coefficient β is only one of many possible estimates, and conclusions drawn from that estimate must take the entire distribution into account. As a result, the classical approach to hypothesis testing, which is what we present in this chapter, consists of three steps:

1. The development of hypotheses about the truth. These are usually the result of the application of economic theory or common sense to the details of the particular equation being estimated.

2. The calculation of estimates of the coefficients and their standard errors. This has been the subject of the previous four chapters.

3. The testing of the implications of the estimates obtained in #2 above for the hypotheses stated in #1 above. This usually involves inferring whether the estimated coefficient is significantly different from the population value that was hypothesized.

Hypothesis testing and the *t*-test should be familiar topics to readers with strong backgrounds in statistics, who are encouraged to skim this chapter and focus only on those applications that seem somewhat new. The development of hypothesis testing procedures is explained here in terms of the regression model, however, so parts of the chapter may be instructive even to those already skilled in statistics.

5.1 What Is Hypothesis Testing?

Hypothesis testing is used in a variety of settings. The Food and Drug Administration, for example, requires testing of new products before allowing their sale. If the sample of people exposed to the new product shows some side-effect significantly more frequently than would have been expected to occur by chance, the FDA is likely to withhold approval of the marketing of the product. Similarly, economists have been statistically testing various relationships between consumption and income for half a century; theories developed by John Maynard Keynes and Milton Friedman, among others, have all been tested on macroeconomic and microeconomic data sets.

Although researchers are always interested in learning whether the theory in question is supported by estimates generated from a sample of real-world observations, it is almost impossible to prove that a given hypothesis is correct. All that can be done is to state that a particular sample conforms to a particular hypothesis. Even though we cannot prove that a given theory is "correct" using hypothesis testing, we *can* often reject a given hypothesis with a certain degree of confidence. In such a case, the researcher concludes that the sample result would be very unlikely to have been observed if the hypothesized theory were correct. If there is conflicting evidence on the validity of a theory, the question is often put aside until additional data or a new approach sheds more light on the issue.

Let's begin by investigating three topics that are central to the application of hypothesis testing to regression analysis:

1. The specification of the hypothesis to be tested.

2. The choice of a particular decision rule for deciding whether to reject the hypothesis in question.

3. The kinds of errors that might be encountered if the application of the decision rule to the appropriate statistics yields an incorrect inference.

5.1.1 Classical Null and Alternative Hypotheses

The first step in hypothesis testing is to state explicitly the hypothesis to be tested; and to insure fairness, the researcher should specify the hypothesis *before* the equation is estimated. The purpose of prior theoretical work is to match the hypothesis to the underlying theory as completely as possible. Hypotheses formulated after generation of the estimates are at times justifications of particular results rather than tests of their validity. As a result, most econometricians take pains to specify hypotheses before estimation.

In making a hypothesis, you must state carefully what you think is not true and what you think is true. These reflections of the researcher's expectations about a particular regression coefficient (or coefficients) are summarized in the null and alternative hypotheses. The **null hypothesis** is typically a statement of the range of values of the regression coefficient that could be expected to occur if the researcher's theory is *not* correct. The **alternative hypothesis** is used to specify the range of values of the coefficient that could be expected to occur if the researcher's theory is correct. The word "null" also means "zero," and the null hypothesis can be thought of as the hypothesis that the researcher does *not* believe. The reason that zero is typically the value that the researcher does not expect is that a variable would not be included in an equation if its expected coefficient were zero.

We set up the null and alternative hypotheses in this way so we can make rather strong statements when we reject the null hypothesis. In particular, only if we define the null hypothesis as the result we do *not* expect (or the "strawman" result) can we control the probability of accidentally rejecting the null hypothesis when it is in fact true. The converse does not hold. That is, we can never actually know the probability of accidentally agreeing that the null hypothesis is correct when it is in fact false. As a result, we can never say that we *accept* the null hypothesis; we always must say that we *cannot reject* the null hypothesis, or we put the word "accept" in quotes.

Researchers occasionally will switch the null and alternative hypotheses. For instance, some tests of the rational expectations theory have put the preferred hypothesis as the null hypothesis in order to make the null hypothesis a specific value. In such cases of tests of specific nonzero values, the reversal of the null and alternative hypotheses is regrettable but unavoidable; an example of this kind of reversal is in Section 5.4. Except for these rare cases, all null hypotheses in this text will be the result we expect not to occur.

The notation used to refer to a null hypothesis is "H_0:", and this notation is followed by a statement of the value or range of values you do *not* expect the particular parameter to take. For example:

$$H_0: \beta = S \quad \text{(where S is the specific value you do not expect)}$$

If the estimated coefficient is significantly different from S, then we reject the null hypothesis. If the estimated coefficient is not significantly different from S, then we cannot reject H_0.

The alternative hypothesis is expressed by "H_A:" followed by the parameter value or values you expect to observe:

H_A: β = T   (where T is the value you expect to be true)

Hypotheses in econometrics often do not specify particular values, but rather particular signs that the researcher expects the estimated coefficients to take. We frequently hypothesize that a particular coefficient will be positive (or negative); in such cases, the null hypothesis still represents what is expected not to occur, but that expectation is now a range; the same is true for the alternative hypothesis. If, for example, you expect a negative coefficient then the correct null and alternative hypotheses would be:

$$H_0: \beta \geq 0$$
$$H_A: \beta < 0$$

Note that the null hypothesis is the "strawman" and the alternative hypothesis is your "pet theory."

Let's look at a more complete example of making such null and alternative hypotheses. Suppose you are about to estimate an equation to explain aggregate retail sales of new cars (Y) as a function of disposable income (X_1) and the average retail price of a new car deflated by the consumer price index (X_2):

$$Y_i = f(\overset{+}{X_1}, \overset{-}{X_2}) = \beta_0 + \beta_1 X_{1i} + \beta_2 X_{2i} + \epsilon_i \qquad (5.1)$$

As was discussed in Section 3.2, the positive sign above X_1 in the functional notation on the left side of Equation 5.1 indicates that you expect income to have a positive impact on car sales, holding prices constant. Because you expect X_1 to have a positive impact on Y, you have already made a hypothesis. That is, you have already stated that you expect β_1 to be greater than zero. Since the null hypothesis contains that which you are hoping to reject, it would be:

$$H_0: \beta_1 \leq 0$$

The alternative hypothesis (which should correspond to your expected sign) would be:

$$H_A: \beta_1 > 0$$

To test yourself, go back to Equation 5.1 and attempt to create null and alternative hypotheses for X_2. Do you see that the answer is H_0: $\beta_2 \geq 0$ and H_A: $\beta_2 < 0$? This answer is correct because you have stated in the signs above Equation 5.1 that you expect price to have a negative impact on car sales, holding disposable income constant, and because you should place your expected coefficient values in the alternative hypothesis.[1]

Another way to state the null and alternative hypotheses for the same equation and underlying theory would be to test the null hypothesis that β_1 is not significantly different from zero in either direction. In this second approach, the null and alternative hypotheses would be:

$$H_0: \beta_1 = 0$$
$$H_A: \beta_1 \neq 0$$

Since the alternative hypothesis has values on both sides of the null hypothesis, this approach is called a **two-sided test** (or *two-tailed test*) to distinguish it from the **one-sided test** of the previous example (where the alternative hypothesis was only on one side of the null hypothesis).

One difficulty with the two-sided approach in the new car sales model is that you expect β_1 to be positive, but the alternative hypothesis does not distinguish between highly positive values, which support your theory, and highly negative values, which do not. Such difficulties do not apply if there are conflicting theories about which sign the coefficient is expected to take, because then dramatically large positive *or* negative values would fit your expectations. Since the expected sign of a coefficient (such as for price or income) is usually predicted by the underlying theory, most null hypotheses involving zero tend to be one-tailed tests. Null hypotheses involving nonzero values can be either one-tailed or two-tailed depending on the underlying theory.[2]

5.1.2 Type I and Type II Errors

The typical testing technique in econometrics is to hypothesize an expected sign (or value) for each regression coefficient (except the constant term) and then to determine whether to reject the null hypothesis. Since the regression coefficients are only estimates of the true population parameters, it would be unrealistic to think that conclusions drawn from regression analysis will always be right.

There are two kinds of errors we can make in such hypothesis testing:

Type I. We reject a true null hypothesis

Type II. We do not reject a false null hypothesis

We will refer to these errors as **Type I and Type II Errors** respectively.[3]

We shall now return to the new car sales model to get a better understanding of these errors. In particular, recall that the null and alternative hypotheses to test the impact of disposable income on new car sales (holding prices constant) are:

$$H_0: \beta_1 \leq 0$$
$$H_A: \beta_1 > 0$$

There are two distinct possibilities. The first is that the true β_1 in the population is equal to or less than zero, as specified by the null hypothesis; this is the same as saying that income does *not* have a positive effect on car sales. When the true β_1 is not positive, unbiased estimates of β_1 will be distributed around zero or some negative number, but any given estimate is very unlikely to be exactly equal to that number. Any single sample (and therefore any estimate of β calculated from that sample) might be quite different from the mean of the distribution. As a result, even if the true parameter β_1 is not positive, the particular estimate obtained by a researcher may be sufficiently positive to lead to the rejection of the null hypothesis that $\beta_1 \leq 0$. This is a Type I Error. For the new car sales model this would mean rejecting the null hypothesis of a nonpositive impact of income on sales even though it is true. A Type I Error is graphed in Figure 5.1.

The second possibility is that the true β_1 is greater than 0, as stated in the alternative hypothesis; this is the same as saying that the impact of income on new car sales is indeed positive. Depending on the specific value of the population

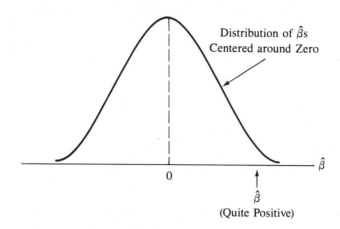

FIGURE 5.1 *Rejecting a True Null Hypothesis Is a Type I Error.*
If $\beta = 0$ but you observe a $\hat{\beta}$ that is very positive, you might reject a true null hypothesis $H_0: \beta \leq 0$ and conclude incorrectly that the alternative hypothesis $H_A: \beta > 0$ is true.

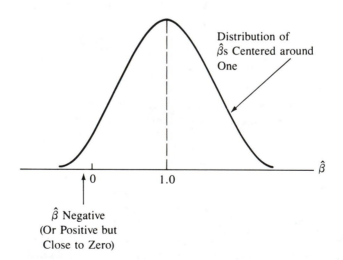

FIGURE 5.2 *Failure To Reject a False Null Hypothesis Is a Type II Error.*
If $\beta = 1$ but you observe a $\hat{\beta}$ that is negative or close to zero, you might fail to reject a false null hypothesis $H_0: \beta \leq 0$ and incorrectly ignore that the alternative hypothesis $H_A: \beta > 0$ is true.

β_1 (and other factors) it is possible to obtain an estimate of β_1 that is close enough to zero (or negative) to be considered "not significantly positive." This occurs because the sampling distribution of $\hat{\beta}_1$, even if unbiased, has a portion of its area in the region of $\beta_1 \leq 0$. Such a result may lead the researcher to "accept" the hypothesis that $\beta_1 \leq 0$ when in truth $\beta_1 > 0$. This is a Type II Error. In the new car sales model this would mean accepting the null hypothesis of a nonpositive impact of price on sales even though it is false. A Type II Error is graphed in Figure 5.2. (The specific value of $\beta_1 = 1$ was selected as the true value in that figure simply for illustrative purposes.)

The following Chart summarizes this example when the null hypothesis being tested is that $\beta_1 \leq 0$ and the alternative hypothesis is that $\beta_1 > 0$.

		The Truth about the Coefficient β_1	
		$\beta_1 \leq 0$ ("Strawman")	$\beta_1 > 0$ ("Pet Theory")
Inference	$\beta_1 \leq 0$	no error	Type II Error
from the Test	$\beta_1 > 0$	Type I Error	no error

5.1.3 Decision Rules of Hypothesis Testing

In testing a hypothesis, a sample statistic must be calculated that allows the null hypothesis to be "accepted" or rejected depending on the magnitude of that sample statistic compared to a "critical" value found in tables such as those at the end of this text. This procedure is referred to as a **decision rule.** There are several approaches to establishing decision rules, including the classical and the Bayesian approaches. The majority of this text will take the classical approach, but the Bayesian approach is briefly examined in Section 6.6.

A decision rule is formulated before regression estimates are obtained. The range of possible values of $\hat{\beta}$ is divided into two regions, an *"acceptance" region* and a *rejection region* where the terms are expressed relative to the null hypothesis. In order to define these regions, we must determine a *critical value* (or, for a two-tailed test, two critical values) of β. A **critical value** is thus a $\hat{\beta}$ value that divides the acceptance region from the rejection region when testing a null hypothesis.

Look again at the example of the new car demand model in Equation 5.1, H_0: $\beta_1 \leq 0$ and H_A: $\beta_1 > 0$. Once we've chosen a critical value, let's call it β_C, then the decision rules becomes:

$$\text{Do not reject } H_0 \text{ if } \hat{\beta}_1 \leq \beta_C$$
$$\text{Reject } H_0 \text{ if } \hat{\beta}_1 > \beta_C$$

A graph of these "acceptance" and rejection regions is presented in Figure 5.3. For a two-tailed test that H_0: $\beta_1 = 0$ and H_A: $\beta_1 \neq 0$, there would be two critical values and the graph would have two different rejection regions as shown in Figure 5.4, but the principle would be identical.

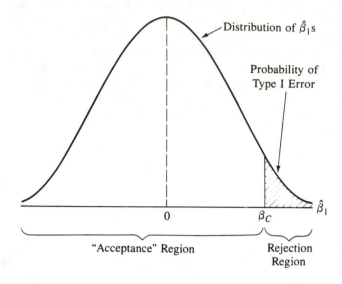

FIGURE 5.3 *"Acceptance" and Rejection Regions for a One-Sided Test of* β.
For a one-sided test of H_0: $\beta \leq 0$ vs. H_A: $\beta > 0$, the critical value β_C divides
the distribution of $\hat{\beta}$ (centered around zero on the assumption that H_0 is true) into
"acceptance" and rejection regions.

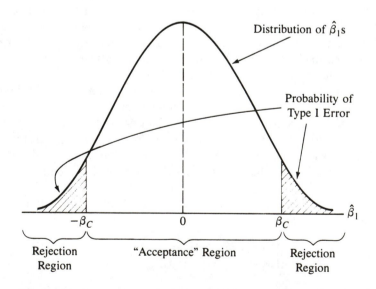

FIGURE 5.4 *"Acceptance" and Rejection Regions for a Two-Sided Test of* β.
For a two-sided test of H_0: $\beta = 0$ vs. H_A: $\beta \neq 0$, the critical values $+\beta_C$ and $-\beta_C$ divide
the distribution of $\hat{\beta}$ into an "acceptance" region and *two* rejection regions.

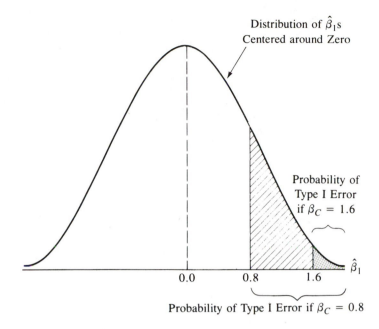

FIGURE 5.5 *Type I Error Decreases as the Critical Value* β_C *Increases.*
For a distribution of $\hat{\beta}_1$s centered around zero for the one-sided test of H_0: $\beta_1 \leq 0$ vs. H_A: $\beta_1 > 0$, the probability of a Type I Error (rejection of a true H_0) decreases as the critical value is increased from 0.8 to 1.6. For this particular null hypothesis, the probability of a Type I Error is represented by the area under the curve to the right of the critical value.

To use a decision rule, we need to select the critical value β_C. Let's suppose that we arbitrarily select a $\beta_C = 0.8$. If the observed $\hat{\beta}_1$ is greater than 0.8 but the true $\beta_1 \leq 0$, then we would reject H_0 when in fact it is true, thus making a Type I Error. Suppose we now increased β_C from 0.8 to 1.6, what would happen to the probability of a Type I Error? Since we make a Type I Error only when a $\hat{\beta}_1$ coming from a distribution centered around zero (or a negative number) exceeds β_C, then increasing β_C would *decrease* the probability of Type I Error. As can be seen in Figure 5.5, the probability of a Type I Error decreases by more than tenfold. Thus, if Type I Errors were the only possible kind (or the only kind that mattered to the researcher) then it would make sense to set β_C quite high. What would such a decision do to the probability of making a Type II Error?

Well, when the observed $\hat{\beta}_1$ is less than 0.8 but the true $\beta_1 > 0$, then we "accept" H_0 when in fact it is false, thus making a Type II Error. If we increase β_c to 1.6, this would increase the likelihood of making a Type II Error because more $\hat{\beta}_1$s centered around a positive value would fall below 1.6 than would fall below 0.8. In Figure 5.6, Type II Error more than doubles if we increase β_C from 0.8 to 1.6 when the true β_1 equals one instead of zero.

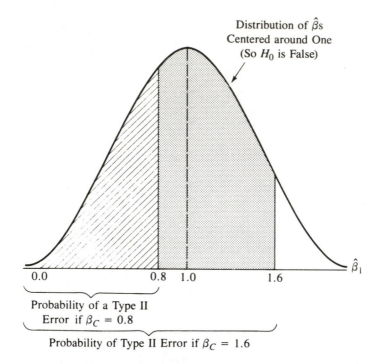

FIGURE 5.6 *Type II Error Increases as the Critical Value* β_C *Increases.*
For a distribution of $\hat{\beta}_1$s centered around one for the one-sided test of H_0: $\beta_1 \leq 0$ vs H_A: $\beta_1 \leq 0$, the probability of a Type II Error ("acceptance" of a false H_0) increases as the critical value is increased from 0.8 to 1.6. For this particular null hypothesis, the probability of a Type II Error is represented by the area under the curve to the left of the critical value.

Thus, to decrease the probability of a Type II Error, we should keep β_C low, but this will increase the probability of a Type I Error, as shown above. What should we do? We should never consider trying to eliminate Type I Error completely because to do so would increase Type II Error considerably; similarly, it is foolhardy to try to eliminate Type II Error totally (by moving β_C to the left) because such a decision rule would mean rejecting virtually every null hypothesis that comes along.

Since it seems clear that we must make a trade-off between Type I and Type II Errors, how would we go about choosing β_C? Is there some easy rule to always follow? Unfortunately, the answer is no; the choice of a critical value depends on the details of the equation and variable in question. One important factor is the costs to you of making each kind of error. In some circumstances, you might want to be extremely confident that you have not "accepted" a false null hypothesis (which, in the example of the FDA, would permit the marketing of a potentially harmful product); here, you would want to be quite conservative because even a hint of harmful side-effects would be enough to reject the product. On the other hand, there might be situations in which you would be more concerned with not rejecting a true null hypothesis (for instance, when dealing with a new approach to the consumption function). In such cases, you would want to be fairly liberal for fear of rejecting a potentially valuable new theory before giving it a fair test. Either way, the appropriate test to apply to single regression coefficients is the *t*-test.

5.2   The *t*-Test

Rather than comparing $\hat{\beta}$s with critical β-values, the *t*-test is the method usually used by econometricians to test hypotheses about individual regression slope coefficients. Tests of more than one coefficient at a time (joint hypotheses) are typically done with the *F*-test, presented in Section 5.8.

The *t*-test is easy to use because it accounts for differences in the units of measurement of the variables and in the standard deviations of the estimated coefficients (both of which would affect the shape of the distribution of $\hat{\beta}$ and the location of the critical value β_C). More importantly, the t-statistic is the appropriate test to use when the stochastic error terms are normally distributed and when the variance of that distribution must be estimated. Since these usually are the case, the use of the *t*-test for hypothesis testing has become standard practice in econometrics.

5.2.1   The t-Statistic

For a typical multiple regression equation:

$$Y_i = \beta_0 + \beta_1 X_{1i} + \beta_2 X_{2i} + \epsilon_i \tag{5.2}$$

we can calculate t-values for each of the estimated coefficients in the equation. For reasons that will be explained in Section 6.3, *t*-tests are usually done only on the slope coefficients; for these, the relevant general form of the **t-statistic** for the *k*th coefficient is:

$$t_k = (\hat{\beta}_k - \beta_{H_0})/SE(\hat{\beta}_k) \qquad (k = 1,2,\ldots,K) \tag{5.3}$$

where: $\hat{\beta}_k$ = the estimated regression coefficient of the *k*th variable

β_{H_0} = the border value (usually zero) implied by the null hypothesis for β_k

$SE(\hat{\beta}_k)$ = the estimated standard error of $\hat{\beta}_k$ (i.e., the square root of the estimated variance of the distribution of the $\hat{\beta}_k$; note that there is no "hat" attached to SE because SE is already defined as an estimate).

How do you decide what *border* is implied by the null hypothesis? Some null hypotheses specify a particular value. For these, β_{H_0} is simply that value;

if H_0: β = S, then β_{H_0} = S. Other null hypotheses involve ranges, but we are concerned only with the value in the null hypothesis that is closest to the border between the acceptance region and the rejection region. This "border" value then becomes the β_{H_0}; for example, if H_0: $\beta \geq 0$ and H_A: $\beta < 0$, then the value in the null hypothesis closest to the border is zero, and β_{H_0} = 0.

Since most regression hypotheses test whether a particular regression coefficient is significantly different from zero, β_{H_0} is typically zero, and the most-used form of the t-statistic becomes

$$t_k = (\hat{\beta}_k - 0)/SE(\hat{\beta}_k) \qquad (k = 1,2,...,K)$$

which simplifies to

$$t_k = \hat{\beta}_k/SE(\hat{\beta}_k) \qquad (k = 1,2,...,K) \qquad (5.4)$$

or the estimated coefficient divided by the estimate of its standard error. This is the t-statistic formula used by most computer programs.

For an example of this calculation, let's reconsider the equation for the check volume at Woody's restaurants from Section 3.3. In that section, we presented only the estimated regression coefficients in the discussion of the model, but now that we have introduced the concept of the t-statistic, we can use the typical regression equation format originally specified in the documentation discussion in Section 3.2:

$$\hat{Y}_i = 102,192 - 9075C_i + 0.3547P_i + 1.288I_i \qquad (5.5)$$
$$(2053) \qquad (0.0727) \qquad (0.543)$$
$$t = \qquad -4.42 \qquad 4.88 \qquad 2.37$$
$$n = 33 \qquad \bar{R}^2 = .579 \qquad F = 15.65$$

In Equation 5.5, the numbers in parentheses underneath the estimated regression coefficients are the estimated standard errors of the estimated $\hat{\beta}$s, and the numbers below them are t-values calculated according to Equation 5.4. The format used to document Equation 5.5 above is the one we will use whenever possible throughout this text, and it is one of two standard notations. A second format sometimes used omits the estimated standard errors and simply put the t-values in parentheses underneath the estimated coefficients. Because of the existence of two different systems, it is often necessary to define the values in parentheses. Note that the sign of the t-value is always the same as that of the estimated regression coefficient, while the standard error is always positive. Thus an inspection of the results can sometimes allow a careful reader to determine definitions even if they were omitted by the researcher.

Starting from the regression results in Equation 5.5, let's calculate the t-value for the estimated coefficient of the population variable. Given the values in Equation 5.5 of 0.3547 for $\hat{\beta}_P$ and 0.0727 for $SE(\hat{\beta}_P)$, and given H_0: $\beta \leq 0$, the relevant t-value is indeed 4.88 as specified in Equation 5.5:

$$t_P = \hat{\beta}_P/SE(\hat{\beta}_P) = 0.3547/0.0727 = 4.88$$

The larger in absolute value this t-value is, the greater the likelihood is that the estimated regression coefficient is significantly different from zero.

5.2.2   The Critical t-Value and the *t*-Test Decision Rule

In order to reject a null hypothesis based on a calculated t-value, we use a critical t-value (which parallels the critical β-value discussed in Section 5.1). A **critical t-value** is the value that distinguishes the "acceptance" region from the rejection region. The critical t-value, t_c, is obtained from a t-table (see Statistical Table B-1 in the back of the book) depending on whether the test is one-sided or two-sided, on the level of Type I Error you specify, and on the degrees of freedom, which we have defined as the number of observations minus the number of coefficients estimated (including the constant) or $n-K-1$. The level of Type I Error in a hypothesis test is also called the **level of significance** of that test and will be discussed in more detail later in this section. The t-table was created to save time during research; it consists of the area underneath curves such as those in Figure 5.5 for Type I Errors of specified amounts; a critical t-value is thus a function of the probability of Type I Error that the researcher wants to specify.

Once you have obtained a calculated t-value and a critical t-value, you reject the null hypothesis if the calculated t-value is greater in absolute value than the critical t-value and if the calculated t-value has the sign implied by H_A.

The rule to apply when testing a single regression coefficient is that you should:

Reject H_0 if $|t_k| > t_c$ and if t_k also has the sign implied by H_A.
Do Not Reject H_0 otherwise.

This decision rule works for calculated t-values and critical t-values for one-sided hypotheses around zero:

$$H_0: \beta_k \leq 0$$
$$H_A: \beta_k > 0$$

or

$$H_0: \beta_k \geq 0$$
$$H_A: \beta_k < 0$$

for two-sided hypotheses around zero:

$$H_0: \beta_k = 0$$
$$H_A: \beta_k \neq 0$$

for one-sided hypotheses based on hypothesized values other than zero:

$$H_0: \beta_k \leq S$$
$$H_A: \beta_k > S$$

or

$$H_0: \beta_k \geq S$$
$$H_A: \beta_k < S$$

and for two-sided hypotheses based on hypothesized values other than zero:

$$H_0: \beta_k = S$$
$$H_A: \beta_k \neq S$$

The decision rule is the same; reject the null hypothesis if the appropriately calculated t-value, t_k, is greater in absolute value than the critical t-value t_c (chosen from Table B-1 in the back of the book) as long as the sign of t_k is the same as the sign of the coefficient implied in H_A. Otherwise, "accept" H_0. Always use Equation 5.3 whenever the hypothesized value is not zero.

Statistical Table B-1 contains the critical values t_c for varying degrees of freedom and levels of significance. The column headings indicate the levels of significance according to whether the test is one-sided or two-sided, and the rows indicate the degrees of freedom. For an example of the use of this table and the decision rule, let's return once again to the estimated model of gross check volume at Woody's restaurant and, in particular, to the t-value for β_p calculated in Section 5.2.1 above. Recall that we hypothesized that population's coefficient would be positive, so this is a one-sided test:

$$H_0: \beta_p \leq 0$$
$$H_A: \beta_p > 0$$

There are 29 degrees of freedom (equal to n − K − 1, or 33 − 3 − 1) in this regression, so the appropriate critical t-value with which to test the calculated t-value is a one-tailed critical t-value with 29 degrees of freedom. To find this value, pick a level of significance, say 5 percent, and turn to Statistical Table B-1. The number there is 1.699; should you reject the null hypothesis?

The decision rule is to reject H_0 if $|t_k| > t_c$ and if t_k has the sign implied by H_A; since the 5 percent, one-sided, 29 degrees of freedom critical t-value is 1.699, and since the sign implied by H_A is positive, that decision rule (for this specific case) becomes:

Reject H_0: if $|t_p| > 1.699$ and if t_p is positive

or, combining the two conditions:

Reject H_0 if $t_p > 1.699$

What was t_p? In the previous section, we found that t_p was +4.88, so we would reject the null hypothesis and conclude that population does indeed tend to have a positive relationship with Woody's check volume (holding constant the other variables in the equation).

This decision rule is based on the fact that, since both $\hat{\beta}$ and $SE(\hat{\beta})$ have known sampling distributions, so does their ratio, the t-statistic. The sampling distribution of $\hat{\beta}$ was shown in Chapter 4 and is based on the assumption of the normality of the error term ϵ_i and on the other classical assumptions. Consequently, the sampling distribution of the t-statistic is also based on the same assumption of the normality of the error term and the classical assumptions. If any of these assumptions are violated, t_c will not necessarily follow the t-distribution detailed in Statistical Table B-1. In many cases, however, the t-table is used as a reasonable approximation of the true distribution of the t-statistic even when some of these assumptions do not hold.

In addition, as was mentioned above, the critical t-value depends on the number of degrees of freedom, on the level of Type I Error (referred to as the level of statistical significance), and on whether the hypothesis is a one-tailed or two-tailed one. Figure 5.7 illustrates the dependence of the critical value t_c on two of these factors. For the simple regression model with 30 observations and two coefficients to estimate (the slope and the intercept) there are 28 degrees of freedom. The "acceptance" and rejection regions are stated in terms of the decision rule for several levels of statistical significance and for one-sided (H_A: $\beta > 0$) and two-sided (H_A: $\beta \neq 0$) alternatives. Note from Statistical Table B-1 that the critical t-value for a one-tailed test at a given level of significance is exactly equal to the critical t-value for a two-tailed test at twice the level of significance as the one-tailed test. This property arises because the t-statistic is symmetrical. For example, if 5 percent of the area under the curve is to the right of t_c, then 5 percent will also be to the left of $-t_c$, and the two tails will sum to 10 percent. This relationship between one-sided and two-sided tests is illustrated in Figure 5.7. The critical value $t_c = 1.701$ is for a one-sided, 5 percent level of significance, but it also represents a two-sided, 10 percent level of significance because if one tail represents 5 percent, then both tails added together represent 10 percent.

5.2.3 Level of Significance and Level of Confidence

To complete the previous example, it was necessary to pick a level of significance before a critical t-value could be found in Statistical Table B-1. The words "significantly positive" usually carry the statistical interpretation that H_0 ($\beta \leq$ 0) was rejected in favor of H_A ($\beta > 0$) according to the pre-established decision rule, which was set up with a given level of significance. The **level of significance** indicates the probability of observing an estimated t-value greater than the critical t-value if the null hypothesis were correct. It measures the amount of Type I Error implied by a particular critical t-value. If the level of significance is 10 percent and we reject the null hypothesis at that level, then this result would have occurred only 10 percent of the time that the null hypothesis was indeed correct.

If a 10 percent chance of Type I Error was specified in the decision rule, then the level of significance is 10 percent. Another way of stating this is to convert the "level of significance" into a degree or **level of confidence** which is exactly 100 percent minus the level of significance. A 10 percent level of significance can

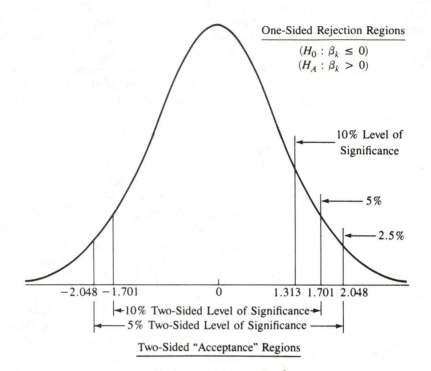

FIGURE 5.7 *One-Sided and Two-Sided* t-*Tests for Various Levels of Significance, for 28 Degrees of Freedom.*
The critical t-value depends on whether the *t*-test is two-sided or one-sided and on the chosen level of significance. In particular, the t_c for a one-sided test at a given level of significance is equal exactly to the t_c for a two-sided test with twice the level of significance of the one-sided test. For example, $t_c = 1.701$ for a 10 percent two-sided *and* a 5 percent one-sided test.

---

also be stated as a 90 percent level of confidence, and results can be summarized by saying that a coefficient has been shown to be "statistically significantly positive," or just "statistically significant" at the 10 percent level of significance or the 90 percent level of confidence. If the alternative hypothesis is accepted, we have 90 percent confidence that the alternative hypothesis is correct.

Many economists use an arbitrary value of two for the critical value of the t-statistic. For a two-tailed test, a value of $t_c = 2$ provides approximately a 5 percent chance of a Type I Error for 10 or more degrees of freedom, and for a one-tailed test, a value of $t_c = 2$ produces a probability of Type I Error equal to about 2.5 percent for 20 or more degrees of freedom. Although the choice of the permissible level of Type I Error and therefore the choice of t_c is essentially arbitrary, beginners are advised to use the more "scientific" classical approach outlined here rather than the rule of thumb $t_c = 2$; though it often saves quite a bit of time to use $t_c = 2$ as a preliminary benchmark when judging the significance of a particular estimated regression coefficient. Some researchers do not even choose a level of significance or a critical t-value before running the regression. Instead, they simply state the highest degree of confidence possible for any given estimated regression coefficient. Such a use of the critical t-value should be regarded as a descriptive, rather than hypothesis testing, use of statistics.

5.3   Examples of One-Sided *t*-Tests

Researchers usually wish to know whether the regression results indicate that β is of the particular sign they have hypothesized; this is a one-sided test. After all, given a positive expected sign, a negative $\hat{\beta}$ of any size would cause a researcher to question whether the results are consistent with theory even without the use of the *t*-test. If the observed $\hat{\beta}$ is positive but fairly close to zero, however, then a one-sided *t*-test should be used to determine whether the $\hat{\beta}$ is different enough from zero to allow the rejection of the null hypothesis. Recall that in order to be able to control the amount of Type I Error we make, such a theory requires an alternative hypothesis of $H_A: \beta > 0$ (the expected sign) and a null hypothesis of $H_0: \beta \leq 0$. Let's look at some complete examples of these kinds of one-sided *t*-tests.

Return one last time to the model of aggregate retail sales of new cars first discussed in Section 5.1. The original model hypothesized was that sales of new cars (Y) was a function of disposable income (X_1) and the average retail price of a new car adjusted by the consumer price index (X_2). Suppose you spend some time reviewing the literature on the automobile industry and are inspired to test a new theory. You decide to add a third independent variable, the number of four-wheel drive trucks sold (X_3) to take into account the fact some potential new car buyers now buy car-like trucks instead. You hypothesize the following model:

$$Y = f(\overset{+}{X_1}, \overset{-}{X_2}, \overset{-}{X_3}) \tag{5.6}$$

β_1 is expected to be positive and β_2 and β_3, negative. This makes sense, since you'd expect higher incomes, lower prices, or lower numbers of four-wheel trucks sold to increase new car sales (holding the other variables in the equation constant). Although in theory a single test for all three slope coefficients could be applied here, nearly every researcher examines each coefficient separately with the *t*-test. The four steps to use when working with the *t*-test are:

1. Set up the null and alternative hypotheses.
2. Choose a level of significance and therefore a critical t-value.
3. Run the regression and obtain an estimated t-value (or t-score).
4. Apply the decision rule by comparing the calculated t-value to the critical t-value in order to reject or "accept" the null hypothesis.

1. Set up the null and alternative hypotheses.[4] From Equation 5.6, the one-sided hypotheses are set up as:

1. H_0: $\beta_1 \leq 0$
   H_A: $\beta_1 > 0$

2. H_0: $\beta_2 \geq 0$
   H_A: $\beta_2 < 0$

3. H_0: $\beta_3 \geq 0$
   H_A: $\beta_3 < 0$

Note that a *t*-test is not typically run on the estimate of the constant term β_0.

2. Choose a level of significance and therefore a critical t-value. Assume that you have considered the various costs involved in making Type I and Type II Errors and have chosen 5 percent as the level of significance with which you want to test. There are ten observations in the data set that is going to be used to test these hypotheses, and so there are $10 - 4 = 6$ degrees of freedom. At a 5 percent level of significance (or a 95 percent level of confidence) the critical t-value, t_c, can be found in Statistical Table B-1 to be 1.943. Note that the level of significance does not have to be the same for all the coefficients in the same regression equation. It could well be that the costs involved in an incorrectly rejected null hypothesis for one coefficient are much higher than for another, and so lower levels of significance would be used. In this equation, though, for all three variables:

$$t_c = 1.943$$

3. Run the regression and obtain estimated t-value. You now use the data (annual from 1971 to 1980) and run the regression on your computer's OLS package, getting:

$$\hat{Y}_t = 1.30 + 4.91X_{1t} + 0.00123X_{2t} - 7.14X_{3t} \tag{5.7}$$
$$\phantom{\hat{Y}_t = 1.30 + } (2.38) \quad\ (0.00022) \quad\ (71.38)$$
$$\phantom{\hat{Y}_t = 1.30 } t= \quad\ 2.1 \qquad\quad 5.6 \qquad\quad -0.1$$

where: Y = new car sales (in hundreds of thousands of units) in year *t*

X_1 = real U.S. disposable income (in hundreds of billions of dollars)

X_2 = the average retail real price of a new car in year *t* (in dollars)

X_3 = the number of four-wheel drive trucks sold in year *t* (in millions)

Once again, we use our standard documentation notation, so the figures in parentheses are the estimated standard errors of the $\hat{\beta}$s. The t-values to be used in these hypothesis tests are printed out by most standard OLS programs, because the programs are written to test the null hypothesis that $\beta = 0$ (or, equivalently, $\beta \leq$ or ≥ 0). If the program does not calculate the t-scores automatically, one may plug the $\hat{\beta}$s and their estimated standard errors into Equation 5.4, repeated here for convenience:

$$t_k = \hat{\beta}_k / SE(\hat{\beta}_k) \qquad (k = 1, 2, \ldots, K)$$

For example, the estimated coefficient of X_3 divided by its estimated standard error is $- 7.14/71.38 = -0.1$. Note that since standard errors are always positive, a negative estimated coefficient implies a negative t-value.

4. Apply the decision rule by comparing the calculated t-value to the critical t-value in order to reject or "accept" the null hypothesis. As we stated in Section 5.1, the decision rule for the *t*-test is to

> Reject H_0 if $|t_k| > t_c$ and if t_k also has the sign implied by H_A.
> Do Not Reject H_0 otherwise.

Note what these decision rules would be for the three hypotheses, the relevant critical t-value (1.943), and the calculated t-values:

> For β_1: Reject H_0 if 2.1 > 1.943 and if 2.1 is positive.

In the case of disposable income, you reject the null hypothesis that $\beta_1 \leq 0$ with 95 percent confidence since 2.1 is indeed greater than 1.943. This result (i.e., H_A: $\beta_1 > 0$) is as you expected on the basis of theory since the more income in the country, the more new car sales you'd expect.

> For β_2: Reject H_0: if 5.6 > 1.943 and if 5.6 is negative.

For prices, the t-statistic is large in absolute value (being greater than 1.943) but has a sign that is contrary to our expectations, since the alternative hypothesis implies a negative sign. Since both conditions in the decision rule must be met before we can reject H_0, you cannot reject the null hypothesis that $\beta_2 \geq 0$. That is, you cannot reject the hypothesis that prices have a zero or positive effect on new car sales! This is an extremely small data set that covers a time-period of dramatic economic swings (and the oil crisis), but even then, you're surprised by this result. Despite your surprise, you stick with your contention that prices belong in the equation and that their expected impact should be negative.

Notice that the coefficient of X_2 is quite small, 0.00123, but that this size has no effect on the t-calculation other than its relationship to the standard error of the estimated coefficient. In other words, the absolute magnitude of any $\hat{\beta}$ is of no particular importance in determining statistical significance because a change in the units of measurement of X_2 will change both $\hat{\beta}_2$ and $SE(\hat{\beta}_2)$ in exactly the same way, so the calculated t-value (the ratio of the two) is unchanged.

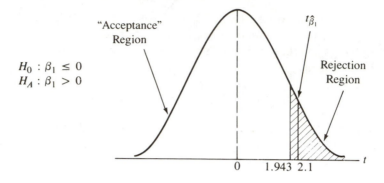

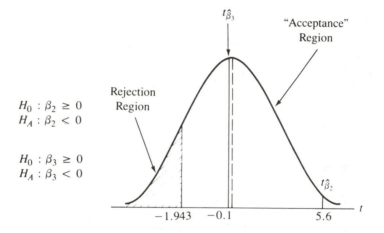

FIGURE 5.8 *One-Sided t-Tests of the Coefficients of the New Car Sales Model.*
Given the estimates in Equation 5.7 and the critical t-value of 1.943 for a 5 percent level of significance, one-sided, 6 degree of freedom *t*-test, we can reject the null hypothesis for $\hat{\beta}_1$, but not for $\hat{\beta}_2$ or $\hat{\beta}_3$.

For β_3: Reject H_0 if $0.1 > 1.943$ and if -0.1 is negative.

For sales of four-wheel drive trucks, the coefficient $\hat{\beta}_3$ is not statistically different from zero since $|-0.1| < 1.943$, and you cannot reject the null hypothesis that $\beta \geq 0$ even though the estimated coefficient has the sign implied by the alternative hypothesis. After thinking this model over again, you come to the conclusion that you were hasty in adding the four-wheel drive variable to this equation.

Figure 5.8 illustrates all three of these outcomes by plotting the critical t-value and the calculated t-values for all three null hypotheses on a t-distribution that is centered around zero (the value in the null hypothesis closest to the border between the acceptance and rejection regions). Students are urged to analyze the results of tests on the estimated coefficients of Equation 5.7 assuming different numbers of observations and different levels of significance. Exercise 4 has a number of such specific combinations, with answers in the back of the book.

Researchers sometimes note in their results the maximum level of confidence achieved by an estimated coefficient. For example, in Figure 5.8, the area under the t-statistic curve to the right of 1.943 for β_1 is the level of significance (about 4 percent in this case). Since the level of significance chosen is subjective, such an approach allows readers to form their own conclusions about the acceptance or rejection of hypotheses. It also conveys the information that the null hypothesis can be rejected with more confidence for some estimated coefficients than for others. Computer programs often give such probabilities of significance for t-values, and if the probability given is less than or equal to the pre-selected level of significance, then the null hypothesis can be rejected. The availability of such probabilities should not deceive a beginning researcher into waiting to state the levels of significance to be used until after the regressions are run, however, because the researcher runs the risk of adapting his or her desired significance levels to the results rather than vice versa.

The purpose of this example was to get practice in the testing of hypotheses, and the results of such a poorly thought-through equation for such a small number of observations should not be taken too seriously. Given all that, however, it is still instructive to note that you did not react the same way to your inability to reject the null hypotheses for the price and four-wheel drive truck variables. That is, the failure of the four-wheel drive variable's coefficient to be significantly negative caused you to realize that perhaps the addition of this variable was ill-advised, but the failure of the price variable's coefficient to be significantly negative did not cause you to consider the possibility that price has no effect on new car sales. Put differently, estimation results should never be allowed to cause you to want to adjust theoretically sound variables or hypotheses, but if they make you realize you have made a serious mistake, then it would be foolhardy to ignore that mistake. What to do about the positive coefficient of price, on the other hand, is what the "art" of econometrics is all about. Surely a positive coefficient is unsatisfactory, but throwing the price variable out of the equation seems even more so. Possible answers to such issues are addressed more than once in the chapters that follow.

5.4   Examples of Two-Sided *t*-Tests

As mentioned above, most hypotheses in regression analysis can be tested with one-sided *t*-tests, but in particular situations, two-sided tests on a single coefficient are appropriate. Researchers sometimes encounter hypotheses that should be rejected if estimated coefficients are significantly different from β in either direction. This situation requires a two-sided *t*-test. The kinds of circumstances in which a two-sided test is called for fall into two categories:

1. Two-sided tests of whether an estimated coefficient is "significantly different from zero," and

2. Two-sided tests of whether an estimated coefficient is significantly different from a specific nonzero value

5.4.1 Testing Whether a $\hat{\beta}$ Is Statistically Different from Zero

One case for a two-sided test of $\hat{\beta}$ arises when there are two or more conflicting hypotheses about the expected sign of a coefficient. For example, in the Woody's restaurant equation of Section 3.3, the impact of the average income of an area on the expected number of Woody's customers in that area is ambiguous. A high-income neighborhood might have more total customers going out to dinner, but those customers might decide to eat at a more formal restaurant than Woody's. As a result, you should run a two-sided *t*-test around zero to determine whether or not the estimated coefficient of income is significantly different from zero in *either* direction. In other words, since there are reasonable cases to be made for either a positive or a negative coefficient, it is appropriate to test the $\hat{\beta}$ for income with a two-sided *t*-test:

$$H_0: \beta_I = 0$$
$$H_A: \beta_I \neq 0$$

As Figure 5.9 illustrates, a two-sided test implies two different rejection regions (one positive and one negative) surrounding the acceptance region. A critical t-value, t_c, must be increased in order to achieve the same level of significance with a two-sided test as can be achieved with a one-sided test.[5] As a result, there is an advantage to testing hypotheses with a one-sided test if the underlying theory allows, because for the same t-values, the possibility of Type I Error is half as much for a one-sided test as for a two-sided test. In cases where there are power-ful theoretical arguments on both sides, however, the researcher has no alternative to using a two-sided *t*-test around zero. To see how this works, we shall follow through the Woody's income variable example in more detail.

1. *Set up the null and alternative hypotheses.*

$$H_0: \beta_I = 0$$
$$H_A: \beta_I \neq 0$$

2. *Choose a level of significance and a critical t-value.* You decide to keep the level of significance at 5 percent, but now this amount must be distributed between two rejection regions for 29 degrees of freedom, and so the correct critical t-value is 2.045 (found in Statistical Table B-1 for 29 degrees of freedom and a 5 per-cent, two-sided test). Note that technically there now are two critical t-values, $+2.045$ and -2.045.

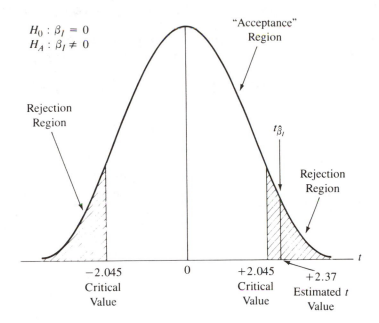

$H_0 : \beta_I = 0$
$H_A : \beta_I \neq 0$

"Acceptance"
Region

Rejection
Region

$t_{\hat{\beta}_I}$

Rejection
Region

t

-2.045
Critical
Value

0

$+2.045$
Critical
Value

$+2.37$
Estimated t
Value

FIGURE 5.9 *A Two-Sided* t-*Test of the Coefficient of Income in the Woody's Model.*
Given the estimates of Equation 5.5 and the critical t-values of ±2.045 for 5 percent level
significance, two-sided, 29 degree of freedom t-test, we can reject the null hypothesis that
$\beta_I = 0$.

3. Run the regression and obtain an estimated t-value. Since the value implied
by the null hypothesis is still zero, the estimated t-value of $+2.37$ given in Equation 5.5 is applicable.

*4. Apply the decision rule by comparing the calculated t-value to the critical
t-value in order to reject or "accept" the null hypothesis.* We once again use the
decision rule stated in Section 5.1, but since the alternative hypothesis specifies
either sign, that decision rule simplifies to:

For β_I: Reject H_0 if $|2.37| > 2.045$

In this case, you reject the null hypothesis that β_I equals zero because 2.37 is
greater than 2.045 (see Figure 5.9). Note that the positive sign implies that, at
least for Woody's restaurants, income increases customer volume (holding constant population and competition). Given this result, we might well choose to run
a one-sided t-test on the next year's Woody's data set. For more practice with two-
sided t-tests, see Exercise 6.

5.4.2   Two-Sided *t*-Tests of a Specific Nonzero Coefficient Value

The second case for a two-sided *t*-test arises when there is reason to expect a specific nonzero value for an estimated coefficient. For example, if a previous researcher has stated that the true value of some coefficient almost surely equals a particular number, β_{H_0}, then that number would be the one to test by creating a two-sided *t*-test around the hypothesized value, β_{H_0}. To the extent that you feel that the hypothesized value is theoretically correct, you also violate the normal practice of using the null hypothesis to state the hypothesis you expect to reject, or the "strawman" approach.[6]

In such a case, the null and alternative hypotheses become:

$$H_0: \beta_k = \beta_{H_0}$$
$$H_A: \beta_k \neq \beta_{H_0}$$

where β_{H_0} is the specific nonzero value hypothesized.

Since the hypothesized β value is no longer zero, the formula with which to calculate the estimated t-value is Equation 5.3, repeated here for convenience:

$$t_k = (\hat{\beta}_k - \beta_{H_0})/SE(\hat{\beta}_k) \qquad (k = 1,2,\ldots,K) \qquad (5.3)$$

This t-statistic is still distributed around zero if the null hypothesis is correct, because we have subtracted β_{H_0} from the estimated regression coefficient whose expected value is supposed to be β_{H_0} when H_0 is true. Since the t-statistic is still centered around zero, the decision rules developed above are still applicable. In other words, the techniques used in Section 5.4.1 above are precisely the same as for a two-sided *t*-test of a specific nonzero coefficient. For practice in this kind of *t*-test, see Exercise 6.

5.5   Limitations of the *t*-Test

A problem with the *t*-test is that it is easy to misuse; t-scores are so frequently printed out by computer regression packages and the *t*-test seems so easy to work with that beginning researchers sometimes attempt to use the *t*-test to "prove" things that it was never intended to even test. For that reason, it is probably just as important to know the limitations of the *t*-test as it is to know the applications of that test. Perhaps the most important of these, that the usefulness of the *t*-test diminishes rapidly as more and more different specifications are estimated and tested, is the subject of Section 6.4. The purpose of the present section is to give a few other examples of how the *t*-test should *not* be used.

5.5.1   The *t*-Test Does Not Test Theoretical Validity

Recall that the purpose of the *t*-test is to help the researcher make inferences about a particular population parameter based on an estimate obtained from a sample of that population. Some beginning researchers conclude that any *statistically* significant result is also a *theoretically* correct one. This is dangerous, because such a conclusion confuses statistical significance with theoretical validity.

Consider for instance, the following estimated regression[7] that explains the consumer price index in the United Kingdom:

$$\hat{P} = \begin{array}{ccc} 10.9 & - & 3.2C & + & 0.39C^2 \\ & & (0.23) & & (0.02) \\ t = & & 13.9 & & 19.5 \end{array} \qquad R^2 = .982 \qquad n = 21$$

Apply the *t*-test to these estimates. Do you agree that the two slope coefficients are statistically significant? As a quick check of Statistical Table B-1 shows, the critical t-value for 18 degrees of freedom and a 5 percent two-tailed level of significance is 2.101, so we can reject the null hypothesis of no effect in these cases and conclude that C and C^2 are indeed statistically significant variables in explaining P.

The catch is that P is the consumer price index and C is the cumulative amount of rainfall in the United Kingdom! We have just shown that rain is statistically significant in explaining consumer prices; does that also show that the underlying theory is valid? Of course not. Why is the statistical result so significant? The answer is that at a 5 percent level of significance, there is a 1 in 20 chance of rejecting a true null hypothesis. If we try 20 or more different tests, the odds are good that eventually we will be able to reject a correct null hypothesis. This almost always inappropriate technique (called data-mining) was used to obtain the unrealistic results above. The moral should be clear; never conclude that statistical significance, as shown by the *t*-test, is the same as theoretical validity.

Once in a while, estimated coefficients will be significant in the direction opposite from that hypothesized, and some beginning researchers may be tempted to change their hypotheses; for example, a student might run a regression in which the hypothesized sign is positive, get a "statistically significant" negative sign, and be tempted to change the theoretical expectations to "expect" a negative sign! Naturally, changed hypotheses would be accompanied by detailed explanations of how the particular result makes sense. Although it is admirable to be willing to reexamine incorrect theories on the basis of new evidence, that evidence should be, for the most part, theoretical in nature. In the case cited above, the student should have been concerned that the evidence did not support the theory, but that lack of support should not have caused the theory itself to change completely. If the evidence causes a researcher to go back to the theoretical underpinnings of a model and find a mistake, then the null hypothesis should be changed, but then this new hypothesis should be tested using a completely different data set— after all, we already know what the result will be if the hypothesis is tested on the old one.

5.5.2   The *t*-Test Does Not Test "Importance"

One possible use of a regression equation is to help determine which independent variable has the largest relative effect (importance) on the dependent variable.

For example, a macroeconomic study might attempt to determine the importance of fiscal and monetary policy in making budgetary recommendations. Some beginning researchers draw the unwarranted conclusion that the most statistically significant variable in their estimated regression is also the most important in terms of explaining the largest portion of the movement of the dependent variable. Statistical significance indicates the likelihood that a particular sample result could have been obtained by chance, but it says little if anything about which variables determine the major portion of the variation in the dependent variable. In order to determine importance, a measure such as the size of the coefficient multiplied by the average size of the independent variable would make much more sense.[8] Consider the following hypothetical equation:

$$\hat{Y} = \underset{(1.0)}{30.0 + 10.0X_1} + \underset{(25.0)}{200.0X_2} \qquad \bar{R}^2 = .90 \quad n = 30$$
$$t = \qquad 10.0 \qquad 8.0$$

where all three variables are measured in dollars:

Y = mail order sales of "O'Henry's Oyster Recipes"
X_1 = advertising expenditures for "The Arlington Gourmet"
X_2 = advertising expenditures for "How to Lose 20 Pounds in a Week" (assume prices did not change during the estimation period)

Where should O'Henry be spending its advertising money? That is, which independent variable has the biggest impact per dollar on Y? Given that X_2's coefficient is twenty times X_1's coefficient, you'd have to agree that X_2 was more important as defined above, and yet which one is more statistically significantly different from zero? With a t-statistic of 10.0, X_1 is clearly more statistically significant than X_2 and its 8.0, but all that means is that we have more confidence that the coefficient is positive, not that the variable itself is necessarily more important in determining Y. The theoretical underpinnings of a result and the actual result itself are at least as important as the statistical significance of that result.

5.5.3   The *t*-Test Is Not Intended for Tests of the Entire Population

The *t*-test helps make inferences about the true value of a parameter from an estimate calculated from a sample of the *population* (the group from which the sample is being drawn). As the size of the sample approaches the size of the population, an unbiased estimated coefficient approaches the true population value; if a coefficient is calculated from the entire population, then an unbiased estimate already measures the population value and a significant *t*-test adds nothing to this knowledge. One might forget this property and attach too much importance to t-scores that have been obtained from samples that approximate the population in size. All the *t*-test does is help decide how likely it is that a particular small sample will cause a researcher to make a mistake in rejecting hypotheses about the true population parameters.

This point can perhaps best be seen by remembering that the t-statistic is the estimated regression coefficient divided by the standard error of that estimated regression coefficient. If the sample size is large enough to approach the population, then the standard error will fall to just about zero because the distribution of estimates will become more and more narrowly distributed around the true parameter (if this is an unbiased estimate). The standard error will approach zero as the sample size approaches infinity. Thus the t-statistic will eventually become:

$$t = \hat{\beta}/0 = \infty$$

The mere existence of a large t-score for a huge sample has no real substantive significance because if the sample size is large enough, you can reject almost any null hypothesis! It is true that sample sizes in econometrics can never approach infinity, but many are quite large; and others, even though fairly small, are not really samples of a population but contain the entire population in one data set.[9]

5.6 The Simple Correlation Coefficient, r

The **simple correlation coefficient, r,** is a measure of the strength and direction of the linear relationship between two variables; the simple correlation coefficient between X_1 and X_2 is:

$$r_{12} = \Sigma[(X_{1i} - \bar{X}_1)(X_{2i} - \bar{X}_2)]/\sqrt{\Sigma(X_{1i} - \bar{X}_1)^2 \Sigma(X_{2i} - \bar{X}_2)^2} \qquad (5.8)$$

If two variables are perfectly positively correlated, then r = +1. To see this, assume that $X_1 = X_2$. In this case, Equation 5.8 would equal:

$$r_{12} = \Sigma[(X_{1i} - \bar{X}_1)(X_{1i} - \bar{X}_1)]/\sqrt{\Sigma(X_{1i} - \bar{X}_1)^2 \Sigma(X_{1i} - \bar{X}_1)^2}$$

$$= \Sigma[(X_{1i} - \bar{X}_1)^2)]/[\Sigma(X_{1i} - \bar{X}_1)^2] = +1$$

If two variables are perfectly negatively correlated, then r = −1. To see that this is so, substitute $X_1 = -X_2$ into Equation 5.8 and verify that r = −1. If two variables are totally uncorrelated, then r = 0.

One of the major uses of the simple correlation coefficient r is to test the hypothesis that two explanatory variables are correlated in a less than perfect but still significant (multicollinear) way. For imperfect multicollinearity to occur in this two-variable case, the simple correlation coefficient must be fairly large in the direction indicated by theory. In order to test this hypothesis, r can be converted into a t-statistic using:

$$t = r\sqrt{n - 2} / \sqrt{(1 - r^2)} \qquad (5.9)$$

where n is the size of the sample. The statistic defined in Equation 5.9 follows the t-distribution with $n - 2$ degrees of freedom. Since t is directly related to r, a large positive r will convert into a large positive t, and so on.

Tests of hypotheses about t (and therefore about r) can be undertaken using the critical t-values and decision rules outlined in Section 5.2 and Table B-1. For example, suppose you encounter a simple correlation coefficient of 0.946 between two variables you expect to be positively correlated in a data set with 28 observations. In this case,

$$H_0: r \leq 0$$
$$H_A: r > 0$$

and we can reject the null hypothesis of no positive collinearity if the calculated t-score is larger in absolute value than the critical t-value of 1.706 (for 26 degrees of freedom at the 5 percent, one-sided level of significance) and if t has the positive sign implied by the alternative hypothesis. If we substitute $r = 0.946$ and $n = 28$ into Equation 5.9, we obtain 14.880, and so the null hypothesis of no positive collinearity can be rejected. (If theory provides no expected direction, a two-sided test should be used.) For practice in hypothesis tests of simple correlation coefficients, see Exercise 10.

5.7   Summary

1. Hypothesis testing makes inferences about the validity of specific economic (or other) theories from a sample of the population for which the theories are supposed to be true. The four basic steps of hypothesis testing (using a *t*-test as an example) are:
   a. Set up the null and alternative hypotheses
   b. Choose a level of significance and therefore a critical t-value
   c. Run the regression and obtain an estimated t-value
   d. Apply the decision rule by comparing the calculated t-value to the critical t-value in order to reject or "accept" the null hypothesis.

2. The null hypothesis states the range of values that the regression coefficient is expected to take on if the researcher's theory is not correct. The alternative hypothesis is a statement of the range of values that the regression coefficient is expected to take if the researcher's theory is correct.

3. The two kinds of errors we can make in such hypothesis testing are:
   Type I : We reject a null hypothesis that is true
   Type II: We do not reject a null hypothesis that is false.

4. A decision rule states critical t-values above or below which observed sample t-values will lead to the rejection or "acceptance" of hypotheses concerning population parameters. Critical values are determined from a t-distribution table depending on the chosen level of significance, the degrees of freedom involved, and the specifics of the particular hypothesis.

5. The *t*-test tests hypotheses about individual coefficients from regression equations. The general form for the t-statistic is

$$t_k = (\hat{\beta}_k - \beta_{H_0})/SE(\hat{\beta}_k) \qquad (k = 1,2,...,K)$$

but in many regression applications, β_{H_0} is zero. Once you have calculated a t-value and chosen a critical t-value, you reject the null hypothesis if the t-value is greater in absolute value than the critical t-value and if (for a one-sided test) the t-value has the sign implied by the alternative hypothesis.

6. The *t*-test is easy to use for a number of reasons, but care should be taken when using the *t*-test to avoid confusing statistical significance with theoretical validity or empirical importance.

Exercises

(Answers to even-numbered exercises are in Appendix A.)

1. Write out the meaning of each of the following terms without reference to the book (or your notes) and then compare your definition with the version in the text for each.
   a. alternative hypothesis
   b. level of significance
   c. Type I Error
   d. two-sided test
   e. decision rule
   f. critical value
   g. t-statistic
   h. simple correlation coefficient

2. Create null and alternative hypotheses for the following coefficients:
   a. The impact of height on weight (Section 1.3).
   b. All the coefficients in Equation A in Exercise 5 in Chapter 2.
   c. All the coefficients in $Y = f(X_1, X_2, $ and $X_3)$ where Y is total gasoline used on a particular trip, X_1 is miles traveled, X_2 is the weight of the car, and X_3 is the average speed you traveled.
   d. The impact of the decibel level of the grunt of a shot-putter on the length of the throw involved (shot-putters are known to make loud noises when they throw, but there is little theory about the impact of this yelling on the length of the put). Assume all relevant "non-grunt" variables are included in the equation.

3. Think of examples other than the ones in Section 5.1 in which:
   a. It would be more important to keep Type I Error low than to keep Type II Error low.

   b. It would be more important to keep Type II Error low than to keep Type I Error low.
(Hint: For example, what about a murder trial? What would the null hypothesis be in our society? What kind of error would be more costly?)

4. Return to Section 5.3 and test the hypotheses in Equation 5.6 with the results in Equation 5.7 for all three coefficients under the following circumstances:
  a. 10 percent significance and 15 observations.
  b. 90 percent confidence and 28 observations.
  c. 99 percent confidence and 10 observations.

5. Return to Section 5.2 and test the appropriate hypotheses with the results in Equation 5.5 for all three coefficients under the following circumstances:
  a. 5 percent significance and 6 degrees of freedom.
  b. 90 percent confidence and 29 degrees of freedom.
  c. 99 percent confidence and 2 degrees of freedom.

6. Using the techniques of Section 5.4, test the following two-sided hypotheses:
  a. For the "O'Henry's Oyster Recipes" equation in Section 5.5.2, test the hypothesis that:

$$H_0: \beta_2 = 160.0$$
$$H_A: \beta_2 \neq 160.0$$

  at the 5 percent level of significance. What special difficulty would this null hypothesis cause?
  b. For Equation 5.5, test the hypothesis that:

$$H_0: \beta_3 = 0$$
$$H_A: \beta_3 \neq 0$$

  at the 99 percent level of confidence.
  c. For Equation 5.7, test the hypothesis that:

$$H_0: \beta_2 = 0$$
$$H_A: \beta_2 \neq 0$$

  at the 5 percent level of significance.

7. For all three tests in Exercise 6 above, under what circumstances would you worry about possible violations of the strawman approach? In particular, what would your theoretical expectations have to be in order to avoid violating the strawman approach on Exercise 6a?

8. A study of hotel investments in Waikiki between 1965 and 1973 estimated this revenue production function:

$$R = AL^{\alpha}K^{\beta}e^{\epsilon}$$

where A = a constant term
     R = annual net revenue of the hotel (in thousands of dollars)
     L = land input (site area in square feet)

K = capital input (construction cost in thousands of dollars)
ϵ = the classical error term
e = the base of the natural log

a. State your general expectations for the population values of α and β; what are their theoretical interpretations?
b. Create specific null and alternative hypotheses for this equation.
c. Create specific decision rules for the two sets of hypotheses in 8b above (5 percent level with 25 degrees of freedom).
d. Calculate the appropriate t-values and run *t*-tests given the following regression result (estimated standard errors in parentheses):

$$\widehat{\ln R} = -0.91750 + \underset{(0.135)}{0.273} \ln L + \underset{(0.125)}{0.733} \ln K$$

Did you reject or "accept" your null hypotheses?
e. Is this result surprising? If you were going to build a Waikiki hotel, what input would you most want to use for investment? Is there an additional piece of information you would need to know before you could answer such a question?

9. Consider the following equation (estimated standard errors in parentheses):[10]

$$\widehat{W}_t = 8.562 + \underset{(0.080)}{0.364P_t} + \underset{(0.072)}{0.004P_{t-1}} - \underset{(0.658)}{2.560U_t}$$
$$R^2 = .873 \qquad n = 19$$

where: W = wages and salaries per employee in year t
P = the price level in year t
U = the unemployment rate in year t

a. Develop and test your own hypotheses with respect to the individual estimated slope coefficients (try to do this without looking at the results).
b. Discuss the theoretical validity of P_{t-1} and how your opinion of that validity in this equation might be changed by your answer to Exercise 9a above. Should P_{t-1} be dropped from the equation? Why or why not?

10. Given the following simple correlation coefficients between two explanatory variables, use the *t*-test (and Equation 5.9) to test the possibility of significant collinearity in the specified circumstances:
a. r = .905, n = 18, 5 percent level, positive expected relationship.
b. r = .958, n = 27, 2.5 percent level, positive expected relationship.
c. r = .821, n = 7, 1 percent level, positive expected relationship.
d. r = -.753, n = 42, 10 percent level, negative expected relationship.
e. r = .519, n = 30, 5 percent level, ambiguous expected relationship.

5.8 Appendix: The *F*-Test on More Than One Coefficient at a Time

As Section 2.2 noted, the *F*-test is most commonly used to test the overall significance of a regression,[11] but the *F*-test has many more uses than just tests of overall fit, however. Indeed, the *F*-test can be used to conduct tests of any (linear) hypothesis that involves more than one coefficient at a time. Such tests should be used whenever the underlying economic theory implies a hypothesis that simultaneously specifies values for more than one coefficient. Hypotheses on more than one coefficient at a time are sometimes referred to as "joint" or "compound" hypotheses.

For example, in a Cobb-Douglas production function:

$$Q = AL^\alpha K^\beta e^\epsilon$$

where Q is output, L is labor input, K is capital input, and ϵ is a classical error term, economists often talk about "constant returns to scale." Constant returns to scale would exist if the sum of α and β were one. That is, the production function can be shown to have constant returns to scale if:

$$\alpha + \beta = 1 \tag{5.10}$$

When a Cobb-Douglas production function is estimated, Equation 5.10 becomes a null hypothesis that should be tested with the results of the estimation to determine if constant returns to scale exist. Since the hypothesis involves more than one coefficient, it cannot be tested with the usual *t*-test. The *t*-test is not applicable because its use assumes that other coefficients are unrestricted, which is not true in a joint hypothesis. Instead, such joint hypotheses must be tested with the *F*-test. Note that if the null hypothesis is stated as H_0: $\alpha + \beta = 1$, we have violated the strawman approach. In this case, as in any in which the suspected true value is a particular constant, we have little alternative but to do so.

The way in which the *F*-test evaluates hypotheses about more than one coefficient at a time is fairly ingenious. The first step is to translate the particular null hypothesis in question into constraints that will be placed on the equation. Such a constrained equation can be thought of as what the equation would look like if the null hypothesis were correct; you substitute the hypothesized values into the regression equation in order to see what would happen if the equation was constrained to agree with the null hypothesis. As a result, in the *F*-test, the null hypothesis always leads to a constrained equation, whether or not the constrained equation is the one which corresponds to the researcher's strawman hypothesis.

The second step in a *F*-test is then to estimate this constrained equation with OLS and compare the fit of the constrained equation with the fit of the unconstrained equation. If the fit of the constrained equation and the unconstrained equation are not significantly different, the null hypothesis should not be rejected. If the fit of the unconstrained equation is significantly better than that of the constrained equation, then we reject the null hypothesis. The fit of the constrained equation is never superior to the fit of the unconstrained equation, since if the constrained equation provided the best possible fit, then the unconstrained equation would produce coefficient values exactly equal to those hypothesized in the constrained equation, because OLS chooses the coefficients that maximize precisely that same fit.

Let's continue with the test for constant returns to scale mentioned above by examining the null and alternative hypotheses:

$$H_0: \alpha + \beta = 1$$
$$H_A: \alpha + \beta \neq 1$$

in a Cobb-Douglas production function $Q = AL^\alpha K^\beta e^\epsilon$

In order to run an OLS equation on such an equation, we must take the log of both sides of the equation, obtaining:

$$\ln Q = A' + \alpha \ln L + \beta \ln K + \epsilon \tag{5.11}$$

where A' is the log of A. Since A is a constant, so too is the log of A, and Equation 5.11 is a typical linear-in-the-parameters equation that can be estimated with OLS. To obtain the constrained equation, we solve the null hypothesis for α:

$$\alpha = 1 - \beta$$

and substitute this constraint into Equation 5.11, obtaining:

$$\ln Q = A' + \ln L + \beta(\ln K - \ln L) + \epsilon$$

or

$$(\ln Q - \ln L) = A' + \beta(\ln K - \ln L) + \epsilon \tag{5.12}$$

That is, $Y^* = \ln Q - \ln L$ is regressed on $X^* = \ln K - \ln L$ to obtain an estimated β.

Equation 5.12 is the constrained equation; it would hold if the null hypothesis was correct. To test the null hypothesis, we estimate both Equations 5.12 and 5.11 with OLS and compare the fit of the constrained Equation 5.12 to the fit of the unconstrained Equation 5.11. If the two provide fits that are not significantly different, then we do not reject the null hypothesis.

The F-statistic provides a statistical measure of whether or not the fits of two equations on a particular sample of data are significantly different at various levels of significance. The second step in running an F-test is to run regressions on the constrained and unconstrained equations. Let's label the statistics generated by the constrained equation with the subscript M, where M is the number of such constraints. The next step is to calculate a special F-statistic:

$$F = \frac{(RSS_M - RSS)/M}{RSS/(n - K - 1)} \tag{5.13}$$

where: RSS   is the residual sum of squares from the unconstrained equation
RSS_M is the residual sum of squares from the constrained equation
M   is the number of constraints placed on the equation (usually equal
        to the number of βs eliminated from the unconstrained equation)
(n − K − 1) is the degrees of freedom in the unconstrained equation.

This F-statistic has two different levels of degrees of freedom; it is said to have
M degrees of freedom in the numerator and (n − K − 1) degrees of freedom
in the denominator. In order to test the null hypothesis, we compare the calculated
F-statistic with the appropriate critical F-value from Statistical Tables B-2 or B-3
in the back of the book; these tables are for five and one percent levels of
significance respectively. In using these tables, note that the numerator degrees
of freedom is the column heading and the denominator degrees of freedom is the
row heading. If the calculated F-statistic *exceeds* the critical F-value for M and
(n − K − 1) degrees of freedom at the selected level of significance, we reject
the null hypothesis. If the calculated F-statistic is less than the critical F-value
found in the appropriate table, then we cannot reject the null hypothesis.

RSS_M is always greater than or equal to RSS; imposing constraints on the coefficients instead of allowing OLS to select their values can never decrease the
summed squared residuals. (Recall that OLS selects that combination of values
of the coefficients that minimizes RSS.) At the extreme, if the unconstrained
regression yields exactly the same estimated coefficients as does the constrained
regression, then the RSS are equal, and the F-statistic is zero. In this case, H_0
is not rejected because the data indicate that the constraints appear to be correct.
As the difference between the constrained coefficients and the unconstrained coefficients increases, the data indicate that the null hypothesis is less likely to be
true. Thus when F gets larger than the critical F-value, the hypothesized restrictions specified in the null hypothesis are rejected by the test.

The decision rule for the *F*-test is:

$$\text{Reject } H_0 \text{ if } F \geq F_c$$
$$\text{Do Not Reject } H_0 \text{ if } F < F_c$$

where F_c is the critical F-value found in the appropriate F-table.

To continue with our example of the test of constant returns to scale, we can
now finally estimate a simple log-linear production function for the U.S. economy,
producing the following results (annual data from 1950 to 1970):

$$\widehat{\ln(GNP)} = -2.28 + 1.48\ln L + 0.422\ln K \qquad (5.14)$$
$$(0.14) \qquad (0.036)$$
$$t = \quad 10.33 \qquad 11.77$$
$$n = 21 \quad \bar{R}^2 = .996$$

To test the null hypothesis of constant returns to scale, we must also estimate
the constrained Equation 5.12 on the same set of data and then calculate an
F-statistic that compares the fit of 5.14 with that of 5.12. The F-statistic that results

is 15.30, and Statistical Table B-2 indicates that the critical F-value for 5 percent significance with 1 and 17 degrees of freedom is 4.45. Thus we are forced to reject the hypothesis that constant returns to scale characterized the U.S. economy in the 1960s and 1970s. In fact, the point estimate of $\alpha + \beta$ is $1.48 + 0.42 = 1.90$, which indicates increasing returns to scale. Does this surprise you? In addition, economic theory suggests that α and β should be between zero and one. A result similar to that in Equation 5.14 should make you concerned that there are problems in the equation that must be resolved before you can feel comfortable with your conclusion.

Since the null hypothesis in this particular example potentially violates the strawman approach, it is important here to remember that there is an unknown amount of Type II Error if the above null hypothesis is not rejected. Unfortunately, there is usually no solution to the problem of "accepting" an explicit value of the sum of the two coefficients (or any other linear combination). In the example, though, we rejected the null hypothesis, so we know the maximum chance of error is 5 percent (the level of significance).

The *F*-test can be used with null hypotheses and constrained equations that apply to only a subset of the coefficients in the equation rather than to all the slope coefficients. For example, if

$$Y_i = \beta_0 + \beta_1 X_{1i} + \beta_2 X_{2i} + \beta_3 X_{3i} + \epsilon_i$$

then the only way to test a null hypothesis involving two of the slope coefficients (for example $H_0: \beta_1 = \beta_2$) would be to estimate constrained and unconstrained equations and to compare their fits with the *F*-test.

An illustration of the use of the *F*-test to test null hypotheses that involve only a subset of the slope coefficients can be obtained by looking at the problem of testing the significance of *seasonal dummies*. When a researcher is using quarterly (or monthly) data, it is common, as mentioned in Chapter 3, to include dummy variables that are equal to one in a given quarter (or month) and equal to zero otherwise. Since only three dummies are included in a quarterly model (to avoid perfect multicollinearity), the coefficients of the dummies are the expected difference between the effect of the specified quarter and the base quarter on the dependent variable, holding constant all the variables in the equation. As a result, to test the hypothesis of significant seasonality in the data, one must test the hypothesis that all the dummies equal zero simultaneously rather than test the dummies one at a time. In other words, the appropriate test of seasonality in a regression model using seasonal dummies involves the use of the *F*-test instead of the *t*-test.

Suppose the original equation was

$$Y = \beta_0 + \beta_1 D_1 + \beta_2 D_2 + \beta_3 D_3 + \beta_4 X + \epsilon \qquad (5.15$$

where: Y and X are typical dependent and independent variables respecti·
ϵ is a classical error term

D_1, D_2, and D_3 are seasonal dummies equal to one in the first, second and third quarters of the year and equal to zero otherwise (note that the fourth quarter is the base quarter in this model).

In this case, the null hypothesis is that there is *no* seasonality:

$$H_0: \beta_1 = \beta_2 = \beta_3 = 0$$
$$H_A: H_0 \text{ is not true}$$

The constrained equation would then be $Y = \beta_0 + \beta_4 X + \epsilon$. To determine whether the whole set of seasonal dummies should be included, the fit of the estimated constrained equation would be compared to the fit of the estimated unconstrained equation by using the *F*-test. Note that this example does indeed use the *F*-test to measure null hypotheses that include only a subset of the slope coefficients.

The exclusion of some seasonal dummies because their estimated coefficients have low t-scores for statistics is not recommended. Instead, testing seasonal dummy coefficients should be done with the *F*-test instead of with the *t*-test, because seasonality is usually a single compound hypothesis rather than three (or eleven with monthly data) individual hypotheses having to do with each quarter (or month). To the extent that a hypothesis is a joint one, it should be tested with the *F*-test. If the hypothesis of seasonal variation can be summarized into a single dummy variable, then the use of the *t*-test will cause no problems. Often, where seasonal dummies are unambiguously called for, no hypothesis testing at all is undertaken.

Another common use of the *F*-test is to test the equivalence of regression coefficients between two sets of data, that is, whether two sets of data contain significantly different regression coefficients for the same theoretical equation. This can be helpful when deciding if it is appropriate to combine two data sets. For example, the null hypothesis may be that the slope coefficients are the same in two samples, such as before and after a major war. The concern is whether there has been a major structural shift in the economy from one set of data to the other. This application of the *F*-test is often referred to as a *Chow test*, [12] and it can be set up by using dummy variables that distinguish between data sets.

Finally, it is important to note that whenever any kind of constrained estimation is put forth, the documentation should include the result of applying regression analysis to the unconstrained case. Readers then can judge for themselves the appropriateness and the consequences of the prior expectations implied by the constraints. Without such documentation, readers are potentially left with the feeling that the researcher is trying to deceive them by making the answers come out when the data or the unconstrained estimating technique do not support the priors. For more on a related topic, see the discussion of Bayesian Econometrics in Section 6.6.

[1.] It should be noted at this point that instead of using $\beta \leq 0$ as your null hypothesis, you can also use $\beta = 0$ as long as you don't change the alternative hypothesis of H_A: $\beta > 0$. These two versions of the null hypothesis give identical answers because in order to test a null hypothesis that is a range like $\beta \leq 0$, you must focus on the value in that range which is closest to the range implied by the alternative hypothesis. If you can reject that value, you can reject values that are farther away as well. Truncating the range of the null hypothesis in this way has no practical importance because you are really asking on which side of zero is the true parameter.

[2.] The reason that null hypotheses involving nonzero values can sometimes involve two-tailed tests is that if your "pet theory" is $\beta = 1$ (or any other nonzero value) then you have no alternative but to violate the "strawman" approach and put $\beta = 1$ in the null hypothesis. For more on this, see Section 5.4.2.

[3.] Some authors refer to these as α and β errors respectively, but no matter which titles are used, many beginning students understandably have trouble remembering which error is which. Such students might be helped by thinking of a Type I Error as an error of short-sightedness (not seeing that a null hypothesis is actually true) and a Type II Error as an error of over-imagination (imagining that a null hypothesis is true when it actually is false). Those with poor memories but vivid imaginations seem to remember this most easily by recalling that someone with only one eye (one I) would probably be short-sighted.

[4.] Recall from Section 5.1 that a one-sided hypothesis can be stated either as H_0: $\beta \leq 0$ *or* H_0: $\beta = 0$ because the value used to test H_0: $\beta \leq 0$ is the value in the null hypothesis closest to the border between the acceptance and the rejection regions. When the amount of Type I Error is calculated, this border value of β is the one that is used because over the whole range of $\beta \leq 0$, the value $\beta = 0$ gives the maximum amount of Type I Error. The classical approach limits this maximum amount to a pre-assigned level, the chosen level of significance.

[5.] See Figure 5.7 in Section 5.2. In that figure, the same critical t-value has twice as large a level of significance for a two-sided test as for a one-sided test.

[6.] Instead of being able to reject an incorrect theory based on the evidence, the researcher who violates the strawman approach is reduced to "not rejecting" the β value expected to be true. This makes a big difference, because to "accept" H_0 is merely to say that H_0 is not rejected by the data, but there are many theories that are not rejected by the data, and so the researcher is left with a regrettably weak conclusion. One way to accommodate violations of the strawman approach is to increase the level of significance (increasing the likelihood of a Type I Error). By doing this you decrease the probability of making a Type II Error when "accepting" the null hypothesis.

[7.] These results, and other similar to them, can be found in David F. Hendry, "Econometrics—Alchemy or Science?," *Economica,* Nov. 1980, pp. 383-406.

[8.] Some useful statistical measures of "importance" have been developed, but none is fully satisfactory because of the presence of multicollinearity (to be discussed in Chapter 8). See J. M. Shanks, "The Importance of Importance," (Berkeley: Survey Research Center, University of California, 1982).

[9.] Donald N. McCloskey, "The Loss Function Has Been Mislaid: The Rhetoric of Significance Tests," *American Economic Review,* May, 1985, p. 204.

[10.] *Prices and Earnings in 1951-1969; An Econometric Assessment,* U. K. Department of Employment, 1971, p. 35.

[11.] This appendix is intended for those who have reviewed the material in Section 2.2 on testing the overall significance of a regression and have at least looked over Exercises 6 and 7 from Chapter 2.

[12.] See Gregory C. Chow, "Tests on Equality Between Sets of Coefficients in Two Linear Regressions," *Econometrica,* Vol. 28, No. 3, July 1960, pp. 591-605 or any advanced econometrics textbook for the details of this test.

6

Specification: Choosing the Independent Variables

Before any equation can be estimated, it must be completely *specified*. Specifying an econometric equation consists of three parts: choosing the correct independent variables, the correct functional form, and the correct form of the stochastic error term.

A **specification error** results when any one of these choices is made incorrectly. This chapter is concerned with only the first of these, choosing the variables; the second and third will be taken up in subsequent chapters.

That researchers can decide which independent variables to include in regression equations is a source of both strength and weakness in econometrics; the strength is that the equations can be formulated to fit individual needs, but the weakness comes from researchers being able to estimate many different specifications until they find the one that "proves" their point even if many other results disprove it. A major goal of this chapter is to help you understand how to choose variables for your regressions without falling prey to the various errors that result from misusing the choice.

The primary consideration in deciding if an independent variable belongs in an equation is whether the variable is essential to the regression on the basis of theory. If the answer is an unambiguous yes, then the variable definitely should be included in the equation even if it seems to be lacking in statistical significance. If theory is ambivalent or less emphatic, a dilemma arises. Leaving a relevant variable out of an equation is likely to bias the remaining estimates, but including an irrelevant variable leads to higher variances of the estimated coefficients. Although we will develop statistical tools to help us deal with this decision, it is difficult in practice to be sure that a variable is relevant, and so the problem often remains unresolved.

We devote the fourth section of the chapter to specification searches and the pros and cons of various approaches to such searches. For example, techniques like stepwise regression procedures or sequential specification searches often cause bias or make the usual tests of significance inapplicable, and we do not recommend them. Instead, we suggest trying to minimize the number of regressions estimated and using theory rather than statistical fit as much as possible when choosing variables. There are no pat answers, however, and so the final decisions must be left to each individual researcher.

6.1 Omitted Variables

Suppose that you forget to include all the relevant independent variables when you first specify an equation (after all, no one's perfect!). Or suppose that you can't get data (or a good proxy) for one of the variables that you *do* think of. The result in both of these situations is an **omitted variable,** defined as an important explanatory variable that has been left out of a regression equation.

Whenever you have an omitted (or *left-out*) variable, the interpretation and use of your estimated equation becomes suspect. Leaving out a relevant variable like price from a demand equation not only prevents you from getting an estimate of the coefficient of price, it also usually causes bias in the estimated coefficients of the variables that are in the equation.

The bias caused by leaving a variable out of an equation is called **specification bias** (or more casually, *omitted variable bias*). In an equation with more than one independent variable, the coefficient β_k is the change in the dependent variable Y caused by a one-unit change in the independent variable X_k holding the values of all the other independent variables in the equation constant. If a variable is omitted, then it is not included as an independent variable, and it is not held constant for the calculation and interpretation of $\hat{\beta}_k$. This omission can cause bias: It can change the expected value of the estimated coefficient away from the true value of the population coefficient.

The estimated value of a regression coefficient can change depending on the other variables that are in the equation. Thus, omitting a relevant variable is usually evidence that the entire estimated equation is suspect because of the likely bias in the coefficients of the variables that remain in the equation. Let's look at this issue in more detail.

6.1.1 The Consequences of an Omitted Variable

Suppose the true regression model is

$$Y_i = \beta_0 + \beta_1 X_{1i} + \beta_2 X_{2i} + \epsilon_i \tag{6.1}$$

where ϵ_i is a classical error term. If a researcher inadvertently omits an important independent variable (or can't get data on that variable), then the equation becomes:

$$Y_i = \beta_0 + \beta_1 X_{1i} + \epsilon_i^* \tag{6.2}$$

where the error term of the mis-specified equation can be seen to be:

$$\epsilon_i^* = \beta_2 X_{2i} + \epsilon_i \tag{6.3}$$

In Equation 6.2, the error term ϵ_i^* is no longer independent of the explanatory variable X_{1i}, as long as X_{1i} and X_{2i} are correlated, because if X_{2i} changes, both X_{1i} and ϵ_i^* will move together. In other words, if we leave an important variable out of an equation, we violate Classical Assumption III (that the explanatory variables are independent of the error term), unless the omitted variable is totally uncorrelated with all the included independent variables (which is extremely unlikely). Recall that the correlation between X_1 and X_2 can be measured by the simple correlation coefficient between the two variables (r_{12}) using Equation 5.8.

In general, when there is a violation of one of the classical assumptions, the Gauss-Markov Theorem on Ordinary Least Squares does not hold, and the OLS estimates are not BLUE. Given linear estimators, this means that the estimated coefficients are no longer unbiased or are no longer minimum variance (for all linear unbiased estimators) or both. In such a circumstance, econometricians first determine the exact property (unbiasedness or minimum variance) that no longer holds and then suggest an alternative estimation technique that might, in some sense, be better than OLS.

An omitted variable causes the classical assumptions to be violated in a way that causes bias. In the case mentioned above, the estimation of Equation 6.2 when Equation 6.1 is the truth will cause bias in the estimates of Equation 6.2. This means that:

$$E(\hat{\beta}_1) \neq \beta_1$$

Instead of having an expected value equal to the true β_1, the estimate $\hat{\beta}_1$ will compensate for the fact that X_2 is missing from the equation. If X_1 and X_2 are correlated and X_2 is omitted from the equation, then the OLS program will attribute to X_1 variations in Y actually caused by X_2, and a biased $\hat{\beta}_1$ will result.

To see how a left-out variable might cause bias, picture a production function that states that output (Y) depends on the amount of labor (X_1) and capital (X_2) used. What would happen if data on capital were unavailable for some reason and X_2 was omitted from the equation? In this case, we would be leaving out the impact of capital on output in our model. This omission would almost surely bias the estimate of the coefficient of labor because it is likely that capital and labor are positively correlated (an increase in capital usually requires at least some labor to utilize it and vice versa). As a result, the OLS program would attribute to labor the increase in output actually caused by capital to the extent that labor and capital were correlated. Thus the bias would be a function of the impact of capital on output (β_2) and the correlation between capital and labor (r_{12}).

To generalize for a model with two independent variables, the expected value of the coefficient of an included variable (β_1) when a relevant variable (X_2) is omitted from the equation equals:

$$E(\hat{\beta}_1) = \beta_1 + \beta_2 \cdot f(r_{12}) \tag{6.4}$$

This states that the expected value of the included variable's coefficient is equal to its true value plus the excluded variable's true coefficient times a function of the simple correlation coefficient between the included and excluded variables.[1] Thus bias exists unless:

(a) the true β_2 is zero

    (i.e. X_2 is not a relevant variable in the true model), or

(b) r_{12}, the simple correlation coefficient between X_1 and X_2, is zero

    (the excluded and included variables are perfectly uncorrelated).

The term $\beta_2 \cdot f(r_{12})$ is the amount of specification bias introduced into the estimate of β_1 by leaving out X_2. For the production function example above, this term would equal the coefficient of capital (β_2) times a function of the simple correlation coefficient between labor and capital (r_{12}). If the included and excluded variables are uncorrelated, there will be no bias, but there is almost always some correlation between any two variables in the real world (even if it is just random), and so bias is almost always caused by the omission of a relevant variable.[2]

6.1.2   An Example of Specification Bias

Consider the following equation for the annual consumption of chicken in the United States:[3]

$$\hat{Y}_t = -49.6 - 0.54PC_t + 0.22PB_t + 10.6LYD_t \tag{6.5}$$
$$\phantom{\hat{Y}_t = -49.6 - }(0.07)\quad\ (0.06)\qquad (1.3)$$
$$t = \quad\ -7.6\qquad\ 3.5\qquad\ 8.3$$
$$\bar{R}^2 = .979 \quad n = 29 \quad \text{(Annual: 1950 through 1978)}$$

where: Y_t = per capita chicken consumption (in pounds) in year t
        PC_t = the price of chicken (in cents per pound) in year t
        PB_t = the price of beef (cents per pound) in year t
        LYD_t = the log of U.S. per capita disposable income (in dollars) in year t

This equation is a simple demand for chicken equation that includes the prices of chicken and a close substitute (beef) and a logged income variable. (The log allows the impact of a one-unit increase in income to be less at higher levels of income that at lower ones.) Note that the signs of the estimated coefficients agree with the signs you would have hypothesized before seeing any regression results.

If we estimate this equation without the price of the substitute, we obtain:

$$\hat{Y}_t = -77.9 - 0.38PC_t + 14.7LYD_t \tag{6.6}$$
$$\phantom{\hat{Y}_t = -77.9 - }(0.07)\qquad (0.68)$$
$$t = \quad\ -5.8\qquad\ 21.5 \quad \bar{R}^2 = .970$$

Comparing Equations 6.5 and 6.6 to see what impact on the estimates the omission of the price of beef variable had, we notice that $\bar{R}^2$ fell slightly from .979 to .970 when the price of beef variable was dropped from the equation. This fits with our perception of how $\bar{R}^2$ should act when a relevant variable is omitted.

More importantly, the estimated coefficients of the remaining variables changed. $\hat{\beta}_{PC}$ went from $- 0.54$ to $- 0.38$, while $\hat{\beta}_{LYD}$ went from 10.6 to 14.7. The direction of this bias, by the way, is called positive because the biased coefficient of PC of $- 0.38$ is more positive (less negative) than the suspected unbiased one of $- 0.54$ and because the biased coefficient of LYD of 14.7 is more positive than the suspected unbiased one of 10.6.

The fact that the bias was positive could have been guessed before any regressions were run if Equation 6.4 had been used. The specification bias caused by omitting the price of beef is expected[4] to be positive because the expected sign of the coefficient of PB is positive and because the expected correlation between the price of beef and the price of chicken itself is positive:

$$\text{expected bias in } \hat{\beta}_{PC} = \beta_{PB} \cdot f(r_{PC,PB}) = (+) \cdot (+) = (+)$$

Similarly for LYD:

$$\text{expected bias in } \hat{\beta}_{LYD} = \beta_{PB} \cdot f(r_{LYD,PB}) = (+) \cdot (+) = (+)$$

Note that both correlation coefficients are anticipated to be (and actually are) positive. (To see this, think of the impact of an increase in the price of chicken on the price of beef and then follow through the impact of an increase in income on the price of beef.)

To sum, if a relevant variable is left out of a regression equation,

1. there is no longer an estimate of the coefficient of that variable in the equation, and
2. the coefficients of the remaining variables are likely to be biased.

While the amount of the bias might not be very large in some cases (when, for instance, there is little correlation between the included and excluded variables), it is extremely likely that at least a small amount of specification bias will be present in all such situations.

6.1.3   Correcting for an Omitted Variable

In theory, the solution to a problem of specification bias seems easy: simply add the omitted variable to the equation. Unfortunately, that is more easily said than done.

First, omitted variable bias is hard to detect. As mentioned above, the amount of bias introduced can be small and not immediately detectable. This is especially true when there is no reason to believe that you have mis-specified the model. While some indications of specification bias are obvious (such as an estimated coefficient that is significant in the direction opposite from that which was expected), others are not so clear. Could you tell from Equation 6.6 alone that a variable was missing? The best indicators of an omitted relevant variable are the theoretical underpinnings of the model itself. What variables *must* be included? What signs do you expect? Do you have any notions about the range into which the coefficient values should fall? Have you accidentally left out a variable that most researchers would agree is important? The best way to avoid omitting an important variable is to invest the time to think carefully through the equation before the data are submitted to the computer.

A second source of complexity is the problem of choosing which variable to add to an equation once you decide that it is suffering from omitted variable bias. That is, a researcher faced with a clear case of specification bias (like an estimated $\hat{\beta}$ that is significantly different from zero in the unexpected direction) will often have no clue as to what variable could be causing the problem. Some beginning researchers, when faced with the dilemma, will add all the possible relevant variables to the equation at once, but this process leads to less precise estimates, as will be discussed in the next section. Other beginning researchers will test a number of different variables and keep the one in the equation that does the best statistical job of appearing to reduce the bias (by giving plausible signs and satisfactory t-values). This technique, adding a "left-out" variable to "fix" a strange-looking regression result, is invalid because the variable that best corrects a case of specification bias might do so only by chance rather than by being the true solution to the problem. In such an instance, the fixed equation may apparently give superb statistical results for the sample at hand but then do terribly when applied to other samples, because it does not describe the characteristics of the true population.

Dropping a variable will not help cure omitted variable bias. If the sign of an estimated coefficient is different from that which was expected, it cannot be changed to the expected direction by dropping a variable that has a lower t-score (in absolute value) than the t-score of the coefficient estimate that has the unexpected sign. Furthermore, the sign in general will not likely change even if the variable to be deleted has a larger t-score.[5]

If the estimated coefficient is significantly different from expectation (either in sign or magnitude), then it is likely that some sort of specification bias exists in our model. Although it is true that a poor sample of data or a poorly theorized expectation may also yield statistically significant unexpected signs or magnitudes, these possibilities can be eliminated in some cases.

A legitimate technique for reducing the number of theoretically sound candidate omitted variables is the investigation of the direction of the bias caused by the omission of a variable from an equation. If the sign of the expected bias can be shown to be in a direction opposite that which is observed, then that variable can be eliminated from consideration. The direction of the expected bias can be determined from the second term in Equation 6.4:

$$\text{expected bias in } \hat{\beta}_1 = \beta_2 \cdot f(r_{12})$$

In the example of omitting the price of beef from the chicken demand equation, the expected direction of the bias was positive since both the expected coefficient and the expected correlation between PB and PC were positive:

$$\text{expected bias in } \hat{\beta}_{PC} = \beta_{PB} \cdot f(r_{PC,PB}) = (+) \cdot (+) = (+)$$

Thus the price of beef was a reasonable candidate to be the omitted variable in Equation 6.6.

A bad choice for the omitted variable in the same equation would be the price of a good that is a complement to the consumption of chicken (such as dumplings) because the expected bias is negative. To see this, calculate the sign of the expected bias in the coefficient of the price of chicken due to the omission of the price of dumplings (PD) from the chicken demand equation:

$$\text{expected bias in } \hat{\beta}_{PC} = \beta_{PD} \cdot f(r_{PC,PD}) = (-) \cdot (+) = (-)$$

The expected sign of the price of dumplings in the chicken demand equation is negative because a high price of dumplings (the complement) would make it more expensive to consume mass quantities of chicken, shifting the demand curve for chicken downward. In addition, the prices of complements generally move together, because a change in the underlying demand for one would change the underlying demand for the other in the same direction (if the supply conditions of the complements were characterized by violent swings caused by different factors, such a positive correlation would not be so likely).

The possible combinations of the expected signs of the coefficients and simple correlation coefficients (due to the omission of a single independent variable) are matched with the expected sign of the resultant specification bias in Table 6.1. To use this table, find the row that contains the expected sign of the coefficient of the candidate omitted variable (for price of dumplings, this was negative) and match it with the column that contains the expected sign of the simple correlation coefficient between the included and excluded variables (for price of dumplings, this was positive). The sign at the intersection of the appropriate row and column is the sign of the expected bias in the coefficient of the particular included variable due to leaving out the particular candidate excluded variable (for price of dumplings, this was negative). While you can never actually observe bias

Table 6.1   The Expected Sign of the Bias Caused by an Omitted Variable

		Expected Sign of the Simple Correlation Coefficient between the included (in) and omitted (o) variables, $r_{in,o}$	
		$r_{in,o}$	
		+	−
Expected Sign of the Coefficient of the Omitted Variable, β_o (Based on Theory)	β_o +	+	−
	−	−	+

(since you don't know the true β), the use of this technique to screen potential causes of specification bias should reduce the number of regressions run and therefore increase the statistical validity of the results. This technique will work best when only one (or one kind) of variable is omitted from the equation in question. With a number of different kinds of variables omitted simultaneously, the impact on the equation's coefficients is quite hard to specify.

A brief warning: It may be tempting to conduct what might be called "residual analysis" by examining a plot of the residuals in an attempt to find patterns that could suggest variables that have been accidentally omitted. A major problem with this approach is that the coefficients of the estimated equation will possibly have some of the effects of the left-out variable already altering their estimated values. Thus, residuals from this equation may show a pattern that only vaguely resembles the pattern of the actual omitted variable. The chances are high that the pattern shown in the residuals may lead to the selection of an incorrect variable. In addition, care should be taken to use residual analysis only to choose between theoretically sound candidate variables rather than as a method of trying to generate those candidates.

6.2   Irrelevant Variables

Irrelevant variables are the converse of omitted variables and can be analyzed using the model developed in Section 6.1. Whereas the omitted variable model has more independent variables in the "true" model than in the estimated equation, the irrelevant variable model has more independent variables in the estimated equation than in the true one.

The addition of a variable to an equation where it doesn't belong does not cause bias, but it does increase the variances of the included variables' regression coefficients.

6.2.1   Impact of Irrelevant Variables

If the true regression specification is

$$Y_i = \beta_0 + \beta_1 X_{1i} + \epsilon_i \tag{6.7}$$

but the researcher for some reason includes an extra variable,

$$Y_i = \beta_0 + \beta_1 X_{1i} + \beta_2 X_{2i} + \epsilon_i^{**} \tag{6.8}$$

the mis-specified equation's error term can be seen to be:

$$\epsilon_i^{**} = \epsilon_i - \beta_2 X_{2i} \tag{6.9}$$

Such a mistake will not cause bias if the true coefficient of the extra (or irrelevant) variable is zero. In that case, $\epsilon_i = \epsilon_i^{**}$. Whereas $\hat{\beta}_1$ in Equation 6.7 is usually biased when $\beta_2 \neq 0$, $\hat{\beta}_1$ in Equation 6.8 is unbiased when $\beta_2 = 0$.

The inclusion of an irrelevant variable will increase the variance of the estimated coefficients, and this increased variance will tend to decrease the absolute magnitude of their t-scores. Also, an irrelevant variable usually decreases the $\bar{R}^2$ (but not the R^2). In a model of Y on X_1 and X_2, the variance of the OLS estimator of β_1 is:

$$\text{VAR}(\hat{\beta}_1) = \frac{\sigma^2}{(1-r_{12}^2) \cdot \Sigma(X_1-\bar{X}_1)^2} \tag{6.10}$$

But when $r_{12} = 0$ (or in the single-independent variable model), then:

$$\text{VAR}(\hat{\beta}_1) = \frac{\sigma^2}{\Sigma(X_1-\bar{X}_1)^2} \tag{6.11}$$

Thus, while the irrelevant variable causes no bias, it causes problems for the regression, because it reduces the precision of the regression. To see why this is so, try plugging a nonzero value (between $+1.0$ and -1.0) for r_{12} into Equation 6.10 and note that $\text{VAR}(\hat{\beta}_1)$ has increased when compared to Equation 6.11. The equation with an included variable that does not belong in the equation usually has lower t-scores and a lower $\bar{R}^2$ than it otherwise would. This property holds, by the way, only when $r_{12} \neq 0$, but since this is the case in virtually every sample, the conclusion of increased variance due to irrelevant variables is a valid one. Table 6.2 summarizes the consequences of the omitted variable and the included irrelevant variable cases:

Table 6.2   Summary of the Impacts of an Omitted Variable or an Included Irrelevant Variable on the Remaining Coefficients

Effect on Remaining Coefficient Estimates	Omitted Variable	Included Irrelevant Variable
Bias?	Yes*	No
Increases or Decreases Variance?	Decreases*	Increases*

*unless $r_{12} = 0$

6.2.2   An Example of an Irrelevant Variable

Let's return to Section 6.1.2 and the equation for the annual consumption of chicken, and see what happens when we add an irrelevant variable to the equation. For convenience, the original equation is:

$$\hat{Y}_t = -49.6 - 0.54PC_t + 0.22PB_t + 10.6LYD_t \qquad (6.12)$$
$$\phantom{\hat{Y}_t = -49.6}\ (0.07)\qquad (0.06)\qquad (1.3)$$
$$\phantom{\hat{Y}_t = }\ t = \qquad -7.6\qquad\ 3.5\qquad\ 8.3$$
$$\bar{R}^2 = .979 \qquad\qquad\qquad\qquad n = 29$$

Suppose you hypothesize that the demand for chicken also depends on INT, the interest rate (which perhaps confuses the demand for a nondurable good with an equation you saw for a consumer durable). If you now estimate the equation with the interest rate included, the result is:

$$\hat{Y} = -52.0 - 0.55PC + 0.23PB + 11.1LYD - 0.17INT \qquad (6.13)$$
$$\phantom{\hat{Y} = -52.0}\ (0.08)\qquad (0.07)\qquad (1.42)\qquad (0.24)$$
$$\phantom{\hat{Y} = }\ t = \qquad -7.3\qquad\ 3.5\qquad\ 7.8\qquad -0.7$$
$$\bar{R}^2 = .978$$

A comparison of Equations 6.12 and 6.13 will make the theory in Section 6.2.1 come to life. First of all, $\bar{R}^2$ has fallen slightly, indicating the reduction in fit adjusted for degrees of freedom. Second, none of the regression coefficients from the original equation changed significantly; compare these results with the larger differences between Equations 6.5 and 6.6. Further, slight increases in the standard errors of the estimated coefficients can be observed. In addition, the t-score for the potential variable (the interest rate) is very small, indicating that it is not significantly different from zero. Given the theoretical shakiness of the new variable, these results indicate that it is irrelevant and never should have been included in the regression.

6.2.3 Making Correct Specification Choices

It seems clear that at least four valid tests exist to help decide whether a given variable belongs in the equation.

1. *Theory:* Is the variable's place in the equation unambiguous and theoretically sound?
2. *t-test:* Is the variable's estimated coefficient significantly different from zero?
3. $\bar{R}^2$: Does the overall fit of the equation (adjusted for degrees of freedom) improve when the variable is added to the equation?
4. *Bias:* Do other variables' coefficients change significantly when the variable is added to the equation?

If all these conditions hold, the variable belongs in the equation; if none of them do, the variable is irrelevant and can be safely excluded from the equation. For a typical omitted relevant variable, for example, its inclusion probably would increase $\bar{R}^2$ and change other coefficients while having a significant t-score. An irrelevant variable, on the other hand, would reduce $\bar{R}^2$, have an insignificant t-score, and have little impact on the other variables' coefficients.

In many cases, all four tests do not agree. It is possible for a variable to have an insignificant t-score that is greater than one, for example. In such a case $\bar{R}^2$

would go up and yet the t-score would still be insignificant. In another case, the variable might be fairly uncorrelated with the included variables and thus have little effect on their coefficients or standard errors. What do you do in such circumstances?

Whenever the four tests of whether or not a variable should be included in an equation disagree, the econometrician must use careful judgment. Researchers should not misuse this freedom by testing various combinations of variables until they find the results that appear to statistically support the point they want to make. All such decisions are a bit easier when you realize that the single most important determinant of a variable's relevance is its theoretical justification. No amount of statistical evidence should make a theoretical necessity into an "irrelevant" variable. Once in a while, a researcher is forced to leave a theoretically important variable out of an equation for lack of a better alternative; in such cases, the usefulness of the equation is limited.

6.3   Illustration of Misuse of the *t*-Test

At times, the rules outlined in the previous section will lead the researcher to an incorrect conclusion if those rules are blindly applied to a problem without the proper concern for common sense or economic principles. In particular, a t-score can often be fairly insignificant for reasons other than the presence of an irrelevant variable. Since economic theory is the most important test for including a variable, an example of why a variable should not be dropped from an equation simply because it has an insignificant t-score is in order.

Suppose you believe that the demand for Brazilian coffee in the United States is a function of the real price of Brazilian coffee (P_{bc}), the real price of tea (P_t) and the real disposable income in the United States (Y_d).[6] Suppose further that you obtain the data, run the implied regression, and observe the following results:

$$\widehat{COFFEE} = 9.1 + 7.8P_{bc} + 2.4P_t + 0.0035Y_d \qquad (6.14)$$

$$(15.6) \quad (1.2) \quad (0.0010)$$

$$t = 0.5 \quad 2.0 \quad 3.5$$

$$\bar{R}^2 = .60 n = 25$$

The coefficients of the second and third variables, P_t and Y_d, appear to be fairly significant in the direction you hypothesized, but the first variable, P_{bc}, appears to have an insignificant coefficient with an unexpected sign. If you think that there is a possibility that the demand for Brazilian coffee is perfectly price-inelastic (i.e., its coefficient is zero), you might decide to run the same equation without the price variable, obtaining:

$$\widehat{COFFEE} = 9.3 + 2.6P_t + 0.0036Y_d \quad\quad (6.15)$$
$$(1.0) \quad\quad (0.0009)$$
$$t = \quad 2.6 \quad\quad 4.0$$
$$\bar{R}^2 = .61$$

By comparing Equations 6.14 and 6.15, we can apply the four tests for the inclusion of a variable in an equation that were outlined in the previous section:

1. *Theory:* Since the demand for coffee could possibly be perfectly price-inelastic, the theory behind dropping the variable seems plausible.
2. *t-test:* The t-score of the possibly irrelevant variable is 0.5, insignificant at any level.
3. *$\bar{R}^2$:* $\bar{R}^2$ increases when the variable is dropped, indicating that the variable is irrelevant. (Since the t-score was less than one, this is to be expected.)
4. *Bias:* The remaining coefficients change only a small amount when P_{bc} is dropped, suggesting that there is little if any bias caused by excluding the variable.

Based upon the analysis summarized above, you might easily conclude that the demand for Brazilian coffee is perfectly price-inelastic and that the variable is therefore irrelevant and should be dropped from the model. As it turns out, this conclusion would be unwarranted. While the demand for coffee in general might be price-inelastic (actually, the evidence suggests that it is inelastic only over a particular range of prices), it is hard to believe that Brazilian coffee is immune to price competition from other kinds of coffee. Indeed, one would expect quite a bit of sensitivity in the demand for Brazilian coffee with respect to the price of, for example, Colombian coffee. In order to test this hypothesis, the price of Colombian coffee (P_{cc}) should be added to the original Equation 6.14:

$$\widehat{COFFEE} = 10.0 + 8.0P_{cc} - 5.6P_{bc} + 2.6P_t + 0.0030Y_d \quad (6.16)$$
$$(4.0) \quad (2.0) \quad (1.3) \quad (0.0010)$$
$$\bar{R}^2 = .65 \quad t = \quad 2.0 \quad\quad -2.8 \quad 2.0 \quad\quad 3.0$$

By comparing Equations 6.14 and 6.16, we can once again apply the four tests:

1. *Theory:* Both prices should always have been included in the model; their logical justification is quite strong.
2. *t-test:* The t-score of the new variable, the price of Colombian coffee, is 2.0, significant at most levels.
3. *$\bar{R}^2$:* $\bar{R}^2$ increases with the addition of the variable, indicating that the variable was an omitted variable.
4. *Bias:* While two of the coefficients remain virtually unchanged, indicating that the correlations between these variables and the price of Colombian coffee variable are low, the coefficient for the price of Brazilian coffee did change significantly, indicating bias in the original result.

An examination of the bias question will also help us understand Equation 6.4, the equation for bias. Since the expected sign of the coefficient of the omitted variable (P_{cc}) is positive and since the simple correlation coefficient between the two competitive prices ($r_{P_{cc},P_{bc}}$) is also positive, the expected direction of the bias in $\hat{\beta}_{bc}$ in the estimation of Equation 6.14 is positive. If you compare Equations 6.14 and 6.16, that positive bias can be clearly seen, because the coefficient of X_{bc} is $+7.8$ instead of -5.6. The increase from -5.6 to $+7.8$ may be due to the positive bias that results from leaving out P_{cc}.

The moral to be drawn from this example is that theoretical considerations should never be discarded even in the face of statistical insignificance. If a variable known to be extremely important from a theoretical point of view turns out to be insignificant in a particular sample, that variable should be left in the equation despite the fact that it makes the results look bad.

Do not conclude that the particular path outlined in this example is the correct way to specify an equation. Trying a long string of possible variables until you get the particular one that makes P_{bc} turn negative and significant is not the way to obtain a result that will stand up well to other samples or alternative hypotheses. The original equation should never have been run without the Colombian coffee variable. Instead, the problem should have been analyzed enough so that such errors of omission were unlikely before any regressions were attempted at all. The more thinking that is done before the first regression is run and the fewer alternative specifications that are estimated, the better the regression results are likely to be.

6.4   Specification Searches

One of the weaknesses of econometrics is that a researcher can potentially manipulate a data set to produce almost *any* results by specifying different regressions until estimates with the desired properties are obtained. Thus, the integrity of all empirical work is potentially open to question.

Although the problem is a difficult one, it does make sense to attempt to minimize the number of equations estimated and to rely on theory rather than statistical fit as much as possible when choosing variables. We will try to illustrate this by discussing three of the most commonly used *incorrect* techniques for specifying a regression equation. These techniques produce the best specification only by chance and at worst are possibly unethical in that they misrepresent the methods used to obtain the regression results and the significance of those results.

6.4.1   Data Mining

Almost surely the worst way to choose a specification is to simultaneously try a whole series of possible regression formulations and to then choose the equation that conforms the most to what the researcher wants the results to look like. In such a situation, the researcher would estimate virtually every possible combination of the various alternative independent variables, and the choice between them would be made on the basis of the results. This practice of simultaneously estimating a number of combinations of independent variables and selecting the best from them does not account for the fact that a number of specifications have been examined before the final one. Thus, their reported t-scores overstate the degree of statistical significance of the estimated coefficients.

Furthermore, "data mining" and "fishing expeditions" to obtain desired statistics for the final regression equation are potentially unethical methods of empirical research. These procedures include using not only many alternative combinations of independent variables, but also many functional forms, lag structures, and what are offered as "sophisticated" or "advanced" estimating techniques. "If you just torture the data long enough, they will confess."[7] In other words, if enough alternatives are tried, the chances of obtaining the results desired by the researcher are increased tremendously, but the final result is essentially worthless. The researcher has not found any scientific evidence to support the original hypothesis; rather, he or she has imposed prior expectations on the data in a way that is essentially misleading.

6.4.2   Stepwise Regression Procedures

A **stepwise regression** involves the use of a computer program to choose the independent variables to be used in the estimation of a particular equation. The computer program is given a "shopping list" of possible independent variables, and then it builds the equation in steps. It chooses as the first explanatory variable the one that by itself explains the largest amount of the variation of the dependent variable around its mean. It then chooses as the second variable the one that adds the most to R^2, given that the first variable is already in the equation. The stepwise procedure continues until the next variable to be added fails to achieve some researcher-specified increase in R^2 (or all the variables are added). The measure of the supposed contribution of each independent variable is the increase in R^2 (which is sometimes called the "R^2 delete") caused by the addition of the variable.

Unfortunately, any correlation among the independent variables (called multicollinearity, which we will take up in more detail in Chapter 8) causes this procedure to be deficient. To the extent that the variables are related, it becomes difficult to tell the impact of one variable from another. As a result, in the presence of multicollinearity, it is impossible to determine unambiguously the individual contribution of each variable enough to say which one is more important and thus should be included first.[8] Even worse, there is no necessity that the particular combination of variables chosen has any theoretical justification.

Because of these problems, most researchers avoid stepwise procedures. The major pitfalls of such procedures are that the coefficients may be biased; the calculated t-values no longer follow the t-distribution; such procedures may result in the exclusion of a relevant variable just because of the arbitrary order in which the selection takes place (according to the contribution to the R^2); and the signs of the estimated coefficients at intermediate or final stages of the routine may be incorrect. Using a stepwise procedure is an admission of ignorance concerning which variables should be entered.

6.4.3   Sequential Specification Searches

To their credit, most econometricians avoid "data-mining" and stepwise regressions. Instead, they tend to specify equations by estimating an initial equation and then sequentially dropping or adding variables (or changing functional forms) until a plausible equation is found with "good statistics." Faced with a situation of perhaps knowing that a few variables are relevant (on the basis of theory) but not knowing whether other, additional variables are relevant, recourse to the usual t-tests for all variables (both before and after selection or exclusion of some independent variables) appears to be the generally accepted practice. Indeed, it would be easy to draw from a casual reading of the previous sections the impression that such a sequential specification search is the best way to go about finding the "truth." Instead, as we shall see, there is a vast difference in approach between a sequential specification search and our recommended approach.

The sequential specification search technique allows a researcher to estimate an undisclosed number of regressions and then present a final choice (which is based upon some unknown set of expectations about the signs and significance of the coefficients) as if it were the only specification estimated. Such a method misstates the statistical validity of the regression results for two reasons:

1. The statistical significance of the results is overestimated, because the estimations of the previous regressions are ignored.
2. The set of expectations used by the researcher to choose between various regression results is rarely if ever disclosed.[9] Thus the reader has no way of knowing whether or not all the other regression results had opposite signs or insignificant coefficients for the important variables.

Unfortunately, there is no universally accepted way of conducting sequential searches, primarily because the appropriate test at one stage in the procedure depends on which tests were previously conducted, and also because the tests have been very difficult to invent. One possibility that has been suggested is to reduce the degrees of freedom in the "final" equation by one for each alternative specification attempted. This procedure is far from exact, but it does impose an explicit penalty for specification searches. More generally, we recommend trying to keep the number of regressions estimated as low as possible, to focus on theoretical considerations when choosing variables, functional forms and the like, and to reveal all the various specifications investigated. That is, we recommend combining parsimony (using theory and analysis to limit the number of specifications estimated) with disclosure (reporting all the equations estimated).

There is another side to this story, however. Some researchers feel that the true model will show through if it is given the chance and that the best statistical results (including signs of coefficients, etc.) are most likely to have come from the true specification. The problem with this philosophy is that the element of chance is ordinarily quite strong in any given application. In addition, reasonable people often disagree as to what the "true" model should look like. As a result, different researchers can look at the same data set and come up with very different "best" equations. Because this can happen, the distinction between good and bad econometrics is not always clear-cut. As long as researchers have a healthy respect for the dangers inherent in specification searches, they are very likely to proceed in a reasonable way.

The lesson to be learned from this section should be quite clear. Most of the work of specifying an equation should be done before even attempting to estimate the equation on the computer. Since it is unreasonable to expect researchers to be perfect, there will be times when additional specifications must be estimated; however, these new estimates should be thoroughly grounded in theory and explicitly taken into account when testing for significance or summarizing results. In this way, the danger of misleading the reader about the statistical properties of estimates is reduced.

6.4.4   The Impact of Sequential Specification Searches

In the previous section, we stated that sequential specification searches are likely to mislead researchers about the statistical properties of the results. This section presents an example of a problem that can be encountered with a particular kind of sequential specification search. The example will illustrate the fact that dropping variables from a model on the basis of t-tests alone will introduce systematic bias into the estimated equation.[10]

Say the hypothesized model for a particular dependent variable is:

$$Y_i = \beta_0 + \beta_1 X_{1i} + \beta_2 X_{2i} + \epsilon_i \qquad (6.17)$$

Assume further that, on the basis of theory, we are certain that X_1 belongs in the equation but that we are not as certain that X_2 belongs. Even though we have stressed four tests to determine whether X_2 should be included, many inexperienced researchers just use the t-test on $\hat{\beta}_2$ to determine whether X_2 should be included. If this preliminary t-test indicates that $\hat{\beta}_2$ is significantly different from zero, then these researchers leave X_2 in the equation, and they choose Equation 6.17 as their final model; if, however, the t-test does *not* indicate that $\hat{\beta}_2$ is significantly different from zero, then such researchers drop X_2 from the equation and consider Y as a function of X_1.

Using such a system, two kinds of mistakes can be made. First, X_2 can sometimes be left in the equation when it does not belong there, but such a mistake does not change the expected value of $\hat{\beta}_1$. Second, X_2 can be sometimes dropped from the equation when it belongs, and then the estimated coefficient of X_1 will be biased by the value of the true β_2 to the extent that X_1 and X_2 are correlated. In other words, $\hat{\beta}_1$ will be biased every time X_2 belongs in the equation and is left out, and X_2 will be left out every time that this estimated coefficient is not significantly different from zero. That is, the expected value of $\hat{\beta}_1$ will not equal the true β_1, and we will have systematic bias in our equation:

$$E(\hat{\beta}_1) = \beta_1 + \beta_2 \cdot f(r_{x1,x2}) \cdot P(t_{\hat{\beta}_2} < t_c) \neq \beta_1$$

Where $P(t_{\hat{\beta}_2} < t_c)$ indicates the probability of an insignifcant t-score. It is also the case that the t-score of $\hat{\beta}_1$ no longer follows the t-distribution. In other words, the *t*-test is also biased by sequential specification searches.

Since most projects consider a number of different variables before settling on the final model, someone who relies on the *t*-test alone is likely to encounter this problem on a systematic basis. That is, the practice of dropping a potential independent variable simply because its t-score indicates that its estimated coefficient is insignificantly different from zero will cause systematic bias in the estimated coefficients (and their t-scores) of the remaining variables.

6.5 Summary

1. The omission of a variable from an equation will cause bias in the estimates of the remaining coefficients to the extent that the omitted variable is correlated with included variables.

2. The bias to be expected from leaving a variable out of an equation equals the coefficient of the excluded variable times a function of the simple correlation coefficient between the excluded variable and the particular included variable in question.

3. Including a variable in an equation in which it is actually irrelevant does not cause bias, but it will usually increase the variances of the included variables' estimated coefficients, thus lowering their t-values.

4. Four useful tests for the inclusion of a variable in an equation are:
   a. Theory
   b. *t*-test
   c. $\bar{R}^2$
   d. Bias

5. Theory, not statistical fit, should be the most important criterion for the inclusion of a variable in a regression equation. To do otherwise runs the risk of producing incorrect and/or disbelieved results. For example, stepwise regression routines will generally give biased estimates and will almost always have test statistics that will not follow the distribution necessary to use standard t-tables.

Exercises

(Answers to even-numbered questions are in Appendix A.)

1. Write out the meaning of each of the following terms without reference to the book (or your notes) and then compare your definition with the version in the text for each:
   a. omitted variable
   b. irrelevant variable
   c. specification bias
   d. stepwise regression
   e. sequential specification search

2. For each of the following situations, determine the *sign* (and if possible comment on the likely size) of the bias introduced by leaving a variable out of an equation:
   a. In an equation for the demand for peanut butter, the impact on the coefficient of disposable income of omitting the price of peanut butter variable. (Hint: start by hypothesizing signs.)
   b. In an earnings equation for workers, the impact on the coefficient of experience of omitting the variable for age.
   c. In a production function for airplanes, the impact on the coefficient of labor of omitting the capital variable.
   d. In an equation for daily attendance at Philadelphia Phillies baseball games, the impact on the coefficient of the weekend dummy variable (1 = weekend) of omitting a variable that measures the probability of precipitation at game time (as estimated by the weather bureau).

3. If a particular variable belongs in your equation, what impacts will omitting it have on the four tests outlined in the section on irrelevant variables (and summarized in item 4 in the summary above)? Be specific.

4. The "term structure of interest rates" describes the effect that maturity (the length of time before the principal of the bond is to be repaid) has on the yield of debt instruments. The yield curve, which plots the yield of bonds against their terms to maturity (the bonds on any given curve differ only in their terms to maturity), graphically illustrates the term structure for any given point in time. Suppose you were given a cross-sectional set of data that included all available information on 25 different bonds. Unfortunately, the bonds differ with respect to more than just their terms to maturity; they have different amounts of risk, taxability, and so on. Is there a way you could still estimate the slope of the yield curve that existed at the point in time the data were collected? How?

5. The attached data set is the one that was used to estimate the chicken demand examples of Section 6.1.2 and 6.2.2.

	Y	PC	YD	PB	INT
1950	20.6	22.2	1362	23.30	2.07
1951	21.7	25.0	1465	28.70	2.56
1952	22.1	22.1	1515	24.30	3.00
1953	21.9	22.1	1581	16.30	3.17
1954	22.8	16.8	1583	16.00	3.05
1955	21.4	18.6	1664	15.60	3.16
1956	24.4	16.0	1741	14.90	3.77
1957	25.5	13.7	1802	17.20	4.20
1958	28.1	14.0	1832	21.90	3.83
1959	28.9	11.0	1903	22.60	4.48
1960	28.1	12.2	1947	20.40	4.82
1961	30.2	10.1	1991	20.20	4.50
1962	30.0	10.2	2073	21.30	4.50
1963	30.8	10.0	2144	19.90	4.50
1964	31.2	9.2	2296	18.00	4.50
1965	33.3	8.9	2448	19.80	4.54
1966	35.6	9.7	2613	22.29	5.63
1967	36.5	7.9	2757	22.30	5.61
1968	36.7	8.2	2956	23.40	6.30
1969	38.4	9.7	3152	26.20	7.96
1970	40.5	8.8	3393	27.10	7.91
1971	40.5	7.7	3630	29.00	5.72
1972	42.0	9.0	3880	33.50	5.25
1973	40.7	15.1	4346	42.80	8.03
1974	41.1	9.7	4710	35.60	10.81
1975	40.6	9.9	5132	32.30	7.86
1976	43.3	12.9	5550	33.70	6.84
1977	44.8	12.0	6046	34.50	6.83
1978	47.5	12.4	6688	48.50	9.06

Sources: U.S. Department of Agriculture, *Agricultural Statistics*
U.S. Bureau of the Census, *Historical Statistics of the United States*
U.S. Bureau of the Census, *Statistical Abstract of the United States*

a. Read these data into your computer and attempt to reproduce the specifications in the chapter.

b. Find data for the price of another substitute for chicken and add that variable to your version of Equation 6.5. Analyze your result. In particular, apply the four tests for the inclusion of a variable to determine whether the price of the substitute is an irrelevant variable or previously was an omitted variable.

6. You have been retained by the "Expressive Expresso" company to help them decide where to build their next "Expresso and Cream Cheese" store. You decide to run a regression on the sales of the 30 existing "Expresso and

Cream Cheese" stores as a function of the characteristics of the locations they are in and then use the equation to predict the sales at the various locations you are considering for the newest store. You end up estimating (standard errors in parentheses):

$$\hat{Y}_i = 30 + 0.1X_{1i} + 0.01X_{2i} + 10.0X_{3i} + 3.0X_{4i}$$
$$\quad\quad\quad (0.02) \quad\quad (0.01) \quad\quad (1.0) \quad\quad (1.0)$$

where: Y_i = average daily sales (in hundreds of dollars) of the ith store
$\quad\quad X_{1i}$ = the number of cars that pass in the ith location per hour
$\quad\quad X_{2i}$ = average income in the area of the ith store
$\quad\quad X_{3i}$ = number of tables in the ith store
$\quad\quad X_{4i}$ = number of competing shops in the area of the ith store

a. Hypothesize expected signs, calculate the correct t-scores, and test the significance at the one percent level for each of the coefficients.
b. What problems appear to exist in the equation? What evidence of the existence of these problems do you have?
c. What suggestions would you make for a possible second run of this admittedly hypothetical equation? (Hint: Before recommending the inclusion of a potentially left-out variable, consider whether the exclusion of that variable could possibly have caused any observed bias.

7. Discuss the topic of specification searches with various members of your econometrics class. What is so wrong with not mentioning previous (probably incorrect) estimates? Why should readers be suspicious when researchers attempt to find results that support their hypotheses; for who would try to do the opposite? Do these concerns have any meaning in the world of business? In particular, if you're not trying to publish a paper, couldn't you use any specification search techniques you want in order to find the best equation?

8. Suppose you run a regression explaining the number of hamburgers that the campus fast-food store (let's call it "The Bucket") sells per day as a function of the price of their hamburgers (in dollars), the weather (in degrees F), the price of hamburgers at a national chain nearby (also in dollars), and the number of students (in thousands) on campus that day. Assume that The Bucket stays open whether or not school is in session (for staff, etc.). Unfortunately, a lightning bolt strikes the computer and wipes out all the memory and you cannot tell which independent variable is which! Given the following regression results (standard errors in parentheses):

$$\hat{Y}_i = 10.6 + 28.4S_{1i} + 12.7X_{2i} + 0.61X_{3i} - 5.9X_{4i}$$
$$\quad\quad\quad (2.6) \quad\quad (6.3) \quad\quad (0.61) \quad\quad (5.9)$$
$$\bar{R}^2 = .63 \quad\quad\quad\quad n = 35$$

a. Attempt to identify which result corresponds to which variable.
b. Explain your reasoning for Part a above.

    c. Develop and test hypotheses about the coefficients assuming that your answer to Part a is correct. What suggestions would you have for changes in the equation for a rerun when the computer is back up again?

9. Many of the examples in the text so far have been demand-side equations or production functions, but economists often also have to quantify supply-side equations that are not true production functions. These equations attempt to explain the production of a product (an example is Brazilian coffee) as a function of the price of the product and various other attributes of the market that might have an impact on the total output of growers.

    a. What sign would you expect the coefficient of price to have in a supply-side equation? Why?

    b. What other variables can you think of that might be important in a supply-side equation?

    c. Many agricultural decisions are made months (if not a full year) before the results of those decisions appear in the market. How would you adjust your hypothesized equation to take account of these lags?

    d. Given all the above, carefully specify the exact equation you would use to attempt to explain Brazilian coffee production. Be sure to hypothesize the expected signs, be specific with respect to lags, and try to make sure you have not omitted an important independent variable.

10. If you think about the previous question, you will realize that the same dependent variable (quantity of Brazilian coffee) can have different expected signs for the coefficient of the *same* independent variable (the price of Brazilian coffee) depending on what other variables are in the regression.

    a. How is this possible? That is, how is it possible to expect different signs in demand-side equations from what you would expect in supply-side ones?

    b. Given that we will not discuss how to estimate simultaneous equations until Chapter 12, what can be done to avoid the "simultaneity bias" of getting the price coefficient from the demand equation in the supply equation and vice versa?

    c. What can you do to systematically insure that you do not have "supply-side" variables in your demand equation or "demand-side" variables in the supply equation?

6.6   Appendix: Bayesian Econometrics

While all our coefficient estimates so far have been based entirely on sample data, such a limitation is not necessary. A different perspective on the specification issues of this chapter can be obtained from a brief investigation of the Bayesian approach, which makes use of this fact. **Bayesian econometrics** combines estimates generated from samples with estimates based on prior theory or research. For example, suppose you attempt to estimate the marginal propensity to consume (MPC) with the coefficient of income in an appropriately specified consumption regression equation. If your prior belief is that the MPC is 0.9 and if the estimated coefficient from your sample data is 0.8, then a Bayesian estimate of the MPC would be somewhere between the two (say, 0.85 or even 0.88). Bayesian estimates are mixtures of estimates generated from prior expectations with estimates generated from the sample data.[11]

To calculate a Bayesian estimate for the MPC example, you must specify not only your prior estimate of the value of the coefficient, but also the strength of your belief in that prior estimate. If you are 50 percent sure that 0.9 is correct, for example, then the mixed estimate would be based 50 percent on your prior estimate and 50 percent on the sample estimate. In such a case, a prior estimate of 0.9 and a sample estimate of 0.8 would yield a Bayesian estimate of 0.85. The stronger your belief in the validity of your prior estimate, the closer the Bayesian estimate will be to it. At the extreme, if you were 100 percent sure, then you could discard the data completely and just use 0.9 as your estimate. In its simplest form, then, the Bayesian estimate of a coefficient is a weighted average of the sample and prior estimates:

$$\hat{\beta}_{Bayesian} = S \cdot (\beta_p) + (1 - S) \cdot (\hat{\beta}) \tag{6.18}$$

where: $\hat{\beta}$ = the coefficient estimate obtained from your sample
  β_p = your prior estimate of the value of the coefficient
  S = the strength of your belief in this prior estimate (the percentage strength measured as a decimal).

While a number of different estimation techniques exist that are significantly more complex[12] than Equation 6.18, this equation captures the essence of Bayesian regression.

If we expect a coefficient of 0.9 and we actually get a sample coefficient estimate of 0.8, then all we need in order to calculate the Bayesian estimated coefficient is S, the strength of our belief that 0.9 is correct. If $S = 0.80$, indicating that the strength of our belief in 0.9 is 80 percent, then the Bayesian estimate would be:

$$\hat{\beta}_{Bayesian} = 0.80(0.9) + 0.20(0.8) = 0.72 + 0.16 = 0.88 \tag{6.19}$$

If $S = 0.80$ but our prior estimate of the MPC was 0.95, then:

$$\hat{\beta}_{Bayesian} = 0.80(0.95) + 0.20(0.8) = 0.76 + 0.16 = 0.92 \tag{6.20}$$

Note that the Bayesian estimated coefficient changes depending on the values of the prior estimate and on the strength of your belief in that prior estimate. Indeed, you can make a Bayesian estimate come out to *any* number simply by manipulating S and β_p.

For coefficients such as the MPC in a consumption function, there often is plenty of theory and research upon which to base a prior. For other coefficients, where there is much less theory than there is for the MPC, the best prior estimate often had little to do with theory (except the sign) and is set equal to the results of a previous study. In such cases, the strength of this belief, S, might be set fairly low. In other situations, it is quite difficult to choose the strength of your belief in a particular expected coefficient value.

This discussion simplifies the complications involved in Bayesian estimation rather significantly. In actual practice, Bayesian regression is often complex to apply, particularly in the face of some of the econometric diseases to be discussed in the following chapters. For example, there are usually many different coefficients in any given equation, so Bayesians end up with a number of conditions that must be met simultaneously. The most well-known variation from the strict Bayesian approach is *mixed* estimation, which treats prior estimates (complete with estimated variances) as extra observations.[13] In addition, Bayesians often take the result of one estimation as the prior for the next (called a *posterior* estimate) and continue from one estimate to another. This can continue as new data become available.

Bayesians rarely test hypotheses; instead, they tend to make extensive use of loss functions, or their expected values, called risk functions. **Loss functions** represent the costs of being wrong (choosing the wrong hypothesis) and are used by Bayesians to make decisions, such as selecting among hypotheses. By comparing loss functions (weighted by their probabilities), Bayesians often can shed light on a decision when ordinary empirical analysis cannot. In such situations, though, the strength of the priors can at times determine the outcome of the test.

It might seem as though Bayesians, since they are capable of changing their coefficient estimates just by changing their priors, are potentially guilty of "data mining" or manipulating statistics to produce the results they desire. Instead, the opposite is the case. Bayesians, by being forced to state explicitly their prior expectations (and the strength of their belief in those expectations) before any regressions are run, tend to do most of their thinking before estimation and tend to run only a few regressions (except to test the fragility of their sample estimates by changing specifications). By being above-board, Bayesians solve the problems we raised about specification searches in Section 6.4. In that sense, we consider Bayesian econometrics to have the potential to become the estimation procedure of choice in the near future.

At present, however, Bayesian regression is practiced only by a small portion of the users of econometrics because Bayesian estimation procedures involve at least three difficult tasks for a typical user: deciding on the prior estimates of the coefficients, choosing the strength of the belief that the prior estimates were correct, and coping with the additional complexity of the estimation process. Of these, the second seems the most important, since information contained in the data can be made meaningless by the choice of a particularly high S. In addition, the theoretical bases on which to decide on S seem at present to have significant room for improvement. As a result, the Bayesian approach has not gained the popularity that it deserves (and will probably eventually get) on the basis of its ethical and statistical advantages.

Still, most of us are already Bayesians in some degree or another. For instance, throughout this text we stress the importance of prior theory in developing econometric models; in addition, we urge researchers to avoid continually re-estimating equations in search of good-looking statistical results. These two tendencies, a reliance on prior theory and an aversion to continual respecifications of equations, are inherently Bayesian, though real Bayesians go one step further by actually incorporating their prior expectations into the estimates themselves.

---

[1] This function, $f(r_{12})$, is: $f(r_{12}) = r_{12}\sqrt{\Sigma x_2{}^2/\Sigma x_1{}^2}$ where $x_1 = (X_1 - \bar{X}_1)$ and $x_2 = (X_2 - \bar{X}_2)$. This turns out to equal the slope coefficient of the linear regression that relates X_2 to X_1. Note that Equation 6.4 only holds when there are exactly two independent variables, but the more general equation is quite similar.

[2] While the omission of a relevant variable almost always produces bias in the estimators of the coefficients of the included variables, the variances of these estimators are generally lower than they otherwise would be. One method of deciding whether this decreased variance in the distribution of the $\hat{\beta}$s is valuable enough to offset the bias is to compare different estimation techniques by using a measure called Mean Square Error (MSE), which is equal to the variance plus the square of the bias. The lower the MSE, the better. For more on the use of MSE and some statistics associated with it, see Takeshi Amemiya, "Selection of Regressors," *International Economic Review,* June 1980, pp. 331-354.

[3] The data for this example are included in Exercise 5; t-scores differ due to rounding.

[4] It is important to note the distinction between expected bias and the actual difference between observed coefficient estimates. Because of the random nature of the error term (and hence the $\hat{\beta}$s), the change in an estimated coefficient brought about by dropping a relevant variable from the equation will not necessarily be in the expected direction. Biasedness refers to the central tendency of the sampling distribution of the $\hat{\beta}$s, not to every single drawing from that distribution. However, we usually (and justifiably) rely on these general tendencies.

[5] See Ignazio Visco, "On Obtaining the Right Sign of a Coefficient Estimate by Omitting a Variable from the Regression," *Journal of Econometrics,* Feb. 1978, pp. 115-117.

[6] This example was inspired by a similar one concerning Ceylonese tea published in Potluri Rao and Roger LeRoy Miller, *Applied Econometrics* (Belmont, California: Wadsworth, 1971) pp. 38-40. This book is now out of print.

[7] Thomas Mayer, "Economics as a Hard Science: Realistic Goal or Wishful Thinking?" *Economic Inquiry,* April 1980, p. 175.

[8] Some programs compute standardized beta coefficients, which are the estimated coefficients for an equation in which all variables are in a deviation-from-the-mean form and all variables have been divided by their own standard deviations. The higher the beta of an independent variable is in absolute value, the more important it is thought to be in explaining the movements in the dependent variable. But, like the R^2 delete, the beta coefficients are deficient in the presence of multicollinearity. So are the partial coefficients of correlation, which are like simple coefficients of correlation between an independent variable and the dependent variable but with all other independent variables "held constant."

[9] Bayesian regression, a technique for dealing systematically with these prior expectations, is discussed in Section 6.6.

[10] For a thorough discussion of sequential or "pre-test" estimators and "Stein-rule" estimators that have improved properties, see George G. Judge, W. E. Griffiths, R. Carter Hill, Helmut Lutkepohl, and Tsoung-Chao Lee. *The Theory and Practice of Econometrics* (New York: Wiley, 1985).

[11] For more, see A. Zellner, *An Introduction to Bayesian Analysis in Econometrics* (New York: Wiley, 1971), and Edward E. Leamer, *Specification Searches* (New York: Wiley, 1978).

[12] A more difficult (at least for beginners) but basically equivalent method of calculating $\hat{\beta}_{Bayesian}$ is based on choosing an expected variance for the prior coefficient value and specifying the probability distribution of the coefficient estimates (normal distributions typically are assumed for both the prior and sample estimate distributions). Given the mean and variance for a prior distribution of the regression coefficient, Equation 6.18 can also be expressed as $\hat{\beta}_{Bayesian} = (n_p \beta_p + n\hat{\beta})/(n_p + n)$ where n is the size of the sample used to estimate $\hat{\beta}$ is calculated as the estimated variance of the estimated coefficient ($s^2_{\hat{\beta}}$) divided by your prior expected variance ($\hat{\sigma}^2_p$).

[13] See H. Theil and A. S. Goldberger, "On Pure and Mixed Statistical Estimation in Econometrics," *International Economic Review,* January 1961, pp. 65-78.

7

Specification: Choosing a Functional Form

Even after you have chosen your independent variables, the job of specifying the equation is not over. The next step is to choose the functional form of the relationship between each independent variable and the dependent variable. Should the equation go through the origin? Do you expect a curve instead of a straight line? Does the impact of a variable peak at some point and then start to decline? An affirmative answer to any of these questions suggests that an equation different from the standard "linear in the variables" model of the previous chapters might be appropriate. Such alternative specifications are important because a correct explanatory variable may well appear to be insignificant or to have an unexpected sign if an inappropriate functional form is used, and the consequences for interpretation and forecasting of an incorrect functional form can be severe.

Theoretical considerations usually dictate the form of a regression model. The basic technique involved in deciding on a functional form is to choose the shape that best exemplifies the expected underlying economic or business principles and then to use the mathematical form that produces that shape. To help with that choice, this chapter contains plots of the most commonly used functional forms along with the mathematical equations that correspond to each.

One may use dummy variables to allow the coefficients of independent variables to differ for qualitative conditions (slope dummies) or to actually change as the independent variable changes ("jack-knifing"). These techniques are fairly innovative ways to use dummy variables to create nonlinear-in-the-variables functional forms that are still linear in the coefficients. The chapter also includes a brief discussion of the constant term. In particular, we suggest that the constant term should be retained in equations even if theory suggests otherwise and that estimates of the constant term should not be relied upon for inference or analysis.

7.1 Alternative Functional Forms

The choice of a functional form for an equation is a vital part of the specification of that equation. The use of ordinary least squares requires that the equation be linear in the coefficients, but there is a wide variety of functional forms that are linear in the coefficients while being nonlinear in the variables. Indeed, in previous chapters we have already used a number of equations that are linear in the coefficients and nonlinear in the variables, but we have said little about how to choose when to use such nonlinear equations. The purpose of the current section is to present the details of the most frequently used functional forms in order to help develop the ability to choose the correct one when specifying an equation.

The choice of a functional form almost always should be based on an examination of the underlying economic or business theory and only rarely on which form provides the best fit. The logical form of the relationship between the dependent variable and the independent variable in question should be compared with the properties of various functional forms, and the one that comes closest to that underlying theory should be chosen for the equation. To allow such a comparison, the paragraphs that follow characterize the most frequently used functional forms in terms of graphs, equations, and examples.

7.1.1 Linear Form

The linear regression model, used extensively to this point in the text, is based on the assumption that the slope of the relationship between the independent variable and the dependent variable is constant:[1]

$$\frac{\Delta Y}{\Delta X_k} = \beta_k \qquad k = 1, 2, \ldots, K \tag{7.1}$$

The slope is constant, so the **elasticity** of Y with respect to X (the percentage change in the dependent variable caused by a one percent change in the independent variable, holding the other variables in the equation constant) is not constant:

$$\eta_{Y,X_k} = \frac{\Delta Y/Y}{\Delta X_k/X_k} = \frac{\Delta Y}{\Delta X_k} \cdot \frac{X_k}{Y} = \beta_k \frac{X_k}{Y} \tag{7.2}$$

If the hypothesized relationship between Y and X is such that the slope of the relationship can be expected to be constant and the elasticity can therefore be expected not to be constant, then the linear functional form should be used.

Unfortunately, theory frequently predicts only the sign of a relationship and not its functional form. When there is little theory on which to base an expected functional form, the linear form should be used until strong evidence that it is inappropriate is found. Unless theory, common sense, or experience justifies using some other functional form, you should use the linear model. Because it is in effect being used by default, this model is sometimes referred to as the *default* functional form. (Some use the log-linear model as the default functional form.)

7.1.2   Log-Linear or Exponential Form

The most common functional form that is nonlinear in the variables (but still linear in the coefficients) is the log-linear form. A log-linear form is often used because a researcher has specified that, contrary to the linear model, the elasticities and not the slopes are constant. If an elasticity is assumed to be constant, that means:

$$\eta_{Y,X_k} = \beta_k = \text{a constant} \tag{7.3}$$

Given the assumption of a constant elasticity, the proper form is the **exponential functional form:**

$$Y = e^{\beta_0} X_1^{\beta_1} X_2^{\beta_2} e^{\epsilon} \tag{7.4}$$

where e is the base of the natural logarithm. A logarithmic transformation can be applied to Equation 7.4 by taking the log of both sides of the equation to make it linear in the coefficients. This transformation converts Equation 7.4 into Equation 7.5, the **log-linear functional form:**

$$\ln Y_i = \beta_0 + \beta_1 \ln X_{1i} + \beta_2 \ln X_{2i} + \epsilon_i \tag{7.5}$$

Where "$\ln Y_i$" refers to the natural log of Y_i, etc. In a log-linear equation, an individual regression coefficient, for example β_k, can be interpreted as an elasticity because:

$$\beta_k = \frac{\Delta(\ln Y)}{\Delta(\ln X_k)} \approx \frac{\Delta Y/Y}{\Delta X_k/X_k} = \eta_{Y,X_k} \tag{7.6}$$

Since regression coefficients are constant, the condition that the model have a constant elasticity is met by the log-linear equation.[2]

The way to interpret β_k in a log-linear equation is that if X_k changes by one percent while the other Xs are held constant, then Y will change by β_k percent. Since elasticities are constant, the slopes are now no longer constant.

Figure 7.1 is a graph of the log-linear or exponential function (ignoring the error term). The panel on the left shows the economic concept of a production function (or an indifference curve). Isoquants from production functions show the different combinations of factors X_1 and X_2, probably capital and labor, that can be used to produce a given level of output Y. This kind of log-linear production function is called a Cobb-Douglas production function; for an example of the estimation of such a function, see Exercise 7. The panel on the right of Figure 7.1 shows the relationship between Y and X_1 that would exist if X_2 were held constant or were not included in the model. Note that the shape of the curve depends on the sign and magnitude of coefficient β_1.

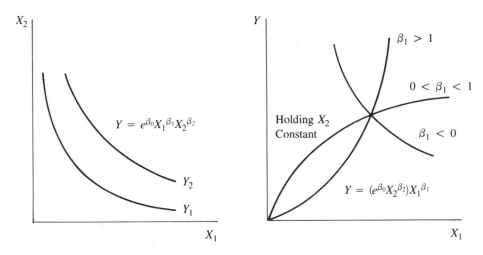

FIGURE 7.1 *Log-Linear Functions*
Depending on the values of the regression coefficients, the log-linear functional form can take on a number of shapes. The left panel shows the use of a log-linear function to depict a shape useful in describing the economic concept of a production function (or an indifference curve). The right panel shows various shapes that can be achieved with a log-linear function if X_2 is held constant or is not included in the equation.

Before using a log-linear model, make sure that there are no negative or zero observations in the data set. Since the log of a non-positive number is undefined, a regression cannot be run. Log-linear models should be run only when all the variables take on positive values. Dummy variables, which take on the value of zero, should not be logged even if they are in a log-linear equation.[3]

7.1.3 Semi-Log Form

The **semi-log functional form** is a variant of the log-linear equation in which some but not all of the variables (dependent and independent) are expressed in terms of their logs. For example, you might choose to use as explanatory variables the logarithms of one or more of the original independent variables as in:

$$Y_i = \beta_0 + \beta_1 \ln X_{1i} + \beta_2 X_{2i} + \epsilon_i \tag{7.7}$$

In this case, the economic meanings of the two slope coefficients are different, since X_2 is linearly related to Y while X_1 is nonlinearly related to Y. In particular, calculus can be used to show that:

$$\Delta Y / \Delta X_1 = \beta_1 / X_1 \tag{7.8}$$

or, solving for β_1:

$$\beta_1 = \Delta Y / (\Delta X_1 / X_1) \tag{7.9}$$

In words, if X_1 changes by one percent, then Y will change by $\beta_1/100$ units (to see this, substitute a one percent change in X_1 into Equation 7.9; recall that values of X_1 must be positive in order to take a log). The elasticity of Y with respect to X_1 is thus:

$$\eta_{Y,X_k} = \frac{\Delta Y}{\Delta X_1} \cdot \frac{X_1}{Y} = \frac{\beta_1}{Y} \tag{7.10}$$

which decreases as Y increases.

Figure 7.2 shows the relationship between Y and X_1 when X_2 is held constant. Note that if β_1 is greater than zero, the impact of changes in X_1 on Y decreases as X_1 gets bigger. Thus the semi-log functional form should be used when the relationship between X_1 and Y is hypothesized to have this "tailing off" form.

Applications of the semi-log form are quite frequent in economics and business. For example, most consumption functions tend to increase at a decreasing rate past some level of income. These *Engel curves* tend to flatten out because as incomes get higher, a smaller percentage of income goes to consumption and a greater percentage goes to saving. Consumption thus increases at a decreasing rate. If Y is the consumption of an item and X_1 is disposable income (with X_2 standing for all the other independent variables), then the use of the semi-log functional form is justified whenever the item's consumption can be expected to tail off as income increases.

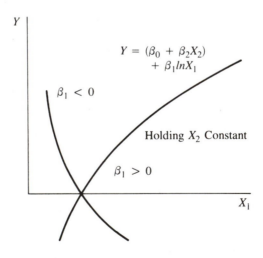

FIGURE 7.2 *Semi-Log Functions*
The semi-log functional form (in the case of taking the log of one of the independent variables) can be used to depict a situation in which the impact of X_1 on Y is expected to tail off as X_1 gets bigger as long as β_1 is greater than zero (holding X_2 constant). An application of this type of semi-log model is a curve that describes quantity consumed as a function of income.

For example, recall the chicken consumption Equation 6.5 from the previous chapter (repeated here for convenience):

$$\hat{Y}_i = -49.6 - 0.54PC_i + 0.22PB_i + 10.6LYD_i \qquad (6.5)$$

In this equation, the independent variables include the two price variables (PC and PB) and the *log* of disposable income, because it was hypothesized that as income rose, consumption would increase at a decreasing rate. For other products, perhaps like yachts or summer homes, no such decreasing rate could be hypothesized, and the semi-log function would not be appropriate.

Note from Equations 6.5 and 7.7 that various combinations of the functional forms are possible. Thus the form taken by X_1 may be different from the form taken by X_2. In addition, Y may assume yet another different functional form. Remember that the researcher should attempt to specify the equation in a way that represents the theory as well as possible. If the theory is not clear, the fancier functional forms may be just curve-fitting devices and should be avoided. The theoretical basis for any functional form other than the standard linear form should be based on grounds that have been well documented in the presentation of the regression project.[4]

An example of a situation in which the functional form of Y is different from that of the rest of the equation is a kind of semi-log function that is derived by taking the log of the dependent variable while leaving the independent variables in linear form:

$$\ln Y_i = \beta_0 + \beta_1 X_{1i} + \beta_2 X_{2i} + \epsilon_i \qquad (7.11)$$

This model has neither a constant slope nor a constant elasticity. If X_1 changes by one *unit*, then Y will change by β_1 (times 100) percent, holding X_2 constant. For an example of this version of the semi-log function, see Exercise 4.

7.1.4 Polynomial Form

In most cost functions, the slope of the cost curve changes as output changes. If the slopes of a relationship are expected to depend on the level of the variable itself (for example, get steeper as output increases) then a polynomial model should be considered. **Polynomial functional forms** express Y as a function of independent variables some of which are raised to powers other than one. For example, in a second-degree polynomial (also called a quadratic) equation, at least one independent variable is squared:

$$Y_i = \beta_0 + \beta_1 X_{1i} + \beta_2 (X_{1i})^2 + \beta_3 X_{2i} + \epsilon_i \qquad (7.12)$$

Such a model does indeed produce slopes that change as the independent variables change. The slopes of Y with respect to the Xs in Equation 7.12 are:

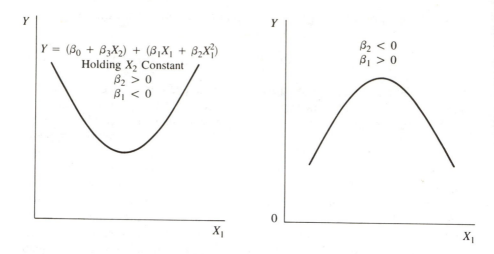

FIGURE 7.3 *Quadratic (Polynomial) Functions*
Second-order quadratic functional forms (polynomials with squared terms) take on U or inverted U shapes depending on the values of the coefficients (holding X_2 constant). The left panel shows the shape of a quadratic function that could be used to show a typical cost curve, while the right panel allows the description of an impact that rises and then falls (like the impact of age on earnings).

$$\frac{\Delta Y}{\Delta X_1} = \beta_1 + 2\beta_2 X_1 \quad \text{and} \quad \frac{\Delta Y}{\Delta X_2} = \beta_3 \tag{7.13}$$

Thus the first slope depends on the level of X_1 and the second slope is a typical linear constant. If this were a cost function, with Y being the average cost of production and X_1 being the level of output of the firm, then we would expect β_2 to be positive if the firm has the typical U-shaped cost curve depicted in the left half of Figure 7.3.

For another example, consider a model of annual employee earnings as a function of the age of each employee and a number of other measures of productivity such as education. What is the expected impact of age on earnings? As a young worker gets older, his or her earnings will typically increase. Beyond some point, however, an increase in age will not increase earnings by very much at all, and around retirement, we expect earnings to start to decrease with age. As a result, a logical relationship between earnings and age might look something like the right half of Figure 7.3; earnings would rise, level out, and then fall as age increased. Such a theoretical relationship could be modeled with a quadratic equation:

$$\text{Earnings}_i = \beta_0 + \beta_1 \text{Age}_i + \beta_2 \text{Age}_i^2 + \cdots + \epsilon_i \tag{7.14}$$

What would the expected signs of $\hat{\beta}_1$ and $\hat{\beta}_2$ be? As a worker got older, the difference between "Age" and "Age²" would increase dramatically, because "Age²" would become quite large. As a result, the coefficient of "Age" would be more important at lower ages than it would be at higher ages. Conversely, the coefficient of "Age^2" would be more important at higher ages. Since you expect the impact of age to rise and fall, you'd thus expect $\hat{\beta}_1$ to be positive and $\hat{\beta}_2$ to be negative (all else being equal). In fact, this is exactly what many researchers in labor economics have observed.

Unfortunately, polynomials can be used as a curve-fitting device. In fact, any n observations can be fitted exactly (that is, all residuals would be zero) to a regression curve that is a polynomial of degree n $-$ 1 (i.e., having as independent variables X, X^2, X^3,..., X^{n-1}). Here, regression becomes a mathematical tautology instead of a statistical relationship and gives false pictures of reality. As a result, the use of higher degree polynomials in regression analysis should be avoided unless the underlying theory specifically calls for such a functional form.

With polynomial regressions, the interpretation of the individual regression coefficients becomes difficult, and the equation may produce unwanted results for particular ranges of X. For example, the slope for a third-degree polynomial will be positive over some range of X, then negative over the next range, and then positive again. Unless such a relationship is called for by theory, it would be inappropriate to use such a polynomial. Even a second-degree polynomial, as in Equation 7.12, imposes a particular symmetric shape (a U-shape or its inverse) that might be unreasonable in some cases. For example, review the rain equation in Section 5.5, where it seems obvious that the squared term was added solely to provide a better fit to this admittedly cooked-up equation. To avoid such curve-fitting, some researchers just use the square of the independent variable and exclude from the equation its linear form. In any event, great care must be taken when using a polynomial regression equation to insure that the functional form will achieve what is intended by the researcher and no more.

7.1.5 Inverse Form

The **inverse functional form** expresses Y as a function of the reciprocal (or inverse) of one or more of the independent variables (in this case, X_1):

$$Y_i = \beta_0 + \beta_1(1/X_{1i}) + \beta_2 X_{2i} + \epsilon_i \qquad (7.15)$$

The inverse (or reciprocal) functional form should be used when the impact of a particular independent variable is expected to approach zero as that independent variable increases and eventually approaches infinity. To see this, note that as X_1 gets larger, its impact on Y decreases.

In Equation 7.15, X_1 must be always positive or always negative in value, since if X_1 equaled zero, dividing it into anything would result in undefined values. The slopes are:

$$\frac{\Delta Y}{\Delta X_1} = \frac{-\beta_1}{X_1^2} \quad \text{and} \quad \frac{\Delta Y}{\Delta X_2} = \beta_2 \qquad (7.16)$$

The slopes for X_1 fall into two categories, both of which are depicted in Figure 7.4:

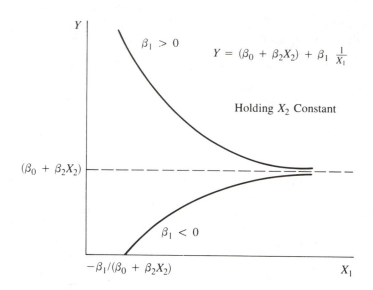

FIGURE 7.4 *Inverse Functions*
Inverse (or reciprocal) functional forms allow the impact of an X_1 on Y to approach zero as X_1 increases in size. The inverse functions approach the same value (the asymptote) from the top or bottom depending on the sign of β_1. A reciprocal function could be used to describe any other model that involves inversely related variables.

1. When β_1 is positive, the slope with respect to X_1 is negative and decreases in absolute value as X_1 increases. As a result, the partial relationship between Y and X_1 holding X_2 constant approaches $\beta_0 + \beta_2 X_2$ as X_1 increases (ignoring the error term).

2. When β_1 is negative, the partial relationship intersects the X_1 axis at $-\beta_1/(\beta_0 + \beta_2 X_2)$ and slopes upward toward the same horizontal line (called an asymptote) that it approaches when β_1 is positive.

Applications of reciprocals or inverses exist in a number of areas in economic theory and the real world. For example, one way to think of the once-popular Phillips Curve (a nonlinear relationship between the rate of unemployment and the percentage change in wages) is to posit that the percentage change in wages (W) is negatively related to the rate of unemployment (U), but that past some level of unemployment, further increases in the unemployment rate would not reduce the level of wage increases any further because of institutional or other reasons. Such a hypothesis could be tested with an inverse functional form:

$$W_t = \beta_0 + \beta_1(1/U_t) + \epsilon_t \tag{7.17}$$

Estimating this equation using OLS gives the following:

$$\hat{W}_t = 0.00679 + 0.1842(1/U_t) \qquad R^2 = .397 \qquad (7.18)$$
$$(0.0590)$$
$$t = \qquad 3.20$$

This indicates that W and U are related in a way similar to that hypothesized (as shown in Figure 7.4 when β_1 is positive), but it does not provide any evidence that the inverse functional form is the best way to depict this particular theory. For more on this example, see Exercise 5.

7.2   Problems with Incorrect Functional Forms

The best way to choose a functional form for a regression model is to choose a specification that matches the underlying theory of the equation. In a majority of cases, the linear form will be adequate, and for most of the rest, common sense will point out a fairly easy choice from among the alternatives outlined above. Once in a while, however, a circumstance will arise in which the model is logically nonlinear in the variables, but the exact form of this nonlinearity is hard to specify. In such a case, the linear form is not correct, and yet a choice between the various nonlinear forms cannot be made on the basis of economic theory. Even in these cases, however, it still pays (in terms of understanding the true relationships) to avoid choosing a functional form on the basis of fit alone.

Recall the estimated Phillips curve in Equation 7.18. While the negative relationship between unemployment and inflation (using the percentage increase in wages as a proxy) implied by the Phillips curve suggests a downward-sloping nonlinear curve, there are a number of different functional forms that could produce such a curve. In addition to the inverse relationship that was actually used, the log-linear form and various semi-log and exponential forms could also give shapes that would fit the hypothesis fairly well. If all the functional forms are so similar and if theory does not specify exactly which form to use, why should we try to avoid using goodness of fit over the sample to determine which equation to use? This section will highlight two answers to this question:

1. R^2s are difficult to compare if the dependent variable is transformed.

2. An incorrect functional form may provide a reasonable fit but not provide accurate inferences about the real world, and so an incorrect functional form has the potential to have large forecasting errors when used outside the range of the sample.

7.2.1 R^2s Are Difficult To Compare When Y Is Transformed

When the dependent variable is transformed from its linear version, the overall measure of fit, the R^2, cannot be used for comparing the fit of the nonlinear equation with the original linear one This problem is not especially important in most cases, because the emphasis in applied regression analysis is usually on the coefficient estimates, etc., but if R^2s (or $\bar{R}^2$s) are ever used to compare the fit of two different functional forms, then it becomes crucial that this lack of comparability be remembered. For example, suppose you were trying to compare a linear equation

$$Y = \beta_0 + \beta_1 X_1 + \beta_2 X_2 + \epsilon \tag{7.19}$$

with a semi-log version of the same equation (using the version of a semi-log function that takes the log of the dependent variable):

$$\ln Y = \beta_0 + \beta_1 X_1 + \beta_2 X_2 + \epsilon \tag{7.20}$$

Notice that the only difference between Equations 7.19 and 7.20 is the functional form of the dependent variable. The reason that the R^2s of the respective equations cannot be used to compare overall fits of the two equations is that the total sum of squares (TSS) of the dependent variable around its mean is different in the two formulations. That is, the R^2s are not comparable because the dependent variables are different. There is no reason to expect that different dependent variables will have the identical (or easily comparable) degrees of dispersion around their means. Since the total sums of squares are different, the R^2s (or $\bar{R}^2$s) will not be comparable.

The way to get around this problem is to create a "quasi-R^2" by transforming the predicted values of the nonlinear dependent variable into a form that is directly comparable to the original dependent variable. This transformed dependent variable is then used to calculate the "quasi-R^2." In essence, then, a **quasi-R^2** is an R^2 that allows the comparison of the overall fits of equations with different functional forms by transforming the predicted values of one of the dependent variables into the functional form of the other dependent variable.

For the example of the previous paragraph, this would mean taking the following steps:

1. Estimate Equation 7.20 and create a set of $\widehat{\ln Y}$s for the sample.

2. Transform the $\widehat{\ln Y}$s by taking their anti-logs (an anti-log reverses the log function: anti-log[$\ln Y$] = Y).

3. Calculate quasi-R^2 (or quasi-$\bar{R}^2$) by using the newly calculated anti-logs as $\hat{Y}$s to get the residuals needed in the R^2 equation:

$$\text{quasi-}R^2 = 1 - \Sigma[Y_i - \text{anti-log}(\widehat{\ln Y_i})]^2 / \Sigma[Y_i - \bar{Y}]^2 \tag{7.21}$$

This quasi-R^2 for Equation 7.20 is directly comparable to the conventional R^2 for Equation 7.19. Do not merely apply Equation 7.21 automatically, however, for each different functional form (of the dependent variable) requires a different transformation to calculate the appropriate quasi-R^2. Whenever the dependent variable is logged, though, Equation 7.21 should be used.[5]

Let's try an example of the comparison of the overall fit of two different functional forms for the Woody's restaurant model originally estimated on data presented in Chapter 3 and analyzed more fully in Equation 5.5, repeated here for convenience:

$$\hat{Y}_i = 102{,}192 - 9075C_i + 0.3547P_i + 1.288I_i \qquad (5.5)$$
$$\phantom{\hat{Y}_i = 102{,}192} (2053) \quad\ (0.0727) \quad\ (0.543)$$
$$t = \quad -4.42 \qquad 4.88 \qquad\ 2.37$$
$$n = 33 \quad \bar{R}^2 = .579 \quad R^2 = .618$$

If, for instance, we estimated a log-linear version of this equation (perhaps because of an idea that the impacts of C, P, and I were nonlinear, with constant elasticities) then:

$$\widehat{\ln Y}_i = 6.66 - 0.378\ln C_i + 0.352\ln P_i + 0.159\ln I_i \qquad (7.22)$$
$$\phantom{\widehat{\ln Y}_i = 6.66} (0.065) \qquad (0.056) \qquad (0.085)$$
$$t = \quad -5.82 \qquad\ 6.29 \qquad\ 1.88$$
$$n = 33 \quad \bar{R}^2 = .674 \quad R^2 = .705$$

Note that the R^2 in Equation 7.22 is quite a bit higher than that in 5.5. This result does not mean that the log-linear equation fits substantially better; all a higher R^2 means is that the log-linear equation explains a higher portion of the variation of the movement of the log of Y around its mean than the portion of the variation of the movement of Y around its mean that is explained by the linear equation.

To compare the fits, we need to calculate a quasi-R^2 for Equation 7.22. We take the 33 $\widehat{\ln Y}$s obtained by plugging the values for C, P, and I into Equation 7.22 and then using those $\widehat{\ln Y}$s to calculate the quasi-R^2 as in Equation 7.21. The quasi-R^2 for Equation 7.22 is .688, implying that the log-linear equation actually provides a better overall fit than the linear one. In deciding which equation to use, of course, this overall fit would not be the most important factor. For more practice with this procedure, see Exercise 6.

7.2.2 Incorrect Functional Forms Outside the Range of the Sample

If an incorrect functional form is used, then the probability of mistaken inferences about the true population parameters will increase. Using an incorrect functional form is a kind of specification error that is very similar to the omitted variable bias discussed in Section 6.1. Although the characteristics of any specification errors depend on the exact details of the particular situation, there is no reason to expect that coefficient estimates obtained from an incorrect functional form will necessarily be unbiased and minimum variance. Even if an incorrect functional form provides good statistics within a sample, though, large residuals almost surely will arise when the misspecified equation is used on data that were not part of the sample used to estimate the coefficients.

In general, the extrapolation of a regression equation to data that are outside the range over which the equation was estimated runs increased risks of large forecasting errors and incorrect conclusions about population values. This risk is heightened if the regression uses a functional form that is inappropriate for the particular variables being studied; nonlinear functional forms should be used with extreme caution for data outside the range of the sample because nonlinear functional forms by definition change their slopes. It is entirely possible that the slope of a particular nonlinear function could change to an unrealistic value outside the range of the sample even if the form produced reasonable slopes within the

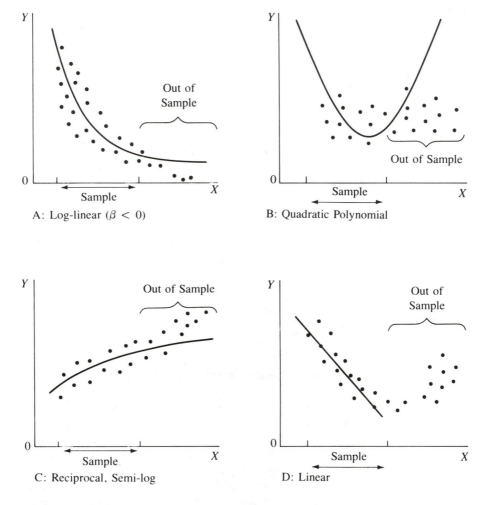

FIGURE 7.5 *Incorrect Functional Forms Outside the Sample*
If an incorrect functional form is applied to data outside the range of the sample on which it was estimated, the probability of large mistakes increases. In particular, note how the polynomial functional form can change slope rapidly outside the sample range (Panel B) and that even a linear form can cause large mistakes if the true functional form is nonlinear (Panel D).

sample. Of course, even a linear function could be inappropriate in this way. If the true relationship changed slope outside the sample range, the linear functional form's constant slope would be quite likely to lead to large forecasting errors outside the sample.

As a result, two functional forms that behave very similarly over the range of the sample may behave quite differently outside that range. If the functional form is chosen on the basis of theory, then the researcher can take into account how the equation will act over any range of values, even if some of those values are outside the range of the sample. If functional forms are chosen on the basis of fit, then extrapolating outside the sample becomes tenuous.

Figure 7.5 contains a number of hypothetical examples. As can be seen, some functional forms (like the quadratic) have the potential to fit quite poorly outside the sample range. Others seem less likely to encounter this problem. Such graphs are meant as examples of what could happen, not as statements of what will necessarily happen, when incorrect functional forms are pushed outside the range of the sample over which they were estimated. Do not conclude from these diagrams that nonlinear functions should be avoided completely, since if the true relationship is nonlinear, then the linear functional form will have large forecasting errors outside the sample. Instead, the researcher must take the time to think through how the equation will act for values both inside and outside the sample before choosing a functional form to use to estimate the equation. If the theoretically appropriate nonlinear equation appears to work well over the relevant range of possible values, then it should be used without concern over this issue.

7.3   Slope Dummies and Jack-knifing

In Section 3.1.3, we introduced the concept of a dummy variable, which we defined as taking the values of 0 or 1 depending on a qualitative attribute such as gender. In that section, our sole focus was on the use of a dummy variable as an **intercept dummy,** a dummy variable that changes the constant or intercept term depending on whether the qualitative condition is met. These take the general form:

$$Y_i = \beta_0 + \beta_1 X_{1i} + \beta_2 X_{2i} + \beta_3 D_i + \epsilon_i \tag{7.23}$$

where: $D_i = \begin{cases} 1 \text{ if the } i\text{th observation meets a particular condition and} \\ 0 \text{ if it does not} \end{cases}$

As can be seen in Figure 7.6, the intercept dummy does indeed change the intercept depending on the value of D, but the slope remains constant no matter what value D takes (holding X_1 constant). Note that in Equation 7.23 the dummy variable stands alone as an independent variable; it is multiplied by its regression coefficient but not by any other independent variable.

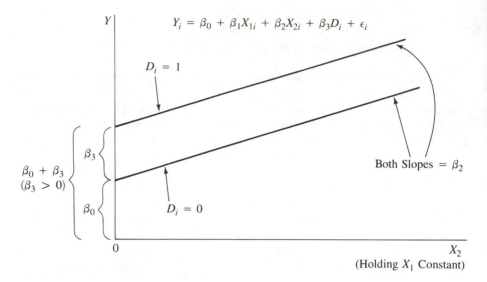

FIGURE 7.6 *An Intercept Dummy*
If an intercept dummy ($\beta_3 D_i$) is added to an equation, a graph of the equation will have different intercepts for the two qualitative conditions specified by the dummy variable. The difference between the two intercepts is β_3. The slopes between the quantitative independent variables and the dependent variable are constant with respect to the qualitative condition.

The purpose of this section is to introduce two extremely useful alternate functional forms that involve dummy variables that are not intercept dummies:

1. **Slope dummies** — the use of dummy variables to allow slopes to be different depending on whether the condition specified by the dummy variable is met.

2. **Jack-knifing** — the use of dummy variables to allow slopes to be different depending on whether a particular non-dummy independent variable exceeds a specified value.

Another possibility, the use of dummy variables as dependent variables, is presented in Section 7.7.

7.3.1 Slope Dummies

Slope dummies can be employed whenever the slope that measures an independent variable's impact on the dependent variable is hypothesized to change if some qualitative condition is met. For example, in the weight-height model of Chapter 1, if being a football player changed the increase in weight caused by a one-inch increase in height, then one way to model that relationship would be with a slope dummy variable. Similarly, if being in a war decreased a country's marginal propensity to consume, this change in the coefficient of income in the consumption function could be modeled with a slope dummy that was equal to one during war years and equal to zero otherwise (or vice versa).

In general a slope dummy is introduced by adding to the equation a variable that is the multiple of an independent variable already in the equation times a dummy variable that does not depend on that independent variable:

$$Y_i = \beta_0 + \beta_1 X_{1i} + \beta_2 X_{2i} + \beta_3 D_i + \beta_4 X_{2i} D_i + \epsilon_i \qquad (7.24)$$

where D is as defined above. Note the difference between Equation 7.23 and 7.24. In Equation 7.24, we have added a variable in which the dummy variable is multiplied[6] by one of the independent variables but not by the other. Such a model is appropriate when the underlying theory suggests that the coefficient of X_2 *changes* when the condition specified by D is met:

$$\text{When } D = 0, \quad \Delta Y/\Delta X_2 = \beta_2$$
$$\text{When } D = 1, \quad \Delta Y/\Delta X_2 = \beta_2 + \beta_4$$
$$\text{In both cases,} \quad \Delta Y/\Delta X_1 = \beta_1$$

To see this, substitute $D = 1$ and $D = 0$ respectively into Equation 7.24. Note that X_1's relationship with Y is not hypothesized to depend on D.

Such a dummy term $(X_{2i}D_i)$ is called a slope dummy because, as can be seen in Figure 7.7, the slope of X_2 changes depending on the value of D. Note that when a slope dummy is used, the researcher will almost always hypothesize that both a slope dummy and an intercept dummy are appropriate. Such a specification

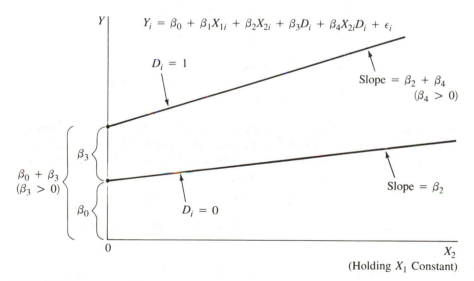

FIGURE 7.7 *Slope and Intercept Dummies*
If slope dummy $(\beta_4 X_{2i} D_i)$ and intercept dummy $(\beta_3 D_i)$ terms are added to an equation, a graph of the equation will have different intercepts and different slopes depending on the value of the qualitative condition specified by the dummy variable. The difference between the two intercepts is β_3, while the difference between the two slopes is β_4.

should be used in all but highly unusual and forced conditions. Using both dummies allows both the intercept and also the slope with respect to X_2 to change with D, but using just the slope dummy constrains its coefficient.

In Figure 7.7, with both a slope dummy and an intercept dummy, the intercept will be β_0 when D = 0 and $\beta_0 + \beta_3$ when D = 1. In addition, the slope of Y with respect to X_2 (holding X_1 constant) will be β_2 when D = 0 and $\beta_2 + \beta_4$ when D = 1. As a result, there really are two equations that have only the $\beta_1 X_{1i}$ term in common:

$$Y_i = \beta_0 \qquad + \beta_1 X_{1i} + \qquad \beta_2 X_{2i} + \epsilon_i \qquad \text{[when D = 0]}$$
$$Y_i = (\beta_0 + \beta_3) + \beta_1 X_{1i} + (\beta_2 + \beta_4)X_{2i} + \epsilon_i \qquad \text{[when D = 1]}$$

As can be seen in Figure 7.8, an equation with both a slope and an intercept dummy can take on a number of different shapes depending on the signs and absolute values of the coefficients. As a result, slope dummies can be used to model a wide variety of relationships.

For example, consider the question of earnings differentials between men and women. While there is little argument that these differentials exist, there is quite a bit of controversy over the extent to which these differentials are caused by sexual discrimination (as opposed to other factors). Suppose you decide to build a model of earnings to get a better view of this controversy. If you hypothesized that men earn more than women on average, then you would want to use an intercept dummy variable for gender in an earnings equation that included measures of experience, special skills, education, etc. as independent variables:

$$\text{Earnings}_i = \beta_0 + \beta_1 D_i + \beta_2 EXP_i + \cdots + \epsilon_i \qquad (7.25)$$

where: D_i = 1 if the ith worker is female and 0 otherwise
         EXP_i = the years experience of the ith worker
         ϵ_i = a classical error term.

In Equation 7.25, $\hat{\beta}_1$ would be an estimate of the average difference between males and females holding constant their experience and the other factors in the equation. Equation 7.25 also forces the impact of increases in experience (and the other factors in the equation) to have the same effect for females that they have for males because the slopes are the same for both genders.

If you hypothesized that men also increase their earnings more per year of experience than women, then you would include a slope dummy as well as an intercept dummy in such a model:

$$\text{Earnings}_i = \beta_0 + \beta_1 D_i + \beta_2 EXP_i + \beta_3 D_i EXP_i + \cdots + \epsilon_i \qquad (7.26)$$

In Equation 7.26, $\hat{\beta}_3$ would be an estimate of the differential impact of an extra year of experience on earnings between men and women. We could test the possibility of a negative true β_3 by running a one-tailed t-test on $\hat{\beta}_3$. If $\hat{\beta}_3$ were

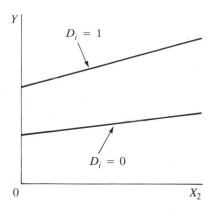

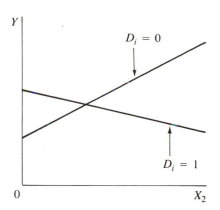

Panel A. All βs > 0

Panel B. All βs > 0 except β_4, $|\beta_4| > |\beta_2|$

$$Y_i = \beta_0 + \beta_1 X_{1i} + \beta_2 X_{2i} + \beta_3 D_i + \beta_4 X_{2i} D_i + \epsilon_i$$

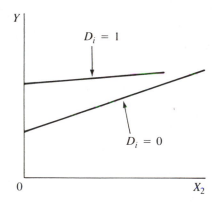

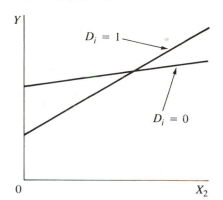

Panel C. $\beta_4 < 0$, $|\beta_4| < |\beta_2|$, $\beta_3 > 0$

Panel D. All βs > 0 except β_3, $|\beta_3| < |\beta_0|$

FIGURE 7.8 *Various Shapes of Equations with Slope and Intercept Dummies*
Depending on the values of the coefficients of the slope (β_4) and intercept (β_3) dummies, equations with both slope and intercept dummies in them can take on a number of different shapes (holding X_1 constant). When using such equations, it is therefore necessary to be fairly specific when hypothesizing values of the coefficients of the various dummy terms.

---

significantly different from zero in a negative direction, then we could reject the null hypothesis of no difference due to gender in the impact of experience of earnings holding constant the other variables in the equation.[7]

7.3.2 Jack-knifing

A second use of dummy variables that goes beyond the concept of a simple intercept dummy to create a new functional form is jack-knifing. **Jack-knifing** is the use

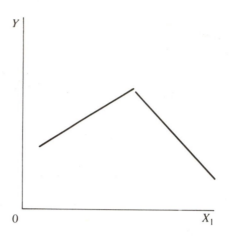

FIGURE 7.9 *A Jack-knifed Equation*
The use of the jack-knife functional form allows the equation to actually change slope for different values of the quantitative independent variable, thus forming a shape that resembles a partially opened jack-knife.

of dummy variables to allow slopes to be different depending on whether a particular non-dummy independent variable exceeds a specified threshold value. This formulation allows the impact of X on Y to change as X itself changes. The name jack-knife comes from the fact that this use of dummy variables allows "bent" regression lines that can sometimes take on the shape of a partially opened jack-knife[8] as in Figure 7.9.

If X is larger than the threshold value, then one slope is expected, but if X is less than the threshold value, then a different slope is expected. The definition of the dummy variable to be used in a jack-knifed equation is thus fairly unusual:

$$D_i = \begin{cases} 1 \text{ if } X_{1i} > X_1^* \\ 0 \text{ if } X_{1i} \le X_1^* \end{cases}$$

where X_1 is the independent variable in the equation whose slope will change and X_1^* is the threshold value at which the slope change takes place. Researchers should resist the urge to estimate a large number of jack-knifed equations in order to choose X* on the basis of fit, because a good fit in one sample does not assure a good fit in other samples, unless sample-specific inference is their goal.

Except for the change in the definition of the dummy variable, the equation to be used in jack-knifing is similar to Equation 7.24:

$$Y_i = \beta_0 + \beta_1 X_{1i} + \beta_2 X_{2i} + \beta_3 D_i + \beta_4 X_{1i} D_i + \epsilon_i$$

It is vital, as with slope dummy equations, that jack-knifed equations include both the intercept dummy term and the slope dummy term.

If the particulars of the equation are carefully investigated, a number of fairly detailed hypotheses about the coefficients of jack-knifed equations can be developed. For example, if the slope below X_1^* is expected to be positive but the slope above X_1^* is expected to be negative, then it is not enough to hypothesize that $\beta_4 < 0$, because it must be negative and greater in absolute value than $\hat{\beta}_1$ for their sum (the new slope) to also be negative.

7.4   The Use and Interpretation of the Constant Term

In the linear regression model, β_0 is the intercept or constant term. It is the expected value of Y when all the explanatory variables (and the error term) equal zero. At times, β_0 is of theoretical importance. Consider, for example, the following cost equation:

$$C_i = \beta_0 + \beta_1 Q_i + \epsilon_i$$

where C_i is the total operating cost of a production process that is producing the level of output Q_i. The term $\beta_1 Q_i$ represents the total variable cost associated with output level Q_i, and β_0 represents the total fixed cost, defined as the cost when output $Q_i = 0$. Thus, a regression equation might seem useful to a researcher who wanted to determine the relative magnitudes of fixed and variable costs. This would be an example of relying on the constant term for inference.

On the other hand, the product involved might be one for which it is known that there are few if any fixed costs. In such a case, a researcher might want to set the constant term to zero, because to do so would conform to the notion of zero fixed costs and would conserve a degree of freedom (which would presumably make the estimate of β_1 more precise). Fairly obviously, this would be an example of suppressing the constant term.

Neither suppressing the constant term nor relying on it for inference is advisable, however, and the reasons for these conclusions are explained in the following sections.

7.4.1   Do Not Suppress the Constant Term

Chapter 4 explained that one of the rationales behind the assumption of the normality of the error term is that the error term absorbs the effects of a number of variables, each of which is not important enough to be included as an independent variable in the equation. Chapter 4 stressed that Assumption II (the error term has an expected value of zero) requires that the constant term absorb the mean effect of all these variables. Thus, suppressing the constant term can lead to a violation of this classical assumption. The only time that this assumption would not be violated by leaving out the intercept term is when the mean effect of the unobserved error term (without a constant term) is zero over all the observations.

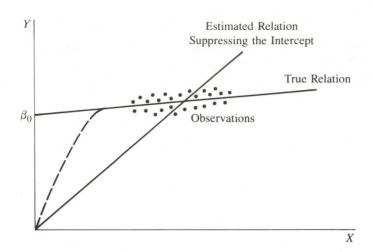

FIGURE 7.10 *The Harmful Effect of Suppressing the Constant Term*
If the constant or intercept term is suppressed, the estimated regression will go through the origin. Such an effect potentially biases the $\hat{\beta}$s and inflates their t-scores. In this particular example, the true β is close to zero in the range of the sample, but forcing the regression through the origin makes $\hat{\beta}$ appear to be significantly positive. In other examples, though, the difference might not be so pronounced.

The consequence of suppressing the constant term is that the slope coefficient estimates are potentially biased with their t-scores inflated. This is demonstrated in Figure 7.10. Given the pattern of the X, Y observations, estimating a regression equation with a constant term would likely produce an estimated regression line very similar to the true regression line, which has a constant term (β_0) quite different from zero. The slope of this estimated line is very low, and the t-scores of the estimated slope coefficient may be very close to zero, implying that the slope coefficient is statistically insignificant, i.e., it does not differ much from zero.

These results should be accepted by the researcher because in this case the true relationship has this appearance. However, if the researcher were to suppress the constant term, which implies that the estimated regression line must pass through the origin, then the estimated regression line shown in Figure 7.10 would result. The slope coefficient is now large, i.e., it is biased upward compared with the true slope coefficient, and the t-score is biased, and it may very well be large enough to indicate that the estimated slope coefficient is statistically significantly positive. Such a conclusion would be incorrect.

On the other hand, it is possible that the true relationship is nonlinear and passes through the origin. In Figure 7.10, such a relation is shown by the appended dashed line that deviates from the straight portion of the true line and passes through the origin. If this nonlinear relationship were to be approximated by a linear regression line, it would be important not to suppress the constant term. Over the relevant range of the observations (i.e., the sample range), the estimated regression line with the constant suppressed does not provide an adequate approximation of the true regression line, compared with an estimated regression equation that includes the constant term. It is a legitimate exercise in applied econometrics to use linear approximations of nonlinear functional forms; suppressing the constant term does not permit an accurate approximation over the sample range of observations.

Thus, even though some regression packages allow the constant term to be suppressed (set to zero), the general rule is: do not do so even if theory specifically calls for it.

7.4.2   Do Not Rely on Estimates of the Constant Term

It would seem logical that if it is a bad idea to suppress the constant term from a regression, then the constant term must be an important analytical tool to use in evaluating the results of the regression. Unfortunately, there are at least two reasons that suggest that the intercept should *not* be relied upon for purposes of analysis or inference.

First, the error term is generated, in part, by the omission of a number of marginal independent variables, the mean effect of which is placed in the constant term. The constant term acts as a garbage collector, with an unknown amount of this mean effect being dumped into it. The constant term's value may be different from what it would have been without performing this task, which is done for the sake of the equation as a whole.

Second, while the constant term is the value of the dependent variable when all the independent variables and the error term are zero, often the values of variables used for economic analysis are positive. Thus, the origin often lies *outside* the range of sample observations (as can be seen in Figure 7.10). Since the constant term is an estimate of Y when the Xs are outside the range of the sample observations, estimates of it are tenuous. Estimating the constant term is like forecasting beyond the range of the sample data, a procedure that inherently contains more likelihood of error than within-sample forecasts. For more on this, see Figure 7.5 and also Chapter 13.

7.5   Summary

1. The choice of a functional form should be based on the underlying economic theory to the extent to which theory suggests a shape similar to that provided by a particular functional form. A form that is linear in the variables should be used unless a specific hypothesis suggests otherwise.

2. Functional forms that are nonlinear in the variables include the log-linear form, the semi-log form, the polynomial form, and the inverse form. The log-linear form is especially useful if the elasticities involved are expected to be constant. The semi-log and inverse forms have the advantage of allow-

ing the effect of an independent variable to tail off as that variable increases. The polynomial form is useful if the slopes are expected to depend on the level of an independent variable, but polynomials of degree higher than two should be avoided unless the underlying theory specifically calls for them.

3. The use of nonlinear functional forms has a number of potential problems. In particular, the R^2s are difficult to compare if Y has been transformed, and the residuals are potentially large if an incorrect functional form is used for forecasting outside the range of the sample.

4. A slope dummy is a dummy variable that is multiplied by an independent variable in order to allow the slope of the relationship between the dependent variable and the particular independent variable to change depending on whether or not a particular condition is met. A similar technique, called jack-knifing, bases the slope dummy's condition on the value of the independent variable in question and allows the slope to "kink" as the X changes.

5. Do not suppress the constant term even if it appears to be theoretically likely to equal zero. On the other hand, do not rely on estimates of the constant term for inference even if it appears to be statistically significant.

Exercises

(Answers to even numbered exercises are in Appendix A.)

1. Write out the meaning of each of the following terms without reference to the book (or your notes) and then compare your definition with the version in the text for each:
   a. elasticity
   b. log-linear or exponential functional form
   c. semi-log functional form
   d. polynomial functional form
   e. reciprocal or inverse functional form
   f. slope dummy
   g. jack-knifing

2. For each of the following pairs of dependent (Y) and independent (X) variables, pick the functional form that you think is likely to be appropriate, and then explain your reasoning (assume that all other relevant independent variables are included in the equation):
   a. Y = sales of shoes; X = disposable income
   b. Y = the attendance at Dodger Stadium on a given night;
      X = whether or not the Dodgers' most famous pitcher, Fernando, was scheduled to pitch that night
   c. Y = aggregate consumption of goods and services in the U.S.;
      X = aggregate disposable income in the U.S.

d. Y = the money supply in the U.S.;
   X = the interest rate on Treasury Bills (in a demand function)
e. Y = average cost of production of a box of pasta;
   X = number of boxes of pasta produced
f. How would your answer to Part e above change if you knew there was a significant outlier due to a capacity constraint and a rush order one year?

3. Can either (or both) of the following equations be estimated with OLS? Why?

a. $Y_i = \beta_0 \, X_{1i}^{\beta_1} \, X_{2i}^{\beta_2} \, e^{u_i}$

b. $Y_i = e^{\beta_0} X_{1i}^{\beta_1} \, X_{2i}^{\beta_2} + u_i$

   where u_i is a typical classical error term and e is the base of the natural logarithm.

4. Consider the following estimated semi-log equation:

$$\widehat{\ln SAL_i} = -5.10 + 0.100ED_i + 0.110EXP_i$$
$$(0.025) \qquad (0.050)$$
$$\bar{R}^2 = .48 \qquad n = 28$$

   where: $\widehat{\ln SAL_i}$ = the log of the salary of the *i*th worker
   ED_i = the years education of the *i*th worker
   EXP_i = the years experience of the *i*th worker

a. Make appropriate hypotheses for signs, calculate t-scores (standard errors are in parentheses), and test your hypotheses.
b. What is the economic meaning of the constant in this equation?
c. Why do you think this particular semi-log functional form is used in this model? More specifically, what are the elasticities of salary with respect to education and experience? What happens to the slopes of the independent variables as they increase?
d. Suppose you ran the linear version of this equation and obtained an $\bar{R}^2$ of .46. What can you conclude from this result?

5. The Phillips curve discussed in Section 7.1.5 is a good example of the use of econometrics to develop, refine and test theory. The curve was originally "discovered" in an empirical study and once was firmly believed to be true. Today, the Phillips curve is not as highly regarded as it used to be in part because of empirical results. Since data for estimating a Phillips curve are readily available, you can test the validity of the Phillips curve yourself.

a. Search the literature (starting with the *Journal of Economic Literature*) and follow the controversy surrounding the topic of the Phillips curve and its estimation.
b. Review the possible functional forms summarized in Section 7.1. What else besides an inverse function could have been used to estimate the function? If possible, collect data and compare alternative functional forms for the Phillips curve.

c. From the middle 1970s to the early 1980s, a Phillips curve estimated for the U.S. economy might have shown a positive slope. What inference should you draw from such an unexpected sign? Why?

6. Given the following data on personal consumption and personal income of various students at "Tiger College" last year:

Student Name	Consumption per week	Income per week
Roxanne	$180	$200
Cindy	100	120
Mike	60	80
Betty	50	80
Dan	40	80
Pete	30	50
Bill	20	40
Terri	10	30

a. Run linear and log-linear regressions to explain weekly consumption as a function of weekly income.
b. Compare the R^2s from the two equations. Which fits better?
c. Calculate a "quasi-R^2" for the log-linear equation and compare it to the R^2 for the same equation.
d. Suppose one of your sexist friends suggested that women spent their income at a higher *rate* than did men. How could you test this hypothesis with a slope dummy? Run the regression and test the hypothesis. (Hint: Terri is a female.)

7. In their 1957 study,[9] Murti and Sastri investigated the production characteristics of seven Indian manufacturing industries including cotton and sugar. They specified Cobb-Douglas production functions for output (Q) as a log-linear function of labor (L) and capital (K)

$$\ln Q_i = \beta_0 + \beta_1 \ln L_i + \beta_2 \ln K_i + \epsilon_i$$

and obtained the following estimates (standard errors in parentheses):

Industry	$\hat{\beta}_0$	$\hat{\beta}_1$	$\hat{\beta}_2$	R^2
Cotton	0.97	0.92	0.12	.98
		(0.03)	(0.04)	
Sugar	2.70	0.59	0.33	.80
		(0.14)	(0.17)	

a. Hypothesize and test appropriate null hypotheses at the 5 percent level of significance.
b. Graph the involved relationships. Does a log-linear function seem theoretically justified in this case?
c. What are the elasticities of output with respect to labor and capital for each industry?
d. What economic significance does the sum $(\hat{\beta}_1 + \hat{\beta}_2)$ have?

8. Suppose you are studying the relationship among the rate of growth of income in a country, the rate of growth of capital in that country, and the per capita income of the country in a cross-sectional data set that includes both developed and developing countries. Suppose further that the underlying theory suggests that income growth rates will increase as per capita income increases and then start decreasing past a particular point. Describe how you would model this relationship with each of the following functional forms:

a. Jack-knifing (assume that the threshold occurs at $2,000)

b. a quadratic function

c. a semi-log function

9. Besides a production function, another typical application of a log-linear regression is an indifference curve from a utility function that includes the consumption of two different products as independent variables. Review the discussion of log-linear production functions in Section 7.1.2 and then:

a. Specify how you would model an indifference curve assuming you had information about a person's utility given various combinations of the consumption of two goods.

b. Give the economic interpretation of the property of constant elasticity that you have assumed.

c. Give the economic interpretations of the regression coefficients.

10. Comanor and Wilson specified the following regression in their study of advertising's effect on the profit rates of 41 consumer goods firms:[10]

$$PR_i = \beta_0 + \beta_1 ADV_i/SALES_i + \beta_2 \ln CAP_i + \beta_3 \ln ES_i + \beta_4 \ln DG_i + \epsilon_i$$

where:
PR_i	= a variable measuring the profit rate of the ith firm
ADV_i	= the advertising expenditures in the ith firm (in dollars)
$SALES_i$	= the total gross sales of the ith firm (in dollars)
CAP_i	= a variable measuring the capital needed to enter the ith firm's market at an efficient size
ES_i	= a variable measuring the degree to which economies of scale exist in the ith firm's industry
DG_i	= the percent growth in sales (demand) of the ith firm over the last ten years
$\ln$	= natural logarithm
ϵ_i	= a classical error term

a. Hypothesize expected signs for each of the slope coefficients.

b. Note that there are two different kinds of nonlinear (in the variables) relationships in this equation. For each independent variable, determine the shape that the chosen functional form implies and state whether you agree or disagree with this shape. Explain your reasoning in each case.

c. Comanor and Wilson state that the simple correlation coefficient between $ADV_i/SALES_i$ and each of the other independent variables is positive.

If one of these remaining variables were omitted, in which direction would $\hat{\beta}_1$ likely be biased?

11. Suppose that one of your friends estimates the following consumption function for the United States:

$$\widehat{NDC}_t = \underset{(10.77)}{29.19} + \underset{(0.0154)}{0.7481 YDR_t}$$
$$t = \underset{}{2.71} \qquad 48.58$$
$$\bar{R}^2 = .98$$

where NDC_t = non-durable consumption in year t and
$\qquad YDR_t$ = disposable income in year t (both in billions of 1972 dollars).

If this friend goes on to infer that autonomous non-durable consumption is \$29.19 billion a year (in 1972 dollars) and further asserts that autonomous consumption has not been significantly different from that value more than 5 percent of the time, what mistakes is he or she making?

7.6   Appendix: Nonlinear (in the Coefficients) Regression

Unfortunately, economic theory sometimes leads to equations that are inherently nonlinear in the coefficients, such as:

$$Y_i = \beta_0 + \beta_1 X_{1i}^{\beta_2} + \beta_3 X_{2i}^{\beta_4} + \epsilon_i \tag{7.27}$$

or

$$Y_i = \alpha(1 - 1/[1 + X_i]^{\beta}) + \epsilon_i \tag{7.28}$$

Neither of these equations can be estimated by OLS, because they cannot be easily transformed into equations that are linear in the coefficients.

7.6.1   Estimating Nonlinear (in the Coefficients) Equations

Given an equation that is nonlinear in the coefficients such as Equation 7.27 or 7.28, estimates can be obtained through either nonlinear least squares or maximum likelihood techniques.

Nonlinear least squares estimates coefficients by iteratively minimizing the summed squared residuals. To use this technique, derivatives[11] of Σe^2 with respect to each coefficient are calculated. The derivatives are functions of the coefficients as well as the data. Values of the coefficients that make all the derivatives zero (and therefore minimize the summed squared residuals) are found by iterating through a number of different sets of $\hat{\beta}$ estimates before arriving at the best $\hat{\beta}$. The iterative estimation procedure starts with an initial set of $\hat{\beta}$ coefficients, calculates Σe^2 for those $\hat{\beta}$s, uses the derivatives to find $\hat{\beta}$s that will decrease Σe^2, and then starts over again with the new set of $\hat{\beta}$s. When further changes in the $\hat{\beta}$s will no longer improve things, the program stops and prints out the last set of $\hat{\beta}$s.[12]

An alternative approach to estimating equations that are nonlinear in the coefficients is to apply **maximum likelihood** (ML) estimation. This approach is inherently different from least squares in that it chooses coefficient estimates that *maximize* the *likelihood* of the sample data set being observed.

The first step in ML estimation is to explicitly assume a particular probability distribution (typically the normal distribution) for the error terms of the equation to be estimated. Once this has been completed a *likelihood function* for the equation is created. The **likelihood function** measures the probability of observing the particular set of dependent variable values (Y_1, Y_2, . . . , Y_n) that occurred in the sample. It is written as the probability of the product of the observed Y_is:

$$\text{Likelihood Function:} \quad L = \text{Pr}(Y_1 \cdot Y_2 \cdot Y_3 \cdots \cdot Y_n) \quad (7.29)$$

where $\text{Pr}(Y_1 \cdot Y_2)$ refers to the joint probability that both Y_1 and Y_2 will occur.[13] The higher L is, the higher the probability of observing the set of Ys found in the sample.

The final step in ML estimation is to find the set of coefficient values ($\hat{\beta}$s) that makes L, the likelihood function, as high as possible given the sample observations. Maximizing L means maximizing the probability of observing the particular set of Ys that was in the sample (given the error term distribution chosen). Computational reasons often incline researchers to maximize the logarithm of the likelihood function, called a log-likelihood function, rather than the likelihood function itself, but the underlying principles are identical in either case.

One of the reasons that maximum likelihood is frequently used is that, in general, it has desirable large sample properties. In particular, ML has better large sample properties than does least squares for a number of advanced estimation problems.[14] Interestingly, the OLS estimation procedure and the ML estimation procedure do not necessarily produce different $\hat{\beta}$s; for a linear equation that meets the Classical Assumptions (including the normality assumption), the OLS estimates are identical to the ML estimates. Indeed, one of the reasons that OLS estimation is attractive is because it is maximum likelihood in this case.

The estimation of maximum likelihood equations is fairly complicated and usually takes a considerable amount of computer time. Luckily, continuing developments in computer programming and the recent decreases in the dollar cost of computer time have now made maximum likelihood estimation procedures reasonably inexpensive. Some fairly general computer packages have been developed to estimate equations using the ML approach, and some specific computer packages have been developed to calculate ML estimates. Interestingly, if the error term ϵ of the inherently nonlinear equation is normally distributed, the maximum likelihood estimates and the nonlinear least squares estimates are identical, leading most researchers to use whichever method is computationally easier given their computer system.

Indeed, many software packages for nonlinear regression now are available. Given the information specified above, these programs iterate and attempt to converge on a set of coefficient estimates. Since these programs also usually provide standard evaluation statistics like R^2 and t-scores, coefficient estimates produced by nonlinear (in the coefficients) regression packages can be analyzed using the tools presented in previous chapters without regard to the estimation procedure, with the exception of the likelihood ratio test, to be discussed in the example that follows.

7.6.2   An Example of Nonlinear (in the Coefficients) Estimation

Let's look at an example of the application of a maximum likelihood estimation technique to an inherently nonlinear equation. It can be shown that Equation 7.30 is the theoretically appropriate functional form to use in a cross-sectional study of aggregate capital requirements by country:[15]

$$Y_1 = \alpha(1 - 1/[1 + X_i]^\beta) + \epsilon_i \qquad (7.30)$$

where: Y_i = the gross incremental output/capital ratio for country i,
X_i = the rate of growth of output for country i, and
ϵ_i = a classical normal error term.

The gross incremental output/capital ratio (the change in output in a country during a particular time period divided by the gross investment during that time period) is useful in determining the capital needs of a country. To quantify the movement of Y with respect to X, data for a sample of 62 countries were collected, and Equation 7.30 was estimated using maximum likelihood estimation with the following results:

$$\hat{Y}_i = 0.56(1 - 1/[1 + X_i]^{17.0}) \qquad (7.31)$$
$$(0.14) \qquad\qquad (6.8)$$
$$t = \quad 4.0 \qquad\qquad\quad 2.5$$
$$LL = 60.28 \quad n = 62 \quad \text{iterations} = 13 \quad \bar{R}^2 = .37$$

where LL refers to -2 times the log of the likelihood ratio (to be discussed shortly) that tests the overall significance of the equation.

Given maximum likelihood estimates, Equation 7.31 can be used and analyzed in much the same way that we have treated other estimated equations throughout this text. For example, both estimated coefficients are significantly different from zero in the direction hypothesized in the article, as shown by t-scores greater than the 5 percent one-tailed critical t-value of approximately 1.645.

Note, however, that tests of the overall significance of an equation estimated with maximum likelihood are done with the **likelihood ratio test,** which consists of comparing the value of a likelihood function for an unrestricted equation with one that has been restricted by the joint hypothesis in question. If the two likelihood functions are significantly different, then the joint hypothesis can be rejected because the imposition of the hypothesis has significantly reduced the fit. If the two likelihood functions are not significantly different, then the null hypothesis cannot be rejected. This likelihood ratio turns out to be distributed according to the Chi-Square distribution (Statistical Table B-8) with degrees of freedom equal to the number of restrictions in the hypothesis. In Equation 7.31, the joint null hypothesis that $\alpha = 0$ and $\beta = 0$ simultaneously (versus the alternative hypothesis that this is not the case) can be rejected at the 5 percent level of significance, because the LL of 60.28 is greater than the critical Chi-Square value of 5.99 for two degrees of freedom as found in Table B-8.

7.7 Appendix: Dummy Dependent Variable Techniques

Until now, our use of dummy variables (variables that take on only the values of 0 and 1, depending on the presence or absence of a particular condition) has been restricted to dummy independent variables. However, there are many important research topics for which the *dependent* variable to be studied is appropriately a dummy. Researchers analyzing consumer choices often have to cope with dummy dependent variables. For example, what distinguishes Pepsi drinkers from Coke drinkers? How do students decide whether to go to college? What influences the decision to take public transportation to work instead of driving? In an examination of such discrete choice questions through econometric analysis, the dependent variable should be a dummy variable.

7.7.1 The Linear Probability Model

The **linear probability model** is the use of a linear-in-the-coefficients equation to explain a dummy dependent variable:

$$D_i = \beta_0 + \beta_1 X_{1i} + \beta_2 X_{2i} + \epsilon_i \qquad (7.32)$$

where D is a dummy variable and the Xs, βs, and ϵ are independent variables, regression coefficients, and an error term, respectively. The name *linear probability model* comes from the fact that the right side of the equation is linear, while the expected value of the left side can be thought of as a probability.

The expected value of D equals the probability that the value of the dummy variable will equal one. To see this, define the probability of D equalling one as P; then the expected value of D is the outcome *1* times its probability P, plus the outcome *0* times its probability $1 - P$. Note that after a choice between two alternatives is made, we can observe only the outcome of that choice, and so the dependent variable can take on only the values of zero or one even though its expected value is the probability of making that choice.

The use of OLS on Equation 7.32 when D is a dummy variable encounters three significant problems:

1. *The error terms are inherently heteroskedastic.* In particular, the variance of ϵ equals $P(1 - P)$, where P is the probability that D equals 1. The values of P depend on X, which varies from observation to observation. Thus, Classical Assumption V is violated.
2. *The error terms are not normally distributed.* Because the dependent variable takes on only two values, the error term is bimodal for small samples and approaches the normal distribution only for large samples. Thus Classical Assumption VII is violated.
3. *The expected value of D is not limited by 0 and 1.* Since the expected value of D is a probability, that value should be limited to a range bounded by 0 and 1. After all, a prediction of a probability of 2.6 (or -2.6, for that matter) would be meaningless. However, depending on the values of the Xs and the $\hat{\beta}$s, the right side of Equation 7.32 might well take on predicted values outside of the meaningful range, and so it is not bounded by 0 and 1.

Since none of these problems causes bias, some researchers disregard them and use the linear probability model with dummy dependent variables. This may not cause insurmountable difficulties; indeed, the signs and general significance of the coefficients of the linear probability model are usually quite similar to those of any maximum likelihood replacement. To avoid the problem of the unboundedness of the expected values of D, these researchers often assign 1.0 to all values above one and assign 0.0 to all negative values. This approach copes with the problem by ignoring it. A person for whom the linear probability model predicts a probability of 2.0 has been judged to be more likely to make the choice in question than a person for whom the model predicts a 1.0, and yet they are lumped together. It is also unrealistic to predict that anything will happen with probability of one or zero unless there are no random elements involved at all. Thus the unboundedness of the expected values of D is a difficult problem when the goal of the research is an analysis of individual choices. In such cases, an alternative should be used.

7.7.2 Binomial Logit Analysis

The most frequently used alternative to the linear probability model is called *binomial (or binary) logit analysis.* The **logit** function is based on the cumulative logistic function and can be expressed as:

$$\ln[P_i/(1 - P_i)] = \beta_0 + \beta_1 X_{1i} + \beta_2 X_{2i} + \epsilon_i \tag{7.33}$$

where P_i is the probability that the *i*th person will make a particular choice. Note that the dependent variable in this nonlinear equation is the log of the odds[16] that a particular choice will be made. Given that, the meaning of a typical logit coefficient in Equation 7.33 differs from the meaning of a linear probability model coefficient in Equation 7.32. For instance, β_1 in Equation 7.33 measures the impact of a change in X_1 on the log of the odds, holding constant X_2. As a result, the absolute sizes of estimated logit coefficients tend to be quite different from the absolute sizes of estimated linear probability model coefficients for the same variables. Interestingly, as mentioned above, the signs and significance levels of the estimated coefficients from the two models are quite similar.

The logit[17] (Equation 7.33) is quite satisfying to most researchers because it turns out that real-world data are often distributed logistically. In addition, both sides are unbounded, and the expected value of D is bounded by zero and one. To see this, note that if $P_i = 1$, then $(1 - P_i) = 0$, and $Ln[P_i/(1 - P_i)]$ approaches infinity, while if $P_i = 0$, then $(1 - P_i) = 1$, and $Ln[P_i/(1 - P_i)]$ approaches negative infinity (the log of zero approaches negative infinity). In other words, this equation solves the most important problem with the linear probability model, that of boundedness.

We can estimate Equation 7.33 through the use of a maximum likelihood iterative process such as that discussed in the previous section. ML has the added advantage of having asymptotically normal coefficient estimates, allowing the use of normal-distribution hypothesis testing techniques. Note that when observed $P_i = 1$, the left side approaches infinity, but this fact does not cause a problem for the ML approach. Because maximum likelihood estimation works best with large samples, and because only two different values of the dependent variable can actually be observed, minimum sample sizes for logit analysis should be substantially larger than for linear regression. It also is important to make sure that the sample contains a reasonable representation of both alternative choices.

Once the binary logit has been estimated, hypothesis testing and econometric analysis can be undertaken in much the same way as for linear equations. When interpreting coefficients, however, be careful to recall that they represent the impact of a one-unit change in the independent variable in question (holding the other explanatory variables constant) on the log of the odds of a given choice, not on the impact on the probability itself.[18]

7.7.3 An Example of the Use of the Binomial Logit

As an example of the binomial logit, let's look at a model of the probability of passing the California State Department of Motor Vehicles Driver's License test. To obtain a license, each driver must pass a written and a "behind the wheel" test, and while the tests are scored from zero to one hundred, all that matters is that you pass and get your license.

Since the test actually involves some boning up on traffic and safety laws, driving students have to decide how much time to spend studying. If you don't study enough, you waste time because the time and effort of waiting in line and retaking the test will outweigh the extra studying. If you study too much, however, you're also wasting time, because there is no bonus for scoring above the minimum, especially since there is no evidence that doing well on the test has much to do with driving well after the test (this, of course, might be worth its own econometric study).

Recently, two students decided to collect data on test-takers in order to build an equation estimating the coefficient of study time in explaining the probability of passing the Department of Motor Vehicles test. (Of course, it took more time to collect the data and run the model than it would have to memorize the entire traffic code, but that's another story.) After reviewing the literature, choosing variables, and hypothesizing signs, the students realized that the appropriate functional form was a binomial logit because their dependent variable was a dummy variable:

$$D_i = \begin{cases} 1 \text{ if the } i\text{th test-taker passed the test on the first try.} \\ 0 \text{ if the } i\text{th test-taker did not pass the test on the first try.} \end{cases}$$

After collecting data from 480 test-takers, the students estimated the following equation:

$$\overset{+ \quad + \quad + \quad +}{D_i = f(A_i, H_i, E_i, C_i)}$$

and obtained:

$$\mathrm{Ln}[D_i/(1 - D_i)] = -1.18 + 0.011A_i + 2.70H_i + 1.62E_i + 3.97C_i \quad (7.34)$$
$$(0.009) \quad (0.54) \quad (0.34) \quad (0.99)$$
$$t = \quad 1.23 \quad 4.97 \quad 4.65 \quad 4.00$$

$$n = 480 \quad LR = 90.59 \quad \text{quasi-}R^2 = .18 \quad \text{iterations} = 5$$

where: A_i = the age of the ith test taker
H_i = the number of hours the ith test-taker studied (usually less than one hour!)
E_i = a dummy variable equal to one if the ith test-taker's primary language was English and zero otherwise
C_i = a dummy variable equal to one if the ith test-taker had any college experience and zero otherwise
quasi-R^2 = a nonlinear estimate of R^2 calculated as discussed in Section 7.2.1.

Note how similar this result looks to a typical linear regression result. Remember, though, that the coefficient estimates have a different meaning than in a regression model. For example, 2.70 is the impact of an extra hour of studying would have had on the log of the odds of passing the test holding constant the other three variables. The quasi-R^2 of .18 might seem fairly low, but it really isn't that bad. Logit is extremely unlikely to provide a very strong overall fit because D_i takes on only two values both of which are at the extremes of the range of the right side of the equation.

What did the students find? They found that given their age, college experience and English-speaking heritage, the expected value of D_i for each of them was quite high even if H was set equal to zero. So what did they actually do? They studied for a half hour "just to be on the safe side" and passed easily, having devoted more time to passing the test than anyone else in the history of the state.

[1.] Throughout this section, the "delta" notation (Δ) will be used instead of the proper calculus notation to make for easier reading. The specific definition of Δ is "change," and it implies a small change in the variable it is attached to. For example, the term ΔX should be read as "change in X." Since a regression coefficient represents the change in the expected value of Y brought about by a one-unit change in X (holding constant all other variables in the equation), then $\beta_k = \Delta Y / \Delta X_k$. Those comfortable with calculus should substitute partial derivative signs for Δs.

[2.] The $\approx$ means "approximately equal to," and the equivalence denoted by the sign is justified by the fact that the derivative of lnY with respect to Y equals $\Delta Y / Y$.

[3.] If it is necessary to take the log of a dummy variable, that variable also needs to be transformed to avoid the possibility of taking the log of zero. The best way is to redefine the entire dummy variable so that, instead of taking on the values of zero and one, it takes on the values of one and e (the base of the natural logarithm). The log of this newly defined dummy then takes on the values of zero and one, and the interpretation of β remains the same as in a linear equation. Such a transformation changes the coefficient value but not the usefulness or theoretical validity of the dummy variable.

[4.] One example of such a combination functional form is called the *translog function*. The translog function combines three different functional forms to come up with an equation perfectly general for estimating various kinds of cost functions. For more on the translog function, see Laurits R. Christensen and William H. Greene, "Economies of Scale in U.S. Electrical Power Generation," *Journal of Political Economy*, August 1976, pp. 655-676.

[5.] One other problem with the quasi-R^2 should be mentioned. It is possible to find examples where the use of the quasi-R^2 to compare the overall fits of equations with different functional forms can give different answers depending on which functional form is considered the "original" functional form and which is considered the "transformed" functional form. In terms of Equation 7.21, this would mean that the R^2 from the linear equation could be greater than the quasi-R^2 obtained by using the logged equation and taking anti-logs, but that the R^2 from the log equation could be greater than the quasi-R^2 obtained by using the linear equation and converting to logs. Happily, such a circumstance is not frequent. In such a case, we advise choosing whichever functional form is easier to work with (i.e., linear, if it is one of the two involved functions). For more, see H. Theil, *Introduction to Econometrics* (Englewood Cliffs, N.J., Prentice-Hall, 1978), pp. 271-277.

[6.] Such a multiple between the slope dummy and X_2 is a specific case of a general group of variables called *interaction terms*. Interaction terms involve multiples of independent variables as in Equation 7.24. They are used when the change in Y with respect to one independent variable (in this case, X_2) depends on the level of the other independent variable (in this case, D). For an example of interaction terms involving wages as a function of unionism and concentration, see F. M. Scherer, *Industrial Market Structure and Economic Performance* (Chicago: Rand McNally, 1977), pp. 298-302.

[7.] Another approach to this problem is to use the Chow test suggested at the very end of Section 5.7 (the appendix on the F-test). To apply the Chow test to the question of earnings differentials between genders, use Equation 7.26 as the unconstrained equation (with all independent variables also having slope dummy formulations) and

$$\text{Earnings}_i = \beta_0 + \beta_1 \text{EXP}_i + \cdots + \epsilon_i \tag{7.26a}$$

as the constrained equation. If the F-test shows that the fit of Equation 7.26 is significantly better than the fit of Equation 7.26a, then we would reject the null hypothesis of equivalence between the male and female slope coefficients in the earnings equation.

[8.] Note that the two portions of the solid line do not quite touch each other. There is no certainty that they will intersect unless constrained to do so by specifying an equation like:

$$Y_i = \beta_0 + \beta_1 X_{1i} + \beta_2 X_{2i} + \beta_3 D_i X_3 + \epsilon_i$$
$$\text{where } D_i = 1 \text{ if } X_{1i} > X_1^* \text{ and } = 0 \text{ if } X_{1i} \leq X_1^*$$
$$\text{and } X_{3i} = (X_{1i} - X_1^*)$$

This constraint works because as X_{1i} approaches X_1^* (either from above or below X_1^*), Y_i approaches $\beta_0 + \beta_1 X_1^* + \beta_2 X_{2i} + \epsilon_i$. Unless disjoint functions need to be avoided for interpretation purposes, however, such constraints are interesting but not required.

[9.] V. N. Murti and V. K. Sastri, "Production Functions for Indian Industry," *Econometrica*, April 1957, pp. 205-221.

[10.] William S. Comanor and Thomas A. Wilson, "Advertising, Market Structure and Performance." *Review of Economics and Statistics*. Nov. 1967, p. 432.

[11.] Derivatives are calculus notations similar to the delta (Δ) notation used in this chapter. If these derivatives are set equal to zero and solved simultaneously, the resulting coefficient values will be those that minimize Σe^2. Thus to use nonlinear least squares, the derivatives, which are functions of the coefficients as well as the data, must be known.

[12.] Another least squares approach is to "linearize" the continuous nonlinear curve into a series of linked (and extremely short) straight lines. This is usually done with a "Taylor series expansion," which utilizes first and second derivatives of the function in question with respect to the coefficients. In such a case, OLS can be applied to the individual equation estimations within the iteration. For more on this approach and a number of other useful techniques, see S. M. Goldfeld and R. E. Quandt, *Nonlinear Methods in Econometrics* (Amsterdam: North-Holland, 1972), or A. R. Gallant, "Nonlinear Regression," *The American Statistician*, May, 1975, pp. 73-81.

[13.] Such likelihood functions can also be equivalently stated in terms of error terms, as in $L = \Pr(\epsilon_1 \cdot \epsilon_2 \cdot \epsilon_3 \cdots \cdot \epsilon_n)$. This is because Y is a function of the Xs, the βs, and the ϵs. Note that if the Ys (or ϵs) are independent of each other, as they should be, then L can be restated as the product of the probabilities.

[14.] Maximum likelihood estimators have three desirable large sample properties: consistency, asymptotic efficiency, and asymptotic normality. Consistency means that the probability that the $\hat{\beta}$s equal the true βs approaches one as the sample size gets larger. Asymptotic efficiency means that the estimator is consistent and has the smallest $\hat{\beta}$ variance of all the consistent estimators. Asymptotic normality means that the distribution of the estimates approaches the normal distribution as the sample size approaches infinity. For more on maximum likelihood, see G. S. Maddala, *Econometrics* (New York: McGraw-Hill, 1977).

[15.] J. Vanek et.al., "Towards a Better Understanding of the Incremental Capital-Output Ratio," *Quarterly Journal of Economics*, October 1968, pp. 452-464. This article also contains the data set used for the example in this section. While we do not derive Equation 7.30 here, we can interpret α as the long-run (or "golden age") net incremental output/capital ratio and β as the average length of time that a typical capital asset lasts before it is scrapped.

[16.] *Odds* refers to the ratio of the number of times a choice will be made divided by the number of times it will not. In today's world, odds are used most frequently with respect to sporting events, such as horse races, on which bets are made. For example, if a horse's odds are quoted as "4 to 1 against winning," then the horse is expected by the odds-maker to lose four times for every time it wins.

[17.] Logit analysis is not the only method of solving the problems of dealing with discrete choice models. Other possibilities include probit analysis, Tobit analysis, and discriminant analysis, but such techniques are beyond the scope of this text. For more on these other possibilities, see G. S. Maddala, *Limited Dependent Variables and Qualitative Variables in Econometrics* (Cambridge: Cambridge University Press, 1983). For more on the binary logit, see J. Berkson, "Application of the Logistic Function to Bio-Assay," *Journal of the American Statistical Association*, 1944, pp. 357-365 and D. R. Cox, *The Analysis of Binary Data* (London: Methuen, 1970).

[18.] If there are more than two possible alternatives to choose from, an alternative approach is to use the *multinomial* logit or probit. A multinomial model allows several alternatives to be considered simultaneously. One alternative is chosen as a base alternative, and then each other possibility is compared to that base with a logit equation. Thus if there were n alternatives, there would be n − 1 different equations in the multinomial system. For more on this, see T. Amemiya, "Qualitative Response Models: A Survey," *Journal of Economic Literature*, 1981, pp. 1483-1536.

8

Multicollinearity

The next three chapters deal with violations of the classical assumptions and remedies for the violations. This chapter addresses multicollinearity; the next two chapters are on serial correlation and heteroskedasticity. For each of the three problems, we will attempt to answer the following questions:

1. What is the nature of the problem?

2. What are the consequences of the problem?

3. How is the problem diagnosed?

4. What remedies for the problem are available?

Strictly speaking, **multicollinearity** is the violation of the assumption that no independent variable is a perfect linear function of one or more other independent variables (Classical Assumption VI). Perfect multicollinearity is rare, but severe imperfect multicollinearity (where two or more independent variables are highly correlated in the particular data set being studied), while not violating Classical Assumption VI, still causes substantial problems.

Recall that the coefficient β_k can be thought of as the impact on the dependent variable of a change in a particular independent variable (X_k), holding constant the impact of the other independent variables in the equation. But if two explanatory variables are significantly related in a particular sample, whenever one changes, the other will tend to change too, and the OLS computer program will find it difficult to distinguish the effects of one variable from the effects of the other. Since the Xs can move together more in one sample than they do in another, the severity of multicollinearity can vary tremendously.

In essence, the more highly correlated two (or more) independent variables are, the more difficult it becomes to accurately estimate the coefficients of the true model. We are usually less concerned about the existence of multicollinearity in a sample (it almost always exists to some degree) than with how severe the multicollinearity is. If two variables move identically, then there is no hope of distinguishing between the impacts of the two, but if the variables are only roughly correlated, then we still might be able to accurately estimate the two impacts.

8.1   Perfect vs. Imperfect Multicollinearity

8.1.1   Perfect Multicollinearity

Perfect multicollinearity[1] violates Classical Assumption VI, which specifies that no explanatory variable is a perfect linear function of any other explanatory variable. The word perfect in this context implies that the variation in one explanatory variable can be completely explained by movements in the other. Such a perfect linear function between two independent variables would be:

$$X_{1i} = \alpha_0 + \alpha_1 X_{2i} \tag{8.1}$$

where the αs are constants; the Xs are independent variables in:

$$Y_i = \beta_0 + \beta_1 X_{1i} + \beta_2 X_{2i} + \epsilon_i \tag{8.2}$$

Notice that there is no error term in Equation 8.1. This implies that X_1 can be calculated exactly given X_2 and the equation. Examples of such perfect linear relationships would be:

$$X_{1i} = 3X_{2i} \quad \text{or} \quad X_{1i} = 6 + X_{2i} \quad \text{or} \quad X_{1i} = 2 + 4X_{2i} \tag{8.3}$$

Figure 8.1 shows a graph of explanatory variables that are perfectly correlated. As can be seen in Figure 8.1, a perfect linear function has all data points on the

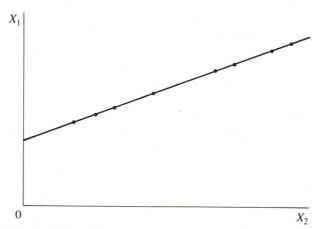

FIGURE 8.1 *Perfect Multicollinearity*
With perfect multicollinearity, an independent variable can be completely explained by the movements of one or more other independent variables. Perfect multicollinearity can usually be avoided by careful screening of the independent variables before a regression is run.

same straight line. There is none of the variation that accompanies the data set from a typical regression.

Some examples of perfect multicollinearity were briefly mentioned in Section 4.1. Recall what happens when nominal and real interest rates are both included as explanatory variables in an equation. Usually, the relationship between nominal and real interest rates continually changes because the difference between the two, the expected rate of inflation, is always changing. If the expected rate of inflation somehow was constant (during extremely strict price controls, for instance) then the difference between the two would be constant, the two would be perfectly linearly related, and perfect multicollinearity would result:

$$in_t = ir_t + inf_t = ir_t + \alpha \qquad (8.4)$$

where: in_t = the nominal (or money) interest rate in time t
             ir_t = the real interest rate in time t
            inf_t = the expected rate of inflation in time t
            α = a constant

What happens to the estimation of an econometric equation where there is perfect multicollinearity? Ordinary least squares is incapable of generating estimates of the regression coefficients. Using Equation 8.2 as an example, we would theoretically obtain the following estimated coefficients and standard errors:

$$\hat{\beta}_1 = \text{indeterminate} \qquad SE(\hat{\beta}_1) = \infty$$
$$\hat{\beta}_2 = \text{indeterminate} \qquad SE(\hat{\beta}_2) = \infty \qquad (8.5)$$

Perfect multicollinearity ruins our ability to estimate the coefficients because the two variables cannot be distinguished. You cannot "hold all the other independent variables in the equation constant" if every time one variable changes, another changes in an identical manner.[2]

Fortunately, instances in which one explanatory variable is a perfect linear function of another are rare. More importantly, perfect multicollinearity should be fairly easy to discover before a regression is run. One can detect perfect multicollinearity by asking whether one variable equals a multiple of another or if one variable can be derived by adding a constant to another. If so, then one of the variables should be dropped because there is no essential difference between the two.

A special case related to perfect multicollinearity occurs when a variable that is definitionally related to the dependent variable is included as an independent variable in a regression equation. Such a **dominant variable** is so highly correlated with the dependent variable that it completely masks the effects of all other independent variables in the equation. In a sense, this is a case of perfect collinearity between the dependent and an independent variable.

For example, if you include a variable measuring the amount of raw materials used by the shoe industry in a production function for that industry, that variable would have an extremely high t-score, but otherwise important variables like labor and capital would have quite insignificant t-scores. Why? In essence, if you knew how much leather was used by a shoe factory, you could predict the number of pairs of shoes produced without knowing *anything* about labor or capital. The relationship is definitional, and the dominant variable should be dropped from the equation to get reasonable estimates of the coefficients of the other variables.

A dominant variable involves a tautology; it is defined in such a way that you can calculate the dependent variable from it without any knowledge of the underlying theory. As such, dominant variables should not be confused with highly significant or important explanatory variables. Instead, they should be recognized as virtually identical to the dependent variable. While the fit between the two is superb, knowledge of that fit could have been obtained from the definitions of the variables without any econometric estimation.

8.1.2 Imperfect Multicollinearity

Since perfect multicollinearity is fairly easy to avoid, econometricians almost never talk about perfect multicollinearity. Instead, when we use the word multicollinearity, we are really talking about severe imperfect multicollinearity. **Imperfect multicollinearity** can be defined as a linear functional relationship between two or more independent variables that is so strong that it can affect the estimation of the coefficients of the variables.

In other words, imperfect multicollinearity occurs when two (or more) explanatory variables are imperfectly linearly related as in:

$$X_{1t} = \alpha_0 + \alpha_1 X_{2t} + u_t \tag{8.6}$$

Notice that Equation 8.6 includes u_t, a stochastic error term. This implies that while the relationship between X_1 and X_2 might be fairly strong, it is not strong

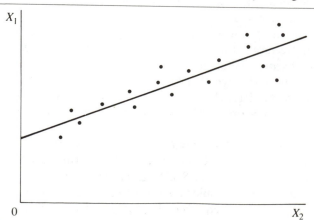

FIGURE 8.2 *Imperfect Multicollinearity*
With imperfect multicollinearity, an independent variable is a strong but not perfectly linear function of one or more other independent variables. Imperfect multicollinearity varies in degree from sample to sample.

enough to allow X_1 to be completely explained by X_2; some unexplained variation still remains. Figure 8.2 shows the graph of two explanatory variables that might be considered multicollinear. Notice that while all the observations in the sample are fairly close to the straight line, there is still some variation in X_1 that has not been explained by X_2.

Imperfect multicollinearity is a strong but imprecise relationship between the explanatory variables. The stronger the relationship between the two (or more) explanatory variables, the more likely it is that they will be considered significantly multicollinear. Whether explanatory variables are multicollinear in a given equation depends on the particular sample chosen. Two variables that might be only slightly related in one sample might be so strongly related in another that they could be considered to be imperfectly multicollinear. In this sense, it is fair to say that multicollinearity is a sample phenomenon. Whether the data are correlated enough to have an effect on the estimation of the equation depends on the particular sample drawn, and each sample must be investigated (using, for example, the simple correlation coefficient to measure collinearity) before multicollinearity can be diagnosed. This contrasts with perfect multicollinearity, for two variables that are perfectly related probably can be detected on a logical basis. The detection of multicollinearity will be discussed in more detail in Section 8.3.

Some research projects are inherently more likely to suffer from multicollinearity than others. For example, almost all macroeconomic time-series data sets have potential multicollinearity in them because aggregates have tended to rise unambiguously over the past half century. Labor force, income, consumption, taxes, and almost every other measure of economic activity have increased as the years have gone by. In addition, increases in productivity and the general rise in prices have augmented this tendency towards co-movement.

Consider a model of the impact of taxes on savings over the last thirty years:

$$S_t = f(\overset{+}{Yd_t}, \overset{+}{i_t}, \overset{-}{T_t}, \overset{-}{SS_t}) \tag{8.7}$$

where: S_t = Savings in year t (nominal, excluding Social Security)
Yd_t = Disposable Income in year t (nominal)
i_t = the nominal interest rate on savings in year t
T_t = the nominal tax rate in year t
SS_t = contributions to Social Security in year t (nominal)

In such a model, savings are hypothesized to rise as disposable income rises. In addition, the incentive to save is hypothesized to increase as the interest rate paid on savings increases but decrease as the tax rate on income from savings increases. To the extent that Social Security is considered saving by the average individual, then contributions to Social Security would tend to reduce the perceived need for saving.

Given the growth in the economy over the years, almost all the variables in this savings model have probably increased over time; the increase in population, in prices, in tax rates, and in the rate of Social Security deductions make it seem quite likely that all the independent variables in Equation 8.7 will be highly correlated (with the possible exception of the interest rate, depending on the precise time period being studied). In such a model, multicollinearity is quite likely to be fairly severe, and the consequences of such severe imperfect multicollinearity need to be investigated.

8.2   The Consequences of Multicollinearity

If the multicollinearity in a particular sample is severe, what will happen to estimates calculated from that sample? Since perfect multicollinearity means that the estimation of an equation is impossible, what consequences does significant imperfect multicollinearity imply? The purpose of this section is to explain the consequences of multicollinearity and then to explore some examples of such consequences.

We should briefly recall the properties of ordinary least squares estimators that might be affected by this or some other econometric problem. In Chapter 4, we stated that the OLS estimators are BLUE (or MvLUE) if the Classical Assumptions hold. This means that OLS estimates can be thought of as being unbiased and having the minimum variance possible for unbiased linear estimators.

8.2.1   An Overview of the Consequences of Multicollinearity

The general consequences of multicollinearity are:

1. *Estimates will remain unbiased.* Even if an equation has significant multicollinearity, the estimates of the βs will still be centered around the true population βs if all the other classical assumptions are met for a correctly specified equation.

2. *The variances of the estimates will increase.* This is the major consequence of multicollinearity. Since two or more of the explanatory variables are significantly related, it becomes very difficult to precisely identify the separate effects of the multicollinear variables. When it becomes hard to tell the effect of one variable from the effect of another, then we are much more likely to make large errors in estimating the βs than we were before we encountered multicollinearity. As a result, the estimated coefficients, while still unbiased, now come from distributions with much larger variances.[3]

Figure 8.3 compares the distribution of a $\hat{\beta}$ with severe multicollinearity to one with virtually no correlation between any of the independent variables. Notice that the two distributions have the same mean, indicating that multicollinearity does not cause bias. Also note how much wider the distribution of $\hat{\beta}$ becomes when multicollinearity is severe; this is the result of the increase in the variance of $\hat{\beta}$ that is caused by multicollinearity.

In particular, the $\hat{\beta}$ distribution with multicollinearity now has a higher probability of obtaining a $\hat{\beta}$ that is significantly different from the true β. For example,

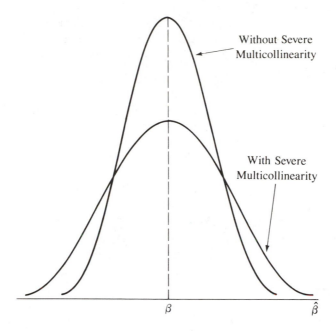

FIGURE 8.3 *Severe Multicollinearity Increases the Variances of the $\hat{\beta}s$*
Severe multicollinearity produces a distribution of the $\hat{\beta}s$ that is centered around the true β but which has a much larger variance. Thus the distribution of $\hat{\beta}s$ with multicollinearity is much wider than otherwise.

it turns out that multicollinearity increases the likelihood of obtaining an unexpected sign[4] for a coefficient even though, as mentioned above, multicollinearity causes no bias. For more on this see Exercise 6.

3. *The computed t-scores will fall.* Multicollinearity tends to decrease the t-scores of the estimated coefficients mainly because of the formula for the t-statistic:

$$t_k = (\hat{\beta}_k - \hat{\beta}_{H_0})/SE(\hat{\beta}_k) \qquad (8.8)$$

Notice that this equation is divided by the standard error of the estimated coefficient. Multicollinearity increases the variance, estimated variance, and therefore the standard error of the estimated coefficient. If the standard error increases, then the t-score must fall, as can be seen from Equation 8.8. Not surprisingly, it is quite common to observe low t-scores in equations with severe multicollinearity.

A second factor also tends to cause more insignificant t-scores to be observed with severe multicollinearity than without. Because multicollinearity increases the variance of the $\hat{\beta}s$, the coefficient estimates are likely to be farther from the true parameter value than they would have been with less multicollinearity. This "pushes" a portion of the distribution of the $\hat{\beta}s$ towards zero, making it more likely that a t-score will be insignificantly different from zero (or will have an unexpected sign). This "pushing" goes in both directions, so multicollinearity is also likely to cause some higher-than-expected $\hat{\beta}$s (and therefore t-scores). This effect is often overshadowed by the larger standard errors mentioned in the previous paragraph.

4. *Estimates will become very sensitive to changes in specification.* The addition or deletion of an explanatory variable or of a few observations will often cause major changes in the values of the $\hat{\beta}$s when significant multicollinearity exists. If you drop a variable, even one that appears to be statistically insignificant, the coefficients of the remaining variables in the equation will sometimes change dramatically.

These large changes occur because OLS estimation is sometimes forced to emphasize small differences between variables in order to distinguish the effect of one multicollinear variable from another. Thus, even a minor specification change can cause a major change in the attribute that the computer program had "focused on," and the estimated coefficients can change significantly. If two variables are virtually identical throughout most of the sample, the estimation procedure relies on the observations in which the variables move differently in order to distinguish between them. As a result, a specification change that drops a variable that had an unusual value for one of these crucial observations can cause the estimated coefficients of the multicollinear variables to change dramatically.

5. *The overall fit of the equation will be largely unaffected.* Even though the individual t-scores are often quite low in a multicollinear equation, the overall fit of the equation, as measured by R^2 or the F-test, will not change much, if at all, in the face of significant multicollinearity. As a result, it is not uncommon to encounter multicollinear equations that have quite high R^2s and yet have no individual independent variable even close to being statistically significantly different from zero.

Because multicollinearity has little effect on the overall fit of the equation, it will also have little effect on the use of that equation for prediction or forecasting as long as the independent variables maintain the same pattern of multicollinearity in the forecast period that they demonstrated in the sample.

6. *The estimation of non-multicollinear (orthogonal) variables will be unaffected.* If an explanatory variable in an equation is not multicollinear (also called orthogonal) with the other variables, then the estimation of its coefficient and standard error usually will not be affected. It is unusual to find an explanatory variable that is totally uncorrelated with any other explanatory variable. If this were to occur, though, then the multicollinearity in the rest of the equation would not change the estimated coefficient or the t-score of the non-multicollinear variable.

7. *The severity of multicollinearity worsens its consequences.* It is intuitively logical that the more severe the multicollinearity, the more severe the impact on the estimates. After all, if perfect multicollinearity makes the estimation of the

equation impossible, then almost perfect multicollinearity should cause more damage to estimates than virtually nonexistent multicollinearity.

Indeed, the higher the simple correlation between the multicollinear variables (in the two-variable case), the higher the estimated variances and the lower the calculated t-values; the variances of the $\hat{\beta}$s calculated with OLS increase as the simple correlation coefficient between the two independent variables increases. When $r = 0$ (no multicollinearity), the variance of $\hat{\beta}$ equals its minimum (i.e., non-multicollinear) value. As the absolute value of r increases from 0 to 1, holding other things constant, the variance slowly increases to infinity, and the t-score goes to zero. For example, if a t-score of 4.00 were observed when $r = 0$, it may fall to 1.75 if $r = 0.90$ and to 1.25 if $r = 0.95$. The same tendency also holds (only more so) when there are three or more multicollinear explanatory variables.

8.2.2   Two Examples of the Consequences of Multicollinearity

To see what severe multicollinearity does to an estimated equation, let's look at a hypothetical example. Suppose you decide to estimate a "student consumption function" that relates better to student problems than some of the aggregate macroeconomic consumption functions you have read about. After the appropriate preliminary work, you come up with the following hypothesized equation:

$$C_i = f(Yd, LA) = \overset{+}{\beta_0} + \overset{+}{\beta_1} Yd_i + \beta_2 LA_i + \epsilon_i \qquad (8.9)$$

where: C_i = the annual consumption expenditures of the ith student
Yd_i = the annual disposable income (including gifts) of that student
LA_i = the liquid assets (savings, etc.) of the ith student's family
ϵ_i = a stochastic error term

You then collect a small amount of data from people who are sitting near you in class:

Student	C_i	Yd_i	LA_i
Howard	$2000	$2500	$25000
Ruth	2300	3000	31000
James	2800	3500	33000
Morgan	3800	4000	39000
Duncan	3500	4500	48000
Allen	5000	5000	54000
Reed	4500	5500	55000

If you run an OLS regression on your data set for Equation 8.9, you obtain:

$$\hat{C}_i = -367.83 + 0.5113 Yd_i + 0.0427 LA_i \qquad (8.10)$$
$$(1.0307)(0.0942)$$
$$t = 0.496 0.453 \bar{R}^2 = .835$$

On the other hand, if you had consumption as a function of disposable income alone, then you would have obtained:

$$\hat{C}_i = -471.43 + 0.9714Yd_i \tag{8.11}$$
$$(0.0157)$$
$$t = \quad 6.187 \qquad \bar{R}^2 = .861$$

Notice from Equations 8.10 and 8.11 that the t-score for disposable income increases more than tenfold when the liquid assets variable is dropped from the equation. Why does this happen? First of all, the simple correlation coefficient between Yd and LA is quite high: $r_{Yd,LA} = .986$. This high degree of correlation causes the standard errors of the estimated coefficients to increase dramatically. In the case of $\hat{\beta}_{Yd}$, the standard error goes from 0.015 to 1.03! In addition, the coefficient estimate itself changes somewhat. Further, note that the $\bar{R}^2$s of the two equations are quite similar despite the large differences in the significance of the explanatory variables in the two equations. It is quite common for $\bar{R}^2$ to stay virtually unchanged when multicollinear variables are dropped. All of these results are typical of equations with multicollinearity.

Which equation is better? If the liquid assets variable theoretically belongs in the equation, then to drop it will run the risk of left-out variable bias, but to include the variable will mean certain multicollinearity. There is no automatic answer when dealing with multicollinearity. We will discuss this issue in more detail in Sections 8.4 and 8.5.

A second example of the consequences of multicollinearity is based on actual, rather than hypothetical, data. Suppose you've decided to build a cross-sectional model of the demand for gasoline by state:

$$PCON_i = f(\overset{+}{UHM}_i, \overset{-}{TAX}_i, \overset{+}{REG}_i) \tag{8.12}$$

where: $PCON_i$ = Petroleum consumption in the ith state (trillions of BTU's)
   UHM_1 = Urban highway miles within the ith state
   TAX_i = The gasoline tax rate in the ith state (cents per gallon)
   REG_i = Motor vehicle registrations in the ith state (thousands)

A complete listing of the data for this model is contained in Section 10.5, so let's move on to the estimation of Equation 8.12 in a linear functional form (assuming a stochastic error term):

$$\widehat{PCON}_i = 389.6 + 60.8UHM_i - 36.5TAX_i - 0.061REG_i \tag{8.13}$$
$$(10.3) \qquad (13.2) \qquad (0.043)$$
$$t = \quad 5.92 \qquad -2.77 \qquad -1.43$$
$$n = 50 \qquad \bar{R}^2 = .919$$

What's wrong with this equation? Motor vehicle registrations has an insignificant coefficient with an unexpected sign, but it's hard to believe that the variable is irrelevant. Is a left-out variable causing bias? It is possible, but adding a variable is unlikely to fix things. Does it help to know that the simple correlation coefficient between REG and UHM is 0.98? Given that, it seems fair to say that one of the two variables is redundant; both variables are really measuring the *size* of the state, so we have multicollinearity.

Notice the impact of the multicollinearity on the equation. The coefficient of a variable such as motor vehicle registrations, which has a very strong theoretical relationship to petroleum consumption, is insignificant and has a sign contrary to our expectations. This is mainly because the multicollinearity has increased the variance of the distribution of the estimated $\hat{\beta}$s.

What would happen if we were to drop one of the multicollinear variables?

$$\widehat{PCON}_i = 551.7 - 53.6TAX_i + 0.186REG_i \qquad (8.14)$$
$$(16.9) \qquad (0.012)$$
$$t = \quad -3.18 \qquad 15.88$$
$$n = 50 \qquad \bar{R}^2 = .861$$

Dropping UHM has made REG extremely significant. Why did this occur? The answer is the standard error of the coefficient of REG has fallen substantially (from 0.043 to 0.012) now that the multicollinearity has been removed from the equation. Also note that the sign of the estimated coefficient has now become positive as hypothesized. The reason is that REG and UHM are virtually indistinguishable from an empirical point of view, and so the OLS program latched onto minor differences between the variables to explain the movements of PCON. Once the multicollinearity was removed, the direct positive relationship between REG and PCON was obvious. Note, however, that the coefficient of the REG variable now measures the effect of both REG and UHM on PCON. Since we've dropped a variable, the remaining coefficient soaks up the effect of the left-out variable.

Note that either UHM or REG could have been dropped with similar results because the two variables are, in a quantitative sense, virtually identical as indicated by the high simple correlation coefficient between them. In this case, REG was judged to be theoretically superior to UHM. Note also that $\bar{R}^2$ fell when UHM was dropped, and yet Equation 8.14 should be considered superior to Equation 8.13. This is an example of the point, originally made in Chapter 3, that the fit of an equation is not the most important criterion to be used in determining its overall quality.

8.3   The Detection of Multicollinearity

We now will discuss methods that can be used to decide whether significant multicollinearity exists in a particular equation. Our main purpose in doing so is to decide how much multicollinearity exists in an equation, not whether any multicollinearity exists. In essence, we know that the explanatory variables are going to be at least slightly related to each other, and so the important consideration is the degree of multicollinearity.

Since multicollinearity is not the kind of problem that an equation either has or doesn't have, many of the methods used to detect multicollinearity are not formal tests with critical values or levels of significance. In fact, there is no universally accepted test of multicollinearity. Instead, most researchers develop a general feeling for the severity and importance of multicollinearity in an equation by looking at a number of the characteristics of the estimated equation.

1. *Is $\bar{R}^2$ high with low t-scores?* One of the unique consequences of multicollinearity is that the overall level of significance of an equation is affected far less than are the levels of significance of the individual regression coefficients. In other words, multicollinearity that is severe enough to substantially lower t-scores does very little to decrease $\bar{R}^2$ or the F-statistic. Given this fact, one of the first indications of the possible presence of severe multicollinearity is the combination of a high $\bar{R}^2$ with low calculated t-values for the individual regression coefficients.

For example, return to Equation 8.10 above and note that the $\bar{R}^2$ is .835 even though no individual t-score is higher than 0.5. Such a combination is a sure sign of fairly severe multicollinearity. It is almost impossible to get an $\bar{R}^2$ greater than .7 if all the individual regression coefficients are insignificantly different from zero without some sort of multicollinearity in the data set.

This approach has its flaws, however; most importantly, a non-multicollinear explanatory variable may still have a significant coefficient even if there is multicollinearity between two or more other explanatory variables. As a result, equations with high levels of multicollinearity will often have one or two regression coefficients significantly different from zero, thus making the "high $\bar{R}^2$, low t" rule a poor indicator in such cases. The existence of a high $\bar{R}^2$ with low t-scores must be considered a sufficient but not necessary test for severe multicollinearity. While all equations with these characteristics will have multicollinearity of some sort, the absence of them will not imply its absence.

2. *Are the Simple Correlation Coefficients High?* Another way to detect severe multicollinearity is to examine all the simple correlation coefficients between the explanatory variables. If the r's are high in absolute value, then we know that the particular Xs are highly correlated and that multicollinearity is a potential problem. For example, in Equation 8.10, the simple correlation coefficient between disposable income and liquid assets is 0.986. A simple correlation coefficient this high is a certain indication of multicollinearity.

How high an r is high? One proposed rule of thumb is that multicollinearity is a potential problem when the squared simple correlation coefficient is greater than the unadjusted R^2:

$$\text{Two Xs are severely multicollinear if } (r_{xi,xj})^2 \geq R^2$$

This approach has a number of problems.[5] In particular, the lower the R^2, the worse an indicator of the severity of the multicollinearity this rule of thumb is. The reason that this comparison works poorly with low R^2s is that if R^2 is low, various r's posing no real multicollinear threat might still be higher than the R^2. For an equation with a good fit, though, this general indicator might be a reasonable first measure of the severity of multicollinearity. A second possibility is to test the individual simple correlation coefficients using the t-test as described in Equation 5.8 in Section 5.6. For practice in these kinds of tests, see Exercise 10 of Chapter Five.

All tests of simple correlation coefficients as indications of the extent of multicollinearity share a major loophole. It is quite possible for groups of explanatory variables, acting together, to cause multicollinearity without any single simple correlation coefficient being high enough to prove that multicollinearity is indeed severe. A given explanatory variable could be jointly determined by a number of other explanatory variables in a way that would cause significant multicollinear consequences without causing any particular r to be high. As a result, tests of simple correlation coefficients must also be considered to be sufficient but not necessary tests for multicollinearity. While a high r does indeed imply severe multicollinearity, a low r by no means proves otherwise.

Even the study of the partial correlation coefficient between two variables (the correlation between two explanatory variables, holding constant the effect of the other explanatory variables in the equation) does not solve the problem. While the use of partial correlation coefficients sheds more light on the question of the severity of multicollinearity, it too is subject to a number of exceptions that make it impossible to be sure that severe multicollinearity does not exist.

3. *What Do More Formal Tests for Multicollinearity Indicate?* The use of tests to give any indication of the severity of the multicollinearity in a particular sample is controversial. Some econometricians reject even the simple indicators developed above, mainly because of the limitations cited. Others tend to use a number of more formal tests; unfortunately, none of these is accepted as the best, and most involve a level of complexity that is beyond the scope of this text and may not be justified by the additional insight that the knowledge of the existence of multicollinearity would bring to the researcher.[6]

8.4 Remedies for Multicollinearity

What can be done to minimize the consequences that severe multicollinearity might have on your estimated equation? There is no automatic answer to this question, because multicollinearity is a phenomenon that could change from sample to sample even for the same specification of a regression equation. The purpose of this section is to outline a number of alternative remedies for multicollinearity that might be appropriate under certain circumstances.

8.4.1 Do Nothing

The first step to take once severe multicollinearity has been diagnosed is to decide whether anything should be done at all. As we will see, it turns out that every remedy for multicollinearity has a drawback of some sort, and so it often happens that doing nothing is the correct course of action.

The major reason for seriously considering doing nothing is that multicollinearity in an equation will not always reduce the t-scores enough to make them insignificant or change the $\hat{\beta}$s enough to make them differ significantly from expectations. In other words, the mere existence of multicollinearity does not necessarily mean anything. A remedy for multicollinearity should only be considered if and when the consequences cause insignificant t-scores or wildly unreliable estimated coefficients. For example, it is possible to observe a simple correlation coefficient of .97 between two explanatory variables each of which have individual t-scores that are significant at the 95 percent level of confidence. It makes no sense to consider remedial action in such a case, because any remedy for multicollinearity could potentially cause other problems for the equation. In a sense, multicollinearity is similar to a non-life-threatening human disease that requires general anesthesia to operate on; the risk of the operation should only be undertaken if the disease is causing a significant problem.

The easiest remedy for severe multicollinearity is to drop one or more of the multicollinear variables from the equation; however, the deletion of a multicollinear variable that theoretically belongs in an equation is fairly dangerous, because now the equation will be subject to specification bias. If we drop such a variable, then we are *purposely* creating bias. Given all the effort typically expended to avoid omitted variables, it seems foolhardy to consider running that risk on purpose. As a result, experienced econometricians often will leave multicollinear variables in equations despite potential decreases in t-scores.

The final reason for considering doing nothing to offset multicollinearity is a theoretical one that would apply to all equations. Every time a regression is rerun, we are running the risk of encountering a specification that fits because it accidentally works for the particular data set involved, not because it is the truth. The larger the number of experiments, the greater the chances of finding the accidental result. When there is significant multicollinearity in the sample, the odds of strange results increase rapidly because of the sensitivity of the coefficient estimates to slight specification changes. Thus the case against sequential specification searches outlined in Chapter 6 is even stronger in the face of severe multicollinearity.

To sum, it is often best to leave an equation unadjusted in the face of all but extreme multicollinearity. Such advice might be difficult for beginning researchers to take, however, if they think that it is embarrassing to report that their final regression is one with insignificant t-scores. Compared to the alternatives of possible omitted variable bias or accidentally significant regression results, the low t-scores seem like a minor problem. For an example of "doing nothing" in the face of severe multicollinearity, see Section 8.5.

8.4.2   Drop One or More of the Multicollinear Variables

Perhaps the surest way to rid an equation of significant multicollinearity is to drop all but one of the multicollinear variables. Multicollinearity is caused by correlation between the explanatory variables; without all the multicollinear variables in the equation, the correlation no longer exists, and any multicollinear consequences also cease to exist. The coefficient of the remaining included variable also now measures the joint impact on the dependent variable of the excluded multicollinear explanatory variables.

To see how this solution would work, let's return to the student consumption function example of Equation 8.10, reproduced here for convenience:

$$\hat{C}_i = -367.83 + 0.5113 Yd_i + 0.0427 LA_i \qquad (8.10)$$
$$(1.0307) \qquad (0.0942)$$
$$t = \quad 0.496 \qquad\qquad 0.453 \qquad \bar{R}^2 = .835$$

where C = consumption, Yd = disposable income, and LA = liquid assets. When we first discussed this example, we compared this result to the same equation without the liquid assets variable (also reproduced):

$$\hat{C}_i = -471.43 + 0.9714 Yd_i \qquad (8.11)$$
$$(0.0157)$$
$$t = \quad 6.187 \qquad \bar{R}^2 = .861$$

If we had instead dropped the disposable income variable, we would have obtained:

$$\hat{C}_i = -199.44 + 0.08876 LA_i \qquad (8.15)$$
$$(0.01443)$$
$$t = \quad 6.153 \qquad \bar{R}^2 = .860$$

Note that dropping one of the multicollinear variables has eliminated both the multicollinearity between the two explanatory variables and also the low t-score of the coefficient of the remaining variable. By dropping Yd, we were able to increase t_{LA} from 0.453 to 6.153.

Assuming you wish to drop a variable, how do you decide which variable to drop? In cases of severe multicollinearity, it makes no statistical difference which variable is dropped. To see this, compare the $\bar{R}^2$ and the t-score from Equation 8.11 with those in 8.15. Note that they are virtually identical. This is hardly a surprise, since the variables themselves move in virtually identical patterns. As a result, it does not make sense to pick the variable to be dropped on the basis of which one gives superior fit or which one is more significant (or has the expected sign) in the original equation. Instead, the theoretical underpinnings of the model should be the basis for such a decision. In the example of the student consumption function, there is more theoretical support for the hypothesis that disposable income determines consumption than there is for the liquid assets hypothesis. Therefore, Equation 8.11 should be preferred to Equation 8.15.

On occasion, the simple solution of dropping one of the multicollinear variables is a good one. For example, some inexperienced researchers include too many variables in their regressions, not wanting to have to face left-out variable bias.

As a result, they often have two or more variables in their equations that are measuring essentially the same thing. In such a case, the multicollinear variables are not irrelevant, since any one of them is quite probably theoretically and statistically sound. Instead, the variables might be called *redundant;* only one of them is needed to represent the effect on the dependent variable that all of them currently represent. For example, in an aggregate demand function, it would not make sense to include disposable income and GNP because both are measuring the same thing: income. A bit more subtle is the inference that population and disposable income should not both be included in the same aggregate demand function, because once again they really are measuring the same thing: the size of the aggregate market. As population rises, so too will income. Dropping these kinds of redundant multicollinear variables is doing nothing more than making up for a specification error; the variables should never have been included in the first place.

8.4.3 Transform the Multicollinear Variables

The consequences of multicollinearity are often serious enough to warrant the consideration of remedial action, but the variables involved are all extremely important on theoretical grounds. In these cases, neither inaction nor dropping a variable is especially helpful; however, it is sometimes possible to transform the variables in the equation to get rid of at least some of the multicollinearity. The two most common such transformations are to:

1. Form a linear combination of the multicollinear variables.

2. Transform the equation into first differences (or logs).

The technique of forming a **linear combination** of two or more of the multicollinear variables consists of:

A.   creating a new variable that is a function of the multicollinear variables

B.   using the new variable to replace the old ones in the regression equation.

For example, if X_1 and X_2 are highly multicollinear, a new variable, $X_3 = X_1 + X_2$ (or more generally, any linear combination of the two variables like $k_1 X_1 + k_2 X_2$) might be substituted for both of the multicollinear variables in a re-estimation of the model. This technique is especially useful if the equation is going to be applied to data outside the sample, for the multicollinearity outside the sample might not exist or might not follow the same pattern that it did inside the sample.

A major disadvantage of the technique is that both portions of the linear combination are forced to have the same coefficient in the re-estimated equation. For example, if $X_{3i} = X_{1i} + X_{2i}$:

$$Y_i = \beta_0 + \beta_3 X_{3i} + \epsilon_i = \beta_0 + \beta_3(X_{1i} + X_{2i}) + \epsilon_i \qquad (8.16)$$

Care must therefore be taken not to include, in a linear combination, variables with dramatically different expected coefficients (such as different expected signs) or dramatically different values (such as different orders of magnitude) without adjusting for these differences by using appropriate constants (ks) in the more general equation $X_3 = k_1X_1 + k_2X_2$. For example, if the two multicollinear variables were GNP and the rate of inflation, then a simple sum might completely swamp the inflation variable (depending on the units of measurement of the variables):

$$X_{3i} = GNP_i + INF_i = 3,250 + 0.08 = 3,250.08 \qquad (8.17)$$

Consider how X_3 changes as GNP or INF change. If GNP doubles, so too does X_3, but if INF doubles, X_3 hardly changes at all. In most linear combinations, then, careful account must be taken of the average size and expected coefficients of the variables used to form the combination. Otherwise, the variables might cancel each other out or swamp one another in magnitude.

To see an example of this, let's form a linear combination of disposable income and liquid assets in the student consumption function and then re-run Equation 8.10 with the linear combination as the explanatory variable. As can be seen from an examination of the original data in Section 8.2.2 or from the regression run in Exercise 5, liquid assets are about ten times the size of disposable income in the sample. To bring the two into balance, disposable income could be multiplied by 10, yielding:

$$X_{3i} = 10(Yd_i) + LA_i \qquad (8.18)$$

The constants in such linear combinations end up being arbitrary, but they can work fairly well. If X_3 is used to replace both explanatory variables in Equation 8.10 and a regression estimated, we obtain:

$$\hat{C}_i = -355.43 + 0.0467X_{3i} \qquad (8.19)$$
$$(0.0073)$$
$$t = \quad 6.362 \qquad \bar{R}^2 = .868$$

Compare this equation with Equations 8.11 and 8.15 above. Notice that once again the deletion of the multicollinearity has significantly raised the t-score of the explanatory variable while having little effect on the overall significance of the equation. Interestingly, the estimated coefficients of Equation 8.19 can be calculated from the previous estimates and the equation of the linear combination. For more on this possibility, see Exercise 5.

The second kind of transformation to consider as a possible remedy for severe multicollinearity is to change the functional form of the equation. Look how the conversion of an equation to first differences might decrease the amount of multicollinearity in the sample. (While we will not discuss conversions to log-linear or other functional forms, the principles involved are quite similar.) A **first difference** is nothing more than the change in a variable from the previous time-period (which we've referred to as "delta" or Δ). That is, we shall define a first difference as:

$$\Delta X_t = X_t - X_{t-1}$$

If an equation (or some of the variables in an equation) is switched from its normal specification to a first difference specification, it is quite likely that the degree of multicollinearity will be significantly reduced for two reasons. First, since multicollinearity is a sample phenomenon, any change in the definitions of the variables in that sample (except a simple linear change) will change the degree of multicollinearity. Second, multicollinearity takes place most frequently (although certainly not exclusively) in time-series data, in which first differences are far less likely to move steadily upward than are the aggregates from which they are calculated. For example, while GNP might grow only five or six percent from year to year, the *change in GNP* (or the first difference) could fluctuate severely. As a result, switching an equation to a first difference specification is likely to decrease the possibility of multicollinearity in a time-series model.

On occasion, the severity of multicollinearity can be diminished by switching to a first difference (or other) format. In other situations, changing the functional form of an equation simply to avoid multicollinearity is not worth the possible theoretical complications. For example, modeling capital stock is not the same as modeling the change in capital stock, which is investment, even though one equation can be derived from the other. If the basic purpose of running the regression were to model first differences, then the model should have been specified that way. Note that one observation will be used up to calculate the first differences, and so the degrees of freedom will fall by one.

8.4.4   Increase the Size of the Sample

Since multicollinearity is a sample phenomenon, perhaps the most honest way to deal with it is to attempt to increase the size of the sample so as to reduce the degree of multicollinearity. While such increases may be impossible when limitations of some sort exist, they are useful alternatives to be considered when they are feasible.

The idea behind increasing the size of the sample is that a larger data set (often requiring new data collection) will allow more accurate estimates than a small one, since the large sample normally will reduce somewhat the variance of the estimated coefficients, diminishing the impact of the multicollinearity even if the degree of multicollinearity remains the same.

For most economic and business applications, however, this solution is not feasible. After all, samples are typically drawn by getting all the available data that seem comparable. As a result, new data are generally impossible or quite expensive to find. Going out and generating new data is much easier in an experimental situation than it is when the samples must be generated by the passage of time.

One way to increase the sample is to pool cross-sectional and time series data. Such a combination of data sources usually consists of the addition of cross-sectional data (typically non-multicollinear) to multicollinear time series data, thus potentially reducing the multicollinearity in the total sample. The major problem with this pooling is in the interpretation and use of estimates generated; unless there is reason to believe that the underlying theoretical model is the same in both settings, the parameter estimates obtained will somehow be joint functions of the true time series model and the true cross-sectional model. In general, such combining of different kinds of data is not recommended as a means of avoiding multicollinearity. In most cases, the unknown interpretation difficulties are worse than the known consequences of the multicollinearity.

8.5 Choosing the Proper Remedy

Of all the possibilities listed, how do you go about making a choice? There is no automatic answer to this question; an adjustment for multicollinearity that might be useful in one equation could be inappropriate to another. As a result, all that this section can accomplish is to illustrate general guidelines to follow when attempting to rid an equation of severe multicollinearity.

8.5.1 An Example of Multicollinearity Left Unadjusted

Our first case provides an example of the idea that multicollinearity is often best left unadjusted. Suppose you work in the marketing department of a hypothetical soft drink company, Mr. T's, and you build a model of the impact on sales of your firm's advertising (which is centered around the slogan, "It Packs a Punch"):

$$\hat{S}_t = 3080 - 75{,}000P_t + 4.23A_t - 1.04B_t \qquad (8.20)$$
$$\phantom{\hat{S}_t = 3080 -} (25{,}000) \quad (1.06) \quad (0.51)$$
$$t = \quad -3.00 \quad 3.99 \quad -2.04$$
$$\bar{R}^2 = \quad .825 \qquad n = \quad 28$$

where S_t = Sales of Mr. T's soft drink in year t
P_t = Average relative price of Mr. T's in year t
A_t = Advertising expenditures for Mr. T's in year t
B_t = Advertising expenditures for Mr. T's main competitor in year t

(Assume that there are no left-out variables. All variables are measured in real dollars; that is, the nominal values are divided, or deflated, by a price index.)

On the face of it, this is a reasonable-looking result. Estimated coefficients are significant in the directions implied by the underlying theory, and both the overall fit and the size of the coefficients seem acceptable. Suppose you now were told that advertising in the soft drink industry was cutthroat in nature and that firms tended to match their main competitor's advertising expenditures. This would lead you to suspect that significant multicollinearity was possible. Further suppose that the simple correlation coefficient between the two advertising variables was over .97:

$$r_{A,B} = .974$$

Such a correlation coefficient is evidence that there is significant multicollinearity in the equation, but there is no reason even to consider doing anything about it, because the coefficients are so powerful that their t-scores remain significant even in the face of severe multicollinearity. Unless multicollinearity causes problems in the equation, it should not be adjusted for. To change the specification might give us better looking results, but the adjustment would be likely to decrease our chances of obtaining the best possible estimates of the true coefficients. While it certainly is lucky that there were no major problems due to multicollinearity in this example, that luck is no reason to try to fix something that isn't broken.

Similarly, remember that when a variable is dropped from an equation, its effect will be absorbed by the other explanatory variables (in the form of specification bias) to the extent that they are correlated with the (now) omitted variable. In the case of multicollinear variables, it is likely that the remaining multicollinear variable(s) will absorb virtually all the bias. This bias may destroy whatever usefulness the estimates had before the variable was dropped. For example, if a variable, say B, was dropped from the Mr. T's equation to fix the multicollinearity, then the following would occur:

$$\hat{S}_t = 2586 - 78{,}000P_t + 0.52A_t \qquad (8.21)$$
$$(24{,}000) \qquad (4.32)$$
$$t = \qquad -3.25 \qquad 0.12$$
$$\bar{R}^2 = .531 \qquad n = 28$$

What's going on here? The Mr. T's advertising coefficient has become less instead of more significant when the multicollinear variable is dropped. To see why, first note that the expected bias on $\hat{\beta}_A$ is negative since the product of the correlation between A and B (positive) and the expected sign of the coefficient of B (negative) is negative:

$$\text{bias} = \beta_B \cdot f(r_{A,B}) = (-) \cdot (+) = - \qquad (8.22)$$

and this negative bias is strong enough to decrease the estimated coefficient of A until it is insignificant even without multicollinearity in the equation. While this problem could have been avoided by using a relative advertising variable (A divided by B, for instance), that formulation would have forced identical absolute coefficients on the two advertising effects. Such identical coefficients will sometimes be theoretically expected or empirically reasonable, but in most cases these kinds of constraints will force bias onto an equation that previously had none.

This example is simplistic, but its results are typical of cases in which equations are adjusted for multicollinearity without regard to the effect that the deletion is going to have. The point here is that it is quite often theoretically or operationally unwise to drop a variable from an equation and that multicollinearity in such cases is best left unadjusted.

8.5.2 A Complete Example of Multicollinearity

Finally, let's work through a more complete example of dealing with significant multicollinearity, a model of the annual demand for fish in the U.S. from 1946 to 1970.[7] Suppose that you decide to try to confirm your idea that the Pope's 1966 decision to allow Catholics to eat meat on (non-Lent) Fridays caused a shift in the demand function for fish (instead of just changing the days of the week when fish was eaten without changing the total amount of fish consumed). Let's say your hypothesized equation was:

$$F_t = f(\overset{-}{PF_t}, \overset{+}{PB_t}, \overset{+}{Yd_t}, \overset{+}{C_t}, \overset{-}{D_t}) \tag{8.23}$$

where: F_t = Average pounds of fish consumed per capita in year t
  PF_t = Price index for fish in year t
  PB_t = Price index for beef in year t
  Yd_t = Real per capita disposable income in year t (in billions of dollars)
  C_t = Number of Catholics in the U.S. in year t (tens of thousands)
  D_t = A dummy variable equal to zero before the Pope's 1966 decision and one afterwards

and that you chose the following functional form:

$$F_t = \beta_0 + \beta_1 PF_t + \beta_2 PB_t + \beta_3 \ln Yd_t + \beta_4 C_t + \beta_5 D_t + \epsilon_t \tag{8.24}$$

A few words about this specification are in order. First, note that the method you have chosen to test your hypothesis is an intercept dummy. Since you've stated that you expect this coefficient to be negative, the null hypothesis should be the "strawman" H_0: $\beta_5 \geq 0$. Second, you've chosen a semilog function to relate disposable income to the quantity of fish consumed; this is consistent with the theory that as income rises, the portion of that extra income devoted to the consumption of fish will decrease. Third, notice that you make no mention of any aggregate supply function for fish; you have perhaps assumed that "fish" is an internationally competitive market in which the U.S. price plays little role (thus there is no simultaneity problem). Leaving other valid criticisms of the model aside, let's investigate the model and the consequences of multicollinearity for it.

After collecting the data (which are in Table 8.1 at the end of this section), you obtain the following OLS estimates:

$$\hat{F}_t = -1.99 - 0.039 PF_t - 0.00077 PB_t + 1.77 \ln Yd_t - 0.0031 C_t - 0.355 D_t$$
$$\quad\quad (0.031) \quad\quad (0.02020) \quad\quad (1.87) \quad\quad (0.0033) \quad (0.353)$$
$$t = \quad 1.27 \quad\quad\quad -0.0384 \quad\quad 0.945 \quad\quad -0.958 \quad -1.01$$
$$\bar{R}^2 = .666 \quad\quad\quad n = 25 \tag{8.25}$$

This result is not encouraging, since you do not have to look at the t-table to know that none of your estimated coefficients is significantly different from zero with 19 degrees of freedom. In addition, three of your coefficients have unexpected signs. Your problems could have been caused, for example, by omitted variables (biasing the coefficients), irrelevant variables (not belonging in the equation), or multicollinearity (a good guess, since this is the topic of the current chapter).

Where do you start? If you have confidence in your literature review and the theoretical work you did before estimating the equation, a good place would be to see if there are any signs of multicollinearity. Sure enough, the $\bar{R}^2$ of .666 seems fairly high for such unanimously low t-scores. Thus the first of our "sufficient but not necessary" characteristics of severe multicollinearity appears to exist.

The second aspect of severe multicollinearity we mentioned has to do with the simple correlation coefficients. Looking at the variables without knowing those statistics, which pairs (or sets) of variables look likely to be significantly correlated? It appears that both per capita disposable income and the number of Catholics are quite likely to be highly correlated in virtually any time-series sample from the United States, and both appear to have been included in the equation to measure buying power. Sure enough, the simple correlation coefficient between C_t and $LnYd_t$ is .946.

It is not unreasonable to think that food prices might move together. Since the prices that we observe are equilibrium prices, supply and demand shocks might affect beef and fish price indices in similar ways. For example, an oil spill that makes fish unmarketable will admittedly raise the price of fish, but that fish price rise will almost surely shift the demand for beef upward, thus increasing the price of beef. Thus it is quite possible for prices of substitutes to tend to move together. As it turns out, the simple correlation coefficient between the two price variables is .958. With multicollinearity this severe between two variables with opposite expected signs, it is no surprise that the two coefficients "switched signs." As the multicollinearity increases, the distribution of the $\hat{\beta}$s widens, and the probability of observing an unexpected sign increases.

Now there appear to be at least two cases of significant multicollinearity in your model. What, if anything, should you do about it? Before going on with this section, go back over Equation 8.25 and review not only the estimates but also what of the underlying theory we have discussed.

The easiest multicollinearity to cope with is between income and the number of Catholics. Independently, either variable is quite likely to be significant because each represents the increase in the buying power of the market over time. Together, however, they ruin each other's chances because of multicollinearity. As a result, one should be dropped as a "redundant" multicollinear variable. Given that the logic behind including the number of Catholics in a per capita fish demand equation is fairly weak, you decide to drop C_t.

At this point, you could decide to rerun the equation without C to see if the low t-scores were in part caused by multicollinearity with C (this turns out to be the case). Indeed, it seems obvious that the two price variables are so theoretically important to the model that neither can be dropped. One alternative would be to create a transformation of the two by dividing one by the other to form a relative price variable:

$$RP_t = PF_t/PB_t$$

Such a variable would make sense only if theory called for keeping both variables in the equation and if the two coefficients could be expected to be close in absolute value but of opposite signs.[8] Choosing to use a relative price variable in effect would be hypothesizing that while consumers might not be sophisticated enough always to consider real prices, they do compare prices of substitutes before making their purchases. Depending on your perception of the underlying theory, you could make a strong case for either approach (that is, dropping C and shifting to real prices or dropping C and replacing both prices with a relative price variable). For the purpose of discussion, suppose you decide to estimate the latter equation:

$$F = f(\overset{-}{RP}, \overset{+}{Yd}, \overset{-}{D})$$ (8.26)

obtaining

$$\hat{F}_t = -5.17 - 1.93RP_t + 2.71 \ln Yd_t + 0.0052D_t$$ (8.27)
$$\quad\quad\quad (1.43) \quad\quad (0.66) \quad\quad (0.2801)$$
$$t = \quad 1.35 \quad\quad 4.13 \quad\quad -0.019$$
$$\bar{R}^2 = .588 \quad\quad\quad\quad n = 25$$

Although these are all questions of judgment, the two changes appear to have worked reasonably well in terms of ridding the equation of much of its severe

Table 8.1 *Data for the Fish/Pope Example*

Year	F	PF	PB	Yd
1946	12.8	56.0	50.1	1606
1947	12.3	64.3	71.3	1513
1948	13.1	74.1	81.0	1567
1949	12.9	74.5	76.2	1547
1950	13.8	73.1	80.3	1646
1951	13.2	83.4	91.0	1657
1952	13.3	81.3	90.2	1678
1953	13.6	78.2	84.2	1726
1954	13.5	78.7	83.7	1714
1955	12.9	77.1	77.1	1795
1956	12.9	77.0	74.5	1839
1957	12.8	78.0	82.8	1844
1958	13.3	83.4	92.2	1831
1959	13.7	84.9	88.8	1881
1960	13.2	85.0	87.2	1883
1961	13.7	86.9	88.3	1909
1962	13.6	90.5	90.1	1969
1963	13.7	90.3	88.7	2015
1964	13.5	88.2	87.3	2126
1965	13.9	90.8	93.9	2239
1966	13.9	96.7	102.6	2335
1967	13.6	100.0	100.0	2403
1968	14.0	101.6	102.3	2486
1969	14.2	107.2	111.4	2534
1970	14.8	118.0	117.6	2610

Source: *Historical Statistics of the U.S., Colonial Times to 1970 Part 1*

multicollinearity. More importantly, once we decide that this specification is good enough, we can now test the hypothesis that was the real reason for the research project. What was the result? If this specification is at all close to the best one, then the null hypothesis of no effect cannot be rejected. For all intents and purposes, it appears that the Pope's decision did not cut down on consumption of fish (the coefficient is quite insignificant).[9]

Finally, notice that someone else might take a completely different approach to alleviating the severe multicollinearity in this sample. There is no obviously correct remedy. Indeed, if you want to be sure that your choice of a specification did not influence your inability to reject the null hypothesis about β_D, you might see how sensitive that conclusion is to an alternative approach towards fixing the multicollinearity. (In such a case, both results would have to be part of the research report.)

8.6   Summary

1. Perfect multicollinearity is the violation of the assumption that no explanatory variable is a perfect linear function of any other explanatory variable. Perfect multicollinearity results in indeterminate estimates of the regression coefficients and infinite standard errors of those estimates.

2. Imperfect multicollinearity, which is what is typically meant when the word "multicollinearity" is used, is a functional relationship between two or more independent variables that is so strong that it can affect the estimation of that equation. Multicollinearity is a sample phenomenon; different samples will result in different degrees of multicollinearity.

3. The major consequence of severe multicollinearity is to increase the variances of the estimated regression coefficients and therefore decrease the calculated t-scores of those coefficients. Multicollinearity causes no bias in the estimated coefficients, and it has little effect on the overall significance of the regression or on the estimates (or variances) of any non-multicollinear explanatory variables.

4. Severe multicollinearity causes difficulty in the identification of the separate effects of the multicollinear variables in a regression equation. In addition, coefficient estimates will become very sensitive to changes in specification in the presence of multicollinearity.

5. The more severe the multicollinearity is (as measured by the simple correlation coefficient between the explanatory variables, for example) the worse the consequences of that multicollinearity are. In addition, multicollinearity exists, to one degree or another, in virtually every data set. The question to be asked in detection is whether severe multicollinearity exists in a particular sample.

6. A useful method for the detection of severe multicollinearity consists of two questions:

a. Is $\bar{R}^2$ high with low individual t-scores?

b. Are the simple correlation coefficients between the explanatory variables high (usually higher in absolute value than the square root of the equation's R^2)?

If the answers to both are yes, then multicollinearity certainly exists, but multicollinearity can also exist even if the answer to one or both questions is no.

7. The four most common remedies for multicollinearity are:

a. Do nothing (and thus avoid specification bias).

b. Drop some multicollinear variables (especially "redundant" ones).

c. Transform the multicollinear variables or the equation.

d. Increase the sample.

8. Quite often, doing nothing is the best remedy for multicollinearity. If the multicollinearity has not decreased t-scores to the point of insignificance, then no remedy should even be considered. Even if the t-scores are insignificant, remedies should be undertaken cautiously, because all impose costs on the estimation that may be greater than the potential benefit of ridding the equation of multicollinearity.

Exercises

(Answers to even-numbered exercises are in Appendix A.)

1. Write out the meaning of each of the following terms without reference to the book (or your notes) and then compare your definition with the version in the text for each:

   a. perfect multicollinearity

   b. severe imperfect multicollinearity

   c. dominant variable

   d. linear combination

   e. first difference

2. Beginning researchers quite often believe that they have multicollinearity when they have accidentally included in their equation two or more explanatory variables that basically serve the same purpose or are in essence measuring the same thing. Which of the following pairs of variables are the most likely to include such a "redundant" variable?

   a. GNP and NNP in a macroeconomic equation of some sort.

   b. the price of refrigerators and the price of washing machines in a durable-goods demand function.

   c. the number of acres harvested and the amount of seed used in an agricultural supply function.

   d. long-term interest rates and the money supply in an investment function.

   e. hits and batting average (the ratio of hits to at bats) in an equation built to explain the number of all-star votes received by a baseball player.

3. A researcher once attempted to estimate an asset-demand equation that included the following three explanatory variables; current wealth W_t, wealth in the previous quarter W_{t-1}, and the change in wealth $\Delta W_t = W_t - W_{t-1}$. What problem did this researcher encounter? What should have been done to solve this problem?

4. In each of the following situations, determine whether the variable involved is a "dominant variable":
   a. "Games lost in year t" in an equation for the number of games won in year t by a baseball team that plays the same number of games each year.
   b. "Number of Woody's restaurants" in a model of the total sales of the entire Woody's chain of restaurants.
   c. "Disposable Income" in an equation for aggregate consumption expenditures.
   d. "Number of tires purchased" in an annual model of the production of automobiles for a "Big Four" auto maker that does not make its own tires.
   e. "Number of acres planted" in an agricultural supply function.

5. The formation of linear combinations is an arbitrary process. The linear combination used between liquid assets and disposable income in Section 8.4.3 ($X_{3i} = 10(Yd_i) + LA_i$) could have been justified in two ways. First, the mean of the liquid assets variable is almost exactly ten times the mean of the disposable income variable. To insure that one does not overwhelm the other, an adjustment by a factor of ten makes sense. Other researchers prefer to regress one of the explanatory variables on the other. In this case, we also obtain evidence that a multiple of ten makes sense:

$$\hat{LA}_t = -2428.6 + 10.786Yd_t$$
$$(0.8125)$$
$$t = \quad 13.274 \qquad \bar{R}^2 = .967$$

Use this same general technique to form linear combinations of the following variables:
   a. Height and Weight in Table 1.1 (assume both are explanatory variables).
   b. P and I from the Woody's data set in Table 3.1.
   c. Y and Yd from Exercise 6.5 (assume both are explanatory Xs).

6. You've been hired by the Dean of Students' Office to help reduce damage done to dorms by rowdy students, and your first step is to build a cross-sectional model of last term's damage to each dorm as a function of the attributes of that dorm:

$$\hat{D}_i = 210 + 733F_i - 0.805S_i + 74.0A_i$$
$$(253) \quad (0.752) \quad (12.4)$$
$$n = 33 \qquad \bar{R}^2 = .84$$

where D_i = The amount of damage (in dollars) done to the ith dorm last term

F_i = The percentage of the *i*th dorm residents who are freshmen
S_i = The number of students who live in the *i*th dorm
A_i = The number of incidents involving alcohol that were reported to the Dean of Students' Office from the *i*th dorm last term (incidents involving alcohol may or may not involve damage to the dorm).

a. Hypothesize signs, calculate t-scores, and test hypotheses for this result (5 percent level).
b. What problems (out of left-out variables, irrelevant variables, and multicollinearity) appear to exist in this equation? Why?
c. Suppose you were now told that the simple correlation coefficient between S_i and A_i was .94; would that change your answer? How?
d. Is it possible that the unexpected sign of $\hat{\beta}_s$ could have been caused by multicollinearity? Why?

7. Suppose your friend was modeling the impact that changes in income had on consumption in a quarterly model and discovered that increases in income do not complete their impact on consumption until at least a year has gone by. As a result, your friend estimated the following model:

$$C_t = \beta_0 + \beta_1 Yd_t + \beta_2 Yd_{t-1} + \beta_3 Yd_{t-2} + \beta_4 Yd_{t-3} + \epsilon_t$$

a. Would this equation be subject to perfect multicollinearity?
b. Would this equation be subject to imperfect multicollinearity?
c. What, if anything, could be done to rid this equation of any multicollinearity it might have? (One answer to this question, the autoregressive approach to distributed lags, will be covered in Section 9.6).

8. You decide to see if the number of votes a baseball player receives in the Most Valuable Player election is more a function of batting average than it is of home runs or runs batted in, and you collect the following data set from the 1983 National League:

Name	Votes	BA	HR	RBI
Murphy	371	.302	36	121
Dawson	249	.299	32	113
Schmidt	223	.255	40	109
Guererro	212	.298	32	103
Raines	97	.298	11	71
Cruz	87	.318	14	92
Thon	78	.286	20	79
Madlock	52	.323	12	68

Just as you are about to run the regression, your friend (trying to get back at you for your comments on Exercise 7) warns you that you probably have multicollinearity in the data set.

a. What should you do about your friend's warning before running the regression?

b. Run the regression implied above: $V = f(\overset{+}{BA}, \overset{+}{HR}, \overset{+}{RBI})$ on the data set above. What signs of multicollinearity are there?

c. What suggestions would you make for another run of this equation? (If you did not get a chance to run the equation yourself, refer to Appendix A before answering this part of the question.) In particular, what would you do about multicollinearity?

9. A full-scale regression model for the total annual gross sales in thousands of dollars of J. C. Quarter's durable goods for the years 1960-1985 produces the following result (all measurements are in real dollars—or billions of real dollars). Standard errors are in parentheses:

$$\widehat{SQ}_t = -7.2 + 200.3PC_t - 150.6PQ_t + 20.6Y_t + 15.8C_t + 201.1N_t$$
$$\qquad\quad (250.1) \qquad (125.6) \qquad (40.1) \quad (10.6) \quad (103.8)$$

where: SQ_t = Sales of durable goods at J. C. Quarter's in year t
   PC_t = Average price of durables in year t at J. C. Quarter's main competition
   PQ_t = Average price of durables at J. C. Quarter's in year t
   Y_t = United States gross national product in year t
   C_t = United States aggregate consumption in year t
   N_t = Number of J. C. Quarter's stores open in year t

a. Hypothesize signs, calculate t-scores, and test hypotheses for this result (5 percent level).

b. What problems (out of omitted variables, irrelevant variables, and multicollinearity) appear to exist in this equation?

c. Suppose you were now told that the $\bar{R}^2$ was .821, that $r_{Y,C}$ was .993, and that $r_{PC,PQ}$ was .813. Would this change your answer to the above question? How?

d. What recommendation would you make for a rerun of this equation with different explanatory variables? Why?

10. A cross-sectional regression was run on a sample of 44 states in an effort to understand Federal defense spending by state (standard errors in parentheses):

$$\hat{S}_i = -148.0 + 0.841C_i - 0.0115P_i - 0.0078E_i$$
$$\qquad\quad (0.027) \qquad (0.1664) \qquad (0.0092)$$

where: S_i = Spending (millions of dollars) on defense in the ith state in 1982
   C_i = Contracts (millions of dollars) awarded in the ith state in 1982 (contracts are often for many years of service)
   P_i = Payroll (millions of dollars) for workers in defense-oriented industries in the ith state in 1982

E_i = Number of civilians employed in defense-oriented industries in the ith state in 1982.

a. Hypothesize signs, calculate t-scores, and test hypotheses for this result (5 percent level).

b. What problems (out of omitted variables, irrelevant variables, and multicollinearity) appear to exist in this equation?

c. Suppose you were not told that the $\bar{R}^2$ was .981, that $r_{P,E}$ was .964, and that $r_{S,C}$ was .990. Would this change your answer to the above question? How?

d. What recommendation would you make for a rerun of this equation with different explanatory variables? Why?

[1.] The word *collinearity* describes a linear correlation between two independent variables, and *multicollinearity* indicates that more than two independent variables are involved. In common usage, multicollinearity is used to apply to both cases, and so we will only use that term in this text even though many of the examples and techniques discussed relate, strictly speaking, to collinearity.

[2.] Most OLS estimation programs will print out an error message when faced with perfect multicollinearity rather than fruitlessly attempt to calculate something indeterminate. A few computer programs contain rounding errors that will produce estimates (admittedly highly unreliable estimates) in the face of perfect multicollinearity, but these programs are in the minority. In such circumstances, the standard errors would not be infinite, they would merely be very large, and the resulting t-scores would still be quite low.

[3.] Even though the variances are larger with multicollinearity than they are without it, OLS is still BLUE when multicollinearity exists. That is, no other linear unbiased estimation technique can get lower variances than ordinary least squares even in the presence of multicollinearity. Thus, while the effect of multicollinearity is to increase the variances of the estimated coefficients, OLS still has the property of minimum variance (these "minimum variances" are just fairly large).

[4.] These unexpected signs generally occur because the distribution of the $\hat{\beta}$s with multicollinearity is wider than without it, increasing the chance that a particular observed $\hat{\beta}$ will be on the other side of zero (have an unexpected sign) from the true β. More specifically, particular combinations of multicollinear variables can make such unexpected signs occur quite frequently. For instance, if two independent variables both have positive true coefficients and positive simple correlation coefficients with Y in the observed sample, and if the simple correlation coefficient between the independent variables in the sample is higher than either of the two simple correlation coefficients between Y and the Xs, then one of the two slope coefficients is virtually assured of having an unexpected sign.

[5.] See D. E. Farrar and R. R. Glauber, "Multicollinearity in Regression Analysis: The Problem Revisited." *Review of Economics and Statistics,* 1967, pp. 92-107.

[6.] The *Farrar-Glauber Test* is perhaps the best known of the formal tests for multicollinearity. It actually consists of three tests of the simple and partial correlation coefficients of a data set:
1. a Chi-square test for the general presence of multicollinearity.
2. an F-test to find the multicollinear explanatory variables.
3. a t-test to find the exact pattern of the multicollinearity.
In each part, a test statistic is calculated, and if the calculated statistic exceeds its critical value, then the null hypothesis of no multicollinearity can be rejected for the particular equation or variable being tested. Researchers who expect multicollinearity to be an important problem, and for whom reasonable remedies appear to exist, are encouraged to consider using the Farrr-Glauber test. For more, see Farrar and Glauber, cited in note 5 above.

[7.] The data used in this study were obtained from *Historical Statistics of the U.S., Colonial Times to 1970 Part 1* (Washington, D.C.: U.S. Bureau of the Census, 1975).

[8.] To see why opposite signs are required, note that an increase in PF will increase RP while an increase in PB will decrease it. Unless PF and PB are hypothesized to have opposite effects on the dependent variable, this relative price variable will not work at all. To test your understanding of this point, attempt to figure out the expected sign of the coefficient of RP in this equation before going on with this example. Note, by the way, that a relative price ratio like RP is a real variable even if PF and PB are not.

[9.]This is in contrast with the findings of the original empirical work on the issue, Frederick Bell's "The Pope and the Price of Fish," *American Economic Review,* Dec. 1968, pp. 1346-1350. Bell built monthly models of the price of seven different species of fish and determined that the Pope's decision had a significant negative impact on the demand for fish in New England in the first nine months after the decision. Since our example was purposely misspecified to cause multicollinearity and then respecified in part to allow an example of the use of a relative price variable, Equation 8.27 should not be considered to refute Bell's result. It is interesting, however, that none of the specifications considered in constructing this example included a significantly negative coefficient of the dummy variable.

9

Serial Correlation

In the next two chapters, we will investigate the final component of the specification of a regression equation—choosing the correct form of the stochastic error term. Our first topic, serial correlation, is the violation of the classical assumption that different observations of the error term are independent of each other. Serial correlation, also called autocorrelation, can exist in any research study in which the order of the observations has some meaning, and it therefore occurs most frequently in time series data sets. In essence, serial correlation implies that the error term from one time period depends in some systematic way on error terms from other time periods. Since time series data are used in many applications of econometrics, it is important to understand serial correlation and its consequences for OLS estimators.

The approach of this chapter to the problem of serial correlation will be similar to that used in the previous chapter to study multicollinearity. We will attempt to answer the same four questions:

1. What is the nature of the problem?

2. What are the consequences of the problem?

3. How is the problem diagnosed?

4. What remedies for the problem are available?

9.1 Pure vs. Impure Serial Correlation

The correlation of observations of the error term with others over time is what gives rise to the name serial correlation. This section gives a fuller description of the nature of serial correlation and distinguishes between two forms of the disease, "pure" and "impure" serial correlation.

9.1.1 Pure Serial Correlation

Pure serial correlation occurs when Classical Assumption IV, which assumes independent error terms, is violated in a correctly specified equation. Recall that Assumption IV states that:

$$\text{IV.}\quad E(\epsilon_i \cdot \epsilon_j) = 0 \quad (i \neq j)$$

If the expected value of the multiple of any two error terms is not equal to zero, then the error terms are said to be serially correlated. When econometricians use the term serial correlation without any modifier, they are referring to pure serial correlation.

The most common kind of serial correlation is **first order serial correlation** in which this time's error term is a function of the previous time period's error term:

$$\epsilon_t = \rho\epsilon_{t-1} + u_t \tag{9.1}$$

where: ϵ is the error term of the equation in question,
ρ is the parameter depicting the functional relationship between the error terms, and
u is a classical (non-serially correlated) error term

The functional form in Equation 9.1 is called a first-order Markov scheme, and the new symbol, ρ (rho, pronounced "row"), is called the **first-order autocorrelation coefficient.** For this kind of serial correlation, all that is needed is for the level of one error term to affect directly the level of the next error term.

The magnitude of ρ indicates the strength of the serial correlation in an equation. If ρ is zero, then there is no serial correlation (because ϵ would equal u, a classical error term). As ρ approaches 1 in absolute value, the value of the previous error term becomes more important in determining the current value of ϵ_t, and a high degree of serial correlation exists. For ρ to be greater than one in absolute value is unreasonable because it implies that the error term has a tendency to continually increase in absolute value over time ("explode"). As a result of the above, we can state that:

$$-1 < \rho < +1$$

The sign of ρ indicates the nature of the serial correlation in an equation. A positive value for ρ implies that the error term tends to have the same sign as the error term from the previous time period. Such a tendency means that if ϵ_t happens by chance to take on a large value in one time period, subsequent error terms would tend to retain a portion of this original large value and would have the same sign as the original error term. For example, in time series models, a large external shock to an economy in one period may linger on for several time periods. If this occurs now and then, the error term will tend to be positive for a number of observations, then negative for several more, and then back again. This is called **positive serial correlation.** Figure 9.1 shows two different examples.

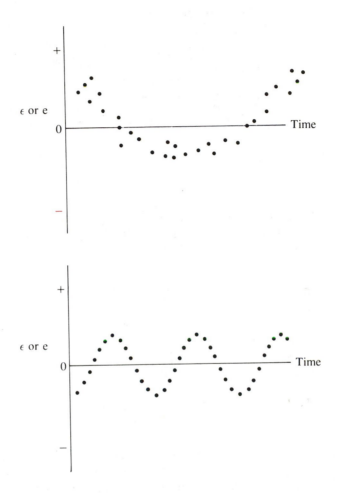

FIGURE 9.1 *Positive Serial Correlation*
With positive first-order serial correlation, this time's observation of the error term tends to have the same sign as last time's observation of the error term. An example of positive serial correlation would be external shocks to an economy that take more than one time period to completely work through the system.

The error terms plotted in Figure 9.1 are arranged in chronological order, with the first observation being the first period for which data are available, the second being the second, and so on. To see the difference between error terms with and without positive serial correlation, compare the patterns in Figure 9.1 with the depiction of no serial correlation ($\rho = 0$) in Figure 9.2.

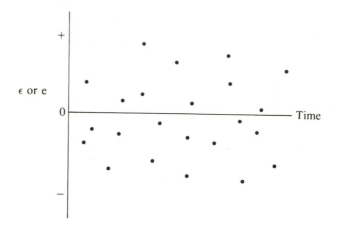

FIGURE 9.2 *No Serial Correlation*
With no serial correlation, different observations of the error term are completely independent of each other. Such error terms would likely conform to Classical Assumption IV.

A negative value of ρ implies that the error term has a tendency to switch signs from negative to positive and back again in consecutive observations. This is called **negative serial correlation** and implies that there is some sort of cycle of error terms (like a pendulum) behind the drawing of stochastic disturbances. Figure 9.3 shows two different examples of negative serial correlation. For example, negative serial correlation might exist in the error terms of a semi-annual equation for the demand for some seasonal item (like Christmas lights) that had no seasonal dummy. In most time series applications, however, negative pure serial correlation is much less likely than positive pure serial correlation. As a result, most econometricians analyzing pure serial correlation concern themselves primarily with positive serial correlation.

Serial correlation can take on many forms other than first-order serial correlation. For example, in a quarterly model, this quarter's error term may be functionally related to the error term from the same quarter in the previous year. This is called seasonally based serial correlation:

$$\epsilon_t = \rho \epsilon_{t-4} + u_t$$

Similarly, it is possible that the error term in an equation might be a function of more than one previous error term:

$$\epsilon_t = \rho_1 \epsilon_{t-1} + \rho_2 \epsilon_{t-2} + u_t$$

Such a formulation is called second-order serial correlation. Higher-order expressions are similarly formed, but the justifications for assuming these higher-order forms are usually much weaker than the justification for the first-order form, which itself is not always all that strong.

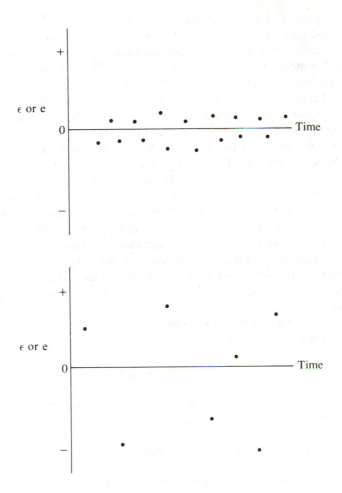

FIGURE 9.3 *Negative Serial Correlation*
With negative first-order serial correlation, this time's observation of the error term tends
to have the opposite sign from last time's observation of the error term. In most time series
applications, negative serial correlation is much less likely than positive serial correlation.

9.1.2 Impure Serial Correlation

By **impure serial correlation** we mean serial correlation that is caused by a specification error such as an omitted variable or an incorrect functional form. While
pure serial correlation is caused by the underlying distribution of the error term
of the true specification of an equation (which cannot be changed by the
researcher), impure serial correlation is caused by a specification error that often
can be corrected.

How is it possible for a specification error to cause serial correlation? Recall that the error term can be thought of as the effect of omitted variables, non-linearities, measurement errors and pure stochastic disturbances on the dependent variable. This means that if we omit a relevant variable or use the wrong functional form, then the portion of that omitted effect that cannot be represented by the included explanatory variables must be absorbed by the error term. The error term for an incorrectly specified equation thus includes a portion of the effect of any omitted variables and/or a portion of the effect of the difference between the proper functional form and the one chosen by the researcher. This new error term might be serially correlated even if the true one is not. If this is the case, the serial correlation has been caused by the researcher's choice of a specification and not by the pure error term associated with the correct specification.

As we shall see in Section 9.4, the proper remedy for serial correlation depends upon whether the serial correlation is likely to be pure or impure. Not surprisingly, the best remedy for impure serial correlation usually is to attempt to find the omitted variable (or at least a good proxy) or the correct functional form for the equation. As a result, most econometricians try to make sure they have the best specification possible before they spend too much time worrying about pure serial correlation.

To see how a left-out variable can cause the error terms to be serially correlated, suppose that the true equation is:

$$Y_t = \beta_0 + \beta_1 X_{1t} + \beta_2 X_{2t} + \epsilon_t \tag{9.2}$$

Where ϵ_t is a classical error term. As shown in Section 6.1, if X_2 is accidentally omitted from the equation (or if data for X_2 are unavailable), then:

$$Y_t = \beta_0 + \beta_1 X_{1t} + \epsilon_t^* \quad \text{where } \epsilon_t^* = \beta_2 X_{2t} + \epsilon_t \tag{9.3}$$

Thus the error term being used in the omitted variable case is not the classical error term ϵ. Instead, it is also a function of one of the independent variables, X_2. As a result, the new error term, ϵ^*, can be serially correlated even if the true error term ϵ is not. In particular, the new error term ϵ^* will tend to be serially correlated when:

1. X_2 itself is serially correlated (this is quite likely in a time series).

2. The size of ϵ is small compared to the size[1] of $\beta_2 X_2$.

These tendencies hold even if there are a number of included and/or omitted variables.

An example of how an omitted variable might cause serial correlation in the error term of the incorrectly specified equation involves the the fish-demand equation of Section 8.5:

$$F_t = \beta_0 + \beta_1 RP_t + \beta_2 \ln Yd_t + \beta_3 D_t + \epsilon_t \tag{9.4}$$

where F_t is per capita pounds of fish consumed in year t, RP_t is the price of fish relative to beef in year t, Yd_t is real per capita disposable income in year t, D_t is a dummy variable equal to zero in years before the Pope's decision and one thereafter, and ϵ_t is a classical (non-serially correlated) error term. Assume that Equation 9.4 is the "correct" specification. What would happen to this equation if disposable income, Yd, were omitted?

$$F_t = \beta_0 + \beta_1 RP_t + \beta_3 D_t + \epsilon_t^* \qquad (9.5)$$

The most obvious effect would be that the estimated coefficients of RP and D would be biased depending on the correlation of RP and D with Yd. A secondary effect would be that the error term would now include a large portion of the left-out effect of disposable income on the consumption of fish; that is, ϵ_t^* would equal $\epsilon_t + \beta_2 \ln Yd_t$. It is reasonable to expect that disposable income (and therefore its log) might follow a fairly serially correlated pattern:

$$\ln Yd_t = f(\ln Yd_{t-1}) + u_t \qquad (9.6)$$

Why is this likely? Observe Figure 9.4, which plots the log of U.S. disposable income over time. Note that the continual rise of disposable income over time makes it (and its log) act in a serially correlated or *autoregressive* manner. But if disposable income is serially correlated (and if its impact is not small relative to ϵ) then ϵ^* is likely to also be serially correlated, which can be expressed as:

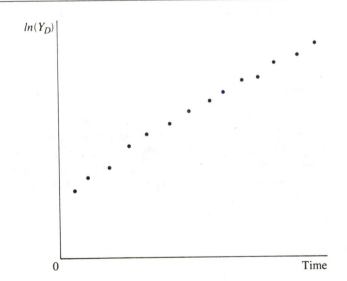

FIGURE 9.4 *U.S. Disposable Income as a Function of Time*
U.S. disposable income (and most other national aggregates) tends to increase steadily over time. As a result, such variables are serially correlated (or autocorrelated), and the omission of such a variable from an equation could potentially introduce impure serial correlation into the residuals of that equation.

$$\epsilon_t^* = \rho\epsilon_{t-1}^* + u_t$$

where ρ is the coefficient of serial correlation and u is a classical error term. This example has shown that it is indeed possible for a left-out variable to introduce "impure" serial correlation into an equation. For more on this example, see Exercise 10.

Another common kind of impure serial correlation is that caused by an incorrect functional form. In this kind of situation, the choice of the wrong functional form can cause the error terms to be serially correlated. Let's suppose that the true equation is log-linear in nature:

$$LnY_t = \beta_0 + \beta_1 lnX_{1t} + \epsilon_t \tag{9.7}$$

but that instead a linear regression is run:

$$Y_t = \alpha_0 + \alpha_1 X_{1t} + \epsilon_t^* \tag{9.8}$$

The new error term ϵ^* is now a function of the true error term ϵ and of the differences between the linear and the log-linear functional forms. As can be seen in Figure 9.5, these differences often follow fairly autoregressive patterns. That is, positive differences tend to be followed by positive differences, and negative differences tend to be followed by negative differences. As a result, using a linear functional form when a nonlinear one is appropriate will usually result in positive impure serial correlation. Unfortunately, when the observations are ordered according to time instead of according to the size of X (when such orders differ), then it becomes very difficult to detect this kind of impure serial correlation.

9.2   The Consequences of Serial Correlation

The consequences of serial correlation are quite different in nature from the consequences of the problems discussed so far in this text. Omitted variables, irrelevant variables, and multicollinearity all have fairly recognizable external symptoms. Each problem changes the estimated coefficients and standard errors in a particular way, and an examination of these changes (and the underlying theory) often provides enough information for the problem to be detected. As we shall see, serial correlation is more likely to have internal symptoms; it affects the estimated equation in a way that is not easily observable from an examination of just the results themselves.

There are three major consequences of serial correlation:

1. Serial correlation does not cause bias in the coefficient estimates.

2. Serial correlation increases the variances of the $\hat{\beta}$ distributions.[2]

3. Serial correlation causes OLS to underestimate the variances (and standard errors) of the coefficients.

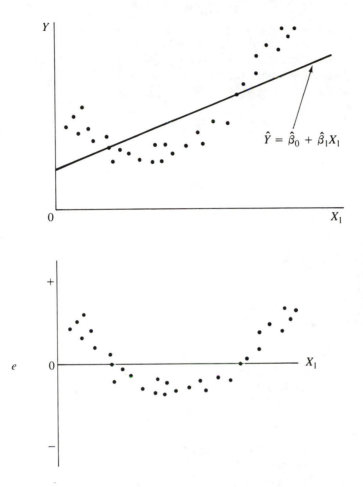

FIGURE 9.5 *Incorrect Functional Form as a Source of Impure Serial Correlation*
The use of an incorrect functional form tends to group positive and negative residuals
together, causing positive impure serial correlation.

Let's now go on to explain these consequences in more detail and to then work
through a hypothetical example of how serially correlated errors affect the estimation of an equation. In the process we will focus mainly on positive pure
first-order serial correlation because it is the kind of autocorrelation most frequently assumed in economic analysis.

9.2.1   An Overview of the Consequences of Serial Correlation

The existence of serial correlation in the error terms of an equation violates the
Classical Assumption IV, and the estimation of the equation with OLS will potentially have at least three consequences.

1. Serial correlation does not cause bias in the coefficient estimates.

Recall that the most important property of the OLS estimation technique is that it is minimum variance for the class of linear unbiased estimators. If the errors are serially correlated, one of the assumptions of the Gauss-Markov Theorem is violated, but this violation does not cause the coefficient estimates to be biased. Suppose that the error term of the following equation:

$$Y_t = \beta_0 + \beta_1 X_{1t} + \beta_2 X_{2t} + \epsilon_t \tag{9.9}$$

is known to have first order serial correlation:

$$\epsilon_t = \rho\epsilon_{t-1} + u_t \tag{9.10}$$

where u_t is a classical (non-serially correlated) error term.

If Equation 9.9 is correctly specified and is estimated with Ordinary Least Squares, then the estimates of the coefficients of the equation obtained from the OLS estimation will be unbiased. That is,

$$E(\hat{\beta}_1) = \beta_1 \quad \text{and} \quad E(\hat{\beta}_2) = \beta_2$$

Serial correlation introduces no bias into the estimation procedure. This conclusion does not depend on whether the serial correlation is positive or negative or first-order. If the serial correlation is impure, however, bias may be introduced by the use of an incorrect specification.

This lack of bias does not necessarily mean that the OLS estimates of the coefficients of a serially correlated equation will be close to the true coefficient values; the single estimate observed in practice can come from a wide range of possible values. In addition, the standard errors of these estimates will typically be increased by the serial correlation. This increase will raise the probability that a $\hat{\beta}$ will differ significantly from the true β value. What unbiased means in this case is that the distribution of the $\hat{\beta}$s is still centered around the true β.

2. Serial correlation increases the variances of the $\hat{\beta}$ distributions.

While the violation of Classical Assumption IV causes no bias, it does affect the main conclusion of the Gauss-Markov Theorem, that of minimum variance. If the error terms are serially correlated, then OLS no longer provides minimum variance estimates of the coefficients.

The serially correlated error terms cause the dependent variable to fluctuate in a way that the OLS estimation procedure attributes to the independent variables. Thus OLS is more likely to mis-estimate the true β in the face of serial correlation. On balance, the $\hat{\beta}$s are still unbiased, because overestimates are just as likely as underestimates; however, these errors increase the variance of the distribution of the estimates, increasing the amount that any given estimate is likely to differ from the true β. Indeed, it can be shown that if the error terms are distributed as in Equation 9.10, then the variance of the $\hat{\beta}$s is a function of ρ. The larger the ρ, the larger the variance of the $\hat{\beta}$s.

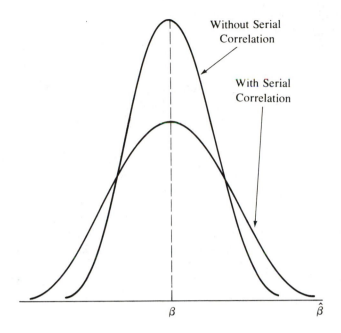

FIGURE 9.6 *Distribution of $\hat{\beta}$s with and without Serial Correlation*
The distribution of $\hat{\beta}$s from a serially correlated equation is centered around the true β, but it is often much wider than the distribution from an equation without serial correlation because serial correlation increases the variances of the $\hat{\beta}$ distributions. Unfortunately, OLS underestimates these variances, masking this effect.

The effect of serial correlation on the distribution of the coefficient estimates is shown in Figure 9.6, which shows that the distribution of $\hat{\beta}$s from a serially correlated equation is centered around the true β but is much wider than the distribution from an equation without serial correlation.

3. Serial correlation causes OLS to underestimate the variances (and standard errors) of the coefficients.

If serial correlation increases the variances (and also the standard deviations) of the $\hat{\beta}$s, then one might guess that the OLS SE($\hat{\beta}$)s would also increase, but this is not usually the case. Instead, these SE($\hat{\beta}$)s tend to be too low. As a result, serial correlation increases the standard deviations of the estimated coefficients, but it does so in a way that is masked by the OLS estimates.

OLS tends to underestimate the standard errors of the coefficients of serially correlated equations, because serial correlation usually results in a pattern of observations that allows a better fit than the actual non-serially correlated observations would justify. This better fit results in underestimates not only of the standard errors of the $\hat{\beta}$s but also of the standard error of the residuals, so neither the t-statistic nor the F-statistic can be relied on in the face of uncorrected serial correlation.

In particular, the tendency of OLS to underestimate the $SE(\hat{\beta})$s will cause it to overestimate the t-statistics of the estimated coefficients since:

$$t = (\hat{\beta} - \beta_{H_0})/SE(\hat{\beta}) \tag{9.11}$$

If a too low $SE(\hat{\beta})$ causes a high t-score for a particular coefficient, then it becomes more likely that we will reject a null hypothesis ($\beta = 0$) when it is true. In a sense, then, OLS misleads the researcher about the significance of a particular result. Serial correlation not only increases the standard deviations but also causes mistaken conclusions by making it difficult for OLS to capture this increase.

9.2.2   An Example of the Consequences of Serial Correlation

Error terms can never be observed, so one cannot examine an existing "real world" data set and be sure what kind of serial correlation, if any, exists. Examples of serial correlation therefore are always clouded by lack of knowledge about the true degree of serial correlation in the error terms. Let's look at a hypothetical example of serial correlation and its effects on OLS estimates. After we have explored the detection and correction of serial correlation, we will be better able to deal with real world situations.

Suppose you are studying the relationship between the real interest rate and the budget deficit. You read the literature on the topic, finding many theoretical articles mostly in favor (at least until recently) of such a link but finding no empirical studies that show a direct, significant, positive relationship between the deficit and real interest rates in the United States.[3]

After some mainly Keynesian consideration, you decide to specify the following equation:

$$\overset{+ \quad -}{r_t = f(D_t, M_t) = \beta_0 + \beta_D D_t + \beta_M M_t + \epsilon_t} \tag{9.12}$$

where: r_t = the short-term real interest rate in year t
D_t = the budget deficit in year t (percent of GNP)
M_t = the nominal money growth rate in year t
ϵ_t = a classical error term

You then estimate Equation 9.12 on annual U.S. data from 1960 through 1984:

$$\hat{r}_t = 0.050 + 0.008D_t - 0.002M_t \tag{9.13}$$
$$(0.002) \quad (0.001)$$
$$t = \quad 4.00 \quad\quad -2.00 \quad\quad \bar{R}^2 = .60$$

You are excited because it appears that you have shown that the deficit is a significant positive factor in the determination of short-term real interest rates. You worry, however, that serial correlation might invalidate your results. Your concern is in part due to the possibility that many of the involved relationships might take years to fully work through the macroeconomy. This would mean that shocks to the system would work their way through slowly, causing positive first-order serial correlation. In addition, it seems likely that any omitted variables (of which there could be many in such a simplistic equation) in a time series would have some "autocorrelated" pattern over time, causing impure serial correlation.

Since your concern is with the estimated coefficient and standard error of the deficit variable, you decide to investigate what your results (with respect to the D variable only) would have looked like if serial correlation had been present in your equation:

A. *With no serial correlation:*

$\hat{\beta}_D$ = 0.008

$SE(\hat{\beta}_D)$ = 0.002

t-score = 4.00

With no serial correlation, valid inferences about the statistical significance of $\hat{\beta}$ can be drawn from Equation 9.13's t-scores.

B. *With serial correlation but a correct estimate of the standard error:*

$\hat{\beta}_D$ = 0.008

$SE(\hat{\beta}_D)$ = 0.006

t-score = 1.33

With serial correlation, the standard deviation increases, and a correct estimate of it would decrease the t-score. This is the result that would be printed out if there were a computer program capable of estimating "correct" $SE(\hat{\beta})$s and t-scores.

C. *With serial correlation and the OLS underestimate of the standard error:*

$\hat{\beta}_D$ = 0.008

$SE(\hat{\beta}_D)$ = 0.003

t-score = 2.66

OLS will underestimate the standard error, giving an unrealistically high t-score. This is the result that will actually be printed out by the OLS computer program. It masks what should be a decreased t-score.

In the real world, you would never see results A or B, only result C; in this hypothetical example, however, we have been able to do what can never be done in an actual regression. We have separated the increase in the standard deviation due to serial correlation from the simultaneous underestimate of that standard deviation by OLS. As a result, we can see that the OLS result (t = 2.66) is not a good indication of the actual significance of a particular coefficient in the face of serial correlation (t = 1.33). In order to decide what to do, it is clear that we need to be able to test for the existence of serial correlation.

9.3   The Durbin-Watson d Test

The test for serial correlation that is most widely used is the Durbin-Watson d test.

9.3.1 The Durbin-Watson d Statistic

The **Durbin-Watson d statistic**[4] is used to determine if there is first-order serial correlation in the error terms of an equation by examining the *residuals* of a particular estimation of that equation. It is important to use the Durbin-Watson d statistic only when the assumptions that underlie its derivation are met:

1. The regression model includes an intercept term.

2. The serial correlation is first-order in nature:

$$\epsilon_t = \rho\epsilon_{t-1} + u_t$$

   where ρ is the coefficient of serial correlation and u is a classical (non-serially correlated) error term.

3. The regression model does not include a lagged dependent variable as an independent variable.[5]

The equation for the *Durbin-Watson d statistic* for T observations is:

$$d = \sum_{2}^{T}(e_t - e_{t-1})^2 / \sum_{1}^{T}e_t^2 \qquad (9.14)$$

where the e_ts are the OLS residuals.[6] Note that the numerator has one fewer observation than the denominator because an observation must be used to calculate e_{t-1}. The Durbin-Watson d statistic equals zero if there is extreme positive serial correlation, two if there is no serial correlation, and four if there is extreme negative serial correlation. To see this, put appropriate residual values into Equation 9.14 for these cases:

1. Extreme Positive Serial Correlation: $d \approx 0$

   In this case, $e_t = e_{t-1}$, so $(e_t - e_{t-1}) \approx 0$ and $d \approx 0$.

2. Extreme Negative Serial Correlation: $d \approx 4$

   In this case, $e_t = -e_{t-1}$, and $(e_t - e_{t-1}) = (2e_t)$. Substituting into Equation 9.14, we obtain $d = \Sigma(2e_t)^2/\Sigma(e_t)^2$ and $d \approx 4$.

3. No Serial Correlation: $d \approx 2$

   When there is no serial correlation, the mean of the distribution is equal to two, since d is symmetrically distributed between 0 and 4.[7] That is, if there is no serial correlation, $d \approx 2$.

9.3.2 Using the Durbin-Watson Test

The techniques required by the Durbin-Watson d test are unusual in two respects. First, econometricians almost never test the one-sided null hypothesis that there is negative serial correlation in the residuals, because negative serial correlation, as mentioned above, is quite difficult to theoretically explain in economic or business analysis. Its existence means that impure serial correlation probably has been caused by some error of specification.

The second reason that the techniques are unusual is that the Durbin-Watson test is sometimes inconclusive. While previously explained decision rules have always had only acceptance regions and rejection regions, the Durbin-Watson test has a third possibility, called the inconclusive region. We shall discuss what to do when the test is inconclusive in Section 9.4.

With these exceptions, the use of the Durbin-Watson d test is quite similar to the use of the *t*- or *F*-tests. In order to test for positive serial correlation, the following steps are required:

1. Obtain the OLS residuals from the equation to be tested and calculate the d statistic by using Equation 9.14.

2. Determine the sample size and the number of explanatory variables and then consult Statistical Tables B-4, B-5, or B-6 in Appendix B to find the upper critical d value, d_U, and the lower critical d value, d_L, respectively. Instructions for the use of that table are also in the appendix.

3. Given the null hypothesis of no positive serial correlation and a one-sided alternative hypothesis:

$$H_0: \rho \leq 0 \quad \text{(no positive serial correlation)}$$
$$H_A: \rho > 0 \quad \text{(positive serial correlation)}$$

the appropriate decision rule is:

$$
\begin{array}{ll}
\text{if } d < d_L & \text{Reject } H_0 \\
\text{if } d > d_U & \text{Do Not Reject } H_0 \\
\text{if } d_L \leq d \leq d_U & \text{Inconclusive}
\end{array}
$$

In some circumstances, a two-sided d test will be appropriate. In such a case, steps 1 and 2 above are still used, but step 3 is now:

3A. Given the null hypothesis of no serial correlation and a two-sided alternative hypothesis:

$$H_0: \rho = 0 \quad \text{(no serial correlation)}$$
$$H_A: \rho \neq 0 \quad \text{(serial correlation)}$$

the appropriate decision rule is:

$$
\begin{array}{ll}
\text{if } d < d_L & \text{Reject } H_0 \\
\text{if } d > 4 - d_L & \text{Reject } H_0 \\
\text{if } 4 - d_U > d > d_U & \text{Do Not Reject } H_0 \\
\text{otherwise} & \text{Inconclusive}
\end{array}
$$

Figure 9.7 presents a graphic illustration of the rejection, acceptance, and inconclusive regions for a two-sided hypothesis of no serial correlation. A graphical

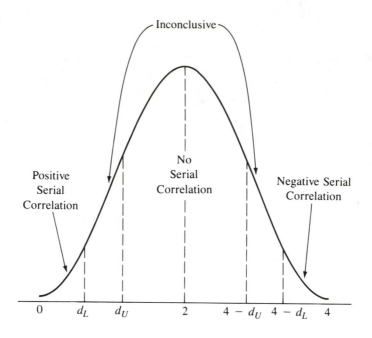

Inconclusive

Positive
Serial
Correlation

No
Serial
Correlation

Negative Serial
Correlation

$0 \quad d_L \quad d_U \quad 2 \quad 4 - d_U \quad 4 - d_L \quad 4$

FIGURE 9.7 *A Two-Sided Durbin-Watson d Test*
The Durbin-Watson d statistic is symmetrically distributed around its mean of 2. In a two-sided test, the farther that the observed d is from 2, the more likely is serial correlation. Note the inconclusive region between the upper and lower critical values of d.

illustration of these regions for one-sided hypotheses is given in the example that follows.

9.3.3 Examples of the Use of the Durbin-Watson d Statistic

Let's work through some applications of the Durbin-Watson test. First, turn to Statistical Tables B-4, B-5, and B-6. Note that the upper and lower critical d values (d_U and d_L) depend on the number of explanatory variables (do not count the constant term), the sample size, and the level of significance of the test. Only a limited set of critical values of d_L and d_U have been constructed; at least 15 observations are required, and values have not been constructed for more than 5 independent variables. Critical values for more than 5 independent variables can usually be approximated by extrapolating from the table data.

Now set up a one-sided 95 percent confidence test for a regression with three explanatory variables and 25 observations. As can be seen from the 5 percent table (B-4), the critical d values are $d_L = 1.12$ and $d_U = 1.66$. As a result, if the hypotheses are:

$H_0: \rho \leq 0$ (no positive serial correlation)
$H_A: \rho > 0$ (positive serial correlation)

the appropriate decision rule is:

if d < 1.12   Reject H_0
if d > 1.66   Do Not Reject H_0
if 1.12 ≤ d ≤ 1.66   Inconclusive

A computed d statistic of 1.78, for example, would indicate that there was no evidence of positive serial correlation, a value of 1.28 would be inconclusive, and a value of 0.60 would imply positive serial correlation. Figure 9.8 provides a graph of the acceptance, rejection, and inconclusive regions for this example.

For a more familiar example, we return to the chicken demand model of Equation 6.5. As can be confirmed with the data provided in Exercise 6.5, the Durbin-Watson

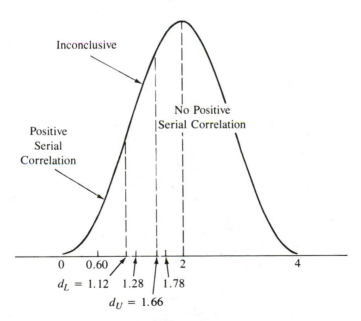

95% Confidence
$k' = 3$ (Explanatory Variables)
$n = 25$ (Observations)
$d_L = 1.12$
$d_U = 1.66$

Inconclusive

No Positive
Serial Correlation

Positive
Serial
Correlation

0   0.60   2   4
$d_L = 1.12$ 1.28 | 1.78
$d_U = 1.66$

FIGURE 9.8 *An Example of a One-Sided Durbin-Watson d Test*
In a one-sided Durbin-Watson test for positive serial correlation, only values of d significantly below 2 cause the null hypothesis of no positive serial correlation to be rejected. In this example, a d of 1.78 would indicate no positive serial correlation, a d of 0.60 would indicate positive serial correlation, and a d of 1.28 would be inconclusive.

statistic from Equation 6.5 is 1.16. Is that cause to be concerned about serial correlation? What would be the result of a one-sided 95 percent test of the null hypothesis of no positive serial correlation? Our first step would be to consult Statistical Table B-4. In that table, with k' (the number of explanatory variables, K) equal to 3 and n (the number of observations) equal to 29, we would find the critical d values $d_L = 1.20$ and $d_U = 1.65$.

The decision rule would thus be:

$$\text{if } d < 1.20 \quad \text{Reject } H_0$$
$$\text{if } d > 1.65 \quad \text{Do Not Reject } H_0$$
$$\text{if } 1.20 \leq d \leq 1.65 \quad \text{Inconclusive}$$

Since 1.16 is less than the critical lower limit of the d statistic, we would reject the null hypothesis of no positive serial correlation, and we would have to decide how to cope with that serial correlation.

9.4   Generalized Least Squares

Suppose that the Durbin-Watson d statistic detects serial correlation in the residuals of your equation. Is there a remedy? Some students suggest reordering the observations of Y and the Xs to avoid serial correlation. That is, if this time's error term appears to be affected by last time's error term, why not reorder the data randomly to get rid of the problem? The answer is that the reordering of the data does not get rid of the serial correlation; it just makes the problem harder to detect. If $\epsilon_2 = f(\epsilon_1)$ and we reorder the data, then the error terms are still related to each other, but they now no longer follow each other, and it becomes almost impossible to discover the serial correlation. Interestingly, reordering the data changes the Durbin-Watson d statistic but does not change the estimates of the coefficients or their standard errors at all.[8]

Instead, the place to start in correcting a serial correlation problem is to look carefully at the specification of the equation for possible errors that might be causing impure serial correlation. Is the functional form correct? Are you sure that there are no omitted variables? In particular, are there specification errors that might have some pattern over time that could have introduced impure serial correlation into the residuals? Only after the specification of the equation has been carefully reviewed should the possibility of an adjustment for pure serial correlation be considered.

It is worth noting that if one or more of the variables increases or decreases steadily over time, as is often the case, or if the data set is logically reordered (say, according to the magnitude of one of the variables), then the Durbin-Watson statistic can help detect impure serial correlation. A significant Durbin-Watson statistic can easily be caused by a left-out variable or an incorrect functional form. In such circumstances, the Durbin-Watson test does not distinguish between pure and impure serial correlation, but the detection of negative serial correlation is often a strong hint that the serial correlation is impure. If you conclude that you have pure serial correlation, then the appropriate response is to consider the application of generalized least squares.

9.4.1 What Is Generalized Least Squares?

Generalized Least Squares (GLS) is a method of ridding an equation of pure first-order serial correlation and in the process restoring the minimum variance property to its estimation. Also called the Aitken estimator, generalized least squares starts with an equation that does not meet the classical assumptions (due in this case to the pure serial correlation in the error term) and transforms it into one (Equation 9.19) that does meet those assumptions.

At this point, you could skip directly to Equation 9.19, but it is easier to understand the GLS estimator by examining the arithmetic transformation from which it comes. Start with an equation that has first-order serial correlation:

$$Y_t = \beta_0 + \beta_1 X_{1t} + \epsilon_t \qquad (9.15)$$

which, if $\epsilon_t = \rho\epsilon_{t-1} + u_t$ (due to pure serial correlation) also equals:

$$Y_t = \beta_0 + \beta_1 X_{1t} + \rho\epsilon_{t-1} + u_t \qquad (9.16)$$

where ϵ is the serially correlated error term, ρ is the coefficient of serial correlation, and u is a classical (non-serially correlated) error term.

If we could get the $\rho\epsilon_{t-1}$ term out of Equation 9.16, the serial correlation would be gone, because the remaining portion of the error term (u_t) has no serial correlation in it. In order to rid $\rho\epsilon_{t-1}$ from Equation 9.16, multiply Equation 9.15 by ρ and then lag the new equation by one time period, obtaining

$$\rho Y_{t-1} = \rho\beta_0 + \rho\beta_1 X_{1\,t-1} + \rho\epsilon_{t-1} \qquad (9.17)$$

Notice that we now have an equation with a $\rho\epsilon_{t-1}$ term in it. If we now subtract Equation 9.17 from Equation 9.15, the equivalent equation that remains no longer contains the serially correlated component of the error term:

$$Y_t - \rho Y_{t-1} = \beta_0(1 - \rho) + \beta_1(X_{1t} - \rho X_{1\,t-1}) + u_t \qquad (9.18)$$

Equation 9.18 can be rewritten as:

$$Y_t^* = \beta_0^* + \beta_1 X_{1t}^* + u_t \qquad (9.19)$$

where

$$Y_t^* = Y_t - \rho Y_{t-1},\ X_{1t}^* = X_{1t} - \rho X_{1\,t-1},\ \text{and}\ \beta_0^* = \beta_0 - \rho\beta_0 \qquad (9.20)$$

Equation 9.19 is called a generalized least squares version of Equation 9.16; notice that:

1. The error term is not serially correlated. As a result, OLS estimation of Equation 9.19 will be minimum variance.

2. The slope coefficient β_1 is the same as the slope coefficient of the original serially correlated equation, Equation 9.15.

As a result, if we substitute $\hat{\rho}$ for ρ, we can estimate Equation 9.19 to obtain estimates of Equation 9.15 or Equation 9.16. One typical question at this point is, "If the slope coefficients are the same for both equations, will the estimated coefficients also be the same?" The answer is that, as always, there is no reason for different unbiased estimates to be identical. In addition, the variances of the two estimates are different, further increasing the likelihood of different $\hat{\beta}$s.

9.4.2 How to Obtain Estimates of ρ

To get rid of pure serial correlation you have to redefine your variables as in Equation 9.20, substitute $\hat{\rho}$ for ρ, and run OLS on Equation 9.19. This will give you unbiased, minimum variance (if $\rho = \hat{\rho}$) estimates of the βs. There's only one problem with all this; where does the $\hat{\rho}$ come from? Since it is quite unlikely that the true ρ will be known theoretically, how do you go about obtaining estimates of the coefficient of serial correlation?

The simplest way to obtain estimates of ρ is to use an approximation formula roughly based on the Durbin-Watson statistic:

$$\hat{\rho} \approx 1 - \frac{d}{2} \tag{9.21}$$

where d is the Durbin-Watson statistic in Equation 9.13 and the "approximately equal" sign indicates that the relationship is inexact. That this equation works for at least some points can be seen by plugging in the three best-known values of d:

With extreme positive serial correlation, $d = 0$, and $\hat{\rho} \approx 1$.

With extreme negative serial correlation, $d = 4$, and $\hat{\rho} \approx -1$.

With no serial correlation, $d = 2$, and $\hat{\rho} \approx 0$.

In each of these three cases, Equation 9.21 gives exactly the right value for $\hat{\rho}$.

To obtain more accurate estimates of ρ, particularly for small samples, there are a number of more complicated methods, including the *Cochrane-Orcutt iterative method*,[9] a two-step iterative procedure:

Step 1: Estimate $\hat{\rho}$ by running a regression based on the residuals of the equation suspected of having serial correlation:

$$e_t = \rho e_{t-1} + u_t \tag{9.22}$$

where the e_ts are the OLS residuals from the equation suspected of having pure serial correlation and u is a classical (non-serially correlated) error term.

Step 2: Use this $\hat{\rho}$ to run (estimated) generalized least squares by substituting it into Equation 9.20 and then using OLS to estimate Equation 9.19 with the adjusted data.

In practice, these two steps are repeated (iterated) until further iteration results in little change in $\hat{\rho}$. Once $\hat{\rho}$ has converged (usually in only a few iterations), the results of the last estimate of Step 2 are printed out (often along with a listing of all the intermediate $\hat{\rho}$s computed in the process). While other methods for estimating ρ are available (Hildreth-Lu, Theil-Nagar, Durbin, among others) the Cochrane-Orcutt method is commonly used and meets our needs quite well, so we will limit our coverage to that method.

Let's examine the application of (estimated) generalized least squares (using the Cochrane-Orcutt method) to the chicken demand example that was found to have positive serial correlation in the previous section. Recall what Equation 6.5 looked like:

$$\hat{Y} = -49.6 - 0.54PC + 0.22PB + 10.6\ln Yd \qquad (6.5)$$
$$(0.07) \qquad (0.06) \qquad (1.3)$$
$$t \; = \qquad -7.6 \qquad 3.5 \qquad 8.3$$
$$\bar{R}^2 = .979 \qquad n = 29 \qquad DW = 1.16$$

where: Y   = annual per capita chicken consumption (in pounds)
        PC   = the price of chicken (cents per pound)
        PB   = the price of beef (cents per pound)
        lnYd = the log of per capita disposable income (dollars)

Note that we have added the Durbin-Watson d statistic to the documentation with the notation "DW." All future time series results will include the DW statistic, but cross-sectional documentation of the DW is not required unless the observations are ordered in some logical manner.

If Equation 6.5 is re-estimated with generalized least squares, we obtain:

$$\hat{Y} = -59.7 - 0.42PC + 0.17PB + 11.9\ln Yd \qquad (9.23)$$
$$(0.09) \qquad (0.06) \qquad (1.5)$$
$$t \; = \qquad -4.7 \qquad 2.7 \qquad 7.9$$
$$\bar{R}^2 = .984 \qquad n = 29 \qquad \hat{\rho} = 0.54$$

Compare these two results. First, note that the $\hat{\rho}$ used in Equation 9.23 was 0.54. That means that Y was actually run as $Y_t^* = Y_t - 0.54Y_{t-1}$, PC as $PC_t^* = PC_t - 0.54PC_{t-1}$, etc. Second, note that the t-scores have decreased (mainly due to increased estimates of the standard errors). This makes sense since one of the consequences of serial correlation is that OLS underestimates the standard errors of the $\hat{\beta}$s. Indeed, one reason for adjusting for serial correlation is to avoid making mistakes of inference because of t-scores that are too high. Finally, note that even though serial correlation causes no bias in the estimates of the βs, the GLS estimates of the slope coefficients still differ somewhat from the OLS ones. To compare intercepts, we would divide $\hat{\beta}_0^*$ by $[1 - \hat{\rho}]$.

With respect to documentation, note that the $\hat{\rho}$ replaces the DW in the documentation of a GLS result since the DW statistic of Equation 9.23 is not strictly comparable with non-GLS DWs (it is biased towards 2). In fact, if any Durbin-Watson statistic should be presented, it should be the one from the OLS estimation (in order to document the need for GLS). Also note that the estimated model is typically presented without the asterisks attached to the transformed Y* and X* variables. This sometimes causes confusion if the reader cannot tell whether the variables in Equation 9.23 are actually Xs or X*s. Since the only difference between the two results is the constant term (remember, the slope coefficients are estimates of the same βs), and since the constant term is usually of little interest to researchers, the common practice is to present the results of GLS with the variables in their transformed state. To forecast with GLS, adjustments like those discussed in Section 13.2 need to be made.

9.4.3   Why Generalized Least Squares Shouldn't Automatically Be Used

There are a number of reasons why generalized least squares should not be applied every time that the Durbin-Watson test indicates the likelihood of serial correlation in the residuals of an equation.

1. The significant DW may be caused by impure serial correlation. When autocorrelation is detected, the cause may be an omitted variable or a poor choice of functional form. In such a case, the best solution is to find the missing variable or the proper form. Even if these easy answers cannot be found, the application of GLS to the mis-specified equation is not necessarily superior to OLS. Impure serial correlation justifies using generalized least squares only when the cause is an omitted variable that is at least reasonably correlated with one of the included variables. In this case, if the left-out variable cannot be found, GLS will reduce the bias somewhat, because the procedure proxies for the autocorrelated portion of the omitted variable. In cases of uncorrelated omitted variables or improper functional form, it can be shown that OLS is superior to GLS for estimating an incorrectly specified equation. In all cases, of course, the best course of action is the use of the correct specification.

2. The serial correlation may be fixed by timewise aggregation. In general, we should expect pure autocorrelation to be more likely in weekly, monthly, or quarterly data than in annual or cross-sectional data. This is because the lag between a shock and its final impact on a system is more likely to be included in a particular time period the longer that time period is. Therefore, it is possible to reduce serial correlation in the data set by aggregating quarterly data (say) into annual data (called "timewise aggregation"). While this new data set will have fewer degrees of freedom, it will not necessarily contain substantially less information. In particular, if the reason for running the regression is to measure the effect of a single policy change (like the Pope's decision to allow Catholics to eat meat on Fridays), then timewise aggregation will better capture that effect because short-run "noise" is less likely to interfere with the estimation of a longer-run phenomenon.

3. The consequences of the serial correlation may be minor. Generalized least squares works well if $\hat{\rho}$ is close to the actual ρ, but $\hat{\rho}$ is biased in small samples, potentially causing estimation problems. Since serial correlation causes no bias, it is possible that the harm done to the equation by the serial correlation may be less than the damage done by attempting to fix that problem with a biased $\hat{\rho}$. In particular, when coefficient estimates seem theoretically reasonable, and when the t-scores of the various coefficients are not being relied upon for the retention of independent variables, the harm caused by serial correlation may be minor.

As a result of these reasons, many econometricians try to avoid the use of generalized least squares when the Durbin-Watson test is inconclusive.

9.4.4 A Complete Example of the Application of Generalized Least Squares

To illustrate the generalized least squares technique, let's make up an example of the serial correlation problem. We will choose a "true" equation, force the error terms to be serially correlated, and generate a data set from the equation. We will first estimate the equation with OLS to see if the Durbin-Watson statistic will detect the serial correlation. We will then apply generalized least squares to the equation to see if GLS can estimate the actual $\hat{\rho}$, rid the equation of the serial correlation, and thus come close to the values we used to generate the observations.

Think how you might act if you received occasional gifts of money from an uncle with the instruction that you should "go out and have a nice dinner," and build a model of the amount of money (in dollars) you would spend on dinner (Y) as a function of the size of the gift you received from your uncle (X). In such a case, the following equation might make sense:

$$Y_t = 4.00 + 0.90X_t + \epsilon_t \tag{9.24}$$

Let's further assume that the error terms are serially correlated

$$\epsilon_t = 0.80\epsilon_{t-1} + u_t \tag{9.25}$$

That is, your behavior follows a pattern of positive serial correlation with an autocorrelation coefficient of 0.80. If one time you spend more than normal, then you tend to spend more than normal the next time, and if you spend less than normal on a gift dinner, you tend to spend less subsequently. (If your behavior instead followed a pattern of negative serial correlation, then you would tend to correct your overspending one time by underspending the next, and the error terms would be negatively related.)

To create the data set, we need to create a set of error terms and then use these error terms to generate observations of Y. For this example's error terms, we randomly selected values u_t from N(0,3), and then plugged the randomly picked *us* into Equation 9.25 above. For the first time period, for example, we randomly drew a u of + 1.56, and then we calculated ϵ_1 (assuming $\epsilon_0 = 0$):

$$\epsilon_1 = 0.80\epsilon_0 + u_1 = 0.80(0) + 1.56 = 1.56$$

For the second time period, we randomly drew u = 0.00, and ϵ_2 was:

$$\epsilon_2 = 0.80\epsilon_1 + u_2 = 0.80(1.56) + 0.00 = 1.25$$

For the generation of the rest of the error terms (ϵ) see Table 9.1.

Table 9.1 The Generation of the Hypothetical Data Set Used in the Serial Correlation Example

X_t	$u_t \sim N(0,3)$	$\epsilon_t = u_t + 0.8\epsilon_{t-1}$	$Y_t = 4.0 + 0.9X_t + \epsilon_t$
1	1.56	1.56	6.46
2	0.00	1.25	7.05
3	−0.54	0.46	7.16
4	2.76	3.13	10.73
5	0.84	3.34	11.84
6	−2.43	0.24	9.64
7	4.02	4.21	14.51
8	1.32	4.69	15.89
9	2.76	6.51	18.61
10	−0.69	4.52	17.52
11	−1.50	2.12	16.02
12	−1.92	−0.22	14.58
13	0.45	0.27	15.97
14	0.54	−0.32	16.28
15	−0.93	−1.19	16.31

We then selected a set of fixed Xs (1 to 15) and combined these with the now serially correlated ϵs to generate the Ys from Equation 9.24. For example, Y_1 was calculated by plugging $X_1 = 1.0$ and $\epsilon_1 = 1.56$ (as calculated above) into Equation 9.24:

$$Y_1 = 4.00 + 0.90X_1 + \epsilon_1 = 4.00 + 0.90(1.0) + 1.56 = 6.46$$

For the generation of the rest of the dependent variables (Y), see Table 9.1.
Our next step was to estimate the serially correlated equation with OLS:

$$\hat{Y} = 7.06 + 0.772X \tag{9.26}$$
$$(0.136)$$
$$t = 5.691$$
$$DW = 0.789$$

This is a reasonable result, since the estimates (7.06 and 0.772) are fairly close to the true values (4.0 and 0.90). Does the Durbin-Watson statistic indicate likely serial correlation? For a 99 percent one-sided test, Table B-6 indicates that d_L is 0.81. Since the observed DW is *less* than 0.81, the test indicates the presence of serial correlation.

Given this, and given that we believe that there are no specification errors, the next step was to re-estimate Equation 9.26 with generalized least squares using the Cochrane-Orcutt method:

$$\hat{Y} = 7.00 + 0.748X \tag{9.27}$$
$$(0.193)$$
$$t = \quad 3.884$$
$$\hat{\rho} = 0.542$$

How did GLS do? First of all, the $\hat{\rho}$ of 0.542 is fairly close to the actual value of 0.80, but note that it still is off by a third or so. Second, the GLS estimate of the standard error is higher than the OLS estimate, which is logical when you recall that the OLS estimate of the standard error is biased. Because of this increased standard error, the t-score falls; in general, this decreased t-score will help lower the chance of errors of inference. Finally, note that while the estimate of the slope coefficient changed hardly at all in this example, such changes do sometimes occur when GLS is used.

9.5   Summary

1. Serial correlation, or autocorrelation, is the violation of the classical assumption that the error terms are independent of each other. Usually, econometricians focus on first-order serial correlation, in which this time's error term is assumed to be a function of last time's error term and a non-serially correlated error term (u):

$$\epsilon_t = \rho\epsilon_{t-1} + u_t \qquad -1 < \rho < 1$$

where ρ is "rho," the coefficient of serial correlation.

2. Pure serial correlation is serial correlation that is a function of the error term of the correctly specified regression equation. Impure serial correlation is caused by specification errors such as an omitted variable or an incorrect functional form. While impure serial correlation can be positive ($0 < \rho < 1$) or negative ($-1 < \rho < 0$), pure serial correlation in economics or business situations is almost always positive.

3. The major consequence of serial correlation is an increase in the variances of the $\hat{\beta}$ distributions that is masked by an underestimation of those variances (and the standard errors) by Ordinary Least Squares. Serial correlation does not cause bias in the estimates of the βs.

4. The most commonly used method of detecting first-order serial correlation is the Durbin-Watson d test, which uses the residuals of an estimated regression to test the possibility of serial correlation in the error terms. A d value of 0 indicates extreme positive serial correlation, a d value of 2 indicates no serial correlation, and a d value of 4 indicates extreme negative serial correlation.

5. The first step in ridding an equation of serial correlation is to check for possible specification errors. Only once the possibility of impure serial correlation has been reduced to a minimum should remedies for pure serial correlation be considered.

6. Generalized least squares (GLS) is a method of transforming an equation to rid it of pure first-order serial correlation. The use of GLS requires the estimation of ρ, which is most commonly accomplished through a two-step iterative method devised by Cochrane and Orcutt. GLS should not be automatically applied every time the Durbin-Watson test indicates the possibility of serial correlation in an equation.

Exercises

(Answers to even-numbered questions are in Appendix A.)

1. Write out the meaning of each of the following terms without reference to the book (or your notes) and then compare your definition with the version in the text for each:
   a. impure serial correlation
   b. first-order serial correlation
   c. first-order autocorrelation coefficient
   d. Durbin-Watson d statistic
   e. Generalized Least Squares
   f. positive serial correlation

2. Use Statistical Tables B-4, B-5, and B-6 to test for serial correlation given the following Durbin-Watson d statistics for serial correlation.

   a. $d = 0.81$, $k' = 3$, $n = 21$, 95 percent, one-sided positive test

   b. $d = 3.48$, $k' = 2$, $n = 15$, 99 percent, one-sided positive test

   c. $d = 1.56$, $k' = 5$, $n = 30$, 90 percent, two-sided test

   d. $d = 2.84$, $k' = 4$, $n = 35$, 95 percent, two-sided test

   e. $d = 1.75$, $k' = 1$, $n = 45$, 95 percent, one-sided positive test

   f. $d = 0.91$, $k' = 2$, $n = 28$, 98 percent, two-sided test

   g. $d = 1.03$, $k' = 6$, $n = 26$, 95 percent, one-sided positive test

3. Recall from Section 9.4 that switching the order of a data set will not change its coefficient estimates. A changed order will change the Durbin-Watson statistic, however. To see both these points, run regressions ($HS = \beta_0 + \beta_1 P + \epsilon$) and compare the coefficient estimates and DW d statistics for different orders of this data set:

Year	Housing Starts	Population
1	9090	2200
2	8942	2222
3	9755	2244
4	10327	2289
5	10513	2290

in the following three orders (in terms of year):
   a. 1,2,3,4,5
   b. 5,4,3,2,1
   c. 2,4,3,5,1

4. After GLS has been run on an equation, the $\hat{\beta}$s are still good estimates of the original (non-transformed) equation except for the constant term:
   a. What must be done to the estimate of the constant term generated by GLS to compare it with the one estimated by OLS?
   b. Why is such an adjustment necessary?
   c. Return to Equation 9.23 and calculate the $\hat{\beta}_0$ that would be comparable to the one in Equation 6.5.
   d. Return to Equation 9.27 and calculate the $\hat{\beta}_0$ that would be comparable to the one in Equation 9.26.
   e. In both cases, the two estimates are fairly different. Why are the estimates so different? Would such a difference concern you?

5. Carefully distinguish between the following concepts:
   a. positive and negative serial correlation.
   b. pure and impure serial correlation.
   c. serially correlated error terms and serially correlated residuals.
   d. generalized least squares and the Cochrane-Orcutt method.

6. In Statistical Table B-4, column $k' = 5$, d_U is greater than two for the five smallest sample sizes in the table. What does it mean if $d_U > 2$?

7. Recall the example of the relationship between the short-term real interest rate and the budget deficit discussed at the end of Section 9.2. The hypothetical results in that section were extrapolated from a cross-sectional study[10] that found at least some evidence of such a link in a sample that pools annual time series and cross-sectional data from six countries.
   a. Suppose you were told that the Durbin-Watson d from their best regression was 0.81. Test this DW for indications of serial correlation ($n = 70$, $k' = 4$, 95 percent one-sided positive test for serial correlation).
   b. Based on this result, would you conclude that serial correlation existed in their study? Why or why not? (Hint: the six countries were the U.K.,

France, Japan, Canada, Italy, and the U.S.; assume that the order of the data was U.K. 1973-82, followed by France 1973-82, etc.)

c. How would you use generalized least squares to correct for serial correlation in this case?

8. Suppose the data in a time series study were entered in reverse chronological order. Would this change in any way the testing or adjusting for serial correlation? How? In particular:

a. What happens to the Durbin-Watson statistic's ability to detect serial correlation if the order is reversed?

b. What happens to the generalized least squares method's ability to adjust for serial correlation if the order is reversed?

c. What is the intuitive economic explanation of reverse serial correlation?

9. Suppose that a plotting of the residuals of a regression with respect to time indicated a significant outlier in the residuals. (Be careful here, this is not an outlier in the original data but is an outlier in the *residuals* of a regression.)

a. How could such an outlier occur? What does it mean?

b. Is the Durbin-Watson d applicable in the presence of such an outlier? Why or why not?

10. Recall the discussion of impure serial correlation caused by leaving out the log of disposable income variable from the fish-demand equation of the previous chapter (see Equations 8.27 and 9.4-7).

a. Return to that data set and estimate Equation 9.5; that is, leave out the lnYd variable and estimate:

$$F = \beta_0 + \beta_1 RP_t + \beta_3 D_t + \epsilon_t^*$$

(If you do not have access to a computer, or if you do not have time to estimate the equation yourself, look up the result in the answer to this question in Appendix A and then attempt to do the rest of the question on your own.)

b. Analyze the results. In particular, test the coefficients for 5 percent statistical significance, test for serial correlation, and decide whether or not the result confirms our original expectation that the Pope's decision did indeed decrease per capita fish consumption.

c. How would you have gone about analyzing this problem if you had not known that the omission of the lnYd variable was the cause? In particular, how would you have determined whether the potential serial correlation was pure or impure?

9.6 Appendix: Distributed Lags

9.6.1 The Use of Lags in Economics and Econometrics

Most of the regressions studied so far have been "instantaneous" in nature. In other words, they have included independent and dependent variables from the same time period as in

$$Y_t = \beta_0 + \beta_1 X_{1t} + \beta_2 X_{2t} + \epsilon_t \qquad (9.28)$$

The subscript t is used to refer to a particular point in time, and if all variables have the same subscript value, then the equation is instantaneous. Not all economic or business situations imply such instantaneous relationships between the dependent and independent variables, however. In many cases we must allow for the possibility that time might elapse between a change in the independent variable and the resulting change in the dependent variable. The length of this time between cause and effect is called a **lag.** Many econometric equations include one or more *lagged independent variables* like X_{1t-1}, where the subscript t−1 indicates that the observation of X_1 is from the time period previous to time period t, in the following equation:

$$Y_t = \beta_0 + \beta_1 X_{1t-1} + \beta_2 X_{2t} + \epsilon_t \qquad (9.29)$$

In this equation, X_1 has been lagged by one time period, but the relationship between Y and X_2 is still instantaneous.

Think about the process by which the supply of an agricultural product is determined. Since agricultural goods take time to grow, decisions on how many acres to plant or how many eggs to let hatch into egg-producing hens (instead of selling them immediately) must be made months if not years before the product is actually supplied to the consumer. Any change in an agricultural market, such as an increase in the price that the farmer can earn for providing the produce, has no effect on the supply of that product for some time:

$$\text{Quantity Supplied}_t = f(\text{Price}_{t-1}, \text{etc.})$$

Similarly, many macroeconomic theories have explicit lag structures built into them. The length of time between the decision to undertake a macroeconomic policy (like a cut in government spending or an increase in the money supply) and the impact of that policy on GNP, employment or prices is usually measured in years. An increase in the money supply stimulates GNP in part by stimulating investment; but investment cannot be increased overnight, because decisions need to be made, plans need to be designed, additional workers need to be hired, and so on. Indeed, noted economist Milton Friedman once estimated that it takes between 6 and 30 months for a monetary policy change to be fully felt in the economy.

If a *simple lag* is hypothesized, there is little difficulty in using lags in econometric equations. The lagged independent variable is simply added to the equation as another independent variable. For example, in studying the demand for farm tractors, Griliches[11] estimated the following equation:

$$\widehat{\ln Y_t} = -0.519\ln P_{t-1} - 4.933\ln INT_{t-1} \qquad (9.30)$$
$$\quad\quad\quad (0.231) \qquad\qquad (0.477)$$
$$\quad t = \quad -2.25 \qquad\qquad -10.34 \qquad R^2 = .793$$

where: Y_t = the real value of the stock of tractors in time t
         P_{t-1} = an index of tractor prices in time $t-1$ divided by average crop prices in time $t-1$
         INT_{t-1} = the interest rate prevailing in time $t-1$

Note that in this equation there is a lag between a change in any of the independent variables and a change in the dependent variable. In this case, it seems reasonable to think that if crop prices changed, then farmers wouldn't react immediately. After all, it would take quite some time for the crop price change to require more tractors. What about the impact of tractor prices or interest rates, though? First, it is likely that the demand for durable goods like tractors does indeed take a while to develop. After all, you expect to own the good for a considerable length of time. Notice also that the dependent variable is not total tractors *sold* in time period t, it is total tractors *owned*. Thus, purchases from previous years are important in determining this year's stock of tractors, because many of the tractors in use today were purchased last year or in years before.

The meaning of the regression coefficient that is attached to a lagged variable is not the same as the meaning of the coefficient of an unlagged variable. In particular, the estimated coefficient attached to a lagged X measures the change in *this year's* Y attributed to a one-unit change in *last year's* X (holding constant all the other Xs in the equation). For example, the coefficient of the lagged interest rate variable in Equation 9.30 indicates that there will be a decrease of 4.933 units in the log of this year's value of the stock of tractors as a result of a one unit increase in the log of last year's interest rate, holding constant last year's tractor prices.[12]

9.6.2 Distributed Lags

A case that is more complicated than the simple lag model occurs when the impact of an independent variable is expected to spread out over a number of different time periods. For example, suppose that a change in the money supply has some impact in the first year, some more in the second year, and so on. In such a case, the appropriate econometric model to use would be a distributed lag model:

$$Y_t = \alpha + \beta_0 X_{1t} + \beta_1 X_{1t-1} + \cdots + \beta_k X_{1\ t-k} + \epsilon_t \qquad (9.31)$$

A **distributed lag model** therefore explains the current value of Y as a function of the current and a number of past values of X, thus "distributing" the impact of X over time. Take a careful look at Equation 9.31. The coefficients β_0, β_1, . . . , β_k show the impacts of the various lagged values of X_1 on the current value of Y. In most economic examples, we would expect the impact of X on Y to diminish as the lag increases, so we would expect the values of the βs to decrease as the length of the lag (indicated by the subscript of the β) increases. That is, while β_0 might be larger or smaller than β_1, we certainly would expect either β_0 or β_1 to be larger in absolute value than β_6 or β_7, for example.

Unfortunately, the estimation of Equation 9.31 with ordinary least squares causes a number of problems:

1. The various lagged values of X are likely to be severely multicollinear, making coefficient estimates imprecise.

2. In part because of this multicollinearity, there is no guarantee that the estimated $\hat{\beta}$s will follow the smoothly declining pattern that economic theory would suggest. Instead, it is quite typical for the estimated coefficients of Equation 9.31 to follow a fairly irregular pattern, for example:

$$\hat{\beta}_0 = 0.26 \quad \hat{\beta}_1 = 0.18 \quad \hat{\beta}_2 = 0.07 \quad \hat{\beta}_3 = 0.17 \quad \hat{\beta}_4 = -0.03 \quad \hat{\beta}_5 = 0.08$$

3. The large number of coefficients estimated to measure the impact of one independent variable and the observations used up to calculate the lagged X values both tend to decrease the number of degrees of freedom.

As a result of the problems that the OLS estimation of distributed lag functions like Equation 9.31 encounters, it is standard practice to use a simplifying assumption to avoid these problems. The most commonly used simplification is the **Koyck distributed lag model**, which assumes that the coefficients decrease in a geometric fashion the longer the lag is:

$$\beta_i = \beta_0\lambda^i \tag{9.32}$$

where i is the length of the lag, 1, 2, . . . , k, and $0 < \lambda < 1$. For example, $\beta_3 = \beta_0\lambda^3$.

If we substitute Equation 9.32 for each coefficient in Equation 9.31 and factor out β_0, we obtain:

$$Y_t = \alpha + \beta_0(X_t + \lambda X_{t-1} + \lambda^2 X_{t-2} + \lambda^3 X_{t-3} + \cdots) + \epsilon_t \tag{9.33}$$

Since we have assumed that λ is between zero and one, λ to the $(n + 1)$th power is smaller than λ to the nth power. As a result, each successive lagged term has a smaller coefficient than the previous term. For example, if $\lambda = 0.2$, then Equation 9.33 becomes:

$$Y_t = \alpha + \beta_0(X_t + 0.2X_{t-1} + 0.04X_{t-2} + 0.008X_{t-3} + \cdots) + \epsilon_t \tag{9.34}$$

To see this, note that $(0.2)^1 = 0.2$, $(0.2)^2 = 0.04$, etc. Thus, as can be seen in Figure 9.9, each successive lagged value has relatively less weight in determining the current value of Y.

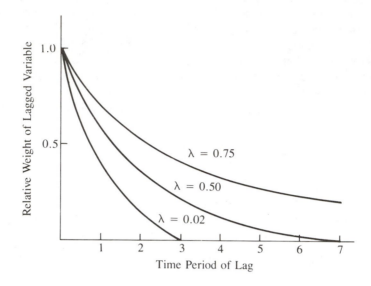

FIGURE 9.9 *Geometric Weighting Schemes for Various* λs

No matter what λ is used, a Koyck distributed lag model has the impact of the independent variable declining as the length of the lag increases.

How can we estimate Equation 9.33? To do this, we must derive an equivalent equation that is linear in the coefficients α, β_0, and λ. It turns out that such a derivation yields:[13]

$$Y_t = \alpha + \beta_0 X_t + \lambda Y_{t-1} + \epsilon_t \qquad (9.35)$$

This, then, becomes the estimating equation. Note that the existence of a lagged dependent variable as an independent variable implies that every other independent variable in the equation is related to the dependent variable by a declining geometric (Koyck) distributed lag function. Such equations are much easier to estimate than Equation 9.31, but if the error term ϵ is serially correlated, then Equation 9.35 produces biased and inconsistent estimates of the regression coefficients. In such a case, a technique called instrumental variables, to be explained in Section 12.3, is often useful in avoiding the bias.

An aggregate consumption function from a macroeconomic equilibrium GNP model can be an example of a distributed lag equation. In such an equation, many economists argue that consumption is not an instantaneous function of income, but rather that current purchases of goods and services (C_t) are influenced by past levels of disposable income (Yd_{t-1}, Yd_{t-2}, etc.) as well as current levels of disposable income (Yd_t):

$$C_t = f(\overset{+}{Yd_t}, \overset{+}{Yd_{t-1}}, \overset{+}{Yd_{t-2}}, \text{ etc.}) \qquad (9.36)$$

Such an equation fits well with simplistic adaptation models of consumption, but it only fits if the weights given to past income levels decrease as the length of the lag increases. That is, we would expect the coefficient of Yd_{t-2} to be less than the coefficient of Yd_{t-1}, and so on. Given that, most econometricians would model Equation 9.36 with a Koyck distributed lag equation:

$$C_t = \alpha + \beta_0 Yd_t + \lambda C_{t-1} + \epsilon_t \qquad (9.37)$$

This equation not only fits a simplistic adaptation model of aggregate consumption, it also is quite close to that suggested by Milton Friedman in his permanent income hypothesis.[14] In that hypothesis, Friedman suggested that consumption was based not on current income but instead on some perception of lifetime income; thus changes in transitory income would not change consumption. Since perceptions of permanent income can be hypothesized to be formed from past levels of income, the simple adaptation model and the more sophisticated permanent income model have quite similar functions.

To estimate equation 9.37, we use the data presented in Section 12.3, where a small simultaneous macro model of the U.S. economy from 1946 through 1970 is built. The OLS estimates of Equation 9.37 for this data set are:

$$\hat{C}_t = -17.89 + 0.67 Yd_t + 0.34 C_{t-1} \qquad (9.38)$$
$$(0.09) \qquad (0.09)$$
$$t = \qquad 7.65 \qquad 3.65$$
$$\bar{R}^2 = .999 \qquad n = 25 \qquad DW = 1.53$$

Before we can interpret this equation, however, we need to convert it back into the format of Equation 9.36 by using the Koyck distributed lag definitions of the individual coefficients: $\beta_i = \beta_0 \lambda^i$ where in the case of Equation 9.38, $\hat{\beta}_0$ is 0.67 and $\hat{\lambda}$ is 0.34. For example, $\hat{\beta}_1 = \beta_0 \hat{\lambda}^1 = (0.67)(0.34)^1 = 0.2278$. If we continue this process, it turns out that Equation 9.38 is equivalent to:

$$\hat{C}_t = -17.69 + 0.67 Yd_t + 0.23 Yd_{t-1} + 0.08 Yd_{t-2} + 0.03 Yd_{t-3} \qquad (9.39)$$

In actuality, this equation keeps going out to an infinitely long lag, but since the coefficient of Yd_{t-4} is less than 0.01, it is close enough to zero to be disregarded. To compare this estimate with an OLS estimate without the Koyck distributed lag format, let us estimate, for the same data set,

$$\hat{C}_t = \beta_0 + \beta_1 Yd_t + \beta_2 Yd_{t-1} + \beta_3 Yd_{t-2} + \beta_4 Yd_{t-3} + \epsilon_t \qquad (9.40)$$

without the constraints of the Koyck distributed lag function. We would correctly expect the estimates to no longer follow the same smoothly declining pattern of the Koyck function:

$$\hat{C}_t = -32.69 + 1.01 Yd_t - 0.10 Yd_{t-1} - 0.21 Yd_{t-2} + 0.32 Yd_{t-3} \qquad (9.41)$$
$$(0.09) \qquad (0.15) \qquad (0.14) \qquad (0.10)$$
$$t = \qquad 10.75 \qquad -0.63 \qquad -1.45 \qquad 3.25$$
$$\bar{R}^2 = .998 \qquad n = 25 \qquad DW = 2.10$$

Compare Equations 9.41 and 9.39. Note that in Equation 9.41, the one-year and two-year lagged impacts are negative and insignificantly different from zero, while the three-year lagged impact is positive and significant. Neither economic theory nor common sense leads us to expect this pattern. Such a poor result is likely in the face of severe multicollinearity, and most econometricians therefore estimate distributed lag models with a lagged dependent variable simplification like the Koyck function in Equation 9.38. For more on this particular example, see Section 12.3.

[1] If typical values of ϵ are significantly larger in absolute value than $\beta_2 X_2$, then even a serially correlated omitted variable (X_2) will not change ϵ very much. In addition, recall that the left-out variable, X_2, will cause bias in the estimate of β_1 depending on the correlation between the two Xs. If $\hat{\beta}_1$ is biased because of this correlation, then a portion of the $\beta_2 X_2$ effect has been absorbed by an included variable and will not end up in the residuals. As a result, tests for serial correlation based on those residuals may give incorrect readings for the existence of serial correlation in the model. Just as importantly, such residuals may leave incorrect clues as to possible specification errors. This is only one of many reasons why an analysis of the residuals should not be the only procedure used to determine the nature of possible specification errors.

[2] This holds as long as the serial correlation is positive, as is typically the case in economic examples. In addition, if the regression includes a lagged dependent variable as an independent variable, then the problems worsen significantly. For more on this topic, see Section 9.6, which is an appendix to this chapter that covers a topic called distributed lags.

[3] See Martin S. Feldstein and Otto Eckstein, "The Fundamental Determinants of the Interest Rate," *Review of Economics and Statistics,* Nov. 1970, pp. 363-375, Gregory P. Hoelscher, "Federal Borrowing and Short-Term Interest Rates," *Southern Economic Journal,* Oct. 1983, pp. 319-333, or any one of a number of more recent studies.

[4] J. Durbin and G.S. Watson, "Testing for Serial Correlation in Least-Squares Regression," *Biometrika,* 1951, pp. 159-177.

[5] In such a circumstance, the Durbin-Watson d is biased towards 2, but the Durbin h test can be used instead, as shown in Appendix B. See J. Durbin, "Testing for Serial Correlation in Least-Squares Regression When Some of the Regressors are Lagged Dependent Variables," *Econometrica,* May 1970, pp. 410-421.

[6] Another approach to the calculation of the Durbin-Watson statistic is:

$$d = 2(1 - \hat{\rho})$$

where $\hat{\rho}$ is the coefficient of a regression of the residuals as a function of their lagged values. This $\hat{\rho}$ is also a rough estimate of rho, the coefficient of serial correlation.

[7] To see this, multiply out the numerator of Equation 9.14, obtaining

$$d = \left[\sum_{2}^{T} e_t^2 - 2\sum_{2}^{T}(e_t e_{t-1}) + \sum_{2}^{T} e_{t-1}^2\right]/\sum_{1}^{T} e_t^2 \approx \left[\sum_{2}^{T} e_t^2 + \sum_{2}^{T} e_{t-1}^2\right]/\sum_{1}^{T} e_t^2 \approx 2$$

If there is no serial correlation, then e_t and e_{t-1} are not related, and, on average, $\sum(e_t e_{t-1}) = 0$.

[8] This can be proven mathematically, but is usually more instructive to estimate a regression yourself, change the order of the observations, and then re-estimate the regression. See Exercise 3.

[9] D. Cochrane and G.H. Orcutt, "Application of Least Squares Regressions to Relationships Containing Autocorrelated Error Terms," *Journal of the American Statistical Association,* 1949, pp. 32-61.

[10] M.M. Hutchinson and D.H. Pyle, "The Real Interest Rate/Budget Deficit Link: International Evidence, 1973-82," *Federal Reserve Bank of San Francisco Economic Review,* Fall 1984, pp. 26-35.

[11] Z. Griliches, "The Demand for a Durable Input: Farm Tractors in the United States 1921-1957," in Arnold C. Harberger (ed.) *The Demand for Durable Goods* (Chicago: The University of Chicago Press, 1960) p. 192. Griliches' results do not include an estimate of the constant term.

[12.]In this particular case, since the equation is log-linear, the coefficients are elasticities (as discussed in Section 7.1). These elasticities thus measure the percentage change in this time's dependent variable as a function of a one-percent change in last time's independent variable.

[13.]To see this, multiply both sides of Equation 9.33 by λ and lag it once (i.e., substitute $t-1$ for t in every instance that it appears) and then subtract the resulting equation from Equation 9.33, which produces, with some rewriting, Equation 9.35.

[14.]M. Friedman, *A Theory of the Consumption Function* (Princeton, N.J.: Princeton University Press/National Bureau of Economic Research, 1957). It is interesting to note, however, that Friedman's original function did not have a constant term in it because of the nature of his derivation of permanent income.

10

Heteroskedasticity

Heteroskedasticity[1] is the violation of Classical Assumption V, which states that the error terms are drawn from a distribution that has a constant variance. The assumption of constant variances for different observations of the error term (homoskedasticity) is not always realistic. For example, in a model explaining heights, compare a one-inch error in measuring the height of a basketball player with a one-inch error in measuring the height of a mouse. It is likely that error terms associated with the height of a basketball player would come from distributions with larger variances than those associated with the height of a mouse. As we will see, the distinction between heteroskedasticity and homoskedasticity is important because Ordinary Least Squares, when applied to heteroskedastic models, is no longer the minimum variance estimator (it still is unbiased, however).

Heteroskedasticity often occurs in data sets in which there is a wide disparity between the largest and smallest observed values. The larger the disparity between the size of observations in a sample, the larger the likelihood that the error terms associated with them will have different variances and therefore be heteroskedastic. That is, we'd expect that the error terms for very large observations might be drawn from distributions with large variances, while the error terms for small observations might be drawn from distributions with smaller variances.

One can easily get such a large range between the highest and lowest values of the variables in cross-sectional data sets. Recall that in cross-sectional models, the observations are all from the same time period (a given month or year, for example), but are from different entities (individuals, states, or countries, for example). The difference between the size of California's labor force and Rhode Island's, for instance, is quite large (comparable in percentage terms to the difference between the heights of a basketball player and a mouse). Since cross-sectional models often include observations of widely different size in the same sample (cross-state studies of the United States usually include California and Rhode Island as individual observations, for example), heteroskedasticity is hard to avoid if economic topics are going to be studied cross-sectionally.

This focus on cross-sectional models is not to say that heteroskedasticity in time series models is impossible, nor to deny the possibility that an omitted variable could cause impure heteroskedasticity in any kind of data. In general, though, heteroskedasticity is more likely to take place in cross-sectional models than in time series models.

Within this context, we will attempt to answer the same four questions for heteroskedasticity that we answered for multicollinearity and serial correlation in the previous two chapters:

1. What is the nature of the problem?

2. What are the consequences of the problem?

3. How is the problem diagnosed?

4. What remedies for the problem are available?

10.1 Pure vs. Impure Heteroskedasticity

Heteroskedasticity, like serial correlation, can be divided into pure and impure versions. Pure heteroskedasticity is that caused by the error term of the correctly specified equation, while impure heteroskedasticity is caused by a specification error such as a left-out variable.

10.1.1 Pure Heteroskedasticity

Pure heteroskedasticity refers to heteroskedasticity that is a function of the error term of a correctly specified regression equation. As with serial correlation, use of the word "heteroskedasticity" without any modifier (like pure or impure) implies *pure* heteroskedasticity.

Such **pure heteroskedasticity** occurs when Classical Assumption V, which assumes that the variance of the error terms is constant, is violated in a correctly specified equation. Recall that Assumption V assumes that:

$$\text{V.} \quad \text{VAR}(\epsilon_i) = \sigma^2 \quad (i = 1,2,\ldots,n) \tag{10.1}$$

If this assumption is met, all the error terms can be thought of as being drawn from the same distribution: a distribution with a mean of zero and a variance of σ^2. This σ^2 does not change for different observations of the error term; this property is called homoskedasticity. A homoskedastic error term distribution is pictured in the top half of Figure 10.1; note that the variance of the distribution of error terms is constant (even though individual observations drawn from that sample will vary quite a bit).

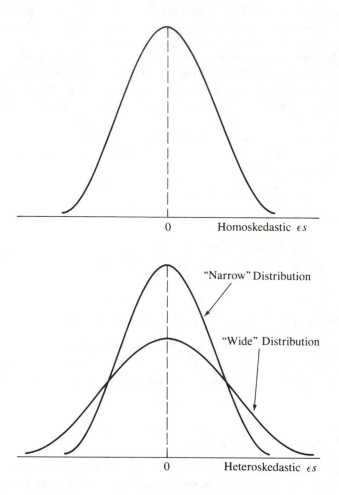

FIGURE 10.1 *Homoskedasticity vs. Discrete Heteroskedasticity*
In homoskedasticity, the distribution of the error terms has a constant variance, so the
error terms are continually drawn from the same distribution (shown in the top panel). In
the simplest heteroskedastic case, discrete heteroskedasticity, there would be two different
error term variances and therefore two different distributions (one wider than the other, as
in the bottom panel) from which the error terms could be drawn.

With heteroskedasticity, this error term variance is not constant; instead, the
variance of the distribution of the error term depends on exactly which observation is being discussed:

$$\text{VAR}(\epsilon_i) = \sigma_i^2 \quad (i = 1,2,\dots,n) \tag{10.2}$$

Note that the only difference between Equation 10.1 and Equation 10.2 is the subscript "i" attached to σ^2, which implies that instead of being constant over all

the observations, a heteroskedastic error term's variance can change depending on the observation (hence the subscript).

Another way to visualize heteroskedasticity is to picture a world in which some of the observations of the error terms are drawn from much wider distributions than are others. The simplest situation would be that the observations of the error terms could be grouped into just two different distributions, "wide" and "narrow." We will call this simplistic version of the problem *discrete heteroskedasticity.* Here, both distributions would be centered around zero, but one would have a larger variance than the other, as indicated in the bottom half of Figure 10.1. Note the difference between the two halves of the figure. With homoskedasticity, all the error terms come from the same distribution, but with heteroskedasticity, they come from different distributions.

Heteroskedasticity takes on many more complex forms, however; the number of different models of heteroskedasticity is virtually limitless, and an analysis of even a small number of these alternatives would be a huge task. Instead, we would like to address the general principles of heteroskedasticity by focusing on the most frequently specified model of pure heteroskedasticity, just as we focused on positive first-order serial correlation in the previous chapter. Don't let this focus mislead you into concluding that econometricians are concerned only with one kind of heteroskedasticity, however.

In this model of heteroskedasticity, the variance of the error term is related to an exogenous variable Z_i. For a typical regression equation:

$$Y_i = \beta_0 + \beta_1 X_{1i} + \beta_2 X_{2i} + \epsilon_i \tag{10.3}$$

the variance of the otherwise classical error term ϵ might be equal to:

$$VAR(\epsilon_i) = \sigma^2 Z_i^2 \tag{10.4}$$

where Z may or may not equal one of the Xs in the equation. The variable Z is called a **proportionality factor** because the variance of the error term changes proportionally to the square of Z_i. The higher the value of Z_i, the higher the variance of the distribution of the ith observation of the error term. There could be n different distributions, one for each observation, from which the error terms could be drawn depending on the number of different values that Z takes. To see what homoskedastic and heteroskedastic distributions of the error terms look like with respect to Z, examine Figures 10.2 and 10.3. Note that the heteroskedastic distribution gets wider as Z increases but that the homoskedastic distribution maintains the same width no matter what value Z takes.

What is an example of a proportionality factor Z? How is it possible for an exogenous variable such as Z to change the whole distribution of an error term? Think about a function that relates the consumption of a household to its income. The expenditures of a low-income household are not likely to be as variable in absolute value as the expenditures of high-income ones because the proportion of the low-income budget that must be spent on necessities is much higher than that of the high-income household. In such a case, the Y_i would be consump-

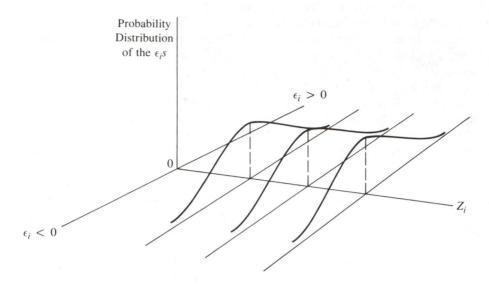

FIGURE 10.2 *Homoskedastic Error Terms with Respect to* Z_i

If an error term is homoskedastic with respect to Z_i, the variance of the distribution of the error terms is the same (constant) no matter what the value of Z_i is: $VAR(\epsilon_i) = \sigma^2$.

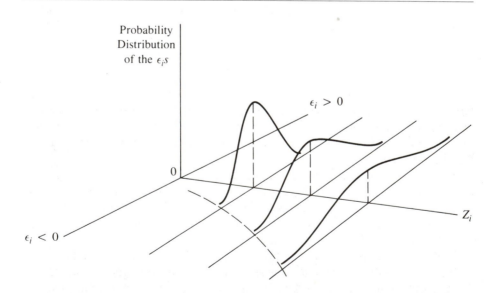

FIGURE 10.3 *Heteroskedastic Error Terms with Respect to* Z_i

If an error term is heteroskedastic with respect to Z_i, the variance of the distribution of the error terms changes systematically as a function of Z_i. In this example, the variance is an increasing function of Z_i, as in $VAR(\epsilon_i) = \sigma^2 Z_i^2$.

tion expenditures and the proportionality factor, Z, would be household income. As household income rose, so too would the variance of the error term of an equation built to explain expenditures. The error term distributions would look something like those in Figure 10.3, where the Z in Figure 10.3 is household income, one of the independent variables in the function.

This example helps emphasize that heteroskedasticity is likely to occur in cross-sectional models because of the large variation in the size of the dependent variable involved. An exogenous disturbance that might seem huge to a low-income household could seem miniscule to a high-income one, for instance.

Heteroskedasticity can occur in at least two situations other than a cross-sectional data set with a large amount of variation in the size of the dependent variable:

1. Heteroskedasticity can occur in a time series model with a significant amount of change in the dependent variable. If you were modeling sales of videotape cassettes from 1970 to 1980, it is quite possible that you would have heteroskedastic error terms. As the phenomenal growth of the industry took place, the variance of the error term is quite likely to also have increased as well. Such a possibility is unlikely in time series data that have low rates of change, however.

2. Heteroskedasticity can occur in any model, time series or cross-sectional, where the quality of data collection changes dramatically within the sample. As data collection techniques get better, the variance of the error term should fall because measurement errors are included in the error term. As measurement errors decrease in size, so should the variance of the error term. For more on this topic (called "errors in the variables"), see Section 12.6.

10.1.2   Impure Heteroskedasticity

Heteroskedasticity that is caused by an error in specification, such as an omitted variable, is referred to as **impure heteroskedasticity.** While improper functional form is less likely to cause impure heteroskedasticity than it is to cause impure serial correlation, the two concepts are similar in most other ways.

An omitted variable can cause a heteroskedastic error term because the portion of the omitted effect not represented by one of the included explanatory variables must be absorbed by the error term. If this effect has a heteroskedastic component, the error term of the misspecified equation might be heteroskedastic even if the error term of the true equation is not. This distinction is important because with impure heteroskedasticity, the correct remedy is to attempt to find the left-out variable and include it in the regression. It is important to be sure that your specification is correct before trying to detect or remedy pure heteroskedasticity.[2]

For example, consider a cross-sectional study of the 1980 imports of a number of variously sized nations. For simplicity, assume that the best model of a nation's imports in such a cross-sectional setting includes a positive function of its Gross National Product and a positive function of the relative price ratio (including the impact of exchange rates) between it and the rest of the world. In such a case, the "true" model would look like:

$$M_i = f(GNP, PR) = \overset{+}{\beta_0} + \overset{+}{\beta_1}GNP_i + \beta_2 PR_i + \epsilon_i \qquad (10.5)$$

where: M_i = the imports (in dollars) of the ith nation
GNP_i = the Gross National Product (in dollars) of the ith nation
PR_i = the ratio of the domestic price of normally traded goods (converted to dollars by the exchange rate) to the world price of those goods (measured in dollars)
ϵ_i = a classical error term

Now suppose that the equation is run without GNP. Since GNP is left out, the equation would become:

$$M_i = \beta_0 + \beta_2 PR_i + \epsilon_i^* \qquad (10.6)$$

where the error term of the misspecified equation, ϵ_i^*, is a function of the left-out variable (GNP) and a non-heteroskedastic error term ϵ:

$$\epsilon_i^* = \epsilon_i + \beta_1 GNP_i$$

To the extent that the relative price ratio does not act as a proxy for GNP, the error term has to incorporate the effect of the omitted variable. If this new effect has a larger variance for larger values of GNP, which seems likely, the new error term, ϵ_i^* is heteroskedastic. The impact of such an effect also depends on the size of the $\beta_1 GNP_i$ component compared with the absolute value of the typical ϵ_i component. The larger the omitted variable portion of ϵ_i^*, the more likely it is to have impure heteroskedasticity. In such a case, the error terms, ϵ_i^*, when plotted with respect to GNP, appear as in Figure 10.4. As can be seen, the larger the GNP, the larger the variance of the error terms.

10.2   The Consequences of Heteroskedasticity

If the error term of your equation is known to be heteroskedastic, what does that mean for the estimation of your coefficients? It turns out that the consequences of heteroskedasticity are almost identical in general framework to those of serial correlation,[3] though the two problems are quite different.

   If the error terms of an equation are heteroskedastic, there are three major consequences:

1. *Heteroskedasticity does not cause bias in the coefficient estimates.*
    Even if the error terms of an equation are known to be purely heteroskedastic, that heteroskedasticity will not cause bias in the OLS estimates of the

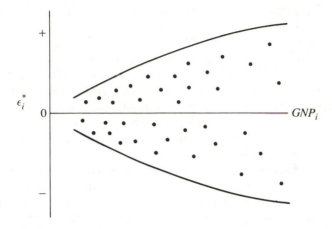

FIGURE 10.4 *Impure Heteroskedasticity Caused by the Omission of GNP*
Impure heteroskedasticity is a nonconstant variance of the distribution of the error terms
that is caused by an incorrect specification. In this case, the omission of GNP from the
equation has forced the error term to incorporate the impact of GNP, causing the distribution of the error term to be wider (higher variance) for large values of GNP than for
small ones.

coefficients. As a result, we can say that an otherwise correctly specified equation that has pure heteroskedasticity still has the property that:

$$E(\hat{\beta}) = \beta \text{ for all } \beta s$$

Lack of bias does not guarantee "accurate" coefficient estimates, especially
since heteroskedasticity increases the variance of the estimates, but the distribution of the estimates is still centered around the true β. Equations with
impure heteroskedasticity caused by an omitted variable, of course, will have
possible specification bias.

2. *Heteroskedasticity increases the variances of the $\hat{\beta}$ distributions.*
Pure heteroskedasticity causes no bias in the estimates of the OLS coefficients, but it does affect the minimum variance property. If the error terms
of an equation are heteroskedastic with respect to a proportionality factor Z:

$$VAR(\epsilon_i) = \sigma^2 Z_i^2 \tag{10.7}$$

then the variance of the $\hat{\beta}$s is a function of Z:

$$VAR^{**}(\hat{\beta}_k) = f(Z^2) \cdot [VAR(\hat{\beta}_k)] \tag{10.8}$$

where $VAR^{**}(\hat{\beta})$ is the variance with heteroskedasticity; $f(Z^2)$ indicates a
positive function of Z, the proportionality factor that is "causing" the heteroskedasticity in Equation 10.7, and $VAR(\hat{\beta})$ is the variance without
heteroskedasticity (see Figure 10.5).

3. *Heteroskedasticity causes OLS to underestimate the variances (and standard errors) of the coefficients.*

Even though heteroskedasticity increases the variances of the coefficients, heteroskedasticity turns out to increase the variances of the $\hat{\beta}$s in a way that is masked by the OLS estimates of them, and OLS nearly always underestimates[4] those variances. As a result, neither the t-statistic nor the F-statistic can be relied on in the face of uncorrected heteroskedasticity. In fact, OLS usually ends up with higher t-scores than would be obtained if the error terms were homoskedastic, sometimes leading researchers to reject null hypotheses that should not be rejected.

Why does heteroskedasticity cause this particular pattern of consequences? As Z and the variance of the distribution of the error term increase, so does the probability of drawing a large (in absolute value) error term. If the pattern of these large error terms happens to be positive when one of the independent variables is substantially above average, the OLS $\hat{\beta}$ for that variable will tend to be greater than it would have been otherwise. On the other hand, if the pattern of these large error terms accidentally happens to be negative when one of the Xs is substantially above average, then the OLS $\hat{\beta}$ for that variable will tend to be less than it would have been. Since the error term is still assumed to be independent of all the explanatory variables, overestimates are just as likely as underestimates, and the OLS estimator is still unbiased in the face of heteroskedasticity. The heteroskedasticity has caused $\hat{\beta}$s to be farther from the true value, however, and so the variance of the distribution of the $\hat{\beta}$s has increased.

For example, the real interest rate/budget deficit study of Section 9.2.2 could just as well be a hypothetical example of the consequences of heteroskedasticity. The OLS-estimated t-scores are too high, leading to potential mistakes of inference whenever t-tests are used in heteroskedastic equations. Before we can get rid of heteroskedasticity, however, we must detect it.

10.3 Testing for Heteroskedasticity

There is no universally agreed-upon method of testing for heteroskedasticity; econometrics textbooks list as many as five different methods of such testing. Econometricians do not all use the same test for heteroskedasticity, because heteroskedasticity takes a number of different forms, and its precise manifestation in a given equation is almost never known. The "Z_i proportionality factor" approach of this chapter, for example, is only one of many specifications of the form of heteroskedasticity.

Because of this wide variety, and because it is difficult to eliminate heteroskedasticity in an equation even if it is identified, we will describe the use of two tests for heteroskedasticity in this book: the *Park test* and the *Goldfeld-Quandt test*. Other tests abound, however, and readers interested in this topic are encouraged to research them.[5] No test for heteroskedasticity can "prove"

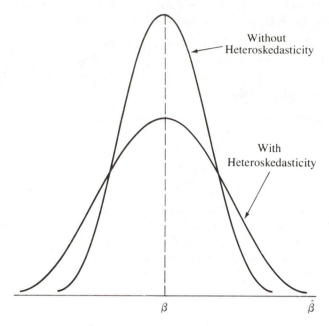

FIGURE 10.5 *Distribution of $\hat{\beta}s$ with and without Heteroskedasticity*
Heteroskedasticity increases the variance of the $\hat{\beta}s$, widening the $\hat{\beta}$ distribution. It does not cause bias, however, so the $\hat{\beta}$ distribution is centered around the true β whether or not there is heteroskedasticity.

---

heteroskedasticity exists in an equation, though, so the best we can do is to get a general indication of its likelihood.

10.3.1 The Park Test

How do we test for pure heteroskedasticity of the form that is most often assumed, the form that we outlined in the previous section:

$$\text{VAR}(\epsilon_i) = \sigma^2 Z_i^2$$

where ϵ is the error term of the equation being estimated, σ^2 is the variance of the homoskedastic error term, and Z is the proportionality factor.

The **Park Test**[6] is a formal procedure that attempts to test for this heteroskedasticity in a manner similar to the way that the Durbin-Watson d statistic tests residuals for serially correlated error terms. The Park test has three basic steps. First, the regression equation is estimated by OLS and the residuals are calculated. Second, the log of the squared residuals is used as the dependent variable of an equation whose sole explanatory variable is the log of the proportionality factor Z. Finally, the results of this second regression are tested to see if there is any evidence of heteroskedasticity.

There is no need to run a Park test for every equation estimated, however, so before using the Park test, it's a good idea to ask some preliminary questions:

1. Are there any obvious specification errors? If the estimated equation is suspected of having an omitted variable or is about to be re-run for some other specification reason, the Park test should be delayed until the specification is as good as possible.

2. Is the subject of the research often afflicted with heteroskedasticity? Not only are cross-sectional studies the most likely source of heteroskedasticity, but some cross-sectional studies (with large variations in the size of the variables, for instance) are more susceptible to heteroskedasticity than are others.

3. Finally, does a graph of the residuals show any evidence of heteroskedasticity? It sometimes saves time to plot the residuals with respect to a potential Z proportionality factor. In such cases, the graphs can often show that heteroskedasticity is or is not likely without a Park test. Figure 10.4 above shows an example of what to look for: an expanding (or contracting) *range* of the residuals.

If there is some reason to suspect heteroskedasticity, it is appropriate to run a Park test. Since the Park test is not run automatically by computer regression packages, you should know how to run the test yourself:

1. *Obtain the residuals of the estimated regression equation.* The first step is to estimate the equation with Ordinary Least Squares and then find the residuals from that estimation:

$$e_i = Y_i - \hat{\beta}_0 - \hat{\beta}_1 X_{1i} - \hat{\beta}_2 X_{2i} \qquad (10.9)$$

These residuals, which are printed out by most computer regression packages, are the same ones used to calculate the Durbin-Watson d statistic we used to test for serial correlation.

2. *Use these residuals to form the dependent variable in a second regression.* In particular, the Park test suggests that you run the following log-linear regression:

$$\ln(e_i^2) = \alpha_0 + \alpha_1 \ln Z_i + u_i \qquad (10.10)$$

where: e_i = the residual from the *i*th observation from Equation 10.9
   Z_i = your best choice as to the possible proportionality factor (Z) that might be causing heteroskedasticity
   u_i = a classical (homoskedastic) error term.[7]

3. *Test the significance of the coefficient of Z in Equation 10.10 with a t-test.* The last step is to use the t-statistic to test the significance of lnZ in explaining $\ln(e^2)$ in Equation 10.10. If the coefficient of Z is significantly different from zero, this is evidence of heteroskedastic patterns in the residuals with

respect to Z; otherwise, heteroskedasticity related to this particular Z is not supported by the evidence in these residuals. However, it is impossible to prove that a particular equation's error terms are homoskedastic.

The Park test is not always easy to use. The major problem with most methods of testing for heteroskedasticity is the identification of the proportionality factor Z. Although Z is often an explanatory variable in the original regression equation, there is no guarantee of that. A particular Z should be chosen for your Park test only after investigation of the type of potential heteroskedasticity in your equation.[8]

In a cross-sectional model of countries or states, a good Z would be one that measured the size of the observation relative to the dependent variable in question. For a dependent variable such as gallons of gasoline consumed, the number of registered drivers or automobiles might be a better measure of size than the population. While it is difficult to identify the best Z for a particular equation, it is often easier to distinguish good Zs from bad Zs. In the gasoline consumption equation, for example, a bad Z might be the speed limit in the state because while the speed limit might be important in determining how much gasoline is used, it is unlikely to "cause" any heteroskedasticity, because the speed limit in a state does not vary in size in the same way that gasoline consumption does (that is, the states likely to have large error term variances are not also likely to have high speed limits). For more on this fairly thorny issue, see Exercise 4.

10.3.2 An Example of the Use of the Park Test

Let's return to the Woody's Restaurants example of Section 3.3 and test for heteroskedasticity in the residuals of Equation 3.14. Recall that regression explained the number of customers, as measured by the check volume (Y) at a cross-section of 33 different Woody's restaurants as a function of the number of nearby competitors (C), the nearby population (P), and the average household income of the local area (I):

$$\hat{Y}_i = 102{,}192 - 9075C_i + 0.3547P_i + 1.288I_i \qquad (3.14)$$
$$(2053) \qquad (0.0727) \qquad (0.543)$$
$$t \quad = \quad -4.42 \qquad 4.88 \qquad 2.37$$

$$n = 33 \qquad \bar{R}^2 = .579 \qquad F = 15.65$$

This equation is cross-sectional, so heteroskedasticity is a theoretical possibility, but the dependent variable does not change much in size from restaurant to restaurant, so heteroskedasticity is not likely to be a major problem. As a result, the assumption of a constant variance of the error term (homoskedasticity) seems to be reasonable.

To judge whether this tentative conclusion is correct, let's use the Park test to see if the residuals from Equation 3.14 give any indication of heteroskedasticity.

1. *Calculate the residuals:* First, obtain the residuals from the equation you want to test. In the Woody's example, these residuals have already been calculated. They are at the end of Section 3.3.

2. *Use these residuals as the dependent variable in a second regression:* Run a regression with the log of the squared residual as the dependent variable as a function of the log of the suspected proportionality factor Z as first outlined in Equation 10.10:

$$\ln(e_i^2) = \alpha_0 + \alpha_1 \ln Z_i + u_i \tag{10.10}$$

It is possible that no Z exists, but if one does, it seems likely that it would somehow be related to the size of the market that the particular Woody's restaurant serves. It's possible that larger error term variances might exist in more heavily populated areas, so population (P) is a reasonable choice as a Z to try in our Park test. Any other variable related to the size of the market or of the particular restaurant would also be a reasonable possibility.

If the logged and squared residuals from Equation 3.14 are regressed as a function of the log of P, we obtain:

$$\widehat{\ln(\hat{e}_i^2)} = 21.05 - 0.2865 \ln P_i \tag{10.11}$$
$$(0.6263)$$
$$t = -0.457$$

$$n = 33 \quad R^2 = .0067 \quad F = 0.209$$

3. *Test the significance of $\hat{\alpha}_1$ in Equation 10.10:* As can be seen from the calculated t-score, there is virtually no measurable relationship between the squared residuals of Equation 3.14 and population. The calculated t-score of -0.457 is quite a bit smaller in absolute value than 2.750, the critical t-value (from Statistical Table B-1) for a two-tailed one-percent test with 30 degrees of freedom. As a result, we would not be able to reject[9] the null hypothesis of homoskedasticity:

$$H_0: \alpha_1 = 0$$
$$H_A: \alpha_1 \neq 0$$

For more practice in the use of the Park test, see Exercise 4.

10.3.3   The Goldfeld-Quandt Test

Perhaps the most commonly used test for heteroskedasticity is the **Goldfeld-Quandt test**[10], which reorders the data according to the value of a potential proportionality factor Z (which might not be an independent variable in the equation) and then tests to see if the variance of the residuals from the first third of the newly reordered data set differs significantly from that of the residuals from the last third. This test is fairly easy to use and is particularly useful to test for heteroskedasticity related to a proportionality factor when the specific form of that relationship is unknown.

To use the Goldfeld-Quandt test:

1. Reorder the observations according to the size of Z, the particular proportionality factor suspected of being related to any possible heteroskedasticity.

2. Omit the middle third of the reordered observations, and use OLS to estimate separate regressions on the first and last thirds of the data set. Use the specification of the original equation.

3. Calculate GQ $= RSS_3/RSS_1$, where RSS_1 is the residual sum of squares from the first third of the reordered data set, and RSS_3 is the residual sum of squares from the last third.

4. Use the F-test to test the hypothesis that GQ is significantly different from zero by comparing GQ to the critical F-value for K and ("n"$-$K$-$1) degrees of freedom in the numerator and denominator respectively and where "n" is the sample size of each of the new smaller data sets.

   If GQ is greater than the critical F-value, the summed squared residuals from the last third of the estimated equation are significantly greater than those from the first third, and you would reject the hypothesis of homoskedasticity. If GQ is less than the critical F-value, you cannot reject the null hypothesis. For an example of and practice in the use of the Goldfeld-Quandt test, see Exercise 7.

10.4   Remedies for Heteroskedasticity

This section presents some remedies for heteroskedasticity, but it will also imply that there are times when the problem should be left unadjusted. Part of the art of econometrics is learning to tell one situation from the other.

There are three general approaches to ridding an equation of heteroskedasticity:

1. *Include a previously omitted variable.* If the heteroskedasticity is impure, determine and include the left-out variable that is causing the impure heteroskedasticity.

2. *Use Weighted Least Squares.* If there is pure heteroskedasticity, weighted least squares (a form of generalized least squares) should be considered. Divide the equation through by the proportionality factor Z (or a function of Z) that appears to be related to the heteroskedasticity. After this division, re-estimate the equation with the newly adjusted dependent and independent variables.

3. *Redefine the variables.* The effects of heteroskedastic residuals can often be negated by redefining the variables. This is a direct approach to correcting heteroskedasticity rather than the indirect approach of weighted least squares.

The redefinition of the variables should be based on the underlying theory and refocusing the equation on the basic behavior it is supposed to explain.

The first thing to do if the Park test (or other tests such as Goldfeld-Quandt) indicates the possibility of heteroskedasticity is to carefully examine the equation for specification errors. Although you should not include an explanatory variable simply because the Park test indicates the possibility of heteroskedasticity, you ought to rigorously think through the specification of the equation. If this rethinking allows you to discover a variable that should have been in the regression from the beginning, then that variable should be added to the equation. If there are no obvious specification errors, however, the heteroskedasticity may be pure in nature and one of the other remedies of this section should be considered.

10.4.1 Weighted Least Squares

Take an equation with pure heteroskedasticity caused by a proportionality factor Z:

$$Y_i = \beta_0 + \beta_1 X_{1i} + \beta_2 X_{2i} + \epsilon_i \tag{10.12}$$

where the variance of the error term, instead of being constant, is

$$\text{VAR}(\epsilon_i) = \sigma_i^2 = \sigma^2 Z_i^2 \tag{10.13}$$

where σ^2 is the constant variance of a classical (homoskedastic) error term u_i and Z_i is the proportionality factor. Given that pure heteroskedasticity exists, then Equation 10.13 can be shown[11] to be equal to:

$$Y_i = \beta_0 + \beta_1 X_{1i} + \beta_2 X_{2i} + Z_i u_i \tag{10.14}$$

The error term in Equation 10.14, $Z_i u_i$, is heteroskedastic because $\sigma^2 Z_i^2$ is not constant. How could we adjust Equation 10.14 to make the error term homoskedastic? That is, what should be done to $Z_i u_i$ to make it turn into u_i? The easiest method is to divide the entire equation through by the proportionality factor Z_i, resulting in an error term, u_i, that has a constant variance σ^2. The new equation thus satisfies the classical assumptions, and a regression run on this new equation would no longer be expected to have heteroskedastic error terms. This general remedy to heteroskedasticity is called weighted least squares, which is actually a version of generalized least squares.

Weighted least squares involves dividing Equation 10.14 through by whatever will make the error term once again homoskedastic and then rerunning the regression on the transformed variables. Given the commonly assumed form of heteroskedasticity in Equation 10.13, this means that the technique consists of three steps:

1. Divide Equation 10.14 through by the proportionality factor Z, obtaining:

$$Y_i/Z_i = \beta_0/Z_i + \beta_1 X_{1i}/Z_i + \beta_2 X_{2i}/Z_i + u_i \tag{10.15}$$

The error term of Equation 10.15 is now u_i, which is homoskedastic.

2. Recalculate the data for the variables to conform to Equation 10.15.

3. Estimate Equation 10.15 with Ordinary Least Squares.

This third step in weighted least squares, the estimation of the transformed equation, is fairly tricky, because the exact details of how to complete this regression depend on whether the proportionality factor Z is also an explanatory variable in Equation 10.12. If Z is not an explanatory variable in Equation 10.15, then the regression to be run in step 3 would be:

$$Y_i/Z_i = \beta_0/Z_i + \beta_1 X_{1i}/Z_i + \beta_2 X_{2i}/Z_i + u_i \qquad (10.16)$$

Note that this equation has no constant term. Most OLS computer packages can run such a regression only if the equation is forced through the origin by specifically suppressing the intercept with an instruction to the computer.

As pointed out in Section 7.4, however, the omission of the constant term forces the constant effect of omitted variables, nonlinearities, and measurement error into the other coefficient estimates. To avoid having these constant term elements forced into the slope coefficient estimates, one alternative approach to Equation 10.16 is to add a constant term[12] to Equation 10.15 before the transformed equation is estimated. If Z is not identical to one of the Xs in the original equation, then either Equation 10.16 or the following specification can be run as step 3 in weighted least squares:

$$Y_i/Z_i = \alpha_0 + \beta_0/Z_i + \beta_1 X_{1i}/Z_i + \beta_2 X_{2i}/Z_i + u_i \qquad (10.17)$$

If Z is also an explanatory variable X in Equation 10.15, then no constant term need be added because one already exists. Look again at Equation 10.15. If $Z = X_1$ (or, similarly, if $Z = X_2$), then one of the slope coefficients becomes the constant term in the transformed equation because $X_1/Z = 1$:

$$Y_i/Z_i = \beta_0/Z_i + \beta_1 + \beta_2 X_{2i}/Z_i + u_i \qquad (10.18)$$

If this form of weighted least squares is used, however, coefficients obtained from an estimation of Equation 10.17 must be interpreted very carefully. Notice that β_1 is now the intercept term of Equation 10.18 even though it is the slope coefficient of Equation 10.14 and that β_0 is a slope coefficient in Equation 10.18 even though it is the intercept in Equation 10.14. As a result, a researcher interested in an estimate of the coefficient of X_1 in Equation 10.14 would have to examine the intercept of Equation 10.18, and a researcher interested in an estimate of the intercept term of Equation 10.14 would have to examine the coefficient of $1/Z_i$ in Equation 10.18. The computer will print out $\hat{\beta}_0$ as a "slope coefficient" and $\hat{\beta}_1$ as a "constant term" when in reality they are estimates of the opposite coefficients in the original Equation 10.14.

There are three other major problems with using weighted least squares:

1. The job of identifying the proportionality factor Z is, as has been pointed out already, quite difficult.

2. The functional form that relates the Z factor to the variance of the error term of the original equation may not be the commonly assumed squared function of Equation 10.13. When some other functional relationship is involved, a different transformation is required. For more on these advanced transformations, see Exercise 8.

3. Sometimes weighted least squares is applied to an equation with impure heteroskedasticity. In such cases, it can be shown that the estimates reduce somewhat the bias from an omitted variable, but the estimates are inferior to those obtained from the correctly specified equation.

Given these uncertainties, it makes sense to consider returning to the original theory and attempting to formulate the project in a way that is not so susceptible to heteroskedasticity.

10.4.2   The Direct Approach: Redefining the Variables

Another approach to ridding an equation of heteroskedasticity is to go back to the basic underlying theory of the equation and redefine the variables in a way that avoids heteroskedasticity. A redefinition of the variables often is useful in allowing the estimated equation to focus more on the behavioral aspects of the relationship. Such a rethinking is a difficult and discouraging process, because it appears to dismiss all the work already done, but once the theoretical work has been reviewed, the alternative approaches that are discovered are often exciting in that they offer possible ways to avoid problems that had previously seemed insurmountable.

Unfortunately, it is difficult to specify procedures for something as general as "completely rethinking the research project," so we would like to present a nonnumerical example of what we mean. When we get to the example of the next section, the direct approach of redefining the variables will then be compared to the more formal method of weighted least squares.

Consider a cross-sectional model of the total expenditures by the governments of different cities. Logical explanatory variables to consider in such an analysis are the aggregate income, the population, and the average wage in each city. The larger the total income of a city's residents and businesses, for example, the larger the city government's expenditures (see Figure 10.6). In this case, it is not very enlightening that the larger cities have larger incomes and also have larger expenditures (in absolute magnitude) than the smaller ones do.

Fitting a regression line to such data (see the line in Figure 10.6) also gives undue weight to the larger cities because they would otherwise give rise to large squared residuals. That is, since OLS minimizes the summed squared residuals, and since the residuals from the large cities are likely to be large due simply to the size of

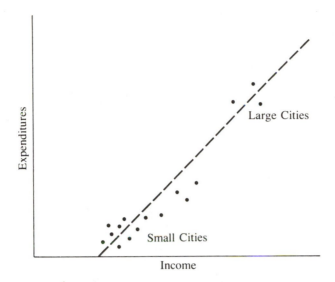

FIGURE 10.6 *City Expenditures as a Function of Income, Aggregate Terms*
If city expenditures are explained in an aggregate model, the larger cities play a major
role in the determination of the coefficient values. Note how the slope would be somewhat
lower without the heavy influence of the larger cities. In addition, heteroskedasticity is a
potential problem in an aggregate model, because the wide range of sizes of the dependent
variable makes different error term variances more likely.

the city, the regression estimation will be especially sensitive to the residuals from
the larger cities. This is often called "spurious correlation" due to size.

In addition, the residuals may indicate heteroskedasticity. The remedy for this
kind of heteroskedasticity is not to automatically use weighted least squares, however, nor is it to throw out the observations from large cities. It makes sense to
consider reformulating the model in a way that will discount the scale factor (the
size of the cities) and emphasize the underlying behavior. In this case, per capita
expenditures would be a logical dependent variable and per capita income a logical explanatory variable. Such a transformation is shown in Figure 10.7. This form
of the equation places New York and Los Angeles on the same scale as, say,
Pasadena or New Brunswick and thus gives them the same weight in estimation.
If an explanatory variable happened not to be a function of the size of the city,
however, it would not need to be adjusted to per capita terms. If the equation
included the average wage of city workers, for example, that wage would not be
divided through by population in the transformed equation.

Note that this transformation is very similar in some ways to weighted least
squares, since both independent and dependent variables have been divided by
population. The difference is that there is no term equal to the reciprocal of population (as there is in weighted least squares) and that not all explanatory variables
are divided by population. For the original equation,

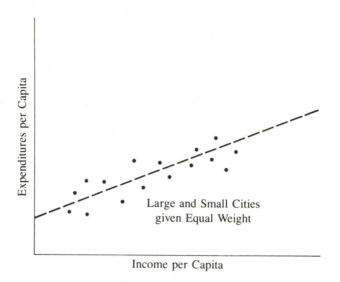

FIGURE 10.7 *City Expenditures as a Function of Income, per Capita Terms*
If city expenditures are explained in a per capita model, then large and small cities have equal weights. In addition, heteroskedasticity is less likely, because the dependent variable does not vary over a wide range of sizes.

$$EXP_i = \beta_0 + \beta_1 POP_i + \beta_2 INC_i + \beta_3 WAGE_i + \epsilon_i \qquad (10.19)$$

the weighted least squares version would be

$$EXP_i/POP_i = \beta_1 + \beta_0/POP_i + \beta_2 INC_i/POP_i + \beta_3 WAGE_i/POP_i + u_i$$

$$(10.20)$$

while the directly transformed equation would be

$$EXP_i/POP_i = \alpha_0 + \alpha_1 INC_i/POP_i + \alpha_2 WAGE_i + u_i \qquad (10.21)$$

where EXP_i refers to the expenditures, INC_i refers to the income, $WAGE_i$ refers to the average wage, and POP_i refers to population of the ith city. As can be seen, the weighted least squares Equation 10.20 divides through the entire equation by population, while the theoretically transformed one divides only expenditures and income by population. While the directly transformed Equation 10.21 does indeed solve any potential heteroskedasticity in the model, such a solution should be considered incidental to the benefits of rethinking the equation in a way that focuses on the basic behavior being examined.

Note that it is possible that the *reformulated* Equation 10.21 could have heteroskedasticity; the error variances might be larger for the observations having the larger per capita values for income and expenditures than they are for smaller per capita values. Thus it is legitimate to suspect and test for heteroskedasticity even in this transformed model. If heteroskedasticity is detected, it does not usually make sense to apply weighted least squares to the equation, since the resulting variables (for example, income divided by population squared) would be hard to interpret. Instead, the model may be transformed once again (into percentage change terms or another appropriate reformulation). Such heteroskedasticity in the transformed equation is unlikely, however, because there will be little of the variation in size normally associated with heteroskedasticity.

A thoughtful transformation of the variables that corrects for heteroskedasticity while at the same time avoiding the spurious correlation due to size may sometimes be the best approach to solving these problems. Note however, that not every variable in the equation is treated the same (unlike weighted least squares). With some thought, each variable in a cross-sectional model can be examined for possible transformations that will facilitate a useful and properly interpreted regression equation.

10.5   A More Complete Example

Let's work through a complete example that involves a cross-sectional data set, potential heteroskedasticity, and the use of the Park test and weighted least squares. Back in the mid-1970s, the United States Department of Energy attempted to allocate gasoline to regions, states, and even individual retailers on the basis of past usage, changing demographics, and other factors. Underlying these allocations must have been some sort of model of the usage of petroleum by state (or region) as a function of a number of factors. It seems likely that such a cross-sectional model, if ever estimated, would have had to cope with the problem of heteroskedasticity.

In a model where the dependent variable is petroleum consumption by state, possible explanatory variables include functions of the size of the state (such as the number of miles of roadway, the number of motor vehicle registrations, or the population), and variables that are *not* functions of the size of the state (such as the gasoline tax *rate* or the speed limit). Since there is little to be gained by including more than one variable that measures the size of the state (because such an addition would be theoretically redundant and likely to cause needless multicollinearity), and since the speed limit is the same for all states (it would be a useful variable in a time series model, however) a reasonable model to consider might be:

$$PCON_i = f(REG, TAX) = \overset{+}{\beta_0} + \overset{-}{\beta_1}REG_i + \beta_2 TAX_i + \epsilon_i \qquad (10.22)$$

where: $PCON_i$ = Petroleum consumption in the ith state (trillions of BTUs)
   REG_i = Motor Vehicle Registrations in the ith state (thousands)
   TAX_i = Gasoline Tax Rate in the ith state (cents per gallon)
   ϵ_i = A classical error term

The more cars registered in a state, we would think, the more petroleum consumed, while a high tax rate on gasoline would decrease aggregate gasoline purchases in that state. If we now collect the data for this example (see Table 10.1) we can estimate Equation 10.22, obtaining

$$\widehat{PCON}_i = 551.7 + 0.1861REG_i - 53.59TAX_i \qquad (10.23)$$
$$(0.0117) \qquad (16.86)$$
$$t = \qquad 15.88 \qquad -3.18$$
$$\bar{R}^2 = .861 \qquad n = 50$$

This equation seems to have no problems—the coefficients are significant in the hypothesized directions, and the overall equation is statistically significant. No Durbin-Watson d statistic is shown, because there is no "natural" order of the observations to test for serial correlation (if you're curious, the DW for the order in Table 10.1 is 2.19). Given the discussion in the previous sections, we wish to investigate the possibility of heteroskedasticity caused by variation in the size of the states.

To test this possibility, we obtain the residuals from Equation 10.23, which are listed in Table 10.1, and run a Park Test on them. Before we can run a Park test, we must decide what possible proportionality factor Z to investigate.

Most variables related to market size would be appropriate, but motor vehicle registrations (REG) is certainly a reasonable choice. Note that to run a Park test with the gasoline tax rate (TAX) as the proportionality factor Z would be a mistake, since there is little evidence that the rate varies significantly with the size of the state. Total tax receipts, on the other hand, would be a possible alternative to motor vehicle registrations. To see what the residuals look like if plotted against REG, see Figure 10.8; note that the residuals do indeed look potentially heteroskedastic. The next step would be to run a Park test:

$$\ln(e_i^2) = \alpha_0 + \alpha_1 \ln REG_i + u_i \qquad (10.24)$$

where e_i is the residual for the ith state from Equation 10.23, and u_i is a classical (homoskedastic) error term.

If we run this Park test regression, we obtain:

$$\widehat{\ln(e_i^2)} = 1.650 + 0.952\ln REG_i \qquad (10.25)$$
$$(0.308)$$
$$t = \qquad 3.09$$
$$\bar{R}^2 = .148 \qquad n = 50 \qquad F = 9.533$$

Since the critical t-value for a 99 percent two-tailed *t*-test is about 2.7 in Statistical Table B-1[13], we can reject the null hypothesis of homoskedasticity, because the appropriate decision rule is:

$$\text{Reject } H_0: \alpha_1 = 0 \quad \text{if } t_{PARK} > 2.7$$
$$\text{Do Not Reject } H_0 \quad \text{if } t_{PARK} \leq 2.7$$

Table 10.1 Data for the Petroleum Consumption Example (1982)

PCON	UHM	TAX	REG	POP	e	STATE
270	2.2	9	743	1136	62.335	Maine
122	2.4	14	774	948	176.52	New Hampshire
58	0.7	11	351	520	30.481	Vermont
821	20.6	9.9	3750	5750	101.87	Massachusetts
98	3.6	13	586	953	133.92	Rhode Island
450	10.1	11	2258	3126	67.527	Connecticut
1819	36.4	8	8235	17567	163.24	New York
1229	22.2	8	4917	7427	190.83	New Jersey
1200	27.9	11	6725	11879	−13.924	Pennsylvania
1205	29.2	11.7	7636	10772	−140.98	Ohio
650	17.6	11.1	3884	5482	−29.764	Indiana
1198	30.3	7.5	7242	11466	−299.72	Illinois
760	25.1	13	6250	9116	−258.33	Michigan
460	13.8	13	3162	4745	16.446	Wisconsin
503	13.0	13	3278	4133	37.855	Minnesota
371	8.1	13	2346	2906	79.330	Iowa
571	13.9	7	3412	4942	−240.63	Missouri
136	1.6	8	653	672	−108.50	North Dakota
109	1.6	13	615	694	139.52	South Dakota
203	4.3	13.9	1215	1589	170.08	Nebraska
349	8.4	8	2061	2408	−157.58	Kansas
118	1.4	11	415	600	78.568	Delaware
487	9.8	13.5	2893	4270	120.31	Maryland
628	12.4	11	3705	5485	−23.806	Virginia
192	2.9	10.5	1142	1961	−9.5451	West Virginia
642	17.1	12	4583	6019	−119.64	North Carolina
320	7.1	13	1975	3227	97.385	South Carolina
677	15.6	7.5	3916	5648	−201.65	Georgia
1459	28.5	8	8335	10466	−215.37	Florida
434	6.9	10	2615	3692	−68.513	Kentucky
482	11.9	9	3381	4656	−216.68	Tennessee
457	13.7	11	3039	3941	−70.842	Alabama
325	6.3	9	1593	2569	−40.877	Mississippi
300	7.4	9.5	1481	2307	−18.235	Arkansas
1417	10.1	8	2800	4383	772.87	Louisiana
451	11.4	6.58	2780	3226	−265.51	Oklahoma
3572	59.9	5	11388	15329	1168.6	Texas
131	2.3	9	758	805	−79.457	Montana
105	2.2	7.5	873	977	−207.25	Idaho
163	1.5	8	508	509	−54.515	Wyoming
323	9.2	9	2502	3071	−212.07	Colorado
192	4.4	11	1193	1367	7.7577	New Mexico
291	8.9	10	2216	2892	−137.25	Arizona
169	5.0	11	1038	1571	13.608	Utah
133	2.4	12	710	876	92.250	Nevada
562	14.8	12	3237	4276	50.895	Washington
364	8.4	8	2075	2668	−145.18	Oregon
2840	62.5	9	17130	24697	−417.81	California
155	1.2	8	319	444	−27.336	Alaska
214	1.3	8.5	586	997	8.7623	Hawaii

SOURCE: *1985 Statistical Abstract* (U.S. Department of Commerce), except the residual.

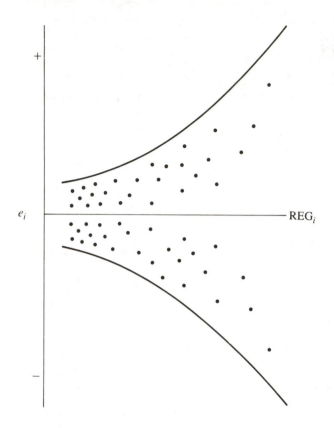

FIGURE 10.8 *Heteroskedastic Residuals from Equation 10.23*
If the residuals from Equation 10.23 and Table 10.1 are plotted with respect to Motor Vehicle Registrations by state (REG), they appear to follow a wider distribution for large values of REG than for small values of REG. Such a pattern is preliminary evidence of heteroskedasticity that should be tested more formally with a test like the Park test.

Since there appears to be heteroskedasticity in the residuals of Equation 10.23, what should we do? First we think through the specification of the equation in search of an omitted variable. While there are a number of possible ones for this equation, it turns out that all of the ones we tried involve either significant multicollinearity (as shown in Chapter 8) or do not cure the heteroskedasticity.

As a result, we will re-estimate Equation 10.22 with weighted least squares, using motor vehicle registrations[14] as the proportionality factor Z:

$$PCON_i/REG_i = \beta_0/REG_i + \beta_1 + \beta_2 TAX_i/REG_i + u_i \qquad (10.26)$$

which results in the following estimates:

$$\overparen{PCON_i/REG_i} = 218.54/REG_i + 0.168 - 17.389TAX_i/REG_i \quad (10.27)$$
$$\phantom{\overparen{PCON_i/REG_i} = 218.54/REG_i +}(0.014) \quad\;\; (4.682)$$
$$t = \quad 12.27 \quad\quad -3.71$$
$$\bar{R}^2 = .333 \quad n = 50$$

Compare this result carefully with Equation 10.23. Note that:

1. The coefficient of the reciprocal of motor vehicle registrations in Equation 10.27 is really an estimate of the intercept of Equation 10.23, and therefore no t-test is conducted even though the OLS regression program will indicate that it is a slope coefficient.

2. What appears to be the intercept of Equation 10.27 is an estimate of the coefficient of motor vehicle registrations in Equation 10.23. Note that this particular estimate is quite close in magnitude and significance to the original results in Equation 10.23.

3. The t-score of the coefficient of the proportionality factor, REG, is lower in the weighted least squares estimate than it is in the potentially heteroskedastic Equation 10.23. The overall fit is also worse, but this has no particular importance because the dependent variables are different in the two equations.

As mentioned in Section 10.4.2, however, it is not always theoretically reasonable to divide all the independent variables by the suspected Z. The variable TAX/REG in Equation 10.27 is the tax rate in cents per gallon divided by the number of registered motor vehicles. While that variable certainly has meaning if the dependent variable is divided by REG as well, it is not an obvious one to choose on its own merits. Alternatively, we can rethink the purpose of the regression and reformulate the variables of the equation to try to avoid heteroskedasticity resulting from spurious correlation due to size. If we were to rethink Equation 10.22, we might decide to attempt to explain per capita petroleum consumption, coming up with:

$$PCON_i/POP_i = f(\overset{+}{REG/POP}, \overset{-}{TAX}) = \beta_0 + \beta_1 REG_i/POP_i + \beta_2 TAX_i + \epsilon_i$$
$$(10.28)$$

where POP_i is the population of the ith state in thousands of people.

We have now reformulated the equation in a way similar to weighted least squares, but we now have an equation that can stand on its own from a theoretical point of view. If we estimate Equation 10.28, we obtain:

$$\overparen{PCON_i/POP_i} = 0.168 + 0.1082REG_i/POP_i - 0.0103TAX_i \quad (10.29)$$
$$\phantom{\overparen{PCON_i/POP_i} = 0.168 +}(0.0716) \quad\quad\;\; (0.0035)$$
$$t = \quad 1.51 \quad\quad\quad -2.95$$
$$\bar{R}^2 = .165 \quad n = 50$$

If we compare Equation 10.29 with Equations 10.27 and 10.23, we see that this third approach is not necessarily better, but it is quite different. The statistical properties of Equation 10.29, though not directly comparable to the other equations, do not appear as strong as they ought to be, but this is not necessarily an important factor.

Which is better, the unadjusted potentially heteroskedastic equation, the one derived from weighted least squares, or the reformulated one? It depends on the purposes of your research. If your goal is to determine the impact of tax rates on gasoline consumption, all three models give virtually the same results in terms of the sign and significance of the coefficient, but the latter two models avoid the heteroskedasticity. If your goal is to allocate petroleum in aggregate amounts to states, then the original equation may be just fine. In most cases of severe heteroskedasticity, some remedial action is necessary, but whether weighted least squares or a reformulation is called for depends on the particular equation in question. We generally find that if reformulation makes intuitive sense, it is usually the best remedy to apply. It more easily avoids the arbitrary process of choosing a Z and produces coefficients with more obvious economic interpretations than does weighted least squares.

10.6   Summary

1. Heteroskedasticity is the violation of the classical assumption that the error terms are drawn from a distribution with a constant variance. While homoskedastic error terms are drawn from a distribution that has a constant variance for all observations, heteroskedastic error terms are drawn from distributions whose variances differ with different observations. Heteroskedasticity occurs most frequently in cross-sectional data sets.

2. The variance of a heteroskedastic error term is not equal to σ^2, a constant. Instead, it equals σ_i^2, where the subscript i indicates that the variance can change from observation to observation. Many different kinds of heteroskedasticity are possible, but a common model is one in which the variance changes systematically as a function of some other variable, a proportionality factor Z:

$$\text{VAR}(\epsilon_i) = \sigma^2 Z_i^2$$

The proportionality factor Z is usually a variable related in some way to the size or accuracy of the dependent variable.

3. Pure heteroskedasticity is a function of the error term of the correctly specified regression equation. Impure heteroskedasticity is caused by a specification error such as an omitted variable.

4. The major consequence of heteroskedasticity is an increase in the variance of the $\hat{\beta}$s that is masked by an underestimation of the standard errors by ordinary least squares. As a result, OLS tends to overestimate t-scores in the face

of heteroskedasticity, sometimes leading to errors of inference. Hetero-skedasticity does not cause bias in the estimates of the βs themselves.

5. Many tests use the residuals of an equation to test for the possibility of het-eroskedasticity in the error terms. The Park test uses a function of these residuals as the dependent variable of a second regression whose explana-tory variable is a function of the suspected proportionality factor Z:

$$\ln(e_i^2) = \alpha_0 + \alpha_1 \ln Z_i + u_i$$

If $\hat{\alpha}_1$ is significantly different from zero, then we reject the null hypothesis of homoskedasticity.

6. The first step in correcting heteroskedasticity is to check for an omitted vari-able that might be causing impure heteroskedasticity. If the specification is as good as possible, then solutions such as weighted least squares or a refor-mulation of the variables of the equation should be considered.

7. Weighted least squares is a method of ridding an equation of heteroskedasticity by dividing it through by a function of the proportionality factor Z and then re-estimating the equation with OLS. In some circumstances, it is more appropriate to completely rethink the underlying theory of the equation and to reformulate the variables, for example by converting them to a per capita basis, before rerunning the equation.

Exercises

(Answers to even-numbered questions are in Appendix A):

1. Write out the meaning of each of the following terms without reference to the book (or your notes) and then compare your definition with the version in the text for each:
   a. impure heteroskedasticity
   b. proportionality factor Z
   c. the Park test
   d. the Goldfeld-Quandt test
   e. weighted least squares

2. In the most common model of heteroskedasticity ($VAR(\epsilon_i) = \sigma^2 Z_i^2$), one of the major difficulties is making good choices for potential proportionality factors (Zs). In each of the following equations, separate the listed explana-tory variables into those that are likely or unlikely to be proportionality factors.
   a. The number of economics majors in a cross-section of various sized col-leges and universities as a function of the number of undergraduates attending a school, the number of required courses in that school's eco-nomics major, the average grade-point average in the major, and the number of economics professors there.

b. Gross National Product in a cross-section of various sized countries as a function of the aggregate gross investment in a nation, the percentage growth of its money supply, the maximum marginal tax rate on capital gains there, and its population.

c. The demand for carrots in a time series model of the United States as a function of the real price of carrots, U.S. disposable income, U.S. per capita disposable income, population, the percentage error in carrot sales measurement, and the real price of celery.

3. Of all the econometric problems we have encountered, heteroskedasticity is the one that seems more difficult to understand intuitively than the others. Close your book and attempt to write out an explanation of heteroskedasticity in your own words. Be sure to include a diagram in your description.

4. Use the Park test to test the null hypothesis of homoskedasticity in each of the following situations (1 percent level of significance):
a. The calculated t-score of your suspected proportionality factor Z is 3.561 from a Park test regression with 25 degrees of freedom.
b. The following residuals and values for the potential Z:

Observation	Residual	Proportionality factor Z
1	3.147	120
2	9.394	240
3	-2.344	900
4	-1.034	50
5	5.678	600
6	2.113	20
7	-4.356	200

c. How would your answer to the above change if the 7th observation of Z was minus 200? How would you even take the log of Z?
d. Test the first column of error terms in Table 9.1. Use X as the potential proportionality factor Z.

5. Ando and Modigliani collected the following data on the income and consumption of non-self-employed homeowners:[15]

Income bracket ($)	Average income ($)	Average consumption ($)
0-999	556	2760
1000-1999	1622	1930
2000-2999	2664	2740
3000-3999	3587	3515
4000-4999	4535	4350
5000-5999	5538	5320
6000-7499	6585	6250
7500-9999	8582	7460
10000-above	14033	11500

a. Run a regression attempting to explain average consumption as a function of average income.

b. Use the Park test to test the residuals from the equation you ran in Part a for heteroskedasticity, using income as the potential proportionality factor Z (5 percent).

c. If there is only one explanatory variable, what does the equation for weighted least squares look like? Does running weighted least squares have any effect on the estimation? Why or why not?

d. If the Park test run in Part b above shows evidence of heteroskedasticity, then what, if anything, should be done about it?

6. Show that Equation 10.14 is true by showing that the variance of an error term that equals a classical error term multiplied times a proportionality constant Z is that shown in Equation 10.13. That is, show that if $\epsilon_i = u_i Z_i$, then $VAR(\epsilon_i) = \sigma^2 Z_i^2$ if $VAR(u_i) = \sigma^2$ (a constant). Hint: go back to the definition of a variance and then calculate the variance for an error term $Z_i u_i$.

7. The best way to feel comfortable with the Goldfeld-Quandt test is to apply that test to a set of residuals to which we have already applied the Park test. Find residuals for and apply the Goldfeld-Quandt test to the following situations (1 percent):

a. The residuals of the Woody's example from Section 3.3 with P as the proportionality factor Z; be sure to compare your conclusion to that in Section 10.3.2.

b. The residuals of the state cross-sectional example of Section 10.5 with P as the proportionality factor Z, once again comparing your conclusion with that of the section.

8. Given the most commonly used functional form for the relationship between the proportionality factor Z and the error term ($\epsilon_i = Z_i u_i$ where u_i is a homoskedastic error term), we can derive the appropriate weighted least squares equation of:

$$Y/Z_i = \beta_0/Z_i + \beta_1 + \beta_2 X_{2i}/Z_i + u_i$$

when $Z = X_1$, an explanatory variable already in the equation. This is accomplished by dividing the equation by the precise value (Z_i) necessary to make the error term homoskedastic in nature. Find the appropriate weighted least squares equations to be used in the following situations:

a. $\epsilon_i = u_i \sqrt{Z_i}$ where $Z = X_1$, an explanatory variable already in the equation.

b. $\epsilon_i = u_i Z_i$ where $Z = X_3$, a variable not in the equation.

c. $\epsilon_i = u_i \hat{Y}_i$, where $\hat{Y}_i$ is the estimated value of the dependent variable obtained from the regression equation.

9. Is it really possible to decide whether to adjust an equation for heteroskedasticity if we can never actually observe the error terms (just the residuals), have no way of knowing whether we have the right proportionality factor, and have no way of knowing whether we have the right functional relationship between the proportionality factor and the error term? Are there any circumstances in which you could feel confident about having used weighted least squares? Are there any circumstances in which you could feel confident about having reformulated the equation? Why?

10. Consider the following log-linear equation (standard errors in parentheses):[16]

$$\hat{Y}_i = 0.442X_{1i} + 0.092X_{2i} + 0.045X_{3i} + 0.259X_{4i}$$
$$\phantom{\hat{Y}_i =} (0.058) \quad\;\; (0.042) \quad\;\; (0.014) \quad\;\; (0.034)$$
$$R^2 = .620 \qquad n = 430$$

where: Y_i = the log of the gross value of agricultural output (in drachmas) of the ith Greek farm in a given year.

X_{1i} = the log of man-workdays in a year on the ith farm.

X_{2i} = the log of the amount of land on the ith farm (in stremmata, equal to a quarter of an acre).

X_{3i} = the log of the value of the plant and equipment (plus operating expenses for plant and equipment) on the ith farm that year (in drachmas).

X_{4i} = the log of the value of livestock (including trees) plus operating expenses on livestock (in drachmas) in the ith farm that year.

a. Create hypotheses about the signs of the various coefficients and then calculate the t-scores to test those hypotheses at the 5 percent level of significance.

b. Suppose you were now told that the Park Test, using X_1 as a potential proportionality factor Z, indicated the likelihood of heteroskedasticity in the residuals of this equation. Is it likely that there actually is heteroskedasticity in such a log-linear equation? Why or why not?

c. If there is a logical reformulation of the equation that might rid the model of heteroskedasticity?

d. If you decided to apply weighted least squares to the equation, what equation would you estimate?

[1.] Various authors spell this "heteroscedasticity," but a recent article by Huston McCulloch appears to settle this controversy in favor of "heteroskedasticity" because of the word's Greek origin. See J. Huston McCulloch, "On Heteros*edasticity," *Econometrica*, March 1985, p. 483. While heteroskedasticity is a difficult word to spell, at least it's an impressive comeback when parents ask "what'd you learn for all that money?"

[2.] If this paragraph sounds vaguely familiar, that's because our discussion of impure heteroskedasticity parallels our previous discussion of impure serial correlation. If this paragraph doesn't sound at all familiar (or if you skipped Section 9.1), then you might consider briefly reading Section 9.1.2 for a fuller explanation of these ideas.

[3.] The consequences of heteroskedasticity are so similar to those of serial correlation that the following section assumes at least some familiarity with them. As long as you have read Section 9.2, the following discussion can stand on its own. If you did not read Section 9.2, you should do so before continuing with this chapter.

[4.] Actually, the OLS estimates of the variance and the standard error of the coefficient estimates β_k are biased, but the bias is negative as long as σ_i^2 and $(X_{ki} - \bar{X}_k)^2$ are positively correlated. The SE($\hat{\beta}$)s will be underestimated as long as an increase in X is related to an increase in the variance of the error terms. In economic examples, such a positive correlation would almost always be expected in cases when a sizable correlation is likely to exist. For some variables, no correlation at all might exist, but a negative correlation would occur quite infrequently. As a result, the statement that OLS underestimates the variances, while a simplification, is almost always true.

[5.] In particular, see tests suggested by T. H. Glejser, "A New Test for Heteroscedasticity," *Journal of the American Statistical Association,* 1969, pp. 316-323; T.S. Breusch and A.R. Pagan, "A Simple Test for Heteroskedasticity and Random Coefficient Variation," *Econometrica,* 1979, pp. 1287-1294; and Halbert White, "A Heteroskedasticity-Consistent Covariance Matrix Estimator and a Direct Test for Heteroskedasticity," *Econometrica,* 1980, pp. 817-838. The first test assumes a generalization of the "Z_i proportionality factor" approach that allows for alternate formulations, the second is applicable to a wide range of heteroskedastic situations, and the last has the distinct advantage of not assuming any particular form of heteroskedasticity at all. The White test is more complex for a beginning researcher to use than either the Park or Goldfeld-Quandt tests, but it is rapidly gaining support as the best test yet devised to apply to all types of heteroskedasticity.

[6.] R.E. Park, "Estimation with Heteroscedastic Error Terms," *Econometrica,* October 1966, p. 888.

[7.] One criticism of the Park test is that this error term is not necessarily homoskedastic. See S. M. Goldfeld and R.E. Quandt, *Nonlinear Methods in Econometrics* (Amsterdam: North-Holland Publishing Company, 1972), pp. 93-94.

[8.] Some econometricians suggest using the Park test for insight into the form of the heteroskedasticity. If $VAR(\epsilon_i) = \sigma^2 Z_i^2$, then $\ln(e_i^2)$ should be equal to $\alpha_0 + 2\ln Z_i$ plus an error term. Thus the estimate of the coefficient of $\ln Z$ in the Park test implies whether the proportionality factor should be squared or raised to some other power. For more on this and its implications for deciding which form to use to adjust for heteroskedasticity, see R.S. Pindyck and D.L. Rubinfeld, *Econometric Models and Economic Forecasts* (New York: McGraw-Hill, 1981), pp. 150-152.

[9.] Recall that not being able to reject the null hypothesis of homoskedasticity does not prove that the error terms are homoskedastic. In addition, note that *this* Park test says nothing about *other* proportionality factors or other forms of heteroskedasticity. While heteroskedasticity of any kind is unlikely in this example because of the nature of the dependent variable, it is possible to find homoskedasticity with respect to one proportionality factor (or form) but heteroskedasticity with respect to some other proportionality factor (or form). Careful thinking is necessary before a potential Z can be chosen. Running a Park test on every conceivable variable would do little but increase the chance of Type I Error (rejecting the null hypothesis of homoskedasticity when it is true).

[10.] S.M. Goldfeld and R.E. Quandt, "Some Tests for Homoscedasticity," *Journal of the American Statistical Association,* September 1965, pp. 539-547. Goldfeld and Quandt do not explicitly specify that exactly a third of the sample should be omitted, but since the power of the test increases as more observations are omitted, the use of one-third has become almost standard practice. The Goldfeld-Quandt test avoids the potential heteroskedasticity (and, it turns out, serial correlation) of the Park test referred to in footnote 7.

[11.] The key is to show that the error term $Z_i u_i$ has a variance equal to $\sigma^2 Z_i^2$. For more, see Exercise 6.

[12.] The suggestion of adding a constant term is also made by Potluri Rao and Roger LeRoy Miller, *Applied Econometrics* (Belmont, California: Wadsworth, 1971) p. 121, and others.

[13.] Note that Statistical Table B-1 does not have critical values for exactly 50 observations. In such cases, most researchers either use the number of observations closest to the value they are looking for or else they interpolate and attempt to approximate the critical values.

[14.] Note that we have divided the equation through by REG_i. This assumes that the error term $\epsilon_i = Z_i u_i$. The coefficient of $\ln REG$ in the Park test is approximately 1 which is evidence that the appropriate functional form may be $\epsilon_i = u_i \sqrt{Z}$, but such a transformation should not be adopted simply on the basis of the Park test coefficient alone. If the underlying theory gives evidence in support of such a change, which is not the case in this example, then we would divide the equation through by the square root of Z_i. For more on this, reread footnote 8 above.

[15.] Albert Ando and Franco Modigliani, "The 'Permanent Income' and 'Life-Cycle' Hypotheses of Saving Behavior: Comparisons and Tests," in I. Friend and R. Jones, eds. *Consumption and Saving,* Vol. II. 1960, p. 154.

[16.] Adapted from Pan A. Yotopoulos and Jeffrey B. Nugent, *Economics of Development* (New York: Harper & Row, 1976), p. 82.

11

A Regression User's Handbook

The real world problems that a regression user encounters are not so neatly labeled and compartmentalized as the previous ten chapters might imply. Instead, researchers must consider all the possible difficulties in an equation in order to decide which specification and estimation techniques to use. As a result, it is useful to have summaries of the definitions, problems, solutions, and statistical tests that are central to basic single-equation linear regression models. The first two sections of this chapter contain such summaries; while you should certainly read these now, we also hope that you will benefit from using them as a reference whenever you are undertaking econometric research.

Frequently, even the best planned and executed regression analysis will not produce the expected set of estimated coefficients and their accompanying statistics the first time it is applied—something is deficient. When this happens, econometrics becomes an art; the core of the problem is that we never know what the true model is. There is a fine line between curve fitting and searching for the truth by formulating and estimating alternative regression equations or using alternative estimating techniques. Some regression results may very well be strictly a product of chance, because the researchers might have experimented with a number of models and estimators until they obtained the results that came closest to what they wanted; such an approach is unscientific. On the other hand, it would be foolhardy to go to the opposite extreme and ignore obvious estimation or specification errors in a first regression run; that would also be unscientific. The last four sections of this chapter help beginning researchers strike a balance between these two positions by providing advice on econometric ethics and by giving some hands-on regression experience. The interactive regression examples in Sections 11.4 and 11.6 are "half-way houses" between reading someone else's regression results (and having no input) and doing one's own regression analysis (and getting no feedback). We strongly encourage the reader to take the exercises seriously and make use of the examples rather than just read them through from beginning to end.

11.1   A Regression User's Checklist

Table 11.1 contains a list of the items that a researcher checks when reviewing the output from a computer regression package. Not every item in the checklist will be produced by your computer package, and not every item in your computer output will be in the checklist, but the checklist can be a generally useful reference. In most cases, a quick glance at the checklist will remind you of the text sections that deal with the item, but if this is not the case, the fairly minimal explanations in the checklist should not be relied upon to cover everything needed for complete analysis and judgment. Instead, you should look up the item in the index. In addition, note that the actions in the right-hand column are merely suggestions. The circumstances of each individual research project are much more reliable guides than any dogmatic list of actions.

There are two ways to use the checklist. First, you can refer to it as a "glossary of packaged computer output terms" when you encounter something in your regression result that you don't understand. Second, you can work your way through the checklist in order, finding the items in your computer output and marking them. This latter use of the checklist will help ensure that you do not forget to note some important item (such as the Durbin-Watson statistic for a time series or the simple correlation matrix for a model with likely collinearity). As with the Regression User's Guide (Table 11.2), the use of the Regression User's Checklist will be most helpful for beginning researchers, but we also find ourselves referring back to it once in a while even after years of experience.

Be careful. All simplified tables, like the two in this chapter, must trade completeness for ease of use. As a result, strict adherence to a set of rules is not recommended even if the rules come from one of our tables. Someone who understands the purpose of the research, the exact definitions of the variables, and the problems in the data is much more likely to make a correct judgment than is someone equipped with a set of rules created to apply to a wide variety of possible applications.

Table 11.1   Regression User's Checklist

Symbol	Checkpoint	Reference	Decision
N. A.	Data	Check for data errors, especially outliers, in computer printout of the data. Spot check transformations of variables.	Correct any errors. If the quality of the data is poor, may want to avoid regression analysis or to use just OLS.
d. f.	Degrees of freedom	$n - K - 1 > 0$ n = number of observations K = number of explanatory variables	If $n - K - 1 \leq 0$, equation cannot be estimated, and if the degrees of freedom is low, precision is low. In such a case, try to include more observations.
$\hat{\beta}$	Estimated Coefficient	Compare signs and magnitudes to expected values.	If they are unexpected, respecify model if appropriate or assess other statistics for possible corrective procedures.
t	t-statistic $$t_k = \frac{\hat{\beta}_k - \beta_{H_0}}{SE(\hat{\beta}_k)}$$ or $$t_k = \frac{\hat{\beta}_k}{SE(\hat{\beta}_k)}$$ for computer-supplied t-scores	Two-sided test: H_0: $\beta_k = \beta_{H_0}$ H_A: $\beta_k \neq \beta_{H_0}$ One-sided test: H_0: $\beta_k \leq \beta_{H_0}$ H_A: $\beta_k > \beta_{H_0}$ β_{H_0}, the hypothesized β, is supplied by the researcher, and is zero for the t-statistic supplied by the computer.	Reject H_0 if $|t_k| > t_c$ t_c is the critical value found in the t-table for α level of significance (the column in the table) and $n - K - 1$ degrees of freedom (the row). The estimate must be of the expected sign to reject H_0.
R^2	Coefficient of Determination	Measures the degree of overall statistical fit of the model to the data.	Just a guide to the overall fit.
$\bar{R}^2$	R^2 adjusted for degrees of freedom	Same as R^2. Also attempts to show the contribution of an additional explanatory variable.	An explanatory variable is irrelevant if theory is unclear as to its inclusion, other coefficients do not change much when it is included, and the $\bar{R}^2$ falls when it is included.

Table 11.1 Regression User's Checklist (continued)

Symbol	Checkpoint	Reference	Decision
F	F-Statistic	To test $H_0: \beta_1 = \beta_2 = \cdots = \beta_K = 0$ $H_A:$ H_0 not true. Construct special F-statistic to test joint hypotheses.	Reject H_0 if $F > F_c$ where F_c is the critical value found in the F-Table for α level of significance and K numerator (for the column designation in the table) and $n - K - 1$ denominator (for the row designation) degrees of freedom.
DW	Durbin-Watson d statistic	Tests: $H_0: p \leq 0$ $H_A: p > 0$ For positive serial correlation	Reject H_0 if $DW < d_L$. Accept H_0 if $DW > d_U$. Inconclusive if $d_L \leq DW \leq d_U$. (d_L and d_U are the critical values of the Durbin-Watson statistic.)
e_i	Residual	Check for transcription errors, especially outliers.	Correct the data.
		Check for heteroskedasticity by examining the pattern of the residuals.	If evidence is clear, may want to take appropriate corrective action, but test first.
SEE	Standard error of the equation	An estimate of σ. Compare with $\bar{Y}$ for a measure of overall degree of fit.	Just a guide to the overall fit.
TSS	Total sum of squares	$TSS = \sum_i (Y_i - \bar{Y})^2$	No direct use. Used to compute F-statistic.
ESS	Explained sum of squares	$ESS = \sum_i (\hat{Y}_i - \bar{Y})^2$	Same as above.
RSS	Residual sum of squares	$RSS = \sum_i (Y_i - \hat{Y}_i)^2$	Same as above. Also used in hypothesis testing.
$SE(\hat{\beta}_k)$	Standard error of $\hat{\beta}_k$	Used in t-statistic.	A "rule of thumb" is if $|\hat{\beta}_k| > 2SE(\hat{\beta}_k)$ reject $H_0: \hat{\beta}_k = 0$.
$\hat{p}$	Estimated first-order autocorrelation coefficient	Usually the estimate is provided by an autoregressive routine.	N.A.
r_{12}	Simple correlation coefficient between X_1 and X_2	Examines collinearity.	If $r_{12}^2 > R^2$, suspect serious multicollinearity and use t-test to see if r_{12} is statistically significant.

11.2   A Regression User's Guide

Table 11.2 contains a brief summary of the major econometric maladies discussed so far in this text. For each econometric problem, we list:

1. Its nature.
2. Its consequences for Ordinary Least Squares estimation.
3. How to detect it.
4. How to attempt to get rid of it.

How might you use the guide? If an estimated equation has a particular problem, such as a significant unexpected sign for a coefficient estimate or a correct but insignificant coefficient estimate, a quick glance at the guide can give some idea of what econometric problems might be causing that symptom. Both multicollinearity and irrelevant variables can cause regression coefficients to have insignificant t-scores, for example, and someone who remembered only one of these potential causes might take the wrong corrective action. After some practice, the use of this guide will decrease until it eventually will seem fairly limiting and simplistic. Until then, however, our experience is that those about to undertake their first econometric research can benefit by referring to this guide.

11.3   The Ethical Econometrician

In Section 11.4, we will present an opportunity to practice the art of econometrics. The interactive regression learning example of that section will give the reader some "hands-on" experience with regression analysis without requiring the use of a computer and will allow the kind of feedback that is usually possible only in one-on-one sessions with an experienced econometrician. Unfortunately, the format of the section also has the potential to mislead, because the interactive example includes a large number of alternative specifications of the same regression project. One conclusion that a casual reader might draw from this large number of specifications is that we encourage the estimation of numerous regression results as a way of insuring the discovery of the best possible estimates.

Nothing could be further from the truth!

As every reader of this book should know by now, our opinion is that the best models are those on which much care has been spent to develop the best theoretical underpinnings and only a short time spent pursuing alternative estimations of that equation. Many econometricians, ourselves included, would hope to be able to estimate only *one* specification of an equation for each data set. Econometricians are fallible and our data are sometimes imperfect, however, so it is unusual for a first attempt at estimation to be totally problem-free. As a result, two or even more regressions are often necessary to rid an estimation of fairly simple difficulties that perhaps could have been avoided in a world of perfect foresight.

The difficulty is that a beginning researcher usually has little motivation to stop running regressions until he or she likes the way the result looks. If running another

Table 11.2   A Regression User's Guide

What can go wrong?	What are the consequences?	How can it be detected?	How can it be corrected?
Omitted Variable The omission of a relevant independent variable.	Bias and inconsistency in the coefficient estimates (the $\hat{\beta}$s) of the included Xs.	On the basis of theory, significant unexpected signs or surprisingly poor fits.	Include the left-out variable or a proxy.
Irrelevant Variable The inclusion of a variable that does not belong in the equation.	Decreased precision in the form of lower $\bar{R}^2$, higher standard errors, and lower t-scores.	1. Theory 2. t-test on $\hat{\beta}$ 3. $\bar{R}^2$ 4. Impact on other coefficients if X is dropped.	Delete the variable if its inclusion is not required by the underlying theory.
No Constant Term The supression of the intercept term.	Biased coefficient estimates and t-scores.	Examine the equation.	Include the constant term to act as a ''garbage term.''
Incorrect Function The functional form is inappropriate.	Biased and inconsistent estimates, poor fit, and difficult interpretation.	Examine the theory carefully; think about the underlying relationship between X and Y.	Transform the variable or the equation to a different functional form.
Multicollinearity Some of the independent variables are (imperfectly) correlated.	No biased $\hat{\beta}$s, but estimates of the separate effects of the Xs are not reliable, i.e. high SEs (and low t-scores).	No universally accepted rule or test is available. Use the t-test or the $\bar{R}^2 < (r)^2$ rule of thumb for collinearity.	Drop redundant variables, but to drop others might introduce bias. A combination variable may be useful, but often doing nothing is best.
Serial Correlation The error terms for different observations are correlated, as in: $\epsilon_t = \rho\epsilon_{t-1} + u_t$	No biased βs, but the variances of the $\hat{\beta}$s increase in a way not captured by OLS (and t-scores fall).	Use Durbin-Watson d test; if significantly less than 2, positive serial correlation exists.	If impure, add the omitted variable or change the functional form. Otherwise, consider generalized least squares.
Heteroskedasticity The variance of the error term is not constant for all observations, as in: $VAR(\epsilon_i) = \sigma^2 z_i^2$	Same as for serial correlation	Plot the spread or contraction of the residuals (against one of the Xs, for example) or use the Park or Goldfeld-Quandt tests.	Redefine the variables (as in percentage terms) or apply a weighted least squares correction by dividing through by the proportionality factor Z.

regression provides a result with a better fit, why shouldn't one more specification be tested?

The reason is a compelling one. Every time an extra regression is run and a specification choice is made on the basis of fit or statistical significance, the chances of making a mistake of inference increase dramatically. This can happen in at least two ways:

1. If you consistently drop a variable when its coefficient is insignificant but keep it when it is significant, it can be shown, as discussed in Section 6.4, that you bias your estimates of the coefficients of the equation and of the t-scores.

2. If you choose to use a lag structure, or a functional form, or an estimation procedure other than OLS on the basis of fit[1] rather than on the basis of previously theorized hypotheses, you run the risk that your equation will work poorly when it is applied to data outside your sample. If you restructure your equation to work well on one data set, you might decrease the chance of it working well on another.

What might be thought of as "ethical econometrics" is also in reality "good econometrics." That is, the real reason to avoid running too many different specifications is that the fewer regressions you run, the more reliable and more consistently trustworthy are your results. The instance in which professional ethics come into play is when a number of changes are made (different variables, lag structures, functional forms, estimation procedures, data sets, dropped outliers, and so on), but the regression results are presented to colleagues, clients, editors, or journals as if the final and best equation had been the first and only one estimated. Our recommendation is that all estimated equations be reported even if footnotes or an appendix have to be added to the documentation.

We think that there are two reasonable goals for beginning econometricians estimating models:

1. Run as few different specifications as possible while still attempting to avoid the major econometric problems.

2. Report honestly the number and type of different specifications estimated so that readers of the research can evaluate how much weight to give to your results.

Therefore, the art of econometrics boils down to attempting to find the best possible equation in the fewest possible number of regression runs. Only careful thinking and reading before the first regression can bring this about. An ethical econometrician is honest and complete in reporting the different specifications and/or data set used.

11.4 An Interactive Regression Learning Example

Econometrics is difficult to learn by reading examples, no matter how expertly done and explained they are. Most econometricians, the authors included, had trouble understanding how to use econometrics, particularly in the area of specification choice, until they had a chance to run their own regression projects. There is an element of econometric understanding that is better learned by doing than by reading about someone else's doing.

Mastering the art of econometrics by running your own regression projects without feedback is also difficult, unfortunately, because it takes quite a while to consistently avoid some fairly simple mistakes. Probably the best way to learn is to work on your own regression project, analyzing your own problems and making your own decisions, but with a more experienced econometrician nearby to give you one-on-one feedback on exactly which of your decisions were inspired and which were flawed (and why).

This section is an attempt to give the reader the opportunity to make independent specification decisions and to then get feedback on the advantages or disadvantages of those decisions. Using the interactive learning example of this section requires neither a computer nor a tutor, although either would certainly be useful. Instead, we have designed an example that can be used on its own to help to bridge the gap between the typical econometrics examples (which require no decisionmaking) and the typical econometrics projects (which give little feedback). A second interactive learning example is presented in the Appendix.

Stop!

In order to get the most out of the example, *you should not read any portion of this section until you are ready to work through the entire exercise.* Reading the pages "in order" as with any other example will waste your time, because once you have seen even a few of the results, the benefits to you of making specification decisions will diminish. *Until you are ready to completely follow the instructions of the example, you should stop now and come back to this section later.* The same warning applies to the interactive learning example in Section 11.6.

11.4.1 Building a Model of U.S. Savings and Loan Passbook Deposits

The dependent variable for our first interactive learning example is total deposits in passbook accounts (savings accounts) in Savings and Loan Associations (S & Ls) in the United States. The data are quarterly for the 1970s, so there are forty observations. For each quarter, the dependent variable, QDPASS, measures the quarterly (hence Q) aggregate current (nominal) dollars on deposit (D) in passbook (PASS) accounts in Savings and Loan Associations in the U.S. Deposits in checking accounts, money market accounts, certificates of deposit, NOW accounts, commercial bank accounts, or brokerage house accounts are not included. Instead, the QDPASS just measures the stock of deposits in traditional savings accounts in Savings and Loans (S & Ls). The term "passbook" comes from the small books that often document such accounts.

What is the basic financial theory on which a model of passbook deposits can be built? What kinds of variables should be considered for inclusion as explanatory variables? It is important to note that while they are called savings accounts by many people, passbook accounts should not be considered a measure of aggregate savings. Instead, the stock of passbook deposits is only one component of wealth. As such, the main theoretical work to be done before choosing variables should investigate how people decide what portion of their assets to keep in passbook accounts. The different levels of sophistication of such models in the literature are impressive, and any reader interested in reviewing a portion of the applicable articles should do so now before continuing on with the section.[2]

If you were going to build a single-equation linear model of passbook deposits, what factors should you consider? During any quarter, new deposits can be generated by individuals wishing to save a portion of their income in that quarter, so any reasonable specification ought to include some measure of income or wealth.

Two such variables are quarterly disposable income in the U.S. (QYDUS) and permanent income (QYPERM), defined below. Indeed, passbook savings accounts bear a lower rate of interest and are more liquid than any other financial asset except demand deposits (checking accounts), so there is some reason to believe that people might treat passbook holdings as interim transaction accounts. If this is true, then the income/wealth variables should be quite important.

A second set of important factors refers to the competition from other assets for existing wealth—the rate of interest paid on passbooks, the rate on other comparable assets, and the existence of competitive new forms of asset accounts. Variables specifically aimed at this competition for existing funds are the interest rate on passbook accounts (QRDPASS), the interest rate on 3-month treasure bills (QRTB3Y), and a dummy variable (MMCDUM) equal to zero before the legalization in 1978 of a money market certificate account paying higher "money market" rates. In addition, a fourth variable, equal to the difference (SPREAD) between the two interest rate variables might also be specified.

A third set of factors measures the environment within which the deposits are operating. If high inflation is expected, for example, holdings in all low interest accounts might fall, so an "adaptive expectations" measure of expected inflation (EXPINF) is a possible explanatory variable. This is last quarter's level of inflation; it is based on the theory that individuals form their expectation of future inflation rates by extrapolating from past inflation rates. In addition, convenience of depositing funds may be relevant, so the total number of branches of S & Ls open nationwide (BRANCH) is also a possible variable.

To sum, the variables available for you to choose for your model are:

$QDPASS_t$ The aggregate stock of deposits held in passbook accounts in Savings and Loan Associations in the U.S. in quarter t (millions of nominal dollars).

$QYDUS_t$ U.S. disposable income in quarter t (millions of nominal dollars).

$QYPERM_t$ U.S. "permanent" income in quarter t (millions of nominal dollars). This variable was formed by taking a four-quarter linearly-declining weighted moving average of disposable income in previous quarters.

QRDPASS$_t$ The average rate of return (in percentage points) on passbook accounts in S & Ls in quarter t.

QRTB3Y$_t$ The interest rate on 3-month treasury bills in quarter t.

SPREAD$_t$ QRDPASS − QRTB3Y.

MMCDUM$_t$ A dummy variable equal to zero before the third-quarter 1978 legalization of money market certificates and equal to one thereafter.

EXPINF$_t$ The expected percentage rate of inflation in quarter t (equal to the previous quarter's inflation rate).

BRANCH$_t$ The number of S & L branches operating in the U.S. in quarter t.

The data for these variables are contained in Table 11.3, but a few comments are in order. First, the data are quarterly from 1970 through 1979. More recent data are available, but the deregulation of the financial services industry makes that data not easily comparable to the data from the 1970s. Second, the interest rate on passbook accounts was controlled by "Regulation Q" and did not change much during the 1970s. In particular, QRDPASS was 5 percent until the fourth quarter of 1973, when it changed to 5.25 percent, where it remained until the third quarter of 1979 when it rose to 5.50 percent. Third, two of the variables were formed using data from previous quarters. QYPERM, a measure of "permanent" income, is a function of the four previous quarters' disposable income, this gives more weight to the last quarter than to quarters a year ago. EXPINF uses a simplified adaptive expectations model of the formation of inflationary expectations by using last quarter's inflation rate (specifically, the percentage rate of change of the fixed-weight GNP deflator) as the rate that will be expected. Finally, data on Savings and Loan branches (technically, total facilities) were not available for every quarter. While a smooth series could have been formed by interpolating between known observations to calculate the missing observations, we simply used the most recent known value as a proxy for the missing observations. As a result of the made-up nature of some of the observations of this variable, it will be potentially unreliable.

Now:

1. Hypothesize expected signs for all these variables in an equation for passbook deposits in the 1970s. Examine each variable carefully; what is the economic content of your hypotheses?

2. Choose carefully the best set of explanatory variables. Assume every model should have QYDUS and either the two interest rate variables or the spread variable. Don't simply include all the variables, intending to drop the insignificant ones. Instead, think through the problem carefully and find the best possible equation you can. For example, using SPREAD instead of both of the rate variables imposes a constraint on the interest rate coefficients; what is that constraint? Does the constraint make sense in our case? Why or why not? Or what about the permanent income hypothesis? Does it mean we should include QYPERM? Why or why not?

Once you have specified your equation, you are ready to begin the interactive example in Section 11.4.2. Keep following the instructions in the example until

Table 11.3   Data for the Passbook Deposits Interactive Learning Example

OBSERV	QDPASS	QYDUS	QYPERM	BRANCH	QRTB3Y	EXPINF
1970:1	84312	671.5	646.39	8498	7.501241	4.8
1970:2	83141	692.4	659.41	8498	6.964994	5.8
1970:3	82754	705.8	675.30	8498	6.569049	4.9
1970:4	84120	711.5	690.33	8372	5.507346	3.5
1971:1	85525	732.7	701.97	8722	3.955616	5.9
1971:2	89286	749.3	716.93	8722	4.310242	5.7
1971:3	90618	757.6	732.41	8722	5.186687	5.1
1971:4	92310	767.4	745.52	8862	4.339589	4.1
1972:1	95112	782.2	757.37	8862	3.513554	3.2
1972:2	97361	794.5	769.55	8862	3.836743	5.4
1972:3	99317	815.6	781.70	8862	4.346840	2.6
1972:4	101634	849.0	797.77	9584	4.979777	3.6
1973:1	103884	878.9	821.40	9977	5.800682	4.8
1973:2	104905	903.5	848.83	9977	6.813935	6.3
1973:3	102782	925.3	876.43	10547	8.689076	7.2
1973:4	103231	950.3	901.85	10547	7.710729	7.7
1974:1	104492	963.9	926.30	11324	7.856835	8.6
1974:2	104675	988.6	946.06	11324	8.561761	10.8
1974:3	102871	1012.7	967.20	12123	8.581159	11.2
1974:4	104386	1028.1	989.47	12123	7.578421	12.4
1975:1	109321	1035.2	1009.16	13056	6.044646	12.6
1975:2	114970	1105.2	1023.91	13056	5.551466	8.2
1975:3	117018	1109.4	1059.53	13839	6.529253	6.6
1975:4	119006	1134.5	1085.17	13839	5.847297	7.8
1976:1	124515	1163.7	1111.18	14479	5.085805	6.6
1976:2	127351	1180.8	1138.23	14479	5.309831	4.2
1976:3	129752	1203.3	1159.27	15108	5.309831	4.4
1976:4	132282	1229.6	1181.75	15108	4.820496	5.5
1977:1	136636	1255.2	1205.36	15835	4.743668	6.7
1977:2	139378	1291.9	1229.70	15835	4.956230	7.4
1977:3	142246	1335.5	1259.57	16439	5.625816	6.6
1977:4	143466	1373.5	1295.77	16439	6.301799	5.1
1978:1	146005	1405.7	1333.95	16955	6.603971	7.2
1978:2	144368	1451.3	1370.62	16955	6.680457	6.8
1978:3	141777	1496.2	1410.48	17492	7.556666	9.6
1978:4	134460	1542.7	1452.36	17492	8.998331	8.3
1979:1	130017	1587.5	1496.77	18100	9.717486	8.9
1979:2	129480	1624.0	1542.18	18100	9.737695	9.9
1979:3	125824	1674.3	1584.01	18676	10.00877	9.5
1979:4	116100	1714.9	1628.69	18676	12.33570	10.0

you have completely specified your equation and have been instructed to go to the discussion of serial correlation and heteroskedasticity in Section 11.4.3. You may take some time to think over the questions contained in Section 11.4.2 or take a break, but when you return to the interactive example, make sure to return to the exact point from which you left rather than starting all over again. To the extent you can do it, you should avoid looking at the hints until after completion of the entire project. The hints are there to help you if you get stuck, not to check every decision you make.

One final bit of advice: Take the time to answer all the questions. Rushing through this interactive example will lessen its effectiveness.

11.4.2 The Passbook Deposits Interactive Regression Example

Start by turning to the regression result[3] that corresponds to the specification you would like to estimate (note that the simple correlation coefficient matrix for this data set is in Table 11.4 just before the results begin). To find your regression result, carefully follow these instructions:

All the equations include QDPASS as the dependent variable, QYDUS as one of the explanatory variables, and either SPREAD or both interest rate variables (QRDPASS and QRTB3Y) as explanatory variables. If you chose SPREAD as one of your variables, continue to question number 1; if you instead chose both interest rate variables, jump to question number 4 below.

1. Do you want to include QYPERM? If yes, continue to question number 2; if no, skip to question number 3.

2. MMCDUM is in all QYPERM equations. Do you want also to include EXPINF? If yes, go to regression 11.9; if no, go to regression 11.10.

3. Find below the combination of explanatory variables (from EXPINF, BRANCH, and MMCDUM) that you wish to include and go to the indicated regression: None of them, go to regression 11.8
     MMCDUM only, go to regression 11.4
     EXPINF only, go to regression 11.7
     BRANCH only, go to regression 11.6
     MMCDUM and BRANCH, go to regression 11.2
     MMCDUM and EXPINF, go to regression 11.3
     BRANCH and EXPINF, go to regression 11.5
     All three, go to regression 11.1

4. Do you want to include QYPERM? If yes, continue to question number 5; if no, skip to question number 6.

5. MMCDUM is in all QYPERM equations. Do you want also to include EXPINF? If yes, go to regression 11.17; if no, go to regression 11.18.

6. Find below the combination of explanatory variables (from EXPINF, BRANCH, and MMCDUM) that you wish to include and go to the indicated regression: None of them, go to regression 11.16
     MMCDUM only, go to regression 11.12
     EXPINF only, go to regression 11.15
     BRANCH only, go to regression 11.14
     MMCDUM and BRANCH, go to regression 11.20
     MMCDUM and EXPINF, go to regression 11.11
     BRANCH and EXPINF, go to regression 11.13
     All three, go to regression 11.19

Table 11.4   Means, Variances, and Simple Correlation Coefficients for the
Passbook Deposits Interactive Learning Example

Means, Variances, and Correlations

Sample Range: 1-40

Variable	Mean	Standard Dev	Variance
QDPASS	113017.2	19655.37	3.8633E + 08
QYDUS	1089.880	303.5133	92120.32
QYPERM	1038.246	284.1240	80726.44
BRANCH	12824.10	3521.420	1.24004E + 07
QRDPASS	5.175000	0.139194	0.019375
QRTB3Y	6.509237	1.944990	3.782986
SPREAD	−1.334237	1.861988	3.466998
EXPINF	6.887500	2.476710	6.134094
MMCDUM	0.150000	0.357071	0.127500

	Correlation Coeff		Correlation Coeff
QYPERM,QYDUS	0.999	QYDUS,QDPASS	0.867
BRANCH, QDPASS	0.911	QYPERM,QDPASS	0.867
BRANCH, QYPERM	0.987	BRANCH,QYDUS	0.985
QRDPASS,QDPASS	0.694	QRDPASS,QYDUS	0.836
QRDPASS,QYPERM	0.841	QRDPASS,BRANCH	0.844
QRTB3Y,QYDUS	0.565	QRTB3Y,QDPASS	0.191
QRTB3Y,BRANCH	0.488	QRTB3Y,QYPERM	0.560
SPREAD,QYDUS	−0.528	QRTB3Y,QRDPASS	0.619
SPREAD,BRANCH	−0.447	SPREAD,QDPASS	−0.148
SPREAD,QRT3BY	−0.998	SPREAD,QYPERM	−0.522
EXPINF,QDPASS	0.270	SPREAD,QRDPASS	−0.572
EXPINF,QYPERM	0.489	EXPINF,QYDUS	0.486
EXPINF,QRDPASS	0.660	EXPINF,BRANCH	0.472
EXPINF,SPREAD	−0.634	EXPINF,QRTB3Y	0.654
MMCDUM,QDPASS	0.354	MMCDUM,QYDUS	0.715
MMCDUM,QYPERM	0.710	MMCDUM,BRANCH	0.628
MMCDUM,QRDPASS	0.477	MMCDUM,QRTB3Y	0.694
MMCDUM,SPREAD	−0.689	MMCDUM,EXPINF	0.420

Regression Run 11.1

```
ORDINARY LEAST SQUARES                    DEPENDENT VARIABLE IS QDPASS
SAMPLE RANGE:        1-40

                      COEFFICIENT      STANDARD ERROR     T-STATISTIC
      CONST            34318.26          4577.597          7.497004
      QYDUS            37.71483          25.19174          1.497111
      SPREAD           2085.763          759.5224          2.746150
      MMCDUM          -16836.48          4539.872         -3.708579
      BRANCH           3.621914          1.966156          1.842129
      EXPINF          -514.7155          457.7060         -1.124555

R-squared              0.941625      Mean of depend var     113017.2
Adjusted R-squared     0.933040      Std dev depend var     19905.77
Std err of regress     5150.947      Residual sum        -1.09673E-05
Durbin Watson stat     0.573681      Sum squared resid    9.02096E+08
F Statistic            109.6873
```

Answer each of the following questions for the above regression run.

a. Evaluate this result with respect to its economic meaning, overall fit, and the signs and significance of the individual coefficients.

b. What econometric problems does this regression have? Why? If you need feedback on your answer, see hint #17 in the material on this chapter in Appendix A.

c. Which of the following statements comes closest to your recommendation for further action to be taken in the estimation of this equation?

i.   No further specification changes are advisable (go to Section 11.4.3).

ii. No further variable changes are advisable, but I am concerned about heteroskedasticity or serial correlation (go to Section 11.4.3).

iii. I would like to drop BRANCH from the equation (go to run #11.3).

iv. I would like to drop EXPINF from the equation (go to run #11.2).

v.   I would like to change away from the spread interest rate formulation (go to run #11.19).

If you need feedback on your answer, see hint #18 in the material on this chapter in Appendix A.

Regression Run 11.2

```
ORDINARY LEAST SQUARES                DEPENDENT VARIABLE IS QDPASS
SAMPLE RANGE:        1-40

                     COEFFICIENT      STANDARD ERROR    T-STATISTIC
        CONST         32355.77           4247.861         7.616956
        QYDUS         42.54051           24.91723         1.707273
        SPREAD        2563.729           631.8402         4.057559
        MMCDUM       -16532.77           4548.932        -3.634429
        BRANCH        3.134560           1.925036         1.628313

R-squared             0.939453      Mean of depend var      113017.2
Adjusted R-squared    0.932534      Std dev depend var      19905.77
Std err of regress    5170.382      Residual sum          -1.74940E-05
Durbin Watson stat    0.524572      Sum squared resid      9.35649E+08
F Statistic           135.7664
```

Answer each of the following questions for the above regression run.

a. Evaluate this result with respect to its economic meaning, overall fit, and the signs and significance of the individual coefficients.

b. What econometric problems does this regression have? Why? If you need feedback on your answer, see hint #17 in the material on this chapter in Appendix A.

c. Which of the following statements comes closest to your recommendation for further action to be taken in the estimation of this equation?

    i.   No further specification changes are advisable (go to Section 11.4.3).

    ii. No further variable changes are advisable, but I am concerned about heteroskedasticity or serial correlation (go to Section 11.4.3).

    iii. I would like to drop BRANCH from the equation (go to run #11.4).

    iv. I would like to add EXPINF to the equation (go to run #11.1).

    v. I would like to change away from the spread interest rate formulation (go to run #11.20).

If you need feedback on your answer, see hint #18 in the material on this chapter in Appendix A.

Regression Run 11.3

```
ORDINARY LEAST SQUARES              DEPENDENT VARIABLE IS QDPASS
SAMPLE RANGE:        1-40

                  COEFFICIENT      STANDARD ERROR      T-STATISTIC
       CONST       30836.71          4309.422           7.155648
       QYDUS       83.52150          4.172854           20.01544
       SPREAD      2565.976          737.3738           3.479885
       MMCDUM      -21061.36         4049.704           -5.200717
       EXPINF      -328.8701         461.4616           -0.712671

R-squared            0.935798     Mean of depend var      113017.2
Adjusted R-squared   0.928461     Std dev depend var      19905.77
Std err of regress   5324.155     Residual sum            -2.22921E-05
Durbin Watson stat   0.729307     Sum squared resid       9.92132E+08
F Statistic          127.5391
```

Answer each of the following questions for the above regression run.

a. Evaluate this result with respect to its economic meaning, overall fit, and the signs and significance of the individual coefficients.

b. What econometric problems does this regression have? Why? If you need feedback on your answer, see hint #17 in the material on this chapter in Appendix A.

c. Which of the following statements comes closest to your recommendation for further action to be taken in the estimation of this equation?

    i.   No further specification changes are advisable (go to Section 11.4.3).

    ii. No further variable changes are advisable, but I am concerned about heteroskedasticity or serial correlation (go to Section 11.4.3).

    iii. I would like to drop EXPINF from the equation (go to run #11.4).

    iv. I would like to add BRANCH to the equation (go to run #11.1).

    v. I would like to change away from the spread interest rate formulation (go to run #11.11).

If you need feedback on your answer, see hint #15 in the material on this chapter in Appendix A.

Regression Run 11.4

```
ORDINARY LEAST SQUARES                DEPENDENT VARIABLE IS QDPASS
SAMPLE RANGE:        1-40

                   COEFFICIENT      STANDARD ERROR     T-STATISTIC
      CONST         29833.37           4045.035          7.375306
      QYDUS         82.62301           3.950564         20.91423
      SPREAD        2843.567           621.8082          4.573061
      MMCDUM       -20475.63           3938.230         -5.199196

  R-squared          0.934867     Mean of depend var      113017.2
  Adjusted R-squared 0.929439     Std dev depend var      19905.77
  Std err of regress 5287.641     Residual sum         -2.88188E-05
  Durbin Watson stat 0.676537     Sum squared resid    1.00652E+09
  F Statistic        172.2372
```

Answer each of the following questions for the above regression run.

a. Evaluate this result with respect to its economic meaning, overall fit, and the signs and significance of the individual coefficients.

b. What econometric problems does this regression have? Why? If you need feedback on your answer, see hint #13 in the material on this chapter in Appendix A.

c. Which of the following statements comes closest to your recommendation for further action to be taken in the estimation of this equation?

   i.   No further specification changes are advisable (go to Section 11.4.3).

   ii. No further variable changes are advisable, but I am concerned about heteroskedasticity or serial correlation (go to Section 11.4.3).

   iii. I would like to add BRANCH to the equation (go to run #11.2).

   iv. I would like to add EXPINF to the equation (go to run #11.3).

   v.   I would like to change away from the spread interest rate formulation (go to run #11.12).

   If you need feedback on your answer, see hint #15 in the material on this chapter in Appendix A.

Regression Run 11.5

```
ORDINARY LEAST SQUARES                DEPENDENT VARIABLE IS QDPASS
SAMPLE RANGE:        1-40

                    COEFFICIENT       STANDARD ERROR     T-STATISTIC
        CONST        44000.71           4392.003          10.01837
        QYDUS       -16.54446           23.95441          -0.690664
        SPREAD        2840.254          854.7564           3.322881
        BRANCH        7.305554          1.981996           3.685958
        EXPINF       -413.7377          533.6858          -0.775246

    R-squared          0.918011    Mean of depend var     113017.2
    Adjusted R-squared 0.908640    Std dev depend var     19905.77
    Std err of regress 6016.666    Residual sum           1.29938E-05
    Durbin Watson stat 0.319973    Sum squared resid      1.26700E+09
    F Statistic        97.97121
```

Answer each of the following questions for the above regression run.

a. Evaluate this result with respect to its economic meaning, overall fit, and the signs and significance of the individual coefficients.

b. What econometric problems does this regression have? Why? If you need feedback on your answer, see hint #12 in the material on this chapter in Appendix A.

c. Which of the following statements comes closest to your recommendation for further action to be taken in the estimation of this equation?

  i.   No further specification changes are advisable (go to Section 11.4.3).

  ii. No further variable changes are advisable, but I am concerned about heteroskedasticity or serial correlation (go to Section 11.4.3).

  iii. I would like to drop EXPINF from the equation (go to run #11.6).

  iv. I would like to add MMCDUM to the equation (go to run #11.1).

  v.   I would like to change away from the spread interest rate formulation (go to run #11.13).

  If you need feedback on your answer, see hint #8 in the material on this chapter in Appendix A.

Regression Run 11.6

```
ORDINARY LEAST SQUARES                DEPENDENT VARIABLE IS QDPASS
SAMPLE RANGE:      1-40

                    COEFFICIENT     STANDARD ERROR    T-STATISTIC
        CONST        42276.73         3766.360         11.22482
        QYDUS       -11.86216        23.05168          -0.514590
        SPREAD       3214.838         701.1670          4.584981
        BRANCH       6.858817         1.885838          3.637013

R-squared            0.916603     Mean of depend var     113017.2
Adjusted R-squared   0.909653     Std dev depend var     19905.77
Std err of regress   5983.231     Residual sum        -5.60284E-06
Durbin Watson stat   0.337198     Sum squared resid    1.28876E+09
F Statistic          131.8897
```

Answer each of the following questions for the above regression run.

a. Evaluate this result with respect to its economic meaning, overall fit, and the signs and significance of the individual coefficients.

b. What econometric problems does this regression have? Why? If you need feedback on your answer, see hint #12 in the material on this chapter in Appendix A.

c. Which of the following statements comes closest to your recommendation for further action to be taken in the estimation of this equation?

    i.   No further specification changes are advisable (go to Section 11.4.3).

    ii. No further variable changes are advisable, but I am concerned about heteroskedasticity or serial correlation (go to Section 11.4.3).

    iii. I would like to drop BRANCH from the equation (go to run #11.8).

    iv. I would like to add MMCDUM to the equation (go to run #11.2).

    v.   I would like to change away from the spread interest rate formulation (go to run #11.14).

If you need feedback on your answer, see hint #8 in the material on this chapter in Appendix A.

Regression Run 11.7

```
ORDINARY LEAST SQUARES              DEPENDENT VARIABLE IS QDPASS
SAMPLE RANGE:       1-40

                COEFFICIENT        STANDARD ERROR    T-STATISTIC
    CONST        41152.02            5022.709        8.193192
    QYDUS        70.63577            4.408044        16.02429
    SPREAD       4653.520            812.0529        5.730563
    EXPINF       158.1950            593.2161        0.266674

R-squared           0.886184      Mean of depend var     113017.2
Adjusted R-squared  0.876699      Std dev depend var      19905.77
Std err of regress  6989.748      Residual sum         -2.64049E-05
Durbin Watson stat  0.293023      Sum squared resid     1.75883E+09
F Statistic         93.43341
```

Answer each of the following questions for the above regression run.

a. Evaluate this result with respect to its economic meaning, overall fit, and the signs and significance of the individual coefficients.

b. What econometric problems does this regression have? Why? If you need feedback on your answer, see hint #12 in the material on this chapter in Appendix A.

c. Which of the following statements comes closest to your recommendation for further action to be taken in the estimation of this equation?

   i.   No further specification changes are advisable (go to Section 11.4.3).

   ii. No further variable changes are advisable, but I am concerned about heteroskedasticity or serial correlation (go to Section 11.4.3).

  iii. I would like to drop EXPINF from the equation (go to run #11.8).

  iv. I would like to add MMCDUM to the equation (go to run #11.3).

   v. I would like to change away from the spread interest rate formulation (go to run #11.15).

If you need feedback on your answer, see hint #8 in the material on this chapter in Appendix A.

Regression Run 11.8

```
ORDINARY LEAST SQUARES              DEPENDENT VARIABLE IS QDPASS
SAMPLE RANGE:        1-40

                   COEFFICIENT        STANDARD ERROR      T-STATISTIC
        CONST      41799.30             4341.727           9.627344
        QYDUS      70.90675             4.235142          16.74247
        SPREAD     4543.382             690.3493           6.581281

R-squared          0.885959       Mean of depend var       113017.2
Adjusted R-squared 0.879795       Std dev depend var        19905.77
Std err of regress 6901.451       Residual sum            -3.25441E-05
Durbin Watson stat 0.280912       Sum squared resid       1.76231E+09
F Statistic        143.7227
```

Answer each of the following questions for the above regression run.

a. Evaluate this result with respect to its economic meaning, overall fit, and the signs and significance of the individual coefficients.

b. What econometric problems does this regression have? Why? If you need feedback on your answer, see hint #14 in the material on this chapter in Appendix A.

c. Which of the following statements comes closest to your recommendation for further action to be taken in the estimation of this equation?

  i.   No further specification changes are advisable (go to Section 11.4.3).

  ii. No further variable changes are advisable, but I am concerned about heteroskedasticity or serial correlation (go to Section 11.4.3).

  iii. I would like to add EXPINF to the equation (go to run #11.7).

  iv. I would like to add MMCDUM to the equation (go to run #11.4).

  v.   I would like to change away from the spread interest rate formulation (go to run #11.16).

If you need feedback on your answer, see hint #8 in the material on this chapter in Appendix A.

Regression Run 11.9

```
ORDINARY LEAST SQUARES                 DEPENDENT VARIABLE IS QDPASS
SAMPLE RANGE:        1-40

                   COEFFICIENT      STANDARD ERROR    T-STATISTIC
     CONST           32416.73          4288.033        7.559814
     QYDUS           224.5774          81.32012        2.761647
     QYPERM         -150.3951          86.59623       -1.736739
     SPREAD          2859.399          736.6466        3.881644
     MMCDUM         -21205.30          3938.738       -5.383780
     EXPINF         -147.9428          460.6521       -0.321159

  R-squared          0.941030      Mean of depend var     113017.2
  Adjusted R-squared 0.932358      Std dev depend var     19905.77
  Std err of regress 5177.123      Residual sum          -1.23978E-05
  Durbin Watson stat 0.995422      Sum squared resid      9.11288E+08
  F Statistic        108.5123
```

Answer each of the following questions for the above regression run.

a. Evaluate this result with respect to its economic meaning, overall fit, and the signs and significance of the individual coefficients.

b. What econometric problems does this regression have? Why? If you need feedback on your answer, see hint #1 in the material on this chapter in Appendix A.

c. Which of the following statements comes closest to your recommendation for further action to be taken in the estimation of this equation?

   i.   No further specification changes are advisable (go to Section 11.4.3).

   ii. No further variable changes are advisable, but I am concerned about heteroskedasticity or serial correlation (go to Section 11.4.3).

   iii. I would like to drop QYPERM from the equation (go to run #11.3).

   iv. I would like to drop EXPINF from the equation (go to run #11.10).

   v. I would like to change away from the spread interest rate formulation (go to run #11.17).

If you need feedback on your answer, see hint #3 in the material on this chapter in Appendix A.

Regression Run 11.10

```
ORDINARY LEAST SQUARES                    DEPENDENT VARIABLE IS QDPASS
SAMPLE RANGE:         1-40

                     COEFFICIENT        STANDARD ERROR      T-STATISTIC
        CONST          32054.54            4083.725           7.849338
        QYDUS          230.0929            78.46106           2.932574
        QYPERM        -156.6846            83.26497          -1.881758
        SPREAD         2990.158            605.9888           4.934346
        MMCDUM        -20961.30            3814.933          -5.494540

R-squared              0.940851        Mean of depend var      113017.2
Adjusted R-squared     0.934091        Std dev depend var      19905.77
Std err of regress     5110.362        Residual sum         -2.31266E-05
Durbin Watson stat     0.983859        Sum squared resid     9.14052E+08
F Statistic            139.1810
```

Answer each of the following questions for the above regression run.

a. Evaluate this result with respect to its economic meaning, overall fit, and the signs and significance of the individual coefficients.

b. What econometric problems does this regression have? Why? If you need feedback on your answer, see hint #1 in the material on this chapter in Appendix A.

c. Which of the following statements comes closest to your recommendation for further action to be taken in the estimation of this equation?

   i.   No further specification changes are advisable (go to Section 11.4.3).

   ii. No further variable changes are advisable, but I am concerned about heteroskedasticity or serial correlation (go to Section 11.4.3).

   iii. I would like to drop QYPERM from the equation (go to run #11.4).

   iv. I would like to add EXPINF to the equation (go to run #11.9).

   v.   I would like to change away from the spread interest rate formulation (go to run #11.18).

   If you need feedback on your answer, see hint #3 in the material on this chapter in Appendix A.

Regression Run 11.11

```
ORDINARY LEAST SQUARES              DEPENDENT VARIABLE IS QDPASS
SAMPLE RANGE:        1-40

                    COEFFICIENT      STANDARD ERROR    T-STATISTIC
    CONST            184591.2          68093.77          2.710838
    QYDUS            97.20543          7.223235          13.45733
    QRDPASS         -31233.99          14958.53         -2.088039
    QRTB3Y           -1987.620         742.8786         -2.675565
    MMCDUM          -26680.35          4565.580         -5.843803
    EXPINF           153.8465          485.8750          0.316638

    R-squared           0.944196    Mean of depend var     113017.2
    Adjusted R-squared  0.935990    Std dev depend var     19905.77
    Std err of regress  5036.200    Residual sum          -2.39313E-05
    Durbin Watson stat  1.038720    Sum squared resid     8.62352E+08
    F Statistic         115.0559
```

Answer each of the following questions for the above regression run.

a. Evaluate this result with respect to its economic meaning, overall fit, and the signs and significance of the individual coefficients.

b. What econometric problems does this regression have? Why? If you need feedback on your answer, see hint #2 in the material on this chapter in Appendix A.

c. Which of the following statements comes closest to your recommendation for further action to be taken in the estimation of this equation?

   i.   No further specification changes are advisable (go to Section 11.4.3).

   ii. No further variable changes are advisable, but I am concerned about heteroskedasticity or serial correlation (go to Section 11.4.3).

   iii. I would like to drop EXPINF from the equation (go to run #11.12).

   iv. I would like to add BRANCH to the equation (go to run #11.19).

   v.   I would like to change to the spread interest rate formulation (go to run #11.3).

If you need feedback on your answer, see hint #5 in the material on this chapter in Appendix A.

Regression Run 11.12

```
ORDINARY LEAST SQUARES                    DEPENDENT VARIABLE IS QDPASS
SAMPLE RANGE:        1-40

                       COEFFICIENT       STANDARD ERROR     T-STATISTIC
          CONST          175517.2           60970.86         2.878707
          QYDUS          96.70339           6.955899        13.90236
          QRDPASS       -29260.79          13422.73         -2.179944
          QRTB3Y        -1918.369           700.7701        -2.737516
          MMCDUM        -26556.05           4489.825         -5.914718

     R-squared           0.944032      Mean of depend var     113017.2
     Adjusted R-squared  0.937635      Std dev depend var     19905.77
     Std err of regress  4971.046      Residual sum          -3.13222E-05
     Durbin Watson stat  1.034733      Sum squared resid      8.64895E+08
     F Statistic         147.5888
```

Answer each of the following questions for the above regression run.

a. Evaluate this result with respect to its economic meaning, overall fit, and the signs and significance of the individual coefficients.

b. What econometric problems does this regression have? Why? If you need feedback on your answer, see hint #2 in the material on this chapter in Appendix A.

c. Which of the following statements comes closest to your recommendation for further action to be taken in the estimation of this equation?

    i.   No further specification changes are advisable (go to Section 11.4.3).

    ii. No further variable changes are advisable, but I am concerned about heteroskedasticity or serial correlation (go to Section 11.4.3).

    iii. I would like to add BRANCH to the equation (go to run #11.20).

    iv. I would like to add EXPINF to the equation (go to run #11.11).

    v. I would like to change to the spread interest rate formulation (go to run #11.4).

If you need feedback on your answer, see hint #6 in the material on this chapter in Appendix A.

Regression Run 11.13

```
ORDINARY LEAST SQUARES                 DEPENDENT VARIABLE IS QDPASS
SAMPLE RANGE:        1-40

                     COEFFICIENT      STANDARD ERROR    T-STATISTIC
    CONST             75571.63          75526.37         1.000599
    QYDUS            -18.30103          24.60198        -0.743884
    QRDPASS          -3918.495          16163.94        -0.242422
    QRTB3Y           -2756.596          887.7795        -3.105046
    BRANCH            7.625268          2.146174         3.552960
    EXPINF           -315.6676          588.6806        -0.536229

    R-squared          0.918431      Mean of depend var   113017.2
    Adjusted R-squared 0.906436      Std dev depend var   19905.77
    Std err of regress 6088.825      Residual sum         5.60284E-06
    Durbin Watson stat 0.317307      Sum squared resid    1.26050E+09
    F Statistic        76.56534
```

Answer each of the following questions for the above regression run.

a. Evaluate this result with respect to its economic meaning, overall fit, and the signs and significance of the individual coefficients.

b. What econometric problems does this regression have? Why? If you need feedback on your answer, see hint #7 in the material on this chapter in Appendix A.

c. Which of the following statements comes closest to your recommendation for further action to be taken in the estimation of this equation?

   i.   No further specification changes are advisable (go to Section 11.4.3).

   ii. No further variable changes are advisable, but I am concerned about heteroskedasticity or serial correlation (go to Section 11.4.3).

   iii. I would like to drop EXPINF from the equation (go to run #11.14).

   iv. I would like to add MMCDUM to the equation (go to run #11.19).

   v. I would like to change to the spread interest rate formulation (go to run #11.5).

If you need feedback on your answer, see hint #10 in the material on this chapter in Appendix A.

Regression Run 11.14

```
ORDINARY LEAST SQUARES                    DEPENDENT VARIABLE IS QDPASS
SAMPLE RANGE:        1-40

                        COEFFICIENT       STANDARD ERROR      T-STATISTIC
        CONST             90549.10           69453.96           1.303728
        QYDUS            -16.18897            24.03620          -0.673525
        QRDPASS         -7121.353            14866.23           -0.479029
        QRTB3Y          -2954.533              799.1416         -3.697133
        BRANCH              7.501259            2.111849          3.551986

    R-squared             0.917741     Mean of depend var        113017.2
    Adjusted R-squared    0.908341     Std dev depend var         19905.77
    Std err of regress    6026.534     Residual sum            4.17233E-06
    Durbin Watson stat    0.333103     Sum squared resid      1.27116E+09
    F Statistic          97.62198
```

Answer each of the following questions for the above regression run.

a. Evaluate this result with respect to its economic meaning, overall fit, and the signs and significance of the individual coefficients.

b. What econometric problems does this regression have? Why? If you need feedback on your answer, see hint #7 in the material on this chapter in Appendix A.

c. Which of the following statements comes closest to your recommendation for further action to be taken in the estimation of this equation?

    i.   No further specification changes are advisable (go to Section 11.4.3).

    ii. No further variable changes are advisable, but I am concerned about heteroskedasticity or serial correlation (go to Section 11.4.3).

    iii. I would like to drop BRANCH from the equation (go to run #11.16).

    iv. I would like to add MMCDUM to the equation (go to run #11.20).

    v.   I would like to change to the spread interest rate formulation (go to run #11.6).

If you need feedback on your answer, see hint #10 in the material on this chapter in Appendix A.

Regression Run 11.15

```
ORDINARY LEAST SQUARES              DEPENDENT VARIABLE IS QDPASS
SAMPLE RANGE:        1-40

                     COEFFICIENT     STANDARD ERROR     T-STATISTIC
     CONST            -22324.93        81162.10         -0.275066
     QYDUS             66.48008         6.911253         9.619107
     QRDPASS         18136.45          17225.33          1.052894
     QRTB3Y           -4662.207          816.5163       -5.709877
     EXPINF             -90.29219        675.4795        -0.133671

R-squared               0.888147     Mean of depend var      113017.2
Adjusted R-squared      0.875363     Std dev depend var       19905.77
Std err of regress   7027.519        Residual sum         -8.55327E-06
Durbin Watson stat      0.312751     Sum squared resid     1.72851E+09
F Statistic            69.47733
```

Answer each of the following questions for the above regression run.

a. Evaluate this result with respect to its economic meaning, overall fit, and the signs and significance of the individual coefficients.

b. What econometric problems does this regression have? Why? If you need feedback on your answer, see hint #7 in the material on this chapter in Appendix A.

c. Which of the following statements comes closest to your recommendation for further action to be taken in the estimation of this equation?

   i.   No further specification changes are advisable (go to Section 11.4.3).

   ii. No further variable changes are advisable, but I am concerned about heteroskedasticity or serial correlation (go to Section 11.4.3).

   iii. I would like to add BRANCH to the equation (go to run #11.13).

   iv. I would like to add MMCDUM to the equation (go to run #11.11).

   v.   I would like to change to the spread interest rate formulation (go to run #11.7).

If you need feedback on your answer, see hint #9 in the material on this chapter in Appendix A.

Regression Run 11.16

```
ORDINARY LEAST SQUARES                 DEPENDENT VARIABLE IS QDPASS
SAMPLE RANGE:       1-40

                     COEFFICIENT       STANDARD ERROR    T-STATISTIC
      CONST          -17529.78           71804.10         -0.244133
      QYDUS           66.69228            6.634067         10.05300
      QRDPASS         17105.76           15191.61          1.126000
      QRTB3Y         -4710.521            722.1070         -6.523300

   R-squared          0.888089       Mean of depend var     113017.2
   Adjusted R-squared 0.878764       Std dev depend var     19905.77
   Std err of regress 6930.995       Residual sum        -2.06828E-05
   Durbin Watson stat 0.314724       Sum squared resid    1.72939E+09
   F Statistic        95.22845
```

Answer each of the following questions for the above regression run.

a. Evaluate this result with respect to its economic meaning, overall fit, and the signs and significance of the individual coefficients.

b. What econometric problems does this regression have? Why? If you need feedback on your answer, see hint #7 in the material on this chapter in Appendix A.

c. Which of the following statements comes closest to your recommendation for further action to be taken in the estimation of this equation?

   i.   No further specification changes are advisable (go to Section 11.4.3).

   ii. No further variable changes are advisable, but I am concerned about heteroskedasticity or serial correlation (go to Section 11.4.3).

   iii. I would like to add BRANCH to the equation (go to run #11.14).

   iv. I would like to add MMCDUM to the equation (go to run #11.12).

   v.   I would like to change to the spread interest rate formulation (go to run #11.8).

If you need feedback on your answer, see hint #9 in the material on this chapter in Appendix A.

Regression Run 11.17

```
ORDINARY LEAST SQUARES                DEPENDENT VARIABLE IS QDPASS
SAMPLE RANGE:        1-40

                    COEFFICIENT      STANDARD ERROR    T-STATISTIC
        CONST        158889.6          72022.07         2.206123
        QYDUS        185.0812          82.05795         2.255494
        QYPERM      -96.22872          89.51065        -1.075053
        QRDPASS    -25174.00          15953.44         -1.577967
        QRTB3Y      -2275.845          788.1823        -2.887460
        MMCDUM     -25796.23          4628.803         -5.572981
        EXPINF       185.7460          485.6733         0.382451

    R-squared           0.946085    Mean of depend var      113017.2
    Adjusted R-squared  0.936282    Std dev depend var      19905.77
    Std err of regress  5024.705    Residual sum          -1.94907E-05
    Durbin Watson stat  1.118237    Sum squared resid      8.33172E+08
    F Statistic         96.51171
```

Answer each of the following questions for the above regression run.

a. Evaluate this result with respect to its economic meaning, overall fit, and the signs and significance of the individual coefficients.

b. What econometric problems does this regression have? Why? If you need feedback on your answer, see hint #1 in the material on this chapter in Appendix A.

c. Which of the following statements comes closest to your recommendation for further action to be taken in the estimation of this equation?

   i.   No further specification changes are advisable (go to Section 11.4.3).

   ii. No further variable changes are advisable, but I am concerned about heteroskedasticity or serial correlation (go to Section 11.4.3).

  iii. I would like to drop QYPERM from the equation (go to run #11.11).

  iv. I would like to drop EXPINF from the equation (go to run #11.18).

   v. I would like to change to the spread interest rate formulation (go to run #11.9).

If you need feedback on your answer, see hint #3 in the material on this chapter in Appendix A.

Regression Run 11.18

```
ORDINARY LEAST SQUARES                    DEPENDENT VARIABLE IS QDPASS
SAMPLE RANGE:        1-40

                      COEFFICIENT      STANDARD ERROR      T-STATISTIC
        CONST          148533.7          65894.91           2.254099
        QYDUS          182.5674          80.76082           2.260593
        QYPERM        -94.13721          88.21461          -1.067139
        QRDPASS      -22932.27           14650.16          -1.565325
        QRTB3Y        -2186.282          743.0808          -2.942186
        MMCDUM       -25665.93           4557.923          -5.631059

R-squared              0.945846     Mean of depend var      113017.2
Adjusted R-squared     0.937882     Std dev depend var      19905.77
Std err of regress     4961.220     Residual sum           -7.92742E-06
Durbin Watson stat     1.116034     Sum squared resid       8.36865E+08
F Statistic            118.7670
```

Answer each of the following questions for the above regression run.

a. Evaluate this result with respect to its economic meaning, overall fit, and the signs and significance of the individual coefficients.

b. What econometric problems does this regression have? Why? If you need feedback on your answer, see hint #1 in the material on this chapter in Appendix A.

c. Which of the following statements comes closest to your recommendation for further action to be taken in the estimation of this equation?

  i.   No further specification changes are advisable (go to Section 11.4.3).

  ii. No further variable changes are advisable, but I am concerned about heteroskedasticity or serial correlation (go to Section 11.4.3).

  iii. I would like to drop QYPERM from the equation (go to run #11.12).

  iv. I would like to add EXPINF to the equation (go to run #11.17).

  v.   I would like to change to the spread interest rate formulation (go to run #11.10).

If you need feedback on your answer, see hint #3 in the material on this chapter in Appendix A.

Regression Run 11.19

```
ORDINARY LEAST SQUARES              DEPENDENT VARIABLE IS QDPASS
SAMPLE RANGE:        1-40

                    COEFFICIENT      STANDARD ERROR     T-STATISTIC
        CONST       205021.5         64868.81           3.160556
        QYDUS       46.06039         23.45340           1.963911
        QRDPASS     -35397.74        14231.12           -2.487347
        QRTB3Y      -1374.301        750.7925           -1.830467
        MMCDUM      -22428.71        4694.232           -4.777930
        BRANCH      4.159648         1.825168           2.279049
        EXPINF      -8.002370        463.8907           -0.017251

    R-squared           0.951785     Mean of depend var    113017.2
    Adjusted R-squared  0.943019     Std dev depend var    19905.77
    Std err of regress  4751.651     Residual sum          -7.33137E-06
    Durbin Watson stat  0.858614     Sum squared resid     7.45080E+08
    F Statistic         108.5728
```

Answer each of the following questions for the above regression run.

a. Evaluate this result with respect to its economic meaning, overall fit, and the signs and significance of the individual coefficients.

b. What econometric problems does this regression have? Why? If you need feedback on your answer, see hint #2 in the material on this chapter in Appendix A.

c. Which of the following statements comes closest to your recommendation for further action to be taken in the estimation of this equation?

    i.   No further specification changes are advisable (go to Section 11.4.3).

    ii.   No further variable changes are advisable, but I am concerned about heteroskedasticity or serial correlation (go to Section 11.4.3).

    iii. I would like to drop EXPINF from the equation (go to run #11.20).

    iv. I would like to drop BRANCH from the equation (go to run #11.11).

    v.   I would like to change to the spread interest rate formulation (go to run #11.1).

If you need feedback on your answer, see hint #5 in the material on this chapter in Appendix A.

Regression Run 11.20

```
ORDINARY LEAST SQUARES                    DEPENDENT VARIABLE IS QDPASS
SAMPLE RANGE:        1-40

                   COEFFICIENT        STANDARD ERROR     T-STATISTIC
    CONST           205458.8             58827.37          3.492571
    QYDUS           46.14516             22.59320          2.042436
    QRDPASS         -35493.15            12918.26         -2.747517
    QRTB3Y          -1378.529            699.1426         -1.971743
    MMCDUM          -22439.95            4579.932         -4.899625
    BRANCH          4.154828             1.776940          2.338193

  R-squared          0.951785     Mean of depend var       113017.2
  Adjusted R-squared 0.944694     Std dev depend var      19905.77
  Std err of regress 4681.273     Residual sum          -2.50340E-05
  Durbin Watson stat 0.859208     Sum squared resid      7.45086E+08
  F Statistic        134.2342
```

Answer each of the following questions for the above regression run.

a. Evaluate this result with respect to its economic meaning, overall fit, and the signs and significance of the individual coefficients.

b. What econometric problems does this regression have? Why? If you need feedback on your answer, see hint #2 in the material on this chapter in Appendix A.

c. Which of the following statements comes closest to your recommendation for further action to be taken in the estimation of this equation?

    i.   No further specification changes are advisable (go to Section 11.4.3).

    ii.   No further variable changes are advisable, but I am concerned about heteroskedasticity or serial correlation (go to Section 11.4.3).

    iii.   I would like to drop BRANCH from the equation (go to run #11.12).

    iv.   I would like to add EXPINF to the equation (go to run #11.19).

    v.   I would like to change to the spread interest rate formulation (go to run #11.2).

If you need feedback on your answer, see hint #5 in the material on this chapter in Appendix A.

11.4.3 Heteroskedasticity and Serial Correlation in the Interactive Example

Congratulations! You have arrived at this section, which implies that you have completed the specification of your model of passbook deposits. Now that you have chosen your specification, the next step is to consider the possibility that pure heteroskedasticity and/or serial correlation might exist in your residuals. We also need to discuss a few other topics that the strict limitations of the interactive example did not allow; these topics will be covered in the exercises at the end of the chapter.

Heteroskedasticity. Heteroskedasticity is extremely unlikely in this example for a number of reasons. First, it is a time series model, meaning that huge cross-sectional differences in size do not exist. Second, while there was certainly growth in passbook deposits during the 1970s, that growth was not exceptional. Indeed, competition from money market certificates and other newly legal assets actually decreased passbook deposits in the late 1970s. Finally, there is no indication of any dramatic change in the quality of measurement of the data.

As a result, many econometricians would not bother to run a Park test on this example, feeling that even a significant result would indicate impure, rather than pure, heteroskedasticity. (It would be good to get into the habit of examining the residuals of the final specification plotted against a suspected proportionality factor and then running a Park test if the plot indicates heteroskedasticity.) Look over your independent variables; which of them would be candidates to be a potential proportionality factor Z? One good choice is to use either income variable because income is the best measure of size available to us. The interest rate variables are much less likely to be proportionality factors, mainly because of their fluctuations. Fortunately, plots of the residuals of the final specifications most frequently chosen by previous users of this example give no indications of pure heteroskedasticity with respect to disposable income, and so we should not seriously consider adjusting for heteroskedasticity. As it turns out, a Park test using the log of QYDUS to explain the log of the squared residuals from regression run #11.4 shows no evidence of heteroskedasticity at all ($t_z = 0.80$).

Serial Correlation. As you have surely noted, almost all of the regression runs produce Durbin-Watson statistics that indicate positive serial correlation (or inconclusive DW statistics quite close to the lower limit). Does this mean that there is serial correlation in the error terms? How do we tell whether we have pure or impure serial correlation? Should we adjust the equation with generalized least squares?

One way to determine whether the serial correlation indicated by the Durbin-Watson statistic is pure or impure is to examine the degree to which the model matches the underlying theory. The last part of the decade was marked by turmoil in the savings and loan industry (deregulation, high interest rates, some closures of S & Ls, and increasing competition for passbook accounts from other kinds of savings vehicles), but only the MMC dummy attempts to account for this turmoil. To most observers, such a set of circumstances is an indication that

Table 11.5   Generalized Least Squares Estimation of Regression Run # 11.4

FIRST ORDER AUTOCORRELATION
SAMPLE RANGE: 1-40   DEPENDENT VARIABLE IS QDPASS

RHO=   0.777901

	COEFFICIENT	STANDARD ERROR	T-STATISTIC
CONST	50036.95	7041.120	7.106391
QYDUS	61.27675	6.603229	9.279815
SPREAD	2861.502	630.4467	4.538848
MMCDUM	-6234.390	3635.652	-1.714793

R-squared	0.974162	Mean of depend var	113017.2
Adjusted R-squared	0.972009	Std dev depend var	19905.77
Std err of regress	3330.336	Residual sum	-1963.098
Durbin Watson stat	1.000196	Sum squared resid	3.99280E+08
F Statistic	452.4353		

A GLS estimation of Run #11.4 neither rids the equation of serial correlation nor makes any of the estimated coefficients insignificantly different from zero.

---

the residual pattern picked up by the Durbin-Watson statistic might be due to impure serial correlation. That is, the model has not properly captured all the factors that were influencing passbook deposits in the last few years of the decade. Such a result is a strong indication that the introduction of a more sophisticated explanatory variable (somehow measuring increasing competition for passbook accounts from other kinds of savings assets) should be attempted before generalized least squares is run.

Since such a variable is not available in the present data set, we went ahead and ran generalized least squares on the most frequently chosen "best" equation, regression run #11.4. The results of that estimation are in Table 11.5. Note that the estimated coefficient of the spread variable is virtually identical in both the GLS and the OLS versions of run #11.4. In addition, note that even when the supposed serial correlation is "corrected," the Durbin-Watson d is only 1.00, even though it is biased towards 2 after GLS is run. Finally, note that all the independent variables are still significantly different from zero in the hypothesized directions after the GLS adjustment. As a result, we would prefer sticking with the OLS estimate at present and attempting to find the possible omitted variable. Even if that variable is not found, it appears that serial correlation is doing little harm to the OLS results.

Reporting Your Final Equation. When reporting your "final" equation, remember also to report (say, in an appendix or a footnote) the equations estimated previously and subsequently (the order of estimation doesn't matter) to the one you chose. This practice allows readers to make up their own minds as to whether your choice was one with which they would agree. Such complete reporting will also let readers be able to judge for themselves the extent to which the reported t-scores are likely to follow the t-distribution and be comparable to the critical t-values found in the t-table.

11.5   Summary

1. Table 11.1 contains a listing of terms that should be checked when reviewing the output from a computer regression package.

2. Table 11.2 contains a summary of the nature, consequences, detection, and correction procedures for the various econometric problems covered so far in this text. A review of this table is a good way to prepare for the first few attempts at applied regression analysis.

3. The art of econometrics involves finding the best possible equation in the fewest possible number of regression runs. The only way to do this is to spend quite a bit of time thinking through the underlying principles of every research project before the first regression is run.

4. An ethical econometrician is always honest and complete in reporting all the different regressions estimated and/or data sets used before the final results were chosen.

5. The interactive examples of Sections 11.4 and 11.6 are meant to provide a bridge between the structured examples of the previous chapters and the unstructured world of running regressions completely on your own.

Exercises

(Answers to even-numbered exercises are in Appendix A.)

1. Is there a problem with dominant variables in the interactive learning example? Don't the high R^2s and high t-scores associated with QYDUS indicate the possibility of its being a dominant variable? Examine regression run #11.4, for example. Why are we not worried about a dominant variable?

2. Some of the regression results you may not have encountered in working through the interactive example contain important lessons to be learned. Return to the following regression runs and answer the questions attached to those results for each one. (You will gain the most from this exercise if you answer the questions in writing without reference to the hints in Appendix A.)
   a. Regression run #11.1
   b. Regression run #11.9
   c. Regression run #11.12
   d. Regression run #11.16

3. What about real income in the interactive example? Since both QDPASS and QYDUS are measured in nominal terms, some of the correlation between them actually measures changes in prices.
   a. Think through the theory behind the relationship between holding assets in particular accounts and nominal vs. real income. Should a measure of real income be included?

b. Analyze the following regression result, which replaces QYDUS with a new variable, $QYDUSR_t$, in regression run #11.3, where:

$QYDUSR_t$ = real disposable income in the U.S. in quarter t calculated by dividing QYDUS through by the consumer price index in quarter t.

$$\overline{QDPASS}_t = -175680 + 42599QYDUSR_t + 3774SPREAD_t$$
$$(2504)(1067)$$
$$t = 17.013.54$$

$$- 6329MMCDUM_t + 435.1EXPINF_t$$
$$(4192)(610.5)$$
$$t = -1.510.71$$

$$\bar{R}^2 = .909 \quad n = 40 \quad DW = 0.50$$

c. Which specification do you prefer, and why? Be explicit.

d. Would it make a difference if the real disposable income variable had been multiplied through by 100 as is typically done after dividing by a price index? How would the estimated equation be changed?

11.6 Appendix: Another Interactive Example

This second interactive example is another attempt to bridge the gap between textbook and computer. It is a complete exercise that helps you make independent specification decisions and get feedback on those decisions without requiring you to use a computer to do the estimation or have access to an experienced econometrician. When you complete this second interactive example, you should be able to do econometric analysis on your own. As with the other interactive example, we strongly encourage you to:

1. Look over a portion of the reading list before deciding on your specification.

2. Try to estimate as few regression runs as possible. There's nothing wrong with looking at only one regression result.

3. Avoid looking at the "hints" until after you reached what you believe is your best specification.

As before, we urge you to put this interactive exercise aside until you have the time to take it seriously. We believe that the benefits from completing it will be directly proportional to the effort you put into it. In other words, stop reading this section if you do not have the time it will take to get out of it what we have intended.

11.6.1 Building a "Demand-Side" Model for Pork

The dependent variable for the second interactive example is the quantity of pork consumed (pounds per person per year) in the United States. The data[4] are quarterly for 1975 through 1984, so there are 40 observations. For each quarter, the dependent variable, *CONPK*, measures the annual per capita consumption (CON) of pork (PK).

This text has discussed demand-side equations for consumption goods frequently, so the underlying theory will be fairly familiar. In the past, all of our equations have included at least the price of the product, in this case, *PRIPK*, the price (PRI) of pork (PK). In addition, we have usually added some measure of consumer buying power, and in this example we will use *YDUSP*, which is disposable income (YD) in the United States (US) per capita (P). In addition, the price of a substitute, PRIBF, the price of beef (BF) is also available as an explanatory variable.

Since many of the questions about inclusion of variables have been considered already, we now go beyond that choice to include somewhat more complex items than were studied in the first interactive exercise. You will choose whether the functional form of the demand/income relationship should be linear (using YDUSP) or semi-log (using the log of that variable, LYDUSP). In addition, you will have to figure out whether to adjust the intercept of the quarterly model for seasonal variation with the inclusion of quarterly seasonal dummies (D1, D2, and D3). You also will have to decide on the extent to which simultaneity can be dealt with by including a production variable, *PROPK*, the production (PRO) of pork, in the equation. Finally, serial correlation or heteroskedasticity may be a problem.

As even a little reading will show you, attention paid in the literature[5] to the demand for pork is impressive. One question is whether the typical consumer decides to buy a product based on real prices and incomes or on nominal prices and incomes. The more sophisticated the consumer behavior is assumed to be, the more logical it is to use real prices and incomes since the dependent variable in this example (pounds of pork) is in real terms. The variables in this exercise are nominal; however, they could be converted to real prices and incomes by dividing through by the consumer price index (CPI) or GNP deflator of the quarter in question and multiplying by 100:

$$\text{Real } X_i = \text{Nominal } X_i (100/\text{CPI}_i)$$

The variables available for your model are:

$CONPK_t$	Per capita pounds of pork consumed in the U.S. in quarter t
$PRIPK_t$	The price of a pound of pork (in dollars per 100 pounds) in quarter t
$PRIBF_t$	The price of a pound of beef (in dollars per 100 pounds) in quarter t
$YDUSP_t$	Per capita disposable income in the U.S. in quarter t (current dollars)
$LYDUSP_t$	The log of per capita disposable income
$PROPK_t$	Pounds of pork produced (in billions) in the U.S. in quarter t
$D1_t$	Dummy equal to 1 in the first quarter of the year and 0 otherwise
$D2_t$	Dummy equal to 1 in the second quarter of the year and 0 otherwise
$D3_t$	Dummy equal to 1 in the third quarter of the year and 0 otherwise

Table 11.6   Data for the Demand for Pork Interactive Example

OBSERV	CONPK	PRIPK	PRIBF	PROPK	YDUSP	D1	D2	D3
1975:1	13.98	114.1	137.2	3.142	4.182	1	0	0
1975:2	12.90	122.7	155.3	2.992	5.125	0	1	0
1975:3	11.29	148.8	166.0	2.555	5.129	0	0	1
1975:4	12.49	152.9	160.9	2.896	5.232	0	0	0
1976:1	13.01	141.2	151.3	2.958	5.335	1	0	0
1976:2	12.08	138.2	150.8	2.847	5.422	0	1	0
1976:3	12.95	137.1	145.3	3.014	5.511	0	0	1
1976:4	15.68	119.6	145.4	3.669	5.617	0	0	0
1977:1	14.28	120.5	144.6	3.294	5.721	1	0	0
1977:2	13.48	121.7	146.4	3.185	5.873	0	1	0
1977:3	13.25	131.0	149.0	3.073	6.055	0	0	1
1977:4	14.81	128.2	153.4	3.500	6.209	0	0	0
1978:1	13.94	137.0	162.7	3.243	6.340	1	0	0
1978:2	13.60	142.4	185.7	3.265	6.529	0	1	0
1978:3	13.61	144.7	189.4	3.160	6.711	0	0	1
1978:4	14.70	150.1	189.7	3.541	6.900	0	0	0
1979:1	14.50	156.1	215.4	3.395	7.082	1	0	0
1979:2	15.55	148.2	235.5	3.754	7.226	0	1	0
1979:3	16.01	138.0	226.6	3.775	7.427	0	0	1
1979:4	17.75	134.3	227.7	4.346	7.584	0	0	0
1980:1	17.30	133.9	235.2	4.125	7.814	1	0	0
1980:2	17.69	124.4	231.4	4.299	7.871	0	1	0
1980:3	16.04	144.2	241.6	3.756	8.095	0	0	1
1980:4	17.25	154.3	242.3	4.252	8.345	0	0	0
1981:1	16.81	148.7	237.5	4.073	8.606	1	0	0
1981:2	15.87	144.7	234.7	3.881	8.732	0	1	0
1981:3	15.38	157.5	243.1	3.605	9.023	0	0	1
1981:4	16.90	158.7	239.5	4.157	9.134	0	0	0
1982:1	15.33	160.1	237.3	3.693	9.209	1	0	0
1982:2	14.76	169.3	247.2	3.550	9.295	0	1	0
1982:3	13.87	185.0	248.3	3.240	9.439	0	0	1
1982:4	15.06	187.1	237.2	3.638	9.593	0	0	0
1983:1	14.51	183.0	237.9	3.483	9.675	1	0	0
1983:2	15.33	171.1	245.1	3.771	9.832	0	1	0
1983:3	15.42	165.4	238.4	3.657	10.082	0	0	1
1983:4	16.91	159.8	231.1	4.206	10.318	0	0	0
1984:1	15.34	161.5	242.6	3.738	10.608	1	0	0
1984:2	15.14	159.4	242.1	3.670	10.806	0	1	0
1984:3	14.77	164.0	236.2	3.355	11.000	0	0	1
1984:4	16.46	163.3	237.3	3.957	11.133	0	0	0

The data for the variables are in Table 11.6.

Now:

1. Hypothesize expected signs for all these variables in an equation for the consumption of pork. Consider each variable carefully; what is the economic content of each hypothesis?

2. Choose the best combination of explanatory variables for this model. Assume that every model has at least the price of pork variable and one of the two

income variables. Do not take the attitude that you will see what a particular specification looks like before making up your mind. As you surely remember from the Section 6.4 on specification searches, such an attitude leads to possible bias and ruins the applicability of the *t*- and *F*-tests. In addition, this example has been set up in the hope that you will be capable of getting the "perfect" equation after looking at only one regression estimate. Take it as a challenge; try to make your first equation your final equation.

Once you have chosen your best equation, you will be ready to begin. As with the first interactive exercise, keep following the instructions until you have completely specified the equation and have been instructed to go to the discussion of serial correlation and heteroskedasticity in Section 11.6.3. To the extent that you can, avoid looking at the hints until after completion of the project. (If you need to look, you will find that the hints are somewhat more sparse than in the first example in the hope that you will eventually be able to do without such hints.) Try to take the time to actually write out the answers to the questions after each result. Good luck!

11.6.2   The Demand for Pork Interactive Learning Example

To start the example, write out the specification you chose in Section 11.6.1 above. To find that equation's estimates, carefully follow these instructions. (Note that the means and simple correlation coefficients for this data set are in Table 11.7 just before the results begin.)

All the equations include CONPK as the dependent variable and PRIPK as one of the explanatory variables. In addition, all the equations available to you at the beginning of the example include either YDUSP or LYDUSP. If you chose YDUSP as one of your variables, go to question number one, but if you instead chose LYDUSP, jump to question number two below.

1. Find below the combination of explanatory variables (from PROPK, PRIBF, and the seasonal dummies) that you wish to include in your regression and then go to the indicated estimated regression equation:
   none of them, go to regression run #11.21
   the seasonal dummies only, go to regression run #11.22
   PROPK only, go to regression run #11.23
   PRIBF only, go to regression run #11.25
   the seasonal dummies and PROPK, go to regression run #11.24
   the seasonal dummies and PRIBF, go to regression run #11.26
   PROPK and PRIBF, go to regression run #11.27
   all three, go to regression run #11.28.

2. Find below the combination of explanatory variables (from PROPK, PRIBF, and the seasonal dummies) that you wish to include in your regression and then go to the indicated estimated regression equation:
   none of them, go to regression run #11.29
   PROPK only, go to regression run #11.31

the seasonal dummies only, go to regression run #11.30
PRIBF only, go to regression run #11.33
the seasonal dummies and PROPK, go to regression run #11.32
the seasonal dummies and PRIBF, go to regression run #11.34
PROPK and PRIBF, go to regression run #11.35
all three, go to regression run #11.36.

Table 11.7   Means, Variances, and Correlations for the
Demand for Pork Interactive Example

Variable	Mean	Standard Dev	Variance
CONPK	14.90000	1.555892	2.420800
PRIPK	148.0550	18.06813	326.4575
PRIBF	205.6075	40.29446	1623.643
PROPK	3.542750	0.435895	0.190004
YDUSP	7.745500	1.928367	3.718598
LYDUSP	2.014656	0.258263	0.066700
D1	0.250000	0.433013	0.187500
D2	0.250000	0.433013	0.187500
D3	0.250000	0.433013	0.187500

	Correlation Coeff		Correlation Coeff
PRIBF,PRIPK	0.708	PRIPK,CONPK	0.110
PROPK,CONPK	0.988	PRIBF,CONPK	0.682
PROPK,PRIBF	0.707	PROPK,PRIPK	0.165
YDUSP,CONPK	0.573	YDUSP,PRIPK	0.758
YDUSP,PRIBF	0.884	YDUSP,PROPK	0.604
LYDUSP,PRIPK	0.752	LYDUSP,CONPK	0.611
LYDUSP,PROPK	0.643	LYDUSP,PRIBF	0.909
D1,PRIPK	−0.078	LYDUSP,YDUSP	0.993
D1,PROPK	−0.037	D1,CONPK	0.000
D1,LYDUSP	−0.096	D1,PRIBF	−0.077
D2,CONPK	−0.096	D1,YDUSP	−0.086
D2,PRIBF	0.025	D2,PRIPK	−0.122
D2,YDUSP	−0.022	D2,PROPK	−0.028
D2,D1	−0.333	D2,LYDUSP	−0.016
D3,CONPK	−0.237	D3,PRIPK	0.112
D3,PRIBF	0.039	D3,PROPK	−0.296
D3,YDUSP	0.030	D3,LYDUSP	0.033
D3,D1	−0.333	D3,D2	−0.333

Regression Run 11.21

```
ORDINARY LEAST SQUARES              DEPENDENT VARIABLE IS CONPK
SAMPLE RANGE:        1-40

                    COEFFICIENT      STANDARD ERROR     T-STATISTIC
     CONST           17.44424          1.481554          11.77429
     PRIPK           -0.065923         0.014111          -4.671866
     YDUSP            0.931629         0.132211           7.046528

R-squared             0.578213     Mean of depend var     14.90000
Adjusted R-squared    0.555413     Std dev depend var      1.575713
Std err of regress    1.050643     Residual sum          8.11997E-09
Durbin Watson stat    0.891839     Sum squared resid      40.84251
F Statistic          25.36097
```

Answer each of the following questions for the above regression run.

a. Evaluate this result with respect to its economic meaning, overall fit, and the signs and significance of the individual coefficients.

b. What econometric problems does this regression have? Why? If you need feedback on your answer, see hint #19 in the material on this chapter in Appendix A.

c. Which of the following statements comes closest to your recommendation for further action to be taken in the estimation of this equation?

i.   No specification changes are advisable (go to Section 11.6.3).

ii. No variable changes are advisable, but I am concerned about heteroskedasticity or serial correlation (go to Section 11.6.3).

iii. I would like to add PRIBF to the equation (go to run #11.25).

iv. I would like to add seasonal dummies to the equation (go to run #11.22).

v.   I would like to change to LYDUSP from YDUSP (go to run #11.29).

If you need feedback on your answer, see hint #21 in the material on this chapter in Appendix A.

Regression Run 11.22

```
ORDINARY LEAST SQUARES                    DEPENDENT VARIABLE IS CONPK
SAMPLE RANGE:        1-40

                   COEFFICIENT        STANDARD ERROR     T-STATISTIC
     CONST           18.52019            1.373476         13.48418
     PRIPK           -0.067432           0.012656         -5.327895
     YDUSP            0.930689           0.117379          7.928913
     D1              -0.741767           0.416294         -1.781835
     D2              -1.295246           0.418102         -3.097919
     D3              -1.343842           0.414676         -3.240705

R-squared              0.699346      Mean of depend var      14.90000
Adjusted R-squared     0.655132      Std dev depend var       1.575713
Std err of regress     0.925345      Residual sum         8.20364E-09
Durbin Watson stat     0.282212      Sum squared resid       29.11292
F Statistic           15.81736
```

Answer each of the following questions for the above regression run.

a. Evaluate this result with respect to its economic meaning, overall fit, and the signs and significance of the individual coefficients.

b. What econometric problems does this regression have? Why? If you need feedback on your answer, see hint #19 in the material on this chapter in Appendix A.

c. Which of the following statements comes closest to your recommendation for further action to be taken in the estimation of this equation?

   i.   No specification changes are advisable (go to Section 11.6.3).

   ii.   No variable changes are advisable, but I am concerned about heteroskedasticity or serial correlation (go to Section 11.6.3).

   iii. I would like to add PRIBF to the equation (go to run #11.26).

   iv. I would like to add PROPK to the equation (go to run #11.24).

   v.   I would like to change to LYDUSP from YDUSP (go to run #11.30).

If you need feedback on your answer, see hint #21 in the material on this chapter in Appendix A.

Regression Run 11.23

```
ORDINARY LEAST SQUARES              DEPENDENT VARIABLE IS CONPK
SAMPLE RANGE:        1-40

                    COEFFICIENT     STANDARD ERROR    T-STATISTIC
     CONST          3.546665          0.584503          6.067834
     PRIPK         -8.56799E-03       3.61098E-03      -2.372757
     YDUSP          0.053113          0.041881          1.268189
     PROPK          3.446612          0.122414         28.15540

  R-squared         0.981678     Mean of depend var      14.90000
  Adjusted R-squared 0.980151    Std dev depend var       1.575713
  Std err of regress 0.221999    Residual sum             2.83762E-09
  Durbin Watson stat 2.344786    Sum squared resid        1.774204
  F Statistic       642.9325
```

Answer each of the following questions for the above regression run.

a. Evaluate this result with respect to its economic meaning, overall fit, and the signs and significance of the individual coefficients.

b. What econometric problems does this regression have? Why? If you need feedback on your answer, see hint #22 in the material on this chapter in Appendix A.

c. Which of the following statements comes closest to your recommendation for further action to be taken in the estimation of this equation?

    i.   No specification changes are advisable (go to Section 11.6.3).

    ii. No variable changes are advisable, but I am concerned about heteroskedasticity or serial correlation (go to Section 11.6.3).

    iii. I would like to add PRIBF to the equation (go to run #11.27).

    iv. I would like to drop PROPK from the equation (go to run #11.21).

    v. I would like to change to LYDUSP from YDUSP (go to run #11.31).

If you need feedback on your answer, see hint #24 in the material on this chapter in Appendix A.

Regression Run 11.24

```
ORDINARY LEAST SQUARES                      DEPENDENT VARIABLE IS CONPK
SAMPLE RANGE:        1-40

                    COEFFICIENT        STANDARD ERROR      T-STATISTIC
       CONST        3.261089           0.543028            6.005384
       PRIPK        -8.88975E-03       2.94923E-03         -3.014258
       YDUSP        0.041745           0.035263            1.183812
       PROPK        3.549741           0.112243            31.62553
       D1           0.146838           0.080576            1.822349
       D2           -0.159385          0.083920            -1.899245
       D3           0.236159           0.090304            2.615171

R-squared           0.990397        Mean of depend var     14.90000
Adjusted R-squared  0.988651        Std dev depend var     1.575713
Std err of regress  0.167863        Residual sum           2.77032E-09
Durbin Watson stat  1.491153        Sum squared resid      0.929878
F Statistic         567.2373
```

Answer each of the following questions for the above regression run.

a. Evaluate this result with respect to its economic meaning, overall fit, and the signs and significance of the individual coefficients.

b. What econometric problems does this regression have? Why? If you need feedback on your answer, see hint #22 in the material on this chapter in Appendix A.

c. Which of the following statements comes closest to your recommendation for further action to be taken in the estimation of this equation?

   i.   No specification changes are advisable (go to Section 11.6.3).

   ii.   No variable changes are advisable, but I am concerned about heteroskedasticity or serial correlation (go to Section 11.6.3).

   iii. I would like to add PRIBF to the equation (go to run #11.28).

   iv.   I would like to drop PROPK from the equation (go to run #11.22).

   v.   I would like to change to LYDUSP from YDUSP (go to run #11.32).

   If you need feedback on your answer, see hint #24 in the material on this chapter in Appendix A.

Regression Run 11.25

```
ORDINARY LEAST SQUARES                   DEPENDENT VARIABLE IS CONPK
SAMPLE RANGE:         1-40

                     COEFFICIENT      STANDARD ERROR       T-STATISTIC
       CONST          15.81965          1.143847            13.83021
       PRIPK          -0.073081         0.010607            -6.889909
       PRIBF          0.036681          6.64475E-03          5.520233
       YDUSP          0.304513          0.150450             2.024009

  R-squared           0.771571      Mean of depend var        14.90000
  Adjusted R-squared  0.752535      Std dev depend var         1.575713
  Std err of regress  0.783851      Residual sum               7.27596E-09
  Durbin Watson stat  1.895964      Sum squared resid         22.11922
  F Statistic         40.53278
```

Answer each of the following questions for the above regression run.

a. Evaluate this result with respect to its economic meaning, overall fit, and the signs and significance of the individual coefficients.

b. What econometric problems does this regression have? Why? If you need feedback on your answer, see hint #25 in the material on this chapter in Appendix A.

c. Which of the following statements comes closest to your recommendation for further action to be taken in the estimation of this equation?

   i.   No specification changes are advisable (go to Section 11.6.3).

   ii. No variable changes are advisable, but I am concerned about heteroskedasticity or serial correlation (go to Section 11.6.3).

   iii. I would like to add PROPK to the equation (go to run #11.27).

   iv. I would like to add seasonal dummies to the equation (go to run #11.26).

   v.   I would like to change to LYDUSP from YDUSP (go to run #11.33).

If you need feedback on your answer, see hint #27 in the material on this chapter in Appendix A.

Regression Run 11.26

```
ORDINARY LEAST SQUARES                 DEPENDENT VARIABLE IS CONPK
SAMPLE RANGE:         1-40

                     COEFFICIENT      STANDARD ERROR     T-STATISTIC
       CONST          16.99718         0.627607           27.08250
       PRIPK          -0.076756        5.71353E-03        -13.43405
       PRIBF          0.041556         3.54857E-03         11.71067
       YDUSP          0.225024         0.079902            2.816248
       D1             -0.917088        0.186697           -4.912169
       D2             -1.633960        0.189129           -8.639402
       D3             -1.529973        0.186053           -8.223335

R-squared              0.941686      Mean of depend var      14.90000
Adjusted R-squared     0.931083      Std dev depend var       1.575713
Std err of regress     0.413657      Residual sum             6.68115E-09
Durbin Watson stat     1.085841      Sum squared resid        5.646691
F Statistic           88.81648
```

Answer each of the following questions for the above regression run.

a. Evaluate this result with respect to its economic meaning, overall fit, and the signs and significance of the individual coefficients.

b. What econometric problems does this regression have? Why? If you need feedback on your answer, see hint #23 in the material on this chapter in Appendix A.

c. Which of the following statements comes closest to your recommendation for further action to be taken in the estimation of this equation?

   i.   No specification changes are advisable (go to Section 11.6.3).

   ii.   No variable changes are advisable, but I am concerned about heteroskedasticity or serial correlation (go to Section 11.6.3).

   iii.   I would like to add PROPK to the equation (go to run #11.28).

   iv.   I would like to drop the dummies from the equation (go to run #11.25).

   v.   I would like to change to LYDUSP from YDUSP (go to run #11.34).

If you need feedback on your answer, see hint #26 in the material on this chapter in Appendix A.

Regression Run 11.27

```
ORDINARY LEAST SQUARES                 DEPENDENT VARIABLE IS CONPK
SAMPLE RANGE:        1-40

                     COEFFICIENT       STANDARD ERROR      T-STATISTIC
        CONST        4.016224          0.652051            6.159372
        PRIPK        -0.011906         4.17236E-03         -2.853550
        PRIBF        3.70474E-03       2.43832E-03         1.519383
        YDUSP        0.029829          0.043901            0.679453
        PROPK        3.289467          0.158608            20.73957

   R-squared         0.982811       Mean of depend var      14.90000
   Adjusted R-squared 0.980847      Std dev depend var      1.575713
   Std err of regress 0.218071      Residual sum            3.01225E-09
   Durbin Watson stat 2.329738      Sum squared resid       1.664422
   F Statistic        500.3034
```

Answer each of the following questions for the above regression run.

a. Evaluate this result with respect to its economic meaning, overall fit, and the signs and significance of the individual coefficients.

b. What econometric problems does this regression have? Why? If you need feedback on your answer, see hint #22 in the material on this chapter in Appendix A.

c. Which of the following statements comes closest to your recommendation for further action to be taken in the estimation of this equation?

i.   No specification changes are advisable (go to Section 11.6.3).

ii.   No variable changes are advisable, but I am concerned about heteroskedasticity or serial correlation (go to Section 11.6.3).

iii. I would like to add seasonal dummies to the equation (go to run #11.28).

iv.   I would like to drop PROPK from the equation (go to run #11.25).

v.   I would like to drop YDUSP from the equation (go to run #11.40).

If you need feedback on your answer, see hint #24 in the material on this chapter in Appendix A.

Regression Run 11.28

```
ORDINARY LEAST SQUARES                    DEPENDENT VARIABLE IS CONPK
SAMPLE RANGE:        1-40

                      COEFFICIENT       STANDARD ERROR      T-STATISTIC
        CONST         4.981253          0.891043            5.590363
        PRIPK        -0.017923          4.73211E-03         -3.787536
        PRIBF         6.66841E-03       2.83470E-03         2.352423
        YDUSP         0.042957          0.033069            1.299023
        PROPK         3.092723          0.220951            13.99731
        D1            4.29959E-03        0.096849            0.044395
        D2           -0.359976          0.116030            -3.102451
        D3            2.87151E-03        0.130400            0.022021

    R-squared          0.991813         Mean of depend var     14.90000
    Adjusted R-squared 0.990022         Std dev depend var     1.575713
    Std err of regress 0.157399         Residual sum           4.62660E-09
    Durbin Watson stat 1.560405         Sum squared resid      0.792780
    F Statistic        553.7938
```

Answer each of the following questions for the above regression run.

a. Evaluate this result with respect to its economic meaning, overall fit, and the signs and significance of the individual coefficients.

b. What econometric problems does this regression have? Why? If you need feedback on your answer, see hint #22 in the material on this chapter in Appendix A.

c. Which of the following statements comes closest to your recommendation for further action to be taken in the estimation of this equation?

   i.   No specification changes are advisable (go to Section 11.6.3).

   ii.   No variable changes are advisable, but I am concerned about heteroskedasticity or serial correlation (go to Section 11.6.3).

   iii.   I would like to drop PROPK from the equation (go to run #11.26).

   iv.   I would like to drop the dummies from the equation (go to run #11.27).

   v.   I would like to change to LYDUSP from YDUSP (go to run #11.36).

If you need feedback on your answer, see hint #28 in the material on this chapter in Appendix A.

Regression Run 11.29

```
ORDINARY LEAST SQUARES              DEPENDENT VARIABLE IS CONPK
SAMPLE RANGE:        1-40

                    COEFFICIENT        STANDARD ERROR      T-STATISTIC
        CONST       10.39433            1.296443            8.017575
        PRIPK       -0.069247           0.012629           -5.483229
        LYDUSP       7.325311           0.883514            8.291111

R-squared           0.654355       Mean of depend var      14.90000
Adjusted R-squared  0.635672       Std dev depend var       1.575713
Std err of regress  0.951095       Residual sum             3.79805E-09
Durbin Watson stat  1.141044       Sum squared resid       33.46949
F Statistic        35.02313
```

Answer each of the following questions for the above regression run.

a. Evaluate this result with respect to its economic meaning, overall fit, and the signs and significance of the individual coefficients.

b. What econometric problems does this regression have? Why? If you need feedback on your answer, see hint #19 in the material on this chapter in Appendix A.

c. Which of the following statements comes closest to your recommendation for further action to be taken in the estimation of this equation?

   i.   No specification changes are advisable (go to Section 11.6.3).

   ii. No variable changes are advisable, but I am concerned about heteroskedasticity or serial correlation (go to Section 11.6.3).

   iii. I would like to add **PRIBF** to the equation (go to run #11.33).

   iv. I would like to add seasonal dummies to the equation (go to run #11.30).

   v. I would like to change to **YDUSP** from **LYDUSP** (go to run #11.21).

If you need feedback on your answer, see hint #21 in the material on this chapter in Appendix A.

Regression Run 11.30

```
ORDINARY LEAST SQUARES              DEPENDENT VARIABLE IS CONPK
SAMPLE RANGE:        1--40

                 COEFFICIENT      STANDARD ERROR    T-STATISTIC
     CONST        11.45431          1.137026         10.07392
     PR1PK        -0.071056         0.010748         -6.610804
     LYDUSP        7.347385         0.744911          9.863446
     D1           -0.691993         0.357755         -1.934265
     D2           -1.316662         0.359186         -3.665681
     D3           -1.337529         0.356146         -3.755566

R-squared            0.778169    Mean of depend var     14.90000
Adjusted R-squared   0.745547    Std dev depend var      1.575713
Std err of regress   0.794842    Residual sum          3.31420E-09
Durbin Watson stat   0.440596    Sum squared resid      21.48033
F Statistic         23.85397
```

Answer each of the following questions for the above regression run.

a. Evaluate this result with respect to its economic meaning, overall fit, and the signs and significance of the individual coefficients.

b. What econometric problems does this regression have? Why? If you need feedback on your answer, see hint #19 in the material on this chapter in Appendix A.

c. Which of the following statements comes closest to your recommendation for further action to be taken in the estimation of this equation?

   i.   No specification changes are advisable (go to Section 11.6.3).

   ii.   No variable changes are advisable, but I am concerned about heteroskedasticity or serial correlation (go to Section 11.6.3).

   iii. I would like to add PRIBF to the equation (go to run #11.34).

   iv. I would like to add PROPK to the equation (go to run #11.32).

   v.   I would like to change to YDUSP from LYDUSP (go to run #11.22).

If you need feedback on your answer, see hint #21 in the material on this chapter in Appendix A.

Regression Run 11.31

```
ORDINARY LEAST SQUARES                  DEPENDENT VARIABLE IS CONPK
SAMPLE RANGE:      1-40

                    COEFFICIENT        STANDARD ERROR     T-STATISTIC
     CONST          3.174375            0.417704           7.599572
     PRIPK         -8.34067E-03         3.82252E-03       -2.181985
     LYDUSP         0.380609            0.344663           1.104293
     PROPK          3.441876            0.136468          25.22104

  R-squared         0.981486        Mean of depend var    14.90000
  Adjusted R-squared 0.979943       Std dev depend var     1.575713
  Std err of regress 0.223155       Residual sum           2.54659E-09
  Durbin Watson stat 2.325275       Sum squared resid      1.792740
  F Statistic       636.1610
```

Answer each of the following questions for the above regression run.

a. Evaluate this result with respect to its economic meaning, overall fit, and the signs and significance of the individual coefficients.

b. What econometric problems does this regression have? Why? If you need feedback on your answer, see hint #22 in the material on this chapter in Appendix A.

c. Which of the following statements comes closest to your recommendation for further action to be taken in the estimation of this equation?

   i.   No specification changes are advisable (go to Section 11.6.3).

   ii. No variable changes are advisable, but I am concerned about heteroskedasticity or serial correlation (go to Section 11.6.3).

   iii. I would like to add PRIBF to the equation (go to run #11.35).

   iv. I would like to drop LYDUSP from the equation (go to run #11.39).

   v.   I would like to change to YDUSP from LYDUSP (go to run #11.23).

If you need feedback on your answer, see hint #24 in the material on this chapter in Appendix A.

Regression Run 11.32

```
ORDINARY LEAST SQUARES                    DEPENDENT VARIABLE IS CONPK
SAMPLE RANGE:        1-40

                    COEFFICIENT        STANDARD ERROR      T-STATISTIC
       CONST         2.936172           0.400831            7.325214
       PRIPK        -8.27413E-03        3.28514E-03        -2.518655
       LYDUSP        0.253454           0.309608            0.818629
       PROPK         3.561964           0.133387           26.70395
       D1            0.150815           0.082635            1.825064
       D2           -0.154851           0.088159           -1.756486
       D3            0.240371           0.096289            2.496345

  R-squared           0.990188      Mean of depend var      14.90000
  Adjusted R-squared  0.988405      Std dev depend var       1.575713
  Std err of regress  0.169676      Residual sum             3.34876E-09
  Durbin Watson stat  1.480375      Sum squared resid        0.950074
  F Statistic       555.0628
```

Answer each of the following questions for the above regression run.

a. Evaluate this result with respect to its economic meaning, overall fit, and the signs and significance of the individual coefficients.

b. What econometric problems does this regression have? Why? If you need feedback on your answer, see hint #22 in the material on this chapter in Appendix A.

c. Which of the following statements comes closest to your recommendation for further action to be taken in the estimation of this equation?

    i. No specification changes are advisable (go to Section 11.6.3).

    ii. No variable changes are advisable, but I am concerned about heteroskedasticity or serial correlation (go to Section 11.6.3).

    iii. I would like to add PRIBF to the equation (go to run #11.36).

    iv. I would like to drop LYDUSP from the equation (go to run #11.37).

    v. I would like to drop PROPK from the equation (go to run #11.30).

If you need feedback on your answer, see hint #24 in the material on this chapter in Appendix A.

Regression Run 11.33

```
ORDINARY LEAST SQUARES               DEPENDENT VARIABLE IS CONPK
SAMPLE RANGE:        1-40
                   COEFFICIENT      STANDARD ERROR     T-STATISTIC
      CONST         13.21440          1.222610          10.80835
      PRIPK         -0.073307         0.010274          -7.135435
      PRIBF          0.032976         7.31164E-03         4.510051
      LYDUSP         2.858567         1.222097           2.339067

   R-squared         0.779143     Mean of depend var      14.90000
   Adjusted R-squared 0.760738    Std dev depend var       1.575713
   Std err of regress 0.770751    Residual sum          5.45697E-09
   Durbin Watson stat 1.947537    Sum squared resid       21.38605
   F Statistic       42.33374
```

Answer each of the following questions for the above regression run.

a. Evaluate this result with respect to its economic meaning, overall fit, and the signs and significance of the individual coefficients.

b. What econometric problems does this regression have? Why? If you need feedback on your answer, see hint #25 in the material on this chapter in Appendix A.

c. Which of the following statements comes closest to your recommendation for further action to be taken in the estimation of this equation?

    i.   No specification changes are advisable (go to Section 11.6.3).

    ii. No variable changes are advisable, but I am concerned about heteroskedasticity or serial correlation (go to Section 11.6.3).

    iii. I would like to add seasonal dummies to the equation (go to run #11.34).

    iv. I would like to add PROPK to the equation (go to run #11.35).

    v.   I would like to change to YDUSP from LYDUSP (go to run #11.25).

If you need feedback on your answer, see hint #27 in the material on this chapter in Appendix A.

Regression Run 11.34

```
ORDINARY LEAST SQUARES                    DEPENDENT VARIABLE IS CONPK
SAMPLE RANGE:         1-40
                        COEFFICIENT       STANDARD ERROR      T-STATISTIC
        CONST            15.04305           0.671939            22.38754
        PRIPK            -0.076858          5.42260E-03        -14.17362
        PRIBF             0.038758          3.83569E-03         10.10445
        LYDUSP            2.121157          0.638094             3.324208
        D1               -0.891381          0.180554            -4.936923
        D2               -1.616533          0.182618            -8.852001
        D3               -1.516465          0.179541            -8.446366

R-squared                0.945815      Mean of depend var        14.90000
Adjusted R-squared       0.935963      Std dev depend var         1.575713
Std err of regress       0.398743      Residual sum               5.91353E-09
Durbin Watson stat       1.191319      Sum squared resid          5.246862
F Statistic             96.00373
```

Answer each of the following questions for the above regression run.

a. Evaluate this result with respect to its economic meaning, overall fit, and the signs and significance of the individual coefficients.

b. What econometric problems does this regression have? Why? If you need feedback on your answer, see hint #19 in the material on this chapter in Appendix A.

c. Which of the following statements comes closest to your recommendation for further action to be taken in the estimation of this equation?

  i. No specification changes are advisable (go to Section 11.6.3).

  ii. No variable changes are advisable, but I am concerned about heteroskedasticity or serial correlation (go to Section 11.6.3).

  iii. I would like to add PROPK to the equation (go to run #11.36).

  iv. I would like to drop the dummies from the equation (go to run #11.33).

  v. I would like to change to YDUSP from LYDUSP (go to run #11.26).

If you need feedback on your answer, see hint #26 in the material on this chapter in Appendix A.

Regression Run 11.35

```
ORDINARY LEAST SQUARES                    DEPENDENT VARIABLE IS CONPK
SAMPLE RANGE:        1-40

                    COEFFICIENT        STANDARD ERROR      T-STATISTIC
     CONST          3.804671           0.579937            6.560486
     PRIPK         -0.011335           4.22807E-03         -2.681006
     PRIBF          3.88151E-03        2.52570E-03         1.536807
     LYDUSP         0.141817           0.372298            0.380922
     PROPK          3.299647           0.162819            20.26569

  R-squared         0.982656       Mean of depend var      14.90000
  Adjusted R-squared 0.980674      Std dev depend var      1.575713
  Std err of regress 0.219051      Residual sum            2.21189E-09
  Durbin Watson stat 2.321783      Sum squared resid       1.679414
  F Statistic        495.7593
```

Answer each of the following questions for the above regression run.

a. Evaluate this result with respect to its economic meaning, overall fit, and the signs and significance of the individual coefficients.

b. What econometric problems does this regression have? Why? If you need feedback on your answer, see hint #22 in the material on this chapter in Appendix A.

c. Which of the following statements comes closest to your recommendation for further action to be taken in the estimation of this equation?

   i.   No specification changes are advisable (go to Section 11.6.3).

   ii. No variable changes are advisable, but I am concerned about heteroskedasticity or serial correlation (go to Section 11.6.3).

   iii. I would like to add seasonal dummies to the equation (go to run #11.36).

   iv. I would like to drop LYDUSP from the equation (go to run #11.40).

   v.   I would like to drop PROPK from the equation (go to run #11.33).

   If you need feedback on your answer, see hint #24 in the material on this chapter in Appendix A.

Regression Run 11.36

```
ORDINARY LEAST SQUARES                      DEPENDENT VARIABLE IS CONPK
SAMPLE RANGE:        1-40

                    COEFFICIENT        STANDARD ERROR       T-STATISTIC
        CONST        4.659578           0.830265             5.612160
        PRIPK       -0.017415           4.99239E-03         -3.488342
        PRIBF        6.68425E-03        2.87027E-03          2.328791
        LYDUSP       0.271935           0.290844             0.934987
        PROPK        3.100112           0.234566            13.21640
        D1           7.14728E-03        0.099133             0.072098
        D2          -0.357211           0.120017            -2.976325
        D3           4.91706E-03        0.135639             0.036251

   R-squared          0.991610      Mean of depend var      14.90000
   Adjusted R-squared 0.989775      Std dev depend var       1.575713
   Std err of regress 0.159334      Residual sum            4.03998E-09
   Durbin Watson stat 1.545712      Sum squared resid        0.812392
   F Statistic      540.3141
```

Answer each of the following questions for the above regression run.

a. Evaluate this result with respect to its economic meaning, overall fit, and the signs and significance of the individual coefficients.

b. What econometric problems does this regression have? Why? If you need feedback on your answer, see hint #22 in the material on this chapter in Appendix A.

c. Which of the following statements comes closest to your recommendation for further action to be taken in the estimation of this equation?

    i.   No specification changes are advisable (go to Section 11.6.3).

    ii.   No variable changes are advisable, but I am concerned about heteroskedasticity or serial correlation (go to Section 11.6.3).

    iii. I would like to drop LYDUSP from the equation (go to run #11.38).

    iv. I would like to drop the dummies from the equation (go to run #11.35).

    v.   I would like to drop PROPK from the equation (go to run #11.34).

If you need feedback on your answer, see hint #24 in the material on this chapter in Appendix A.

Regression Run 11.37

```
ORDINARY LEAST SQUARES              DEPENDENT VARIABLE IS CONPK
SAMPLE RANGE:       1-40

                   COEFFICIENT      STANDARD ERROR    T-STATISTIC
   CONST            2.739559         0.319348          8.578610
   PRIPK           -5.89585E-03      1.52616E-03      -3.863198
   PROPK            3.655655         0.068176         53.62105
   D1               0.171500         0.078294          2.190458
   D2              -0.122343         0.078327         -1.561955
   D3               0.279955         0.082863          3.378542

R-squared            0.989989     Mean of depend var    14.90000
Adjusted R-squared   0.988517     Std dev depend var     1.575713
Std err of regress   0.168851     Residual sum           1.07593E-09
Durbin Watson stat   1.500170     Sum squared resid      0.969367
F Statistic        672.4652
```

Answer each of the following questions for the above regression run.

a. Evaluate this result with respect to its economic meaning, overall fit, and the signs and significance of the individual coefficients.

b. What econometric problems does this regression have? Why? If you need feedback on your answer, see hint #22 in the material on this chapter in Appendix A.

c. Which of the following statements comes closest to your recommendation for further action to be taken in the estimation of this equation?

   i.   No specification changes are advisable (go to Section 11.6.3).

   ii. No variable changes are advisable, but I am concerned about heteroskedasticity or serial correlation (go to Section 11.6.3).

  iii. I would like to add LYDUSP to the equation (go to run #11.32).

  iv. I would like to drop the dummies from the equation (go to run #11.39).

  v. I would like to replace PROPK with YDUSP (go to run #11.22).

If you need feedback on your answer, see hint #29 in the material on this chapter in Appendix A.

Regression Run 11.38

```
ORDINARY LEAST SQUARES              DEPENDENT VARIABLE IS CONPK
SAMPLE RANGE:      1-40

                    COEFFICIENT       STANDARD ERROR     T-STATISTIC
        CONST        4.429906          0.791582           5.596272
        PRIPK       -0.014765          4.10206E-03        -3.599465
        PRIBF        6.61103E-03       2.86372E-03         2.308541
        PROPK        3.205620          0.205246           15.61843
        D1           0.030899          0.095640            0.323075
        D2          -0.320142          0.113064           -2.831516
        D3           0.049935          0.126564            0.394545

    R-squared            0.991381      Mean of depend var      14.90000
    Adjusted R-squared   0.989814      Std dev depend var       1.575713
    Std err of regress   0.159030      Residual sum             3.89082E-09
    Durbin Watson stat   1.524391      Sum squared resid        0.834585
    F Statistic        632.6324
```

Answer each of the following questions for the above regression run.

a. Evaluate this result with respect to its economic meaning, overall fit, and the signs and significance of the individual coefficients.

b. What econometric problems does this regression have? Why? If you need feedback on your answer, see hint #22 in the material on this chapter in Appendix A.

c. Which of the following statements comes closest to your recommendation for further action to be taken in the estimation of this equation?

    i.   No specification changes are advisable (go to Section 11.6.3).

    ii. No variable changes are advisable, but I am concerned about heteroskedasticity or serial correlation (go to Section 11.6.3).

    iii. I would like to add LYDUSP to the equation (go to run #11.36).

    iv. I would like to drop the dummies from the equation (go to run #11.40).

    v. I would like to replace PROPK with YDUSP (go to run #11.26).

If you need feedback on your answer, see hint #29 in the material on this chapter in Appendix A.

Regression Run 11.39

```
ORDINARY LEAST SQUARES                    DEPENDENT VARIABLE IS CONPK
SAMPLE RANGE:        1-40

                    COEFFICIENT       STANDARD ERROR      T-STATISTIC
     CONST          2.980064            0.379956           7.843186
     PRIPK         -4.73003E-03         1.98604E-03        -2.381641
     PROPK          3.562273            0.082323           43.27210

  R-squared         0.980859        Mean of depend var     14.90000
  Adjusted R-squared 0.979824       Std dev depend var      1.575713
  Std err of regress 0.223816       Residual sum            1.36788E-09
  Durbin Watson stat 2.412963       Sum squared resid       1.853467
  F Statistic        948.0087
```

Answer each of the following questions for the above regression run.

a. Evaluate this result with respect to its economic meaning, overall fit, and the signs and significance of the individual coefficients.

b. What econometric problems does this regression have? Why? If you need feedback on your answer, see hint #22 in the material on this chapter in Appendix A.

c. Which of the following statements comes closest to your recommendation for further action to be taken in the estimation of this equation?

   i.   No specification changes are advisable (go to Section 11.6.3).

   ii. No variable changes are advisable, but I am concerned about heteroskedasticity or serial correlation (go to Section 11.6.3).

   iii. I would like to add LYDUSP to the equation (go to run #11.31).

   iv. I would like to add seasonal dummies to the equation (go to run #11.37).

   v.   I would like to replace PROPK with YDUSP (go to run #11.21).

   If you need feedback on your answer, see hint #30 in the material on this chapter in Appendix A.

Regression Run 11.40

```
ORDINARY LEAST SQUARES                    DEPENDENT VARIABLE IS CONPK
SAMPLE RANGE:        1-40

                    COEFFICIENT        STANDARD ERROR      T-STATISTIC
        CONST        3.810085            0.572838           6.651243
        PRIPK       -0.010534            3.62399E-03        -2.906824
        PRIBF        4.28305E-03         2.26779E-03         1.888643
        PROPK        3.321979            0.150083           22.13423

    R-squared        0.982585        Mean of depend var      14.90000
    Adjusted R-squared   0.981133    Std dev depend var       1.575713
    Std err of regress   0.216434    Residual sum             2.93949E-09
    Durbin Watson stat   2.327164    Sum squared resid        1.686376
    F Statistic      677.0419
```

Answer each of the following questions for the above regression run.

a. Evaluate this result with respect to its economic meaning, overall fit, and the signs and significance of the individual coefficients.

b. What econometric problems does this regression have? Why? If you need feedback on your answer, see hint #22 in the material on this chapter in Appendix A.

c. Which of the following statements comes closest to your recommendation for further action to be taken in the estimation of this equation?

   i.   No specification changes are advisable (go to Section 11.6.3).

   ii. No variable changes are advisable, but I am concerned about heteroskedasticity or serial correlation (go to Section 11.6.3).

   iii. I would like to add YDUSP to the equation (go to run #11.27).

   iv. I would like to add seasonal dummies to the equation (go to run #11.38).

   v.   I would like to replace PROPK with LYDUSP (go to run #11.33).

If you need feedback on your answer, see hint #30 in the material on this chapter in Appendix A.

11.6.3   Heteroskedasticity and Serial Correlation in the Interactive Example

Now that you have chosen your "best" specification, we can discuss the possibility that pure heteroskedasticity or serial correlation might exist in your residuals.

Heteroskedasticity. This dependent variable is already per capita, is time series, and does not change substantially during the sample period. As a result, the possibility of pure heteroskedasticity is so low that most econometricians would not even bother testing for it. (If a Park test were to be run, however, a logical proportionality factor Z might be per capita disposable income.)

Serial Correlation. Serial correlation is quite another matter, however, since the data are time series and a number of the Durbin-Watson d statistics are below the critical d_L value for positive serial correlation. In addition, it seems possible that short-run fads in the consumption of pork, or alternatively, supply shocks, might cause swings in consumption from year to year that would not be completely captured by the price variables or by coefficients estimated over the entire sample.

In particular, if your final equation was either regression run #11.26 or run #11.34, then there is a possibility of serial correlation. Their Durbin-Watson d's of 1.09 and 1.19 respectively are right at the edge of the critical d_L for positive serial correlation for 40 observations and 6 explanatory variables. By the way, the $k' = 6$ column must be extrapolated from the $k' = 4$ and $k' = 5$ columns; for 40 observations, this works out to something like $d_L = 1.00$ and $d_U = 1.64$ for one percent one-sided level of significance (Table B-6).

The application of generalized least squares to regression runs #11.26 and #11.34 are contained in regression runs #11.41 and #11.42 respectively; we include these mainly for instructional purposes, since the inconclusive Durbin-Watson statistics do not justify GLS on their own. As can be seen by comparing the GLS result with the OLS result, the correction with a $\hat{p}$ in the range of 0.43 did indeed decrease the significance of the price and income explanatory variables as would have been expected. The increase in significance of the seasonal dummies with GLS estimation raises the possibility that the seasonal pattern is not as simple as that implied by the three intercept dummies.

Note that most of the lowest Durbin-Watson statistics came with the seasonal dummy group included, supporting the hypothesis that this set of dummies did not properly capture the actual seasonality of the demand for pork; the introduction of the seasonal dummies might have deleted some but not all of the seasonal variation, leaving a serially correlated pattern in the residuals. While the equation was probably better off with the seasonal dummies than without, a better knowledge of the meat industry before estimation might have allowed a more sophisticated seasonal pattern to be chosen. Even using only intercept dummies, for example, a better overall fit might have been obtained by using only one seasonal dummy (D_4, equal to one in the fourth quarter and zero otherwise). To make such a switch (or to drop one of the seasonal dummies while keeping the others) on the sole basis of the attached estimations would be a mistake, however, because the hypothesis would be tested on the same data set from which it was developed.

Finally, note that some of the Durbin-Watson statistics were greater than two when PROPK was included in the regression. This result almost surely occurred because the resulting equation included both demand-side and supply-side variables, and the residuals were no longer the residuals of just the demand-side equation. This result is one of many reasons that most econometricians go to great lengths to avoid including such a production variable in a demand-side equation. In a sense, production acts like a dominant variable; its relationship to the dependent variable is strong but is definitional with little economic content.

Regression Run #11.41

FIRST ORDER AUTOCORRELATION   DEPENDENT VARIABLE IS CONPK
SAMPLE RANGE: 1-40

RHO=   0.455853

	COEFFICIENT	STANDARD ERROR	T-STATISTIC
CONST	17.41381	0.800001	21.76725
PRIPK	-0.079405	7.26075E-03	-10.93616
PRIBF	0.040689	5.18376E-03	7.849304
YDUSP	0.244804	0.107771	2.271525
D1	-0.939562	0.137605	-6.827952
D2	-1.648780	0.159060	-10.36576
D3	-1.524093	0.135052	-11.28527

R-squared	0.953951	Mean of depend var	14.90000
Adjusted R-squared	0.945579	Std dev depend var	1.575713
Std err of regress	0.367587	Residual sum	0.021340
Durbin Watson stat	1.975783	Sum squared resid	4.458970
F Statistic	113.9392		

Regression Run #11.42

FIRST ORDER AUTOCORRELATION   DEPENDENT VARIABLE IS CONPK
SAMPLE RANGE: 1-40

RHO=   0.404150

	COEFFICIENT	STANDARD ERROR	T-STATISTIC
CONST	15.43025	0.904503	17.05938
PRIPK	-0.078753	6.88048E-03	-11.44580
PRIBF	0.038995	5.24579E-03	7.433650
LYDUSP	2.050851	0.815826	2.513834
D1	-0.923854	0.140226	-6.588323
D2	-1.642605	0.159753	-10.28214
D3	-1.522505	0.137216	-11.09566

R-squared	0.954593	Mean of depend var	14.90000
Adjusted R-squared	0.946337	Std dev depend var	1.575713
Std err of regress	0.365017	Residual sum	-0.086148
Durbin Watson stat	1.969632	Sum squared resid	4.396830
F Statistic	115.6273		

[1]Choices on the basis of fit are only valid if two different data sets are used. One data set is used to develop hypotheses by testing the fits of various lag structures or functional forms (this is often called "scanning"). The second is then used to test these hypotheses by estimating the equation involved. The use of such dual data sets is easiest when there is a plethora of data. This is sometimes the case in cross-sectional research projects but rarely for time series research. If the same data set is used both to scan competing hypotheses and also to test them, our typical statistical tests have little meaning in the second use because the researcher knows ahead of time what the result will be.

[2]Background articles include Peter Fortune, "The Effectiveness of Recent Policies to Maintain Thrift-Deposit Flows," *Journal of Money, Credit and Banking*, August 1975, pp. 297-316, and A. Thomas King, "Thrift Institution Deposits: The Influence of MMCs and MMMFs," *Journal of Money, Credit and Banking*, August 1984, pp. 328-333. See also a number of excellent articles in Edward M. Gramlich and Dwight M. Jaffee, eds., *Savings Deposits, Mortgages, and Housing* (Lexington, Mass: Lexington Books, 1972).

[3]All the regression results in this book were obtained using the ECSTAT regression package. ECSTAT, which is produced by Insight Software, 3 Risley Road, Winchester, MA 01890, is an extremely user-friendly software package intended for use on personal computers.

[4]This data set was obtained from Prof. William G. Tomek of Cornell University, who has created an eight-part series of hands-on problem sets (of up to six exercises per problem set) on the demand for pork. Most of the tasks to which he sets his students go beyond what we have covered so far in this text. They include specifications with price as the dependent variable (which is more difficult than the quantity dependent variable model we use), distributed lag equations, forecasting, and a simultaneous model of the pork industry. We are extremely grateful to Professor Tomek for his help in preparing this interactive exercise, but we hasten to point out that since the approach we have taken is different from his, any errors in this example should not be blamed on him. (Don't blame us either, they're probably stochastic errors!)

[5]The place to start is to review the demand for chicken example of Section 6.1 and to consult a typical intermediate microeconomics text regarding the demand for a product. More advanced readings, among many suggested by Professor Tomek, include E.R. Arzac and M. Wilkinson, "A Quarterly Econometric Model of United States Livestock and Feed Grain Markets and Some of Its Policy Implications," *American Journal of Agricultural Economics*, May 1979, pp. 297-308; Giancarlo Moschini and Karl D. Meilke, "Parameter Stability and the U.S. Demand for Beef," *Western Journal of Agricultural Economics*, December 1984, pp. 271-282; and Z.A. Hassen and S.R. Johnson, "Structural Stability and Recursive Residuals: Quarterly Demand for Meat," *Agricultural Economics Research*, October 1979, pp. 20-29.

12

Simultaneous Equations

12.1 Structural and Reduced-Form Equations

12.2 The Bias of Ordinary Least Squares (OLS)

12.3 Two-Stage Least Squares (2SLS)

12.4 The Identification Problem

12.5 Summary and Exercises

12.6 Appendix: Errors in the Variables

12.7 Appendix: Recursive Models, Seemingly Unrelated Regressions and Three-Stage Least Squares

Unfortunately, single-equation models ignore much of the interdependence that characterizes the modern world. The anticipation and analysis of the secondary effects of an action or policy is vital to proper decisionmaking. The best approach to understanding these interdependences is to explicitly acknowledge them with feedback loops in our models. This means hypothesizing and estimating simultaneous equation systems instead of looking at just one equation at a time.

A majority of the applications of econometrics is inherently simultaneous in nature; the most important model in microeconomics, supply and demand, is obviously simultaneous. Virtually all of the major approaches to macroeconomics, from Keynesian aggregate demand models to the rational expectations models currently in vogue, are simultaneous as well. Both the demand for pork and the stock of passbook deposits, the dependent variables for the two interactive examples of the previous chapter, might most appropriately be considered as part of a simultaneous system. To study the demand for pork without also looking at the supply of pork or to study passbook deposits without modeling alternative assets is to take a chance on missing important linkages and thus making significant mistakes.

The estimation of simultaneous equation systems with Ordinary Least Squares causes a number of difficulties that are not encountered with single equations. Classical Assumption III, which states that all explanatory variables should be uncorrelated with the error term, is violated in simultaneous models; mainly because of this, OLS coefficient estimates in simultaneous systems are biased. This problem is explained in more detail in Section 12.2. Alternative estimation techniques aimed at avoiding most of this bias, like the Two-Stage Least Squares method explained in Section 12.3, require an equation to be identified before it can be estimated (see Section 12.4). The identification properties of an equation change every time any equation in the system is changed, however, so a researcher must be well equipped to deal with specification problems like those of the previous six chapters. As a result, it does not make sense to learn how to estimate a simultaneous system until you are fairly adept at estimating a single equation.

12.1   Structural and Reduced-Form Equations

Before we can study the problems encountered in the estimation of simultaneous equations, we need to explain why it is that simultaneous equations systems violate Classical Assumption III and to introduce a few new concepts. We start off with a brief review of the nature of simultaneous systems; readers well versed in the subject are encouraged to skip to Section 12.1.2.

12.1.1   The Nature of Simultaneous Equations Systems

Which came first, the chicken or the egg? This question is impossible to answer satisfactorily because chickens and eggs are *jointly determined;* the more eggs you have, the more chickens you'll get, but the more chickens you have, the more eggs you'll get.[1] More realistically, the economic world is full of the kind of *feedback effects* and *dual causality* that require application of simultaneous equations. Besides the supply and demand and simple macroeconomic model examples mentioned above, we could talk about the dual causality of population size and the food supply, the joint determination of wages and prices, or the interaction between foreign exchange rates and international trade and capital flows. In terms of a typical econometric equation:

$$Y_t = \beta_0 + \beta_1 X_{1t} + \beta_2 X_{2t} + \epsilon_t \tag{12.1}$$

a simultaneous system is one in which Y clearly has an effect on at least one of the Xs in addition to the effect that the Xs have on Y.

Such topics are usually modeled by distinguishing between variables that are simultaneously determined (the Ys, called **endogenous variables**) and those that are not (the Xs, called **exogenous variables**):

$$Y_{1t} = \alpha_0 + \alpha_1 Y_{2t} + \alpha_2 X_{1t} + \alpha_3 X_{2t} + \epsilon_{1t} \tag{12.2}$$

$$Y_{2t} = \beta_0 + \beta_1 Y_{1t} + \beta_2 X_{3t} + \beta_3 X_{2t} + \epsilon_{2t} \tag{12.3}$$

For example, Y_1 and Y_2 might be the quantity and price of chicken (respectively), X_1 the income of consumers, X_2 the price of beef (beef is a substitute for chicken in both consumption and production), and X_3 the price of chicken feed. With these definitions, Equation 12.2 would characterize the behavior of consumers of chickens and Equation 12.3 the behavior of suppliers of chickens. These behavioral equations are also called "structural equations." **Structural equations** characterize the underlying economic theory behind each endogenous variable by expressing it in terms of both endogenous and exogenous variables. Researchers must view them as an entire system in order to see all the feedback loops involved. For example, the Ys are jointly determined, so a change in Y_1 will cause a change in Y_2, which will in turn cause Y_1 to change *again*. Contrast this feedback with a change in X_1, which will not eventually loop back and cause X_1 to change again. The αs and the βs in the equations are *structural coefficients*, and hypotheses should be made about their signs just as we did with the regression coefficients of single equations.

Note that a variable is endogenous because it is jointly determined, not just because it appears in both equations. That is, X_2, which might be the price of beef or some other factor beyond our control, is in both equations as an explanatory variable but is still exogenous in nature, because it is not simultaneously determined within the chicken market. In a general equilibrium model of the entire economy, however, such a price variable would also likely be endogenous. How do you decide whether a particular variable should be endogenous or exogenous? Some variables are almost always exogenous (the weather, for example), but most others can be considered either endogenous or exogenous depending on the other equations in the system. Thus the distinction between endogenous and exogenous variables usually depends on how the researcher defines the scope of the research project.

Also note that the term explanatory variable can be applied to endogenous as well as exogenous variables. In addition, lagged endogenous variables sometimes appear as explanatory variables in simultaneous systems even if the equations involved are not distributed lag equations (described in Section 9.6). To avoid confusion, **predetermined variables** are defined to include all exogenous and lagged endogenous variables. "Predetermined" implies that exogenous and lagged endogenous variables are determined outside the system of specified equations or prior to the current period. Endogenous variables that are not lagged are not predetermined, because they are jointly determined by the system. Therefore, econometricians tend to speak in terms of endogenous and predetermined variables when discussing simultaneous equations systems.

Let's look at the specification of a simple supply and demand model, say for a new soft-drink "Antique Cola":

$$Q_{Dt} = \alpha_0 + \alpha_1 P_t + \alpha_2 X_{1t} + \alpha_3 X_{2t} + \epsilon_{Dt} \tag{12.4}$$

$$Q_{St} = \beta_0 + \beta_1 P_t + \beta_2 X_{3t} + \epsilon_{St} \tag{12.5}$$

$$Q_{St} = Q_{Dt} \quad \text{(equilibrium condition)}$$

where: Q_{Dt} = the quantity of Antique Cola demanded in time period t
   Q_{St} = the quantity of Antique Cola supplied in time period t
   P_t = the price of Antique Cola in time period t
   X_{1t} = dollars of advertising for Antique Cola in time period t
   X_{2t} = another "demand-side" exogenous variable (e.g., income or the prices or advertising of competitors)

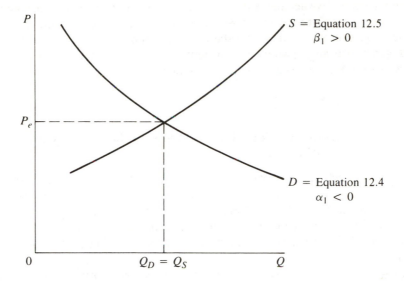

FIGURE 12.1 *Supply and Demand Simultaneous Equations*
An example of simultaneous equations that jointly determine two endogenous variables is the supply and demand for a product. In this case, Equation 12.4, the downward-sloping demand curve, and Equation 12.5, the upward-sloping supply curve, intersect at the equilibrium price and quantity for this market.

X_{3t} = a "supply-side" exogenous variable (e.g., the price of artificial flavors or other factors of production).

ϵ_t = classical error terms (each equation has its own error term, subscripted "D" and "S" for demand and supply).

In this case, price and quantity are simultaneously determined, but price, one of the endogenous variables, is not on the left side of any of the equations. It is incorrect to automatically assume that the endogenous variables are those that appear on the left side of at least one equation; in this case, we could have just as easily written Equation 12.5 with price on the left side and quantity supplied on the right side, as we did in the chicken example above. While the estimated coefficients would be different, the underlying relations would not. Note also that there must be as many equations as there are endogenous variables. In this case, the three endogenous variables are Q_D, Q_S, and P.

What would the expected signs for the coefficients of the price variables in Equations 12.4 and 12.5 be? We would expect price to enter negatively in the demand equation but to enter positively in the supply equation. The higher the price, after all, the less quantity will be demanded, but the more quantity will be supplied. These signs would result in the typical supply and demand diagram (Figure 12.1) that we're all used to. Look at Equations 12.4 and 12.5 again, however, and note that they would be identical but for the different predetermined variables. What would happen if we accidentally put a supply-side predetermined variable in the demand equation or vice versa? We would have a very difficult time identifying which equation was which, and the expected signs for the coefficients of the endogenous variable P would become ambiguous. As a result, we must take care when specifying the structural equations in a system.

12.1.2 Simultaneous Equations Systems Violate Classical Assumption III

Recall from Section 4.4.2 that Classical Assumption III states that the error term and each explanatory variable must be independent of each other, for if there is such a correlation, then the OLS regression estimation program is likely to attribute to the particular explanatory variable any variations in the dependent variable that are actually being caused by variations in the error term. The result will be biased estimates.

To see why simultaneous equations violate the assumption of independence between the error term and the explanatory variables, look again at a simultaneous system, Equations 12.2 and 12.3, repeated here for convenience (with directional arrows):

$$\overset{\uparrow}{Y_{1t}} = \alpha_0 + \overset{\uparrow}{\alpha_1 Y_{2t}} + \alpha_2 X_{1t} + \overset{\uparrow}{\alpha_3 X_{2t}} + \epsilon_{1t} \qquad (12.2)$$

$$\overset{\uparrow}{Y_{2t}} = \beta_0 + \overset{\uparrow}{\beta_1 Y_{1t}} + \beta_2 X_{3t} + \beta_3 X_{2t} + \epsilon_{2t} \qquad (12.3)$$

Let's work through the system and see what happens when one of the error terms increases, holding everything else in the equations constant:

1. If ϵ_1 increases in a particular time period, Y_1 will also increase due to Equation 12.2.

2. If Y_1 increases, Y_2 will also rise[2] due to Equation 12.3.

3. But if Y_2 increases in Equation 12.3, it also increases in Equation 12.2 where it is an explanatory variable.

Thus an increase in the error term of an equation causes an increase in an explanatory variable in that same equation: If ϵ_1 increases, Y_1 increases, and then Y_2 increases, violating the assumption of independence between the error term and explanatory variables.

This is not an isolated result that depends on the particular equations involved. Indeed, as you will find in Exercise 3, this result works for other error terms, equations, and simultaneous systems. All that is required for the violation of Classical Assumption III is that there be endogenous variables that are jointly determined in a system of simultaneous equations.

12.1.3   Reduced-Form Equations

An alternative way of expressing a simultaneous equations system is through the use of **reduced-form equations,** equations that express a particular endogenous variable solely in terms of an error term and all the predetermined (exogenous plus lagged endogenous) variables in the simultaneous system.

The reduced-form equations for the structural Equations 12.2 and 12.3 would thus be:

$$Y_{1t} = \pi_0 + \pi_1 X_{1t} + \pi_2 X_{2t} + \pi_3 X_{3t} + v_{1t} \tag{12.6}$$

$$Y_{2t} = \pi_4 + \pi_5 X_{1t} + \pi_6 X_{2t} + \pi_7 X_{3t} + v_{2t} \tag{12.7}$$

where the vs are stochastic error terms and the πs are called **reduced-form coefficients** because they are the coefficients of the independent variables in the reduced-form equations. Note that each equation includes only one endogenous variable, the dependent variable, and that each equation has exactly the same set of explanatory variables. The reduced-form coefficients, such as π_1 and π_5, are known as **impact multipliers** because they measure the impact on the endogenous variable of a one unit change in the value of the exogenous variable, after allowing for the feedback effects from the entire simultaneous system.

There are at least four reasons for using reduced-form equations:

1. Since the reduced-form equations have no inherent simultaneity, they do not violate Classical Assumption III. Therefore, they can be estimated with Ordinary Least Squares without encountering the problems discussed in this chapter.

2. The reduced-form coefficients estimated in this way can sometimes be mathematically manipulated to allow the estimation of the structural coefficients. That is, estimates of the πs of Equations 12.6 and 12.7 can be used to solve for the αs and βs of Equations 12.2 and 12.3. This method of calculating estimates of the structural coefficients from estimates of the reduced-form coefficients is called **Indirect Least Squares** (ILS). Unfortunately, indirect least squares turns out to be useful only in very limited situations. For more on indirect least squares, see Exercise 4.

3. The interpretation of the reduced-form coefficients as impact multipliers means that they have economic meaning and useful applications of their own. For example, if you wanted to compare a government spending increase with a tax cut in terms of the per dollar impact in the first year, estimates of the impact multipliers (reduced-form coefficients or πs) would allow such a comparison.

4. Perhaps most importantly, reduced-form equations play an important role in the estimation technique most frequently used for simultaneous equations. This technique, Two-Stage Least Squares, will be explained in Section 12.3.

To conclude, let's return to the supply and demand model for Antique Cola and specify the reduced-form equations for that model. (To test yourself, flip back to Equations 12.4 and 12.5 and see if you can get the right answer before going on.) Since the equilibrium condition forces Q_D to be equal to Q_S, we need only two reduced-form equations:

$$Q_t = \pi_0 + \pi_1 X_{1t} + \pi_2 X_{2t} + \pi_3 X_{3t} + v_{1t} \tag{12.8}$$

$$P_t = \pi_4 + \pi_5 X_{1t} + \pi_6 X_{2t} + \pi_7 X_{3t} + v_{2t} \tag{12.9}$$

Even though P never appears on the left side of a structural equation, it is an endogenous variable and should be treated as such.

12.2   The Bias of Ordinary Least Squares (OLS)

All the classical assumptions must be met for OLS estimates to be BLUE; when an assumption is violated, we must determine which of the properties no longer holds. It turns out that applying OLS directly to the structural equations of a simultaneous system, called *Direct Least Squares,* produces biased estimates of the coefficients. Such bias is called simultaneous equations bias or simultaneity bias.

12.2.1   Understanding Simultaneity Bias

Simultaneity bias refers to the fact that in a simultaneous system, the expected values of the OLS-estimated structural coefficients ($\hat{\beta}$s) are not equal to the true βs. These estimated coefficients are also inconsistent. That is, the expected values of the $\hat{\beta}$s do not approach the true βs even if the sample size gets quite large. We are therefore faced with the problem that in a simultaneous system:

$$E(\hat{\beta}) \neq \beta \tag{12.10}$$

Why does this simultaneity bias exist? Recall from Section 12.1.2 that in simultaneous equation systems, the error terms (the ϵs) tend to be correlated with the endogenous variables (the Ys) whenever the Ys appear as explanatory variables. Let's follow through what this correlation means (assuming positive coefficients for simplicity) in typical structural equations like 12.11 and 12.12:

$$Y_{1t} = \beta_0 + \beta_1 Y_{2t} + \beta_2 X_t + \epsilon_{1t} \tag{12.11}$$

$$Y_{2t} = \alpha_0 + \alpha_1 Y_{1t} + \alpha_2 Z_t + \epsilon_{2t} \tag{12.12}$$

Since we cannot observe the error term (ϵ_1) and don't know when ϵ_{1t} is above average, it will appear that if every time Y_1 is above average, so too is Y_2. As a result, the OLS estimation program will tend to attribute increases in Y_1 caused by the error term ϵ_1 to Y_2, thus overestimating β_1. This overestimation is simultaneity bias. If the error term is abnormally negative, Y_{1t} is less than it would have been otherwise, causing Y_{2t} to be less that it would have been otherwise, and the computer program will attribute the decrease in Y_1 to Y_2, once again causing us to overestimate β_1 (i.e., induce upward bias).

Recall that the causation between Y_1 and Y_2 runs in both directions, because the two variables are interdependent. As a result, β_1, when estimated by OLS, can no longer be interpreted as the impact of Y_2 on Y_1, holding X constant. Instead, $\hat{\beta}_1$ now measures some mix of the effects of the two endogenous variables on each other! In addition, consider β_2. It is supposed to be the effect of X on Y_1 holding Y_2 constant, but how can we expect Y_2 to be held constant when a change in Y_1 takes place? As a result, there is potential bias in all the estimated coefficients in a simultaneous system.

What does this bias look like? It is possible to derive an equation[3] for the expected value of the regression coefficients in a simultaneous system that is estimated by OLS. This equation shows that as long as the error term and any of the explanatory variables in the equation are correlated, then the coefficient estimates will be biased. In addition, it also shows that the bias will have the same sign as the correlation between the error term and the endogenous variable that appears as an explanatory variable in that error term's equation. Since that correlation is usually positive[4] in economic and business examples, so is the bias of OLS. The violation of Classical Assumption III will almost always mean bias in the estimation of β_1. In addition, this bias will usually be positive in economic applications, but the direction of the bias will depend on the specific details of the structural equations and the model's underlying theory.

This does not mean that every coefficient from a simultaneous system estimated with OLS will be a bad approximation of the true population coefficient; indeed, most researchers use OLS to estimate equations in simultaneous systems under a number of circumstances. Instead, it is vital at least to consider an alternative to OLS whenever simultaneous equations systems are being estimated. Before we investigate the alternative estimation technique most frequently used (Two-Stage Least Squares), let's look at an example of simultaneity bias.

12.2.2 An Example of Simultaneity Bias

To show how the application of OLS to simultaneous equation estimation causes bias, we generated an example of such biased estimates. Since it is impossible to know whether any bias exists unless you also know the true βs, we picked a set of coefficients arbitrarily considered true, stochastically generated data sets based on these coefficients, and obtained repeated OLS estimates of these coefficients from the generated data sets. The expected value of these estimates turned out to be quite different from the true coefficient values, thus exemplifying the bias in OLS estimates of coefficients in simultaneous systems.

We used a supply and demand model as the basis for our example:

$$Q_t = \beta_0 + \beta_1 P_t + \beta_2 X_t + \epsilon_{Dt} \qquad (12.13)$$

$$Q_t = \alpha_0 + \alpha_1 P_t + \alpha_2 Z_t + \epsilon_{St} \qquad (12.14)$$

where: Q_t = the quantity demanded and supplied in time period t
P_t = the price in time period t
X_t = a "demand-side" exogenous variable, such as income
Z_t = a "supply-side" exogenous variable, such as weather
ϵ_t = classical errors (different for each equation).

The first step was to choose a set of true coefficient values that corresponded to our expectations for this model:

$$\beta_1 = -1 \qquad \beta_2 = +1 \qquad \alpha_1 = +1 \qquad \alpha_2 = +1$$

In other words, we have a negative relationship between price and quantity demanded, a positive relationship between price and quantity supplied, and positive relationships between the exogenous variables and their respective dependent variables.

The next step was to randomly generate a number of data sets based upon the true values. This also meant specifying some other characteristics of the data[5] and then generating the different data sets (5,000 in this case).

The final step was to apply OLS to the generated data sets and to calculate the estimated coefficients of the demand equation (12.13). (Similar results were obtained for the supply equation.) The arithmetic means of the results for the 5000 regressions were:

$$\hat{Q}_{Dt} = -0.37 P_t + 1.84 X_t \qquad (12.15)$$

In other words, the expected value of $\hat{\beta}_1$ should have been -1.00, but instead it was $-.037$, and the expected value of $\hat{\beta}_2$ should have been $+1.00$ but instead it was 1.84:

$$E(\hat{\beta}_1) = -0.37 \neq -1.00$$

$$E(\hat{\beta}_2) = 1.84 \neq 1.00$$

This is simultaneity bias! As the diagram of the sampling distributions of the $\hat{\beta}$s in Figure 12.2 shows, the OLS estimates of β_1 were almost never very close to -1.00, while the OLS estimates of β_2 were distributed over a wide range of values.

The biased estimation in this example did not cause incorrect signs for the majority of the estimates, but any kind of bias is worth avoiding if it is at all possible. The most frequently used method of mitigating the simultaneity bias is a technique called Two-Stage Least Squares (2SLS).

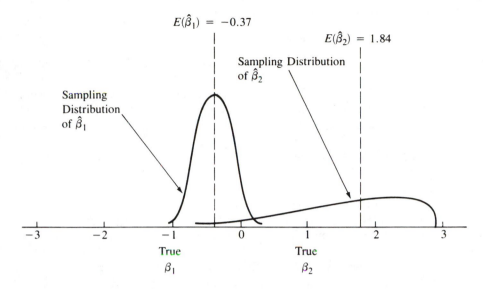

$E(\hat{\beta}_1) = -0.37$

$E(\hat{\beta}_2) = 1.84$

Sampling Distribution of $\hat{\beta}_2$

Sampling Distribution of $\hat{\beta}_1$

FIGURE 12.2 *Sampling Distributions Showing Simultaneity Bias of OLS Estimates*
In the experiment in Section 12.2.2, simultaneity bias is evident in the distribution of the estimates of β_1, which had a mean value of -0.37 compared with a true value of -1.00 and in the estimates of β_2, which had a mean value of 1.84 compared with a true value of 1.00.

12.3 Two-Stage Least Squares (2SLS)

While there are a number of econometric estimation techniques available that help mitigate the bias and avoid the inconsistency inherent in the application of OLS to simultaneous equations systems, the most frequently used alternative to OLS is called Two-Stage Least Squares (2SLS).

12.3.1 What Is Two-Stage Least Squares?

If OLS encounters bias in the estimation of simultaneous equations mainly because such equations violate Classical Assumption III, then one ought as least to explore ways to avoid violating that assumption. We could do this if we could find a variable that is:

1. A good proxy for the endogenous variable and

2. Uncorrelated with the error term.

If we then substitute this new variable for the endogenous variable where it appears as an explanatory variable, our new explanatory variable will be uncorrelated with the error term, and Classical Assumption III will be met. This general approach is called *instrumental variables*.

That is, consider Equation 12.16 in the following system:

$$Y_{1t} = \beta_0 + \beta_1 Y_{2t} + \beta_2 X_t + \epsilon_{1t} \tag{12.16}$$

$$Y_{2t} = \alpha_0 + \alpha_2 Y_{1t} + \alpha_2 Z_t + \epsilon_{2t} \tag{12.17}$$

If we could find a variable that was highly correlated with Y_2 but that was uncorrelated with ϵ_1, then we could substitute this new variable for Y_2 on the right side of Equation 12.16, and we'd conform to Classical Assumption III. An **instrumental variable** replaces an endogenous variable (when it is an explanatory variable); it is a good proxy for the endogenous variable that is independent of the error term.

Since there is no joint causality between the instrumental variable and any endogenous variable, the use of the instrumental variable avoids the violation of Classical Assumption III. The job of finding such a variable is another story, though. How do we go about finding variables with these qualifications? For simultaneous equations systems, Two-Stage Least Squares provides an approximate answer.

Two-Stage Least Squares (2SLS) is a method of systematically creating instrumental variables to replace the endogenous variables where they appear as explanatory variables in simultaneous equations systems. 2SLS does this by running a regression on the reduced form of the right side endogenous variables in need of replacement and then using the $\hat{Y}$s (or fitted values) from those reduced-form regressions as the instrumental variables. More specifically, the two-step procedure consists of:

Stage One: Find the reduced-form equations for each of the endogenous variables that appear as explanatory variables in the structural equations in the system, and then apply OLS to each of these reduced-form equations.

Since the predetermined (exogenous plus lagged endogenous) variables are uncorrelated with the reduced-form error term, the OLS estimates of the reduced-form coefficients (the $\hat{\pi}$s) are unbiased. These $\hat{\pi}$s can then be used to calculate estimates of the endogenous variables:[6]

$$\hat{Y}_{1t} = \hat{\pi}_0 + \hat{\pi}_1 X_t + \hat{\pi}_2 Z_t \tag{12.18}$$

$$\hat{Y}_{2t} = \hat{\pi}_3 + \hat{\pi}_4 X_t + \hat{\pi}_5 Z_t \tag{12.19}$$

These $\hat{Y}$s are the instrumental variables that will be used as proxies in the structural equations of the simultaneous system.

Stage Two: Substitute the reduced-form $\hat{Y}$s (instrumental variables) for the Ys that appear on the right side (only) of the structural equations, and then estimate these revised structural equations with OLS.

That is, Stage Two consists of estimating the following equations with OLS:

$$Y_{1t} = \beta_0 + \beta_1 \hat{Y}_{2t} + \beta_2 X_t + u_{1t} \tag{12.20}$$

$$Y_{2t} = \alpha_0 + \alpha_2 \hat{Y}_{1t} + \alpha_2 Z_t + u_{2t} \tag{12.21}$$

Note that the dependent variable is still the original endogenous variable and that the substitutions are only for the endogenous variables where they appear as explanatory variables in the structural equations.

This description of Two-Stage Least Squares can be generalized to m different simultaneous structural equations with m reduced-form equations for each of the m endogenous variables. Each reduced-form equation has as explanatory variables every predetermined variable in the entire system of equations. The OLS estimates of the reduced-form equations are used to compute the estimated values of all the endogenous variables that appear as explanatory variables in the m structural equations. After substituting these fitted values for the original values of the endogenous regressors, OLS is applied to each equation in the set of structural equations.

12.3.2   The Properties of Two-Stage Least Squares

1. *Two-Stage Least Squares estimates are still biased, but they are now consistent.* That is, for small samples, the expected value of a $\hat{\beta}$ produced by 2SLS is still not equal to the true β,[7] but as the sample size gets larger, the expected value of the $\hat{\beta}$ approaches the true β. As the sample size gets bigger, the variances of both the OLS and the 2SLS estimates decrease. Thus, in the limiting case, OLS estimates are very precise estimates of the wrong number and 2SLS estimates are very precise estimates of the correct number. As a result, the larger the sample size, the better a technique 2SLS is.

   This is called *consistency*; to illustrate, let's look again at the example of Section 12.2. We returned to that example and expanded the data set from 5000 different samples of size 20 each to 5000 different samples of 50 observations each. As expected, the average $\hat{\beta}_1$ for 2SLS moved from -1.25 to -1.06 compared to the "true" value of -1.00. By contrast, the OLS average estimate went from -0.37 to -0.44. Such results are typical; large sample sizes will produce unbiased (and consistent) estimates for 2SLS while still producing biased estimates for OLS.

2. *The bias in 2SLS for small samples is of the opposite sign of the bias in OLS.* Recall that the bias in OLS was positive, indicating that a $\hat{\beta}$ produced by OLS for a simultaneous system is likely to be greater than the true β. For 2SLS, the expected bias is negative, and thus a $\hat{\beta}$ produced by 2SLS is likely to be less than the true β. For any given set of data, the 2SLS estimate can be larger than the OLS estimate, but it can be shown that the majority of 2SLS estimates are likely to be less than the corresponding OLS estimates. For large samples, there is little bias in 2SLS because the estimates are consistent.

   Return to the example of Section 12.2. Compared to the true value of -1.00 for β_1, the small sample 2SLS average estimate was -1.25, as mentioned above. This means that the 2SLS estimates showed negative bias. The OLS estimates, on the other hand, averaged -0.44, so they exhibited positive bias.

Thus the observed bias in the example due to OLS was opposite the observed bias due to 2SLS.

3. *If the fit of the reduced-form equation is quite poor, then 2SLS will not work very well.* Recall that the instrumental variable is supposed to be a good proxy for the endogenous variable. To the extent that the fit (as measured by R^2) of the reduced-form equation is poor, then the instrumental variable is no longer highly correlated with the original endogenous variable, and there is no reason to expect 2SLS to be effective. As the R^2 of the reduced-form equation increases, the usefulness of 2SLS will increase.

4. *If the predetermined variables are highly correlated, 2SLS will not work very well.* The first stage of 2SLS includes explanatory variables from different structural equations in the same reduced-form equation. As a result, severe multicollinearity between explanatory variables from different structural equations is possible in the reduced-form equations. When this happens, the $\hat{Y}$ produced by this reduced-form equation can be highly correlated with the exogenous variables in the structural equation. Consequently, the second stage of 2SLS will also show a high degree of multicollinearity, and the variances of the estimated coefficients will be high. Thus the higher the simple correlation coefficient between exogenous variables, the less precise 2SLS estimates will be.

5. *The use of the t-test for hypothesis testing is far more accurate using 2SLS estimators than it is using OLS estimators.* The *t*-test is not exact for the 2SLS estimators, but it is accurate enough in most circumstances. By contrast, the biasedness of OLS estimators in simultaneous systems implies that its t-statistics are not accurate enough to be relied upon for testing purposes.[8] This means that it may be appropriate to use 2SLS even when the predetermined variables are highly correlated.

On balance, then, 2SLS will almost always be a better estimator of the coefficients of a simultaneous system than OLS will be. The major exception to this general rule is when the fit of the reduced-form equation in question is quite poor for a small sample.

12.3.3   An Example of Two-Stage Least Squares

Let us work through an example of the application of Two-Stage Least Squares to a naive linear Keynesian macroeconomic model of the United States economy. Let us specify the following system:

$$Y_t = C_t + I_t + G_t + NX_t \tag{12.22}$$

$$C_t = \beta_0 + \beta_1 YD_t + \beta_2 C_{t-1} + \epsilon_t \tag{12.23}$$

$$YD_t = Y_t - T_t \tag{12.24}$$

$$I_t = \alpha_0 + \alpha_1 Y_t + \alpha_2 r_{t-1} + u_t \tag{12.25}$$

with G_t, NX_t, T_t, and r_{t-1} being exogenous

where: Y_t = Gross national product in year t
$\quad\quad C_t$ = Total personal consumption in year t
$\quad\quad I_t$ = Total gross private domestic investment in year t
$\quad\quad G_t$ = Government purchases of goods and services in year t
$\quad\quad NX_t$ = Net exports of goods and services (exports minus imports) in year t
$\quad\quad T_t$ = Taxes (actually equal to taxes, depreciation, corporate profits, governments transfers and other adjustments necessary to convert GNP to disposable income) in year t
$\quad\quad r_{t-1}$ = The interest rate on prime commercial paper (4-6 months) in year $t - 1$ (the year before the year t).

All variables are measured in billions of 1958 U.S. dollars with the exception of the interest rate, which is measured in nominal percent per annum. The data for this example are from 1946 through 1970 and are presented in Table 12.1.

Equations 12.22 through 12.25 are the structural equations of the system, but only Equations 12.23 and 12.25 are stochastic (or behavioral) in nature and need to be estimated. The endogenous variables are those that are jointly determined by the system, namely Y_t, YD_t, C_t, and I_t. To see why all four of these variables are jointly determined, try holding one of them constant and let one of the others, say Y_t, change. Note that if Y_t changes, so too must YD_t, C_t, and I_t. On the other hand, G_t, NX_t, T_t, and r_{t-1} are all exogenous and therefore predetermined. In addition, C_{t-1} is a lagged endogenous variable and is also predetermined. To sum, then, we have four structural equations, four endogenous variables, and five predetermined variables.

What is the economic meaning of the coefficients of the stochastic structural equations? Equation 12.23, repeated here for convenience,

$$C_t = \beta_0 + \beta_1 YD_t + \beta_2 C_{t-1} + \epsilon_t \tag{12.23}$$

is a "distributed lag permanent income consumption function." That is, it hypothesizes that consumption depends on "permanent" income:

$$C_t = f(\text{permanent income})$$

and that permanent income depends on past values of disposable income:

$$\text{Permanent income} = f(YD_t, YD_{t-1}, YD_{t-2}, \dots)$$

Table 12.1   Data for the Small Macromodel

YEAR	Y	C	C_{t-1}	I	G	NX	r_{t-1}	Y_d	T
1946	312.6	203.5	183.0	52.3	48.4	8.4	0.75	239.88	72.72
1947	309.9	206.3	203.5	51.5	39.9	12.3	0.81	227.50	82.40
1948	323.7	210.8	206.3	60.4	46.3	6.1	1.03	237.62	86.08
1949	324.1	216.5	210.8	48.0	53.3	6.4	1.44	238.31	85.80
1950	355.3	230.5	216.5	69.3	52.8	2.7	1.49	258.12	97.18
1951	383.4	232.8	230.5	70.0	75.4	5.3	1.45	264.55	118.85
1952	395.1	239.4	232.8	60.5	92.1	3.0	2.16	272.51	122.59
1953	412.8	250.8	239.4	61.2	99.8	1.1	2.33	285.99	126.81
1954	407.0	255.7	250.8	59.4	88.9	3.0	2.52	287.18	119.82
1955	438.0	274.2	255.7	75.4	85.2	3.2	1.58	302.97	135.03
1956	446.1	281.4	274.2	74.3	85.3	5.0	2.18	312.01	134.09
1957	452.5	288.2	281.4	68.8	89.3	6.2	3.31	316.47	136.03
1958	447.3	290.1	288.2	60.9	94.2	2.2	3.81	318.80	128.50
1959	475.9	307.3	290.1	73.6	94.7	0.3	2.46	331.86	144.04
1960	487.7	316.1	307.3	72.4	94.9	4.3	3.97	338.88	148.82
1961	497.2	322.5	316.1	69.0	100.5	5.1	3.85	348.36	148.84
1962	529.8	338.4	322.5	79.4	107.5	4.5	2.97	364.33	165.47
1963	551.0	353.3	338.4	82.5	109.6	5.6	3.26	377.54	173.46
1964	581.1	373.7	353.3	87.8	111.2	8.3	3.55	402.56	178.54
1965	617.8	397.7	373.7	99.2	114.7	6.2	3.97	426.84	190.96
1966	658.1	418.1	397.7	109.3	126.5	4.2	4.38	449.24	208.86
1967	675.2	430.1	418.1	101.2	140.2	3.6	5.55	464.62	210.58
1968	706.6	452.7	430.1	105.2	147.7	1.0	5.10	483.22	223.38
1969	725.6	469.1	452.7	110.5	145.1	0.2	5.90	494.81	230.79
1970	722.5	477.5	469.1	103.4	139.3	2.3	7.83	511.47	211.03

Source: *Historical Statistics of the United States: Colonial Times to 1970*

because we adapt our expectation of what our permanent income will be to past values of our income. As shown in Section 9.6, this distributed lag equation can be transformed[9] (with some simplifications) to Equation 12.23. β_1 in Equation 12.23 measures the dollar change in consumption this year caused by a one-dollar change in income, while β_2 measures the percentage rate of decay of that impact (β_1) a year later. We would expect positive signs for both coefficients, and we would expect β_2 to be between one and zero.

Equation 12.25, repeated here for convenience, is an investment function

$$I_t = \alpha_0 + \alpha_1 Y_t + \alpha_2 r_{t-1} + u_t \tag{12.25}$$

that includes simplified multiplier and cost of capital components. The multiplier term α_1 measures the stimulus to investment that is generated by an increase in GNP. As production rises, investment must rise to allow the production of that output; investment might rise because producers' expectations of future sales rise as well. In a Keynesian model, α_1 would thus be expected to be positive. The higher the cost of capital, the less investment should be undertaken mainly because the expected rate of return on marginal capital investments is no longer sufficient to cover the higher cost of capital. Thus α_2 is expected to be negative. It takes time to plan and start up investment projects, though, and so the interest rate is lagged one year.[10]

If Equations 12.23 and 12.25 are the structural equations of this small macro-model, then what do the reduced-forms look like? Even though there are four endogenous variables, only two of them appear as explanatory variables in stochastic equations, so only two reduced-form equations need to be estimated to apply 2SLS:

$$Y_t = \pi_0 + \pi_1 G_t + \pi_2 NX_t + \pi_3 T_t + \pi_4 C_{t-1} + \pi_5 r_{t-1} + v_{1t} \quad (12.26)$$

$$YD_t = \pi_6 + \pi_7 G_t + \pi_8 NX_t + \pi_9 T_t + \pi_{10} C_{t-1} + \pi_{11} r_{t-1} + v_{2t} \quad (12.27)$$

where the vs are stochastic error terms. Recall that all predetermined variables appear as right-side variables in each of the reduced-form equations.

Two-Stage least squares estimates are produced as follows:

Stage One: If we estimate Equations 12.26 and 12.27 with OLS on the data in Table 12.1, we obtain:

$$\hat{Y}_t = 6.09 + 0.37G_t - 0.099NX_t + 0.78T_t + 1.18C_{t-1} - 7.99r_{t-1} \quad (12.28)$$
$$\phantom{\hat{Y}_t = 6.09 +} (0.34) \quad (0.772) \quad (0.43) \quad (0.23) \quad (5.22)$$
$$\phantom{\hat{Y}_t = 6.09 +} t = 1.08 \quad -0.13 \quad 1.85 \quad 5.11 \quad -1.53$$

$$\bar{R}^2 = .997 \quad n = 25 \quad DW = 1.90$$

$$\widehat{YD}_t = 6.10 + 0.37G_t - 0.099NX_t - 0.21T_t + 1.18C_{t-1} - 7.99r_{t-1} \quad (12.29)$$
$$\phantom{\widehat{YD}_t = 6.10 +} (0.34) \quad (0.773) \quad (0.43) \quad (0.23) \quad (5.22)$$
$$\phantom{\widehat{YD}_t = 6.10 +} t = 1.08 \quad -0.13 \quad -0.49 \quad 5.11 \quad -1.53$$

$$\bar{R}^2 = .992 \quad n = 25 \quad DW = 1.90$$

These reduced forms have very good fits and are virtually identical. Since the only difference between disposable income and GNP is what we have called "taxes," the tax variable's significance is much lower in Equation 12.29 than in Equation 12.28. Note, however, that we do not drop T_t from the YD_t reduced-form even though it is theoretically irrelevant and statistically insignificant. The whole purpose of Stage One of 2SLS is not to get meaningful reduced-form estimated equations, but rather to generate useful instruments ($\hat{Y}$s) to use as independent variables in the second stage. To do that, we calculate the $\hat{Y}$s and $\widehat{YD}$s for all 25 observations by plugging the actual values for the five predetermined variables into Equations 12.28 and 12.29.

Stage Two: We then substitute these $\hat{Y}$s and $\widehat{YD}$s for the endogenous variables where they appear on the right sides of Equations 12.23 and 12.25:

$$C_t = \beta_0 + \beta_1 \widehat{YD}_t + \beta_2 C_{t-1} + \epsilon_t \quad (12.30)$$

$$I_t = \alpha_0 + \alpha_1 \hat{Y}_t + \alpha_2 r_{t-1} + u_t \quad (12.31)$$

If we use OLS to estimate these second stage equations on the data in Table 12.1, we will obtain the final[11] Two-Stage Least Squares results:

$$\hat{C}_t = -23.24 + 0.86\widehat{YD}_t + 0.13C_{t-1} \qquad (12.32)$$
$$(0.19) \qquad (0.20)$$
$$t = \quad 4.58 \qquad 0.68$$

$$\bar{R}^2 = .998 \qquad n = 25 \qquad DW = 1.36$$

$$\hat{I}_t = -2.87 + 0.19\hat{Y}_t - 4.61r_{t-1} \qquad (12.33)$$
$$(0.018) \qquad (1.40)$$
$$t = \quad 10.41 \qquad -3.30$$

$$\bar{R}^2 = .940 \qquad n = 25 \qquad DW = 1.59$$

Compare these results with what we would have obtained if, instead of using 2SLS, we had estimated the equations with OLS alone:

$$\hat{C}_t = -17.89 + 0.67YD_t + 0.34C_{t-1} \qquad (12.34)$$
$$(0.09) \qquad (0.09)$$
$$t = \quad 7.65 \qquad 3.65$$

$$\bar{R}^2 = .999 \qquad n = 25 \qquad DW = 1.53$$

$$\hat{I}_t = -3.80 + 0.19Y_t - 4.85r_{t-1} \qquad (12.35)$$
$$(0.018) \qquad (1.39)$$
$$t = \qquad 10.69 \qquad -3.50$$

$$\bar{R}^2 = .940 \qquad n = 25 \qquad DW = 1.58$$

For the investment equation, the OLS and 2SLS results are virtually identical. If OLS is biased in small samples, how could this occur? When the fit of the Stage One reduced-form equations is excellent, then Y and $\hat{Y}$ are virtually identical, and the second stage of 2SLS is quite similar to the OLS estimate. Since the fit of the YD reduced form was also quite good, why aren't the OLS and 2SLS consumption equations virtually identical as well? Note that in Equation 12.29, C_{t-1} happens to be the most significant of the reduced-form explanatory variables. Because of this, $\widehat{YD}$ is fairly multicollinear with C_{t-1} in Equation 12.32, causing different estimates.

This model provides us with a complete example of the use of Two-Stage Least Squares to estimate a simultaneous system. However, to apply 2SLS requires that the equation being estimated be "identified," so before concluding our study of simultaneous systems, we need to address the problem of identification.

12.4 The Identification Problem

It is unfortunate that Two-Stage Least Squares cannot be applied to an equation unless that equation is *identified*. Before estimating any equation in a simultaneous system, the researcher must address the identification problem. Once an equation has found to be identified, then it can be estimated with 2SLS, but if an equation is not identified *(underidentified)*, then 2SLS cannot be used no matter how large the sample. It is important to point out that an equation being identified (and therefore capable of being estimated with 2SLS) does not insure that the resulting 2SLS estimates will be good ones. The question being asked is not how good the 2SLS estimates will be but whether the 2SLS estimates can be obtained at all.

12.4.1 What Is the Identification Problem?

Identification is a precondition for the application of 2SLS to equations in simultaneous systems; a structural equation is identified only when enough of the system's predetermined variables are omitted from the equation in question to allow that equation to be distinguished from all the others in the system. Note that one equation in a simultaneous system might be identified while another might not.

How is it possible that we could have equations that we could not identify? To see this, let's consider a supply and demand simultaneous system where only price and quantity are specified:

$$Q_{Dt} = \alpha_0 + \alpha_1 P_t + \epsilon_{Dt} \quad \text{(demand)} \quad (12.36)$$

$$Q_{St} = \beta_0 + \beta_1 P_t + \epsilon_{St} \quad \text{(supply)} \quad (12.37)$$

Although we have labeled one equation as the demand question and the other as the supply equation, the computer will not be able to identify them from the data, because the right side and the left side variables are exactly the same in both equations; without some predetermined variables included to distinguish between the two equations, it would be impossible to distinguish supply from demand.

What if we added a predetermined variable to one of the equations, say the supply equation? Then, Equation 12.37 would become:

$$Q_{St} = \beta_0 + \beta_1 P_t + \beta_2 Z_t + \epsilon_{St} \quad (12.38)$$

In such a circumstance, every time Z changed, the supply curve would shift, but the demand curve would not, so that eventually we would be able to collect a good picture of what the demand curve looked like.

Figure 12.3 demonstrates this. Given four different values of Z, we get four different supply curves, each of which intersects with the constant demand curve at a different equilibrium price and quantity (intersections 1-4). These equilibria are the data that we would be able to observe in the real world and are all that we could feed into the computer. As a result, we would be able to identify the demand curve because we left out at least one exogenous variable; when this exogenous variable changed, but the demand curve did not, the supply curve shifted so that quantity demanded moved along the demand curve and we gathered enough information to estimate the coefficients of the demand curve. The supply curve,

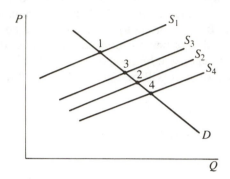

FIGURE 12.3 *A Shifting Supply Curve Allows the Identification of the Demand Curve*
If the supply curve shifts but the demand curve does not, then we move along the demand curve, allowing us to identify and estimate the demand curve (but not the supply curve).

on the other hand, remains as much a mystery as it ever was, because its shifts give us no clue whatsoever about its shape. In essence, the demand curve was identified by the exogenous variable that was included in the system but excluded from the demand equation. The supply curve is not identified because there is no such excluded exogenous variable.

Even if we added Z to the demand curve as well, that would not identify the supply curve. In fact, if we had Z in both equations, the two would be identical again, and while both would shift when Z changed, those shifts would give us no information about either curve! As illustrated in Figure 12.4, the observed equilibrium prices and quantities would be almost random intersections describing neither the demand nor the supply curve. That is, the shifts in the supply curve are the same as before, but now the demand curve also shifts with Z. In this case, it is not possible to identify either the demand curve or the supply curve without prior knowledge of the relative magnitudes of the coefficients of Z in the two equations.

The way to identify both curves is to have at least one exogenous variable in each equation that is not in the other, as in:

$$Q_{Dt} = \alpha_0 + \alpha_1 P_t + \alpha_2 X_t + \epsilon_{Dt} \tag{12.39}$$

$$Q_{St} = \beta_0 + \beta_1 P_t + \beta_2 Z_t + \epsilon_{St} \tag{12.40}$$

Now when Z changes, the supply curve shifts, and we can identify the demand curve from the data on equilibrium prices and quantities. When X changes, the demand curve shifts, and we can identify the supply curve from the data. Of course, if X and Z are perfectly correlated, we still will have problems of estimation, as mentioned in the previous section.

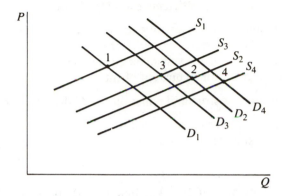

FIGURE 12.4 *If Both the Supply Curve and the Demand Curve Shift, Neither Curve Is Identified*

If both the supply curve and the demand curve shift in response to the same variable, then we move from one equilibrium point to another, and the resulting data points identify neither curve. To allow such an identification, at least one exogenous factor must cause one curve to shift while allowing the other to remain constant.

To sum, identification is a precondition for the application of 2SLS to equations in simultaneous systems. A structural equation is identified only when the predetermined variables are arranged within the system so as to allow the observed data on equilibrium points to make it possible to distinguish the shape of the equation in question. Since most systems are quite a bit more complicated than the ones above, econometricians need a general method by which to determine whether equations are identified, and the method typically used is the order condition of identification.

12.4.2   The Order Condition of Identification

The **order condition** is a systematic method of determining whether a particular equation in a simultaneous system has the potential to be identified. If an equation can meet the order condition, then it is identified in all but a very small number of cases that are beyond the scope of this section. We thus say that the order condition is a necessary but not sufficient condition of identification.[12]

What is the order condition? Recall that we have used the phrases endogenous and predetermined to refer to the two kinds of variables in a simultaneous system. Endogenous variables are those that are jointly determined in the system in the current time period. Predetermined variables are exogenous variables plus any lagged endogenous variables that might be in the model. For each equation in the system, we need to determine:

1. The number of predetermined (exogenous plus lagged endogenous) variables in the entire simultaneous system.

2. The number of slope coefficients estimated in the equation in question.

The Order Condition: A necessary condition for an equation to be identified is that the number of predetermined (exogenous plus lagged
endogenous) variables in the system be greater than or equal to the number
of slope coefficients in the equation of interest.

In equation form, a structural equation meets the order condition[13] if:

> The # of predetermined variables $\geq$ The # of slope coefficients
> (in the simultaneous system) (in the equation)

12.4.3 Two Examples of the Application of the Order Condition

Let's apply the order condition to some of the simultaneous equation systems
encountered in this chapter. For example, consider the supply and demand model
for Antique Cola in Section 12.1.1 (repeated here for convenience):

$$Q_{Dt} = \alpha_0 + \alpha_1 P_t + \alpha_2 X_{1t} + \alpha_3 X_{2t} + \epsilon_{Dt} \qquad (12.4)$$

$$Q_{St} = \beta_0 + \beta_1 P_t + \beta_2 X_{3t} + \epsilon_{St} \qquad (12.5)$$

$$Q_{St} = Q_{Dt}$$

Equation 12.4 is identified by the order condition because the number of predetermined variables in the system (three, X_1, X_2, and X_3) is equal to the number of
slope coefficients in the equation (three, α_1, α_2, and α_3). This particular result
(equality) implies that Equation 12.4 is *exactly identified* by the order condition.
Equation 12.5 is also identified by the order condition, because there still are three
predetermined variables in the system, but there are only two slope coefficients
in the equation; this condition implies that Equation 12.5 is *overidentified*. 2SLS
can be applied to equations that are identified (which includes exactly identified
and overidentified) but not to equations that are underidentified.

A more complicated example is the small macroeconomic model of Section
12.3.3, (also repeated for convenience):

$$Y_t = C_t + I_t + G_t + NX_t \qquad (12.22)$$

$$C_t = \beta_0 + \beta_1 Y_{Dt} + \beta_2 C_{t-1} + \epsilon_t \qquad (12.23)$$

$$YD_t = Y_t - T_t \qquad (12.24)$$

$$I_t = \alpha_0 + \alpha_1 Y_t + \alpha_2 r_{t-1} + u_t \qquad (12.25)$$

As we have noted, there are five predetermined (exogenous plus lagged
endogenous) variables in this system (I_t, G_t, NX_t, T_t, and C_{t-1}). There are two
slope coefficients in Equation 12.23, β_1, and β_2. Since $5 > 2$, this equation
meets the order condition of identification, and it is overidentified. Equation 12.25

also turns out to be overidentified. The 2SLS computer program did indeed come up with estimates of the βs in Section 12.3.3, so we knew this already. Since Equations 12.22 and 12.24 are identities, we are not concerned with their identification properties because we do not estimate them.

12.5   Summary

1. Most economic and business models are inherently simultaneous because of the dual causality, feedback loops, or joint determination of particular variables. These simultaneously determined variables are called endogenous, while nonsimultaneously determined variables are called predetermined.

2. A structural equation characterizes the theory underlying a particular variable and is the kind of equation we have used to date in this text. A reduced-form equation expresses a particular endogenous variable solely in terms of an error term and all the predetermined (exogenous and lagged endogenous) variables in the simultaneous system.

3. Simultaneous equation models violate the classical assumption of independence between the error term and the explanatory variables because of the feedback effects of the endogenous variables. For example, an unusually high observation of an equation's error term works through the simultaneous system and eventually causes a high value for the endogenous variables that appear as explanatory variables in the equation in question, thus violating the assumption of no correlation (Classical Assumption III).

4. If Ordinary Least Squares is applied to the coefficients of a simultaneous system, the resulting estimates are biased and inconsistent. This occurs mainly because of the violation of Classical Assumption III; the OLS regression package attributes to explanatory variables changes in the dependent variable actually caused by the error term (with which the explanatory variables are correlated).

5. Two-Stage Least Squares is a method of decreasing the amount of bias in the estimation of simultaneous equation systems. It works by systematically using the reduced-form equations of the system to create proxies for the endogenous variables that are independent of the error terms (called instrumental variables), and running OLS on the structural equations of the system with the instrumental variables replacing the endogenous variables where they appear as explanatory variables.

6. Two-Stage Least Squares estimates are still biased (with a sign opposite that of the OLS bias) but they are consistent (becoming more unbiased and closer to zero variance as the sample size gets larger). If the fit of the reduced-form estimates is poor or if the exogenous variables are highly correlated, then 2SLS will not work very well. The larger the sample size, the better it is to use 2SLS.

7. 2SLS cannot be applied to an equation that is not identified. A necessary (but not sufficient) requirement for identification is the order condition, which requires that the number of predetermined variables in the system be greater than or equal to the number of slope coefficients in the equation of interest. Sufficiency is usually determined by the ability of 2SLS to estimate the coefficients.

Exercises

(Answers to even-numbered exercises are contained in Appendix A.)

1. Write out the meaning of each of the following terms without reference to the book (or your notes) and then compare your definition with the version in the text for each:
   a. endogenous variables
   b. predetermined variables
   c. structural equations
   d. reduced-form equations
   e. simultaneity bias
   f. Two-Stage Least Squares
   g. identification
   h. order condition for identification

2. Which of the equations in the following systems are simultaneous, and which allow the endogenous variables to be determined sequentially (also called *recursive*)? Be sure to specify which variables are endogenous and which are predetermined (exogenous or lagged endogenous):

   a. $Y_{1t} = f(Y_{2t}, X_{1t}, X_{2t-1})$
   $Y_{2t} = f(Y_{3t}, X_{3t}, X_{4t})$
   $Y_{3t} = f(Y_{1t}, X_{1t-1}, X_{4t-1})$
   b. $Z_t = g(X_t, Y_t, H_t)$
   $X_t = g(Z_t, P_{t-1})$
   $H_t = g(Z_t, B_t, C_t, D_t)$
   c. $Y_{1t} = f(Y_{2t}, X_{1t}, X_{2t})$
   $Y_{2t} = f(Y_{3t}, X_{5t})$

3. Section 12.1.2 works through Equations 12.2 and 12.3 to show the violation of Classical Assumption III by an unexpected increase in ϵ_1. Show the violation of Classical Assumption III by working through the following examples:
   a. A decrease in ϵ_2 in Equation 12.3
   b. An increase in ϵ_D in Equation 12.4
   c. An increase in ϵ in Equation 12.23

4. As mentioned in Section 12.1.3, indirect least squares is a method of calculating the coefficients of the structural equations directly from the coefficients of the reduced-form equations without the necessity of a second-stage regression. This technique, which requires that the equations be exactly identified, can be used because the coefficients of the structural equations can be expressed in terms of the coefficients of the reduced-form equations. These expressions can be derived by solving the structural equations for one of the endogenous variables in terms of the predetermined variables and then substituting.
   a. Return to Equations 12.4 and 12.5 and confirm that the reduced-form equations for that system are Equations 12.8 and 12.9.
   b. By mathematically manipulating the expressions, express the coefficients of Equation 12.4 in terms of the πs of the reduced-form equations.
   c. What disadvantages does the method of indirect least squares have? Why isn't it used very frequently?
   d. What advantages and disadvantages would simply estimating the reduced-form equations have?
   e. Think through the application of indirect least squares to an overidentified equation. What problem would that estimation encounter?

5. Section 12.2.1 makes the statement that the correlation between the ϵs and the Ys (where they appear as explanatory variables) is usually positive in economic examples. To see if this is true, investigate the sign of the error term/explanatory variable correlation in the following cases:
   a. The three examples in Question 3 above.
   b. The more general case of all the equations in a typical supply and demand model (for instance, the model for Antique Cola in Section 12.1.
   c. The more general case of all the equations in a simple macroeconomic model (for instance, the small macroeconomic model in Section 12.3.3).

6. Determine the identification properties of the following equations. In particular, be sure to note the number of predetermined variables in the system, the number of slope coefficients in the equation, and whether the equation is underidentified, overidentified, or exactly identified.
   a. Equations 12.2-3
   b. Equations 12.13-14
   c. Part a of question 2 above (assume all equations are stochastic)
   d. Part b of question 2 above (assume all equations are stochastic)

7. Determine the identification properties of the following equations. In particular, be sure to note the number of predetermined variables in the system, the number of slope coefficients in the equation, and whether the equation is underidentified, overidentified or exactly identified. (Assume all equations are stochastic unless specified otherwise.)
   a. $A_t = f(B_t, C_t, D_t)$
      $B_t = f(A_t, C_t)$

b. $Y_{1t} = f(Y_{2t}, X_{1t}, X_{2t}, X_{3t})$

$Y_{2t} = f(X_{2t})$

$X_{2t} = f(Y_{1t}, X_{4t}, X_{3t})$

c. $C_t = f(Y_t)$

$I_t = f(Y_t, R_t, E_t, D_t)$

$R_t = f(M_t, R_{t-1}, Y_t - Y_{t-1})$

$Y_t = C_t + I_t + G_t$ (non-stochastic)

8. Return to the supply and demand example for Antique Cola in Section 12.1 and explain exactly how Two-Stage Least Squares would estimate the αs and βs of Equations 12.4 and 12.5. Write out the equations to be estimated in both stages, and indicate precisely what, if any, substitutions would be made in the second stage.

9. As an exercise to gain familiarity with the Two-Stage Least Squares program on your computer system, take the data provided for the simply Keynesian model in Section 12.3.3, and:
   a. Estimate the investment function with OLS.
   b. Estimate the reduced-form for Y by OLS.
   c. Substitute the $\hat{Y}$ from your reduced-form into the investment function and run the second stage yourself with OLS.
   d. Estimate the investment function with your computer system's 2SLS program (if there is one) and compare the results with those obtained in Part c above.

10. Suppose that one of your friends recently estimated a simultaneous equation research project and found the OLS results to be virtually identical to the 2SLS results. How would you respond if he or she said "What a waste of time! I shouldn't have bothered with 2SLS in the first place! Besides, this proves that there wasn't any bias in my model anyway."
    a. What is the value of 2SLS in such a case?
    b. Does the similarity between the 2SLS and OLS estimates indicate a lack of bias?

11. Think over the problem of building a model for the supply of and demand for labor (measured in hours worked) as a function of the wage and other variables.
    a. Completely specify labor supply and labor demand equations and hypothesize the expected signs of the coefficients of your variables.
    b. Is this system simultaneous or not? That is, is there likely to be feedback between the wage and hours demanded and supplied? Why or why not?
    c. Is your system likely to encounter biased estimates? Why?
    d. What sort of estimation procedure would you use to obtain your coefficient estimates? (Hint: Be sure to determine the identification properties of your equations.)

12.6   Appendix: Errors in the Variables

Until now, we have implicitly assumed that our data were measured accurately. That is, while the stochastic error term was defined as including measurement error, we never explicitly discussed what the existence of such measurement error did to the coefficient estimates. In the real world, unfortunately, errors of measurement are common. Mismeasurement might result from the data being based on a sample, as are almost all national aggregate statistics, or simply because the data were reported incorrectly. Whatever the cause, these **errors in the variables** are mistakes in the measurement of the dependent and/or one or more of the independent variables that are large enough to potentially have impacts on the estimation of the coefficients. Such errors in the variables might be better called "measurement errors in the data." We will tackle this subject by first examining errors in the dependent variable and then moving on to look at the more serious problem of errors in an independent variable. We assume a single equation model. The reason we have included this section here is that errors in explanatory variables give rise to biased OLS estimates very similar to simultaneity bias.

12.6.1   Measurement Errors in the Data for the Dependent Variable

Suppose that the true regression model is

$$Y_i = \beta_0 + \beta_1 X_i + \epsilon_i \qquad (12.41)$$

and further suppose that the dependent variable, Y_i, is measured incorrectly, so that Y_i^* is observed instead of Y_i, where

$$Y_i^* = Y_i + v_i \qquad (12.42)$$

and where v_i is an error of measurement that has all the properties of a classical error term. What does this mismeasurement do to the estimation of Equation 12.41?

Add v_i to both sides of Equation 12.41, obtaining

$$Y_i + v_i = \beta_0 + \beta_1 X_i + \epsilon_i + v_i \qquad (12.43)$$

which is the same as

$$Y_i^* = \beta_0 + \beta_1 X_i + \epsilon_i^* \qquad (12.44)$$

where $\epsilon_i^* = (\epsilon_i + v_i)$. That is, we estimate equation 12.44 when in reality we want to estimate Equation 12.41. Take another look at Equation 12.44. When v_i changes, both the dependent variable and the error term ϵ_i^* move together. This is no cause for alarm, however, since the dependent variable is always correlated with the error term. While the extra movement will increase the variability of Y and therefore be likely to decrease the overall statistical fit of the equation, an error of measurement in the dependent variable does not cause any bias in the estimates of the βs.

12.6.2 Measurement Errors in the Data for an Independent Variable

This is not the case when the mismeasurement is in the data for one or more of the independent variables. Unfortunately, such errors in the independent variables cause bias that is quite similar in nature (and in remedy) to simultaneity bias. To see this, once again suppose that the true regression model is Equation 12.41, repeated here for convenience:

$$Y_i = \beta_0 + \beta_1 X_i + \epsilon_i \qquad (12.41)$$

and now suppose that the independent variable, X_i, is measured incorrectly, so that X_i^* is observed instead of X_i, where

$$X_i^* = X_i + u_i \qquad (12.45)$$

and where u_i is an error of measurement just like v_i above. To see what this mismeasurement does to the estimation of Equation 12.41, let's add the term $0 = (\beta_1 u_i - \beta_1 u_i)$ to Equation 12.41, obtaining

$$Y_i = \beta_0 + \beta_1 X_i + \epsilon_i + (\beta_1 u_i - \beta_1 u_i) \qquad (12.46)$$

which can be rewritten as

$$Y_i = \beta_0 + \beta_1 (X_i + u_i) + (\epsilon_i - \beta_1 u_i) \qquad (12.47)$$

or

$$Y_i = \beta_0 + \beta_1 X_i^* + \epsilon_i^{**} \qquad (12.48)$$

where $\epsilon_i^{**} = (\epsilon_i - \beta_1 u_i)$. In this case, we estimate Equation 12.48 when we should be trying to estimate Equation 12.41. Notice what happens to Equation 12.48 when u_i changes, however. When u_i changes, the stochastic error term ϵ_i^{**} and the independent variable X_i^* move in opposite directions; they are correlated. Such a correlation is a direct violation of Classical Assumption III in a way that is remarkably similar to the violation described in Section 12.1 of the same assumption in simultaneous equations. Not surprisingly, this violation causes the same problem, bias, for errors-in-the-variables models that it causes for simultaneous equations. That is, because of the measurement error in the independent variable, the OLS estimates of the coefficients of Equation 12.48 are *biased and inconsistent*.

A frequently used technique to rid an equation of the bias caused by measurement errors in the data for one or more of the independent variables is *instrumental variables*. A proxy for X is chosen that is highly correlated with X but is uncorrelated with ϵ. Recall that Two-Stage Least Squares is an instrumental variables technique. Such techniques are only rarely applied to errors in the variables problems, however, because while we may suspect that there are errors in the variables, it is unusual to know positively that they exist, and it is difficult to find an instrumental variable that satisfies both conditions. As a result, X^* is about as good a proxy for X as we usually can find, and no action is taken. If the mismeasurement in X were known to be large, however, some remedy would be required.

To sum, an error of measurement in one or more of the independent variables will cause the error term of Equation 12.48 to be correlated with the independent variable, causing bias analogous to simultaneity bias.[14] While instrumental variables is a possible remedy for this problem, more often than not, corrective steps are not taken.

12.7   Appendix: Recursive Models, Seemingly Unrelated Regressions and Three-Stage Least Squares

In a simultaneous equations model of supply and demand, the current quantity supplied is a function of the current price, but such a model is not appropriate for most agricultural products and many other products that take a long time to produce. In such markets, the quantity supplied can more reasonably be thought of as being a function of the last time period's price because of the length of time it takes producers to react to market changes. This produces what is often called a "cobweb" model, which may be written as:

$$Q_{Dt} = \alpha_0 + \alpha_1 P_t + \alpha_2 X_{1t} + \epsilon_{Dt} \tag{12.49}$$

$$Q_{St} = \beta_0 + \beta_1 P_{t-1} + \beta_2 X_{2t} + \epsilon_{Dt} \tag{12.50}$$

$$Q_{St} = Q_{Dt}$$

Note that the impact of price on quantity supplied has been lagged one time period (usually a growing season for animals or crops).

Such a system is a **recursive** model, which is a system of equations that are linked together though the linkage does not include any feedback effects. Last period's quantity supplied is a function of only predetermined variables, so it can be calculated without reference to either of the other equations (given coefficient estimates). Given a fixed supply of the product, this period's price must be adjusted until the quantity demanded equals the quantity supplied. Note that there is no feedback effect in a recursive model; the causality goes from Equation 12.50 to Equation 12.49 (through the equilibrium condition), but it does not return to Equation 12.50 as would be the case with simultaneous equations.

It would appear that since the equations are no longer simultaneous, OLS could be used to estimate each equation without any problem; unfortunately, there is a distinct possibility that the error terms in such equations will not be independent of each other. That is, if two equations are truly unrelated, then

$$E(\epsilon_{Dt} \cdot \epsilon_{St}) = 0 \tag{12.51}$$

Instead, it seems entirely likely that disturbances in the same market could have an effect on both supply and demand, and the two error terms would be correlated. For example, an unexpected drought that causes the quantity supplied to fall may also stimulate "panic buying" (and therefore increase quantity demanded) as news of the pending shortage spreads around the country and consumers begin to expect higher prices in the future. This is an example of a relationship between equations that are seemingly unrelated.

More generally, systems of **seemingly unrelated equations** are systems in which the error terms of the different equations are related to each other even though the variables of the equations are not. Thus the unrelated equations are related by the error term correlation; for efficient estimation to take place, we need to take this correlation into account. An estimation procedure that does so, using generalized least squares (GLS, previously discussed in Chapter 10) as a base, is Zellner's seemingly unrelated regression estimation technique,[15] which has two major steps:

1. Use OLS on each equation, but only to estimate the variances and covariances of the error terms.

2. Substitute these estimates into a special stacked regression equation that combines all the equations into one (rather large) equation, and then use GLS to estimate all the αs and βs simultaneously.

While the details of Zellner's method are beyond the scope of this text, a number of computer packages include programs expressly written for this purpose. This estimator can be applied to any system in which the error terms are suspected to be correlated.

This general approach can be applied to simultaneous equations systems. Two-stage least squares (2SLS) does not attempt to account for the possibility that the error terms are correlated even if the equations are known to be simultaneous. A simultaneous estimating technique that does so is called **Three-Stage Least Squares** (3SLS). This technique uses 2SLS as its first two stages, but only to calculate estimates of the variances and covariances of the error terms (as above). Then the stacking (GLS) routine of Zellner is used to estimate all the coefficients and their standard errors in all the simultaneous equations at once. Most beginning researchers do not use this technique, but once again it is included in many computer packages.[16]

[1.]This also depends on how hungry you are, which is a function of how hard you're working, which depends on how many chickens you have to take care of. Note that because of the time lags involved, this chicken/egg system is probably best viewed as recursive; for more on this, see Section 12.7.

[2.]This assumes that β_1 is positive. If β_1 is negative, Y_2 will decrease and there will be a negative correlation between ϵ_1 and Y_2, but this negative correlation will still violate Classical Assumption III. Also note that both Equations 12.2 and 12.3 could have Y_{1t} on the left side; if two variables are jointly determined, it does not matter which variable is considered dependent and which independent, because they are actually mutually dependent. We used this kind of simultaneous system in the model of "Antique Cola," as portrayed in Equations 12.4 and 12.5.

[3.]For Equation 12.11, the expected value of $\hat{\beta}_1$ simplifies to:

$$E(\hat{\beta}_1) = \beta_1 + E[\Sigma(Y_{2t} - \bar{Y}_2) \cdot (\epsilon_{1t})/\Sigma(Y_{2t} - \bar{Y}_2)^2]$$

In a nonsimultaneous equation, where Y_2 and ϵ_1 are not correlated, the expected value of $\hat{\beta}_1$ equals the true β_1, because the expected value of the term $\Sigma(Y_{2t} - \bar{Y}_2) \cdot (\epsilon_{1t})$ is zero. If Y_2 and ϵ_1 are positively correlated, as would be true in most simultaneous systems in economics, then the expected value of $\hat{\beta}_1$ is greater than the true β_1 because the expected value of $\Sigma(Y_{2t} - \bar{Y}_2) \cdot (\epsilon_{1t})$ is positive. In the less likely case that Y_2 and ϵ_1 are negatively correlated, the expected value of $\hat{\beta}_1$ is less than the true β_1.

[4.]See Exercise 5 to examine this general statement in more detail for various economic models.

[5.]Other assumptions included a normal distribution for the error term, $\beta_0 = 0$, $\alpha_0 = 0$, $\sigma_S^2 = 3$, $\sigma_D^2 = 2$, $r_{xz}^2 = 0.4$, and n = 20. In addition, it was assumed that the error terms of the two equations were not correlated. This is another example of a "Monte Carlo experiment."

[6.]Because the $\hat{\pi}$s are not uncorrelated with the ϵs, this procedure produces only approximate instrumental variables that provide consistent (for large samples) but biased (for small samples) estimates of the coefficients of the structural equations (the βs).

[7.]This bias is caused by remaining correlation between the $\hat{Y}$s produced by the first stage reduced-form regressions and the ϵs, the error terms of the structural equations. The effect of this correlation tends to decrease as the sample size increases. Even for small samples, though, it is worth noting that the expected bias due to 2SLS is usually smaller than the expected bias due to OLS.

[8.]In our experiments, the 2SLS estimators were found to reject a correct null hypothesis about twice as frequently as would have been expected from distribution theory. In contrast, the OLS estimators rejected the correct null hypothesis over eight times as often as would have been expected from an unbiased procedure.

[9.]For those who did not read Section 9.6 and who are uncomfortable with Equation 12.23, the equivalent equation is:

$$C_t = \beta_0 + \beta_1 YD_t + \beta_2^* YD_{t-1} + \beta_3^* YD_{t-2} + \cdots + \epsilon_t \qquad (12.23a)$$

where the slope coefficients follow a specific declining pattern. In particular, it can be shown that β_2^* in Equation 12.23a can be expressed in terms of the βs of Equation 12.23 as $\beta_1 \cdot \beta_2$. For more on this, see Section 9.6

[10.]This investment equation is a simplified mix of the accelerator and the neoclassical theories of the investment function. The former emphasizes that changes in the level of output are the key determinant of investment, while the latter emphasizes that user cost of capital (the opportunity cost that the firm incurs as a consequence of owning an asset) is the key. For an introduction to the determinants of consumption and investment, see any intermediate macroeconomics textbook. For traditional and modern overviews of the estimation of consumption and investment equations in simultaneous macroeconomic models, see Otto Eckstein, *The DRI Model of the U.S. Economy* (New York: McGraw-Hill, 1983); Michael K. Evans, *Macroeconomic Activity* (New York: Harper and Row, 1969); and Thomas M. Havrilesky, *Modern Concepts in Macroeconomics* (Arlington Heights, Illinois: Harlan Davidson, Inc., 1985).

[11.]A few notes about 2SLS estimation and this model are in order. The 2SLS estimates in Equations 12.32 and 12.33 are correct, but if you were to estimate those equations with OLS (using as instruments $\hat{Y}$s and $\widehat{YD}$s generated from Equations 12.28 and 12.29) you would obtain the same coefficient estimates but a different set of estimates of the standard errors (and t-scores). This difference comes about because running OLS on the second stage alone ignores the fact that the first stage was run at all; to get accurate estimated standard errors and t-scores, the estimation should be done on a complete 2SLS program. Most computer regression packages, including ECSTAT, include such a 2SLS program. As it turns out, however, our estimates were not computed on the ECSTAT program because the ECSTAT 2SLS program was being revised as we went to press; as a result, rounding errors may be encountered if the regression results are compared.

[12.] A sufficient condition for an equation to be identified is called the *rank condition*, but this is so difficult to apply by hand to large systems of simultaneous equations that many researchers tend just to examine the order condition before estimating an equation with 2SLS. As a result, most researchers now let the computer estimation procedure tell them whether the rank condition has been met (by its ability to apply 2SLS to the equation). A rapid increase in the cost of computer time might cause econometricians to reconsider this usage, but for the present a beginning researcher needs to understand only the order condition. Those interested in the rank condition are encouraged to consult an advanced econometrics text.

[13.] A more popular but harder to remember way of stating this condition is that the number of predetermined variables in the system that are excluded from the equation must be greater than or equal to the number of endogenous variables included in the equation minus one.

[14.] If errors exist in the data for the dependent variable and one or more of the independent variables, then both decreased overall statistical fit and bias in the estimated coefficients will result.

[15.] See A. Zellner, "An Efficient Method of Estimating Seemingly Unrelated Regressions and Tests for Aggregation Bias," *Journal of the American Statistical Society,* 1962, pp. 348-368.

[16.] See A. Zellner and H. Theil, "Three-Stage Least Squares: Simultaneous Estimation of Simultaneous Relations," *Econometrica,* 1962, pp. 54-78.

13

Forecasting

Of the uses of econometrics outlined in Chapter 1, we have discussed forecasting the least. Accurate forecasting is vital to successful planning, so it is the primary goal of many business and governmental uses of econometrics. For example, manufacturing firms need sales forecasts, banks need interest rate forecasts, and governments need unemployment and inflation rate forecasts.

To many business and government leaders the words "econometrics" and "forecasting" mean the same thing. Such a simplification gives econometrics a bad name, because some consulting econometricians overestimate their ability to produce accurate forecasts, resulting in unrealistic claims and unhappy clients. Some of these clients would probably applaud the 19th century New York law (luckily unenforced but apparently also unrepealed) that provides that persons "pretending to forecast the future" shall be liable to a $250 fine and/or six months in prison.[1] While many econometricians might wish that such consultants would call themselves "futurists" or "soothsayers," it is impossible to ignore the importance of econometrics in forecasting in today's world.

The ways in which the prediction of future events is accomplished are quite varied. At one extreme, some forecasters use models with hundreds of equations.[2] At the other extreme, quite accurate forecasts can be created with nothing more than a good imagination and a healthy dose of self-confidence.

Unfortunately, it is unrealistic to think we can cover even a small portion of the topic of forecasting in one short chapter. Indeed, there are a number of excellent books on this subject alone.[3] Instead, this chapter is meant to be a brief introduction to the use of econometrics in forecasting. We will begin by using simple linear equations and then move on to investigate a few more complex forecasting situations. The chapter concludes with an introduction to a technique, called ARIMA or time series analysis, that calculates forecasts entirely from past movements of the dependent variable without the use of any independent variables at all.

13.1 What Is Forecasting?

In general, forecasting is the act of predicting the future; in econometrics, **forecasting** is the estimation of the expected value of a dependent variable for observations that are not part of the sample data set. In most forecasts, the values being predicted are for time periods in the future, but cross-sectional predictions of values for countries or people not in the sample are also common. To simplify terminology, the words prediction and forecast will be used interchangeably in this chapter. (Some authors limit the use of the word forecast to out-of-sample prediction for a time series.)

We have already encountered an example of a forecasting equation. Think back to the weight/height example of Section 1.3 and recall that the purpose of that model was to guess the weight of a male customer based on his height. In that example, the first step in building a forecast was to estimate Equation 1.21, repeated here for convenience:

$$\text{Estimated Weight}_i = 103.4 + 6.38 \cdot \text{Height}_i \text{ (inches over five feet)} \quad (1.21)$$

That is, we estimated that a customer's weight on average equaled a base of 103.4 pounds plus 6.38 pounds for each inch over five feet. To actually make the prediction, all we had to do was to substitute the height of the individual whose weight we were trying to predict into the estimated equation. For a male who is 6'1" tall, for example, we'd calculate:

$$\text{Predicted Weight} = 103.4 + 6.38 \cdot (13 \text{ inches over five feet}) \quad (13.1)$$

or $103.4 + 82.9 = 186.3$ pounds.

The weight-guessing equation is a specific example of using a single linear equation to predict or forecast. Our use of such an equation to make a forecast can be summarized in two steps:

1. *Specify and estimate an equation that has as its dependent variable the item that we wish to forecast.* We obtain a forecasting equation by specifying and estimating an equation for the variable we want to predict:

$$\hat{Y}_t = \hat{\beta}_0 + \hat{\beta}_1 X_{1t} + \hat{\beta}_2 X_{2t} \quad (t = 1, 2, \dots, T) \quad (13.2)$$

Such specification and estimation has been the topic of the first eleven chapters of this book. The use of $t = (1, 2, \dots, T)$ to denote the sample size is fairly standard for time series forecasts (t stands for "time").

2. *Obtain values for each of the independent variables for the observations for which we want a forecast and substitute them into our forecasting equation.* To calculate a forecast for Equation 13.2, this would mean finding values for period $T+1$ (for a sample of size T) for X_1 and X_2 and substituting them into the equation:

$$\hat{Y}_{T+1} = \hat{\beta}_0 + \hat{\beta}_1 X_{1T+1} + \hat{\beta}_2 X_{2T+1} \qquad (13.3)$$

What is the meaning of this $\hat{Y}_{T+1}$? It is a prediction of the value that Y will take in observation T+1 (outside the sample) based upon our values of X_{1T+1} and X_{2T+1} and based upon the particular specification and estimation that produced Equation 13.2.

To understand these steps more clearly, look at two applications of this forecasting approach.

Forecasting Chicken Consumption: Let's return to the chicken demand model, Equation 6.5 of Section 6.1, to see how well that equation forecasts aggregate per capita chicken consumption:

$$\hat{Y}_t = -49.6 - 0.54PC_t + 0.22PB_t + 10.6LYD_t \qquad (6.5)$$
$$\phantom{\hat{Y}_t = -49.6} (0.07) \qquad (0.06) \qquad (1.3)$$
$$t = \quad -7.6 \qquad 3.5 \qquad 8.3$$
$$\bar{R}^2 = .979 \qquad n = 29 \text{ (Annual, 1950 to 1978)}$$

where Y is pounds of chicken consumption per capita, PC and PB are the prices of chicken and beef respectively in cents per pound, and LYD is the log of per capita U.S. disposable income (in dollars).

To forecast with this model, we would obtain values for the three independent variables and substitute them into Equation 6.5. For example, in 1979,

$$\hat{Y}_{79} = -49.6 - 0.54(13.9) + 0.22(66.1) + 10.6(\ln 7331) = 51.8 \qquad (13.4)$$

Continuing on through 1982, we'd end up with:

Year	Forecast	Actual	Percent Error
1979	51.8	50.6	2.4
1980	53.5	50.1	6.8
1981	53.6	51.6	3.9
1982	54.3	53.1	2.3

How does the model do? Well, forecasting accuracy, like beauty, is in the eye of the beholder. While the equation consistently overforecasts[4] (see Figure 13.1), it predicts the consumption of chicken to within 3 percent four years beyond the sample period.

Forecasting Stock Prices: Some students react to the previous example by wanting to build a model to forecast stock prices and make a killing on the stock market. "If we could predict the price of a stock four years from now to within 3 percent," they reason, "we'd know which stocks to buy." To see how such a forecast might work, let's look at a simplified model of the quarterly price of a particular individual stock, that of the J. L. Kellogg Company (maker of breakfast cereals and other products):

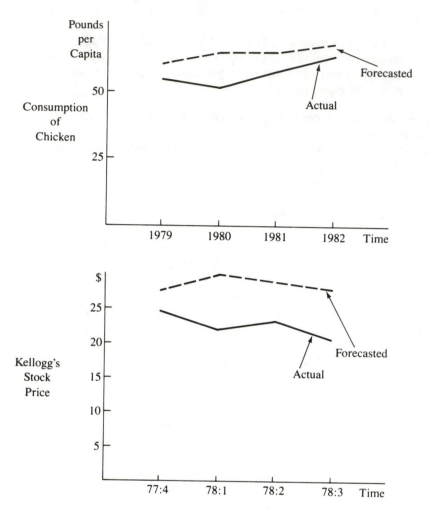

FIGURE 13.1 *Forecasting Examples*
In the chicken consumption example, the equation overforecasted slightly. For the stock price model, even actual values for the independent variables and an excellent fit within the sample could not produce an accurate forecast.

$$\widehat{PK}_t = -7.80 + 0.0096DJIA_t + 2.68LTEG_t + 16.18DIV_t + 4.84BVPS_t \quad (13.5)$$
$$\phantom{\widehat{PK}_t =}(0.0024)\qquad(2.83)\qquad(22.70)\qquad(1.47)$$
$$t =\quad 3.91\qquad\quad 0.95\qquad\quad 0.71\qquad\quad 3.29$$

$$\bar{R}^2 = .95 \quad n = 35 \text{ (Quarterly 69:1 to 77:3)} \quad DW = 1.88$$

where: PK_t = the dollar price of Kellogg's stock in quarter t
$DJIA_t$ = the Dow-Jones Industrial Average in quarter t

$LTEG_t$ = Kellogg's earnings growth (percent change in annual earnings over the previous five years)

DIV_t = Kellogg's declared dividends (in dollars) that quarter

$BVPS_t$ = per-share book value of the Kellogg corporation that quarter

The signs of the estimated coefficients all agree with those hypothesized before the regression was run, $\bar{R}^2$ indicates a reasonably good overall fit, and the Durbin-Watson d statistic indicates that the hypothesis of no serial correlation cannot be rejected. The low t-scores for LTEG and DIV are caused by multicollinearity ($r = .985$), but both variables are left in the equation because of their theoretical importance.

In order to forecast with Equation 13.5, we obtained actual values for all of the independent variables for the next four quarters and substituted them into the right side of the equation, obtaining:

Quarter	Forecast	Actual	Percent Error
77:4	$26.32	$24.38	8.0
78:1	27.37	22.38	22.3
78.2	27.19	23.00	18.2
78:3	27.13	21.88	24.0

How did our forecasting model do? Even though the $\bar{R}^2$ within the sample was .95, even though we used actual values for the independent variables, and even though we only forecasted four quarters beyond our sample, the model was something like 20 percent off. If we had decided to buy Kellogg's stock based on our forecast, we'd have *lost* money! Since other attempts to forecast stock prices have also encountered difficulties, this does not seem like a reasonable use for econometric forecasting. Individual stock prices (and many other items) are simply too variable and depend on too many non-quantifiable items to consistently forecast accurately, even if the forecasting equation has an excellent fit! The reason for this apparent contradiction is that equations that worked in the past may or may not work well in the future.

13.2 More Complex Forecasting Problems

The forecasts generated above are unrealistically simple, however, and most actual forecasting involves one or more additional questions. For example:

1. *Unknown Xs:* It is unrealistic to hope always to know the values for the independent variable outside the sample. For instance, we will almost never know what the Dow-Jones Industrial Average will be in the future when we are making forecasts of the price of a given stock, and yet we assumed that knowledge when making our Kellogg price forecasts. What happens when we don't know the values of the independent variables for the forecast period?

2. *Serial Correlation:* If there is serial correlation involved, the forecasting equation may be estimated with Generalized Least Squares. How should predictions be adjusted when forecasting equations are estimated with GLS?

3. *Confidence Intervals:* All the forecasts above were single values, but such single values are almost never exactly right. Wouldn't it be more helpful if we forecasted an interval within which we were confident that the actual value would fall a certain percentage of the time? How can we develop these confidence intervals?

4. *Simultaneous Equations Models:* As we saw in Chapter 12, many economic and business equations are part of simultaneous models. How can we use an independent variable to forecast a dependent variable when we know that a change in value of the dependent variable will change, in turn, the value of the independent variable that we used to make the forecast?

Even a few questions like these should be enough to convince you that forecasting involves issues that are more complex than implied by Section 13.1.

13.2.1 Conditional Forecasting (Unknown X Values for the Forecast Period)

A forecast in which all values of the independent variables are known with certainty can be called an **unconditional forecast**, but, as mentioned above, the situations in which one can make such unconditional forecasts are rare. More likely, we will have to make a **conditional forecast**, for which actual values of one or more of the independent variables are *not* known. We are forced to obtain forecasts for the independent variables before we can use our equation to forecast the dependent variable, making our forecast of Y conditional on our forecast of the Xs.

One key to an accurate conditional forecast is accurate forecasting of the independent variables. If the forecasts of the independent variables are unbiased, using a conditional forecast will not introduce bias into the forecast of the dependent variable. Anything but a perfect forecast of the independent variables will contain some amount of forecast error, however, and so the expected error variance associated with conditional forecasting will typically be larger than that associated with unconditional forecasting. Thus, one should try to find unbiased, minimum variance forecasts of the independent variables when using conditional forecasting.

To get good forecasts of the independent variables, take the forecastability of a potential independent variable into consideration when making specification choices. For instance, when we choose which of two redundant variables to include in an equation to be used for forecasting, we should choose the one that is easier to forecast accurately. When you can, you should choose an independent variable that is regularly forecasted by someone else (an econometric forecasting firm, for example) so that you do not have to forecast X yourself.

The careful selection of independent variables can sometimes avoid the need for conditional forecasting in the first place. This opportunity can arise when the dependent variable can be expressed as a function of leading indicators. A **leading indicator** is an independent variable whose movements anticipate movements in the dependent variable. For instance, the impact of interest rates on investment is typically not felt until one or two time periods after interest rates have changed, as in the investment function in the small macroeconomic model in Section 12.3.3. That equation was:

$$\hat{I}_t = -2.87 + 0.19\hat{Y}_t - 4.61r_{t-1} \qquad (12.33)$$
$$(0.018) \qquad (1.40)$$
$$t = \quad 10.41 \qquad -3.30$$
$$\bar{R}^2 = .94 \qquad n = 25 \qquad DW = 1.59$$

where I equals gross investment, Y equals GNP, and r equals the interest rate. In this equation, r_T can be used as an independent variable in an equation that is being used to forecast I_{T+1}. Such leading indicators help avoid conditional forecasting only for a time period or two. For long-range forecasts, a conditional forecast is usually necessary.

13.2.2 Forecasting with Serially Correlated Error Terms

Recall from Chapter 9 that pure first-order serial correlation implies that the current observation of the error term ϵ_t is affected by the previous error term and an autocorrelation coefficient, ρ:

$$\epsilon_t = \rho\epsilon_{t-1} + u_t \qquad (13.6)$$

where u_t is a nonserially-correlated error term. Also recall that when serial correlation is severe, one remedy is to run Generalized Least Squares (GLS) as noted in Equation 9.18:

$$Y_t - \rho Y_{t-1} = \beta_0(1 - \rho) + \beta_1(X_t - \rho X_{t-1}) + u_t \qquad (9.18)$$

Unfortunately, whenever the use of GLS is required to rid an equation of pure first-order serial correlation, the procedures used to forecast with that equation become a bit more complex. To see why this is necessary, note that if Equation 9.18 is estimated, the dependent variable will be:

$$Y_t^* = Y_t - \hat{\rho} Y_{t-1} \qquad (13.7)$$

Thus if a GLS equation is used for forecasting, it will produce predictions of Y^*_{T+1} rather than of Y_{T+1}. Such predictions will thus be of the wrong variable.

If forecasts are to be made with a GLS equation, Equation 9.18 should first be rewritten to be solved for Y_t before forecasting is attempted:

$$Y_t = \rho Y_{t-1} + \beta_0(1 - \rho) + \beta_1(X_t - \rho X_{t-1}) + u_t \qquad (13.8)$$

We now can forecast with Equation 13.8 as we would with any other. If we substitute subscript T+1 for t (to forecast time period T+1) and insert estimates for the coefficients, ρs and Xs into the right side of the equation, we obtain:

$$\hat{Y}_{T+1} = \hat{\rho}Y_T + \hat{\beta}_0(1 - \hat{\rho}) + \hat{\beta}_1(\hat{X}_{T+1} - \hat{\rho}X_T) \qquad (13.9)$$

Equation 13.9 thus should be used for forecasting when an equation has been estimated with GLS to correct for serial correlation.

We now turn to an example of such forecasting with serially correlated error terms. In particular, recall from Chapter 9 that the Durbin-Watson statistic of the chicken demand equation used as an example in Section 13.1 above was 1.16, indicating significant positive first-order serial correlation. As a result, we estimated the chicken demand equation with GLS, obtaining Equation 9.23, repeated here for convenience:

$$\hat{Y}_t = -59.7 - 0.42PC_t + 0.17PB_t + 11.9LYD_t \qquad (9.23)$$
$$(0.09) \qquad (0.06) \qquad (1.5)$$
$$t = \quad 4.7 \qquad\quad 2.7 \qquad\quad 7.9$$
$$\bar{R}^2 = .983 \qquad n = 29 \qquad \hat{\rho} = 0.54$$

Since Equation 9.23 was estimated with GLS, though, Y is actually Y^*_t, which equals $(Y_t - \hat{\rho}Y_{t-1})$, PC_t is actually PC^*_t, which equals $PC_t - \hat{\rho}PC_{t-1}$, and so on. Thus, to forecast with Equation 9.23, we have to convert it to the form of Equation 13.9, or:

$$\hat{Y}_{T+1} = 0.54Y_T - 59.7(1 - 0.54) - 0.42(PC_{T+1} - 0.54PC_T)$$
$$+ 0.17(PB_{T+1} - 0.54PB_T) + 11.9(LYD_{T+1} - 0.54LYD_T) \qquad (13.10)$$

Substituting the actual values for the independent variables into Equation 13.10, we obtain:

Year	Forecast	Actual	Percentage Error
1979	51.3	50.6	1.4
1980	53.1	50.1	6.0
1981	53.6	51.6	3.9
1982	54.4	53.1	2.4

Note that these forecasts compare favorably to those that were calculated without taking serial correlation into consideration in Section 13.1. Indeed, GLS often will provide superior forecasting performances to OLS in the presence of serial correlation.

Whether to use GLS is not the topic of this section, however. Instead the point is that if generalized least squares is used to estimate the coefficients of an equation, then Equation 13.9 must be used to forecast with the GLS estimates.

13.2.3 Forecasting Confidence Intervals

Until now, the emphasis in this text has been on obtaining point (or single value) estimates. This has been true whether we have been estimating coefficient values or estimating forecasts. Recall, though, that a point estimate is only one of a whole range of such estimates that could have been obtained from different samples (for coefficient estimates) or different independent variable values or coefficients (for forecasts). The usefulness of such point estimates is improved if we can also generate some idea of the variability of our forecasts. The measure of variability typically used is the **confidence interval,** which is defined as the range of values within which the actual value of the item being estimated is likely to fall some percentage of the time (called the level of confidence). This is the easiest way to warn forecast users that a sampling distribution exists.

Suppose you are trying to decide how many hot dogs to order for your city's July 4th fireworks show and that the best point forecast is that you'll sell 24,000 hot dogs. How many hot dogs should you order? If you order 24,000, you're likely to run out about half the time! This is because a point forecast is the mean of the distribution of possible sales figures; you will sell more than 24,000 about as frequently as less than 24,000. It would be easier to decide how many dogs to order if you also had a confidence interval that told you the range within which hot dog sales would fall 95 percent of the time. This is because the usefulness of the 24,000 hot dog forecast changes dramatically depending on the confidence interval; an interval of 22,000 to 26,000 would pin down the likely sales, while an interval of 4,000 to 44,000 would leave you virtually in the dark about what to do.[5]

The same techniques we use to test hypotheses can also be adapted to create confidence intervals. Given a point forecast, $\hat{Y}_{T+1}$, all we need to generate a confidence interval around that forecast are t_c, the critical t value (for the desired level of confidence) and S_F, the estimated standard error of the forecast:

$$\text{Confidence Interval} = \hat{Y}_{T+1} \pm S_F t_c \tag{13.11}$$

or, equivalently,

$$\hat{Y}_{T+1} - S_F t_c \leq Y_{T+1} \leq \hat{Y}_{T+1} + S_F t_c \tag{13.12}$$

The critical t-value, t_c, can be found in Statistical Table B-1 (for a two-tailed test with $T - K - 1$ degrees of freedom), while the standard error of the forecast, S_F, for an equation with just one independent variable, equals the square root of the forecast error variance:

$$S_F = \sqrt{s^2[1 + 1/T + (\hat{X}_{T+1} - \bar{X})^2 / \sum_{t=1}^{T} (X_t - \bar{X})^2]} \tag{13.13}$$

where s^2 is the estimated variance of the error term, T is the number of observations in the sample, $\hat{X}_{T+1}$ is the forecasted value of the single independent variable, and $\bar{X}$ is the arithmetic mean of the observed Xs in the sample.[6]

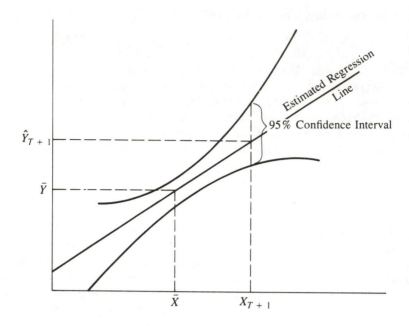

FIGURE 13.2 *A Confidence Interval for* $\hat{Y}_{T+1}$
A 95 percent confidence interval for $\hat{Y}_{T+1}$ includes the range of values within which the actual Y_{T+1} will fall 95 percent of the time. Note that the confidence interval widens as X_{T+1} differs more from its within-sample mean, $\bar{X}$.

Note that Equation 13.13 implies that the forecast error variance decreases the larger the sample, the more X varies within the sample, and the closer $\hat{X}$ is to its within-sample mean. An important implication is that the farther the X used to forecast Y is from the within-sample mean of the Xs, the wider the confidence interval around the $\hat{Y}$ is going to be. This can be seen in Figure 13.2, in which the confidence interval actually gets wider as $\hat{X}_{T+1}$ is farther from $\bar{X}$. Since forecasting outside the sample range is common, researchers should be aware of this phenomenon. Also note that Equation 13.13 is for unconditional forecasting. If there is any forecast error in $\hat{X}_{T+1}$, then the confidence interval is larger and more complicated to calculate.

As mentioned above, Equation 13.13 assumes that there is only one independent variable; the equation to be used with more than one variable is similar but more complicated. Some researchers who must deal with more than one independent variable avoid this complexity by ignoring Equation 13.13 and estimating a confidence interval equal to $\hat{Y}_{T+1} \pm st_c$, where s is the standard error of the equation. Compare this shortcut with Equation 13.13; note that the shortcut confidence interval will work well for large samples and $\hat{X}$s near the within-sample means but will provide only a rough estimate of the confidence interval in other cases. At a minimum in such cases, Equation 13.13 should be modified with a $(\hat{X}_{T+1} - \bar{X})^2/\Sigma(X_t - \bar{X})^2$ term for each X.

Let's look at an example of building a forecast confidence interval by returning to the weight/height example. In particular, let's create a 95 percent confidence interval around the forecast for a 6′1″ male calculated in Equation 13.1 above (repeated for convenience):

$$\text{Predicted Weight}_i = 103.4 + 6.38 \cdot (13 \text{ inches over five feet}) \qquad (13.1)$$

for a predicted weight of 103.4 + 82.9 or 186.3 pounds. In order to calculate a 95 percent confidence interval around this prediction, we substitute Equation 13.13 into Equation 13.11, obtaining a confidence interval of:

$$186.3 \pm (\sqrt{s^2[1 + 1/T + (\hat{X}_{T+1} - \bar{X})^2 / \sum_{t=1}^{T} (X_t - \bar{X})^2]}) t_c \qquad (13.14)$$

We then substitute the actual figures into Equation 13.14. From the data set for the example, we find that T = 20, the mean X = 10.35, the summed squared deviations of X around its mean is 92.50, and s^2 = 65.05. From Statistical Table B-1, we obtain the 95 percent, two-tailed critical t-value for 18 degrees of freedom of 2.101. If we now combine this with the information that our $\hat{X}$ is 13, we obtain:

$$186.3 \pm (\sqrt{65.05[1 + 1/20 + (13.0 - 10.35)^2/92.50]}) t_c \qquad (13.15)$$

$$186.3 \pm 8.558(2.101) = 186.3 \pm 18.0 \qquad (13.16)$$

In other words, our 95 percent confidence interval for a 6′1″ college-age male is from 168.3 to 204.3 pounds. Ask around; are 19 out of 20 of your male friends that tall within that range?

13.2.4   Forecasting with Simultaneous Equations Systems

As we learned in Chapter 12, most economic and business models are actually simultaneous in nature; for example, the investment equation used in Section 13.2 was estimated with Two-Stage Least Squares as a part of our small simultaneous macromodel in Chapter 12. Since GNP is one of the independent variables in the investment equation, when investment rises, so will GNP, causing a feedback effect that is not captured if we just forecast with a single equation. How should forecasting be done in the context of a simultaneous model? There are two approaches to answering this question. The correct approach to forecasting with simultaneous equations depends on whether there are lagged endogenous variables on the right side of any of the equations in the system.

If there are no lagged endogenous variables in the system, then the reduced-form equation for the particular endogenous variable can be used for forecasting, because it represents the simultaneous solution of the system for the endogenous variable being forecasted. Since the reduced-form equation is the endogenous variable expressed entirely in terms of the predetermined variables in the system, it allows the forecasting of the endogenous variable without any feedback or simultaneity impacts. This result explains why some researchers forecast potentially simultaneous dependent variables with single equations that appear to combine supply-side and demand-side predetermined variables; they are actually using modified reduced-form equations to make their forecasts.

If there are lagged endogenous variables in the system, then the approach must be altered to take into account the dynamic interaction caused by the lagged endogenous variables. For simple models, this sometimes can be done by substituting for the lagged endogenous variables where they appear in the reduced-form equations. If such a manipulation is difficult, however, then a technique called simulation analysis can be used. Simulation involves forecasting for the first post-sample period by using the reduced-form equations to forecast all endogenous variables and by using sample values for the lagged endogenous variables where they appear in the reduced-form equations. The forecast for the second postsample period, however, uses the endogenous variable *forecasts* from the first period as lagged values for any endogenous variables that have one-period lags while continuing to use sample values for endogenous variables that have lags of two or more periods. This process continues until all forecasting is done with reduced-form equations that use as data for lagged endogenous variables the forecasts from previous time periods. While such dynamic analyses are beyond the scope of this chapter, they are important to remember when considering forecasting with a simultaneous system.[7]

13.3   Forecasting with ARIMA, or Time-Series Analysis

The forecasting techniques of the previous two sections are applications of familiar regression models. We use linear regression equations to forecast the dependent variable by plugging likely values of the independent variables into the estimated equations and calculating a predicted value for Y; this bases the prediction of the dependent variable on the independent variables (and on their estimated coefficients).

ARIMA or time-series analysis is an increasingly popular forecasting technique that completely ignores independent variables in making forecasts. **ARIMA** is a highly refined curve-fitting device that uses current and past values of the dependent variable to produce often accurate short-term forecasts of that variable. Examples of such forecasts are stock market price predictions created by brokerage analysts (called "chartists" or "technicians") based entirely on past patterns of movement of the stock prices.

Any forecasting technique that ignores independent variables also essentially ignores all potential underlying theories except those that hypothesize repeating patterns in the variable under study. Since we have emphasized the advantages of developing the theoretical underpinnings of particular equations before estimating them, why would we advocate using ARIMA? The answer is that the use of ARIMA is appropriate when little or nothing is known about the dependent variable being forecasted, when the independent variables known to be important really cannot themselves be effectively forecasted, or when all that is needed is a one or two period forecast. In these cases, ARIMA has the potential to provide short-term forecasts that are superior to more theoretically satisfying regression models. In addition, ARIMA can sometimes produce better explanations of the residuals from an existing regression equation (in particular, one with known omitted variables or other problems). In other circumstances, the use of ARIMA is not recommended. This introduction to ARIMA is intentionally brief; a more complete coverage of the topic can be obtained from a number of other sources.[8]

13.3.1 The ARIMA Approach

The ARIMA approach combines two different specifications (called *processes*) into one equation. The first specification is an *autoregressive* process (hence the AR in ARIMA), and the second specification is a *moving average* process (hence the MA).

An **autoregressive process** expresses a dependent variable Y_t as a function of past values of the dependent variable, as in:

$$Y_t = f(Y_{t-1}, Y_{t-2}, \ldots , Y_{t-p}) \tag{13.17}$$

where Y_t is the variable being forecasted and p is the number of past values used. This equation is similar to the serial correlation error term function of Section 9.1 and to the distributed lag equation of Section 9.6. Since there are p different lagged values of Y in this equation, it is often referred to as a "pth-order" autoregressive process.

A **moving-average process** expresses a dependent variable Y_t as a function of past values of the error term, as in:

$$Y_t = f(\epsilon_{t-1}, \epsilon_{t-2}, \ldots , \epsilon_{t-q}) \tag{13.18}$$

where ϵ_t is the error term associated with Y_t and q is the number of past values of the error term used. Such a function is a moving average of past error terms that can be added to the mean of Y to obtain a moving average of past values of Y. Such an equation would be a *q*th-order moving-average process.

To create an ARIMA model, we begin with an econometric equation with no independent variables ($Y_t = \beta_0 + \epsilon_t$) and add to it both the autoregressive and moving average processes:

$$\tag{13.19}$$

$$Y_t = \beta_0 + \underbrace{\theta_1 Y_{t-1} + \theta_2 Y_{t-2} + \cdots + \theta_p Y_{t-p}}_{\text{autoregressive process}} + \epsilon_t + \underbrace{\phi_1 \epsilon_{t-1} + \phi_2 \epsilon_{t-2} + \cdots + \phi_q \epsilon_{t-q}}_{\text{moving-average process}}$$

where the θs and the ϕs are the coefficients of the autoregressive and moving-average processes respectively.

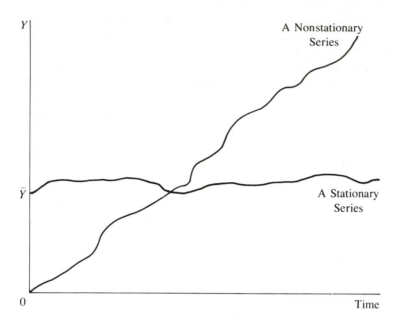

FIGURE 13.3 *Stationary vs. Nonstationary Series*
Whether a series is stationary or nonstationary can usually be determined by plotting Y with respect to time. If the series appears to have a fairly constant mean and variance, then it is stationary. If it exhibits an upward or downward trend over time, it is nonstationary.

Before this equation can be applied to a time series, however, it must be assured that the time series is *stationary*. A **stationary series** is a time series in which the dependent variable has a constant mean and variance over time. A **nonstationary series** is a time series that exhibits some sort of upward or downward trend (or a non-constant variance) over time. Figure 13.3 graphically depicts a stationary and a nonstationary series. If a series is plotted with respect to time and determined to be nonstationary, then steps must be taken to convert the series into a stationary one before the ARIMA technique can be applied. For example, a nonstationary series can often be converted into a stationary one by taking the first difference of the variable in question:

$$Y_t^* = \Delta Y_t = Y_t - Y_{t-1} \tag{13.20}$$

If the first differences do not produce a stationary series, then first differences of this first-differenced series can be taken. The resulting series is a second-difference transformation:

$$Y_t^{**} = (\Delta Y_t^*) = Y_t^* - Y_{t-1}^* = \Delta Y_t - \Delta Y_{t+1} \tag{13.21}$$

In general, successive differences are taken until the series is stationary. The number of differences required to be taken before a series becomes stationary is denoted with the letter d. For example, suppose that GNP is increasing by a fairly consistent amount each year. A plot of GNP with respect to time would depict a nonstationary series, but a plot of the first differences of GNP might depict a fairly stationary series. In such a case, d would be equal to one because one first difference was necessary to convert the nonstationary series into a stationary one.

The dependent variable in Equation 13.19 must be stationary, and so the Y in that equation may be Y, Y* or even Y** depending on the variable in question.[9] If a forecast of Y* or Y** is made, then it must be converted back into Y terms before its use; for example, if d = 1, then

$$\hat{Y}_{T+1} = Y_t + \hat{Y}^*_{T+1} \tag{13.22}$$

This conversion process is similar to integration in mathematics, and so the "I" in ARIMA stands for "integrated." ARIMA thus stands for *Auto*Regressive *Integrated *Moving *Average. (If the original series is stationary and d therefore equals 0, this is sometimes shortened to ARMA.)

As a shorthand, an ARIMA model with p, d, and q specified is usually denoted as ARIMA(p,d,q) with the specific integers chosen inserted for p, d, and q as in ARIMA(2,1,1). ARIMA (2,1,1) would indicate a model with two autoregressive terms, one first difference, and one moving average term:

$$\text{ARIMA(2,1,1):} \quad Y^*_t = \beta_0 + \theta_1 Y^*_{t-1} + \theta_2 Y^*_{t-2} + \epsilon_t + \phi_1 \epsilon_{t-1} \tag{13.23}$$

where $Y^*_t = Y_t - Y_{t-1}$.

13.3.2 Estimating ARIMA Models

The first task in estimating an ARIMA model is to specify p (the number of autoregressive terms), d (the number of first-differences or other transformations) and q (the number of moving-average terms). Generally, the higher the p, d, and q, the better the fit, but the lower the degrees of freedom. Once the parameters p, d, and q have been chosen, the job of specifying the ARIMA equation is complete, and the computer estimation package will then calculate estimates of the appropriate coefficients. Because the error terms in the moving average process are of course not observable, a nonlinear estimation technique must be used instead of OLS.

How are the values for p, d, and q to be chosen? While experience with choosing p, d, and q will make these choices seem fairly routine, there are three diagnostic tests that can be used to determine good (integer) values for these parameters:

Choosing d: The number of first differences is usually found by examining the plot of the series. If Y shows growth over time, then calculate Y*; if Y* shows growth over time, then use Y**. It is rare to find in economic examples a situation calling for d > 2. If the correct d has been chosen, the simple correlation coefficient between the dependent variable and lagged values of the dependent variable should approach zero as the number of lags increases. Such a simple correlation coefficient is called the autocorrelation function (ACF), and is often included as output in ARIMA packages. **Autocorrelation functions (ACFs) are** simple correlation coefficients[10] between a variable and the same variable lagged a number of time periods. If the ACFs approach zero as the number of lags increases, then the series is stationary; a nonstationary series will show little tendency for the ACFs to decrease in size as the number of lags increases. After an examination of the plot and/or the ACFs makes the researcher feel comfortable that enough transformations have been applied to make the resulting series stationary, the next step is to choose integer values for p and q.

Choosing p and q: The number of autoregressive terms (p) and moving-average terms (q) to be included are typically determined at the same time. These are chosen by finding the lowest p and q for which the residuals of the estimated equation are devoid of autoregressive and moving-average components. This is done by:

1. choosing an initial (p, q) set (making them as small as is reasonable),

2. estimating Equation 13.19 for that (p, q) and the d chosen above, and

3. testing the residuals of the estimated equation to see if they are free of autocorrelations. If they are not, then either p or q is increased by one, and the process is begun again.

In order to complete step 1 (choosing an initial (p, q) set), an ARIMA(0,d,0) is run and the residuals from this estimate are analyzed with two statistical measures. These are the ACF, this time applied to the residuals instead of to the variable itself, and a new measure, the partial ACF (PACF), which is similar to the ACF (applied to the residuals) except that it holds the effects of other lagged residuals constant. That is, the **partial autocorrelation function (PACF)** for the *k*th lag is the correlation coefficient between e_t and e_{t-k}, holding constant all other residuals. (Another way to picture a PACF for the *k*th lag is as the coefficient of e_{t-k} in a regression of e_t on $e_{t-1}, e_{t-2}, \ldots, e_{t-k}$.) Almost every different ARIMA model has a unique ACF/PACF combination; the theoretical ACF and PACF patterns are different for different ARIMA(p,d,q) specifications. In particular, the last lag before the PACF tends to zero is typically a good value for p, and the last lag before the ACF tends to zero is typically a good value for q. That is, as can be seen in the examples in Table 13.1, the ACF and PACF for Y can be used as guides[11] to the selection of p and q.

In order to complete step 3, testing the residuals of the estimated equation, a new statistic (called the Q statistic) is added to the measures used in the previous paragraph. The **Q statistic** is a measure of whether the first k ACFs are (jointly) significantly different from zero. If the ACFs and the PACFs are nearly all zero for various lags, and if the Q statistic is less than the critical value of the chi-square statistic for $k - p$ degrees of freedom (found in Statistical Table B-8), then the residuals from the ARIMA(p,d,q) model can be considered free from autoregressive and moving-average components.[12]

Once the (p,d,q) parameters have been chosen, the equation is estimated by the computer's ARIMA estimation package, producing estimates of p different θs, q different ϕs, and $\hat{\beta}_0$ (if appropriate). Since the moving-average process contains

Table 13.1   Unique ACFs and PACFs for the Major ARIMA Models

Model	Match Up Estimated ACF and PACF for Y_t to:		
	Theoretical ACF		*Theoretical PACF*
Nonstationary	Different from zero	or	Different from zero
ARIMA(0,0,0) (white noise)	All are zero	and	All are zero
ARIMA(1,0,0) $Y_t = \theta_0 + \theta_1 Y_{t-1} + \epsilon_t$	Tends to zero	and	Zero after 1 lag
ARIMA(2,0,0) $Y_t = \theta_0 + \theta_1 Y_{t-1} + \theta_2 Y_{t-2} + \epsilon_t$	Tends to zero	and	Zero after 2 lags
ARIMA(0,0,1) $Y_t = \theta_0 + \epsilon_t + \phi_1 \epsilon_{t-1}$	Zero after 1 lag	and	Tends to zero
ARIMA(0,0,2) $Y_t = \theta_0 + \epsilon_t + \phi_1 \epsilon_{t-1} + \phi_2 \epsilon_{t-2}$	Zero after 2 lags	and	Tends to zero
ARIMA(1,0,1) $Y_t = \theta_0 + \theta_1 Y_{t-1} + \epsilon_t + \phi_1 \epsilon_{t-1}$	Zero after 1 lag	and	Zero after 1 lag

error terms that cannot actually be observed, an ARIMA estimation with q > 0 requires the use of a nonlinear estimation procedure rather than OLS. If q = 0, OLS can be used. Once this estimation is complete, you are ready to forecast.

13.3.3   Forecasting with ARIMA

To forecast with an estimated ARIMA (or time-series) model, plug past values of Y and e into the estimated version of Equation 13.19, obtaining a forecast for Y. That is, once p, d and q have been selected and ARIMA(p,d,q) has been estimated, ARIMA forecasts for Y_t can be made using

$$Y_t = \beta_0 + \theta_1 Y_{t-1} + \theta_2 Y_{t-2} + \cdots + \theta_p Y_{t-p} + e_t + \phi_1 e_{t-1} + \phi_2 e_{t-2} + \cdots + \phi_q e_{t-q}$$

$$(13.24)$$

This is done by substituting current and past values of the (possibly transformed) dependent variable and the *residuals* into Equation 13.24. Note that in Equation 13.24, the residuals are used as proxies for the error terms specified in Equation 13.19. After the first value of the dependent variable is forecasted, the second-forecast-period value of Y is computed by using the first forecasted value of Y on the right side of the equation and by assuming that the error terms outside the sample of Equation 13.24 are zero (based on their expected values). In other words, the forecasts are made sequentially, with one forecast value being used to forecast subsequent values.

To illustrate, assume that an ARIMA(2,0,1) has been estimated using the procedures of Section 13.3.2 and that the subscript T denotes the last data point of the sample period. An ARIMA(2,0,1) equation is:

$$Y_t = \beta_0 + \theta_1 Y_{t-1} + \theta_2 Y_{t-2} + \epsilon_t + \phi_1 \epsilon_{t-1} \qquad (13.25)$$

To forecast with this equation for time period T+1, we would estimate Equation 13.25, substitute residuals for the error terms, and substitute (T+1) for t where it appears in Equation 13.25, producing

$$\hat{Y}_{T+1} = \hat{\beta}_0 + \hat{\theta}_1 Y_T + \hat{\theta}_2 Y_{T-1} + \hat{\phi}_1 e_T \qquad (13.26)$$

where the residual from time period T+1 is set equal to zero. To forecast for time period T+2, add one to the subscripts of Equation 13.26, being careful to use the value of $\hat{Y}_{T+1}$ just computed and to set the residual from time period T+1 equal to zero, obtaining:

$$\hat{Y}_{T+2} = \hat{\beta}_0 + \hat{\theta}_1 (\hat{Y}_{T+1}) + \hat{\theta}_2 Y_T \qquad (13.27)$$

Note that the moving-average process has disappeared. Further forecasted values of Y can be computed in essentially the same sequential (or recursive) way.

13.3.4   An Example of Forecasting with ARIMA

Let's look at an example of ARIMA forecasting by building a model of and attempting to predict the quarterly average work week of production workers (for manufacturing). This variable is an important leading economic indicator, so forecasting this variable is of more than academic interest.

Choosing d: The data for this series, which is quarterly from 1951 through 1980, are plotted in Figure 13.4, which appears to show that the series fluctuates around a fixed mean in the sample period. In addition, the sample autocorrelation coefficients (ACFs) of the series (reported in Table 13.2) move towards zero very quickly. These two pieces of evidence (the plot and the sample ACFs) indicate that the series is a stationary time series, and so d should be set equal to zero.

Choosing p and q: From Table 13.2, it is also possible to observe that the sample ACFs[13] follow a damped "sine wave" pattern, which is similar to the theoretical ACF of the second-order autoregressive model summarized in Table 13.1. In addition, note that the sample ACFs and PACFs are all quite close to zero[14] except those for the PACFs for lags of one and two quarters, indicating that a good starting point is p = 2, q = 0, as outlined in Section 13.3.3. The ARIMA(2,0,0) model is:

$$WW_t = \beta_0 + \theta_1 WW_{t-1} + \theta_2 WW_{t-2} + \epsilon_t \qquad (13.28)$$

where WW = the average work week. Estimating Equation 13.28 with OLS, we obtain (standard errors in parentheses):

$$\widehat{WW}_t = 7.497 + 1.115 WW_{t-1} - 0.301 WW_{t-2} \qquad (13.29)$$
$$\qquad\qquad\quad (0.100) \qquad\quad (0.090)$$
$$\qquad t = \quad 11.15 \qquad\quad -3.33$$
$$SEE = 0.275 \quad T = 120 \text{ (quarterly, 1951:1 } - \text{ 1980:4)}$$

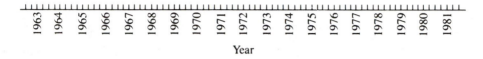

FIGURE 13.4 *The Average Work Week of Production Workers (Manufacturing)*
The average work week of production workers in manufacturing shows no long-term
upward or downward trend when plotted over time. As a result, the variable can be
considered to be stationary and "d" can be set equal to zero.

Table 13.2   Sample ACF and PACF of the Average Work Week of Production Workers
1951:1 to 1980:4

AUTOCORRELATIONS

LAGS

1 to 12	.85	.64	.44	.26	.13	.05	.02	.01	.03	.08	.10	.12
13 to 24	.14	.16	.15	.11	.05	−.03	−.13	−.20	−.25	−.25	−.23	−.19

Standard error $\approx 1/\sqrt{T} = 0.0913$, Q(12) = 178.36 with 12 d.f., Q(24) = 230.61 with 24 d.f.

PARTIAL AUTOCORRELATIONS

LAGS

1 to 12	.85	−.30	−.02	−.13	.06	.01	.10	−.11	.16	−.01	−.01	.03
13 to 24	.07	.02	−.00	−.14	−.01	−.13	−.04	−.07	−.01	.02	−.01	−.02

Standard error ≈ 0.0913

Table 13.3   Sample ACF and PACF of the Residuals from the ARMIA(2,0,0) Model Fitted for the Average Work Week

AUTOCORRELATIONS

LAGS

1 to 12	−.02	−.01	.12	−.09	−.00	−.14	.09	−.11	−.05	.13	−.00	.02
13 to 24	.02	.04	.11	−.03	.08	.00	−.07	−.03	−.13	−.05	−.11	.04

Standard error ≈ 0.0913, Q(12) = 10.98 with 10 d.f., Q(24) = 19.74 with 22 d.f.

PARTIAL AUTOCORRELATIONS

LAGS

1 to 12	−.02	−.01	.12	−.09	−.00	−.16	.12	−.13	−.00	.07	.05	−.02
13 to 24	.02	.01	.14	−.02	.07	−.01	−.02	−.07	−.09	−.07	−.07	.04

Standard error ≈ 0.0913

We now need to check the residuals of Equation 13.29 to make sure that there are no significant autoregressive or moving-average components left. As can be seen from Table 13.3, the sample ACFs of the residuals of Equation 13.29 are all quite close to zero. In addition, the Q statistic is 19.74, less than the critical chi-square value (for k − p = 22 degrees of freedom) of 33.9 (extrapolating from Table B-8). Given these two pieces of evidence, the residuals from Equation 13.29 can be deemed free of autoregressive and moving-average components, and the equation can be used for forecasting.

Most ARIMA estimation programs will also forecast the dependent variable for a specified number of time periods into the future by applying techniques such as those used in Equations 13.25 through 13.27 in the previous section.

Such forecasts for WW with a 95 percent confidence interval and the actual data are presented in Table 13.4. Note that the percentage error, as well as the confidence interval, increase in absolute value the further the forecast goes. This is to be expected, because the standard error increases and the fitted model is less likely to be applicable the further the forecast is pushed.

Table 13.4   Forecasts and Actual Work Weeks

DATE	FORECAST (F)	LOWER CONFIDENCE BOUND	UPPER CONFIDENCE BOUND	ACTUAL (A)	(A − F)	PERCENTAGE ERROR (A − F)/A
1981:1	40.12	39.58	40.66	40.00	−0.12	−0.30%
1981:2	40.22	39.41	41.02	40.10	−0.12	−0.30
1981:3	40.26	39.31	41.21	39.80	−0.46	−1.15
1981:4	40.28	39.25	41.30	39.40	−0.88	−2.22
1982:1	40.28	39.22	41.34	38.70	−1.58	−4.08
1982:2	40.28	39.20	41.36	39.10	−1.18	−3.02
1982:3	40.28	39.20	41.37	39.00	−1.28	−3.28
1982:4	40.28	39.19	41.38	39.00	−1.28	−3.28

13.4 Summary

1. Forecasting is the estimation of the expected value of a dependent variable for observations that are not part of the sample data set. Forecasts are generated (via regressions) by estimating an equation for the dependent variable to be forecasted, and substituting values for each of the independent variables (for the observations to be forecasted) into the equation.

2. An excellent fit within the sample period for a forecasting equation does not guarantee that the equation will forecast well outside the sample period.

3. A forecast in which all the values of the independent variables are known with certainty is called an unconditional forecast, but if one or more of the independent variables have to be forecasted, it is a conditional forecast. Conditional forecasting introduces no bias into the prediction of Y (as long as the X forecasts are unbiased), but increased forecast error variance is virtually unavoidable with conditional forecasting.

4. If the coefficients of an equation have been estimated with Generalized Least Squares (to correct for pure first-order serial correlation), then the forecasting equation is:

$$\hat{Y}_{T+1} = \hat{\rho}Y_T + \hat{\beta}_0(1 - \hat{\rho}) + \hat{\beta}_1(X_{T+1} - \hat{\rho}X_T)$$

    where ρ is the coefficient of autocorrelation, rho.

5. Forecasts are often more useful if they are accompanied by a confidence interval, which is a range within which the actual value of the dependent variable should fall a given percentage of the time (the level of confidence). This is:

$$\hat{Y}_{T+1} \pm S_F t_c$$

    where S_F is the estimated standard error of the forecast and t_c is the critical two-tailed t-value for the desired level of confidence.

6. ARIMA, or time-series analysis, is a highly refined curve-fitting technique that uses current and past values of the dependent variable (and only the dependent variable) to produce often accurate short-term forecasts of that variable. The first step in using ARIMA is to make the dependent variable series stationary by taking d first-differences until the resulting transformed variable has a constant mean and variance. The ARIMA(p,d,q) approach then combines an autoregressive process (with $\theta_1 Y_{t-1}$ terms) of order p with a moving-average process (with $\phi_1 \epsilon_{t-1}$ terms) of order q to explain the dth differenced dependent variable.

7. Specifying an ARIMA model involves choosing the correct p, d, and q. The best d value is the smallest number of first differences (or other transformations) that will produce a stationary series. The best p and q values are the

smallest integer values that produce an equation with residuals that are free of autoregressive and moving-average components. The basic tools used to make such specification choices are the simple (ACF) and partial (PACF) autocorrelation functions, which are correlation coefficients between a variable (or a residual) and itself lagged a number of time periods.

Exercises

(Answers to even-numbered exercises are contained in Appendix A.)

1. Write out the meaning of each of the following terms without reference to the book (or your notes) and then compare your definition with the version in the text for each:
   a. conditional forecast
   b. leading indicator
   c. confidence interval
   d. autoregressive process
   e. moving-average process
   f. ARIMA(p,d,q)
   g. stationary series
   h. simple and partial autocorrelation functions
   i. Q statistic

2. Calculate the following unconditional forecasts:
   a. Bond prices for 1975-78 given the simplified equation in Exercise 5 in Chapter 1 and the following data for the Federal funds rate: 1975: 5.82, 1976: 5.04, 1977: 5.54, 1978: 7.93.
   b. The expected level of check volume at three possible future sites for new Woody's restaurants, given Equation 3.14 and the following data. If you could only build one new eatery, in which of these three sites would you build (all else equal)?

Site	Competition	Population	Income
Richburgh	6	58,000	38,000
Nowheresville	1	14,000	27,000
Slick City	9	190,000	15,000

   c. Per capita consumption of fish in the U.S. for 1971-74 given Equation 8.27 and the following data:

Year	PF	PB	YD
1971	130.2	116.7	2679
1972	141.9	129.2	2767
1973	162.8	161.1	2934
1974	187.7	164.1	2871

   (Hint: Read Section 8.5.2 again before attempting this forecast.)

3. Forecast values for the appropriate independent variables and then calculate the following conditional forecasts:
   a. The weights of the three next males you see using Equation 1.21 and your estimates of their heights. (Remember to forecast, not obtain actual values for, the independent variables.)
   b. Per capita consumption of pork for all four quarters of 1985 given the equation you chose in the interactive exercise in Section 11.6. (Hint: If you didn't do that exercise, this is a good opportunity; if the run you chose involved GLS, then switch to one of the other regression runs.)
   c. Per capita consumption of pork for all four quarters of 1985 given regression run #11.41 and your forecasts for the Xs. (Hint: Note that this regression run was estimated with GLS.) Compare the forecasts you generated in part b above with your GLS forecasts. Which seems more likely to be accurate? Why?

4. Calculate 95 percent confidence interval forecasts for the following:
   a. the weight of a male who is $5\,'9\,''$ tall. (Hint: modify Equation 13.15.)
   b. Next month's sales of ice cream cones at the Campus Cooler given an expected price of 60 cents per cone and:

$$\hat{C}_t = 2{,}000 - 20.0P_t \qquad \bar{R}^2 = .80$$
$$(5.0) \qquad\qquad T = 30$$
$$t = -4.0 \qquad\qquad \bar{P} = 50$$

   where: C_t = number of ice cream cones sold in month t,
   P_t = the price of the Cooler's ice cream cones (in cents) in month t,
   $s^2 = 25{,}000$, and $\Sigma(P_t - \bar{P})^2 = 1000$

   c. Your forecast for first quarter 1985 per capita pork consumption from Question 3b above. (Hint: Use the actual data set in Section 11.6.)

5. Build your own (nonARIMA) forecasting model from scratch: Pick a dependent variable, specify your equation, hypothesize signs, find a data set, estimate your model (leaving a couple of the most current observations out of the sample) and forecast your dependent variable. Now comes the "fun" of comparing your forecast with the actual Ys. How did you do?

6. For each of the following series, calculate and plot Y_t, $Y_t^* = \Delta Y_t$, and $Y_t^{**} = \Delta Y_t^*$, describe the stationarity properties of the series, and choose an appropriate value for d.
   a. 2, 3, 4, 5, 6, 7, 8, 9, 10, 11, 12, 13.
   b. 2, 2, 3, 4, 5, 6, 8, 10, 12, 15, 19, 24.
   c. 2, 3, 6, 3, 4, 2, 3, 5, 1, 4, 4, 6.

7. Take the three Y_t^* series you calculated as part of your answer to Question 6 above and check to see if they are correct by calculating backwards and

seeing if you can derive the original three Y_t series from your three Y^*_t series. (Hint: Equation 13.22 can be adapted for this "integration" purpose.)

8. Suppose you have been given two different ARIMA(1,0,0) fitted time series models of the variable Y_t:

$$\text{Model A: } Y_t = 15.0 + 0.5Y_{t-1} + \epsilon_t$$

$$\text{Model T: } Y_t = 45.0 - 0.5Y_{t-1} + \epsilon_t$$

where ϵ_t is a normally-distributed error term with mean zero and standard deviation equal to one.

a. The final observation in the sample (time period 86) is $Y_{86} = 31$. Determine forecasts for periods 87, 88, and 89 for both models.

b. Suppose you now find out that the actual Y_{87} was equal to 33. Revise your forecasts for periods 88 and 89 to take the new information into account.

c. Based on the fitted time series and your two forecasts, which model (Model A or Model T) do you expect to exhibit smoother behavior? Explain your reasoning.

9. Suppose you have been given an ARIMA(1,0,1) fitted time series model:

$$Y_t = 0.0 + 1.0Y_{t-1} + \epsilon_t - 0.5\epsilon_{t-1}$$

where ϵ_t is a normally-distributed error term with mean zero and standard deviation equal to one and where $T = 99$, $Y_{99} = 27$, and where $\hat{Y}_{99} = 27.5$.

a. Calculate e_{99}.

b. Calculate forecasts for Y_{100}, Y_{101}, and Y_{102}. (Hint: Use your answer to part a.)

10. The actual data used to estimate Equation 13.5 for the Kellogg stock forecasting problem are given below. Calculate an ARIMA forecast for this data set by:

a. choosing p, d, and q,

b. estimating the coefficients of your ARIMA(p, d, q) model,

c. forecasting the Kellogg's stock price four quarters into the future,

d. calculating percent forecast errors and comparing your results with those in Section 13.1. Did you do better or worse than the regression-generated forecasts? Why do you think this happened?

DATA (The dollar price of J. L. Kellogg's stock quarterly from 1969 through third quarter 1977):

Year	First Quarter	Second Quarter	Third Quarter	Fourth Quarter
1969:	10.50	10.44	9.94	10.25
1970:	11.00	9.88	10.50	12.00
1971:	13.94	12.25	12.61	13.50
1972:	13.44	12.44	13.50	15.39

Year	First Quarter	Second Quarter	Third Quarter	Fourth Quarter
1973:	15.75	13.88	14.50	15.50
1974:	16.13	14.75	11.75	15.25
1975:	17.13	20.50	19.00	21.50
1976:	20.25	25.63	26.88	27.63
1977:	23.88	26.38	24.00	—

---

[1] Section 899 of the N.Y. State Criminal Code; the law does not apply to "ecclesiastical bodies acting in good faith and without personal fees."

[2] For example, Data Resources Incorporated, one of the leading econometric forecasting firms in the U.S., has an 800-equation model, and a number of other macroeconomic models are of similar size. For more on this, see Otto Eckstein, *The DRI Model of the U.S. Economy* (New York: McGraw-Hill, 1983).

[3] See, for example, C. W. J. Granger, *Forecasting in Business and Economics.* (New York: Academic Press, 1980) or Hans Levenbach and James P. Cleary, *The Modern Forecaster.* (Belmont, California: Wadsworth, Inc., 1984).

[4] The data for this example are in Exercise 6.5; the actual values of the independent variables for the three other forecast years were PC(11.0, 11.1, 10.3); PB(62.4, 58.6, 56.7); and YD(8012, 8827, 9385). A simplistic way to avoid such consistent over (or under) forecasting in some cases (although not in this case) is to add a dummy variable to the equation (before it is estimated) which equals one in the last time period in the sample and throughout the forecast period but zero otherwise. Such a forecasting dummy constrains the forecasts to link up to the actual data at the beginning of the forecast period, but it is a "one-time dummy" that uses up a degree of freedom, so it should be used with caution.

[5] The decision as to how many hot dogs to order would also depend on the costs of having the wrong number. These may not be the same per hot dog for overestimates as they are for underestimates. For example, if you do not order enough, then you lose the entire retail price of the hot dog minus the wholesale price of the dog (and bun), because your other costs (like hiring employees and building hot dog stands) are essentially fixed. On the other hand, if you order too many, you lose the wholesale cost of the dog and bun minus whatever salvage price you might be able to get for day-old buns, etc. As a result, the right number to order would depend on your profit margin and the importance of non-returnable inputs in your total cost picture.

[6] Equation 13.13 is valid whether Y_t is in the sample period or outside the sample period, but it applies only to point forecasts of individual Y_ts. If a confidence interval for the expected value of Y, $E(Y_t)$, is desired, then the correct equation to use is

$$S_F = \sqrt{s^2[1/T + (\hat{X}_{T+1} - \bar{X})^2/\Sigma(X_t - \bar{X})^2]}.$$

[7] For more on this topic, see pp. 723-731 in Jan Kmenta, *Elements of Econometrics* (New York: Macmillan, 1985); chapters 12-14 in Robert S. Pindyck and Daniel L. Rubinfeld, *Econometric Models and Economic Forecasts* (New York: McGraw-Hill, 1981); or W. J. Baumol, *Economic Dynamics* (New York: Macmillan, 1970).

[8] See, for example, T. M. O'Donovan, *Short-Term Forecasting* (New York: Wiley, 1983); C. W. J. Granger and Paul Newbold, *Forecasting Economic Time Series* (New York: Academic Press, 1977); Walter Vandaele, *Applied Time Series and Box-Jenkins Models* (New York: Academic Press, 1983); and Chapters 16-20 in Robert S. Pindyck and Daniel L. Rubinfeld, *Econometric Models and Economic Forecasts* (New York: McGraw-Hill, 1981).

[9] If Y in Equation 13.19 is Y*, then β_0 represents the coefficient of the linear trend in the original series, and if Y is Y**, the β_0 represents the coefficient of the second-difference trend in the original series. In such cases, for example Equation 13.23, it is not always necessary that β_0 be in the model.

[10] Like simple correlation coefficients, autocorrelation coefficients (ACFs) vary between −1 and +1, with zero indicating no correlation. For more on simple correlation coefficients, see Section 5.6.

[11.]The phrase "tends to zero" in Table 13.1 typically means that the ACF or PACF moves toward zero with an exponential decay, but for ARIMA(2,0,0), a damped sine wave is also possible. In addition, note that the stability of estimated ARIMA models (referred to as stationarity and invertability) depends on the values of the estimated parameters. For example, in ARIMA(1,0,0), $\hat{\theta}$ must be between -1 and $+1$ for the model to be stable.

[12.]The details of the calculation of the PACFs and the Q statistic are beyond the scope of this section. An explanation of the use of the chi-square test is contained in Statistical Table B-8. The ARIMA(p,d,q) model is sometimes additionally tested for adequacy by comparing the variance of ARIMA(p,d,q) to those of ARIMA(p+1,d,q) and ARIMA(p,d,q+1). If ARIMA(p,d,q) has the lowest variance, then it is considered adequate.

[13.]Note that since d = 0, no new ACFs must be calculated. If d had equaled one or more, then the sample ACF analyzed in choosing p and q would be the ACF of the residuals of ARIMA(0,d,0).

[14.]This can be tested using the normal distribution, with $1/\sqrt{T}$ as an estimate of the standard error of the ACFs and PACFs. In this case, since T = 120, $1/\sqrt{120} = 0.0913$. Since the critical value of the normal distribution with a 95 percent level of confidence is 1.96, the 95 percent confidence intervals for the ACFs and PACFs would be:

$$0 \pm 1.96(0.0913) = 0 \pm 0.179$$

Any ACF or PACF less than 0.179 in absolute value can be considered not significantly different from zero.

Appendix A

Answers to Even-Numbered Exercises

Chapter One

1-2. **a.** positive, **b.** negative, **c.** positive, **d.** negative, **e.** ambiguous (although Desmond Morris, human zoologist and author of *Manwatching,* claims there is a negative relationship), f. negative.

1-4. **a.** **b.** and **c.** coefficients, **d.** variables, **e.** and **f.** neither, **g.** both.

1-6. **a.** Customers #3, 4 and 20; no.
b. Weight is determined by more than just height.
c. People who decide to play the weight-guessing game may feel they have a weight that is hard to guess.

Chapter Two

2-2. **a.** $F = [R^2/(K)]/[(1 - R^2)/(n - K - 1)]$.
b. F is a statistical measure of fit while R^2 is a qualitative measure; printing both saves reader time and avoids (human) computation errors.

2-4. **a.** $\hat{\beta}_1 = -0.5477$, $\hat{\beta}_0 = 12.289$
b. $R^2 = .465$, $\bar{R}^2 = .398$, $F = 6.95$ (rounding will cause slight differences)
c. $\widehat{\text{Income}} = 12.289 - 0.5477(8) = 7.907$

2-6. $F = (3764.99/1)/(1305.43/18) = 51.91$; the estimated equation is significant since $51.91 > 4.41$, the critical F-value at the 5% level.

2-8. **a.** Yes, **b.** at first glance, perhaps, but see below.
c. Three dissertations, since $(489 \times 3 = \$1467) > (\$230)$ or $(120 \times 2 = \$240)$.
d. The coefficient of D seems to be too high; perhaps it is absorbing the impact of an independent variable that has been omitted from the regression. For example, students may choose a dissertation advisor on the basis of reputation, a variable not in the equation.

Chapter Three

3-2.   **a.** $D = 1$ if graduate student and $D = 0$ if undergraduate.
      b. Yes, for example $E =$ how many exercises (such as this) the student did.
      c. If D is defined as in answer a., then its coefficient's sign would be expected to be positive. If D is defined as 0 if graduate student, 1 if undergraduate, then the expected sign would be negative.
      d. A coefficient with a value of .5 indicates that, all else equal, a graduate student would be expected to earn half a grade point higher than an undergraduate. If there were only graduate students or only undergraduates in class, the coefficient of D could not be estimated.

3-4.   **a.** There are many possible omitted explanatory variables; for example, the number of parking spaces near the restaurant.
      c. This calculation gives the ratio of checks to population without taking the other variables into consideration. The regression coefficient is an estimate of the impact of a change in population on check volume, holding constant the other variables in the equation.

3-6.   **a.** New $P =$ Old $P/1000$, so β goes from 0.3547 to 354.7; **b.** 286.3; **c.** no.

3-8.   **a.** "Least squares" estimates coefficients that minimize the sum of the squared differences between the actual and predicted Ys. The squares are "least" in the sense that their sum is minimized.
      b. If $R^2 = 0$, the residual sum of squares (RSS) equals the total sum of squares (TSS), and the explained sum of squares (ESS) equals 0. If R^2 is calculated as ESS/TSS, then it cannot be negative. If R^2 is calculated as $1 - \text{RSS/TSS}$, then it will be negative if RSS > TSS, but this can only happen if Y is a *worse* predictor of Y than the mean of Y, which is possible only with a non-OLS estimator or if the constant term is omitted.
      c. Model A: $\bar{R}^2 = 1 - (1)[(56 - 1)/(56 - 1 - 1)] = -.02$

          Model T: $\bar{R}^2 = 1 - (1 - .40)[(38 - 1)/(38 - 2 - 1)] = .37$

      d. Model T has estimated signs that correspond to prior expectations and also includes an important variable (assuming that interest rates are nominal), so it is preferable to Model A, which has an unexpected sign. A higher $\bar{R}^2$ does *not* mean that an equation is automatically preferred.

Chapter Four

4-2.   **a.** β_1, **b.** yes; log-linear production function.

4-4.   c. definitely violates Assumption VI, and a. might for some samples.

4-6. $Z_i = (X_i - \mu)/\sigma = (1.0 - 0.0)/\sqrt{0.5} = 1.414$; for this Z_i, Table B-7 gives 0.0787, which is the probability of observing an X greater than $+ 1$. To also include the probability of an X less than -1, we need to double 0.0787, obtaining a final answer of 0.1574.

4-8. We know that: $\Sigma e_i^2 = \Sigma(Y_i - \hat{Y}_i)^2 = \Sigma(Y_i - \hat{\beta}_0 - \hat{\beta}_1 X_i)^2$. To find the minimum, differentiate Σe_i^2 with respect to $\hat{\beta}_0$ and $\hat{\beta}_1$ and set each derivative equal to zero (these are the "normal equations"):

$$\delta(\Sigma e_i^2)/\delta\hat{\beta}_0 = -2[\Sigma(Y_i - \hat{\beta}_0 - \hat{\beta}_1 X_i)] = 0$$
$$\text{or } \Sigma Y_i = n(\hat{\beta}_0) + \hat{\beta}_1(\Sigma X_i)$$

$$\delta(\Sigma e_i^2)/\delta\hat{\beta}_1 = -2[\Sigma(Y_i - \hat{\beta}_0 - \hat{\beta}_1 X_i)X_i] = 0$$
$$\text{or } \Sigma Y_i X_i = \hat{\beta}_0(\Sigma X_i) + \hat{\beta}_1(\Sigma X_i^2)$$

Solve the two equations simultaneously and rearrange:

$$\hat{\beta}_1 = [n(\Sigma Y_i X_i) - \Sigma Y_i X_i]/[n(\Sigma X_i^2) - (\Sigma X_i)^2]$$

$$= \Sigma(X_i - \bar{X})(Y_i - \bar{Y})/\Sigma(X_i - \bar{X})^2 = \Sigma x_i y_i/\Sigma x_i^2$$

where $x_i = (X_i - \bar{X})$ and $y_i = (Y_i - \bar{Y})$

$$\hat{\beta}_0 = [\Sigma X_i^2 \Sigma Y_i - \Sigma X_i \Sigma X_i Y_i]/[n(\Sigma X_i^2) - (\Sigma X_i)^2] = \bar{Y} - \hat{\beta}_1\bar{X}$$

To prove linearity: $\hat{\beta}_1 = \Sigma x_i y_i/\Sigma x_i^2 = \Sigma x_i(Y_i - \bar{Y})/\Sigma x_i^2$

$$= \Sigma x_i Y_i/\Sigma x_i^2 - \Sigma x_i(\bar{Y})/\Sigma x_i^2$$

$$= \Sigma x_i(Y_i)/\Sigma x_i^2 - \bar{Y}\Sigma x_i/\Sigma x_i^2$$

$$= \Sigma x_i(Y_i)/\Sigma x_i^2 \text{ since } \Sigma x_i = 0$$

$$= \Sigma k_i Y_i \text{ where } k_i = x_i/\Sigma x_i^2$$

$\hat{\beta}_1$ is a linear function of Y; this is how a linear function is defined. It is also a linear function the βs and ϵ, which is the basic interpretation of linearity. $\hat{\beta}_1 = \beta_0\Sigma k_i + \beta_1\Sigma k_i x_i + \Sigma k_i\epsilon_i$. $\hat{\beta}_0 = \bar{Y} - \hat{\beta}_1(\bar{X})$ where $\bar{Y} = \hat{\beta}_0 + \hat{\beta}_1(\bar{X})$, which is also a linear equation.

To prove unbiasedness: $\hat{\beta}_1 = \Sigma k_i Y_i = \Sigma k_i(\beta_0 + \beta_1 X_i + \epsilon_i)$

$$= \Sigma k_i\beta_0 + \Sigma k_i\beta_1 X_i + \Sigma k_i\epsilon_i$$

Since $k_i = x_i/\Sigma x_i^2 = (X_i - \bar{X})/\Sigma(X_i - \bar{X})^2$,

then $\Sigma k_i = 0$, $\Sigma k_i^2 = 1/\Sigma x_i^2$, $\Sigma k_i x_i = \Sigma k_i X_i = 1$.

So, $\hat{\beta}_1 = \beta_1 + \Sigma k_i\epsilon_i$ and given the assumptions of ϵ_i,

$E(\hat{\beta}_1) = \beta_1 + \Sigma k_i E(\epsilon_i) = \beta_1$, proving $\hat{\beta}_1$ is unbiased.

To prove minimum variance (of all linear unbiased estimators):

$\hat{\beta}_1 = \Sigma k_i Y_i$. Since $k_i = x_i/\Sigma x_i^2 = (X_i - \bar{X})/\Sigma(X_i - \bar{X})^2$, $\hat{\beta}_1$ is a weighted average of the Ys, and k_i are the weights. To write an expression for any linear estimator, substitute w_i for k_i, which are also weights but not necessarily equal to k_i:

$$\beta_1^* = \Sigma w_i Y_i, \text{ so } E(\beta_1^*) = \Sigma x_i E(Y_i) = \Sigma w_i (\beta_0 + \beta_1 X_i)$$
$$= \beta_0 \Sigma w_i + \beta_1 \Sigma w_i X_i$$

In order for β_1^* to be unbiased, $\Sigma w_i = 0$ and $\Sigma w_i X_i = 1$. The variance of β_1^*:

$$var(\beta_1^*) = var\Sigma w_i Y_i = \Sigma w_i var Y_i = \sigma^2 \Sigma w_i^2$$
$$[var(Y_i) = var (\epsilon_i) = \sigma^2]$$
$$= \sigma^2 \Sigma(w_i - x_i/\Sigma x_i^2 + x_i/\Sigma x_i^2)^2$$
$$= \sigma^2 \Sigma(w_i - x_i/\Sigma x_i^2)^2 + \sigma^2 \Sigma x_i/(\Sigma x_i^2)^2$$
$$+ 2\sigma^2 \Sigma(w_i - x_i/\Sigma x_i^2) (x_i/\Sigma x_i^2)$$
$$= \sigma^2 \Sigma(w_i - x_i/\Sigma x_i^2)^2 + \sigma^2/(\Sigma x_i^2)$$

The last term in this equation is a constant, so the variance of β_1^* can be minimized only by manipulating the first term. The first term is minimized only by letting $w_i = x_i/\Sigma x_i^2$, then

$$var(\beta_1^*) = \sigma^2/\Sigma x_i^2 = var(\hat{\beta}_1).$$

When the least-squares weights, k_i, equals w_i, the variance of the linear estimator β_1 is equal to the variance of the least-squares estimator, $\hat{\beta}_1$. When they are not equal, $var(\beta_1^*) > var(\hat{\beta}_1)$ Q.E.D.

Chapter Five

5-2.   **a.** $H_0: \beta_1 \leq 0, H_A: \beta_1 > 0$

   b. $H_0: \beta_1 \geq 0, H_A: \beta_1 < 0; H_0: \beta_2 \leq 0; H_A: \beta_2 > 0; H_0: \beta_3 \leq 0,$
   $H_A: \beta_3 > 0$ (The hypothesis for β_3 assumes that it is never too hot to go jogging.)

   c. $H_0: \beta_1 \leq 0, H_A: \beta_1 > 0; H_0: \beta_2 \leq 0, H_A: \beta_2 > 0; H_0: \beta_3 \geq 0,$
   $H_A: \beta_3 < 0$ (The hypothesis for β_3 assumes you're not breaking the speed limit.)

   d. $H_0: \beta_G = 0; H_A: \beta_G \neq 0$ (G for grunt.)

5-4.   **a.** $t_c = 1.363$; reject H_0 for β_1, cannot reject H_0 for β_2 and β_3.

   b. $t_c = 1.318$; reject H_0 for β_1, cannot reject H_0 for β_2 and β_3.

   c. $t_c = 3.413$; cannot reject the null hypothesis for β_1, β_2, and β_3.

5-6. **a.** $t_2 = (200 - 160)/25.0 = 1.6$; $t_c = 2.052$; therefore cannot reject H_0. (Notice the violation of the strawman here.)

b. $t_3 = 2.37$; $t_c = 2.756$; therefore cannot reject the null hypothesis.

c. $t_2 = 5.6$; $t_c = 2.447$; therefore reject H_0 if it is formulated as in the exercise, but this poses a problem because the original hypothesized sign of the coefficient was negative. Thus the alternative hypothesis ought to have been stated: H_A: $\beta_2 < 0$, and H_0 cannot be rejected.

5-8. **a.** α and β both have positive hypothesized signs because as L or K increases holding the other constant, output should increase. As we will see in Chapter 7, they measure the percentage increase in output resulting from a one percent increase in land and capital, holding the other constant, respectively (i.e. elasticities).

b. H_0: $\alpha \leq 0$; H_A: $\alpha > 0$; H_0: $\beta \leq 0$; H_A: $\beta > 0$

c. Reject H_0 if t-value > 1.708 and t-value is positive.

d. α: $t = 0.273/0.135 = 2.022$; therefore reject H_0.

β: $t = 0.733/0.125 = 5.864$; therefore reject H_0.

e. The relative prices of the two inputs need to be known.

5-10 **a.** $t = 8.509$; with $t_c = 1.746$, reject H_0 of no collinearity.

b. $t = 16.703$; with $t_c = 2.060$, reject H_0.

c. $t = 3.126$; with $t_c = 3.365$, cannot reject H_0 of no collinearity.

d. $t = -7.237$; with $t_c = -1.303$, reject H_0.

e. $t = 3.213$; with $t_c = 2.048$, reject H_0.

Chapter Six

6-2. Expected bias in $\hat{\beta} = (\beta_{omitted}) \cdot f(r_{omitted, included})$

a. Expected bias $= (-) \cdot (+) = (-) =$ negative bias.

b. $(+) \cdot (+) = (+) =$ positive bias; this bias will be potentially large since age and experience are highly correlated.

c. $(+) \cdot (+) = (+) =$ positive bias.

d. $(-) \cdot (0) = 0 =$ no bias; it may seem as though it rains more on the weekends, but there is no theoretical relationship between the two.

6-4. Yes; you could run a regression that includes variables for the risk and taxability of the bonds as well as maturity date and interest rate.

6-6.   **a.**   Coefficient:

	β_1	β_2	β_3	β_4
Hypothesized sign:	+	+	+	−
calculated t-score:	5.0	1.0	10.0	3.0

$t_c = 2.485$ (1% level), so: signif.   insig.   signif.   unexpected sign

b.   The significant unexpected sign of $\hat{\beta}_4$ is evidence of a possible omitted variable that is exerting positive bias. The omitted variable must either be correlated positively with X_4 *and* have a positive expected coefficient or else be correlated negatively with X_4 *and* have a negative expected coefficient. The fairly low calculated t-score for β_2 is not strong evidence of a specification error.

c.   A second run might add an independent variable that is theoretically sound and that could have caused positive bias in $\hat{\beta}_4$. For example, $X_5 = $ the number of "attractions" like movie theaters or shopping malls in the area would have a positive expected coefficient and be positively correlated with the number of nearby competing stores.

6-8.   **a.**   Nothing is certain, but the best guess is: $X_1 = $ # of students, $X_2 = $ chain price, $X_3 = $ temperature, $X_4 = $ Bucket price.

b. X_4 has the only negative coefficient, and Bucket price has the only negative expected sign. # of students (in thousands) should be the most significant and have the largest coefficient. Weather should be the least significant and also have a small coefficient (since that variable can be the largest in size). $X_2 = $ chain price by elimination.

c.   Note that developing hypotheses includes determining the desired level of significance. A possible rerun would be to drop (or reformulate to absolute degrees difference from optimal hamburger-eating range, if there is such a thing) the temperature variable. If there is omitted variable bias, it is positive on $\hat{\beta}_4$ (advertising?).

6-10.   **a.**   Consumers and producers can react differently to changes in the same variable. For example, price: a rise in price causes consumers to demand a lower quantity and producers to supply a greater quantity.

b.   Include only variables affecting demand ("demand-side variables") in demand equations and only variables affecting supply ("supply-side variables") in supply equations.

c.   Review the literature, decide whether the equation you wish to estimate is a supply or a demand equation, and, when specifying the model, think carefully about whether an independent variable is appropriate for a demand or a supply equation.

Chapter Seven

7-2. **a.** Semi-log [where $Y = f(\ln X)$]; as income increases, the sales of shoes will increase, but at a declining rate (except for Imelda Marcos).

b. Linear (intercept dummy); there is little theory for any other form.

c. Semi-log (as in **a.** above) or linear are both justifiable.

d. Inverse function [where $Y = f(1/X)$]; as the interest rate gets higher, the demand for money will decrease, but even at very high interest rates there still will be some money held to allow for transactions.

e. Quadratic function [where $Y = f(X, X^2)$]; as output levels are increased, we will encounter diminishing returns to scale.

f. While functional form should be chosen on the basis of theory, one outlier is capable of shifting an estimated quadratic unreasonably; in such cases, a log-linear function might avoid the problem.

7-4. **a.** Coefficient: $\qquad\qquad\quad \beta_1 \qquad\qquad \beta_2$

Hypothesized sign: $+ \qquad\qquad +$

t-value: $\qquad\qquad\quad 3.96 \qquad\quad 2.20$

$t_c = 1.708$ at the 5% level, so $H_0: \beta \le 0$ can be rejected for both.

b. It is the sum of the effect of omitted independent variables and the nonzero mean of a finite sample; it does not mean that salaries (logged) could be negative.

c. For this semi-log function, the elasticities are $\beta_1 ED_i$ and $\beta_2 EXP_i$ and the slopes are $\beta_1 SAL_i$ and $\beta_2 SAL_i$, which both increase as the Xs rise. This implies that a one-unit change in ED_i will cause β_1 *percent* change in SAL_i, which makes sense for salaries.

d. The R^2s cannot be compared because the dependent variables are different. To do so, you would need to calculate a "quasi-R^2."

7-6. **a.** To check your answer, compare your R^2s with those below.

b. The R^2 for the linear equation $= .982$, and the R^2 for the log-linear equation $= .971$, but since the equations have different dependent variables, they are not directly compatible.

c. "Quasi-R^2" for the log-linear equation $= 1 - (511.01/21487.5)$ $= .976$.

d. Run the regression: $C_i = \beta_0 + \beta_1(I_i) + \beta_2 D_i + \beta_3(I_i)D_i + \epsilon_i$

where $D_i = 1$ if female, 0 if male (C_i = consumption and I_i = income).

To test H_0: $\beta_3 \leq 0$ (no difference due to gender) vs.

H_A: $\beta_3 > 0$ (women spend at a higher rate).

we compare the calculated $t_3 = 1.212$ with t_c (5%) = 2.132 and cannot reject the null hypothesis of no difference.

7-8.   Let PCI_i = per capita income in the ith period

GR_i = rate of growth in the ith period (ϵ_i = a classical error term)

a. $GR_i = \beta_0 + \beta_1 PCI_i + \beta_2 D_i + \beta_3 D_i PCI_i + \epsilon_i$

where $D_i = 0$ if $PCI_i \leq \$2,000$ and $D_i = 1$ if $PCI_i > \$2,000$.

b. $GR_i = \alpha_0 + \alpha_1 PCI_i + \alpha_2 PCI_i^2 + \epsilon_i$ where we'd expect $\alpha_1 > 0$ and $\alpha_2 < 0$.

c. A semi-log function alone cannot change from positive to negative slope, so it is not appropriate.

7-10. **a.** The expected signs are β_1, + or ?; β_2, + ; β_3, + ; β_4, + .

b. $ADV_i/SALES_i$: the inverse form implies that the larger sales are, the smaller will be the impact of advertising on profits.
$CAPREQ_i$, ES_i, DG_i: the semi-log functional form implies that as each of these variables increases (holding all others constant), PR increases at a decreasing rate.

c. β_2, β_3, and β_4 all have positive expected signs, so $(+) \cdot (+) = (+)$ = positive expected bias on β_1, if one of the other Xs were omitted.

Chapter Eight

8-2.   **a., c., e.**

8-4.   Likely dominant variables = a and d. In **a.** # of games won = # of games played (which is a constant) − # of games lost, while in **d.**, # of autos = (# of tires bought)/(# of tires per car, which = 4 if no spare is sold with the cars or = 5 if a spare is included).

8-6. **a.**

Coefficient:	β_F	β_S	β_A
Hypothesized sign:	+	+	+
t-value:	2.90	−1.07	5.97
$t_c = 1.699$ at the 5% level, so:	signif.	insig.	signif.
		unexpected sign	

b. All three are possibilities.

c. Multicollinearity is a stronger possibility.

d. Yes; the distribution of the $\hat{\beta}$s is wider with multicollinearity.

8-8. **a.** Don't change your regression just because a fellow student says you are going to have a problem; in particular, even if you do have multicollinearity, you may well end up doing nothing about it.

b. There is a relatively high $\bar{R}^2$ ($\bar{R}^2 = .75$) while all the estimated coefficients are insignificant at the 10% level. Furthermore, the simple correlation coefficient between HR and RBI of .90 is significant at the 1% level ($t = 5.06 > t_c = 3.143$).

c. Since multicollinearity is a sample problem, the best solution here would be to try to increase the sample size (more than eight baseball players received MVP votes).

8-10. **a.** Coefficient:

	β_C	β_P	β_E
Hypothesized sign:	+	+	+
t-value:	31.15	0.07	0.85
$t_c = 1.69$ at the 5% level, so:	signif.	insig.	insig.

b. From the information given, omitted variables, irrelevant variables, and multicollinearity are all possible problems in this equation.

c. Yes; with the high $\bar{R}^2$, the low t-values for $\hat{\beta}_P$ and $\hat{\beta}_E$, and the high simple correlation coefficient between the two, there is definite multicollinearity in the equation. The high correlation coefficient between the dependent variable and C_i would not be evidence of multicollinearity, but it is cause for a reexamination of the definitions of the two variables just to make sure that they are not tautologically related.

d. Since contracts often last for several years and can vary greatly in how much they are worth, C_i does not seem to be a dominant variable. The payroll for defense workers and the number of civilians employed in defense industries are redundant, however; they measure the same thing. As a result, one or the other should be dropped.

Chapter Nine

9-2. **a.** reject H_0 of no positive serial correlation ($d < d_L = 1.03$).

b. cannot reject H_0 of no positive serial correlation ($d > d_U = 1.25$).

c. inconclusive ($d_L = 1.07 < d < 1.83 = d_U$).

d. reject H_0 of no serial correlation ($d > 4 - d_L = 4 - 1.13 = 2.87$).

e. cannot reject H_0 of no positive serial correlation ($d > d_U = 1.57$).

f. reject H_0 of no serial correlation ($d < d_L = 1.04$).

g. inconclusive (extrapolating, $d_L = 0.90 < d < 2.01 = d_U$).

9-4. **a.** $\beta^*_0 = \beta_0(1 - \hat{\rho})$, so to get β_0, divide β^*_0 by $(1 - \hat{\rho})$.

b. To account for the fact that the equation was estimated with GLS.

c. $\hat{\beta}_0 = -60.7/(1 - 0.52) = -126.46$

d. $\hat{\beta}_0 = 6.98/(1 - 0.610) = 17.90$

e. The equations are inherently different, and different equations can have drastically different constant terms, because β_0 acts as a "garbage collector" for the equation it is in. As a result, we should not analyze the estimated values of the constant term.

9-6. The same test applies, but the inconclusive region has expanded because of the small sample size and the large number of explanatory variables. As a result, even if the DW d = 2, you cannot conclude that there is no positive serial correlation.

9-8. **a.** Except for the first and last observations in the sample, the DW test's ability to detect first-order serial correlation is unchanged.

b. GLS can be applied mechanically to correct for serial correlation, but this procedure generally does not make sense; this time's error term is now hypothesized to be a function of *next* time's error term.

c. First-order serial correlation in data that have been entered in reverse chronological order means that this time's error term is a function of next time's error term. This might occur if, for example, the decision makers accurately predict and adjust to future random events before they occur, which would be the case in a world of rational expectations and perfect information.

9-10. **a.** $\hat{F}_t = 13.99 - 0.700RP_t + 0.854D_t$ $\bar{R}^2 = .288$
$$\phantom{\hat{F}_t = 13.99 -} (1.840) (0.250) \quad n = 25$$
$$t = -0.38 3.41 \quad DW = 1.247$$

b. The relative price coefficient is now insignificant, and the dummy variable is now significant in the unanticipated direction (that is, the Pope's decision significantly *increased* the fish consumption). In addition the DW is inconclusive in testing for serial correlation, but the DW of 1.247 is quite close to the d_L of 1.21 (for a 10 percent level of significance). Thus the omitted variable has not only caused bias, it also has moved the DW d just about into the positive serial correlation range.

c. This exercise is a good example of why it makes sense to search for specification errors before adjusting for serial correlation.

Chapter Ten

10-2. **a.** LIKELY: the number of professors, the number of undergraduates.

b. LIKELY: aggregate gross investment, population.

   c.   LIKELY: U.S. disposable income, population, and, less likely, U.S. per capita disposable income.

10-4. a. At the 1 percent level, $t_c = 2.787$; reject the null hypothesis of homoskedasticity.

     b. At the 1 percent level, $t_c = 4.032$; $t = 1.2987$, cannot reject null hypothesis of homoskedasticity.

     c. It depends on the underlying theory that led you to choose Z as a good proportionality factor. If you believe that the absolute value of Z is what makes the variance of ϵ large, then there is no difference between -200 and $+200$. On the other hand, if you believe that the *relative* value of Z is important, then you are forced to add a constant (greater than 200) to each Z (which changes the nature of Z) and run the Park test. If we add 300, for example, we obtain a t of 0.8245 (and we cannot reject the null hypothesis of homoskedasticity).

     d. At the 1 percent level, $t_c = 3.012$; $t = 0.606$ (after setting 0.0 equal to 0.1), and we cannot reject the null hypothesis of homoskedasticity.

10-6. $\epsilon_i = u_i Z_i$, so $VAR(\epsilon_i) = Var(u_i Z_i) = E[u_i Z_i - E(u_i Z_i)]^2$ since u_i is a classical error term, $E(u_i) = 0$ and u_i is independent of Z_i, so $E(u_i Z_i) = 0$ and $VAR(\epsilon_i) = E(u_i Z_i)^2 = E[(u_i^2)(Z_i^2)] = Z_i^2 E(u_i^2) = \sigma^2 Z_i^2$ (since Z_i is constant with respect to ϵ_i.).

10-8. a. $Y_i/\sqrt{X_{1i}} = \beta_0/\sqrt{X_{1i}} + \beta_1\sqrt{X_{1i}} + \beta_2 X_{2i}/\sqrt{X_{1i}} + u_i$

     b. $Y_i/X_{3i} = \beta_0/X_{3i} + \beta_1 X_{1i}/X_{3i} + \beta_2 X_{2i}/X_{3i} + u_i$

     c. $Y_i/\hat{Y}_i = \beta_0/\hat{Y}_i + \beta_1 X_{1i}/\hat{Y}_i + \beta_2 X_{2i}/\hat{Y}_i + u_i$

10-10. a.

Coefficient:	β_1	β_2	β_3	β_4
Hypothesized sign:	+	+	+	+
t-value:	7.62	2.19	3.21	7.62
$t_c = 1.645$ (5% level) so:	signif.	signif.	signif.	signif.

     b. Some authors suggest the use of a log-linear equation to avoid heterosketasticity because the log-linear functional form compresses the scales on which the variables are measured, reducing a tenfold difference between two values to a twofold difference.

     c. A reformulation of the equation in terms of output per acre (well, stremmata) would likely produce homosketastic error terms.

     d. Assuming the heteroskedastic error term is $\epsilon_i = Z_i u_i$, where u_i is a homoskedastic error term, Z_i is the proportionality factor, and $Z_i = X_{1i}$, then the equation to estimate is:

$$Y_i/X_{1i} = \beta_0/X_{1i} + \beta_1 + \beta_2 X_{2i}/X_{1i} + \beta_3 X_{3i}/X_{1i} + \beta_4 X_{4i}/X_{1i} + u_i.$$

Chapter Eleven

Hints for Section 11.4.2: The Passbook Deposits Interactive Example:

1. Serial correlation, omitted variables, and irrelevant variables are all possible, but the obvious problem is severe multicollinearity between QYPUS and QYPERM (the coefficients are much less significant than would have been expected for such important variables, and the simple correlation coefficient is .999). Any expected signs in such circumstances are merely the result of chance correlations.

2. Serial correlation and irrelevant variables are both possible, but the wrong sign for QRDPASS raises the question of an omitted variable or a switch to the spread interest rate formulation. Does economic theory argue in favor of or against the spread formulation? Are there any potential omitted variables that could cause negative bias?

3. If you did anything but drop QYPERM (you're required to keep QYPUS because of the way the example is set up) you probably will not be very happy with your results, and you will have wasted a regression run.

4. Serial correlation, omitted variables, and irrelevant variables are all possible, but the insignificant interest rate variables and the unexpected sign for QRDPASS raise the question of a switch to the spread interest rate formulation. Does economic theory argue in favor of or against such a switch?

5. Dropping EXPINF is not a terrible mistake, but it is too soon to tell, given the potential omitted variable problems. The switch to SPREAD seems much more pressing at this point.

6. Adding BRANCH is a poor idea, since leaving it out is unlikely to have caused the wrong sign (+ · + = + bias), but adding EXPINF at least could potentially solve the unexpected sign on the coefficient of QRDPASS (+ · − = − bias). The switch to SPREAD also seems likely to get at that problem, but this particular choice is not obvious from the regression results. It really comes down to your prior economic thinking: which of the two variables (EXPINF or SPREAD) makes more sense?

7. Serial correlation, omitted variables and irrelevant variables are all possible, but if there is serial correlation, it almost *has* to be at least partly impure serial correlation because the DW is virtually zero. This means we should focus on an omitted variable or a switch to the spread interest rate formulation. Does economic theory argue in favor of or against the spread formulation? Are there any potential omitted variables that could cause negative bias?

8. Adding MMCDUM seems to be the best route from a theoretical point of view; and the empirical results support this choice, since a dummy variable that equals zero for the first part of the sample and one thereafter would be quite likely to cause the kind of positive (impure) serial correlation indicated by the Durbin-Watson statistic.

9. Adding BRANCH is a poor idea, since leaving it out is unlikely to have caused the unexpected sign (+ · + = + bias), but adding MMCDUM could potentially solve the apparent negative bias on the coefficient of QRDPASS (+ · − = − bias). The switch to SPREAD also seems likely to get at that problem, but this particular choice is not obvious from the regression results. It really comes down to your prior economic thinking; which of the two variables (MMCDUM or SPREAD) makes more sense?

10. If one of the variables is irrelevant, dropping it will not fix any bias problem. Adding MMCDUM could potentially solve the apparent negative bias of the coefficient of QRDPASS (+ · − = − bias). The switch to SPREAD also seems likely to get at that problem, but this particular choice is not obvious from the regression results. It really comes down to your prior economic thinking: which of the two variables (MMCDUM or SPREAD) makes more sense?

11. Dropping BRANCH makes more sense than dropping EXPINF because the theory is weaker for BRANCH. While it is true that the coefficient of BRANCH has an unexpected sign, that result is insignificant and should not make you more likely to drop BRANCH than EXPINF for that reason alone. Extra branches would help an individual savings and loan association compete with other associations, but the overall impact might be expected to net out to zero because variations in return and income seem far more important than ease of deposit in choosing a portfolio. In addition, having more branches also makes it easier to withdraw funds as well as to deposit them!

12. Serial correlation, omitted variables and irrelevant variables are all possible, but if there is serial correlation, it almost *has* to be at least partly impure serial correlation because the DW is virtually zero. This means we should focus on an omitted variable instead of worrying about an irrelevant variable right now.

13. Serial correlation and irrelevant variables are both possible.

14. Serial correlation and omitted variables are both possible, but if there is serial correlation it almost *has* to be at least partly impure serial correlation because the DW is virtually zero. This means we should focus on an omitted variable; which one should you consider adding?

15. It is unclear whether EXPINF belongs in the equation. In the final analysis, it depends on whether the expectation of inflation will make asset holders more sensitive to interest rate differentials and therefore less likely to leave a portion of their assets in relatively low-earning passbook accounts. The choice between these two equations becomes a matter of the strength of your prior belief in EXPINF; there is not always a "best" answer in the art of econometrics!

16. It is vital that you drop MMCDUM immediately; as long as you leave it in the equation, you will have higher R^2s and a significant negative sign.

17. Serial correlation, irrelevant variables, and omitted variables are all possible problems.

18. Dropping BRANCH makes a lot of sense, since the theory behind it is weak. While extra branches would help an individual savings and loan association compete with other associations, the overall impact might be expected to net out to zero because variations in return and income seem far more important than ease of deposit in choosing a portfolio. In addition, having more branches also makes it easier to withdraw funds as well as to deposit them!

Hints for Section 11.6.2: The Demand for Pork Interactive Example:

19. Serial correlation and omitted variables are both possible.

20. Serial correlation and irrelevant variables are both possible.

21. Omitted variables should always be tackled before serial correlation because of the possibility of impure serial correlation.

22. Omitted variables and irrelevant variables are both possible.

23. Serial correlation, omitted variables, and irrelevant variables are all possible.

24. Income could be irrelevant, or its coefficient could be negatively biased due to an omitted variable. Before you go too far, though, review the theory behind PROPK.

25. An omitted variable is possible; what is it?

26. Serial correlation may well be the biggest remaining problem.

27. Deciding what to add is not easy, but if you added PROPK you should carefully review the theory behind that variable.

28. Income could be irrelevant, or its coefficient could be negatively biased due to an omitted variable. Before you go too far, though, review the theory behind PROPK. How should insignificant dummy variables be handled?

29. The theory behind choosing PROPK instead of an income variable needs to be reviewed carefully. Does supply create its own demand *without* price changes?

30. Note that DW > 2 indicates negative serial correlation, which is usually a sign of specification error. In addition, the theory behind choosing PROPK instead of an income variable needs to be reviewed carefully. Does supply create its own demand *without* price changes?

Chapter Twelve

12.2. **a.** All three equations are simultaneous.

Endogenous variables $= Y_{1t}, Y_{2t}, Y_{3t}$

Predetermined variables: $X_{1t}, X_{1t-1}, X_{2t-1}, X_{3t}, X_{4t}, X_{4t-1}$

b. All three equations are simultaneous.

Endogenous variables $= Z_t, X_t, H_t$

Predetermined variables: $Y_t, P_{t-1}, B_t, C_t, D_t$

c. The equations are recursive; solve for Y_2 first and use it to get Y_1.

12-4. **a.** $P_t = \pi_0 + \pi_1 X_{1t} + \pi_2 X_{2t} + \pi_3 X_{3t} + Y_{1t}$

$Q_{St} = Q_{Dt} = \pi_4 + \pi_5 X_{1t} + \pi_6 X_{2t} + \pi_7 X_{3t} + v_{2t}$

b. Step one: Set the two structural quantity equations equal to each other and solve for P_t:

$\alpha_0 + \alpha_1 P_t + \alpha_2 X_{1t} + \alpha_3 X_{2t} + \epsilon_{Dt} = \beta_0 + \beta_1 P_t + \beta_2 X_{3t} + \epsilon_{St}$

$P_t = (\beta_0 - \alpha_0)/(\alpha_1 - \beta_1) - [\alpha_2/(\alpha_1 - \beta_1)] X_{1t} - [\alpha_3/(\alpha_1 - \beta_1)]X_{2t}$
$\qquad + [\beta_2/(\alpha_1 - \beta_1)] X_{3t} + [(\epsilon_{St} - \epsilon_{Dt})/(\alpha_1 - \beta_1)]$

Step two: compare this equation with the first reduced-form equation in Part a:

$\pi_0 = (\beta_0 - \alpha_0)/(\alpha_1 - \beta_1); \pi_1 = -\alpha_2/(\alpha_1 - \beta_1);$
$\pi_2 = -\alpha_3/(\alpha_1 - \beta_1); \pi_3 = \beta_2/(\alpha_1 - \beta_1);$
$v_{1t} = (\epsilon_{St} - \epsilon_{Dt})/(\alpha_1 - \beta_1).$

Step three: Substitute P_t into the structural Q_D equation, combine like terms, and compare this equation with the second reduced-form equation in Part a:

$\pi_4 = (\alpha_1 \beta_0 - \alpha_0 \beta_1)/(\alpha_1 - \beta_1); \pi_5 = -\alpha_2 \beta_1/(\alpha_1 - \beta_1);$
$\pi_6 = -\alpha_3 \beta_1/(\alpha_1 - \beta_1); \pi_7 = \alpha_1 \beta_2/(\alpha_1 - \beta_1);$
$v_{2t} = (\alpha_1 \epsilon_{St} - \beta_1 \epsilon_{Dt})/(\alpha_1 - \beta_1).$

Step four: Rearrange and solve simultaneously for the αs:

$$\alpha_0 = \pi_4 - \pi_0\alpha_1; \; \alpha_1 = \pi_7/\pi_3; \; \alpha_2 = \pi_5 - \pi_1\alpha_1; \; \alpha_3 = \pi_6 - \pi_2\alpha_1$$

c. First, the equation needs to be exactly identified; to see why this is so, try to solve for the βs of the overidentified Equation 12.5. Second, for equations with more than one or two slope coefficients, it is very awkward and time-consuming to use indirect least squares. Third, 2SLS gives the same estimates in this case, and 2SLS is much easier to apply.

12-6. a. There are 3 predetermined variables in the system, and both equations have 3 slope coefficients, so both equations are exactly identified. (If the model specified that the price of beef was determined jointly with the price and quantity of chicken, then it would not be predetermined, and the equations would be underidentified.)

b. There are 2 predetermined variables in the system, and both equations have 2 slope coefficients, so both equations are exactly identified.

c. There are 6 predetermined variables in the system, and there are 3 slope coefficients in each equation, so all three equations are overidentified.

d. There are 5 predetermined variables in the system, and there are 3, 2, and 4 slope coefficients in the first, second, and third equations respectively, so all three equations are overidentified.

12-8. Stage One: Apply OLS to the second of the reduced-form equations:

$$Q_{St} = Q_{Dt} = \pi_0 + \pi_1 X_{1t} + \pi_2 X_{2t} + \pi_3 X_{3t} + v_{1t}$$

$$P_t = \pi_4 + \pi_5 X_{1t} + \pi_6 X_{2t} + \pi_7 X_{3t} + v_{2t}.$$

Stage Two: Substitute the reduced-form estimates of the endogenous variables for the endogenous variables that appear on the right side of the structural equations. This would give:

$$Q_{Dt} = \alpha_0 + \alpha_1 \hat{P}_t + \alpha_2 X_{1t} + \alpha_3 X_{2t} + u_{Dt}$$

$$Q_{St} = \beta_0 + \beta_1 \hat{P}_t + \beta_2 X_{3t} + u_{St}$$

To complete stage two, estimate these revised structural equations with OLS.

12-10. a. You don't know that OLS and 2SLS will be the same until the system is estimated with both.

b. Not necessarily. It indicates only that the fit of the reduced-form equation from stage one is excellent and that $\hat{Y}$ and Y are virtually identical. Since bias is only a general tendency, it does not show up in every single estimate; indeed, it is possible to have estimated coefficients in the opposite direction. That is, even though positive bias exists, an estimated coefficient less than the true coefficient can be produced.

Chapter Thirteen

13-2.   **a.**   73.58; 77.31; 74.92; 63.49
   b.   117,259; 132,859; 107,230; Nowheresville
   c.   14.11; 14.23; 14.57; 14.24

13-4.   **a.** 160.82 ± 17.53
   b. 800 ± 344.73

13-6.   **a.** $Y_t^* = 1, 1, 1, 1, 1, 1, 1, 1, 1, 1, 1$
     $Y_t^{**} = 0, 0, 0, 0, 0, 0, 0, 0, 0, 0 \ (d = 1)$
   b. $Y_t^* = 0, 1, 1, 1, 1, 2, 2, 2, 3, 4, 5$
     $Y_t^{**} = 1, 0, 0, 0, 1, 0, 0, 1, 1, 1 \ (d = 2)$
   c. $Y_t^* = 1, 3, -3, 1, -2, 1, 2, -4, 3, 0, 2$
     $Y_t^{**} = 2, -6, 4, -3, 3, 1, -6, 7, -3, 2 \ (d = 0)$

13-8.

		Model A	Model T
a.	1987	30.50	29.50
	1988	30.25	30.25
	1989	30.13	29.87
b.	1988	31.50	28.50
	1989	30.75	30.75

   c.   Model A should exhibit smoother behavior because of the negative coefficient in Model T.

13-10.   **a.**   Before we can forecast with ARIMA, we must:
     a. specify the model by choosing p, d and q, and
     b. then estimate ARIMA(p,d,q).

     The first step in specifying the model is to choose d by checking for stationarity. Based on the upward trend of the stock price data and the fact that the ACF of the series does not decline geometrically to zero, the series appears to be nonstationary. If first differences are taken, then the resulting PK* series does indeed appear to be stationary, indicating that $d = 1$.

     To choose p and q, we examine the ACFs and PACFs of the first-differenced series PK*. The PACFs are all statistically insignificant, which implies $p = 0$. The ACFs have spikes which are significantly different from zero (at the 5 percent level) for lags 3 and 4, indicating that $q = 4$. Thus one reasonable specification is ARIMA(0,1,4). (Another might be to suppress the MA coefficients for one and two lags, but such a specification is beyond this text.)

     If we estimate ARIMA(0,1,4) on the data, we obtain:

$$\widehat{PK}_t^* = 0.198e_{t-1} - 0.008e_{t-2} - 0.017e_{t-3} + 0.686e_{t-4}$$

$$\quad\quad\quad (0.200) \quad\quad (0.149) \quad\quad (0.214) \quad\quad (0.250)$$

$$\quad t = 0.99 \quad\quad -0.06 \quad\quad -0.81 \quad\quad 2.71$$

$$SEE = 1.623$$

If we now forecast with this equation, we obtain:

	Forecast	Actual	Percent Error
1977:4	24.32	24.38	0.3
1978:1	23.10	22.38	3.2
1978:2	23.70	23.00	3.1
1978:3	21.86	21.88	0.1

These results are significantly better than the regression-produced forecasts, indicating the potential of ARIMA for short-term forecasts of variables with little or no strong underlying theory. Not all ARIMA stock-market forecasts are this accurate, of course.

Appendix B

Statistical Tables

The following tables present the critical values of various statistics used primarily for hypothesis testing. The primary applications of each statistic are explained and illustrated. The tables are:

B-1   Critical Values of the *t*-Distribution

B-2   Critical Values of the *F*-Statistic: 5 Percent Level of Significance

B-3   Critical Values of the *F*-Statistic: 1 Percent Level of Significance

B-4   Critical Values of the Durbin-Watson Test Statistics d_L and d_U: 5 Percent Level of Significance

B-5   Critical Values of the Durbin-Watson Test Statistics d_L and d_U: 2.5 Percent Level of Significance

B-6   Critical Values of the Durbin-Watson Test Statistics d_L and d_U: 1 Percent Level of Significance

B-7   The Normal Distribution

B-8   The χ^2 Distribution

Table B-1:   The t-Distribution

The t-distribution is used in regression analysis to test whether an estimated slope coefficient (say $\hat{\beta}_k$) is significantly different from a hypothesized value (such as β_{H_0}). The t-statistic is computed as

$$t_k = (\hat{\beta}_k - \beta_{H_0})/SE(\hat{\beta}_k)$$

where $\hat{\beta}_k$ is the estimated slope coefficient and $SE(\hat{\beta}_k)$ is the estimated standard error of $\hat{\beta}_k$. To test the one-sided hypothesis:

$$H_0: \beta_k \leq \beta_{H_0}$$
$$H_A: \beta_k > \beta_{H_0}$$

the computed t-value is compared with a critical t-value t_c, found in the t-table on the opposite page in the column with the desired level of significance for a one-sided test (usually 5 or 10 percent) and the row with $n-K-1$ degrees of freedom, where n is the number of observations and K is the number of explanatory variables. If $t_k > t_c$ and if t_k has the sign implied by the alternative hypothesis, then reject H_0; otherwise, do not reject H_0. In most econometric applications, β_{H_0} is zero and most computer regression programs will calculate t_k for $\beta_{H_0} = 0$. For example, for a 5 percent one-sided test with 15 degrees of freedom, $t_c = 1.753$, so any positive t_k larger than 1.753 would lead us to reject H_0 and declare that $\hat{\beta}_k$ is statistically significant in the hypothesized direction at the 95 percent level of confidence.

For a two-sided test, $H_0: \beta_k = \beta_{H_0}$ and $H_A: \beta_k \neq \beta_{H_0}$, the procedure is identical except that the column corresponding to the two-sided level of significance is used. For example, for a 5 percent two-sided test with 15 degrees of freedom, $t_c = 2.131$, so any t_k larger in absolute value than 2.131 would lead us to reject H_0 and declare that $\hat{\beta}_k$ is significantly different from β_{H_0} at the 95 percent level of confidence.

Another use of the t-test is to determine whether a simple correlation coefficient (r) between two variables is statistically significant. That is, the null hypothesis of no correlation between two variables can be tested with:

$$t_r = r \sqrt{(n - 2)} / \sqrt{(1 - r^2)}$$

where n is the number of observations. This t_r is then compared to the appropriate t_c (n−2 degrees of freedom) using the methods outlined above. For more on the t-test, see Chapter 5.

Table B-1
Critical Values of the t-Distribution

Degrees of Freedom		*Level of Significance*				
	One Sided:	*10%*	*5%*	*2.5%*	*1%*	*0.5%*
	Two Sided:	*20%*	*10%*	*5%*	*2%*	*1%*
1		3.078	6.314	12.706	31.821	63.657
2		1.886	2.920	4.303	6.965	9.925
3		1.638	2.353	3.182	4.541	5.841
4		1.533	2.132	2.776	3.747	4.604
5		1.476	2.015	2.571	3.365	4.032
6		1.440	1.943	2.447	3.143	3.707
7		1.415	1.895	2.365	2.998	3.499
8		1.397	1.860	2.306	2.896	3.355
9		1.383	1.833	2.262	2.821	3.250
10		1.372	1.812	2.228	2.764	3.169
11		1.363	1.796	2.201	2.718	3.106
12		1.356	1.782	2.179	2.681	3.055
13		1.350	1.771	2.160	2.650	3.012
14		1.345	1.761	2.145	2.624	2.977
15		1.341	1.753	2.131	2.602	2.947
16		1.337	1.746	2.120	2.583	2.921
17		1.333	1.740	2.110	2.567	2.898
18		1.330	1.734	2.101	2.552	2.878
19		1.328	1.729	2.093	2.539	2.861
20		1.325	1.725	2.086	2.528	2.845
21		1.323	1.721	2.080	2.518	2.831
22		1.321	1.717	2.074	2.508	2.819
23		1.319	1.714	2.069	2.500	2.807
24		1.318	1.711	2.064	2.492	2.797
25		1.316	1.708	2.060	2.485	2.787
26		1.315	1.706	2.056	2.479	2.779
27		1.314	1.703	2.052	2.473	2.771
28		1.313	1.701	2.048	2.467	2.763
29		1.311	1.699	2.045	2.462	2.756
30		1.310	1.697	2.042	2.457	2.750
(Normal) ∞		1.282	1.645	1.960	2.326	2.576

Source: Reprinted from Table IV in Sir Ronald A. Fisher, *Statistical Methods for Research Workers,* 14th ed. (copyright © 1970, University of Adelaide) with permission of the Macmillan Publishing Company, Inc.

Table B-2:   The *F*-Distribution

The *F*-distribution is used in regression analysis to test two-sided hypotheses about more than one regression coefficient at a time. To test the most typical joint hypothesis (a test of the overall significance of the regression):

$$H_0: \beta_1 = \beta_2 = \cdots = \beta_K = 0$$
$$H_A: H_0 \text{ is not true}$$

the computed *F*-value is compared with a critical *F*-value, found in one of the two tables that follow. The *F*-statistic has two types of degrees of freedom, one for the numerator (columns) and one for the denominator (rows). For the null and alternative hypotheses above, there are K numerator (the number of restrictions implied by the null hypothesis) and n−K−1 denominator degrees of freedom, where n is the number of observations and K is the number of explanatory variables in the equation. This particular *F*-statistic is printed out by most computer regression programs. For example, if K = 5 and n = 30, there are 5 numerator and 24 denominator degrees of freedom, and the critical *F*-value for a 5 percent level of significance (Table B-2) is 2.62. A computed *F*-value greater than 2.62 would lead us to reject the null hypothesis and declare that the equation is statistically significant at the 95 percent level of confidence. For more on the *F*-test, see Section 5.8.

Table B-2
Critical Values of the F-Statistic: 5 Percent Level of Significance

v_2 = degrees of freedom for denominator

v_1 = degrees of freedom for numerator

v_2	1	2	3	4	5	6	7	8	9	10	12	15	20	24	30	40	60	120	∞
1	161	200	216	225	230	234	237	239	241	242	244	246	248	249	250	251	252	253	254
2	18.5	19.0	19.2	19.2	19.3	19.3	19.4	19.4	19.4	19.4	19.4	19.4	19.4	19.5	19.5	19.5	19.5	19.5	19.5
3	10.1	9.55	9.28	9.12	9.01	8.94	8.89	8.85	8.81	8.79	8.74	8.70	8.66	8.64	8.62	8.59	8.57	8.55	8.53
4	7.71	6.94	6.59	6.39	6.26	6.16	6.09	6.04	6.00	5.96	5.91	5.86	5.80	5.77	5.75	5.72	5.69	5.66	5.63
5	6.61	5.79	5.41	5.19	5.05	4.95	4.88	4.82	4.77	4.74	4.68	4.62	4.56	4.53	4.50	4.46	4.43	4.40	4.37
6	5.99	5.14	4.76	4.53	4.39	4.28	4.21	4.15	4.10	4.06	4.00	3.94	3.87	3.84	3.81	3.77	3.74	3.70	3.67
7	5.59	4.74	4.35	4.12	3.97	3.87	3.79	3.73	3.68	3.64	3.57	3.51	3.44	3.41	3.38	3.34	3.30	3.27	3.23
8	5.32	4.46	4.07	3.84	3.69	3.58	3.50	3.44	3.39	3.35	3.28	3.22	3.15	3.12	3.08	3.04	3.01	2.97	2.93
9	5.12	4.26	3.86	3.63	3.48	3.37	3.29	3.23	3.18	3.14	3.07	3.01	2.94	2.90	2.86	2.83	2.79	2.75	2.71
10	4.96	4.10	3.71	3.48	3.33	3.22	3.14	3.07	3.02	2.98	2.91	2.85	2.77	2.74	2.70	2.66	2.62	2.58	2.54
11	4.84	3.98	3.59	3.36	3.20	3.09	3.01	2.95	2.90	2.85	2.79	2.72	2.65	2.61	2.57	2.53	2.49	2.45	2.40
12	4.75	3.89	3.49	3.26	3.11	3.00	2.91	2.85	2.80	2.75	2.69	2.62	2.54	2.51	2.47	2.43	2.38	2.34	2.30
13	4.67	3.81	3.41	3.18	3.03	2.92	2.83	2.77	2.71	2.67	2.60	2.53	2.46	2.42	2.38	2.34	2.30	2.25	2.21
14	4.60	3.74	3.34	3.11	2.96	2.85	2.76	2.70	2.65	2.60	2.53	2.46	2.39	2.35	2.31	2.27	2.22	2.18	2.13
15	4.54	3.68	3.29	3.06	2.90	2.79	2.71	2.64	2.59	2.54	2.48	2.40	2.33	2.29	2.25	2.20	2.16	2.11	2.07
16	4.49	3.63	3.24	3.01	2.85	2.74	2.66	2.59	2.54	2.49	2.42	2.35	2.28	2.24	2.19	2.15	2.11	2.06	2.01
17	4.45	3.59	3.20	2.96	2.81	2.70	2.61	2.55	2.49	2.45	2.38	2.31	2.23	2.19	2.15	2.10	2.06	2.01	1.96
18	4.41	3.55	3.16	2.93	2.77	2.66	2.58	2.51	2.46	2.41	2.34	2.27	2.19	2.15	2.11	2.06	2.02	1.97	1.92
19	4.38	3.52	3.13	2.90	2.74	2.63	2.54	2.48	2.42	2.38	2.31	2.23	2.16	2.11	2.07	2.03	1.98	1.93	1.88
20	4.35	3.49	3.10	2.87	2.71	2.60	2.51	2.45	2.39	2.35	2.28	2.20	2.12	2.08	2.04	1.99	1.95	1.90	1.84
21	4.32	3.47	3.07	2.84	2.68	2.57	2.49	2.42	2.37	2.32	2.25	2.18	2.10	2.05	2.01	1.96	1.92	1.87	1.81
22	4.30	3.44	3.05	2.82	2.66	2.55	2.46	2.40	2.34	2.30	2.23	2.15	2.07	2.03	1.98	1.94	1.89	1.84	1.78
23	4.28	3.42	3.03	2.80	2.64	2.53	2.44	2.37	2.32	2.27	2.20	2.13	2.05	2.01	1.96	1.91	1.86	1.81	1.76
24	4.26	3.40	3.01	2.78	2.62	2.51	2.42	2.36	2.30	2.25	2.18	2.11	2.03	1.98	1.94	1.89	1.84	1.79	1.73
25	4.24	3.39	2.99	2.76	2.60	2.49	2.40	2.34	2.28	2.24	2.16	2.09	2.01	1.96	1.92	1.87	1.82	1.77	1.71
30	4.17	3.32	2.92	2.69	2.53	2.42	2.33	2.27	2.21	2.16	2.09	2.01	1.93	1.89	1.84	1.79	1.74	1.68	1.62
40	4.08	3.23	2.84	2.61	2.45	2.34	2.25	2.18	2.12	2.08	2.00	1.92	1.84	1.79	1.74	1.69	1.64	1.58	1.51
60	4.00	3.15	2.76	2.53	2.37	2.25	2.17	2.10	2.04	1.99	1.92	1.84	1.75	1.70	1.65	1.59	1.53	1.47	1.39
120	3.92	3.07	2.68	2.45	2.29	2.18	2.09	2.02	1.96	1.91	1.83	1.75	1.66	1.61	1.55	1.50	1.43	1.35	1.25
∞	3.84	3.00	2.60	2.37	2.21	2.10	2.01	1.94	1.88	1.83	1.75	1.67	1.57	1.52	1.46	1.39	1.32	1.22	1.00

Abridged from M. Merrington and C. M. Thompson, "Tables of percentage points of the inverted beta (F) distribution," *Biometrika*, Vol. 33, 1943, p. 73. By permission of the *Biometrika* trustees.

Table B-3: The *F*-Distribution

The *F*-distribution is used in regression analysis to test two-sided hypotheses about more than one regression coefficient at a time. To test the most typical joint hypothesis (a test of the overall significance of the regression):

$$H_0: \beta_1 = \beta_2 = \cdots = \beta_K = 0$$
$$H_A: H_0 \text{ is not true}$$

the computed *F*-value is compared with a critical *F*-value, found in one of the two tables that follow. The *F*-statistic has two types of degrees of freedom, one for the numerator (columns) and one for the denominator (rows). For the null and alternative hypotheses above, there are K numerator (the number of restrictions implied by the null hypothesis) and $n-K-1$ denominator degrees of freedom, where n is the number of observations and K is the number of explanatory variables in the equation. This particular *F*-statistic is printed out by most computer regression programs. For example, if K = 5 and n = 30, there are 5 numerator and 24 denominator degrees of freedom, and the critical *F*-value for a 1 percent level of significance (Table B-3) is 3.90. A computed *F*-value greater than 3.90 would lead us to reject the null hypothesis and declare that the equation is statistically significant at the 99 percent level of confidence. For more on the *F*-test, see Section 5.8.

Table B-3
Critical Values of the F-Statistic: 1 Percent Level of Significance

v_1 = degrees of freedom for numerator

v_2 = degrees of freedom for denominator

v_2	1	2	3	4	5	6	7	8	9	10	12	15	20	24	30	40	60	120	∞
1	4052	5000	5403	5625	5764	5859	5928	5982	6023	6056	6106	6157	6209	6235	6261	6287	6313	6339	6366
2	98.5	99.0	99.2	99.2	99.3	99.3	99.4	99.4	99.4	99.4	99.4	99.4	99.4	99.5	99.5	99.5	99.5	99.5	99.5
3	34.1	30.8	29.5	28.7	28.2	27.9	27.7	27.5	27.3	27.2	27.1	26.9	26.7	26.6	26.5	26.4	26.3	26.2	26.1
4	21.2	18.0	16.7	16.0	15.5	15.2	15.0	14.8	14.7	14.5	14.4	14.2	14.0	13.9	13.8	13.7	13.7	13.6	13.5
5	16.3	13.3	12.1	11.4	11.0	10.7	10.5	10.3	10.2	10.1	9.89	9.72	9.55	9.47	9.38	9.29	9.20	9.11	9.02
6	13.7	10.9	9.78	9.15	8.75	8.47	8.26	8.10	7.98	7.87	7.72	7.56	7.40	7.31	7.23	7.14	7.06	6.97	6.88
7	12.2	9.55	8.45	7.85	7.46	7.19	6.99	6.84	6.72	6.62	6.47	6.31	6.16	6.07	5.99	5.91	5.82	5.74	5.65
8	11.3	8.65	7.59	7.01	6.63	6.37	6.18	6.03	5.91	5.81	5.67	5.52	5.36	5.28	5.20	5.12	5.03	4.95	4.86
9	10.6	8.02	6.99	6.42	6.06	5.80	5.61	5.47	5.35	5.26	5.11	4.96	4.81	4.73	4.65	4.57	4.48	4.40	4.31
10	10.0	7.56	6.55	5.99	5.64	5.39	5.20	5.06	4.94	4.85	4.71	4.56	4.41	4.33	4.25	4.17	4.08	4.00	3.91
11	9.65	7.21	6.22	5.67	5.32	5.07	4.89	4.74	4.63	4.54	4.40	4.25	4.10	4.02	3.94	3.86	3.78	3.69	3.60
12	9.33	6.93	5.95	5.41	5.06	4.82	4.64	4.50	4.39	4.30	4.16	4.01	3.86	3.78	3.70	3.62	3.54	3.45	3.36
13	9.07	6.70	5.74	5.21	4.86	4.62	4.44	4.30	4.19	4.10	3.96	3.82	3.66	3.59	3.51	3.43	3.34	3.25	3.17
14	8.86	6.51	5.56	5.04	4.70	4.46	4.28	4.14	4.03	3.94	3.80	3.66	3.51	3.43	3.35	3.27	3.18	3.09	3.00
15	8.68	6.36	5.42	4.89	4.56	4.32	4.14	4.00	3.89	3.80	3.67	3.52	3.37	3.29	3.21	3.13	3.05	2.96	2.87
16	8.53	6.23	5.29	4.77	4.44	4.20	4.03	3.89	3.78	3.69	3.55	3.41	3.26	3.18	3.10	3.02	2.93	2.84	2.75
17	8.40	6.11	5.19	4.67	4.34	4.10	3.93	3.79	3.68	3.59	3.46	3.31	3.16	3.08	3.00	2.92	2.84	2.75	2.65
18	8.29	6.01	5.09	4.58	4.25	4.01	3.84	3.71	3.60	3.51	3.37	3.23	3.08	3.00	2.92	2.84	2.75	2.66	2.57
19	8.19	5.93	5.01	4.50	4.17	3.94	3.77	3.63	3.52	3.43	3.30	3.15	3.00	2.92	2.84	2.76	2.67	2.58	2.49
20	8.10	5.85	4.94	4.43	4.10	3.87	3.70	3.56	3.46	3.37	3.23	3.09	2.94	2.86	2.78	2.69	2.61	2.52	2.42
21	8.02	5.78	4.87	4.37	4.04	3.81	3.64	3.51	3.40	3.31	3.17	3.03	2.88	2.80	2.72	2.64	2.55	2.46	2.36
22	7.95	5.72	4.82	4.31	3.99	3.76	3.59	3.45	3.35	3.26	3.12	2.98	2.83	2.75	2.67	2.58	2.50	2.40	2.31
23	7.88	5.66	4.76	4.26	3.94	3.71	3.54	3.41	3.30	3.21	3.07	2.93	2.78	2.70	2.62	2.54	2.45	2.35	2.26
24	7.82	5.61	4.72	4.22	3.90	3.67	3.50	3.36	3.26	3.17	3.03	2.89	2.74	2.66	2.58	2.49	2.40	2.31	2.21
25	7.77	5.57	4.68	4.18	3.86	3.63	3.46	3.32	3.22	3.13	2.99	2.85	2.70	2.62	2.53	2.45	2.36	2.27	2.17
30	7.56	5.39	4.51	4.02	3.70	3.47	3.30	3.17	3.07	2.98	2.84	2.70	2.55	2.47	2.39	2.30	2.21	2.11	2.01
40	7.31	5.18	4.31	3.83	3.51	3.29	3.12	2.99	2.89	2.80	2.66	2.52	2.37	2.29	2.20	2.11	2.02	1.92	1.80
60	7.08	4.98	4.13	3.65	3.34	3.12	2.95	2.82	2.72	2.63	2.50	2.35	2.20	2.12	2.03	1.94	1.84	1.73	1.60
120	6.85	4.79	3.95	3.48	3.17	2.96	2.79	2.66	2.56	2.47	2.34	2.19	2.03	1.95	1.86	1.76	1.66	1.53	1.38
∞	6.63	4.61	3.78	3.32	3.02	2.80	2.64	2.51	2.41	2.32	2.18	2.04	1.88	1.79	1.70	1.59	1.47	1.32	1.00

Tables B-4, B-5, and B-6: The Durbin-Watson d Statistic

The Durbin-Watson d statistic is used to test for first-order serial correlation in the residuals. First-order serial correlation is characterized by $\epsilon_t = \rho\epsilon_{t-1} + u_t$, where ϵ_t is the error term found in the regression equation and u_t is a classical (non-serially correlated) error term. Since $\rho = 0$ implies no serial correlation, and since most economic and business models imply positive serial correlation if any pure serial correlation exists, the typical hypotheses are:

$$H_0: \rho \leq 0$$
$$H_A: \rho > 0$$

To test the null hypothesis of no positive serial correlation, the Durbin-Watson d statistic must be compared to two different critical d-values, d_L and d_U found in the tables that follow depending on the level of significance, the number of explanatory variables (K') and the number of observations (n). For example, with 2 explanatory variables and 30 observations, the 1 percent level critical values are $d_L = 1.07$ and $d_U = 1.34$, so any computed Durbin-Watson statistic less than 1.07 would lead to the rejection of the null hypothesis. For computed DW d-values between 1.07 and 1.34, the test is inconclusive, and for values greater than 1.34, we can say that there is no evidence of positive serial correlation at the 99 percent level of confidence. These ranges are illustrated in the diagram below:

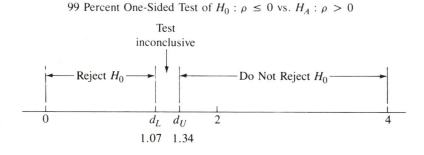

99 Percent One-Sided Test of $H_0 : \rho \leq 0$ vs. $H_A : \rho > 0$

Tables B-4, B-5, and B-6 (for 5, 2.5, and 1 percent levels of significance in a one-sided test) go only up to five explanatory variables, so extrapolation for more variables (and interpolation for observations between listed points) is often in order. Two-sided tests are done similarly, with $4 - d_U$ and $4 - d_L$ being the critical DW d-values between 2 and 4. For more on this, see Chapter 9.

Table B-4
Critical Values of the Durbin-Watson Test Statistics d_L and d_U:
5 Percent One-Sided Level of Significance
(10 Percent, Two-Sided Level of Significance)

n	$k' = 1$		$k' = 2$		$k' = 3$		$k' = 4$		$k' = 5$	
	d_L	d_U	d_L	d_U	d_L	d_U	d_L	d_U	d_L	d_U
15	1.08	1.36	0.95	1.54	0.82	1.75	0.69	1.97	0.56	2.21
16	1.10	1.37	0.98	1.54	0.86	1.73	0.74	1.93	0.62	2.15
17	1.13	1.38	1.02	1.54	0.90	1.71	0.78	1.90	0.67	2.10
18	1.16	1.39	1.05	1.53	0.93	1.69	0.82	1.87	0.71	2.06
19	1.18	1.40	1.08	1.53	0.97	1.68	0.86	1.85	0.75	2.02
20	1.20	1.41	1.10	1.54	1.00	1.68	0.90	1.83	0.79	1.99
21	1.22	1.42	1.13	1.54	1.03	1.67	0.93	1.81	0.83	1.96
22	1.24	1.43	1.15	1.54	1.05	1.66	0.96	1.80	0.86	1.94
23	1.26	1.44	1.17	1.54	1.08	1.66	0.99	1.79	0.90	1.92
24	1.27	1.45	1.19	1.55	1.10	1.66	1.01	1.78	0.93	1.90
25	1.29	1.45	1.21	1.55	1.12	1.66	1.04	1.77	0.95	1.89
26	1.30	1.46	1.22	1.55	1.14	1.65	1.06	1.76	0.98	1.88
27	1.32	1.47	1.24	1.56	1.16	1.65	1.08	1.76	1.01	1.86
28	1.33	1.48	1.26	1.56	1.18	1.65	1.10	1.75	1.03	1.85
29	1.34	1.48	1.27	1.56	1.20	1.65	1.12	1.74	1.05	1.84
30	1.35	1.49	1.28	1.57	1.21	1.65	1.14	1.74	1.07	1.83
31	1.36	1.50	1.30	1.57	1.23	1.65	1.16	1.74	1.09	1.83
32	1.37	1.50	1.31	1.57	1.24	1.65	1.18	1.73	1.11	1.82
33	1.38	1.51	1.32	1.58	1.26	1.65	1.19	1.73	1.13	1.81
34	1.39	1.51	1.33	1.58	1.27	1.65	1.21	1.73	1.15	1.81
35	1.40	1.52	1.34	1.58	1.28	1.65	1.22	1.73	1.16	1.80
36	1.41	1.52	1.35	1.59	1.29	1.65	1.24	1.73	1.18	1.80
37	1.42	1.53	1.36	1.59	1.31	1.66	1.25	1.72	1.19	1.80
38	1.43	1.54	1.37	1.59	1.32	1.66	1.26	1.72	1.21	1.79
39	1.43	1.54	1.38	1.60	1.33	1.66	1.27	1.72	1.22	1.79
40	1.44	1.54	1.39	1.60	1.34	1.66	1.29	1.72	1.23	1.79
45	1.48	1.57	1.43	1.62	1.38	1.67	1.34	1.72	1.29	1.78
50	1.50	1.59	1.46	1.63	1.42	1.67	1.38	1.72	1.34	1.77
55	1.53	1.60	1.49	1.64	1.45	1.68	1.41	1.72	1.38	1.77
60	1.55	1.62	1.51	1.65	1.48	1.69	1.44	1.73	1.41	1.77
65	1.57	1.63	1.54	1.66	1.50	1.70	1.47	1.73	1.44	1.77
70	1.58	1.64	1.55	1.67	1.52	1.70	1.49	1.74	1.46	1.77
75	1.60	1.65	1.57	1.68	1.54	1.71	1.51	1.74	1.49	1.77
80	1.61	1.66	1.59	1.69	1.56	1.72	1.53	1.74	1.51	1.77
85	1.62	1.67	1.60	1.70	1.57	1.72	1.55	1.75	1.52	1.77
90	1.63	1.68	1.61	1.70	1.59	1.73	1.57	1.75	1.54	1.78
95	1.64	1.69	1.62	1.71	1.60	1.73	1.58	1.75	1.56	1.78
100	1.65	1.69	1.63	1.72	1.61	1.74	1.59	1.76	1.57	1.78

NOTE: n = number of observations; k' = number of explanatory variables, excluding the constant term. It is assumed that the equation contains a constant term and no lagged dependent variables (if so, see Table B-7). Source: J. Durbin and G. S. Watson, "Testing for Serial Correlation in Least Squares Regression," *Biometrika*, vol. 38, 1951, pp. 159-77. Reprinted with permission of the *Biometrika* trustees.

Table B-5
Critical Values of the Durbin-Watson Test Statistics of d_L and d_U:
2.5 Percent One-Sided Level of Significance
(5 Percent, Two-Sided Level of Significance)

n	$k' = 1$		$k' = 2$		$k' = 3$		$k' = 4$		$k' = 5$	
	d_L	d_U	d_L	d_U	d_L	d_U	d_L	d_U	d_L	d_U
15	0.95	1.23	0.83	1.40	0.71	1.61	0.59	1.84	0.48	2.09
16	0.98	1.24	0.86	1.40	0.75	1.59	0.64	1.80	0.53	2.03
17	1.01	1.25	0.90	1.40	0.79	1.58	0.68	1.77	0.57	1.98
18	1.03	1.26	0.93	1.40	0.82	1.56	0.72	1.74	0.62	1.93
19	1.06	1.28	0.96	1.41	0.86	1.55	0.76	1.72	0.66	1.90
20	1.08	1.28	0.99	1.41	0.89	1.55	0.79	1.70	0.70	1.87
21	1.10	1.30	1.01	1.41	0.92	1.54	0.83	1.69	0.73	1.84
22	1.12	1.31	1.04	1.42	0.95	1.54	0.86	1.68	0.77	1.82
23	1.14	1.32	1.06	1.42	0.97	1.54	0.89	1.67	0.80	1.80
24	1.16	1.33	1.08	1.43	1.00	1.54	0.91	1.66	0.83	1.79
25	1.18	1.34	1.10	1.43	1.02	1.54	0.94	1.65	0.86	1.77
26	1.19	1.35	1.12	1.44	1.04	1.54	0.96	1.65	0.88	1.76
27	1.21	1.36	1.13	1.44	1.06	1.54	0.99	1.64	0.91	1.75
28	1.22	1.37	1.15	1.45	1.08	1.54	1.01	1.64	0.93	1.74
29	1.24	1.38	1.17	1.45	1.10	1.54	1.03	1.63	0.96	1.73
30	1.25	1.38	1.18	1.46	1.12	1.54	1.05	1.63	0.98	1.73
31	1.26	1.39	1.20	1.47	1.13	1.55	1.07	1.63	1.00	1.72
32	1.27	1.40	1.21	1.47	1.15	1.55	1.08	1.63	1.02	1.71
33	1.28	1.41	1.22	1.48	1.16	1.55	1.10	1.63	1.04	1.71
34	1.29	1.41	1.24	1.48	1.17	1.55	1.12	1.63	1.06	1.70
35	1.30	1.42	1.25	1.48	1.19	1.55	1.13	1.63	1.07	1.70
36	1.31	1.43	1.26	1.49	1.20	1.56	1.15	1.63	1.09	1.70
37	1.32	1.43	1.27	1.49	1.21	1.56	1.16	1.62	1.10	1.70
38	1.33	1.44	1.28	1.50	1.23	1.56	1.17	1.62	1.12	1.70
39	1.34	1.44	1.29	1.50	1.24	1.56	1.19	1.63	1.13	1.69
40	1.35	1.45	1.30	1.51	1.25	1.57	1.20	1.63	1.15	1.69
45	1.39	1.48	1.34	1.53	1.30	1.58	1.25	1.63	1.21	1.69
50	1.42	1.50	1.38	1.54	1.34	1.59	1.30	1.64	1.26	1.69
55	1.45	1.52	1.41	1.56	1.37	1.60	1.33	1.64	1.30	1.69
60	1.47	1.54	1.44	1.57	1.40	1.61	1.37	1.65	1.33	1.69
65	1.49	1.55	1.46	1.59	1.43	1.62	1.40	1.66	1.36	1.69
70	1.51	1.57	1.48	1.60	1.45	1.63	1.42	1.66	1.39	1.70
75	1.53	1.58	1.50	1.61	1.47	1.64	1.45	1.67	1.42	1.70
80	1.54	1.59	1.52	1.62	1.49	1.65	1.47	1.67	1.44	1.70
85	1.56	1.60	1.53	1.63	1.51	1.65	1.49	1.68	1.46	1.71
90	1.57	1.61	1.55	1.64	1.53	1.66	1.50	1.69	1.48	1.71
95	1.58	1.62	1.56	1.65	1.54	1.67	1.52	1.69	1.50	1.71
100	1.59	1.63	1.57	1.65	1.55	1.67	1.53	1.70	1.51	1.72

Source and Notes: See previous table.

Table B-6
Critical Values of the Durbin-Watson Test Statistics d_L and d_U:
1 Percent One-Sided Level of Significance
(2 Percent, Two-Sided Level of Significance)

n	k′ = 1		k′ = 2		k′ = 3		k′ = 4		k′ = 5	
	d_L	d_U	d_L	d_U	d_L	d_U	d_L	d_U	d_L	d_U
15	0.81	1.07	0.70	1.25	0.59	1.46	0.49	1.70	0.39	1.96
16	0.84	1.09	0.74	1.25	0.63	1.44	0.53	1.66	0.44	1.90
17	0.87	1.10	0.77	1.25	0.67	1.43	0.57	1.63	0.48	1.85
18	0.90	1.12	0.80	1.26	0.71	1.42	0.61	1.60	0.52	1.80
19	0.93	1.13	0.83	1.26	0.74	1.41	0.65	1.58	0.56	1.77
20	0.95	1.15	0.86	1.27	0.77	1.41	0.68	1.57	0.60	1.74
21	0.97	1.16	0.89	1.27	0.80	1.41	0.72	1.55	0.63	1.71
22	1.00	1.17	0.91	1.28	0.83	1.40	0.75	1.54	0.66	1.69
23	1.02	1.19	0.94	1.29	0.86	1.40	0.77	1.53	0.70	1.67
24	1.04	1.20	0.96	1.30	0.88	1.41	0.80	1.53	0.72	1.66
25	1.05	1.21	0.98	1.30	0.90	1.41	0.83	1.52	0.75	1.65
26	1.07	1.22	1.00	1.31	0.93	1.41	0.85	1.52	0.78	1.64
27	1.09	1.23	1.02	1.32	0.95	1.41	0.88	1.51	0.81	1.63
28	1.10	1.24	1.04	1.32	0.97	1.41	0.90	1.51	0.83	1.62
29	1.12	1.25	1.05	1.33	0.99	1.42	0.92	1.51	0.85	1.61
30	1.13	1.26	1.07	1.34	1.01	1.42	0.94	1.51	0.88	1.61
31	1.15	1.27	1.08	1.34	1.02	1.42	0.96	1.51	0.90	1.60
32	1.16	1.28	1.10	1.35	1.04	1.43	0.98	1.51	0.92	1.60
33	1.17	1.29	1.11	1.36	1.05	1.43	1.00	1.51	0.94	1.59
34	1.18	1.30	1.13	1.36	1.07	1.43	1.01	1.51	0.95	1.59
35	1.19	1.31	1.14	1.37	1.08	1.44	1.03	1.51	0.97	1.59
36	1.21	1.32	1.15	1.38	1.10	1.44	1.04	1.51	0.99	1.59
37	1.22	1.32	1.16	1.38	1.11	1.45	1.06	1.51	1.00	1.59
38	1.23	1.33	1.18	1.39	1.12	1.45	1.07	1.52	1.02	1.58
39	1.24	1.34	1.19	1.39	1.14	1.45	1.09	1.52	1.03	1.58
40	1.25	1.34	1.20	1.40	1.15	1.46	1.10	1.52	1.05	1.58
45	1.29	1.38	1.24	1.42	1.20	1.48	1.16	1.53	1.11	1.58
50	1.32	1.40	1.28	1.45	1.24	1.49	1.20	1.54	1.16	1.59
55	1.36	1.43	1.32	1.47	1.28	1.51	1.25	1.55	1.21	1.59
60	1.38	1.45	1.35	1.48	1.32	1.52	1.28	1.56	1.25	1.60
65	1.41	1.47	1.38	1.50	1.35	1.53	1.31	1.57	1.28	1.61
70	1.43	1.49	1.40	1.52	1.37	1.55	1.34	1.58	1.31	1.61
75	1.45	1.50	1.42	1.53	1.39	1.56	1.37	1.59	1.34	1.62
80	1.47	1.52	1.44	1.54	1.42	1.57	1.39	1.60	1.36	1.62
85	1.48	1.53	1.46	1.55	1.43	1.58	1.41	1.60	1.39	1.63
90	1.50	1.54	1.47	1.56	1.45	1.59	1.43	1.61	1.41	1.64
95	1.51	1.55	1.49	1.57	1.47	1.60	1.45	1.62	1.42	1.64
100	1.52	1.56	1.50	1.58	1.48	1.60	1.46	1.63	1.44	1.65

Source and Notes: See previous table.

Table B-7:   The Normal Distribution

The normal distribution is usually assumed for the error term in a regression equation. Table B-7 indicates the probability that a randomly drawn number from the standardized normal distribution (mean $= 0$ and variance $= 1$) will be greater than or equal to the number identified in the side tabs, called Z. For a normally distributed variable ϵ with mean μ and variance σ^2, $Z = (\epsilon - \mu)/\sigma$. The row tab gives Z to the first decimal place, and the column tab adds the second decimal place of Z.

The normal distribution is referred to infrequently in the text, but it does come in handy in a number of advanced settings. For instance, testing for serial correlation when there is a lagged dependent variable in the equation (distributed lags) is done with a normally distributed statistic, Durbin's h Statistic:

$$h = (1 - 0.5DW) \sqrt{n/(1 - n \cdot s_{\hat{\beta}_1}^2)}$$

where DW is the Durbin-Watson d Statistic, n is the number of observations, and $s_{\hat{\beta}_1}^2$ is the estimated variance of the estimated coefficient of the lagged dependent variable (Y_{t-1}). The h-statistic is asymptotically distributed as a standard normal variable. To test a one-sided null hypothesis of no positive serial correlation:

$$H_0: \rho \leq 0$$
$$H_A: \rho > 0$$

calculate h and compare it to a critical h-value for the desired level of significance. For a one-sided 2.5 percent test, for example, the critical h-value is 1.96, and if we observed a computed h higher than 1.96, we would reject the null hypothesis of no positive serial correlation at the 97.5 percent level of confidence.

Table B-7
The Normal Distribution

$$Z = \frac{\epsilon - \mu}{\sigma} \quad \text{(Standardized normal)}$$

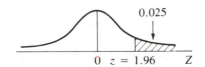

z	.00	.01	.02	.03	.04	.05	.06	.07	.08	.09
0.0	.5000	.4960	.4920	.4880	.4840	.4801	.4761	.4721	.4681	.4641
0.1	.4602	.4562	.4522	.4483	.4443	.4404	.4364	.4325	.4686	.4247
0.2	.4207	.4168	.4129	.4090	.4052	.4013	.3974	.3936	.3897	.3859
0.3	.3821	.3873	.3745	.3707	.3669	.3632	.3594	.3557	.3520	.3483
0.4	.3446	.3409	.3372	.3336	.3300	.3264	.3228	.3192	.3156	.3121
0.5	.3085	.3050	.3015	.2981	.2946	.2912	.2877	.2843	.2810	.2776
0.6	.2743	.2709	.2676	.2643	.2611	.2578	.2546	.2514	.2483	.2451
0.7	.2420	.2389	.2358	.2327	.2296	.2266	.2236	.2206	.2217	.2148
0.8	.2119	.2090	.2061	.2033	.2005	.1977	.1949	.1922	.1894	.1867
0.9	.1841	.1814	.1788	.1762	.1736	.1711	.1685	.1660	.1635	.1611
1.0	.1587	.1562	.1539	.1515	.1492	.1469	.1446	.1423	.1401	.1379
1.1	.1357	.1335	.1314	.1292	.1271	.1251	.1230	.1210	.1190	.1170
1.2	.1151	.1131	.1112	.1093	.1075	.1056	.1038	.1020	.1003	.0985
1.3	.0968	.0951	.0934	.0918	.0901	.0885	.0869	.0853	.0838	.0823
1.4	.0808	.0793	.0778	.0764	.0749	.0735	.0721	.0708	.0694	.0681
1.5	.0668	.0655	.0643	.0630	.0618	.0606	.0594	.0582	.0571	.0559
1.6	.0548	.0537	.0526	.0516	.0505	.0495	.0485	.0475	.0465	.0455
1.7	.0446	.0436	.0427	.0418	.0409	.0401	.0392	.0384	.0375	.0367
1.8	.0359	.0351	.0344	.0366	.0329	.0322	.0314	.0307	.0301	.0294
1.9	.0287	.0281	.0274	.0268	.0262	.0256	.0250	.0244	.0239	.0233
2.0	.0228	.0222	.0217	.0212	.0207	.0202	.0197	.0192	.0188	.0183
2.1	.0179	.0174	.0170	.0166	.0162	.0158	.0154	.0150	.0146	.0143
2.2	.0139	.0136	.0132	.0129	.0125	.0122	.0119	.0116	.0113	.0110
2.3	.0107	.0104	.0102	.0099	.0096	.0094	.0091	.0089	.0087	.0084
2.4	.0082	.0080	.0078	.0075	.0073	.0071	.0069	.0068	.0066	.0064
2.5	.0062	.0060	.0059	.0057	.0055	.0054	.0052	.0051	.0049	.0048
2.6	.0047	.0045	.0044	.0043	.0041	.0040	.0039	.0038	.0037	.0036
2.7	.0035	.0034	.0033	.0032	.0031	.0030	.0029	.0028	.0027	.0026
2.8	.0026	.0025	.0024	.0023	.0023	.0022	.0021	.0020	.0020	.0019
2.9	.0019	.0018	.0018	.0017	.0016	.0016	.0015	.0015	.0014	.0014
3.0	.0013	.0013	.0013	.0012	.0012	.0011	.0011	.0011	.0011	.0010

Source: Based on *Biometrika Tables for Statisticians,* Vol. 1, 3rd ed. (1966), with the permission of the *Biometrika* trustees.
NOTE: The table plots the cumulative probability Z > z.

Table B-8:   The Chi-Square Distribution

The chi-square distribution describes the distribution of the estimate of the variance of the error term and is useful in the "likelihood ratio test" of Section 7.7. The rows represent degrees of freedom, and the columns denote the probability that a number drawn randomly from the chi-square distribution will be greater than or equal to the number shown in the body of the table. For example, the probability is 10 percent that a number drawn randomly from any chi-square distribution will be greater than or equal to 22.3 for 15 degrees of freedom.

   The steps for the likelihood ratio test of a significant difference between the fit of a constrained equation and an unconstrained equation are:

1. Compute LL $= -2\ln(LR)$, where LR is the likelihood ratio, equal to the likelihood function of the constrained equation divided by the likelihood function of the unconstrained equation.

2. Compare LL to the chi-square value found in Table B-8 for the number of degrees of freedom equal to the number of parameters constrained by the null hypothesis at a specific level of significance; if LL $>$ the critical chi-square value, then reject the null hypothesis. For example, with two degrees of freedom and 10 percent level of significance, the critical chi-square value is 4.61. If the observed LL is greater than 4.61, then we can reject the null hypothesis with 90 percent confidence.

Table B-8
The χ^2 Distribution

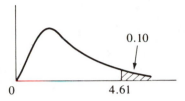

Degrees of Freedom	Level of Significance (Probability of a Value of at Least as Large as the Table Entry)			
	10%	*5%*	*2.5%*	*1%*
1	2.71	3.84	5.02	6.63
2	4.61	5.99	7.38	9.21
3	6.25	7.81	9.35	11.34
4	7.78	9.49	11.14	13.28
5	9.24	11.07	12.83	15.09
6	10.64	12.59	14.45	16.81
7	12.02	14.07	16.01	18.48
8	13.36	15.51	17.53	20.1
9	14.68	16.92	19.02	21.7
10	15.99	18.31	20.5	23.2
11	17.28	19.68	21.9	24.7
12	18.55	21.0	23.3	26.2
13	19.81	22.4	24.7	27.7
14	21.1	23.7	26.1	29.1
15	22.3	25.0	27.5	30.6
16	23.5	26.3	28.8	32.0
17	24.8	27.6	30.2	33.4
18	26.0	28.9	31.5	34.8
19	27.2	30.1	32.9	36.2
20	28.4	31.4	34.2	37.6

Source: See previous table.

Index